INTRODUCING SOCIOLOGY

A Critical Approach

D1303604

INTRODUCING SOCIOLOGY

A Critical Approach

Third Edition

MURRAY KNUTTILA

OXFORD
UNIVERSITY PRESS

OXFORD

UNIVERSITY PRESS

70 Wynford Drive, Don Mills, Ontario M3C 1J9
www.oup.com/ca

Oxford University Press is a department of the University of Oxford.
It furthers the University's objective of excellence in research, scholarship,
and education by publishing worldwide in

Oxford New York

Auckland Cape Town Dar es Salaam Hong Kong Karachi
Kuala Lumpur Madrid Melbourne Mexico City Nairobi
New Delhi Shanghai Taipei Toronto

With offices in

Argentina Austria Brazil Chile Czech Republic France Greece
Guatemala Hungary Italy Japan Poland Portugal Singapore
South Korea Switzerland Thailand Turkey Ukraine Vietnam

Oxford is a trade mark of Oxford University Press
in the UK and in certain other countries

Published in Canada
by Oxford University Press

Statistics Canada information is used with the permission of the Minister of Industry,
as Minister responsible for Statistics Canada. Information on the availability of the wide range
of data from Statistics Canada can be obtained from Statistics Canada's Regional Offices,
its World Wide Web Site at http://www.statcan.ca, and its toll-free access number 1-800-263-1136.

Library and Archives Canada Cataloguing in Publication

Knuttila, Kenneth Murray
Introducing sociology : a critical perspective / Murray
Knuttila. — 3rd ed.

First published as: Sociology revisited : basic concepts and perspectives.
Includes bibliographical references and index.
ISBN-13: 978-0-19-542027-2.—
ISBN-10: 0-19-542027-6

1. Sociology—Textbooks. I. Title.

HM586.K58 2005   301   C2005-901605-1

3 4 - 08 07 06

Cover Design: Brett J. Miller
Cover Image: Children balance on rail © Black Star

This book is printed on permanent (acid-free) paper ∞.

Printed in Canada

Contents

I would like to thank
Wendee Kubik, Erin Knuttila, Lee Knuttila, and Andre Magnan
for all those spirited dinner conversations
that forced me to broaden my horizons
and sharpen my thinking.

For Mäelle—the future.

Preface to the Third Edition

On the occasion of the Second Edition I expressed my gratitude at having an opportunity to address the errors and confusions that I may have made in the first edition. What I said then about society still holds true: society is changing faster than we can contemplate. This means that this book, like every other book, or even the information on your computer, is somewhat out of date by the time you use it. The major changes in this Third Edition include the addition of a new chapter on mass communications, as well as efforts to update data where relevant. I have used my own experiences in the interim to facilitate an introduction to this complex subject and discipline in a manner that will allow the reader a better understanding of the daily developments in the world and the discipline of sociology. The overall objective of stimulating systematic and critical thought remains as the guiding principle of the text.

At the completion of the Third Edition I would like to thank the anonymous reviewers and Lisa Meschino and her staff at Oxford University Press for their assistance. In particular, I would like to thank Jessica Coffey for outstanding editorial assistance. I am, of course, solely responsible for all errors and omissions.

Some of the material in this volume was first presented in an earlier volume, *Sociology Revisited: Basic Concepts and Perspectives.* As well, some of the ideas—particularly in chapters 8, 11, 14, and 15—are shared from *State Theories: Classical, Global and Feminist Perspectives,* co-authored with Wendee

Kubik. Of course, much of this book was presented in the first two editions of *Introducing Sociology: A Critical Perspective.* The title continues to suggest a double entendre because the reader is asked to be critical of sociology while engaging in the study of a critical sociology. The need for critical thinking in every facet of our lives has never been greater.

No single volume can possibly introduce every aspect of a social science discipline; nevertheless, the material presented allows the reader to begin to grasp some of the essential features of sociological thought. The book is organized into three major sections. Part I overviews the basic concepts employed by sociologists in our efforts to understand human beings and our behaviour. Part II provides a critical overview of key developments in sociological theory, suggesting that recent feminist critiques have placed the entire agenda of previous theoretical work in question. Part III illustrates the nature of sociological analysis. It uses the concepts and theories from Parts I and II to introduce a number of the ways in which sociologists look at specific issues such as social inequality, polity, deviance, ethnic and race relations, familial relations, and globalization.

The overarching theme of each section is 'the promise' of the sociological imagination. We must accept the underlying logic of the work of C. Wright Mills and attempt to ensure that sociological thought, analysis, empirical research, and theory contribute to fulfilling the potential of the discipline by facilitating a greater degree of self-understanding.

PART I

The Sociological Perspective and the Basic Language of Sociology

In 1959, the late C. Wright Mills began his classic volume *The Sociological Imagination* with a statement that—if you ignore the gender-specific noun—could have been written today. Mills wrote: 'Nowadays men often feel that their private lives are a series of traps. They sense that within their everyday worlds, they cannot overcome their troubles, and in this feeling, they are often quite correct' (3). For many of us the task of understanding our lives has never seemed more daunting. Perhaps this is because the world seems to be getting more and more complex, or, perhaps it is because some of us just don't try very hard. As a species, we have never had so many opportunities to avoid thinking about our lives in spite of the fact that we have never had so much information, literally, at our fingertips. If we accept the convincing argument that Neil Postman presents in *Amusing Ourselves to Death*, the two phenomena are connected. Postman argues that humans have never had as much access to information as we now do, but that we seem increasingly incapable of translating that information into useful knowledge and understanding, let alone wisdom. Clearly, the survival and well-being of our species requires us to try to make better sense of things.

The book you are about to read has at least two objectives. The first is to stimulate you to think about yourself from the perspective of the discipline of sociology. The second is to provide some concepts, ideas, theories, and data that will facilitate that process. Since the book attempts to introduce you to the discipline of sociology, it starts at the beginning by focusing on the basic language, concepts, assumptions, and premises that the discipline embraces and that sociologists use in their approach to analyzing and understanding the social behaviour of *Homo sapiens*.

As I stated above, a simple yet important assumption informs the material in this volume, namely, that we are interested in and capable of better understanding ourselves, our behaviour and character, and the behaviour and character of others. The well-known American sociologist C. Wright Mills referred to the capacity to understand our behaviour sociologically as the 'sociological imagination'. The first chapter introduces the discipline of sociology, examines how it is different from other disciplines, and explores this notion of the sociological imagination.

In Chapter 2 we begin to encounter the key elements of the sociological approach to understanding humans and their social behaviours when we learn that it is more appropriate to understand humans as cultural, as opposed to instinctual, creatures. Chapter 3 moves from the study of culture to an analysis of human society. When sociologists analyze human society, that is, resolve it into its component parts, they conclude that it can be understood to comprise institutions, roles, statuses, values, norms, groups, and so on. These concepts represent the core language of the discipline. Chapter 4 connects the individual to the social structure by examining the importance of social learning, in sociology known as 'socialization', for human development. In many ways Chapter 4 presents the core idea of the sociological perspective, specifically that our character, personality, and behaviour have been, and constantly are, radically influenced by our social environment and experiences. The last chapter in Part I presents several alternative explanations of the processes by which human personality and character develop. Chapter 5 challenges the reader to consider alternative theories of socialization and personality formation with an eye to synthesizing insights from a variety of perspectives to better account for this complex process.

CHAPTER 1

Understanding Human Behaviour

Ever since 11 September 2001, when two commercial passenger planes were deliberately flown into two of the tallest buildings in New York City, our world has been a different place. The aftermath of this unimaginable event has reintroduced a horrendous modern phrase into our everyday language—death toll. The latest figures on the 11 September 2001 death toll are just over 3,000. In the years that have followed, the invasions of Afghanistan and Iraq have resulted in death tolls that are, of course, much higher. Why do we not recoil in horror every time an innocent life is taken, no matter how valiant the efforts are to justify the cause? Have we somehow become so desensitized that we hear and use this phrase without realizing that it refers to the abrupt end of an individual and alters the lives of someone's mother, father, daughter, son, lover, friends, and co-workers? If so, how did this happen and why? This is, of course, not the first time that terrorists have used aircrafts and innocent victims in their campaigns. But, before we decided that humanity is hopelessly depraved and capable only of violence and hatred, recall that many of the hundreds who died in New York were firefighters who routinely risk their lives for people they do not know. Why do some people wilfully plant bombs while others risk their lives to remove children from burning buildings? Indeed, ask yourself why, in any major North American city, we can see lovers in a city park holding hands, while elsewhere in the same city women are routinely admitted to hospitals after being battered by their spouses?

Staying with the theme of diverse human behaviours, consider this. Across the globe families celebrate special events by feasting on delicacies: food as diverse as raw sea urchins, sheep brains, spicy lentil soup, and partly cooked calf rump. Some of the celebrants eat with their fingers, others use long thin wooden sticks, and still others use odd-shaped silver utensils. Why, in the same city, do two youths impulsively decide to rob a convenience store, while across town two people of the same age debate what clothes they'll wear the next morning, their first day of university classes? Or try to explain this: after a wedding meal in one country, the loud burp of a guest causes considerable embarrassment for those present; in another part of the world a dinner guest's burp is ignored, or possibly understood as a compliment, an indication that the meal was thoroughly satisfying.

For students interested in understanding human behaviour, these snippets of human conduct raise important questions. What is terrorism? Why are terrorists willing to kill and injure people who have no direct connection to their particular grievances? What makes humans risk their lives for others? What is the role of romantic love in society? Why are women the most common victims of domestic violence in our society? What kinds of foods are considered tasty, and what kinds are unpalatable? What modes of conduct are appropriate during and after the consumption of food? Why do some people attend university while others do not? Why do some people commit acts defined as criminal while others do not? What is a criminal act? Above all else, perhaps, why do human beings exhibit so many diverse kinds of behaviour?

To answer questions like these we must be both prepared and able to think systematically about human behaviour, about what is going on, and why we behave and act in certain ways. And when we begin to consider the actions and behaviour of our selves and others, we quickly realize that we are dealing with subject matter that is incredibly complex and wide-ranging.

We find out that all aspects of human behaviour, even the seemingly most trivial and unimportant events, are part of complex social processes that occur within complicated sets of social structures, rules, and conventions. To engage in this task, to

CONCEPTIONS OF SOCIETY

In their book, *Society*, David Frisby and Derek Sayer explain the importance of understanding core concepts such as society, noting that students of sociology are confronted with quite different conceptions of what society is. They point out that three of the important so-called 'founders' each had a radically different view of society. Here is some of what they say.

Emile Durkheim

Frisby and Sayer discuss Durkheim's view of society in Chapter 2 titled 'Society as Object':

Durkheim's claim is that the 'being', society, which is formed out of the association of individuals, is a whole—an object—distinct from and greater than the sum of its parts. It forms a specific order of reality with its own distinctive characteristics. This is what is meant by saying it is *sui generis*. These characteristics of society are not reducible to nor, therefore, explicable from those of its component elements—human individuals taken in isolation. Society has emergent properties, that is, properties which do not derive from its elements considered independently of their combination, but which arise from and do not exist outwith *(sic)* that combination itself *(36)*.

For Durkheim recognition of the *sui generis* reality of society—its distinctive ontological status—is the first, and most indispensable, condition of any scientific sociology. Society is thereby conceived as a 'system of active forces' in its own right, a causally efficacious whole, and sociological explanation is accordingly explanation by specifically social causes.

Durkheim's second essential proposition—that social facts must be studies *(sic)* 'objectively', 'from the outside'—is for him a corollary of the first. He is demarcating himself from two major traditions in social thought here. First, he is distancing himself from aprioristic social philosophy. If, he reasons, the social world is indeed a part (albeit the highest part) of natural reality—a real object, an order of facts—then its characteristics and causes can no more be discovered by philosophical speculation than can any other laws of nature. Sociology must be 'positive', not normative; its object is a world 'out-there' which can only be discovered empirically, not deduced from philosophical first principles *(37)*.

Durkheim's concept of society has undoubted consistency. The *sui generis* thesis, as well as being a methodological postulate, underpins the major substantive dimensions of his concept. Society for Durkheim is primarily a moral . . . community because it is an object which is transcendent *vis-à-vis* individuals, both in space and time, and can therefore both coerce them and command their loyalty and respect. For him neither morality nor conceptual thought, both of which go beyond the individual, can originate with the individual; they both testify to and presuppose the ontological distinctiveness of society. Whatever judgement one might finally come to on Durkheim's conception, we should note its immense fecundity. He could not, for instance, have illuminated the social conditions of suicide as he did without first refusing the reduction of the social to the individual: without, in other words, positing society as object. That fecundity, moreover, stems largely from exactly the counter-intuitive aspects of Durkheim's conception, its deliberate distance-taking from the 'common sense' perception of society as nothing but the totality of individuals and their interactions *(49)*.

Max Weber

The notion that society is a reality out there, a social fact external to us, is radically different from the approach taken by Max Weber. Frisby and Sayer explain Weber's views of society (which are often compared with those of George Simmel, a contemporary of Weber's) in Chapter 3, 'Society as Absent Concept':

A brief examination of Max Weber's grounding of sociology, which has somewhat relatedly provided one of the most powerful traditions in modern sociology, will also confirm the tendency in sociology to abandon the concept of society as the starting point for the study of sociology. In his incomplete assessment of Simmel as a sociologist, Weber pointed to a crucial dimension of Simmel's sociology. Whereas many of those studying social life have been 'dealing with questions of "facticity," empirical questions, Simmel has turned to look at the "meaning" which we can obtain from the phenomenon (or can believe we can)'. This meaning of social interaction, for instance, had been studied by Simmel through that process by which Weber was also to operate, namely, through the construction of social types, the examination of the social scientist's typifications of participants in interaction and more generally, the interpretive understanding of actions' motivations. More significantly, however, Weber, writing over a decade after Simmel's early delineation of sociology, still detects that he himself is reflecting upon sociology within 'a period . . . when sociologists who are to be taken very seriously maintain the thesis that the only task of sociological theory is the definition of the concept of society' *(441)*.

Weber's own grounding of sociology decisively breaks with such a thesis. Weber systematically avoids treating all collectivities and major social aggregates, of which society is one, as *sui generis* entities. Instead, they are all introduced as labels for tendencies towards action. Although one of his major works is entitled *Economy and Society,* it does not discuss 'the definition of the concept of society' but rather societal tendencies to action or sociation *(Vergesellschaftung)* which is contrasted with action motivated by a tendency towards solidarity and communality *(Vergemeinschaftung)*. This becomes intelligible, as we shall see, in the light of Weber's definition of the subject-matter of sociology as the study of social action and its meaning for individual actors. The avoidance of the concept of society is justifiable for Weber given his commitment to the methodological individualist position. Such a commitment is most clearly evident in his statement that 'If I am now a sociologist . . . I am so in order to put an end to the use of collective concepts, a use which still haunts us. In other words: even sociology can only start out from the action of one or a few, or many individuals, i.e., pursue a strictly "individualistic" method! This is why Weber preferred to use verb forms or active nouns in order to delineate the social processes with which he was concerned. At all events, recourse to collective concepts by sociologists was only justified on the grounds that they referred to the actual or possible social actions of individuals. And this means, in contrast to Durkheim, that 'there is no such thing as a collective personality which "acts"'. Society cannot be the starting point of Weber's sociology *(67–8)*.

. . . Sociology is thus a discipline which 'searches for empirical regularities and types' of human action. General sociology will thus attempt to 'systematically classify' social groups—formed, through concerted social action according to the structure, content and means of social action' *(69)*.

Karl Marx

The last major conception of society that Frisby and Sayer discuss is in the work of Karl Marx. The chapter in which we find a discussion of Marx is titled 'Society and Second Nature':

Society is not, then, a self-acting subject *sui generis*: 'its only subjects are the individuals, but individuals in mutual relationships, which they produce and reproduce anew'. But nor is society reducible to these individual subjects as such, considered independently of these relations. That would be to consider individuals abstractly and ahistorically. Society is, rather, the *set of relationships* that links individuals. Individuals—and, as we will see, objects—acquire social characteristics in virtue of their positions within these relations.

Central to this conception of society is an important point that emerges from both of the last two quotations we have given. Because is *(sic)* relational, it is integrally a system of differences, and those characteristics which mark individuals as social are therefore ones which also differentiate them as individuals in definite ways:

for instance, as master or servant, husband or wife. This means that society is not homogeneous. It is rather, in Marx's own concept, a contradictory unity. Where, as in most societies Marx analyses, the contradictions within social relations are antagonistic, society emerges as an entity to which possibilities of conflict, movement and change are inbuilt. It is thus, from the start, implicitly a dynamic whole *(96)*.

For Marx the most basic of social relations are relations of production—those social relations established within the 'production of material life itself'—and an adequate sociology must accordingly be a materialistic one. Unlike for Simmel or Winch, there is a privileged starting-point for sociological analysis. It lies in human needs (and their historical development) *(97)*.

Having said this, Frisby and Sayer warn against simplistic economic determinist readings of Marx in which the economic base somehow determines the character of the rest of society. After arguing that Marx himself presented views of productive relations that were complex, they go on:

Had Marxists taken this seriously, they could have generated neither a universal model of society of the base/superstructure kind nor the sort of restricted category of production relations it sustains. For on this methodology 'the connection of the social and political structure with production'—what, in any given case production relations are—could not properly be the object of a general theory, whether posited *a priori* or arrived at inductively. What is, or is not, a relation of production could only be ascertained through empirical inquiry in each specific case. The only general concept of production relations consistent with this is precisely the one Marx offers—an empirically open-ended one. Production relations are, simply, all those social relations presupposed to a way in which people produce. What in any specific instance these relations will be in an ineluctably empirical question *(101–2)*.

Marx's conception of society remains, nevertheless, grounded in materialist premises:

For Marx, then, people's 'materialistic connection'—their production relations—is the groundwork of society, and different types or historical epochs of society are distinguished by the particular forms this connection takes. The *mode of production,* or 'way' in which people produce their means of subsistence, is therefore his fundamental unit of sociological analysis and historical periodization *(103)*.

From David Frisby and Derek Sayer, *Society* (New York: Tavistock, 1986). Reprinted by permission of the authors.

explore this apparently formidable terrain of human behaviour, we clearly need to use a wide variety of intellectual tools.

The social sciences aim to provide those tools necessary for understanding behaviour and existence. We use the plural form, *social sciences*, because different social science disciplines take different approaches, or use different tools, to answer the same questions. Anthropologists, psychologists, geographers, economists, political scientists, historians, and sociologists focus on different aspects of human social existence. Given the complexities of the subject matter, this is undoubtedly both a necessary and a desirable situation. No one discipline is capable of providing all the insights required for an understanding of the many varied dimensions of human life. Indeed, each discipline is further broken down into subfields—it is next to impossible for any one person to cover any one particular field in its entirety.

Science as a Way of Knowing

Although the various social sciences approach the study of human behaviour differently, they all have at least one thing in common: they make an effort to be scientific. Used in this context, scientific refers to an approach to knowledge production that is systematic and based on specified principles and methods.

There are a number of possible responses to the simple questions, 'Why is that happening?' and 'How do you know that?' You could cite an authority as your source—a special book, a special person, or an oracle. The essence of this way of knowing is the total acceptance of the authority as an unquestioned source of knowledge. The particular authority—in which you have complete trust—defines what you know. Less common these days as a source of knowing is the experience of revelation, in which some unusual, or even mystical, occasion or phenomenon provides certain knowledge.

History is full of individuals who claim to know something because of an experience that brings about a revelation.

We more often say we know things because it is just 'plain old common sense'. Indeed, much of what we call knowledge in our society is based on common sense, defined by one dictionary as 'sound practical judgment that is independent of specialized knowledge or training'. It reflects a kind of 'normal native intelligence'. Common sense might tell us that we should wear a hat when we go out into a cold rain. It tells us to lock our doors when we go out at night. It might warn us that it is wise not to 'burn the candle at both ends'. These bits of advice seem valid enough. But at one time common sense also told Europeans that the Earth was flat.

M.H. Walizer and P.L. Wienir (1978) note that common-sense knowledge is often presented in the form of old sayings. The problem is, some of those sayings—such as 'opposites attract' and 'birds of a feather stick together' or 'he who hesitates is lost' and 'look before you leap'—can directly contradict one another. Although common-sense knowledge is pervasive, it often forms an obstacle to systematic social analysis and investigation because of its inconsistencies and inaccuracies.

In Western society we have come to downplay both the authoritative and the mystical ways of knowing. Instead, we rely on science, a way of knowing and a way of producing knowledge based on a number of basic assumptions or premises—even though these assumptions and premises are not often explicitly spelled out by scientists themselves in their work. First, the scientific method assumes that an external objective world exists outside of and apart from the human individual who is attempting to understand that world. Second, it assumes that we can secure information, knowledge, and an understanding of the world by collecting data through experimentation or observation. Scientists refer to this as empirical data. Third, the practice of science assumes that there is order and regularity in the world—that there is causality. Conditions, phenomena, or events are not created or do not just happen randomly and accidentally; rather, they are caused, and by following proper scientific procedures we can come to know and understand these causes.

While there are continuing debates about how to turn empirical data into knowledge and understanding, the practitioners in most scientific disciplines tend to agree that the production of knowledge requires the use of both empirical data and human reason. Scientists use both inductive and deductive thinking to produce knowledge about the world. Inductive thinking moves from the particular to the general, meaning that a general claim or statement is made after studying individual or particular instances of some phenomenon. Deductive thinking moves from the general to the particular. A conclusion about some particular phenomenon is deduced or drawn on the basis of some established general premise or law. In either case, scientists use knowledge grounded in empirical reality to provide a basis for making generalized statements about that world.

Building on these assumptions, the scientific approach specifies a series of steps or procedures that guide practitioners in their search for knowledge and understanding. The first step involves the selection of a problem, which becomes the centre of the investigation. Since science seeks to answer questions about both what is happening and why things happen, the second step involves the adoption or elaboration of a theory or explanatory framework. The explanation adopted may or may not be correct, so it must be tested through empirical research. After scientists conduct research and analyze the data, they draw conclusions, which seek to provide answers to the initial problem. What is important about this method of knowing is its demands for empirical confirmation and verification of all statements that claim to represent knowledge in a field. If proof and evidence do not support all contentions, the knowledge is not accepted as scientific.

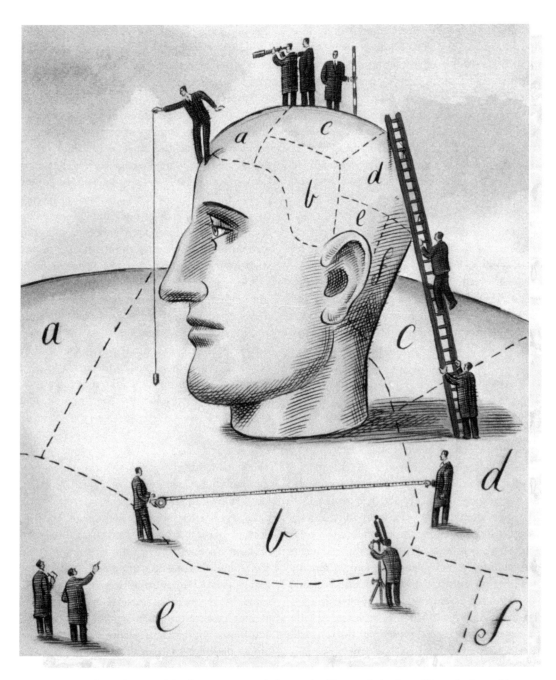

Although the various social sciences approach the study of human behaviour differently, they all have at least one thing in common: they make an effort to be scientific. 'Scientific' refers to an approach to knowledge production that is systematic and based on specified principles and methods. (Copyright © 2000 Peter Till/The Image Bank).

The data and evidence required in various disciplines could be different, so each discipline has its own procedures for gathering data. The one common requirement is that the practitioners in the area recognize the methods used for gathering data as legitimate and that other scientists are able to repeat them—this is referred to as replication. A part of learning about a given discipline is learning about the modes of inquiry and the standards of evidence characteristic of that discipline.

Sociology and the Social Sciences

In their efforts to understand human behaviour, social scientists have developed a diversity of disciplines, of which sociology is only one. By focusing on different aspects of human social existence and behaviour, each discipline contributes in its own way to the project of understanding human behaviour.

Anthropology

There is a common misconception that anthropology and anthropologists are only interested in the study of pre-industrial or non-industrial societies. Indeed, much of the classical literature in anthropology does focus on non-industrial societies or what the practitioners often referred to as 'primitive societies'—thus revealing their own biased sense of cultural or racial superiority. But the discipline is also interested in the modern world. Anthropology is the study of human development and culture in a comparative and systematic manner, with an interest in the physical and cultural structures and development of the human species. The discipline is divided into several branches, with physical anthropology addressing the physical development of the human species and its relationship to the physical environment. Social or cultural anthropology concerns itself with the history, origin, characteristics, and structures of contemporary and past cultures. Linguistics and the study of human communication are also important parts of the anthropological enterprise, along with the study and recovery of physical artifacts, which is also the mandate of archeology.

Economics

The study of material production, consumption, and distribution is the purview of economics. Economics is usually defined as the study of the production, distribution, exchange, and consumption of various goods and services. Because economists deal with many issues, from local pricing structures to patterns of international trade, the discipline is divided into macroeconomics and microeconomics. Macroeconomics focuses on the study of the 'big picture' or the aggregate level, looking at the larger patterns of production, consumption, savings, and investment at the national and international levels, as well as looking at the impact of government actions and policies. Microeconomics concerns itself with economic activity and associated behaviour at the level of individual decision-making units and with associated theories of production, consumption, and distribution.

Geography

The human animal exists in an intimate relationship with the physical environment of the Earth. Geography concentrates on the study of the Earth's physical properties and characteristics and the relationship of these properties and characteristics to the human species, with recent studies ranging from the relationship between time and space to the development of urban areas. Geography is 'located' somewhere between the social and natural sciences; at some universities it is considered a natural science and at others it is a social science. Like other disciplines, there are internal specializations, with the key ones being physical and cultural (or human) geography. In an era of increasingly serious environmental crisis, geography's study of the relationship between the physical environment and the human species has become particularly important.

History

The importance of learning from the past has been a part of the common-sense knowledge of virtually every human society. In the university setting, the discipline of history plays an important role because history is, by definition, the study of human and social development through the ages. When historians study the past record of human social development they do so with an eye to determining if there are patterns or if the events that occurred were unique parts of a larger and longer process.

Political Science

Political science is the social science whose mandate is perhaps most clearly understood by the average person, although most non-specialists do not fully understand the entire gamut of concerns that political scientists address. In focusing on the organization, structure, operation, and administration of the polity, including the operation of the government, political scientists are most often deeply concerned with the history and development of these institutions. While political scientists who appear on television to give commentary on elections and constitutional matters are undoubtedly interested in political parties and voting, they are also likely to be concerned with theories of political power and government and with the comparative study of all aspects of decision-making at the political and social levels.

Psychology

If political scientists get the most media exposure on television news, psychologists are portrayed more often in the movies or on television dramas. As a discipline, psychology focuses on the study of the mind, the personality, individual behaviour, and various mental processes. Psychologists concentrate in various subfields or areas of specialization within the discipline, ranging from behavioural and experimental through clinical and social. Key areas of concern in the behavioural field include learning, intelligence, emotions, thinking, memory, and perception, while applied psychology is concerned with the diagnosis and treatment of personality, learning, and other disorders.

Sociology as the Study of Structure and Agency

How and where does sociology fit into this array of social sciences?

The term *sociology* appears to have been coined by the French thinker Auguste Comte around 1830. The two stems of the word are *socius*, Latin for 'companion', and *logos*, Greek for 'the study of', which together give us 'the study of companionship' as a literal definition. But in its development as a discipline, sociology has come to mean much more than this. The standard dictionary and introductory textbook definitions of sociology refer to it as the scientific and systematic study of human society; this short, general definition is of limited value because it could just as easily apply to most of the other social science disciplines. Even if we extend the definition to include the scientific study of both human society and human behaviour, it is still not clear precisely what ground the discipline covers and how it is different from the other social sciences.

In their sociology dictionary, Nicholas Abercrombie, Stephen Hill, and Bryan S. Turner provide the basis for a useful definition of sociology by suggesting that sociology is not only the 'study of the basis of social membership'—a translation of its literal meaning—but also 'the analysis of the structure of social relationships as constituted by social interaction' (1988: 232). This very general definition is a useful point of departure for understanding just how the sociological enterprise is different from the other social sciences and how it contributes to the main goal of understanding human behaviour and action.

When Auguste Comte first used the term *sociology* he was trying to explain his own grandiose project. Comte was, somewhat immodestly, attempting to establish a new discipline that would represent nothing less than the crowning achievement of Western intellectual development. He was going to provide an approach to human affairs that would assist the establishment of an orderly social world. Such a discipline would have to address an enormous range of social issues. Few sociologists have ever attempted to develop an approach as grand as the one envisioned by Comte, although the discipline of sociology does tend to provide a broader and more holistic approach to human social existence than most of the other disciplines. Sociologists sometimes annoy their colleagues in other disciplines by borrowing ideas, concepts, data, and theories in an attempt to understand the entire social structure and the relationship of the individual to that social structure.

In a real sense, sociology is differentiated from the other social sciences by its insistence that we need to understand the 'larger picture' of how human beings are shaped and moulded by society and how humans in turn are a part of the process by which society is produced and also reproduced through labour power, both in the outside workplace and in the family and domestic labour. While sociologists recognize the importance of the work of the other social scientists, they would argue that the distinct areas covered by those other disciplines only tell part of the story. If we are to understand human behaviour and action, the insights of all the disciplines must be brought to bear on the entire social structure. This holistic, comprehensive focus on social structure is one of sociology's tasks. But sociologists are also interested in studying people as individuals and the relationship of individuals to the larger society. All the various social science disciplines address this issue, but only one of them—sociology—makes it an essential component of its agenda.

Sociology attempts to understand how the structures and processes of the social system influence human development, action, and behaviour. In addition, sociology also seeks to understand how social structures and processes themselves do not necessarily exist on their own but rather emerge out of the actions and behaviour of individuals. Sociology studies how people, acting both as individuals and together, have an impact on the society. Sociologists believe that the holistic approach is the basis of improved self-understanding, and that self-understanding should be an essential objective of the social sciences.

Sociology can be defined, then, as the systematic analysis and investigation of how human beings, as social agents, produce their social structures, and how human beings are produced—and reproduced—by those structures.

To accomplish this task, sociology engages in the systematic and scientific investigation of social structures, social relationships, and social interactions. Before we develop some of the core assumptions that inform sociology, it is useful to have a picture of how and even why this new discipline emerged at the historical moment that it did.

Science, Theory, and the Origins of Sociology

The Historical Background

To understand the emergence of sociology, it may help to look at the insights of one of its subfields, the sociology of knowledge, which is a branch of the discipline that studies the relationship between the social conditions and structures that exist at a given time and place and the process of the production of knowledge. The sociology of knowledge attempts to place the producer of knowledge and the process of knowledge production within its historical, cultural, political, economic, and religious contexts. Perhaps by applying this practice to the discipline of sociology we can better understand its unique perspective.

The French thinker Auguste Comte (1798–1857) first used the term *social physics* to describe the new science he was attempting to establish, later switching to the word *sociology*. In developing his arguments about why a new approach to the understanding of human affairs was needed, Comte was reacting to the conceptions of humanity and society prevalent in his day. In his opinion, the existing conceptions of humanity and society were faulty, and the relationship between them needed reconsideration. This meant a complete revamping of how people explained the workings of the social world—a revamping of the sources and methods of social knowledge.

The Rise of Capitalism

In Comte's era, the modes of thought associated with the term *science* were just gaining dominance. It is important to understand that the emergence of science as the most commonly accepted way of explaining the world was part of a much wider series of changes in Western societies. Underlying many of these changes was the fact that during the seventeenth and eighteenth centuries, Western Europe was being transformed from a feudal to a capitalist society.

The transition from feudalism to capitalism was a radical revolution in the true sense of the word, because it changed every aspect and dimension of society. The emergence of capitalist or market society involved radical and dramatic changes to the political, economic, family, religious, military, and educational orders. In addition, an intellectual revolution changed accepted ideas about the sources of knowledge, about how we come to understand the world we live in.

In feudal society the Church had played a powerful role, and one of its major influences was in knowledge production. The pervasiveness of religious beliefs meant that nearly everyone accepted the authority of the Church as the definitive source for most, if not all, knowledge. They saw God as the prime cause of events in the world, and they understood events in nature as being related to God, God's blessing, God's will, or God's wrath. The fact that not all events could be explained was accounted for by the viewpoint that humans could not possibly know or understand all things, and that this, too, reflected God's will.

As time passed and new ideas and modes of thought from North Africa, the eastern Mediterranean, India, and other parts of Asia began to filter into Western Europe, changes began to occur in the understanding of the relationship between the authority of the Church and the production of knowledge. Among the new ideas were the introduction of Arabic numbers and a revival of interest in the ideas and philosophy of classical antiquity. The emergence of Islam with its interest in a synthesis of ideas drawn from Greek, Roman, and Indian society provided an important challenge to the notion of Christianity as a universal belief system. The Christian response in the form of the Crusades served in the long run only to undermine the power of the Church, because the returning adventurers brought back different forms of thought, including knowledge of classical geometry, new philosophies, and logic. As these diverse streams of thought took hold and merged with local improvements in technology within the context of expanding economic activity, major changes began.

The Copernican Revolution

In his classic study of the intellectual developments of the period, *The Making of the Modern Mind*, J.H. Randall states: 'Two great revolutions in thought had occurred, and the course of intellectual history since that time is primarily the record of the gradual penetration into the beliefs of men of the significant consequences of those revolutions' (1940: 226).

The first of the intellectual transitions was the Copernican revolution, which dramatically altered the popular conception of our physical location in the universe. Before the sixteenth century there was broad acceptance, among Western thinkers at least, of the basic tenets of the Ptolemaic astronomical system. Claudius Ptolemaeus, known as Ptolemy, was a second-century AD Alexandrian astronomer and mathematician who developed an astronomical system based on the premise that the Earth was the centre of the universe and the sun and certain planets revolved around it. The theory received broad support from the Church and theological thinkers because it meshed with their understanding of creation. It made sense, many of them held, that God would put the Earth and humanity, the centrepiece of His creation, at the centre of the universe.

The Ptolemaic system dominated thinking in astronomy and theology for centuries, but by the early sixteenth century it had begun to encounter problems. As new optical technologies were developed and Europeans began to move about the planet making stellar observations from different perspectives, the accepted system, with its explanations of planetary movements and locations, began to be questioned. At first, the discrepancies between the Ptolemaic theory and the new empirical data were addressed by making additions to and placing qualifiers on the system. As a result of these additions and qualifiers the explanatory system used by astronomers eventually became cumbersome and complicated. When Ptolemy's system was used to interpret the data the astronomers were producing, the universe seemed to be a place of chaos. Scientists working in the field were forced to consider one of two possible explanations: either there was no logic and order in God's universe or the basic premises of Ptolemy's system were incorrect.

Nicolaus Copernicus (1473–1543), a Polish astronomer who studied in Italy, was convinced that God's universe was a place of order. Like other thinkers attracted to the new sciences, he believed that creation was governed by logic and that it was mathematical and harmonious. He proposed a radical solution to the problem of the order of the universe, putting the sun into the centre, with the Earth and other planets rotating around the sun. By advocating a heliocentric concept, Copernicus found himself under pressure from the authorities of the day. Church officials were concerned that his theory downplayed the centrality of the Earth and humanity in the structure of the universe. The Vatican declared his ideas to be 'false and altogether opposed to holy scripture' (Barnes, 1965: 677).

In challenging the authority of the Church, Copernicus was advocating an alternative way of knowing and producing knowledge. By the time his work was further developed by Johann Kepler and Galileo, using data produced by the constantly improving telescopes, the correctness of the heliocentric view was firmly established. The Copernican revolution established the importance of empirical data, or information gathered by some manner of observation, in producing knowledge. Empirical proof would increasingly become the means of determining the truth or falsity of a statement.

The Cartesian Revolution

Copernicus firmly believed that the universe was a place of mathematical order and regularity. It was the second major intellectual revolution—the Cartesian revolution—that established logical thought and correct reasoning as an integral part of knowledge production. By the time the French thinker René Descartes (1596–1650) emerged, the absolute authority of the Church as the source of all knowledge was in decline. More and more intellectuals were looking to empirical data as a source of knowledge. Descartes added to the legitimacy of the scientific approach through the arguments made in his *Discourse on Method*, published in 1637. He argued that the first step in knowledge production is to wipe out all existing ideas, including those based on authority, in order to begin with an unbiased mind. The thinker would then start over again with simple and proved statements and, using the rules and procedures of current and formal logical thought, develop more and more complex truths. Knowledge and truth could thus be produced only by the rigorous application of patterns of deductive and rational thought. No statement not arrived at by the use of logical and rational thought would be accepted as knowledge.

The Emergence of Science

Although some intellectuals maintained that knowledge was totally dependent on empirical or sense data (empiricists) and others argued that knowledge came first and foremost from logic and rational thought (rationalists), a union of each of these 'new' ways of knowing was in formation throughout the sixteenth and seventeenth centuries.

Among the first to argue that true knowledge required the use of both correct reason and empirical data was the English essayist Francis Bacon (1561–1626), a contemporary of Descartes. But the first fully systematic exposition of the method of producing knowledge we now call science is commonly attributed to Isaac Newton (1642–1727). Newton's method of 'analysis and synthesis' called on investigators to use both inductive and deductive logic, both observation and reason. Newton maintained that observation is the point of departure because empirical support must be provided before a statement can be accepted. Once a statement is proved to be true, it can be used as the basis for subsequent rational and logical thought, so that conclusions not provided by the immediate empirical or observational data can be arrived at through rigorous logical thought. The method of science thus involved the production of general statements by inductive thought working from data provided by the senses. Knowledge that claimed to be scientific required some form of further or subsequent confirmation or proof; and this was to come through the production of deductive hypotheses that could in turn be verified by still more empirical sense data. Observation, in the broadest sense of the word, and experience, along with reason and logic, were all deemed essential parts of the process of knowledge production. A new way of knowing was born, which was soon to prove itself in the discoveries and findings that paved the way for the transformations of the Industrial Revolution.

The linkage between the capacity of the way of knowing called science and the development of new technology was striking. The standard lists of prerequisites for industrial development always include the presence of machines and technology (Clough and Cole, 1967: 393). While some of the discoveries and findings that came out of the work of people in physics, chemistry, astronomy, and biology might be considered 'pure science' (knowledge produced for its own sake without any direct application), much of the new knowledge was applied, that is, used almost immediately in industry and production. The outcome was an explosion of technology that formed the basis of the mechanization of industry, agriculture, and commerce. The knowledge produced by science, which was often cast in terms of the discovery of universal and natural laws, became the basis of a new economic and social order. A central idea in this new order was progress, and scientific knowledge became linked with this powerful notion.

Given the apparent successes of the scientific method in what we commonly refer to as the natural sciences, it is not surprising that some thinkers argued that this same method of knowing or producing knowledge should be used to provide systematic and assured knowledge in the social world. As the feudal order was declining and being replaced by the emerging market or capitalist system, radical social, political, and economic revolutions were also sweeping the world. Although it was obvious to many thinkers that the old order was on the way out, the nature and characteristics of the new order were not yet apparent. Among the key social, economic, and political questions that emerged was the question of social order.

As the power of the Church declined, social thinkers concerned themselves with determining if the new scientific way of knowing could provide knowledge that would serve as the basis of social order, stability, and solidarity, as religion had in the past. During the feudal era, religion and the power of the Church had provided a strong common set of beliefs and thus an important source of social solidarity. If people in the new capitalist order were to interact as unregulated, isolated individuals in market transactions, with each pursuing his or her own interests, and if each were to be allowed to believe whatever he or she wanted, how could a stable and ongoing community or society be possible? If everyone just acted out of self-interest without an overriding concern for the community, would the situation result in unbridled chaos? Other questions also emerged.

As the political structures of feudal society collapsed and the new nation-states emerged, theorists began to ask fundamental questions about the nature of political power. What precise form should the state take? What is the appropriate role for the monarch and the feudal aristocracy in governing society? In the past those elements had claimed absolute authority and power, but now new classes and groups were contending for power. What role should the governed, especially those involved in business and commerce, play in the operation of the state and government? As the Church declined, questions emerged concerning the basic role of religion in a person's life. Similar fundamental questions were asked about the role of education, the structure of family life, and even the relationships between the sexes. Nothing seemed sure or secure in the way it had before.

Liberalism and Scientific Politics

Among the first thinkers to address these kinds of questions in the modern era was Thomas Hobbes (1588–1679). Hobbes believed that just like the rest of the universe, human society was subject to certain natural laws. He was further convinced that the new method of knowing, called science, was indeed the most appropriate route to the kind of 'assured' knowledge that would allow humans to construct a society in accordance with the laws of nature. The methods of science were deemed to be capable of uncovering the laws of nature that governed human affairs, and once we had discovered these laws all we need do was ensure that our social, economic, and political structures did not contravene the laws.

Much has been written about the actual method that Hobbes used and the extent to which it followed what we would now call science (Macpherson, 1968:

25–8; 1973: 230–50; Nelson, 1982: 138). But the precise method Hobbes used to arrive at his conclusions is of less interest for us here than his conclusions. On the basis of his observations and an intellectual process that Brian Nelson refers to as 'thought experiment' (1982: 139), Hobbes concluded that human beings are by nature selfish, egotistical, individualistic, and possessive. On the basis of this conception of human nature Hobbes went on to develop arguments about what form of social and political organization humans should endeavour to create. He concluded that the 'natural' form of human society was one built on competitive, individualistic market relations overseen by a powerful state governed by an absolute monarch.

For Hobbes and other thinkers who came after him, including political philosopher John Locke (1632–1704) and economists Adam Smith (1732–90) and David Ricardo (1772–1823), the scientific method was the only acceptable method for producing knowledge. For these intellectuals, the scientific method marked an intellectual revolution. The knowledge that was produced by many of them related directly to the issues of social, economic, and political reconstruction. In their own ways the later thinkers suggested that, given their findings, the most appropriate form of social organization was a market economy combined with a more liberal state. Each of them produced knowledge that served social, economic, and political interests engaged in a critique of the old feudal order—interests working for the establishment of a new market-based liberal democratic society. The first fruits of the scientific revolution served as the basis for a critical analysis of the existing order. What was called scientific knowledge became a part of continuing political struggles.

The thinkers of the seventeenth and eighteenth centuries also accepted and used the idea of a fixed and universal human nature. Although the specifics of their conceptions of human nature varied, most of them maintained that there were fundamental, innate human behavioural tendencies that had to be acknowledged as the basis for the structuring of society. That is, most of the thinkers we commonly include in what is called the classic liberal tradition tended to believe that human beings were by nature competitive, acquisitive, possessive, and individualistic. They supported the social relations connected to a market or capitalist economy because they believed those social relations would allow the blossoming of the natural behavioural tendencies of human beings. As we will see in Chapter 7, their particular emphases on the scientific method and the fixed and universal nature of humanity provided a distinct background for the development of Auguste Comte's ideas. Comte objected to a good deal of the logic and assumptions of this line of thought, and he set out to provide an alternative view of humans and society; however, his work followed others who began to develop criticisms of classical liberalism that were to be the precursors of sociology.

The Enlightenment Foundations of Sociology

In his study of the history of sociological thought, Steven Seidman points out that during the period often referred to as the Enlightenment (sometimes called the Age of Reason corresponding approximately to the one hundred years preceding the French Revolution in 1789) many thinkers were critical of the basic ideas of the social contract theorists (1983: 21–5). According to Seidman, philosophers as diverse as Voltaire, Montesquieu, Condorcet, and David Hume disagreed with the notion that there was an eternal fixed human nature and that one could understand social phenomenon by simply studying this human nature. Seidman quotes Condorcet as declaring that humans were coming to know the globe and they were now able to study humanity everywhere in its many modified forms. Seidman notes that Enlightenment had as its object *'all the peoples of the earth, from antiquity to modernity, from East to West'* (28, emphasis in original).

In his study of the emergence of sociology, David Westby makes a similar point. Westby (1991) notes that there were several central issues or philosophical-political problems that conditioned the emergence of sociology. One was how to understand and account for human progress, that is, social change. Social and political change clearly was occurring but pre-Enlightenment philosophy and theology seemed unable to account for it. The second intellectual problem was the notion of a fixed unchanging human nature. Increasing knowledge of other cultures and of history were demonstrating that people were different now than they had been in the past, and they were different in different parts of the world. The last troubling intellectual issue of the day was the question of whether science could be applied to human affairs. Westby goes on to note that a group of thinkers he calls the 'Scottish Moralists' laid out a series of arguments concerning human sociability, progress, and the possibility of creating a science of society that paved the way for Comte, about whom we will read more later.

Westby points out how radical the new view of human beings and the new conception of society were. If indeed humans beings were not bound by some natural propensity to be greedy, selfish, and self-seeking as Hobbes had suggested, or if we are not members of an innately sinful fallen humanity as the Christian theology of the day suggested, then it is possible to improve our condition. On the other hand, if society is not merely the sum of the parts, that is, a mere reflection of human nature in institutional or collective form, then social reform and change is possible. Finally, if the social environment is dramatically impacted by the character and behaviour of humans as Montesquieu, Rousseau, David Hume, Adam Smith, and Adam Ferguson argue, then social and individual human progress were intimately connected. Progress was possible on all fronts because more social justice and more social humans could be created.

These comments provide an initial indication of how and why the perspective that the sociologist brings to humans and society is different. For now, it is enough to keep in mind the fact that sociology arose out of a particular historical context when humans were questioning whether they could know and understand themselves by using the scientific method. It arose in the context of exuberant support for science as a new way of knowing that seemed to be superior to any way of knowing previously developed by humans. New knowledge and understanding of the natural world that science seemed to provide was proving to be the basis of many dramatic changes in the realm of material production. The new technologies and advances in the production of the material goods people need to survive seemed sufficient evidence that science was a superior way of knowing. The application of science to society and human behaviour, it was hoped, would provide the kind of knowledge needed to ensure that the future did indeed bring progress and the betterment of the species.

Modernity is the term commonly used to describe the longer time period ushered in by the intellectual changes associated with the Enlightenment, the rise of science, the emergence and expansion of capitalism, and the expansion of Western Europe. Barry Smart identifies the central political and analytical assumptions of modernity as including the notion that 'knowledge is progressive, cumulative, holistic, universal, and rational' (1996: 397). As we will see, the knowledge that was produced during this period under the sway of these assumptions took the form of systematic grand theories and treatises that attempted to or claimed to explain many aspects and dimensions of the world. These large-scale comprehensive theories—what post-modernists call grand narratives—have become the object of significant criticism, partly on the grounds of their ontological assumptions (their assumptions about the nature of human existence and being) and their epistemological claims (their ideas about how we know).

Whether sociology or any human knowledge to date has accomplished the tasks set out by the Enlightenment is an issue we will defer discussing until we better understand the elementary principles on which sociology is built. We discuss theory in Chapter 6. For now we will return to the sociological imagination.

The Sociological Imagination and Its 'Promise'

For many sociologists the essential mandate of modern sociology comes not from Comte but from an American sociologist, C. Wright Mills. He is perhaps best known for his books *White Collar* (1951) and *The Power Elite* (1956). A third book, *The Sociological Imagination* (1959), is still widely read and remains one of the most important books in the discipline, in part because of the project it lays out for sociology and all the social sciences.

In the first chapter of *The Sociological Imagination*, 'The Promise', Mills argues that the development of the ability or intellectual capacity that he calls the sociological imagination is essential for all citizens of modern complex societies. For Mills, the sociological imagination is an intellectual capacity, an ability or quality of mind—a kind of thinking that is essential if we want to begin to understand ourselves, our behaviour, and the behaviour of others around us, near and far.

Mills uses several different phrases to explain the concept, including 'the quality of mind essential to grasp the interplay of man and society, of biography and history, of self and world'. Elsewhere he notes, 'The sociological imagination enables us to grasp history and biography and the relations between the two within society.' He also states that the sociological imagination promises 'an understanding of the intimate realities of ourselves in connection with larger social realities', an ability that, if developed, will allow human reason 'to play a greater role in human affairs' (1959: 4, 6, 15).

The desire to understand ourselves should not be seen as something new. Indeed, the search for self-understanding has always been a part of what

American sociologist C. Wright Mills' third book, *The Sociological Imagination* (1959) remains one of the most important books in the discipline. In this book, he argues that the sociological imagination is a necessary intellectual capacity if we want to begin to understand ourselves, our behaviour, and the behaviour of others around us, near and far. (Photograph courtesy of Yaroslava Mills.)

makes the human animal distinct. As our world seems to become more complex and more confusing, the task seems more difficult, yet an understanding of the structures and processes of society is more important than ever.

Biography and History

According to Mills, the key to self-understanding is to grapple with the distinction between biography and history. Each of us has an individual biography or life story, and each of these individual biographies is set or located in a larger social and historical context. Each and every one of us was born into, grew up and developed in, and currently exists in a society that itself is part of an emerging and continuing historical process. We cannot understand much about our individual lives without locating ourselves in society and in the historical processes that have shaped, structured, and moulded that society. As Mills points out, although we may not always realize it, the larger developments that take place in society and history have a direct impact on all of us as individuals.

For example, with the outbreak of war a person's entire life can change even if that individual has nothing to do with the causes of the war and is opposed to war. When an economic depression sets in, an entire family's way of life can change, due entirely to forces and factors beyond the members' immediate control. A new tax law has an impact on the country's whole economy, leading to lost jobs or new jobs and dramatic changes in the lives of many citizens. If a student receives failing grades at school, the tendency might be simply to think of the failure as a personal problem—the student didn't work hard enough or isn't intelligent enough. But perhaps the grades are really the product of having to work at two part-time jobs to pay for the university course or help out the folks back home. This factor would place the school performance in a new light. Similarly, a woman who experiences sexual harassment must be able to understand that the root cause of her problem is not to be found in her behaviour, demeanour, or dress, but rather in the social dynamics of a patriarchal and sexist society.

Simple as they are, these examples illustrate Mills' point, namely, that our individual lives are not lived in a vacuum; rather, they unfold within a complex system of social structures, processes, and events. The situating of our lives in this larger context is an essential prerequisite for understanding ourselves, and this situating process is the task of the sociological imagination. The first step in the development of the sociological imagination is therefore to grasp the intimate connection between your own life and the historically developing society around about you.

The Three Vital Questions

The ability to connect our lives and our individual biographies with the larger social structures around us is just the first step in developing the sociological imagination. It should lead us to pose fundamental questions about our society and ourselves. Mills argues that a person's capacity for self-understanding, that is, the sociological imagination, is not complete without the capacity to ask and answer three different but essential kinds of questions (1959: 6–7):

1. What are the structures of my society like? How is my society organized and how does it operate? How is it similar to and different from other societies?
2. Where does my society fit into the broader picture of human history? How does the history of my society influence its current organization? What are the most important aspects of the current historical epoch? Where does my society seem to be going?
3. How do the structures of my society and the historical period of which I am a part influence me and those around me? What social and historical forces have shaped and moulded my character and personality?

If individuals understand that their personal life stories, their biographies, are intimately tied to the history and development—as well as the current state—of their society, and if those individuals are able to ask and answer Mills' three types of questions, then they are well on the road to developing their sociological imaginations. The promise of the sociological imagination is quite simple—with a little thought and intellectual effort we can develop an understanding of ourselves and those around us. Such an understanding is the first step in ensuring that our lives are lived to the fullest and that we do indeed possess a degree of control over our destinies.

Developing the Sociological Perspective

One of the best introductory sociology books is Peter Berger's classic, *Invitation to Sociology: A*

Humanist Perspective. The book is over 40 years old and has a different format than what students are used to today: it lacks pictures, boxes, and learning aids. The reason it is a classic resides in the first two chapters, 'Sociology as an Individual Pastime' and 'Sociology as a Form of Consciousness'. Hidden away in the sometimes-dense text are a set of observations that, if you understand now, will make this book and the course for which you are in all likelihood reading this book much easier to understand. Sociology is, according to Berger, first and foremost 'an *attempt to understand*' (1963, 4, emphasis in original). But you might wonder: to understand what? While Berger offers several answers, the most telling is the most simple: our everyday world and existence in it. Berger explains that coming to understand our everyday lives can actually be very exciting:

> It is not the excitement of coming upon the totally unfamiliar, but rather the excitement of finding the familiar becoming transformed in its meaning. The fascination of sociology lies in the fact that its perspective makes us see in a new light the very world in which we have lived our lives. This also constitutes a transformation of consciousness. (21)

But, you say, surely everyone understands themselves and their lives! The sociologist's response is both yes and no. We may understand our lives at a common sense, 'never thought about systematically' level, but this is not good enough because, as Berger brilliantly puts it: 'It can be said that the first wisdom of sociology is this—things are not what they seem' (23).

For beginning students, the subject matter of sociology often appears to be quite ordinary, mundane, and everyday. Certainly, sociologists do deal with many issues and processes that are a routine part of our everyday lives. Students in their first sociology course already know something about, have read about, thought about, or at least hold opinions about many of the issues and topics normally covered in the course. In some instances students just beginning to study society might even consider themselves experts in a given area, such as politics or religion, because they have been politically active for years or have gone to church all their life.

In sociology, however, we tend to adopt an approach and a perspective that are different from those we use in our everyday lives. The sociological approach is different, in part because it looks at all social issues and processes in a deliberate, systematic, and holistic manner, with an eye to understanding their larger significance and role for society, as well as their impact on individuals and their development. A systematic investigation of what we thought was a simple issue about which we knew nearly everything could produce startling results. Being familiar with something at the level of 'common sense' does not, it turns out, necessarily mean that you are an expert—or even that what you think you know is in fact correct. When there are fundamental differences between what we 'know' at the levels of common sense and scientific knowledge, and when these differences result in a fundamental questioning of what we 'know', the result is often controversial—as most students will quickly discover.

Sociologists maintain that even though we think we know everything about some phenomenon, we can still be wrong and our supposed 'knowledge' can be flawed. What is required if we are to understand our complex social behaviours, they argue, is systematic thinking and research coupled with analytical perspectives. Usually the approach adopted in sociology is to do that work within a particular subfield.

The Subfields of Sociology

Like all the disciplines in the social sciences, sociology is subdivided into fields or areas of specialization. For example, most economists wouldn't dream of studying all aspects of the production, distribution, and consumption of goods and services, and not many historians try to focus on all aspects of human history. Likewise, political scientists usually don't concentrate on every aspect of the polity and the political process. The complexity of human social structures and existence makes it nearly—if not completely—impossible for a practitioner in any field to be an expert or a specialist in all areas.

To understand the basic organization of the discipline, it is necessary first to understand the basis of what is commonly called the sociological perspective. For simplicity's sake, the sociological perspective can be summarized as the argument that the human animal is unique because it cannot exist, develop, or be understood outside of the context of human society. The society into which we are born and within which we develop and exist exercises a profound influence on our characters, personalities, behaviours, and whole beings. Understanding the overall structures, development, and processes of our society is the point of departure for self-understanding.

But human society is so complex and complicated that most of us cannot grasp its operation in its entirety. As a result, sociologists have come to specialize in the study and analysis of particular aspects of society. The following list illustrates some of the areas of specialization, or subfields, that characterize modern sociology:

- sex and gender roles
- crime and criminology
- health and medicine
- education
- religion
- social stratification
- class analysis
- social movements and collective behaviour
- industrial relations
- ethnic group dynamics
- power and domination
- the polity and the political process

- sports and leisure
- population and demography
- art in society
- mass media
- social change
- theories of society
- research and the data-gathering process
- urban development and structures
- rural development and structures
- knowledge
- work
- development and underdevelopment
- family and household
- war and revolution
- deviance and social problems
- the aging process

In essence, what sociologists do is investigate and study many different, and often quite particular, aspects of the social process.

Getting On with Sociological Analysis

Within the approach I am presenting here, sociology is not so much a specific body of knowledge as a mode of thinking. We must be confident that we can untangle and understand the complexities of our social existence, made up as it is of a web of interactions and relationships influenced by, among other factors, class, gender, race, nation, age, culture, religion, and locale or region. Although the task is difficult, we must be prepared to undertake the necessary research and thought to facilitate clarification and understanding.

In the pages that follow you will be encouraged to subject both your social existence and the discipline of sociology to a critical examination. In so doing you must be prepared to place both what you think you know and what sociologists and others have claimed they know under careful scrutiny. As I hope will soon become apparent, the existing approaches in sociology often seem ill-equipped and unable to account for life in the twenty-first century. If this is the case, the criticisms of thinkers influenced by important new approaches such as feminism must be acknowledged, and their insights must be incorporated into a reassessment of how we practise our craft as sociologists.

Throughout this book you will be asked to be critical of what you already know—or think you know. You will be expected to examine and re-examine, to be analytical and critical, and to not accept what you think you know until you have systematically investigated and examined the phenomenon you are interested in. The book emphasizes the centrality of systematic critical thought because the capacity to engage in such a process is one of the defining characteristics of the human species. If we are to realize our potential and better ourselves and our species, we must use our intelligence in a constructive manner; and using our intelligence constructively requires that we know how to think, how to engage in research, and how to arrive at satisfactory conclusions.

As we undertake these activities, we must also realize that the results of our intellectual efforts and the conclusions we reach may not be agreeable to everyone. The process of producing knowledge that is predicated on critical thought has always produced controversy, and even discord. Isn't it true that to live life fully and to make it worth living, you must examine it fully and understand it to the best of your abilities?

Critical Thinking Questions

- What is unique about science as a way of knowing? Is science somehow 'superior' as a way of knowing? Explain.
- Should we be interested in developing a greater degree of self-understanding? What disciplines do you need to study in order to understand yourself?
- Explain the relationship between the emergence of capitalism and the rise of science.
- What is the sociological imagination? What must you know in order to develop this capacity?
- How has history had an impact on your biography/life story? Provide three concrete illustrations of this connection.

Terms and Concepts

Science—a way of knowing or producing knowledge that emphasizes the role of both empirical data and theoretically informed explanation. While scientists insist that all claims to knowledge must be supported by empirical data, they are also aware of empirical data being intimately connected to theoretical frameworks. They use theoretical frameworks and perspectives to order and make sense out of empirical data; thus, the data never simply 'speak for themselves', but must be interpreted.

Sociology—the systematic study, analysis, interpre-

tation, and explanation of how human beings are produced by the social structures within which they develop and exist, and of how human beings in turn produce these social structures. Sociology adopts a holistic approach to the study of humans and society, freely incorporating insights, ideas, and perspectives from a variety of other disciplines.

The sociological imagination—a term that C.W. Mills coined to explain what he sees as the essential task of the social sciences: to facilitate self-understanding. Mills argues that if we are to understand ourselves in particular, and human behaviour in general, we must be able to locate our life stories, our biographies, within the context of our society and its larger historical context. Understanding the interconnection or intersection of biography and history is the first step in self-

understanding. To develop the intellectual capacity or quality of mind we call the sociological imagination, Mills argues that we must be able to understand how society impacts on us, how society is structured and works, and how society changes and develops.

Related Web Sites

http://www.genordell.com/stores/maison/ CWMills.htm

This site contains a short biography, a list of his major works, and links to other works by and about C.W. Mills.

http://www.ucm.es/info/isa/

The International Sociological Association is the major general international professional association for sociologists. The home page includes links to the various major research committees in different areas (over 50 committees in various sub- or applied fields), conferences, job opportunities, and links for the association's major international conference site.

http://alcor.concordia.ca/~csaa1/index.htm

The Canadian Sociology and Anthropology Association is the major national professional association in Canada. In addition to publishing the *Canadian Review of Sociology and Anthropology*, the CRSA provides a range of serv-

ices for the professional community, including a major annual conference somewhere in Canada. This bilingual site contains a wealth of information for sociologists, students, and practising professionals alike, in Canada.

http://www.mcmaster.ca/socscidocs/ w3virtsoclib/index.htm

Maintained by Dr Carl Cuneo of McMaster University, this site provides an impressive range of links to everything from institutions and departments to professional associations, to databases, journals, and theory sites.

http://www.socsciresearch.com/

'Research Resources for the Social Sciences' is a comprehensive social science research Web site with many, many good links and the opportunity to enter keywords as you search for conceptual definitions or issues related to the discipline. Craig McKie at Carleton University deserves our thanks, as does McGraw-Hill.

Suggested Further Readings

Berger, P., and T. Luckmann. 1967. *The Social Construction of Reality*. New York: Doubleday Books. Subtitled *A Treatise in the Sociology of Knowledge*, this remains one of the best treatments of society as an objective and subjective reality.

Burke, J. 1984. *The Day the Universe Changed*. London: British Broadcasting Corporation. A somewhat dated but still excellent and comprehensive history of human knowledge, this book has an emphasis on the rise of science and the modern era.

Hall, S., D. Held, D. Hubert, and K. Thompson, eds. 1966. *Modernity*. Cambridge, MA: Blackwell. This large and multi-authored history of virtually every institution and social practice on our society is a source book that verges on encyclopedic coverage.

Lynd, R.S. 1967. *Knowledge for What: The Place of Social Science in American Culture*. Princeton: Princeton University Press. Lynd asks some questions and raises issues that many social scientists think would be better left undisturbed. What is the role of the critical intellectual in the modern era? Whom do we serve and why?

Mills, C.W. 1959. *The Sociological Imagination.* New York: Oxford University Press. This remains the classic conscience of sociology, offering both a critique of ineffective sociology and the prescription for realizing the potential of critical thought in search of self-understanding.

CHAPTER 2

Homo sapiens:
Biology and Culture

If the general objective of the discipline of sociology is to help bring about a greater degree of self-understanding, how or where do we begin the task? A useful point of departure is to first consider our prime subject matter—human beings—as biological creatures.

For social scientists, this raises elementary questions. First, are there essential characteristics of the human animal, or *Homo sapiens,* that are unique and that differentiate us from other species? And if there are, what are they and what do we know about them?

One reason for beginning by considering the biological side of human beings and human behaviour is the prevalence and popularity of arguments that offer simplistic biologically-based explanations for complex human behaviours. Some social scientists argue that everything, from our eating habits to our sexual conduct, apparent natural competitiveness, and war and male dominance can be explained in terms of biological imperatives (see Morris, 1969; and Cook's rebuttal, 1975). Indeed, as many researchers, including R.C. Lewontin (1991) and Lewontin, Steven Rose, and Leon Kamin (1985) have argued, the re-emergence during the past decade of explanations that offer an essentially biological explanation for many complex social processes and structures must be understood as part of a larger political agenda. This political agenda maintains that there is nothing we can do to redress structural inequities such as sexism, racism, and class domina-

tion, and therefore they must be accepted as natural and inevitable (see Caplan, 1978).

Most sociologists, as well as many other social scientists, reject these simplistic arguments in favour of more complex arguments that draw on the cultural characteristics of *Homo sapiens* to explain our behaviour, while still recognizing the biological foundation of much of human conduct.

Physiological Needs and Drives

Although social scientists are well known for their ability to disagree on almost everything, there is one point they can all accept: that human beings are biological organisms; and that as such they have basic physiological or biological *needs.* The *Harper-Collins Dictionary of Sociology* refers to a need as 'the basic requirements necessary to sustain human life' (Jary and Jary, 1991: 325). The most obvious of our physiological needs is our nutritional or dietary needs. We all require a certain basic amount of food and nourishment if we are to survive physically. We also have a physiological need for liquid intake. In addition, the continued long-term survival of our species is dependent on sexual activity that leads to biological reproduction.

Associated with such physiological needs is what is commonly referred to as *drives.* Whereas a physiological need refers to the basic requirements of survival such as food, oxygen, or sleep, a drive refers to what Gordon Marshall calls the 'energizing forces' that direct an organism to try and provide for the requirements of life (Marshall, 1994: 133). A drive is the internal impulse produced by the need. Drives motivate individuals to activity to reduce the tension or dissatisfaction produced by the need. The need for food manifests itself in the drive we commonly refer to as hunger. The need for liquid appears in what we refer to as thirst, and sexual tension produces the sex drive.

Our individual and species survival is clearly dependent on meeting our basic needs and dealing with our basic drives. In this regard, human beings are no different than other non-human life forms. Your cat, dog, budgie, boa constrictor, or any other life form you live with must also satisfy its basic physical needs for food and liquids if it is to survive. Human beings are different, however, not because we have needs, but because of how we deal with our needs and drives. Because the objective of sociological analysis is to assist in understanding human behaviour, the key issue is not the existence of basic needs and drives—we can assume they exist—but the modes of social conduct or behaviour through which humans meet their needs and deal with their drives.

Instinct

Most non-human animals seem to have been genetically equipped with the ability to deal with their basic needs and drives, and as a result their conduct and behaviour seem automatic—it 'comes naturally'. This is because the conduct and behaviour of many non-human animal life forms are governed by instinct.

The concept of instinct is subject to much controversy, debate, and confusion. One author refers to instinct as 'one of the most ideological concepts science ever operated with' (Heller, 1979: 5). The definition adopted here is a hybrid drawn from a variety of sources in biology and the social sciences and incorporating the basic features of many common definitions (see, for example, Case

and Stiers, 1971; Heller, 1979; Nagle, 1984; Johnson, 1969; and Torrance, 1979).

Behaviour or actions can be considered instinctual if they are:

- relatively complex;
- unlearned, genetically transmitted, innate, inborn;
- species-wide, invariant among members of a species or common to all members of a species;
- manifest full-blown the first time the required level of maturity has been reached and the triggering stimuli is present in the environment.

In addition, an action, behaviour, or mode of conduct is instinctual if a member of a species can be reared without contact with other members of its species and it still exhibits the behaviour in question the first time the animal is presented with the necessary 'triggering' stimulus. While the term 'instinct' is used here in this specific manner, it is common for scholars in psychology to use the designation 'fixed pattern behaviour'. Crider *et al.* note that 'fixed pattern behaviour' is a synonym for 'instinct' (1989: 130).

Imagine, for instance, that a sociologist skilled in the delicate art of securing research grants is able to convince a funding agency to support an international study of rat behaviour. After securing the grant, the researcher's first step is a trip around the world to collect rat specimens from each continent. After returning, our researcher sets up an experiment. He places each of the rats, one by one, in a corner of a confined area, such as a cage or a room, and then thrusts his hand forward in a sudden manner at the rodent. If performed boldly, the action forms a stimulus that registers in the rat's brain and central nervous system as a threat. The result is that the researcher observes a common response from the rats regardless of their country or continent of origin. Each and every rat rears up and fights to defend itself.

If we were to take blood tests from people who had just been startled, we would find high levels of adrenaline, but the mere presence of this hormone in the human bloodstream does not elicit or produce any particular behavioural patterns. There is no evidence that humans are pre-programmed to respond to actions or situations we might perceive as threatening or to behaviour that appears aggressive. Indeed, it is apparent that what we interpret to be aggression or aggressive behaviour is itself something we learn and thus cannot be instinctual. In rats, when we observe a species-wide, invariant, and unlearned response, the concept of instinct is appropriate. In the case of humans, the responses to fear or apparent aggression seem to be diverse, different, and unpredictable; therefore, they are by definition not instinctual.

Let us consider a more specific example of instinctual behaviour. James Torrance (1979) describes two instinctual behaviours of the stickleback fish, one relating to defence of its territory, the other to its reproductive behaviour. During its breeding period, the male stickleback will attack objects if the underside of the object is red, even if the object does not bear a shape that resembles a stickleback fish (79). The red colouring is significant because a male stickleback's belly becomes red prior to mating. The research related to this phenomenon indicates that the colour red acts as a releaser, or stimulus, for the male's fighting behaviour, and this fighting behaviour is elicited, or released, by the simple presence of the colour red on the underside of an object. Experiments further demonstrate that a real stickleback fish lacking red on its underbelly does not elicit the fighting behaviour in males, while any object with the appropriate shade of red does. This indicates that it is the colour red that is the stimulus for this instinctual behaviour.

If all members of a species respond with an identical complex behaviour to some stimulus, we can conclude that the behaviour in question is instinctual. Within the realm of human conduct, it is difficult to provide a similar instance of a specific

colour eliciting a specific unlearned pattern of behaviour. There is no evidence that the human response to various colours is genetically programmed and species-wide. There are, it is true, a variety of different cultural responses to colours and combinations of colours, as in the pride a nationalist might feel for the flag, but these are behaviours and responses that are not instinctual but rather cultural and learned.

Reproductive behaviour is often very complex, not to mention fascinating and interesting to observe, and provides a rich source of data for the study of instincts and behaviour. In his work, Torrance describes the complex patterns of behaviour that both the male and female stickleback fish engage in as the females lay and the males fertilize eggs. The mating ritual involves a series of complex moves, manoeuvres, and dances all repeated in an identical fashion each time the stickleback fish mate. The mating behaviour of many birds, such as the whooping crane's dance, is equally complex, elaborate, and interesting. Perhaps the most significant aspect of these behaviour patterns, especially after you watch them several times, is their similarity among a given species. The elaborate mating dance of the whooping crane is repeated, for example, in a virtually identical manner by each and every whooping crane attempting to entice a partner to reproduce. Similarly, the dances or movements of the stickleback fish partners display an amazing degree of consistency. Indeed, one could argue that if you have seen one sexually aroused whooping crane or stickleback fish you have 'seen them all', in that all sexually aroused members of those species exhibit virtually identical behavioural patterns.

Again, the challenge is to ascertain the extent to which humans exhibit species-wide, invariant complex behavioural patterns in their efforts to secure a compatible sexual partner. Are there standard or similar behavioural patterns, even in our own culture, that characterize the actions of a sexually stimulated human? I have often challenged students to investigate the behaviour of their fellow humans in search of a sexual partner, perhaps at a dance or at the local university pub, to determine the extent to which there are common patterns. After several hours of systematic observation, the students conclude that the 'moves', actions, and countermoves of individuals of both sexes differ radically and are truly different, diverse, and varied, not similar and invariant.

If we consider, on the one hand, the behaviour of various animals in acquiring and dealing with food, a similar pattern emerges. The hunting patterns of animals such as weasels and wolves display amazing similarities, as do the food-gathering techniques of animals such as squirrels. These similarities are explained by the fact that such complex behaviours are unlearned, genetically transmitted, and species-wide; that is, they are instinctual. On the other hand, are there actions that characterize the behaviour of all humans as they attempt to acquire, prepare, or consume food? Indeed, there is perhaps no aspect of human existence that is more varied than our eating behaviour. The diversity of human conduct becomes more apparent if we begin with a simple consideration of what it is that we will accept as satisfaction for our basic nutritional requirements.

What sources of protein will we accept and will we be able to consume? Will we eat fish? If the answer is yes, then what species of fish do we find acceptable? Will we eat our fish cooked or raw? Will we eat the meat of the common domesticated hog? Are we able to tolerate the concept of eating the meat of a cow? What range of rodents do we find palatable? Are members of the trusty canine species legitimate objects of culinary interest? We could ask these questions about a whole range of other potential food sources, including insects, and get no consistent answer across the planet. This fact makes it possible to suggest that, when it comes to the acquiring, preparing, and consuming of food, human beings do not seem to be any more instinctively governed than we are in our sexual behaviour. Erich Goode provides a somewhat different take on

the issue by equating instincts with simpler behaviours; however, even by this understanding of instinct he concludes that 'these few instincts do not take us very far. They do not dictate any specific or complex forms of behaviour. We could not survive at birth on our instincts alone' (1999: 237). Perhaps there is an alternative concept to describe these simple behaviours.

There is also an important distinction to be made between instinct and *reflex*. Human beings exhibit a number of reflex-based actions and reactions such as the blinking of the eye, the movement of the leg when a specific point below the knee is tapped, sneezing when foreign objects invade the nose, and throwing out our arms when we lose our balance. Such behaviours are too simple to be considered the same as the more complex behaviour defined as instinct.

It is also important to differentiate instinct and reflex from other basic voluntary actions and involuntary physical or metabolic processes. Actions such as those involved in breathing, swallowing, digestion, the circulation of blood, and the internal production of bodily wastes are involuntary metabolic processes and not complex behaviours. In his overview of the role of reflexes in human conduct, Thomas Williams (1972) suggests that there are three levels of reflexes: the superficial, the deep, and the visceral. Superficial reflexes refer to such actions as eye blinking, and a deep reflex involves actions like the movement of the leg when an area below the knee is tapped. Visceral reflexes are related to processes such as digestion (29–30).

The central question is: how important are instincts and reflexes in influencing the overall repertoire of human conduct? The sociological answer to this question is 'not very important'. Sociologists maintain that humans are not well endowed with instincts and are therefore willing to make the controversial claim that little of our complex social behaviour can be explained in instinctual terms. But although our biological makeup may not have endowed us well in terms of instinctual behaviours that solve our needs and problems, we do have a unique set of physiological characteristics and features that have allowed us to develop solutions.

Human Physiology

Although sociologists tend to maintain that instincts are not particularly important factors in influencing human conduct, they do recognize that much of what we do and how we go about living our lives has a biological component to it. An argument could be made that we have a number of unique physiological characteristics that have allowed us to survive as a species. (See, for instance, the excellent summary of much of the literature relating to this debate in Robert Endleman's 'Reflections on the Human Revolution', 1977.)

Although numerous efforts have been made to catalogue the precise, unique physiological characteristics of human beings (see, for example, Schusky and Culbert, 1967), according to the classic work of A.M. Rose (1956: 96), humans possess nine important anatomical or physical characteristics:

1. erect posture
2. prehensile hands
3. forward vision
4. large and complex brain
5. complex voice mechanism
6. greater dependency in infancy and slow maturation
7. flexibility of needs and drives
8. constant sex drive
9. longevity

I want to argue that these biological features have clearly allowed human beings to survive and prosper. What is unique about our species is the extent to which we have used these traits to systematically develop ways of meeting our needs, solving our problems, and dealing with our drives. Although we may lack a significant instinctual basis for the

complex behaviour required to survive and prosper as a species, we have survived and prospered because of our tremendous capacities for creativity, innovation, and the development of solutions to problems that confront us. These capacities are predicated on our unique biological traits and characteristics.

Posture and Hands

In addition to allowing us to survey our immediate environment, our nearly perfect upright or erect posture has freed two of our appendages, our arms. Since we do not need our arms for simple locomotion, they have been made available for a variety of other uses, including tool manipulation. Our prehensile hands, with highly moveable fingers and opposable thumbs that can touch the fingers, have in turn allowed humans to become proficient at the construction and use of tools.

Take a moment to think about your hands, and especially your thumbs, and how vital they are to your various daily routines. You might prove this point to yourself by not using your thumbs for a day. Try taping your fingers together with your thumbs across your palms and see just how hard simple everyday tasks become. Clearly, our hands, with their fingers and opposable thumbs, are an important asset in our efforts to survive.

Vision

Our forward vision, though not as keen under some circumstances as in many other creatures, does allow us to perceive the world in a three-dimensional array of many colours. The capacity for three-dimensional vision is important for a creature that also engages in the systematic development of tools to assist its efforts to solve basic problems and meet basic needs.

Large and Complex Brain

Without our large and complex brain, the other listed attributes might not be as important. Indeed, one could argue that none of the other features would have been as decisive if they were not coupled to our huge and complex brain. The human brain is one of the most complex organs within all of the animal kingdom. Its size and degree of complexity plus the highly developed cerebral cortex make it unique among animal life forms.

First, our brain gives us the capacity for 'creative intelligence', the simple ability to think, reason, and generally 'figure things out'. In addition, our brain gives us the capacity to remember and recall what we 'figured out' and how we acted to solve some problem. As a result, the human being, when confronted with a problem or driven by a need, resorts to thought, reflection, deliberation, and the use of reason. Once we 'work out' a solution, we retain it in our memory and revert to that action when we are confronted with a similar problem or situation in the future. It is clear that these attributes have been vital in our species' survival and dominance. Imagine a scene in which some of our earlier ancestors are attempting to get some tree fruit that is beyond their reach. After several hours of jumping and not being able to reach the fruit, one of them picks up a nearby stick and waves it at the tree, accidentally knocking the fruit down. The lesson may not have been learned the first time, but if it were accidentally repeated, the person would probably 'discover' that a stick can be a useful tool when it comes to getting this particular fruit. The stick may very well become a part of that person's learned behavioural repertoire for dealing with the need for food. The lesson here? Humans are tool-users, and we have the capacity to remember how we did something, so the next time we face a similar situation we have a learned solution at hand.

An additional capacity afforded by our large and multifaceted brain is the ability to develop complex and abstract patterns of communication. No other species seems to have developed as varied forms of communication as humans have. This is not to argue that non-human animals do not communicate, for it is clear that they do, through sounds, physical gestures, colour changes, and even

odours. The well-known example of the honeybee communicating the direction and distance of food to other bees through a series of complicated dancing motions illustrates the sophisticated information that animals can pass on to each other. Many animals have ways of communicating with other members of their species to provide information about matters such as the presence of danger or their availability for mating. A variety of animals can also communicate with the members of other species, as in the case of a dog baring its teeth and growling or a cat arching its back and hissing—to indicate to all present that it considers their actions a threat and that it is prepared to take action.

Most of this non-human communication is governed by instinctual processes and is thus quite different from human communication. Animal signals make up what Charles F. Hockett and Robert Ascher (1964) refer to as closed call systems. In a closed call system the reasons for an animal producing a signal, the signal itself, and the response of other animals are often fixed; that is, they are instinctual and not within the conscious control of the animal. Stated differently, the various signals that non-human animals use to communicate are often inborn, species-wide, and unlearned reactions to particular stimuli, and to the extent that other animals respond in some manner, that response is often also inborn, species-wide, and unlearned. No deliberate or conscious thought goes into producing or interpreting the signal.

It is common in the social sciences to refer to the kinds of signals we have been discussing as *gestures*. A gesture is defined as a physical movement or vocal sound that is meant to communicate. The physical gestures utilized in the non-human world are often instinctively based. When, for example, a beaver receives a stimulus from its surroundings that it perceives as a danger or as representing a threat, its instinctual response is to slap its tail on the water. Other beavers hearing or observing the slap receive it as a specific stimulus and respond in an instinctively determined manner by diving, fleeing, or otherwise attempting to move to positions of safety. Similarly, the white-tailed deer indicates the presence of danger with a wave of its tail. Other members of the species know that gesture as a message that danger is present, and they will attempt to flee. Non-human animals also use a variety of vocal gestures, such as a wolf's cry, the song of a bird, or a frog's croak. To the extent that these gestures are instinctual, they are produced automatically by stimuli in the environment, and other animals receiving them likewise respond in a pre-programmed, species-wide, and invariant manner.

Human beings also use gestures; however, the nature of the gestures we use and their significance for our survival make the use patterns among humans qualitatively different. It is clear that as a species we are unique in the extent to which we use gestures and in the kinds of gestures we use. In our communications with each other we do not just use physical movements, although 'body language' can be important in human communication. More than any other species we communicate through the use of vocal gestures, and we are unique in our use of written gestures, like those you are reading now. The special and different dimension to our use of objects and vocal gestures is found in the *symbolic nature of our gestures.*

In his classic 1944 essay on the nature of human beings, Ernst Cassirer (1977) explicitly notes that humans inhabit a symbolic and not just a physical universe. Cassirer's basic point is that there are few, if any, gestures that humans use that have a 'natural', unlearned, or instinctual basis to them. All the gestures we use in the process of our communications are symbolic in nature. This means that, whether they are physical movements, vocalizations, or physical objects, all our gestures have arbitrary meanings attached to them. In this sense the word *arbitrary* refers to the fact that the gestures, symbols, and signs we use to communicate have the meanings that the users assign to them and not any instinctual basis. For example, many four-letter

combinations taken from the English alphabet can be put together in ways that are generally considered to be offensive. Why do people find these particular combinations offensive? It is not because we have an instinctual response to specific combinations. On the contrary, certain words are considered to be offensive, obscene, or profane because some arbitrary and historical process has defined them that way. Our symbols of human communication are arbitrary designations or expressions without some species-wide 'natural' meaning attached to them. After stressing the importance of symbols in human existence, Cassirer argues that we can define humans as *animal symbolicum* because the use of symbols is the key to understanding the human capacity to think, communicate, and respond. Indeed, it is the key to understanding most human behaviour. Leslie White makes a similar point even more forcefully by recounting the story of the transformation of Helen Keller, once her teacher was able to reach her at the symbolic level. White is definitive: 'Human behaviour is symbolic behaviour; if it is not symbolic it is not human' ([1949] 2001: 35). He goes on to claim that it is by being introduced to culture that the 'infant of the genus *Homo* becomes human being' (35).

Consider the difference between human symbolic communication and non-human instinctual communication within the context of a particular process, mating. When a non-human animal is ready to mate, it indicates its state to others by means of an instinctual behaviour we can call a sign. Because the behaviour is instinctual, all other members of that species receiving the sign will respond accordingly, indicating that they are either ready or not ready. Can you think of a similar pattern in human affairs or human conduct? Are there patterns of behaviour, words, body language, or indeed physical objects, such as clothing, that mean the same thing across cultures and historical epochs? Those of us who happen to live in a Western culture know a variety of actions, body movements, or phrases that are used to indicate romantic interest in another individual; but to what extent are these actions and symbolic behaviours understood correctly in other cultures? Cross-cultural studies tell us that the simple act of making eye contact with another person has a broad range of different meanings in different cultures.

In a fascinating essay, 'The Sounds of Silence', Edward Hall and Mildred Reed Hall (1982) examine the cultural-specific uses of various forms of body language, including the use of the eye and eye contact, the meanings of distance (how far we position ourselves from others when we are in conversation with them), and even the meanings attached to different leg positions (83–7). One of their essential conclusions is that the meanings we attach to these various modes of non-verbal communication are learned; that is, they are cultural.

Sociologists argue that there is no evidence that a behaviour or symbol with a particular meaning in one culture is going to have a similar meaning in another. A simple act like the raising of a clenched fist can mean many different things in different cultures. In our culture such a physical gesture can have a variety of meanings, ranging from joking with a friend or indicating 'third down' in the Canadian Football League, to physically threatening someone; or it might even be a sign of defiance and determination to continue some ongoing conflict. Similarly, a series of words such as 'I feel really cool' could mean a number of different things depending on the speaker and the context within which the words are uttered. Human communication is complex, and it is clear that the meanings of the gestures used can only be understood within the social and cultural context of a system that assigns meanings to various kinds of symbols.

The most common forms of gesture used by humans are systems of vocalizations and written symbols. We know that over time, sets and systems of symbols tend to become codified and established into what we call language, and an understanding of the role of language is one further key to the study of human behaviour. The insights of the domain of linguistics, the study of language, are useful in explaining the nature of human communications. Andrew Crider and his co-authors define language as 'a form of communication characterized by semanticality, generativity, and displacement' (1989: 296).

Semanticality refers to the requirement that a language has an established system of meanings to it. We recognize that very young children will vocalize, although we don't accept the sounds as language because they lack the systematized meaning that we assume is essential to language. The distinction between a series of sounds we call a language from another series of sounds that might be randomly produced and called noise is found in the fact that the sounds we call language have systematic meanings attached to them.

Generativity refers to the flexibility of human language. Speaking a human language is a creative process that brings innumerable combinations of words into different arrangements to convey different meanings. In the course of our daily communications we use many words over and over again, but as we arrange and rearrange the order of these words the meaning varies.

Displacement refers to the ability of human languages to transcend a particular time and place. Human languages allow their users to communicate about events that occurred in the past, or that are occurring in the present in distant locations, or that might occur in the future. In short, we communicate about phenomena and events beyond the limits of our immediate existence. We are not confined in our communications to the here and now.

Human beings have developed elaborate systems of vocal and written symbols, and widely understood rules and modes of combining sounds and words govern the use of those systems. Those systems of language allow the creative combination of sounds and words to communicate vast amounts of information. The development and use of such systems of symbolic communications have been an essential part of the process of human survival, an essential part of our human behaviour. Once we have 'worked out' or discovered a solution to one of our many problems, we can pass on that information, thereby enabling others to benefit from our experiences. Because we use these systems, each new generation does not have to solve the same problems all over again, and humans can accumulate knowledge, understanding, skills, tools, and artifacts. We do not have to continually 'reinvent the wheel'.

Vocal Capacities

The human ability to develop symbolic systems of communication is dependent on our large and complex brain; but the emergence and use of language are related to our sound-producing organs. The human larynx, throat structures, tongue, and lips all contribute to our species' capacity to make an enormous variety of sounds. The thousands of existing languages and dialects used around the world in human communication indicate how flexible our sound-producing capacities are. The development of the symbolic codes that make up these languages is a spectacular feat that only a species with an amazing brain could accomplish. The actual vocalization of the many arbitrary sounds that make up the systems of sounds we call language is an equally demanding feat that only a creature with our particular vocal capacities could master. Our domesticated dogs, cats, cows, and horses can make a fair number of different sounds, but no matter how hard we try, or how much time we spend with them, we can't teach a cat to sound like a dog or a cow to sound like a horse. Our children, however, quickly develop the ability to make sounds similar to all of these animals as well as, potentially, the sounds of many different human languages.

Long Dependency Period

It is ironic that the amazing creature we have been describing—mobile, with free appendages, intelligent, communicative, and vocal—should also be so

relatively incompetent at birth. If we were to develop a scale of how competent and capable of looking after themselves various animals are at birth, the human species would rank near the bottom. It is a biological fact that we are incapable of caring for ourselves at birth and that we are dependent on the care and attention of others for a long period of time after birth. Richard Leakey has turned his attention to the question of why humans have such a long dependency period. He concludes that the problem is in part because of the fact that human babies are born too early. His explanation runs as follows:

> This may sound odd, but it has to do with the extraordinary large brain of which we are so proud. The large brain is associated with a slowing down and a lengthening of our species' life history factors such as sexual maturity and longevity. If we were to do the calculations for length of gestation based on our brain size, we would arrive at a figure of twenty-one months, not nine months. As a result, for almost the first year after birth human babies live like embryos, growing very fast but remaining essentially helpless. (Leakey, 1992: 159–60)

Leakey further argues that a gestation of 21 months would produce a baby that is physically incompatible with the size of the human birth canal, and thus the necessity of being born somewhat prematurely. He notes that one of the important post-natal changes is the continued rapid growth of the brain which 'more than triples in size between birth and maturity' (160). Elsewhere, he suggests that our extended dependency period is linked to the emergence of the patterns of social learning that, as we will see, characterize human beings (145). The precise length of this dependency period varies from culture to culture. In Canada, for example, if you asked the parents of a typical first-year university student about the length of the dependency period in our society, you might receive a cry of anguish in return: 'nineteen years and counting!' Apparently, our lack of instincts makes us ill-equipped to survive, while our long period of dependency provides the required time for learning what we need to know to survive.

Flexibility of Needs and Drives

Our biological and physiological makeup gives us the ability to digest and utilize a wide variety of protein sources, illustrating one of our central biological characteristics, the flexibility of our needs satisfaction. The materials that satisfy our basic needs for food, clothing, or shelter are almost infinitely variable, differing radically from location to location and from historical period to historical period.

Constant Sex Drive

The idea of the human sex drive as constant does not mean—depictions of our species in the movies and on television aside—that the human species is in a continuous state of readiness for sexual activity. The point refers instead to the human capacity to reproduce at any time of the year. Unlike most other animals, humans have no particular seasons during which we go 'into heat' and during which time fertilization must take place.

Longevity

Although some animals do live as long or even longer than humans, for the most part our species has a relatively long lifespan. And because we live for quite a long time we have abundant opportunities to use all the other various human characteristics in the pursuit of solutions to our various problems.

What do these unique characteristics have to do with how we as a species meet our needs, solve our problems, and deal with our drives? For one thing, sociologists conclude that human beings are not well equipped instinctively to deal with their needs, drives, and problems; instead, they argue, humans have developed *social modes of conduct* to

satisfy their needs, solve their problems, and allow them to deal with their drives. These patterns of behaviour or modes of conduct are social, that is, they involve social interaction with others. As a discipline, sociology is very much interested in understanding and analyzing these modes of social conduct. In the process of undertaking this task sociologists have adopted an approach that places emphasis on the concept of culture.

Culture: The Work of Ruth Benedict and Margaret Mead

To survive and prosper as a species, humans have developed 'ways of doing things'. This notion will serve as a preliminary definition for a central concept in the study of human behaviour: *culture.* The field of cultural anthropology has provided essential material for anyone seeking to understand human behaviour, and in their work in particular, Margaret Mead and Ruth Benedict have provided valuable examples of cross-cultural studies; that is, of several different sociocultural systems that represent different ways of doing things.

Patterns of Culture

Ruth Benedict's book *Patterns of Culture,* first published in 1934, examines three different peoples who had developed three different modes of organizing their lives and solving their problems—three different ways of doing things.

The first people Benedict discusses are the Pueblo Indians of the American Southwest. She described three groupings, the Acoma, Zuni, and Hopi, who lived in an arid region with poor soil and little wild game yet enjoyed a relatively comfortable material existence. They raised sheep, had developed a system of irrigation to water orchards and cornfields, and had sophisticated bow and arrow technology for hunting game. They had also developed advanced architecture, which they used to construct elaborate cliff dwellings and large, well-planned urban settlements.

For the Pueblo society, as Benedict notes, rituals, ceremonies, dances, and rites associated with strong religious beliefs were central organizing dynamics in yearly social cycles. Much of the adult life of males was spent in preparation for, and actually conducting, religious activities. The religious activities of the Pueblo people were highly ceremonial, involving complex rites and rituals that had to be conducted in a precise manner with little or no room for innovation or variation. Males spent long periods of their lives learning the correct performance of these rites and rituals.

The family structures in traditional Pueblo society were organized along matriarchal lines, so that the women controlled lines of descent and owned and controlled the material assets in the household. The women owned both the house and the corn stored in it, while males may have produced them. Economic activity was organized communally, with much of the produce ending up in a common or communal storehouse that housed the collective property of the women. The communal and co-operative orientation of the society meant that it was rare for individuals or family members to go without having their basic material needs taken care of. Sharing and mutual care were important.

The Pueblo people were peace-loving. Indeed, the avoidance of strife and conflict was of paramount importance. The ideal individual sought to co-operate with others at all times, avoid strong emotions, and never stand out from the crowd. Benedict notes that the statement 'No one ever hears anything from him' (91) was among the highest praise a man could receive. Although the language Benedict used was cast in the masculine, it is safe to assume the same would apply to women. The ideal individual always put the needs and interests of the collectivity first, claiming no personal authority. Individuals attempted to avoid office, agreeing to a position of authority only after their arguments about why they should not hold office had been shown to be inadequate. When they did gain an official position of some sort, individuals demonstrated as little authority and leadership qualities as possible.

For the Pueblo, the universe was essentially a place of harmony. There was a time and a season for everything. Little was made of death because it was widely accepted that death and life were part of a larger cycle of existence in the universe.

The typical Pueblo personality as Benedict saw it, then, was one of dedication to the community and the welfare of others. Such a person would be peace-loving, inoffensive, and subordinate to the group. These people would value sobriety and harmony and go out of their way to avoid conflict, competition, or any behaviour that would make them stand out from the larger collectivity. They would live their lives in the knowledge that the universe was indeed a place of harmony and peace. They would understand that 'The seasons unroll themselves before us, and man's life also.'

Ruth Benedict follows her description of life among the Pueblo with a picture of how another people in a very different part of the world organized their existence: the residents of Dobu Island, located near the shores of New Guinea.

The Dobu also lived in a difficult environment, this one an island that was volcanic and had little good soil. The area also lacked substantial sea-based resources such as fish or other sea life. The Dobu had nevertheless developed elaborate patterns of behaviour to deal with their various needs and were surviving handily when Europeans arrived in the area. These modes of organizing and conducting themselves were radically different from those of the Pueblo.

The Dobu had a reputation for being dangerous. Indeed, Benedict notes that before European colonization of the region the Dobu were cannibals. Whereas the Pueblo valued peace and harmony, the Dobu 'put a premium on ill will and treachery and make of them the recognized virtues of their society'. By the cultural standards of twentieth-century North America the Dobu were 'lawless and treacherous' (121). According to Benedict theirs was a society in which no one trusted anyone and everyone seemed to be only interested in seeking personal gain, at the expense of others if necessary.

The Dobu had no religion in the sense of an acknowledged deity or a series of codified beliefs, although they believed in and practised magic. There were no formal political structures, no acknowledged leaders or chiefs, and no legal system, at least not one formally organized and acknowledged as legitimate by most members of the society.

Personal conduct was essentially governed by the simple principle that you could do almost anything you could get away with. As Benedict notes, this was not a situation of anarchy in that there were limits and rules concerning the expressions of aggressive behaviour. These limits or rules were based on concentric circles of acceptable violence, which start with members of the matriarchal family. As members moved out from the immediate family, differing degrees of hostility and aggression were acceptable for various relatives, fellow villagers, and finally those in neighbouring villages—those located in the outermost imagined circle. The limits were provided by the expected response of others in the community to a gross violation of these boundaries. Each person, knowing that violations of the limits would not be tolerated, recognized limits on personal behaviour. Put more simply, you could not get away with it so you did not do it.

The essential staple of the Dobu diet was the yam. Given the poor soil, crops were meagre and hunger an ever-present problem. Each mature member of the society maintained an individual garden for growing yams, and a person's seed yams were deemed to be a part of their heritage. Husbands and wives each maintained a separate garden and grew their own yams, although they did pool their produce for the purpose of feeding their children. This is one of the few instances of any degree of co-operation among the Dobu.

Relationships between wife and husband were based on considerable hostility and mistrust. The Dobu were sexually active before marriage, with much of this sexual activity occurring in the home of the girl. A formal marriage ceremony took place when the mother of a female prevented a male from leaving her home after he had spent the night, perhaps after the male had become accustomed to spending a lot of time with the particular girl. There was no acknowledged phenomenon equivalent to the Western conception of romantic love, a point Benedict makes clear: 'Faithfulness is not expected between husband and wife, and no Dobuan will admit that a man and a woman are together even for the shortest interval except for sexual purposes' (127).

Dobu culture valued an extreme form of individualism. Individuals did not expect to receive favours from anyone, and they certainly gave none. According to Benedict, 'All existence is cutthroat competition, and every advantage is gained at the expense of a defeated rival' (130). Benedict's final comments on the Dobu summarize their culture and personalities:

> Life in Dobu fosters extreme forms of animosity and malignancy which most societies have minimized by their institutions. Dobuan institutions, on the other hand, exalt them to the highest degree. The Dobuan lives out without repression man's worst nightmares of the ill-will of the universe, and according to his view of life virtue consists in selecting a victim upon whom he can vent the malignancy he attributes alike to human society and to the powers of nature. All existence appears to him as a cutthroat struggle in which deadly antagonists are pitted against one another in a contest for each one of the goods of life. Suspicion and cruelty are his trusted weapons in the strife and he gives no mercy, as he asks none. (159)

Benedict's third society, the Native people of the Northwest Coast of North America, represented a radical contrast to both the Dobu and the Pueblo peoples. The Indians of the Northwest, in particular the Kwakiutl, were a people of great material wealth. The locale they inhabited was bountiful, with a rich variety of resources including abundant marine life, game, timber, and other products of the forest. As a result, the Kwakiutl were a people of great possessions, a commercial people, and they had sophisticated networks of trading relations including a complex system of currency that used shells and sheets of copper as the means of exchange. The commercial aspects of the society were developed to the point that they had arrangements for loans and the charging of interest payable in currency.

In traditional Kwakiutl society wealth was considered strictly private property and tended to belong to males. Two types of possessions were important: material and non-material. On the material side were fishing areas, hunting grounds, berry-picking territories, houses, currency, and other material forms of wealth. But individuals could also own non-material items, including names, rights, myths, songs, and stories. For the men in this society the ownership of possessions, both material and non-material, provided the basis of their position in the society. In Kwakiutl society men were very much concerned with their position in a social hierarchy, and they were constantly attempting to demonstrate their superiority through the accumulation of possessions. For students of twentieth-century North American society, this idea is not at all alien; however, in Kwakiutl society there was a significant difference in how members used their personal wealth to demonstrate superiority.

A central feature of Kwakiutl society was the potlatch, a complex ceremony involving the exchange of massive amounts of wealth. Although there were significant variations in the details of how the potlatch was conducted and what kind of transactions took place, one aspect was common: it was essentially an opportunity for individual men to demonstrate their superiority either by giving more wealth to a rival than the rival would be able to

return, or by publicly destroying their own wealth. The potlatch was an event or ceremony that might be held in conjunction with any number of events: a birth or a death, a high-status marriage, the raising of a carved pole, a naming, or even an accident. Because they occurred frequently, the events had a significant impact on the social distribution of wealth across the society. All participants at a potlatch received some form of gift, although those nearer the bottom of the social hierarchy received less. As a result of the potlatch, no one person or family went without the necessities of life, although because of the society's abundant material wealth, the process went beyond the simple sharing that was more common in Pueblo society.

In her description of the Kwakiutl, Benedict provides rich detail of the exuberant behaviour that characterized many aspects of their culture, including religion. Whereas the Pueblo peoples were deeply religious, their religious rituals were routinized to an extreme degree, with each step being choreographed in detail. The religious activities of the Kwakiutl were characterized by attempts to reach states of ecstasy during which individuals lost control of their behaviour. Indeed, Benedict reports that at times dancers had to be tethered with ropes to prevent them from doing harm to themselves or others around them.

Benedict's Main Thesis

Ruth Benedict's book is a classic in its field and deserves to be read in its entirety because she provides a wealth of detail and an analytical style that is impossible to summarize. For students of sociology, Benedict's study of different cultures raises important questions. First of all, she offers information on an array of diverse cultures, behaviours, and personalities. How are we to make sense of this material? What does her study tell us about human conduct, society, behaviour, and, indeed, 'human nature'? If by human nature we mean biologically based, unlearned, species-wide, and invariant behaviour, is there such a thing?

According to the evidence provided by Benedict, there are few, if any, species-wide, invariant, unlearned, complex behaviours by which humans solve their basic problems and meet their basic needs. One of the central points she makes is that in our attempts to understand human conduct and personalities, the concept of culture is more appropriate than the concept of instinct. She argues that it is possible to understand human beings and human behaviour as flexible, variable, and malleable to the point that we are capable of organizing our societies and developing personalities in a fashion similar to that found in Zuni or Dobu or Kwakiutl society. She says it is possible that other humans can come to *learn* to act in a manner similar to the typical resident of Dobu or Hopi society. Benedict's argument raises important questions about just how 'flexible' or 'malleable' we are.

Sex and Temperament in Three 'Primitive' Societies

Margaret Mead's *Sex and Temperament in Three Primitive Societies* adopts an approach similar to Benedict's. First published in 1935, and reprinted numerous times since, Mead's study also discusses the social organization and behaviour characteristic of three different societies, although her focus is more on a comparative analysis of the general

NATURE/NUTURE

Perhaps no book articulating a rigorous biological determinist point of view has had the impact of *The Naked Ape* by Desmond Morris. Morris is a prolific writer and by any standard *The Naked Ape* has been a commercial success. First published in 1967, it has undergone many subsequent editions. The excerpts presented here are from the introduction, the discussions of sexual behaviour and fighting, and the conclusion.

The Naked Ape

There are one hundred and ninety-three living species of monkeys and apes. One hundred and ninety-two of them are covered with hair. The exception is a naked ape self-named *Homo sapiens*. This unusual and highly successful species spends a great deal of time examining his higher motives and an equal amount of time studiously ignoring his fundamental ones. He is proud that he has the biggest brain of all the primates, but attempts to conceal the fact that he also has the biggest penis, preferring to accord this honour falsely to the mighty gorilla. He is an intensely vocal, acutely exploratory, over-crowded ape, and it is high time we examined his basic behaviour.

I am a zoologist and the naked ape is an animal. He is therefore fair game for my pen and I refuse to avoid him any longer simply because some of his behaviour patterns are rather complex and impressive. My excuse is that, in becoming so erudite, *Homo sapiens* has remained a naked ape nevertheless; in acquiring lofty new motives, he has lost none of the earthy old ones. This is frequently a cause of some embarrassment to him, but his old impulses have been with him for millions of years, his new ones only a few thousand at the most—and there is no hope of quickly shrugging off the accumulated genetic legacy of his whole evolutionary past. He would be a far less worried and more fulfilled animal if only he would face up to this fact. Perhaps this is where the zoologist can help *(9)*.

On Competition and Fighting

Animals fight amongst themselves for one of two very good reasons: either to establish their dominance in a social hierarchy, or to establish their territorial right over a particular piece of ground. Some species are purely hierarchical, with no fixed territories. Some are purely territorial, with no hierarchy problems. Some have hierarchies on their territories and have to contend with both forms of aggression. We belong to the last group: we have it both ways. As primates we were already loaded with the hierarchy system. This is the basic way of primate life *(146–7)*.

On the Fixed Nature of Our Sexual Conduct

Looking back now on the whole sexual scene we can see that our species has remained much more loyal to its basic biological urges than we might at first imagine. Its primate sexual system with carnivore modifications has survived all the fantastic technological advances remarkably well. If one took a group of twenty suburban families and placed them in a primitive sub-tropical environment where the males had to go off hunting for food, the sexual structure of this new tribe would require little or no modification. In fact, what has happened in every large town or city is that the individuals it contains have specialized in their hunting (working) techniques, but have retained their socio-sexual system in more or less its original form *(101)*.

Conclusion

Optimism is expressed by some who feel that since we have evolved a high level of intelligence and a strong inventive urge, we shall be able to twist any situation to our advantage; that we are so flexible that we can re-mould our way of life to fit any of the new demands made by our rapidly rising species-status; that when the time comes, we shall manage to cope with the overcrowding, the stress, the loss of our privacy and independence of action; that we shall re-model our behaviour patterns and live like giant ants; that we shall control our aggressive and territorial feelings, our sexual impulses and our parental tendencies; that if we have to become battery chicken-apes, we can do it; that our intelligence can dominate all our basic biological urges. I submit that this is rubbish. Our raw animal nature will never permit it. Of course, we are flexible. Of course, we are behavioural opportunists, but there are severe limits to the form our opportunism can take *(241)*.

The Naked Ape, by Desmond Morris, published by Jonathan Cape. *Reprinted by permission of The Random House Group Ltd.*

temperament and characteristics of females and males. The cultures she discusses were located physically much closer to each other; all of them were located in New Guinea. Mead provides a wealth of interesting data on the cultures she studies, including social structures, physical organization, and typical patterns of behaviour. Most important for our purposes is what she says about the essential differences between these peoples.

The three cultures Mead discusses are the Arapesh, the Mundugumor, and the Tchambuli. Although each of these peoples inhabited quite different physical environments, it is the differences in their social organization that are striking. The Arapesh, for instance, are a people who lived in a harsh mountain environment and spent a great deal of their time attempting to wrestle the bare necessities of survival out of that difficult terrain. Although

Margaret Mead is a hugely influential anthropologist. Her first work of influence was *Sex and Temperament in Three Primitive Societies*, first published in 1935. This study discussed the social organization and behaviour characteristics of three different societies. Here, Mead is shown on a field trip to Manus, Papua, New Guinea, 1953–4. (CP Picture Archive)

this environment is similar in many ways to that of the Dobu, the mode of social organization developed by the Arapesh was quite different. Mead characterizes the Arapesh as a peace-loving people whose conduct was marked by co-operation and sociability. In her focus on the typical conduct of the female and male members of society, Mead notes that there were few outward personality differences. Indeed, this was a people who had taken virtually every step possible to minimize the differences between the sexes, although certain activities were organized on the basis of sex. Heavy lifting was one. The mountainous environment demanded a lot of lifting and hauling, and women did most of the heavy work because it was common knowledge in this society that women were physically better suited for such work.

In their sexual activities, Mead saw a uniform lack of interest and ambition among both females and males. Indeed, she concludes her discussion of the Arapesh by noting how difficult it is for the Western mind to understand what the Arapesh typically believe about women and men: 'That both men and women are naturally maternal, gentle, responsive and not aggressive' (1971: 157).

The Mundugumor and the Arapesh were, like the Dobu and the Pueblo, a study in contrasts. Whereas the Arapesh were a peace-loving agricultural people, the Mundugumor were hunters and formerly cannibals. Unlike the Arapesh, the Mundugumor were a rich people with abundant natural resources in their region. While the very poor Arapesh valued children and lavished a great amount of love and attention on them, the typical Mundugumor child was not valued; children were ignored and even mistreated. Infanticide, the killing of children, was not uncommon, and as Mead notes, those not hurled into the river after birth were 'treated most summarily and exposed to many risks to which young children are not subjected among the most primitive peoples' (185).

Given the biological connection between sexual activity and reproduction, one of the reasons for the lack of interest and affection for the young might be the Mundugumor's attitudes towards sexual activity. The Mundugumor tendency to be individualistic and violent was carried over to their modes of conduct surrounding sexual intercourse. Both females and males were sexually active and neither simply waited passively for the other to take the initiative. The act of sexual intercourse was marked by extreme passion and even violence, after which each of the participants showed signs of the encounter in the form of scratches and bites.

There were also several forms of marriage among the Mundugumor. In spite of their propensity for sexual activity, the Mundugumor valued virginity: a virgin was highly valued as a marriage partner by both sexes, as testified to by the fact that a virgin could only marry another person who was also a virgin. But the most common form of marriage was between partners who were both known to have had sexual experiences. The final form of marriage was arranged marriages, often as a result of some larger social process such as peacemaking.

If a Western mind has difficulty understanding a society in which both sexes demonstrate little sexual ambition or a society in which both sexes are relatively aggressive, it will reel at the conduct of women and men among Mead's third group, the Tchambuli. Although property among the Tchambuli was organized along patriarchal lines, with men formally owning gardens and household property, women were the central economic actors. The primary source of food for the lake-dwelling Tchambuli was the fishing activity of the women and their work in the gardens. The major activities of the men were related to their ceremonies and their art. As Mead notes: 'Every man is an artist and most men are skilled not in some art alone, but in many: in dancing, carving, plaiting, painting, and so on. Each man is chiefly concerned with his role upon the stage of his society, with the elaboration of his costume, the beauty of the masks that he owns, the skill of his own flute playing, the finish and *élan* of his ceremonies, and upon other people's recognition and valuation of his performance' (231).

The women's position of dominance in economic matters carried over into the realm of personal and sexual matters. The women initiated courtship, mating, and marriage. Men worked hard at their ceremonies and on occasion as traders, hoping that their tasks would receive approval and praise from their wives. The wife, Mead states, controlled the real property required to survive, and her attitude towards her man was one of 'kindly tolerance and appreciation' (239).

The Anthropologists' Central Lesson
The work of Mead, Benedict, and others in the field of cultural anthropology reminds us that while all

COUNTERPOINT: THE POLITICS OF BIOLOGICAL DETERMINISM

Stephen Jay Gould is prominent among the many scientists who have critiqued both the science and the politics of biological determinism. Gould's *The Mismeasure of Man* was one of the first systematic critiques. Although the following article focuses on the issue of biology and IQ, and was published in a journal devoted to educational issues, Gould's introductory comments are an excellent summary of the political and social issues that emerge from the assumptions that we are biologically or genetically fixed in our places in society.

Why the Longing to Attribute Everything to Genes?

I regard the critique of biological determinism as both timeless and timely. It is timeless because the errors of biological determinism are so deep and insidious and appeal to the worst manifestations of our common nature. It is timely because the same bad arguments recur every few years with a predictable and depressing regularity.

No mystery attends the reason for these recurrences. They are not manifestations of some underlying cyclicity, obeying a natural law that might be captured in a mathematical formula as convenient as IQ; nor do these episodes represent any hot item of new data or some previously unconsidered novel twist in argument.

The reasons for recurrence are sociopolitcal and are not hard to find. Resurences of biological determinism correlate with episodes of political retrenchment, particularly with campaigns for reduced government spending on social programs, or at times of fear among ruling elites, when disadvantaged groups sow serious social unrest or even threaten to usurp power.

Twentieth-century America has experienced three major episodes of biological determinism: the first around the introduction of the IQ test in America in the years following World War I; the second beginning in 1969; and most recently in an episode that kicked off in 1994 with the publication of *The Bell Curve*.

These episodes of biological determinism have served useful socio-political purposes. What argument against social change could be more chillingly effective than the claim that established orders, with some groups on top and others at the bottom, exist as an accurate reflection of the innate and unchangeable intellectual capacities of people so ranked? Why struggle and spend to raise the unboostable IQ of races or social classes at the bottom of the economic ladder?—better simply to accept nature's unfortunate dictates and save a passel of federal funds. (We can then more easily sustain tax breaks for the wealthy!) Why bother yourself about underrepresentation of disadvantaged groups in your honored and remunerative bailiwick if such absence records the diminished ability or general immorality, biologically imposed, of most members in the rejected group, and not the legacy or current reality of social prejudice?

The new upsurge of biological determinism in this century constitutes one of the saddest ironies of US history. We like to think of America as a land with generally egalitarian traditions, a nation 'conceived in liberty and dedicated to the proposition that all men are created equal'. We recognize, *au contraire*, that many European nations, with their long histories of monarchy, feudal order, and social stratification, have been less committed to ideas of social justice or equality of opportunity. Since the IQ test originated in France, we might naturally assume that the false hereditarian interpretations, so commonly and so harmfully imposed upon the tests, arose in Europe. Ironically, this reasonable assumption is entirely false.

Alfred Binet, the French inventor, not only avoided a hereditaian interpretation of his test, but explicitly (and fervently) warned against such a reading as a perversion of his desire to use the tests for identifying children who needed special help. (Binet argued that an innatist interpretation would only stigmatize children as unteachable, producing a result opposite to his intent—a fear entirely and tragically justified by later history.)

humans around the world face a series of common problems that must be solved if we are to survive as individuals and as groups, we do not go about solving these problems and meeting our needs in similar ways. Indeed, we have developed incredibly diverse and different ways of solving our problems and dealing with our drives and needs. Each of the societies that Benedict and Mead studied had developed unique and successful modes of conduct for dealing with its individual and species needs and problems. Each of these peoples had developed systems of action and interaction, modes of conduct, sets of beliefs and ideals, as well as tools, technology, and associated skills and knowledge. Each of them had established a culture that formed a basis for its individual and group survival. Each of these cultures was in turn characterized by a set of beliefs, stocks of knowledge, and established practices that allowed its members to exist in their particular environment.

But before we attempt to develop generalized statements concerning human beings on the basis of the cultural anthropologists' studies, we should note that their works have been subject to considerable criticism and debate. Margaret Mead's work in particular has been the subject of systematic criticism—although Lowell Holmes, who extensively studied the criticisms and Mead's work, concluded that there was much to recommend her work as a valid source of knowledge concerning human cultural behaviour (Holmes, 1985). To better appreciate what it is like to have an outsider describe your culture—that is, someone who might not understand the meaning and significance of many of your actions—North American readers might consult Horace Miner's 'Body Rituals Among the Nacirema' (1985). Among the features of the culture Miner describes are practices revolving around the oral cavity:

The Nacirema have an almost pathological horror of and fascination with the mouth, the condition of which is believed to have supernatural influence on all social relationships. Were it not for the rituals of the mouth, they believe their teeth would fall out, their gums bleed, their jaws shrink, their friends desert them, and their lovers reject them. They also believe that a strong relationship exists between oral and moral characteristics. For example, there is a ritual ablution on the mouth for children which is supposed to improve their moral fiber. (150)

By the way, did you brush your teeth or use mouthwash this morning?

The Characteristics of Culture

The concept of culture is widely used in the social sciences and, like many other concepts, is subject to considerable misunderstanding because different thinkers have used the term in different ways. Although social scientists have used a variety of definitions, they agree on one point, namely that the term does not simply apply to art, classical music, and the ballet. Indeed, social scientists tend to argue that eating a hot dog and drinking a soft drink at a football or hockey game is as much a part of Canadian culture as watching the Royal Winnipeg Ballet. In defining cultural activities social scientists follow the lead of Edward Tylor, who, in 1871, defined culture as 'that complex whole which includes knowledge, belief, art, morals, law, custom, and any other capacities and habits acquired by man as a member of society' (quoted in Schusky and Culbert, 1967: 35).

While Tylor's definition still provides a basis for understanding culture as being linked to virtually all aspects of human existence, others have further elaborated on the term. In the early 1950s, Alfred Kroeber and Clyde Kroeber studied various definitions of culture and developed a composite definition that has also become a standard reference in the field. They stated:

> Culture consists of patterns, explicit and implicit, of and for behaviour acquired and transmitted by symbols, constituting the distinctive achievements of human groups, including their embodiments in artifacts; the essential core of culture consists of traditional (i.e., historically derived and selected) ideas and especially their attached values. (quoted in Theodorson and Theodorson, 1969: 95)

In their *Modern Dictionary of Sociology*, the Theodorsons also provide a more compact definition: 'The way of life of a social group; the group's total man-made environment, including all the material and non-material products of group life that are transmitted from one generation to the next' (95).

Teasing a definition out of these various positions, we can conclude that culture is best understood as a group's total way of life, including two aspects of human existence. First, there are the shared *non-material human products* such as beliefs, myths, customs, habits, skills, or knowledge. The second aspect is the *material dimension*, the group's material artifacts and material products that have been developed over time as the group undertook the solving of its problems and the meeting of its needs. The material aspects of North American culture include everything from a Coke bottle to a streetlight, a hockey stick, and the latest high-technology recording of Beethoven's *Fifth Symphony*.

Ernest L. Schusky and T. Patrick Culbert (1967) provide a concise list of the essential features of culture. According to them, culture is shared, learned, cumulative, diverse, and complex. First, it must be *shared* by a group of people. Not every particular or idiosyncratic individual action or belief is cultural. In most Western societies the stamping of your foot when you sneeze and giggling after an inadvertent burp are not considered cultural patterns of behaviour, while using a phrase such as 'excuse me' or 'pardon me' is. One behaviour is widely shared by members of most Western societies while the other is not.

Culture is also *learned*. Human beings seem not to have an instinctual pre-programmed behaviour that leads them to engage in specific behaviour after they sneeze or burp. Indeed, the importance and meaning of a biological or physiological occurrence such as sneezing or burping are themselves cultural, because a loud burp after a meal is entirely appropriate, even complementary, in some cultures. Our attitudes towards such occurrences as well as our responses and behaviours are entirely learned.

As you read these words on a sheet of paper—words that first appeared as an electronic image on the screen of a word processor, consider the third

Culture is learned and developed by shared non-material human products such as beliefs, myths, customs, habit, and skill. It is shared, cumulative, diverse, and complex. Here, Leslie McGarry offers a Native welcoming gesture near a stunningly beautiful totem pole in Beacon Hill Park, British Columbia. The totem pole was actually carved by her great-grandfather Mungo Martin. (Photograph by Diana Nethercott)

characteristic of culture, its *cumulative* nature. The fact that you are in possession of a book made of paper and containing certain gems of wisdom in the English language is testimony to the accumulation of knowledge in Western society. But focus for a moment on the physical product in your hand. The knowledge and skills required to produce such an artifact are staggering, and it is essential to understand that this capacity has emerged out of the accumulation of knowledge stored and passed on from one generation to another, indeed from one century to another. Perhaps a better example might be a jumbo-jet airliner. Consider the accumulated knowledge and skills that made possible that particular physical artifact and its operation. Our culture is, in part, the legacy of thousands of years of history and development, thousands of years of humans accumulating skills, beliefs, and knowledge as well as developing technology and passing these on, largely through language. Cultural phenomenon must thus be understood as the cumulative outcome of the creative efforts of generation after generation of humans.

One of the essential characteristics of culture that emerges from a consideration of the work of anthropologists such as Mead and Benedict is its *diversity*. Any cursory anthropological examination of different cultures indicates the diversity in their organizational patterns, modes of behaviour, and action. What are the common elements in the forms of social organization and behaviour described by Benedict and Mead? The answer surely is that there are few if any common elements other than the fact that each of the peoples had developed social patterns of behaviour and action to solve problems and deal with needs. Indeed, every attempt to describe human behaviour and to make generalizations about common patterns arrives at one conclusion: human culture is incredibly diverse and varied. Added to this is its *complexity*. Culture encompasses every aspect of humanity's socially developed products in both the material and non-material spheres.

For sociologists, culture remains a general concept that serves to draw our attention to the fact that humans develop social solutions to their individual and species problems. The problem with the concept is that it may be too general to aid the analysis of specific behaviours and the development of the sociological imagination. What we need to do is locate culture in its larger context, as a part of human social structures.

Critical Thinking Questions

- Explain the concept of instinct as it is applied to animal studies. If we apply a rigourous definition, do humans have instincts? What evidence would you apply to support your answer?
- Are human needs fixed and unchanging, or are they socially, culturally, and historically conditioned? Or are they both? If they are both, provide examples of each.
- Are there universal cross-cultural and transhistorical human rights that might prohibit certain behaviours and activities? Do members of one culture have the right to criticize the cultural and social practices and conduct of another culture?
- What is cultural and what is natural about your behaviour and actions?
- Is your culture superior to, or 'better than', other cultures in any way? If you answer in the affirmative, how do you know?

Terms and Concepts

Need—a condition that produces a state of tension or dissatisfaction that in turn impels an organism to action; a requirement that must be met or satisfied if an organism is to survive; a condition requiring relief.

Drive—an impulse to action produced by a need. The basis of a drive is an organic condition or state. In sociology we assume most drives are directed by an organism's life-sustaining tendencies.

Instinct—a complex behavioural pattern that is unlearned, genetically transmitted, invariant among members of a species, and manifested the first time a triggering mechanism is present. Some examples of instinctual behaviours are the complex mating behaviours of many animals, nest-building among birds, and hunting behaviours in animals such as weasels. A behaviour is instinctual if an animal raised in isolation from other members of its species exhibits that behaviour the first time the triggering stimulus is in place.

Reflex—a simple involuntary behaviour that is unlearned and species-wide. As opposed to an instinct, a reflex is a simple action such as blinking an eye or moving the leg when tapped below the knee.

Gesture—a physical and audible action used in communication. A beaver slapping its tail on the water is a physical gesture to signal that danger is present, while a human yelling 'watch out' is an audible gesture. The use of and response to gestures in many non-human animals are instinctual.

Symbol—a gesture or sign that has an arbitrary, cultural, learned meaning as opposed to one that is species-wide, unlearned, or instinctual. A beaver slapping its tail on the water is a physical gesture while a human yelling 'watch out' is a form of symbolic communication. There is no unlearned, species-wide, invariant response among humans to the sounds that in English mean 'watch out'.

Language—a system of communication that uses a variety of gestures and symbols. Language is essential to human existence and survival, because social interaction and complex processes, such as socialization and cultural transmission, are dependent upon its use.

Culture—the totality of the various material and non-material aspects of human existence that characterize how a specific people live and 'do things.' The non-material dimension includes beliefs, myths, knowledge, ideas, ideals, values, habits, and traditions, while material artifacts are those human-made and natural products that have acquired a socially defined existence and use among a group of people. Culture is complex, shared, diverse, and cumulative.

Related Web Sites

http://www.interculturalstudies.org/IIS/index.html

    An Institute for Intercultural Studies Web site, it commemorates the centennial of Margaret Mead's birth. Among other things, this site provides extensive links to biographical material, material relating to her fieldwork, and awards in her name.

http://www.webster.edu/~woolflm/women.html

    Dr Linda M. Woolf at Webster University provides an excellent site through which one can access information on women in anthropology, psychology, psychoanalysis, and sociology. The extensive list contains well over one hundred names, some better known than others.

http://www.webster.edu/~woolflm/ruthbenedict.html

One of the many very informative sites accessible through Dr Woolf's site noted above, there is information here on Ruth Benedict's life and work with extensive references.

http://www.blackwellpublishing.com/linguist/Default.asp

Blackwell Publishing maintains a comprehensive site for those interested in the study of language and linguistics. It includes links to a number sources under General Indices as well as links under Theoretical Linguistics, and journal links.

http://www.cycad.com/cgi-bin/Brand/quotes/q05.html?nochoice=y

Chris Brand, Department of Psychology at the University of Edinburgh, has compiled the material on this site. It includes some introductory comments on the nature/nurture debate and a lengthy section of quotes and comments on the subject from a variety of sources.

Suggested Further Readings

Benedict, R. 1934. *Patterns of Culture*. New York: Mentor Books. This book still deserves a full reading after all these years in order to appreciate both the complexities of culture and her treatment of same.

Leakey, R., and R. Lewin. 1933. *Origins Revisited: In Search of What Makes Us Human*. New York: Anchor Books/Doubleday. This text provides an excellent overview of major contemporary issues in paleontology and an opportunity to see the minds of scientists in action as they re-examine the meaning of some important data.

Mead, M. [1935] 1971. *Sex and Temperament in Three Primitive Societies*. New York: William Morrow and Company. Along with Benedict, Mead's work, despite some controversy, remains required reading for both cultural and gender studies.

Segerstrale, U. 2000. *Defenders of Truth*. New York: Oxford University Press. A recent account is given of the ins and outs of the sociobiology debate. Good overviews of key positions are presented with critical insights about the implications for science.

CHAPTER 3

Social Structure and the Language of Sociology

The systematic examination of our selves, our species, and our society often results not only in seemingly mundane questions such as 'Why did I do that?' but also in more profound probing such as 'Why are economic resources unevenly distributed in society?' and 'How is power really distributed?' If we are to answer these questions satisfactorily, we must know something about the basic characteristics of the society. The process of determining the basic characteristics of a phenomenon is commonly referred to as analysis.

The verb *analyze* refers to a process of examining something in order to discover its basic components. If chemists analyzed the substance in the cup of coffee you had this morning they could provide you with a list of compounds and elements present in the liquid. We analyze, that is, resolve things into their elements or constitutive parts, so we can better understand the phenomena around us. The result of the process is an analysis.

The process of analyzing something can produce results that violate our common-sense impressions of the phenomenon. When we throw water on a fire we do not stop to think that we are really adding a combination of two gases, one that is essential for combustion and another that is highly explosive. Yet, chemical analysis tells us that is exactly what water is composed of. When literary critics analyze plays or novels by looking at their characters, formats, settings, dynamics, and composition, they may provide us with new insights into the material. Analysis is often essential to understanding, and this is certainly the case in sociology. Before we can understand the role of a society and its impact on the people within, we must know something about its basic structures, components, and processes.

One last word of warning. When we analyze something, we are often performing a somewhat 'unnatural' act in that we take apart and study the elements of what seems like a 'natural whole'—what already seems familiar and known to us. We may think because we have lived in a society all our lives that we pretty much understand the world around us on the basis of our common sense and lived experience. We may therefore find it unnatural to look at our everyday lived reality and experiences within the context of the basic concepts of the sociological perspective. The wholeness of our lived social reality is very real, but it is also, when systematically examined, too complex to be automatically or simply understood. To assist in making sense of this complex process of social living, sociologists use a specific set of concepts to refer to different parts of that whole, concepts that are the basis of the discipline and its modes of thinking.

Culture and Society

The culture we are born into and in which we develop influences and moulds much of our behaviour. There is virtually no evidence in the field of cultural anthropology of complex behaviours that are species-wide, invariant, and unlearned. All human beings have needs, drives, and problems they must solve if they are to survive, but there appear to be few if any inborn species-wide complex behaviours to deal with these needs, drives, and problems. From the evidence it seems that we are above all else cultural creatures. Still, in the discipline of sociology the concept of culture is usually considered part of something larger: society.

Society is a term used just as much in everyday language as in academic discourse, and it can take on many different meanings depending on the context. If many of you reading this book were asked what society you belong to, the answers might include the university debating club, the engineering students' association, or even the Society for the Prevention of Cruelty to Animals. These answers, in fact, relate to one of the first dictionary definitions: 'an organized group of persons associated together for religious, benevolent, cultural, scientific, political, patriotic, or other purposes'. The definitions in a standard English-language dictionary range widely, from the concept of people living as collective members of a community to the idea of 'the social life of wealthy, prominent, or fashionable persons' (people, for instance, 'step out in society'). The term can be used in the sense of a highly structured, large-scale, national organization ('Canadian society'); in an even more broad sense of a social system characterized by some economic form ('modern industrial society'); or in its older, once-primary meaning, companionship or fellowship (see, for instance, Williams, 1976: 291).

Clearly, sociologists have to begin once again by defining the term as precisely as possible in order to assist our understanding of our social life. *The Modern Dictionary of Sociology* provides a starting point: 'A group of people with a common and at least somewhat distinct culture who occupy a particular territorial area, have a feeling of unity, and regard themselves as a distinguishable entity' (Theodorson and Theodorson, 1969: 398). The

authors note that the concept of society typically applies to groups that have a comprehensive set of social institutions capable of taking care of most of the basic needs of a population over an extended period of time.

In his useful book *Keywords,* Raymond Williams (1976) draws attention to the fact that the term *society* has been used in many different ways over the past several centuries. David Jary and Julia Jary (1991) provide two definitions, both of them useful. First, they say society is 'the totality of human relationships'. Second, it is 'any self-perpetuating human grouping occupying a relatively bounded territory, having its own more or less distinctive CULTURE and INSTITUTIONS' (467). The common points in most definitions of society include notions of territory or geographical locale, enduring and ongoing organized social relationships, a degree of self-sufficiency, and some sharing of culture.

Keeping all of these considerations of meaning in mind, the definition of *society* we will use here is: *the totality of social relationships and interactions among a collectivity of people occupying a territory who, over time, survive by meeting their needs and solving their problems.*

We should note that a society is not necessarily the same thing as a nation-state, although the two are often confused. The established geographic boundaries of a nation-state may or may not be the same boundaries that define a society. It is also important to note that many societies have disappeared when their social relationships and interactions were not able to sustain the lives of the collectivity, while other societies have been absorbed, conquered, and taken over by outsiders. The phenomenon of Western colonialism has been one of the most important processes in defining and redefining the social map of the planet, often with catastrophic results for many indigenous and aboriginal peoples.

Within this framework, Canada or Canadian society, Australia or Australian society, or the United

States or American society represent more than just the shared material and non-material products defined as culture. When we refer to Canadian society we imply some generally accepted territorial boundaries inhabited by a people who share a specific way of organizing and structuring their efforts to solve their various problems and deal with their various needs and drives. Australia is likewise more than the shared products of its inhabitants. When we refer to Australian society we refer to a geographic locale as well as the specific modes of organizing religious, economic, educational, sexual, and other activities—all the factors that make up the unique characteristics distinguishing the people of that continent.

What is more, this definition of society draws our attention to another point: the human actions, interactions, and behaviours that occur as individuals attempt to solve their problems within geographical boundaries are not random and accidental; they are structured and organized. The structured nature of human behaviour is an essential attribute and is at the core of sociological analysis.

The Elements of Social Structure

This sociological definition of society raises a key point: the importance of understanding just how our behaviour, conduct, and actions are organized, patterned, and structured. While most sociologists use the term *society*, it is also appropriate, and helpful, to use the term *social structure*. The concept of social structure draws our attention to the essential characteristic of human social existence: its organized nature. Whatever characteristics human behaviour exhibits, it is, for the most part, not haphazard or random. We rarely act in a totally unpredictable and unorganized manner. Most of our lives are spent within the context of structured, patterned, and regularized social activities, interactions, and practices. Indeed, the discipline of sociology centres on the study of these social arrangements, structures, patterns, and modes of organization.

The Development of Social Structures

A rich and interesting—and often conflicting—literature has addressed the issue of how we as a species came to develop our various social structures. For our purposes, however, the historical origins of our social structures are of less interest than an essential sociological point that is beyond contention and debate: as a species we have developed a great variety of social structures, social behaviours, and social organizations in our ever-continuing efforts to solve individual and species needs, drives, and problems.

Institutions

As a species, human beings meet needs, solve problems, and deal with various drives through conscious, intentional, knowledgeable social action and interaction. These deliberate actions are what we call *social practices*. Over time these social practices become regularized, routinized, patterned, and established as 'the way things are done'. As they become firmly established, the social practices become a solidified part of life in the form of *institutions*.

In everyday English, 'institution' tends to be associated with a specific type of organization, like a prison or a mental health-care facility. But the sociological literature contains a number of different definitions. Many of sociology's definitions stress the importance of norms, values, and rules of conduct in structuring human interaction. Although the concept of structuring or ordering human activity is important, it is necessary to relate the behaviour that is organized or structured to the satisfaction of some need or the solving of some problem. For our purposes, an *institution* is defined as: *a set of organized relationships, structured interactions, patterned behaviour, and regularized and routinized collective actions that are geared to or serve to meet some problem, need, or drive*. Significantly, if we rearrange the modifiers in this definition to read, for example, *organized* instead of *patterned,* or *routinized* instead of *organized,* or *structured* instead of *regularized,* the definition still works. The essence of the definition rests in the idea that institutions are not so much places, physical locations, or buildings as they are *social arrangements* for dealing with our needs, drives, and problems.

Institutionalization

It is possible that the various institutions that are part of modern industrial society developed by accident or 'by chance', that is, as a result of someone discovering that a certain action or practice 'got the job done'. It is also possible that some institutions were planned and deliberately developed as arrangements to help meet some individual or social need or solve some problem. The process, whether accidental or deliberate, by which social actions, behaviours, patterns of interactions, and relationships become routinized, regularized, and ultimately widely accepted and recognized as the appropriate way of dealing with a problem, need, or drive is called *institutionalization.* When we say behaviour is institutionalized we simply mean that the behaviour has come to be structured and organized into widely accepted and recognized patterns. This follows from the sociological position that an institution is not necessarily a place or a physical structure, but is rather a patterned, organized, and structured group behaviour that facilitates the solving of a problem or the meeting of a need.

Peter Berger and Thomas Luckmann note that institutions are essentially habitualized actions that become a form of objective reality (1967: 54–60). They also use the word 'sedimentation' to convey the notion that our behaviours become routinized and regularized into patterns that, in turn, become the traditions that impact the conduct of our everyday lives (67–8). Elsewhere Berger explains how it is that humans, as active creatures, create the reality in which they live. He uses the word 'objectification' to explain how we, through our deeds,

actions, and interactions with others, create the objects that make up our world (1969: 6). Look around you right now and ask how many of the objects that you see exist in their natural state, and are not transformed by humans? My guess is few, if any, do. The material and non-material world you inhabit has been created by humans; it is the objectification of human activity.

Given that humans have a variety of different individual and species needs and problems that must be solved if we are to survive both as individuals and as a species, it follows that we have also developed a number of different institutionalized behaviours to deal with those needs and problems. Because the behaviours and patterns of interaction required to deal with the needs are very complex, it follows that institutions tend to be a complex phenomenon. One way of encouraging the analysis and understanding of such a complex phenomenon is the development of a classification system. Hans Gerth and C.W. Mills provide one such system in their book *Character and Social Structure,* which allows us to classify institutions according to the need they meet or the problem they solve.

Institutions and Institutional Orders

Gerth and Mills distinguish between institutions and institutional orders. An institutional order is essentially a cluster or collection of institutions geared to meeting similar needs or solving similar problems (1964: 25). For instance, the arrangements or behaviours that we engage in when we attempt to provide for our material needs form our *economic institutions,* whereas the *economic order* consists of all those institutions in a given society that are geared to the production and distribution of the material necessities of life. Within the economic order in our society there are particular economic institutions such as the large industrial corporation, the small business, the family farm, or the fishing co-operative. In sociological analysis we draw attention to the fact that when we refer to these entities as institutions we are not focusing on their physical

Religious institutions are those practices and behaviours that surround our efforts to seek the answers to ultimate questions and to celebrate and collectively ritualize the mysteries of life. In seeking to discover the meaning of the events of birth, life, and death we have developed complex and intricate systems of beliefs and associated social practices that include the rites and rituals of various religions. (Photograph courtesy of Michael Rumack)

assets or their geographic locale, but rather on the fact that they represent patterns of behaviour, specific modes of social organization, and structured interactions.

It is well known, to use a familiar phrase, that humans cannot live by bread alone or, put somewhat differently, that we have needs other than those directly tied to material or physical survival.

Human survival depends on solving a host of other problems, such as cultural transmission, biological reproduction, and collective or social decision-making, as well as spiritual questions. In our efforts to address and deal with these problems we have developed numerous modes of conduct and behaviour that have become routinized and regularized— that is to say, institutionalized—into what we refer

Need/problem faced by species	Institutional order	Examples of specific institutions in Canada
Provision and distribution of material necessities	Economic order	The corporation, family farm, trade union, small business
Cultural and knowledge transmission and enhancement	Educational order	University, trade school, public school
Social decision-making, international relations	Political order	Parliament, Senate, courts, provincial and local governments, lobby groups
Spiritual needs, answers to ultimate questions	Religious order	Various and specific churches and sects
Species reproduction and early childcare	Family order	Nuclear and other family forms

to as the educational order, the family order, the religious order, and the political order.

Firstly, the *educational order* or the educational system refers to those structured practices, patterned interactions, and organized relationships that various peoples have developed to facilitate the transmission and enhancement of culture. Included under the rubric of the educational order, in many Western societies at least, is a range of specific institutions such as the kindergarten, the public school system, secondary, private, and alternative schools, universities, community colleges, and technical schools. Each of these specific institutions plays its own part in our overall efforts to enhance and transmit the knowledge and skills that are a part of our culture.

Secondly, the mere meeting of our individual material needs is inadequate to ensure species survival, because without continuing arrangements to support biological reproduction, the future of the species would be limited. In sociology we understand that set of behavioural arrangements and patterns of organized interaction that have developed around the process of biological reproduction and the care and nurturing of the very young as constituting the *family order*. Familial institutions are thus the means by which we facilitate biological reproduction and childcare. The sociological literature tends to view the social arrangements we call 'the family' as also being involved in the provision of various forms of emotional support for its members. According to the analytical logic of sociology, as an institution the family—whether it is nuclear, extended, or same-sex—is not so much a place or a specific set of persons, but rather a method of organizing behaviour and interaction to ensure biological reproduction, relations of mutual support, and the care and training of the young.

Thirdly, although there are various explanations about why this is the case, the human species tends to ask profound and even ultimate questions concerning the meaning of our lives and our position in the larger scale of things. We may never know if we do this because of how we were made by a creator or if it is the product of the considerable intellect we have evolved over the thousands of years we have been on the planet. These considerations are less important for sociologists than our very tendency to ask the ultimate questions and, even more importantly, the interactions and conduct resulting from our attempts to answer them. This realm of human social experience and behaviour is referred to as religion.

The *religious order* and religious institutions are those practices and behaviours that surround our efforts to seek the answers to ultimate questions and to celebrate and collectively ritualize the mysteries of life. In seeking to come to grips with the meaning of issues like birth, life, and death we have developed complex and intricate systems of beliefs and associated social practices that include the rites and rituals of various religions. Although sociologists are more interested in the actual social interactions and conduct of religions than in the doctrinal content of a particular set of beliefs, they do not ignore doctrine and teachings, especially if their acceptance becomes a factor leading to specific kinds of actions and practices.

Fourthly, as societies become more populous and complex they require a means of developing social policy and establishing social goals. As peoples become organized into autonomous nation-states, the establishment of formal relations between and among the various social groupings becomes crucial: this becomes one of the essential aspects of the *political order*. Those social arrangements that we refer to as the political order or the political institutions encompass certain relations and behaviours: for instance, the allocation of leadership roles and the making of decisions about rules and regulations that form social legal codes.

The political order is the entire constellation or configuration of social practices and arrangements that facilitate these objectives. The specific or internal institutions making up the political order vary from place to place and time to time. In a liberal democracy such as Canada the institutions include Parliament, the judiciary, provincial and local government structures, lobby groups, and special coalitions or social movements.

The concepts of institution and institutional order are, sociologists think, useful concepts when it comes to understanding the patterns and relationships that characterize our on-going social life. However to merely designate all of the activities that take place at, for example, a university as merely statuses and roles found within a particular institution may not be refined enough. Pierre Bourdieu's concept of 'field' may allow us to refine this analysis somewhat. Bourdieu refers to a field as 'a network, or a configuration, of objective relations between positions' (1992: 97). His concept of field not only requires us to consider what we are calling institutions in terms of relations, it opens up the possibility of thinking about smaller, more refined, units of organized behaviours. Bourdieu makes it clear that humans act and interact in and across multiple fields. Therefore, in a university we might think about teaching activities, research, administration, student politics, and alumni relations as distinct fields of social activity (94–5).

Institutions, institutional orders, and fields of social practice, then, are the basic building blocks of human society. To grasp the essential character of any human society or social structure, we must have an understanding of its basic institutional structures. Better still, we must also carry the process of analyzing further, by dissecting institutions into their component parts. An analysis is not complete until we have broken down the phenomenon being studied into its smallest, most basic units.

Status

An examination of the behaviour that makes up the patterns of interaction and social organization we call institutions reveals a certain *structure*—in that there are parts within an institution that exist in orderly relationships with each other. For those parts, or positions, within an organization we use the term *status*; and the structure of an institution refers to the specific organization of the statuses that compose it.

As used here, the term *status* does not refer, as it usually does, to a ranking within a hierarchy, or to a position of prestige. A status is, more simply, a position within an institution. Within a Western university, for instance, the statuses include president, caretaker, librarian, secretary, dean, vice-president, instructor, cafeteria worker, carpenter, student, and so on. These statuses, without being ranked in any particular order, indicate that the modern university is in fact a collection of different positions.

Similarly, the various statuses within various religious institutions could include priest or minister, member of congregation, church elder, church council member, or Sunday school teacher. Within a typical Western nuclear family we can find various statuses such as wife, mother, husband, sister, brother, daughter, son, and father. Each institution is composed of a number of different positions or statuses, and attached to each status are certain behavioural expectations that serve to direct the actions and behaviour of those in the status.

Role and Role Set

Just as there are statuses in each institution, within each status there is a role, a generally expected way of behaving, acting, and interacting. A *role* can be defined as a culturally expected or defined behaviour attached to a particular status. In a modern university, for instance, behaviour expected of a librarian or a caretaker is quite different from that expected of a president.

The extent to which these statuses and roles are strictly defined or somewhat flexible varies from one historical period to another and from institution to institution and society to society. In Western society the role of kindergarten teacher is strictly defined, so

that people occupying that role may find they have considerably less flexibility and room for variations in approaching the basic task of teaching than, for instance, university professors. University professors might, for example, argue that it is appropriate to utter a word generally considered to be an obscenity if it accomplishes a particular pedagogical objective. Kindergarten teachers using the same approach would probably be called to account for their actions shortly after any of their pupils relayed the details of the day's activities to their parents.

The very term *role* implies an analogy and draws our attention to certain comparisons with formal theatrical acting. If status represents a person's part in the play, the character itself, role is the more detailed script. The theatrical analogy brings up another essential feature of the term: an individual's role is usually acted out in concert with other roles and statuses.

There is also more than one role attached to each status. In your status as student, do you act or interact in a fundamentally similar manner when you are having coffee with friends, requesting help from library staff, discussing an assignment with your instructor, and meeting the dean of your faculty? The answer for most students is no, because there is no single role attached to the status of student. Rather, there is a set of roles that sociologists call a *role set*, which means a collection or cluster of roles. The concept of role set implies that sociologists expect to see different behaviours within the same status, depending on the status and role of the other party in an interactive situation.

Role Conflict and Role Strain

Two additional concepts associated with the analysis of roles are role conflict and role strain. *Role conflict* refers to instances of conflict between two or more of the roles in a role set. For instance, instructors are usually responsible for the enforcement of standardized, uniform grading criteria for all students, so that in their role as instructors their relationships to all students must be as equal and uniform as possible. Imagine what could happen if an instructor becomes friends with a student, or if a friend enrols in the class. If the friend fails the course, role conflict can emerge as the role of instructor conflicts with the role of friend. Take another example: a supervisor in a formal work environment wants to maintain friendly interpersonal relations with others within the plant but is also responsible for enforcing new directives to speed up the work process and improve productivity. This kind of enforcement can have a negative impact on the workers under supervision, creating conflict. If the expected behaviour of one role conflicts or is at variance with the expected behaviour of another role, role conflict results. Conflict also arises when an individual is involved with two or more roles and the behaviour of one role contradicts the behaviour of another role.

Many of you struggling to read these words are involved in *role strain,* which is commonly described as a situation in which a particular role may involve a set of expectations, and the successful accomplishment of those expectations strains the energy and resources of the status holder to the point that the person is unable to meet all the expectations. A university student may be expected to do the necessary work to get passing—or better—grades, engage in sports, participate in university clubs, plus live a 'normal' social life and fulfill family responsibilities. The person on the other side of the podium could also very well be involved in role strain, because university instructors are expected to teach, contribute to university administration, undertake research, publish, and engage in public service—not to mention maintain their own personal lives. When people complain that there are just not enough hours in the day to do all they have to do, they are most likely in a situation of role strain.

Values and Norms

Our discussion of roles raises questions about the basis or origin of the cultural or social expectations that define the behaviour appropriate for various positions in an institution. Where do these behavioural expectations come from? What is the source of the knowledge that we draw on when deciding how to act in a particular role?

We know that all human societies have certain ideas, ideals, and stocks of knowledge, rules, and regulations that guide the actions and interactions of individuals. Sociologists refer to these elements as values and norms. A *value* is a general and abstract principle or idea about what is good or bad, desirable or undesirable, right or wrong, or appropriate or inappropriate. Discussion of values often refers to qualities of behaviour such as honesty, faithfulness, freedom, patriotism, or equality. A particular value does not contain any specific instructions about how we need to behave in order to live a life according to that value.

What sociologists call norms do provide us with more precise instructions. Indeed, in sociology norms are commonly understood to be more specific expressions of values. If honesty is a part of a society's value system, a command or suggestion such as 'Do not tell lies' represents a normative instruction. A *norm* is a specific rule, regulation, or instruction that indicates specifically how to behave and act or what is appropriate and inappropriate.

Norms indicate what is expected of us in our day-to-day behaviour; they guide our behaviour in our various roles. For example, most men born and raised in North America feel entirely comfortable shaking hands when they meet someone for the first time, especially if the person they are meeting is another man. For men, this is accepted—and practised—as a normal greeting. Many North American men feel equally uncomfortable when a stranger embraces and kisses them. For women in North America, an embrace or a kiss on the cheek is a more common formal greeting, even when meeting strangers. Why do men and women feel that these different forms of behaviour are the appropriate modes of conduct? The answer is that the behavioural forms are a part of the norms or the normative orientation of North American society.

In their analysis of norms, sociologists commonly utilize a further analytical distinction between folkways, mores (pronounced *mor-ays*), and laws. They consider each of these as a type of norm varying in how specific the 'instructions' are and in the implications that follow from violations of the norm. *Folkways* are norms or behavioural instructions that govern a large variety of everyday situations and interactions. Folkways deal with common everyday matters and a violation is considered rude, or bad manners, but not a sign of moral depravity.

Once folkways become established and accepted they tend to govern various aspects of our everyday lives, from how to behave in a supermarket queue to what colours are considered to be appropriate to mix and match in our wardrobe. The violation of a folkway can draw attention to a person's action or personality, but generally most people do not feel that the transgression represents a serious violation of society's morals. Picking your nose in public is usually considered a violation of a folkway because it is generally deemed to be an unpleasant and inappropriate activity, but people who do this are not necessarily considered morally depraved or wanting, nor would they be subject to any formal punishment.

Mores are norms or behavioural instructions that hold great significance, and observance of them is deemed to have moral implications for the well being of individuals and society. The violation of mores is considered to be a much more significant breach of appropriate rules of conduct than the violation of folkways. If a man walks down Yonge Street in Toronto on a hot July afternoon wearing nothing above his waist, some onlookers might consider it a breach of a folkway, but in all likelihood a passing police official would take little notice. If a woman walks down the same street with no clothing above the waist some people would object, and perhaps even call the police. But even if the woman's actions did not contravene a law, for many people it would still be a violation of mores in

Canadian society: women are not supposed to bare their breasts in public.

Consider another example: someone goes to a professional football game and in the heat of the moment yells an angry obscenity at the referee. Others sitting nearby might feel a little uncomfortable, because swearing in public still carries a certain stigma and is often considered to be inappropriate behaviour. Sociologists might consider this behaviour the violation of a folkway. If the same person is in a church service, disagrees with something said, and utters the same obscenity at the same volume, or is on the street and shouts an obscenity at a police officer, nearly everyone would consider this action as a serious violation of proper codes of conduct. Sociologists would consider it to be the violation of mores.

William Graham Sumner in his 1906 classic volume, *Folkways*, developed the original conception of folkways and mores. Sumner also distinguished folkways and mores from *laws,* which for him were norms or more often mores that had been formally codified and enforced. For instance, in many societies the concept of equality is represented by the norm that we should treat all people as equal regardless of their national origins, religion, and sex. These types of norms are often codified into laws prohibiting discrimination and enforced by both the police and human rights commissions.

Like norms and values, folkways and mores are subject to change. There may be groups in society that hold values and subscribe to norms that are different from those of the dominant culture. If such a group accepts some of the values and norms of the dominant culture but has other values and norms as well, they are referred to as a subculture. For instance, to the extent that Finnish Canadians accept the general value system and normative orientations of mainstream Canadian society while maintaining other values and norms unique to Finnish culture, they are said to compose a subculture. A subculture can usually exist with no major conflicts within a society.

In many societies there are groups who reject most if not all of the values and norms of the dominant culture, subscribing instead to alternative beliefs and practices. In sociology these groups are called countercultures. The 'hippies' of the late 1960s and early 1970s who rejected mainstream North America and posited an alternative lifestyle dominated by alternative values and norms represented a counterculture, as do present-day Hutterite and Amish communities. The essence of a counterculture is the advocating of a value system and normative orientations that are distinctly different from the dominant culture and mainstream society.

Much of our conduct is influenced, structured, and prescribed by what we know about how we are expected to act. Indeed, as we go about our normal daily routines of work, shopping, attending classes, going to church, and other social activities, we usually don't have to think about what to do in most situations. We just seem to know what to do. The knowledge that informs our behaviour as we stand in a line-up at the supermarket or wait for our professor to finally come to the point is an important part of the values, folkways, norms, and mores that facilitate the everyday interactions that are so essential to everyday living in society.

Groups

Although we are highly institutionalized creatures, not all of our time is spent engaging in patterns of behaviour and interaction geared to meeting a basic need or solving a basic problem. There is a good chance that many of you reading this text will soon decide you've had enough and will put the book down, call a friend, and go out for a coffee or some other refreshment. If we assume that in this new activity no basic need is involved—that is, the liquid intake is not really related to substantial thirst—and that what you want to do is relax and talk to a friend, your conduct now falls outside the context of an institution. In this case we have to drop the concept of institution as an explanation and refer instead to the behaviour as occurring in a group.

In sociological analysis a *group* refers to people who interact in an orderly or patterned way and share a certain specific set of norms and values. According to Theodorson and Theodorson's classic definition, a group is: 'A plurality of persons who have a common identity, at least some feeling of unity and certain common goals and shared norms' (1969: 176). The key to the sociological conception of a group is the idea of an orderly or regularized interaction among persons who share a normative system and have a sense of their identity and common purposes or goals. When you have coffee with a friend, socialize at the mall with your mates, play a game of pickup basketball on the driveway, go to a bonspiel on the weekend, or just drive around on Sunday afternoon, you are engaging in a group interaction. Although these kinds of activities are an important part of our lives, they are not necessarily related to meeting a particular need, in the way that institutional behaviour is. Rather, they occur because we share goals and values with others, or have a sense of common identity and feelings of unity.

Sociologists make an analytical subdivision between primary and secondary groups. A *primary group* is small in size, cohesive and intimate, and involved in 'face-to-face' interaction that takes place over a relatively long time and in a number of different settings. Perhaps the best example of a primary group is your own collection of friends, or a clique in high school. In all likelihood this kind of 'crowd' is small, perhaps five people or less. These groups tend to be cohesive and intimate, and the members feel extremely close to each other. They know intimate details about each other's lives, things hidden from parents. When you are in this kind of a group the members become your closest friends, and you take their opinions and advice seriously. You interact with them on a daily, indeed hourly, basis—these are the people you might spend all day with and then when you get home you phone them up within 10 minutes to check on what's happening. When you are emotionally

In sociology, the term *formal organization* refers to a collectivity that has a formal structure, specific purposes, and objectives with clearly delineated rules, regulations, and procedures that govern the conduct of its members or volunteers. (M.C. Escher's *Relativity* © 2004 The M.C. Escher Company–Baarn–Holland. All rights reserved.)

involved with members of a primary group, your whole being—your behaviour, your personality—becomes caught up in it.

Compared to a primary group, a *secondary group* is larger in size and less intimate and cohesive. It is more impersonal and usually geared to some specific activity or purpose: a sports team, for

example, or a club that engages in a special activity, such as drama or photography. In this kind of group the various members usually don't know the intimate details of each other's lives. For instance, if you are on a softball team and you have an 'off day' at bat and one of your team mates offers less than constructive criticism, you could most likely shrug off the comments with less difficulty than if your best friend had made critical comments to you. Other examples of secondary groups are church groups, people who regularly meet to play cards or chess, or casual—as opposed to close—friends at work.

The differences between primary and secondary groups can be subtle. A group of casual friends at school or work can become closer and closer as the interaction becomes more personal and intimate, so that a secondary group becomes a primary group. Likewise, a group of close friends can drift apart, becoming more casual acquaintances that only meet occasionally for routine and non-intimate interaction. This group would make a transition from a primary to a secondary group, illustrating an essential characteristic of social life: it is a dynamic, ever-changing process.

The sociological discussion of group also includes two other terms: aggregates and categories. The concept of *aggregate* refers to a collection of people who just happen to be together for a common but temporary purpose. When you stand with others to wait for a bus or a train, attend a course in introductory sociology, or have dinner in a restaurant, you are part of an aggregate. The people who find themselves in these situations don't interact with each other in a manner characteristic of either primary or secondary groups.

A further distinction is made between an aggregate and a *category*. In undertaking their analyses, social scientists often divide and subdivide the populations they study according to various classification schemas. They might, for instance, use the category of university student to analytically differentiate those who attend university from those who do not. In this relationship there is no implication of group interaction or even of an accidental coming together as in an aggregate. As a category, university students simply represent a division of the population based on an arbitrary attribute. Categories can be established on the basis of endless arbitrary divisions, including everything from age to level of education to place of birth.

Formal Organizations

One final component of a typical Western industrial society is the concept of formal organization. Imagine, once again, that you've had enough of reading this book and you want to make an effort to salvage the rest of your day. You decide to do something worthwhile, like engage in a community service. You go out and do some work for the United Way or an AIDS action committee or rape crisis centre. By joining and participating in these formal organizations you are interacting in yet another part of the social structure.

In sociology the term *formal organization* refers to a collectivity that has a formal structure, specific purposes and objectives with clearly delineated rules, and regulations and procedures that govern the conduct of its members or volunteers. People often do not formally join institutions or primary and secondary groups, but they do formally join certain organizations. Within such organizations there might be a formal structure of offices, with formal procedures for selecting persons to fill them as well as definite lengths of tenure.

The essential characteristics of formal organizations are the formal procedures and regulations that govern interaction within them. Some institutions, such as the multinational corporation, share some of these characteristics. But many institutions, such as the family, do not, and because many formal organizations do not relate to basic needs and problems, we make a distinction. One of the most systematic sociological treatments of formal organizations is found in Peter Blau and Richard Scott's book *Formal Organizations* (1963).

In the internal structuring of interaction and behaviour within groups and formal organizations, the concepts of status and role also come back into play. Even in the most intimate primary peer groups there are statuses and roles. In a high school group, for instance, there is often one person who becomes the group 'clown', another who becomes the group 'brain', and perhaps someone who is the group 'toughie'. These statuses and the associated roles can be vital in influencing people's behaviour. Similarly, there are formal statuses with attached roles in many formal organizations.

The Tools of Sociology

The key to understanding what sociologists mean by institutions, groups, and formal organizations resides in the notion of structured or organized behaviour that is determined by the shared common knowledge of the human actors—bearing in mind always that human behaviour and action are not random or unpredictable.

The language of sociology has developed slowly over the years as sociologists have analyzed society. In using this terminology we must take care to avoid assuming that a sociological analysis means merely the naming and labelling of aspects of human life. For sociologists the terms provide the tools necessary for the larger operation: building an understanding of the composition and operation of society.

The act of creating and developing solutions to our needs, problems, and drives is a social act which, by definition, involves other human beings in complex, highly structured modes of action or interactions. Sociologists argue that the structures of these organized interactions can be better understood through the concepts of institution, role, status, value, norm, and group. The analysis of these modes of conduct is an essential project in the discipline of sociology.

Critical Thinking Questions

- How many roles have you already played today? How many more do you anticipate playing? Were you conscious at the time that you were 'playing a role'?
- Have you even been involved in the institutionalization of a behaviour or social practice? Support an affirmative answer with a concrete example.
- What primary groups have been important to you as you have developed? Provide a concrete illustration of how this group had an effect on your character or behaviour.
- Do values and norms change? If so, how and why?
- Who has had a more significant impact on you—your parents or your friends? Explain

Terms and Concepts

Social analysis—both the process of taking society, social processes, and social phenomena apart in order to better understand them and the resulting understanding and knowledge that we acquire. The verb *analyze* refers to examining something by resolving or breaking it down into its component parts. The noun *analysis* refers to the results of the process of analyzing something.

Social structure—sometimes used interchangeably in sociological analysis with *society*. Social structure may be a preferable term because it draws attention to the fact that the human relationships, interactions, actions, and behaviours that make up society are both social and structured, as well as ordered, patterned, routinized, and regularized.

Institution—a pattern of behaviour, a set of organized social relationships, routinized interactions, or structured social relationships geared to solving some basic individual or group need or solving some individual or group problem. In sociological thinking an institution is not to be confused with a physical place such as a building dedicated to some specific activity such as health care. An educational institution is thus not necessarily a specific building or place but a complex set of structured and organized behaviours and patterns of interaction through which we attempt to transmit some aspect of our society's stock of knowledge.

Institutionalization—the process by which behaviour, actions, and interactions become routinized, regularized, organized, and structured into ongoing patterns. Institutionalization is the process of either deliberately or unintentionally 'building' institutions by engaging in recurring and structured behaviour to meet some need or solve some problem.

Institutional order—a cluster of specific institutions that are all related to meeting a basic need or solving a problem. The economic order refers to all those economic institutions, from the family farm to the small main-street business to the chain store and the giant corporation, that are a part of how the material needs of people in our society are met.

Status—a position within an institution, group, or organization. The term does not necessarily imply a hierarchy or ranking of positions, just the existence of different positions. In a university there are typically a number of different statuses, including student, instructor, secretary, librarian, caretaker, and dean.

Role—the set of culturally defined behaviours that is appropriate and expected or inappropriate and unacceptable for a given status. In drama, when we play a role we act according to a set of instructions in the script. In our social behaviour we act according to a set of 'instructions' provided by the society's script: its normative orientations, value systems, and ideological dictates.

Norm—a specific expression of a value. Norms are behavioural prescriptions or instructions that apply to behaviour in various roles and statuses. There are two different kinds of norms. A *folkway* is a norm that is generally accepted and governs a wide range of activities; but it does not involve serious moral considerations, and a violation is more a breach of manners and bad taste than a matter of serious concern. *Mores* are norms that are more strictly adhered to and considered a matter of public morality. The violation of mores is often a violation of a moral dictate and can be punishable in a formal manner by agents of social order such as the police. In Canadian society, picking your nose is generally considered a folkway violation, whereas appearing nude in public is a mores violation.

Value—a general and abstract principle or idea related to what is appropriate and inappropriate behaviour, what is desirable and undesirable, right and wrong, good and bad. Values are by nature general and might include vague and general instructions like 'be honest' or 'be polite' or 'respect your elders'.

Group—two or more individuals who share a set of normative orientations and value commitments, have a sense of identity and/or common goals and purposes, and interact in an ongoing and orderly way over an extended period of time. As opposed to institutional interaction, group interaction may not be directly linked to meeting some basic individual need or solving some problem.

Primary group—a small number of people in an 'intimate', face-to-face, long-lasting, cohesive relationship or pattern of interaction. The actors involved consider primary-group interaction and primary-group members important. An example is a typical high school or adolescent clique or 'gang'.

Secondary group—larger than a primary group, and not involving as much intimate and face-to-face interaction. Primary-group interaction is shorter in duration and has less meaning and significance for the participants. A baseball or hockey team is typically a secondary group.

Formal organization–a formally organized collectivity with a specific purpose or objective. The formal organization typically includes a 'constitution', formal officers, and membership procedures and rules to govern conduct. Many community organizations, charities, and service clubs are formal organizations.

Related Web Sites

http://www.sociologyonline.co.uk/

Hosted by Tony Fitzgerald from Nottingham, England, this is a comprehensive search site that offers newsletters, slide shows, a library link, and even an opportunity to send a 'SocioCard'.

http://www.sociology.org.uk/

This is another good comprehensive site for beginning and experienced sociologists. Listed as a Byteachers.org.uk linked site, 'Sociology Central' is an Association of Teachers Web site and offers an array of links relating to many issues that sociologists study.

http://www.webref.org/

Here is one of the most comprehensive and detailed glossary/dictionaries available on-line. From Iverson Software, the definitions contain links to ensure that you understand the concept.

http://bitbucket.icaap.org/SocialDict.tmpl

Robert Drislane, Gary Parkinson, and Mike Sosteric from Athabasca University, described as 'Canada's Open University', maintain the On Line Dictionary for the Social Sciences, which contains more than one thousand entries.

Suggested Further Readings

Chomsky, N. 1992. *Language and Politics*. Montreal: Black Rose Books. This collection of essays introduces the reader to some of Chomsky's important ideas in linguistics and why language is an essential component of our social existence.

Cooley, C.H. [1909] 1962. *Social Organization: A Study of the Larger Mind*. New York: Schocken Books. The section on 'primary groups' has achieved the stature of a true classic. Reprinted many times over, it is still one of the best accounts of group activity.

Gerth, H., and C.W. Mills. 1964. *Character and Social Structure: The Psychology of Social Institutions*. New York: Harcourt Brace. This remains one of the best overall introductions to the complex relations between the various components of a social structure and human personality dynamics and development.

Postman, N. 1992. *The Disappearance of Childhood*. New York: Vintage Books. In his readable style, Postman explains how and why childhood is a historical and social concept while examining the ways we have treated children over the centuries.

CHAPTER 4

Socialization

The sociological imagination demands more than a thorough analysis of the basic structures of human society, although clearly this is necessary—and a good place to start. The sociological imagination demands that we understand the connections between our social structures, made up of institutions, statuses, roles, values, norms, and so on, and ourselves as individuals. The concept of *socialization* is the essential link between an individual and the social structure. It is one of the most important concepts in the discipline of sociology.

Although, again, there are minor differences in how sociologists define the concept, there is general agreement that socialization refers broadly to the process of social learning. *Socialization,* for our purposes, refers to the lifelong social learning process that is essential to human existence and development. As a result of this lifelong social learning process, we not only learn how we are expected to live our lives, but also acquire a culture and develop a personality.

The Biological Processes

Let's return to a discussion of your physiological being, your physical body, and its various biological processes. When do you get hungry? Are there particular times of the day that you tend to get hungry and then seek out and enjoy food? Usually there are. A key question is why, in most parts of North America, do we tend to feel hungry shortly after we get up in the morning, then again around twelve o'clock noon, and later around 6:00 PM? Do we have a genetically based biological need for nourishment at these specific times in our twenty-four-hour-based time system? There seems to be little evidence that humans as a species are genetically programmed to eat at certain times of the day, because across cultures there are enormous variations as to when people eat. Anyone from North America who visits India or Chile, for example, finds that by the time dinner is served at between 9:00 and 10:30 PM, they are past being hungry. Could it be that, as we grow up and develop in a particular society, we learn or are trained to be hungry at certain times of the day? Could it be that the process of getting hungry and desiring food, which we normally think of as natural and biological, is in some important way influenced by the overall structure and pattern of our social existence? The sociological answer to these questions is a resounding yes, because we know that mealtimes and diets are among the most diverse of cultural features.

Leaving aside the question of when hunger strikes you in the daily cycle of life, let's consider what you will accept as nourishment in the satisfaction of that hunger. We know that the human body needs a certain amount of protein, and we know that most locations around the world contain bountiful sources of protein. Yet most of us are relatively fussy about what we will accept. For many people born and raised in North America, the choices of meat-based protein are limited to certain parts of beef- and pork-producing animals, poultry, certain fish and seafood, and mutton and lamb. For most North Americans, food coming from skunks, snakes, lizards, worms, grubs, insects, rodents, and the friendly feline and canine species is not acceptable. Indeed, many of us might have difficulty putting snake meat in our mouths, let alone swallowing it and keeping it down.

Many foods are considered delicacies in one culture but are not acceptable sources of protein in another. Does your palate allow you to enjoy very spicy flavours, like the ones we find in traditional foods in India? When we consider our ability and willingness to consume certain foods and not consume others we are confronted with the question of why. Is the explanation biological, that is, are some *Homo sapiens* born with a genetic propensity to throw up after eating snake meat while others lack this gene? Do some people have a gene that allows them to consume very spicy foods while others do not? There is no evidence that this is the case, and it seems more likely that for the most part we enjoy and consume foods we have become accustomed to through a long process of learning.

In our physiological processes such as sight, more is involved than the biological processes of light waves striking certain kinds of nerves that stimulate the transmission of electrical messages to the brain. In this case, too, a significant degree of social learning is involved. For instance, Canadians born and raised in most southern parts of the country know what snow is, and they can look out across a snow-covered field and recognize several different kinds of snow. Depending on what they see, they might describe the snow as sticky, wet, powdery, or crusted. Despite these adjectives, the English language has only one word for snow. In Inuit culture, though, there are many words for snow. There are different nouns for falling snow, snow on the ground, snow packed hard like ice, slushy snow, and other forms. Individuals born and raised in that culture commonly have the ability to perceive and recognize the various kinds of snow at great distances. A person born and raised in the southern coastal area of British Columbia, with its year-long moderate temperatures, would in all likelihood be unable to recognize, let alone identify by name, different types of snow.

Once again we must face the why questions. Are the Inuit biologically or genetically programmed with the capacity to perceive and identify different types of snow at great distances while people in the south are not? A more logical and supportable argument is that snow is a dominant factor of life in the North and physical survival there depends on knowing about snow conditions and being able to communicate on this subject with others. Given this fact, a central part of the social learning process in Inuit culture is recognizing types of snow and acquiring the appropriate language to describe them.

Another example illustrating the link between social learning and the process of perception relates to the issue of physical attractiveness or beauty. Have you ever used the phrase 'good looking' or 'attractive' to describe another person? Have you ever noticed that you find certain 'types' of people sexually attractive? If you answered yes to either of these questions, then what particular set of physical characteristics or features do you define as attractive? Furthermore, is there a species-wide, transcultural set of physical attributes that defines 'attractiveness'? The answer to this is no. What is considered attractive or sexually appealing varies radically from historical epoch to epoch and from culture to culture. At a particular time in history a man might be considered attractive if he is slim, bronze in colour, and tall. In that same culture at another historical moment the ideal man could be heavier, with pale skin, and so on. Our definition of what constitutes a beautiful and sexually attractive person is not present in our genes; rather it is a part of a society's values and norms that we are taught and learn through socialization.

In sexual conduct, to take another example, what are the typical behaviours of *Homo sapiens* as they prepare for and engage in sexual activity? The question of what particular physical appearance stimulates the sex drive aside, once the sex drive is stimulated, how do we behave? Are there universal, species-wide, invariant, unlearned behaviours that characterize sexual conduct? On the contrary, the behaviour associated with human sexual activity is as varied and diverse as the characteristics associated with masculinity and femininity. All we need do is think about the various different styles of hair, dress, and makeup that characterize what is defined as masculine and feminine in different cultures at different times. The sexual behaviours that are typical in a given society are cultural in origin, and they are learned at the level of the individual through socialization.

Another aspect of human behaviour is related to a basic physical need, but is still fundamentally influenced by socialization: the need for shelter and clothing. The inhabitants of many regions of the planet require, if they are to survive, shelter and clothing to protect them from the elements; but if we consider the patterns of human dress we are immediately struck by the diversity of apparel that has been developed to deal with this problem. The essential point, at least in understanding the importance of socialization, relates to how we come to accept as 'natural' the norms and values concerning dress. We can all think of clothes we like to wear and feel comfortable in, clothes in which we just feel 'natural'. Conversely, we can all think of clothes we loathe wearing and that we feel uncomfortable in, clothes we would not be caught dead wearing in public. So, what determines the clothing we find acceptable, and what determines the clothes we avoid like the plague? Is it in our genes? The answer is once again 'no'. The types of clothing we prefer and the clothes we feel comfortable in are related to the social learning process that we have experienced over the course of our entire lives. It is our culture and the socialization that goes on within it that

influence how we protect ourselves from the social environment through our dress.

The Human Personality

In stating that there is much more to our personalities and character structures than just our biological processes and how we deal with our basic biological problems, we move into an area of major controversy in the social sciences. Although many volumes have been written on the issue of human personality, authors have had apparent difficulties in defining the concept of personality. One massive introductory psychology text, Gleitman (1986), offers no definition, whereas Andrew Crider and his associates (1989) define personality in terms of the unique patterns of behaviour and mental processes characteristic of individuals and their positions in the environment (471). Frager and Fadiman (1984) discuss a variety of different approaches to personality without venturing a definition. Peterson (1988) adopts an approach that has merit for our purposes here, noting that while personality is by necessity a 'fuzzy term', it can be understood as a 'family' or collection of attributes.

Perhaps the best definition has come from psychologist David Statt (1990), who says human personality is the sum total of how we think, feel, and behave. Statt notes that while all of us share patterns of thought, emotion, and behaviour with others in our society, at the same time we also possess and exhibit unique and individual patterns of thought, emotion, and action. As a result of this, our personalities are composed of the shared and unique traits and characteristics that make us what and who we are.

The concept of *personality* then, refers to those general, individual, characteristic, and integrated attributes of an individual that define his or her uniqueness and distinctive being in the world. Our personalities are composed of extremely complex sets and patterns of traits, attributes, beliefs, and behaviours that relate to a very complex series of issues including, among other things, religion, politics, war, peace, co-operation, competition, relations to persons of the same or opposite sex, sexual behaviour, age and aging, and physical appearance and ability. Our personalities or character structures also have to do with how we experience fear, anger, aggression, or frustration. They are connected to what makes us anxious and how we deal with anxiety. On the other end of the emotional spectrum, what makes us happy, how we express joy, what gives us pleasure and satisfaction, and the sorts of things we really enjoy doing are also important elements of our personalities and characters.

The sociological position holds that key aspects of our personalities—our beliefs and attitudes, our value systems and general attitudes—are better understood by reference to our social environment and experiences than our genetic heritage. Put simply, there is no evidence that some people are born with a genetic propensity to be Christians, Jews, Muslims, or atheists. Similarly, there does not seem to be a gene that makes us sympathetic to left-wing or right-wing ideas or that makes us exhibit any of the other great number of traits that make each of us what we are. In summary, it is clear that the lifelong social learning process called socialization fundamentally influences a good deal of our personality and character structure.

Types of Socialization

Within the discipline of sociology there is a general assumption that socialization has an impact on virtually all aspects of our being. The norms, values, folkways, and mores that we acquire through socialization become important in the development of our personalities and subsequent behaviour. The social environment and the social learning process influence even some aspects of our bodily or biological functions. Our language, our political beliefs, how and what we perceive, and our religious beliefs and practices are all influenced. Indeed, we can argue that who we are and how we act must be understood within the context of the lifelong socialization process we all experience.

Within the discipline of sociology there is a tradition of distinguishing between several different types of socialization. These include primary and secondary socialization, resocialization, and anticipatory socialization.

Primary Socialization

Our survival as individuals, and the long-term survival of our species, depends on our ability to interact successfully with other human beings to solve our basic problems and meet various needs. This continuing interaction, which is the basis of our social existence, is predicated on the sharing of a basic stock of knowledge, part of which is a system of symbols used for communication—language.

The learning of language is an essential aspect of *primary socialization,* which refers to social learning that involves the acquisition or transmission of the basic stock of knowledge essential to social interaction in a particular society. In addition to language, primary socialization in Western society includes the learning of behaviours such as eating habits, table manners, and toilet training. Through primary socialization we also begin to learn about the basic statuses and roles typical of the various institutions in our society, as well as the norms and values that influence behaviour.

As children observe the roles played by their caretakers they begin to learn what it means to be both female and feminine and male and masculine. For instance, by being intensively exposed to the daily routines and patterns of interaction in a middle-class nuclear family, children learn not only about expected roles but also how to deal with emotions such as frustration, anger, and pleasure. Indeed, children learn what causes frustration, anger, and pleasure. Each day, to the extent that there is a rigid division of labour and clearly understood distinctions between male and female roles and clear definitions about what is masculine and what is feminine, children, regardless of their

As they observe the roles played by their caregivers, children also learn sophisticated patterns of interaction and methods of dealing with complex emotions such as frustration, anger, and pleasure. The family is the setting where most children learn this primary socialization. Parents have the key roles. (Harry Cutting Photography—www.harrycutting.com)

gender, learn about what men and women are like, how they act, and even how they view themselves in relationship to the other gender. A young male child who is told, after falling and skinning his knee, not to cry but rather to act like a man and not a girl, is learning about masculinity and toughness and how this supposedly differs from the expected or 'appropriate' feminine response.

If children constantly see women in the house-

hold performing domestic labour and men involved in other tasks such as doing repairs or relaxing while domestic labour is performed, they are being taught lessons about roles in the family and appropriate conduct for men and women. People born and raised in a traditional North American nuclear family in which there is a traditional sex-based division of labour tend to find later on in life that it can be difficult to radically change the patterns of domestic work. Even couples committed to changing sex and gender roles often find that it is a daily, perhaps endless, struggle to avoid falling into traditional roles.

Craig Ramey and Sharon Ramey have studied the issue of intellectual disabilities, and their conclusions bear on this issue. In an essay titled 'Prevention of Intellectual Disabilities: Early Interventions to Improve Cognitive Development' they report that a child's interactions with adults is very important to the child's development. They refer to such interactions as 'priming mechanisms', concluding that sustained and positive interactions between adults and children are very important for the child's development:

> That intensive early intervention can positively alter the cognitive developmental trajectories of socially and biologically vulnerable young children has now been demonstrated and replicated in diverse samples. In principle, therefore, the issue of the efficacy of early intervention is answered in the affirmative for both biologically and socially at-risk infants. Intensive early intervention can have a meaningful positive impact on the cognitive development of vulnerable young children. Importantly, those infants from families with the least formal education derive the greatest cognitive benefits. This finding is an important piece of information in this era of reform concerning health care, education, and welfare. (1999: 161)

Secondary Socialization

As human beings mature and develop, they begin to engage in ever more complex and numerous social interactions. In many Western societies much of the primary socialization occurs within the scope of those patterns of interaction we commonly refer to as the family. As children develop and the range of their interactions becomes more complicated, they enter new institutional and group settings, such as the school or church, where they learn more complicated patterns of language and are introduced to society's norms, values, and behavioural expectations.

Secondary socialization is the name given to the learning of these more complex and subtle aspects of a society's language, symbols, norms, values, folkways, mores, institutional structures, roles, statuses, and group interactive processes.

Resocialization

The process of resocialization refers to deliberate and intentional attempts to modify or replace some aspect of an individual's earlier socialization with new or alternative beliefs, viewpoints, norms, or values. Many of the basic arguments put forward in an introductory sociology course, for instance, could be considered an example of resocialization because they often run counter to much of what students have previously been socialized to believe. For example, it is common for people in our society to believe there is such a thing as human nature, meaning that much human conduct occurs because of basic instincts or biologically based propensities. Many people in Canada would agree with a statement such as 'Human nature being what it is, there will always be war and conflict.' Behind this statement is the argument that there are basic behavioural patterns that are innate, unlearned, and invariant. Moreover, it suggests that humans tend to be pre-programmed to be aggressive, selfish, and competitive. But an introductory sociology course might attempt to resocialize students by teaching them that there is no evidence indicating humans are governed by predetermined, instinctual, and unlearned behavioural tendencies. This book is attempting to resocialize you to accept the idea that in a fundamental way you are the product of your social environment, an argument that may contravene messages you have received from a variety of other sources. Resocialization is also evident in how individuals are treated after they enter the army, where systematic efforts are made to inculcate them with new atti-

As human beings mature and develop, they begin to engage in ever more complex and numerous social interactions. They enter institutions and group settings, such as school or church, where they learn more complicated patterns of language and are introduced to society's norms, values, and behavioural expectations. *Secondary socialization* is the name given to the learning of these more complex aspects, which include symbols, folkways, and values. (Photograph courtesy of V.R. Rajagopalan)

tudes, beliefs, and modes of dress, speech, and behaviour. Similarly, if you are accepted into the Royal Canadian Mounted Police, systematic efforts will be made to change certain behavioural patterns. The same could be said of those who end up being incarcerated in prison, where systematic efforts to rehabilitate inmates are really nothing more than systematic efforts to resocialize them.

Anticipatory Socialization

As supposedly intelligent and knowledgeable creatures, we are often in a position to think about and plan our lives, or at least anticipate what might happen to us. When we realize we might soon be in a new situation, we sometimes try to figure out in advance what will be expected of us, what the dress codes might be, or with whom we might be interacting and what the protocol might be. In addition to just thinking about these issues, we might try to adopt the necessary views, actions, mannerisms, or dress, or we might even try to practise the actions we could be called on to perform.

For many students the first day at a new high school or university is a stressful situation—they do not yet know the rules. As a result, in situations like these some people may try to find out as much as they can in advance so they won't make fools of themselves or commit serious social blunders. If you join an exclusive golf and country club you will likely make sure that you understand and conform to the dress codes and other such rules, again to make your entry as smooth as possible. This process of adapting to a new situation in advance and thereby making adjustment to that situation easier is known as *anticipatory socialization.*

Socialization as Intentional and Unintentional

When we discuss social learning, or socialization, we are dealing with an extremely complex process that is sometimes the result of systematic and deliberate efforts and sometimes the more indirect and less deliberate outcome of social interactions. To fully understand socialization it is necessary to pay attention to this dual aspect.

Much primary socialization is quite intentional and deliberate, as in the systematic teaching of table manners, eating habits, and toilet training. But while parents intentionally attempt to teach their children a specific pattern of behaviour, they may also be unintentionally teaching them how to handle frustration and anger. When parents lose their tempers, for example, the children will, whether we want them to or not, learn about handling emotions.

Although it is often difficult to make a precise distinction between the intentional and unintentional, there is a clear example in the teaching and learning of language. Most of us have either observed or engaged in efforts to teach a young child some part of our language. For example, a child's caretaker holds up a metal or plastic object with a concave-shaped part at one end that is attached to a long, slender part. The caretaker says 'spoon', attempting to get the child to repeat the word. We all learned some of our linguistic skills in this way. But if we consider the very large number of words that a child typically learns during the first two years of life, it is remarkable how few of those words were systematically taught and learned. A great deal, if not most, of the language we learn during our formative years is 'picked up', that is, taught and learned in an unintentional manner as parents or caretakers and children go about their everyday normal routines. The distinction between deliberate, intentional socialization and the learning that occurs outside of intentional instruction will become more apparent as we consider the various agents of socialization.

There is a rich sociological literature dealing with the various deliberate and subtle dimensions of the socialization process. In her article 'Killers of the Dream', Lillian Smith describes the socialization of white Christian females in the American South during the early decades of this century (Smith, 1971). Harry Gracey's ([1977] 1999) essay with the provocative title 'Learning the Student Role: Kindergarten as Academic Boot Camp' provides an excellent overview of the great many things that are 'taught' in kindergarten as well as the methods employed.

Agents or Agencies of Socialization

The concept of socialization as a lifelong process of social learning leads to a further concept: the existence of agents or agencies that do the teaching that results in the learning. In sociology we use the term *agent* or *agency of socialization* to refer to the institutions, groups, organizations, situations, and statuses within the social structures that, in a variety of deliberate and non-intentional ways, mould, shape, and influence our beings, personalities, and development.

The precise and specific array of agents of socialization that are important varies from individual to individual, culture to culture, and historical moment to historical moment. In most modern Western societies the list of important agents of socialization includes family structures, the education system, religion, the media, peer groups, state agencies, and economic institutions.

Family
As suggested earlier, much of the necessary primary socialization that allows us to acquire the basic knowledge and skills necessary for subsequent social interaction takes place within that set of relationships referred to as the family—although we have to take care to avoid discussing 'the family' as if there were only one form or set of relationships that characterizes all activities under the rubric of family interaction. In most situations children's parents have an enormous impact on their development. It is often parents who teach children the rudiments of language and communicative skills, elementary eating habits and manners, culturally defined appropriate conduct for the elimination of bodily wastes, as well as basic norms and values relating to

many aspects of existence. Our first introduction to the female and male roles often occurs in the family. Members of the family, often without realizing it, demonstrate various ways of dealing with anger, frustration, anxiety, and affection.

Because many of our basic norms, values, and ideas about masculinity and femininity are acquired through interaction in the family, the family is one of the most important agents of socialization. But its role in gender socialization raises again the issue of deliberate versus subtle or unintentional socialization. The human infant seems to revel in mimicking (though grownups do this as well), and this is clearly a main method of learning. Despite what they may be trying to formally teach about sexual equality, when parents go about the daily routine of domestic labour (housework) they are instructing the child about sex and gender roles, duties, and behaviour. The almost infinite variety of subtle and unintentional ways by which socialization takes place has been extensively researched. In a study of the transmission of sex roles and gender behaviour, Sandra Bem and Daryl Bem note that even when their children are as young as two days old, there are noticeable differences in how parents treat girls and boys. Girls are touched more, hovered over more, smiled at more, and spoken at more (1982: 56–7). Although we may not know precisely how, such differences will tend to influence subsequent personality development.

Educational Institutions
Perhaps no institutional order is more directly involved in the socialization process in a systematic and deliberate way than the educational order. One dictionary defines education as 'systematic instruction, schooling, or training in preparation for life or some particular task; bringing up'.

The primary task of the educational order is to train, instruct, or school individuals in a variety of aspects of a culture, especially the elements of its formal stocks of knowledge: society's accumulated learning, skills, beliefs, traditions, and wisdom. In

Much of the primary socialization that allows us to acquire the basic knowledge and skills necessary for subsequent social interaction takes place within that set of relationships referred to as the family. (Photograph courtesy of Saskia Mueller)

Western societies this includes an ability to read and write in one or more languages, an elementary knowledge of mathematics and the sciences, as well as an appreciation of the society's history, geography, and physical environment. The educational order attempts to ensure that children acquire the basic skills necessary for interaction and participation in society.

School also introduces other aspects of a society's norms and values. For example, in school an individual is taught about gender roles, both in the formal content of the curriculum and the classroom and in the less formal playground environment. In the content of textbooks and library books as well as in playground interaction, children learn about being a girl or a boy, competition, and what it means to win or lose. Through the actions and words of teachers on the playground they learn about what is appropriate, what is encouraged, what is inappropriate, and what is officially taboo.

The formal school situation might be the first time that a child has to take orders and instruction from an outsider or stranger, that is, from someone not a blood relative. In school, children learn about neatness, punctuality, discipline, respect for others, and respect for authority, as well as patriotism and the role of competition in society. In a discussion of what has become known as the 'hidden curriculum', Canadian sociologist John Harp (1980) notes that a number of studies have focused on the importance of children learning competitive patterns in school, beginning at the kindergarten level. The sense of competition may not be as systematic and formally organized in the early years, but young pupils learn to compete for the attention and even affection of their teachers by demonstrating their skills in painting or printing—or even by encouraging the teachers' interest in their entries in show-and-tell contests. Harry Gracey makes the point even more dramatically, referring to kindergarten as an 'academic boot camp' that includes teaching children to learn 'to go through routines and to follow orders with unquestioning obedience, even when these make no sense to them' (1999: 332). While what we learn at school includes the core content of the basic curriculum, our education goes well beyond this, because most of the time we spend at school is really time spent with peers. In case you are prone to thinking this sort of thing only occurs with young children, see Howard Becker and Blanche Geer's 'The Fate of Idealism in Medical School' (1980).

The lyrics of some popular songs notwithstanding, Stephen J. Ceci suggests that school attendance has a positive impact on IQ. Although Ceci does not necessarily assume that one's score on a standardized IQ test is a measure of intelligence, he does argue that there is strong evidence that the longer one stays in school the higher one's IQ scores are (1999: 169). He offers an explanation:

The most parsimonious explanation of the full corpus of data and findings that I reviewed is that schooling helps prop up IQ because much of what is tapped by IQ tests is either directly taught in school (e.g., information questions on popular IQ tests, such as 'Who wrote Hamlet?' and 'What are hieroglyphics?' are taught in school or confronted in school-related activities such as plays and class trips, as are vocabulary items such as 'What is espionage?') or else indirectly taught by schools (e.g., modes of cognizing that emphasize one form of conceptual organization over another). In addition, schooling fosters disembedded ways of construing the world in terms of hypotheticals, and inculcates attitudes toward testing that may be favored by test manufacturers, such as sitting still for prolonged periods, trying hard, and making certain assumptions about the purposes of testing. (1999: 170)

Peer Groups

Not all socialization takes place within the structures or social arrangements we call institutions. Indeed, during certain periods in their lives, North American adolescents spend large amounts of time with their peers. The peer groups that are important vary as an individual matures and passes through the various stages of life.

During childhood, neighbourhood friends may be the most important peer group, while during adolescence a school-based crowd or clique becomes more important. The peer group is often a child's first experience in a situation that is not dominated by adults, and thus the child has more flexibility to explore interactive processes. Later in life the peer group that plays an important part in socialization may become centred on friends at work, in church or a club, or at university.

The primary group is, by definition, a group of people who really count and are important. The members of a clique in your school can have a profound impact on your conduct. Many of our habits, values, norms, language, and dress codes are acquired as a result of interaction with our peers. The fact that our ways of seeing the world and thinking about it are influenced by these interactions means that we are learning—that is, we are being socialized. These peer groups form an agent of socialization.

Mass Media

North Americans spend a great deal of time with mass media: watching television and videos, reading newspapers and magazines, going to movies, or listening to CDs, tapes, and the radio. In the process of watching, reading, and listening we are exposed to countless messages and signals touching on countless aspects of our social and physical being and behaviour.

For example, we acquire much of our information about events in the world, both locally and internationally, from the mass media. Many of us rely on the mass media for the latest 'news', and this information becomes central to how we understand, interpret, and generally feel about the world. Our sense of optimism or pessimism, joy or despair, relief or anxiety is influenced by what we see, hear, and read. The latest news on international relations, hunger in the Third World, political tensions in Europe, death squads in Central America, the seemingly daily carnage in the Middle East, and US bombing in Afghanistan all impact our understanding of the world and our personalities. Because our attitudes, beliefs, and values are being influenced, we are being socialized even as we simply watch, read, or listen to the news.

For anyone interested in the media, Noam Chomsky's *Necessary Illusions* (1989) is compulsory reading. Chomsky presents a chilling picture of the power of the media and those whose interests are supported by the media to mould our lives and what is commonly called public opinion through the manipulation of information. A similar argument is also developed in another book, Joyce

Nelson's *The Perfect Machine* (1987), a must-read for anyone who watches more than one hour of television a week.

But there is more to the media's role than just providing news. Indeed, a great many people who watch television avoid watching the news programs, preferring instead to be 'entertained' by the dramas, sports, variety and game shows, and situation comedies that make up the bulk of television time. Watching television to escape from the pressures of life is also part of the ongoing social learning process. People do in fact acquire much of their knowledge about how the world works from watching entertainment television. Unfortunately, as sociologists have found, the knowledge acquired can be dubious. All you need do is ask a local police officer how many children think police work is mostly about chasing dangerous criminals at high speeds, making massive drug busts, and collaring murderers. Ask someone who operates a private detective agency, or who is a lawyer, or a medical doctor if they think the television portrayal of his or her occupations is accurate. Nevertheless, it is clear that we do learn as we are being entertained. The learning may be of a subtle and unintentional type, but we are learning about many things, including roles and jobs, men and women, the role of violence in solving problems, minorities and how they behave, and children and aging.

Another component in the socializing content of the media is the role of advertising. Advertising has become an essential part of our lives. It is everywhere we go—not just in commercial mass media, but also on billboards, buses, and T-shirts. The central task of advertisers is to convince us to buy a particular product, and they accomplish this by the direct and indirect manipulation of our norms, values, beliefs, and behaviours. For example, if we become convinced that the perfectly normal human process of perspiring is disgusting and revolting and that we should do everything in our power to avoid that disastrous state of affairs, we become ready, in turn, to cover our bodies with various chemicals that solve the 'problem'. If we can be convinced that the most important thing in life is spotless laundry, we become prime candidates for a new soap product. The advertisements that we see and hear (and even smell now in some magazines) are designed to 'teach' us something. That is, they are designed to be a part of the social processes by which we learn of life's problems and how we should solve them.

Through all of this we are being instructed about what is important and what is not, what it means to be feminine and masculine, and how men and women relate to each other. Advertisements often suggest, for example, that how we appear in a physical sense is far more important than how we feel inside or how we react to others. As typically pictured, men are in command while women are obsessed with domestic cleanliness. As a child watches these images and messages day after day, year after year, the learning takes hold in a powerful way.

Religion

Much of the socialization or social learning that occurs within religious institutions is deliberate and systematic. Churches often have programs of instruction for people of every age, from nursery and Sunday schools for the young through various youth groups, adolescent membership rites, and premarital counselling to groups that help older members cope with the death of a spouse. At all of these stages there is continuing systematic instruction and, presumably, learning regarding various particulars of the church's beliefs, practices, doctrines, and rituals.

Religious socialization is important because of the comprehensive nature of the issues, concerns, or aspects of life covered. The norms, values, beliefs, and behaviours systematically taught by formally organized religions touch on most aspects of an individual's life, including everything from gender roles and sexual conduct and how we dress to our attitudes towards the rich and poor. What we eat, how we see

nature, how we deal with death, and how we respond to others with different beliefs: these are only a few aspects of our personalities that are influenced by religious beliefs and practices. Clearly, socialization plays a fundamental role in the acquisition of religious beliefs: even the most ardent biological determinist is not going to argue that some of us are born with a genetic propensity for Protestantism, Hinduism, or Buddhism. Our religious beliefs are learned, the product of our socialization.

Economic Institutions

Socialization also takes place within economic institutions. People who have had butterflies in their stomachs on the first day of a new job or who have hoped just to get through the first day or week on the job with out making a complete fool of themselves have felt the impact of the workplace on their behaviour. An essential part of the first few days on any new job is learning 'the ropes', that is, learning about the norms and values and language and roles that are a part of the routines of the job. If you learn about the various aspects of a job in advance, that represents a case of anticipatory socialization, while learning about them on the job is simply socialization.

A part of workplace socialization might include obvious things such as learning new and specialized languages, dress styles, codes, and expectations, as well as more subtle aspects of the work environment like obedience to authority, the importance of being punctual, and even making personal sacrifices for the employer. Among the best treatments of the work process and its enormous impact on virtually every facet of people's lives is Studs Terkel's fine book *Working* (1974).

The concept of 'good corporate' material implies a recognition on the part of corporations that certain individuals have the potential to be socialized and resocialized in a way that produces a budding executive. When corporations hire people who have certain basic skills and abilities and mould them to become future executive material, they are engaging in socialization. A person who joins a trade union for the first time also tends to become socialized into accepting a new set of roles, norms, values, and language.

State Agencies

Another type of socialization and resocialization occurs after an individual joins a branch of the military or a police force. In the case of military training, the concept of 'boot camp' is very much about socialization and resocialization. It is common for people joining the military to undergo radical changes in both their physical appearances and their character structures. Changes to physical appearance result from the rigorous physical fitness regimes, cropped hairstyles, improved posture, and new dress codes that accompany military training. Changes to personality could include a strengthened sense of patriotism, a more willing acceptance of authority and responsibility, and the decreased sense of individuality that comes with a stress on teamwork. A systematic account of the personality and character changes that result from several years of military service could well serve to highlight the changeability or plasticity of the human personality.

Internalizing Roles, Values, Norms

In his classic, *Invitation to Sociology: a Humanistic Perspective*, Peter Berger discussed the processes by which roles and identities come to be socially constructed. Berger explains that as we grow and develop we come to understand that there are concentric circles of social control that impact our behaviours. The precise modes of social control vary with the distance of the circle from the individual, meaning that your family and those closest to you, both figuratively in the vision of you at the centre with concentric circles emanating out and in your everyday life, will attempt to use certain modes of control. These will differ from those used by your co-workers or students in your school who are in a subsequent circle further out. Ever further out are those individuals with roles in the various formal legal and judicial systems that will adopt other

different modes of conduct in attempting to control your behaviour. What all these modes of social control tend to have in common is an overarching set of values and norms that prescribe certain behaviours as acceptable and appropriate or unacceptable and inappropriate. How your mom deals with the fact that you missed your curfew will be different from how the police officer deals with you when you violate a state-imposed curfew.

Berger suggests that your understanding, adoption, and adaptation of these various forms amounts to a process of internalization. As was noted above, we do not just learn roles—we *become* them. In Berger's own eloquent words:

> The key term used by sociologists to refer to the phenomena discussed in this chapter is that of internalization. What happens in socialization is that the social world is internalized within the child. The same process, though perhaps weaker in quality, occurs every time the adult is initiated into a new social context or a new social group. Society, then, is not only something 'out there', in the Durkheimian sense, but it is also 'in here', part of our innermost being. Only an understanding of internalization makes sense of the incredible fact that most external controls work most of the time for most of the people in a society. Society not only controls our movements, but shapes our identity, our thought and our emotions. The structures of society become the structures of our own consciousness. Society does not stop at the surface of our skins. Society penetrates us as much as it envelops us. Our bondage to society is not so much established by conquest as by collusion. (1963: 121)

Strong stuff—perhaps too strong. The time has come to take stock of our argument thus far and face up to the consequences of the position that is emerging.

The Cultural Determinist Position

The arguments concerning the central role of social learning in the development and structuring of the human personality take what can be called a *cultural determinist position*. This position holds that most, if not all, of our behavioural patterns and personality characteristics and traits can be accounted for by reference to the process of social learning, or socialization.

Such an approach allows little, if any, room for arguments that attempt to explain human behaviour or personality in terms of biological or genetic factors. Yet the cultural determinist position has distinct shortcomings: much of our human behaviour is directed towards meeting basic needs and dealing with basic drives that are, to the contrary, deeply rooted in our biology. Clearly, biology cannot be ignored.

On one hand, the process of socialization does not create the drives that manifest themselves in hunger or thirst, nor does it cause our sex drive to emerge or give us the mental capacity that leads us to ask the ultimate spiritual questions of religion. On the other hand, it would seem that without socialization and the social context we would be quite unable to deal successfully with our various drives and needs. The human personality, then, must be understood as a unique product of the interaction between biologically or genetically produced physiological and psychological possibilities and socialization.

If I, as an individual, am to survive and if my species is to continue to exist, I must eat, drink, excrete bodily wastes, deal with my sex drive, clothe myself, and take care of my young. What is unique about our species is the important role that social surroundings and socialization play in the development of the modes of conduct through which these needs and drives are addressed.

Our personalities or character structures are composed of a series of norms, values, folkways, mores, ideas, beliefs, roles, behaviours, attitudes, knowledge, and understandings that influence how we conduct ourselves. They are also based on a myriad of beliefs and attitudes relating to everything from politics and sports to religion. What is the origin of these various elements of personality? How do we explain them? The sociological answer comes through connecting our biological beings with the experiences we have had in our families, in the educational system, in religious settings, among various peer groups, through media exposures—and so on. In short, we explain development and personalities by analyzing the entire complex of social institutions, settings, situations, and experiences that have been a part of the socialization process, which has moulded our unique biological possibilities and potentials into what they are at this moment in time.

In their classic work, Logan Wilson and William Kolb (1949) use the term *original nature* to refer to the biological basis of human development. They are careful to note explicitly that the concept of original nature is different from the concept of human nature. The term *human nature* is usually associated with arguments maintaining that there are specific inborn and unlearned behaviours and characteristics that are associated with human beings regardless of their social environment. An example of an argument based on the existence of human nature might be the proposition that all humans, everywhere and always, are violent, selfish, self-centred, and competitive. Wilson and Kolb say that proponents of such a position frequently use the phrase 'you can't change human nature' to argue that such characteristics and behaviours are indeed genetically programmed and unchangeable. The term *original nature* refers to the biologically based potentials, structures, and abilities that the human organism possesses at birth or that emerge as a result of normal physiological growth and maturity.

In an important article, 'The Tangled Skeins of Nature and Nurture in Human Evolution', Paul Ehrlich explained the complex manner in which genetics and environment are intermingled. He noted that 'Every attribute of every organism is, of course, the product of the interactions between its genetic code and its environment' (2000: B9, emphasis in original). He goes on to warn us that 'attempts to dichotomize nature and nurture almost always end in failure' because a realistic examination of the issue should require us to examine 'the contributions of three factors: genes, environment and gene-environment interactions' (B10, emphasis in original). The last point I want to draw out of Ehrlich's work is his claim that if we use the term human nature we have to use it in the plural. What he means by this is that we have to talk about human natures with an emphasis on the fact that they change from society to society. In his words: 'There is no single human nature, any more than there is a single human genome, although there are common features to all human natures and all human genomes' (B11).

So perhaps it is best to think about our original nature as including physiological characteristics and structures such as our reflexes, drives, and intellectual capacities. Physiological features such as skin colour, facial features, natural hair colour, and, to a certain extent, body size, are biologically determined. A particular skin colour does not by itself necessarily have a bearing on personality or character structure; however, if a person's skin is dark and they live in a racist society, the social processes that they are exposed to as a result of having that physiological characteristic could influence their personality in direct ways. In such a case, do we point to the biological basis of personality or to the environmental factors?

The Cases of Feral Children

The interaction between biological givens and environmental or social conditioning becomes most obvious when a human being misses a substantial portion, if not all, of what we call the normal socialization process. The issue of social isolation and primate behaviour has fascinated humans for centuries. Prior to considering some of the literature on humans who have survived in relative isolation it is worthwhile to review some non-human research. Harry and Margaret Harlow are well known for their early experiments with rhesus monkeys (1976; 1976a).

The Harlows work involved the use of two different types of artificial mothers. One was made of uncovered wire with warming lights and a milk bottle while the other was made of wire covered with rubber & soft cloth. They conducted various experiments that demonstrated that infant monkeys preferred the soft figure even when the wire figure had been the only source of food. Other experiments further demonstrated that when frightened infant monkeys fled to the soft figure. In other research they demonstrated that monkeys reared in total isolation and with minimal human contact did not develop normal patterns of sexual interest, contact, or activity. Furthermore, those reared in isolation exhibited a range of abnormal behaviours, from spending an inordinate amount of time clutching themselves while rocking back and forth to excessive aggression. Indeed, many took no interest in their offspring, ignoring, neglecting, and even abusing them.

The word feral, indicating as it does a state of wildness or of being untamed, is not necessarily the most appropriate term to describe what are in essence unsocialized humans, but it has become widely used in sociology. A long mythology surrounds people who, for one reason or another, have been deprived of what sociologists call a normal socialization process. The stories date back at least to antiquity and the accounts of Remus and his twin brother Romulus (legendary founders of Rome), who were set adrift on the Tiber River by enemies, only to be washed ashore and suckled by a wolf. When considering the issue of feral, or wolf, children it is important to be sceptical of the literature. There are many 'wild' claims on web. For example, FeralChildren.com lists over 80 cases. The following are the apparent 'caregivers':

In descending order of mention	Supposed feral children
Not listed	7
Wolves	25
Primates	10
Dogs	8
Bears	7
Gazelles	3
Goats	2
Leopards	2
Sheep	2
Cow, pig, panther, jackal, ostrich, kangaroo	Each listed once

Needless to say, some of these apparent cases are a stretch on one's imagination; imagine some of these creatures caring for a human infant! The site does, however, mention a number of cases in which we have some degree of confidence.

In more modern times, an extensive literature has developed around the subject of feral children. In his book *Wolf Children and the Problem of Human Nature,* Lucien Malson (1972) presents an extensive review of stories and accounts of feral children, finding their origins in everything from ancient mythology to the modern press, some collaborated, some not. As its main focus, Malson's book reprints the diaries of Jean Itard, which provide detailed accounts of the discovery and subsequent development of a feral child called Victor.

Victor

The diaries of Jean Itard are of interest in the study of socialization because they represent one of the few systematic records of the behaviour of a human child who apparently survived for many years without significant human contact. There is no way of knowing at what age or under what circumstances the child Victor was abandoned. He was about 12 years old when he was finally 'captured', though he had been caught and held several times before January 1800, when he was placed in a hospital and subjected to systematic medical and scholarly attention.

The boy was examined by a variety of specialists, including naturalists and the famous psychologist Pinel. Victor, also referred to as the Wild Boy of Aveyron, demonstrated no capacity for language or conceptual thinking. His preferred foods were berries, roots, and raw chestnuts, and he made a murmuring noise while he ate. He seemed to dislike sweet and spicy foods. The boy liked to watch storm clouds and enjoyed rain. At first he constantly tried to escape. He seemed to enjoy cold and damp sleeping conditions, preferring, for example, the floor to a bed. He would sniff at everything that he was presented with and at first seemed not to notice loud noises very close to him, although he did seem to hear sounds like that of nuts being cracked. In his summary of Itard's initial observations, Malson notes that Victor seemed to show none of the characteristics we commonly associate with human civilization.

Victor's behaviour and condition stimulated considerable interest and study, and the overwhelming conclusion of the specialists of the day was that he was a congenital idiot, probably biologically defective. Itard, a medical doctor with a strong interest in psychological development, disagreed, arguing that Victor was most likely a normal child who had experienced an unusual childhood and that childhood experiences explained his condition. Itard took the opportunity to prove his point by working to transform the 'wild child' into a normal human being through an intensive socialization process.

We know a great deal about the work of Itard and his housekeeper Madame Guérin, because Itard wrote two detailed accounts of his work with Victor. Interestingly, although Madame Guérin did a great deal of the actual work and provided essential care for Victor, she has received little credit in the literature. Itard's reports, written to and for the government of the day, form the basis of what are referred to as his diaries.

In the reports Itard described their slow, laborious, and at first seemingly hopeless, work with Victor. At first just preventing Victor from running away was their main concern; however, gradually they were able to begin to teach Victor to follow simple directions, to distinguish between an object and the word that described the object, and to use letters, words, and even sounds. Victor gradually exhibited not only conceptual and intellectual growth but also emotional growth. There is solid evidence that he came to be attached to his caretakers. Although he never mastered speech, he was eventually able to understand words and communicate his simple and basic needs in writing.

Victor was eventually entrusted to the care of Madame Guérin, and he lived with her until his death at the age of 40. There is little systematic data on Victor's subsequent development, but we know from Itard's earlier reports that he was able to help with routine household duties and chores such as chopping wood and gardening.

Victor's case eventually formed the basis of the François Truffaut film *The Wild Child* (1969). But, as interesting as his case is, we might feel the need for more up-to-date data. Indeed, there have been periodic reports in the popular press about abandoned or feral children, and there have been several well-documented North American cases in this century.

Anna and Isabelle

In an article in the *American Journal of Sociology* in January 1940, the well-known US sociologist Kingsley Davis reported on the case of a child who had spent most of her life imprisoned in a single room in the house of her mother's father. This girl, called Anna, was the second illegitimate child born to her mother, and Anna's grandfather was so enraged by what he saw as the indiscretion of her mother that he refused to even look at the child. As a result, Anna was kept in seclusion in a second-floor room and given only enough attention to keep her alive.

Evidence gathered concerning Anna's history indicates that at the time of her birth in a private nurse's home she appeared normal and was even described as beautiful. But, Davis reported, when she was removed from the room in her grandfather's house and brought to a new home about five years later she was suffering from serious malnutrition and was completely apathetic. She lay in a 'limp, supine position, immobile, expressionless, indifferent to everything' (Davis, 1949: 555). She seemed to show little response to various stimuli, so at first the onlookers believed she was deaf and even blind. Anna did not know how to walk or talk; indeed, in a subsequent report Davis noted that she did not do anything that indicated intelligence (1949: 174).

Davis described the treatment Anna received in the various homes in which she was placed and, finally, the private home for mentally handicapped children in which Anna made her greatest strides. She was not given any systematic or particularly rigorous regime of training, but, as Davis noted, two years after her discovery Anna 'could walk, understand simple commands, feed herself, achieve some neatness, remember people, etc.' (1949: 175). About three years later she had learned to talk, although she mainly used phrases. In addition she worked with beads and pictures. She was concerned about keeping clean—she washed her hands habitually—and was able to run. Her general disposition was described as pleasant (176).

Anna's physical health never recovered from the effects of her malnutrition and isolation, and she died in 1942 at the age of 10. In his 1949 article Davis compared Anna's case with that of another girl who had also spent the first years of her life under unusual circumstances. The second girl, given the name Isabelle, was discovered shortly after Anna and had also been kept in seclusion because of her illegitimacy. Isabelle had been looked after by her mother, a deaf mute, and had received considerably more care than Anna. Nevertheless, she spent the first six years of her life secluded in a small room, and when she was removed and placed in an institution she showed few of the characteristics we associate with a child her age. She was in poor physical condition. She suffered from severe bowing of her legs, was unable to talk, and, at first, appeared to be deaf. She was subjected to a series of personality and intelligence tests and the results, predictably, showed little sign of intellect or ability.

Isabelle's treatment program was considerably more systematic and rigorous than the one given Anna. Those caring for her concentrated their efforts on teaching her elementary language skills, and while their efforts produced no results at first, the persistence of the team paid off. Once Isabelle began to learn language her progress took a dramatic leap forward. She moved quickly through a series of learning steps until her measured IQ had tripled in a year and a half. Davis reported that she struck him as 'being a very bright, cheerful, energetic little girl' (1949: 179). She was still behind others of her age in school, but had made such rapid strides that her future seemed no more uncertain than any other child's.

Genie

The 18 November 1970 *Globe and Mail* carried a story with the startling headline: 'Girl, 13, kept like a prisoner'. The story reported that a 13-year-old girl had been taken into Los Angeles police custody after having been kept in virtual seclusion since birth. Thus began the public story of a modern feral child, subsequently given the name Genie.

Genie's story is now documented in books, films, and articles (Rymer, 1992, 1993, 1994; Curtiss, 1977; Pines, 1981, 1997), however, even in a contemporary case, the details can be difficult to establish. In this case, it became clear that Genie's father was a very disturbed man who hated children. (Genie had three brothers and sisters but only one, as a result of the intervention of a grandparent, survived.) Genie's father—convinced that the child would die young—forced his wife to co-operate

with Genie's seclusion in a back room of the house. She was essentially harnessed to a potty chair or in a crib fitted with a wire mesh for her entire life. Genie was fed soft food (baby food, cereal, and sometime soft boiled eggs) and beaten with a piece of wood if she uttered a sound.

Genie's mother—a victim of spousal abuse—had acquiesced to her husband on the condition that if the child lived to be 12 she could get her help. When Genie's father reneged, Genie's mother removed the child from the house while planning to attend a medical appointment for her failing eyesight. Apparently Genie's mother inadvertently walked into a family aid office where the social workers immediately knew something was wrong. They called the police. Genie was taken into custody and her parents were arrested. Genie's father, who Michael Newton, author of the book *Savage Girls and Wild Boys: A History of Feral Children*, describes as 'hating the world' (2002: 211), killed himself before trial and her mother subsequently escaped conviction on the grounds that she, like Genie, was a victim of his violent behaviour.

Various accounts of Genie's condition can be found in the literature; however all of them paint a picture that Newton says 'beggared belief' (214). He writes:

> She was malnourished, thin, incontinent. Her short, dark hair was sparse, her eating habits disgusting; she salivated and spat constantly. She would only glance at you, then look away; she smelled objects by holding them close to her pallid face. Stooped and frail, her gait pigeon-toed, her body was bent at the waist; her shoulders hunched forward, her hands held up before her like a rabbit or comic zombie returned from the dead. She could only make a strange sound in her throat; language was beyond her (214).

Rymer notes that after her arrival at the hospital Genie 'quickly became an object of intense

THE IQ DEBATES

The issue of intelligence, what it means, how it is measured, and the explanation for apparent different 'levels', has been at the centre of the nature/nurture controversy for decades. In a recent book, *Are We Hardwired? The Role of Genes in Human Behaviour*, William R. Clark and Michael Grunstein present the conventional biological argument with reference to some twin-study data.

IQ: **It's in the Genes**

The debate about whether IQ tests measured acquired knowledge (content) or basic mental functioning (ability) continues to this day. At the same time, evidence that variability in performance IQ tests is heritable—whatever it is these tests actually measure—continues to grow. As with the relation of genes to human personality, the best data we have for estimating the relative contributions of genes and the environment to mental function comes from family studies, particularly studies of adopted children, and of monozygotic and dizygotic twins reared together or apart. A few starts in this direction had been made in the 1930; the results were suggestive, but not definitive, and were understandably greeted with suspicion by those becoming alarmed about the social and political implications of eugenics. But a comprehensive reanalysis carried out in 1960 of the existing literature on adoption and twin studies revealed a definite correlation between degree of genetic relatedness and performance on IQ-tests. For example, a parent and an adopted child are no more likely to score the same on an IQ-test than two randomly selected unrelated individuals, even after many years of a close family relationship. A parent and a biological child, on the other hand, are much more likely to score close to one another—even when the child is adopted out at birth, and the parent and child are tested only later in life.

Follow-up studies over the ensuing years have strengthened this correlation. Detailed analyses of monozygotic twins reared together or apart, such as those from the Minnesota Twin Study, have been particularly informative. Thomas Bouchard, in a paper published in 1998, summarized the results from five different, well-controlled twin studies. Genetically identical twins reared together or apart had IQ test score correlations of about 0.75; dizygotic twins reared together or apart had IQ test score correlations of 0.38. Adopted children and their adoptive siblings had IQ test correlations of about 0.28 when they were young, but this correlation essentially disappears by the time the children leave home. According to Bouchard, these correlations allow the conclusion that at least 70 percent of the variability among individuals in performance on IQ tests is due to genetic differences. The results in all of the twin studies, using a variety of testing techniques, were remarkably similar. So while we cannot be entirely sure exactly what aspect of mental function it is that IQ tests measure—perhaps nothing more than the ability to take IQ tests—it seems quite clear that variability in performance on these tests is to a large extent heritable, and thus has a genetic basis *(229–30)*.

From ARE WE HARDWIRED? THE ROLE OF GENES IN HUMAN BEHAVIOR by William R. Clark and Michael Grunstein, copyright © 2001 by Oxford University Press, Inc. Used by permission of Oxford University Press, Inc.

COUNTERPOINT

Orlando Patterson critiques the notion that IQ test results represent some measure of innate ability. His contribution to the debate over *The Bell Curve* includes the following arguments that call into question many of Clark and Grunstein's claims.

Genes or Not: What Are We Really Testing?

Now, recall that, throughout *The Bell Curve,* and indeed among all hereditarian psychologists, it is claimed that intelligence, as measured by IQ tests, is highly hereditary: ranging between .40 and .80, and taken to be .60 by Herrnstein and Murray. If we return to the equation for heredity which is commonly employed—and the one used throughout *The Bell Curve* (h2 = Vg/Vp) in the light of one well established principle of genetic selection, we are immediately faced with what Vale calls a 'nice irony'. The selection principle in question is the fact that any trait which has been under strong selection for a long evolutionary period will demonstrate very little additive genetic variance and should consist mainly of dominance and possibly epistatic variance, the reason being that almost all the additive genetic variance—which is the only component of the three elements of total genetic variance that responds to evolutionary selection—will have been 'used up', so to speak. This being so, the hereditarians are faced with an embarrassing, because inexplicable, dilemma *(195)*.

The problem which Herrnstein, Jensen, and all hereditarian psychologists face then, from the discipline on which they have so heavily drawn, is that IQ scores are too hereditary if they are to sustain the claim that these tests have any significance beyond the test center and classroom. Whatever it is that IQ tests are measuring, whatever it is that g is—whether it be some Platonic ideal, or g for ghost, a pun which Ryle might not have intended when he dismissed the whole thing in his *Concept of Mind* as 'the ghost of the machine'—it could have nothing whatever to do with those vitally important behavioral qualities that meaningfully account for our survival in both broad evolutionary and narrower sociological terms.

I return, then, to my more familiar sociological terrain with this understanding of the problem. Intelligence is not an essence but a process, not some operationally inferred static entity, indicated by IQ tests—and the much beloved analogies with the discovery of gravity and electricity are as pretentious and silly as the tautology that intelligence is whatever it is that IQ tests are testing—but that mode of thinking, symbolizing, acting, and interacting which, in their totality, facilitates survival in, and/or mastery of, its environment by an individual or group. It is acknowledged that cognitive functioning is central to this behavioral configuration, and further, that genetic factors are important in its determination—that, indeed, intelligence was a major factor in our evolution as a species—but that there is absolutely no way in which we can meaningfully separate genetic and environmental effects, and that, given the impossibility of conducting experiments on human populations, it is practically impossible, theoretically misguided, sociologically reprehensible, and morally obtuse to attempt to separate or even talk about the two as distinct processes *(196–7)*.

From Orlando Patterson, 'For Whom the Bell Curves' in Steven Fraser, ed., *The Bell Curve Wars* (New York: Basic Books, 1995).

interest among a host of doctors and scientists' (1992: 43). The reason is understandable—Genie represented the forbidden experiment, a chance to study how humans learn and develop first hand! Myra Pines writes in 'The Civilizing of Genie':

> The discovery of Genie aroused intense curiosity among psychologists, linguists, neurologists, and others who study brain development. They were eager to know what Genie's mental level was at the time she was found and whether she would be capable of developing her faculties. 'It's a terribly important case,' says Harlan Lane, a psycholinguist at Northeastern University who wrote *The Wild Boy of Aveyron*. 'Since our morality doesn't allow us to conduct deprivation experiments with human beings, these unfortunate people are all we have to go on.'

Indeed, Rymer quotes one of the doctors involved with Genie, who noted that she was 'perhaps one of the most tested children in history' (62). As was the case with the other children, and as may be gleaned from the description above, Genie's case seemed quite hopeless at first. Pines describes her in this way:

> Working with Genie was not an easy task. Although she had learned to walk with a jerky motion and became more or less toilet trained during her first seven months at Children's Hospital, Genie still had many disconcerting habits. She salivated and spat constantly, so much so that her body and clothing were filled with spit and 'reeked of a foul odor,' as Curtiss recounts. When excited or agitated, she urinated, leaving her companion to deal with the results. And she masturbated excessively.

Much controversy still surrounds Genie's subsequent treatment and development. One issue revolves around a series of custody battles. It seems that she spent time in and out of the hospital, at the home of one of the special education teachers, with the family of one of the doctors, with her mother, and, finally, in a series of foster homes before she entered an institution for intellectually challenged adults, where she apparently remains today.

As for what those who worked with, and on, her learned, there is debate and disagreement. The matter of most interest was Genie's capacity to learn language after such a long period of silence. Linguists who had debated the role of innate and universal language learning capacities were interested in her case. Equally interested were those who were critical of this notion and believed that there were key periods for learning, which, if missed, might never be recoverable. In his *New Yorker* articles Rymer paints a picture of amazing change and progress:

> Genie, for one, seemed oblivious of the battles behind the scenes. For the first time in her life she was being treated relatively the same as other children, and was, relatively thriving. Her mental and physical development had begun almost immediately on her admission to hospital. By her third day she was able to dress herself and was voluntarily using the toilet, though her incontinence problems were persistent. (64)

He documents equally amazing progress in terms of her acquisition of language in the form of an increased vocabulary. He quotes Curtiss as describing her as 'hungry to learn the words for all the new items filling her senses' (66). On the matter of her actual brain development, Rymer notes that initial tests had indicated that Genie's left hemisphere was almost totally void of activity. As an explanation, he suggests that this was because Genie had not been exposed to language; without language to stimulate it, that portion of the brain remains essentially dormant (68–69).

What we can learn from Genie's tragedy remains an open question. Rymer, for one, is critical of those in charge of Genie for ignoring her emotional and personal needs in their haste to study her (1992: 77). The precise conclusions linguists can draw remain open to debate. Peter Jones has a number of criticisms—reprinted on the web site FeralChildren.com—of the conclusions that Curtiss and others have drawn. What we do know is that Genie had significant, probably what one might call normal, potential to become a functioning member of society but the circumstances of her tragic 'upbringing' robbed her of that.

The Lessons

Although the backgrounds of Victor, Anna, Isabelle, and Genie are different, their cases provide certain insights into human conduct.

Perhaps the first point to consider is the actual behaviour of these children who had been denied a 'normal' socialization process. Are there any common patterns of behaviour or conduct present in humans who are substantially unsocialized? If we are looking for specific characteristics or traits, the answer is no. These four children did not exhibit uniform behaviour that could be defined as aggressive, violent, gregarious, co-operative, loving, competitive, or anything else. They did exhibit the human capacity of locomotive activity, which Thomas Williams (1972) calls gross random movement, meaning that people have the innate physiological capacity, based on our muscle, bone, and tendon structures, for a great many random and different motor movements. Isabelle and Victor each demonstrated this ability early on, and Anna later displayed the ability. Other than this, the children had little in common.

The conclusion we can draw from these studies is that when reared in isolation, or at least under conditions of relative social isolation, human beings do not tend to develop identifiable and distinguishable characteristics. Instead we seem to possess, as Ruth Benedict argued, enormously wide and varied potentials and possibilities. Furthermore, to fully develop our human potentials and possibilities, we require a social environment and social contact with others.

A recent volume, *The Nurture Assumption: Why Children Turn Out the Way They Do* by Judith Harris, has renewed the debate about the role of deliberate nurture. The major theme of the book is that parents are not necessarily *the* most important agent of socialization. What is controversial about the book is the claim that it is peers and peer interactions that are the most important environmental factors. Harris also seems to suggest that genes seem to play a significant role in certain behaviours. Several of the responses to the Harris book, including Joseph LeDoux's review (1998) and a commentary by Stanley Greenspan contradict the Harris thesis, claiming in the words of the title of Greenspan's piece that 'Parents DO Matter'. An issue that both authors raise relates to the interconnection between the environment and the development of the brain and the mind. According to Sara Gable and Melissa Hunting (2000), children pass though a series of important phases of physiological development, and the overall environment during these periods is very important for the subsequent development of both the brain and the mind. So the role of parents as part of the larger environment is, they claim, essential.

Recent data on the impact of childhood deprivation provides some food for thought. Michael Rutter has studied the development of about one hundred babies from Romania who were adopted by English parents. The babies had suffered significant malnutrition and neglect in Romanian orphanages during a period when a repressive government regime was disintegrating. All the children in the study were, by a variety of measures, 'severely developmentally impaired' at the time of entry (1999: 116). The study documents the developmental catch-up using a number of physiological and psychological indicators. Even though the children were in very poor condition as a result of the situation in the institutions in Romania, Rutter notes that 'the degree of cognitive catch-up by the age of four years was spectacular' (127). Those children who were adopted before they were six months old were on par with other adopted children from within England by the time they were four years old. The study concludes that 'the initial developmental deficit was a function of the children's prolonged experience of grossly depriving conditions, and that the subsequent catch-up was a function of the radical improvement in rearing conditions' (129). Ann Clark and Alan Clarke studied the extent to which children can recover from early negative childhood environments and experiences. Their conclusion is that many children are, in fact, able to overcome the potential limitations that result from negative early experiences. They note that 'children rescued from adversity progress on average to normality', although such children might be more vulnerable to regression if they are placed under similar stress later (1999: 143). Of the feral children above, Anna and Victor seem to have had the best treatment and both exhibited amazing progress.

Critical Thinking Questions

- Discuss four ways that your social experiences or environment have influenced your biological being.
- Discuss how the mass media has influenced your values, norms, and patterns of behaviour.
- What does a sociologist mean when he or she says we tend to become our roles?
- What, in your experience, is the most important agent of socialization? Explain your answer.
- Can feral children think and reason? If they do, in what language do they think?

Terms and Concepts

Socialization—the lifelong process of social learning that human beings undergo. As one of the most important concepts in sociology, it is variously defined as everything from the process of cultural transmission to the acquisition of a personality. Socialization influences virtually every aspect of our beings and personalities from key physiological processes to our character structure. Social learning occurs in practically every social setting, and nearly all our social experiences contribute to what and who we are.

Agents of socialization—the institutions, groups, organizations, sources, social situations, and locations within which we are socialized. Agents of socialization include statuses in institutions as well as social and cultural settings in which we learn certain ways of acting and behaving. For example, as you prepare to get a driver's licence you encounter a number of different agents of socialization including driving instructors, teachers, parents, other drivers, and traffic situations. If you learned to drive in a small community and subsequently move to a big city, the traffic situations you encounter on the expressway then literally become a site of social learning and thus an agent of socialization.

Primary socialization—the basic social learning that typically occurs during the first few years of a life. Primary socialization is the acquisition of a basic knowledge of a society's values, norms, folkways, and mores and thus includes learning things like language, eating practices, everyday rules of conduct, and etiquette.

Secondary socialization—the process of acquiring the more complex and subtle knowledge that we need in order to interact and behave appropriately in the many complex roles we engage in as we mature and become involved in more and more institutions and group behaviour. Primary socialization may not teach us how to act in school, a lecture hall, a union meeting, or a boardroom; however, as a result of secondary socialization we acquire this knowledge later in life.

Resocialization—the social learning process that involves deliberate and sometimes systematic efforts to change an aspect of what was previously learned. In an introductory sociology course, efforts may be made to resocialize you in order to have you understand and accept the sociological perspective. If you join the military or the RCMP you will also certainly be resocialized.

Anticipatory socialization—learning values, norms, behaviours, and modes and rules of conduct in anticipation or in advance of some situation when you might need them. Before entering a new social or institutional setting we frequently learn what might be expected of us—how to dress, how to talk—in order to make our entrance into that new setting easier and to avoid embarrassing mistakes.

Feral children—children who have for some reason missed a significant portion of the 'normal' socialization. Sometimes referred to as 'wolf children', feral children typically have survived in a degree of social isolation that usually results in death. Among the well-documented cases are Victor, Anna, Isabelle, and most recently Genie.

Related Web Sites

http://www.library.unr.edu/instruction/courses/hdfs/hdfs435.html

This University of Nevada (Reno) site includes a substantial listing of studies, links, and databases dealing with various aspects and issues relating to child socialization. It includes a select list of Web sources worldwide.

http://www.aber.ac.uk/media/Functions/mcs.html

As you think about the media as an agent of socialization, this site developed by the College of Education at the University of Oregon provides a wealth of information. There are file tab buttons for a range of related issues in media studies ranging from gender and ethnicity to TV, radio, films, popular music, and other search engines.

http://www.pbs.org/wgbh/nova/transcripts/2112gchild.html

The full transcript of the Nova program on Genie

(PBS Television) first broadcast on 4 March 1997 is available here. It's an important source in developing lessons from the feral children studies.

http://www.socialpsychology.org/

Scott Plous maintains this site that includes over five thousand links to sources relating to social psychology. Sociologists can and do learn much from social psychology and the range of resources available here is second to none in my experience.

http://www.familyeducation.com/topic/front/0,1156,3-2482,00.html

Based on the assumption that the relationships between parents and children is important, this site provides interesting research opportunities by linking to articles, idea exchange sites, and current debates.

Suggested Further Readings

Lewontin, R.C. 1993. *Biology as Ideology*. Concord, ON: Anansi. A published transcript of the 1990 CBC Massey Lectures, this text comprises five very tightly packed chapters that address the scientific and political dimensions of the resurgence of biological determinism.

Lewontin, R.C., S. Rose, and L. Kamin. 1986. *Not in Our Genes.* Harmondsworth, UK: Penguin Books. This remains one of the most systematic and detailed critiques of the science and politics of biological determinism.

Macionis, J., and N. Benokraitis, eds. 2001. *Seeing Ourselves,* 4th edn. Upper Saddle, NJ: Prentice-Hall. This comprehensive set of readings drawn from a variety of contemporary and classical and cross-cultural sociological sources covers a range of issues.

Rymer, R. 1993. 'A Silent Childhood, Parts I and II'. *The New Yorker* (13 and 20 April). A two-part article, this is an excellent account of the details of the modern feral child, Genie. The article documents her actual story and the tragic series of events surrounding her 'treatment'.

Wright, L. 1997. *Twins.* New York: John Wiley. This is a very detailed and readable overview of some of the evidence for and against the genetic determination of complex behaviours from the perspective of a journalist.

CHAPTER 5

Theories of Socialization

Most social scientists acknowledge that the concept of socialization is fundamental to understanding how our personalities are formed and our behaviour is structured. But once we've learned the basic tenets—the types of socialization, the possible agents and agencies—further questions arise. Exactly how does socialization take place? How does the process make its distinctive impact on our personalities and social behaviour?

These new questions bring about new theories. Social scientists have spent long hours trying to explain the more intricate workings of socialization and, as always, the answers to 'what makes socialization work' are contentious. Here we will explore several key theories of learning and personality development in order to determine their value in coming to our own understanding of the socialization process. We begin with one of the earliest arguments.

Conditioning Theory

Classical Conditioning

Classical conditioning was one of the first theories developed to explain how animals, including humans, learn.

We commonly, and correctly, associate the term *classical conditioning* with the work of the Russian physiologist Ivan Pavlov—though Pavlov was originally interested not in learning theory but in the study of the digestive processes of dogs. As a part of his research Pavlov presented dogs with food

and measured their salivation response. As he was carefully making his observations he noticed that after a while the dogs would salivate when they saw the food dish, that is, before they actually got to take the food into their mouths. Based on these observations Pavlov concluded that the dogs had learned to associate their dishes with food, and that the dish itself had become a stimulus to produce salivation.

The dogs did not have to be trained to salivate when they were presented with food, because the salivation was a natural response. In other words, the food was a natural or unconditioned stimulus, and salivation was the natural, unconditioned response. What happened was that the dish, as a stimulus to salivation, became a substitute for the food. The dish became a conditioned or learned stimulus, and salivation at the sight of a dish was a learned or conditioned response. A conditioned stimulus is one that has become associated with an original stimulus; and thus it is a learned and not a natural stimulus. Although it is considered natural for a hungry dog to salivate when food is presented, there is nothing in the natural repertoire of a dog's behaviour that causes it to salivate at the sight of a dish. The conditioned response is the one elicited by the conditioned stimulus. To prove his point, Pavlov subsequently conditioned dogs to salivate at the sound of a bell, something that originally would not be associated in any way with food.

While there is debate about the extent to which classical conditioning explains human conduct, it is clear that we do learn some things this way. Imagine a child's first encounter with a hot stove. The child, reaching out and touching the stove, feels the pain at the same time that a parent shouts, 'Hot—don't touch!' After repeating this unfortunate lesson a few times the child comes to associate the words *Hot—don't touch!* with pain. So when the child is about to touch a hot barbecue in the backyard and someone shouts 'hot', the conditioned response is avoidance. The child has come to associate the word *hot* with pain and will avoid objects if others say they are hot.

Imagine another situation involving parents, their children, and a snake. The parents have a pathological and irrational fear of snakes, and each time they encounter even a harmless garter snake they shout out and jump away. After a few such encounters the children come to associate a snake with an unpleasant experience, and the snake becomes a conditioned stimulus that brings on a conditioned response of fear or flight.

The American psychologist John Watson developed the most forceful arguments relating to the usage of conditioned learning for human development. In an oft-quoted statement, Watson declared that there were almost no limits to the capacity of conditioned learning to mould the human personality.

> Give me a dozen healthy infants, well-formed, and my own specified world to bring them up in, and I'll guarantee to take any one at random and train him to become any type of specialist I might select—doctor, lawyer, artist, merchant-chief, and, yes, even beggar, and thief, regardless of his talents, penchants, tendencies, abilities, vocations, and race of his ancestors. (quoted in Robertson, 1981: 107)

Watson, fortunately for the sake of his potential human subjects, never carried out the project. The general approach was subsequently criticized, largely because of its simplicity. Others working in the area of human learning suggested that the classical conditioning approach was not adequate to account for the complex patterns of learning that humans experience.

Operant Conditioning

The most famous proponent of a second school of conditioning theory, operant conditioning, is B.F. Skinner.

Skinner approached human behaviour as if all actions were responses to stimuli. He did not believe we could understand, or that we should try to understand, what went on between a stimulus and a response, because science had to concern itself only with observable phenomena. Skinner's focus therefore is on operant behaviour rather than, like classical conditioning, on respondent behaviour. Operant behaviour can be produced by a stimulus; however, the stimulus may not necessarily precede the behaviour, as it does in classical conditioning. When a chicken pecks on a button and receives food as a reward it eventually learns to peck the button in order to receive food. Skinner is well known for advocating the use of rewards in teaching and for the Skinner box (Schultz, 1975: 245–50).

According to the theory of classical conditioning, an organism learns to associate an 'unnatural' or secondary stimulus with an original stimulus, and as a result the second stimulus or conditioned stimulus becomes enough to elicit a response. Operant conditioning refers to situations in which an organism actually learns to behave in certain ways as a result of the response it receives when it acts or behaves in that way. For example, if an initial action is followed by a positive reward, the organism taking that action will learn that it is the appropriate way to act in order to receive the reward. However, a negative reward (punishment) will deter the organism from taking the action that produces it. If an initial action is followed by a punishment, the organism will learn to avoid that action. For example, if a hungry chicken accidentally pecks a green button in its cage and food is released, the chicken, with a sufficient number of successful repetitions of the action, will come to learn that pecking the green button is the way to acquire food. In a similar fashion, an organism encountering a negative experience or some form of punishment will learn to associate the action with its unpleasant consequences and avoid the behaviour. The proverbial slap on the wrist can be understood as a form of operant conditioning.

These approaches are usually linked under the general heading of behaviouralism (Salkind and Ambron, 1987: 199). A major criticism of the approach from sociologists is that it presents an overly simple view of human personality and human development because the human learning process is said to follow a pattern similar, if not identical, to that in non-human animals. Many social scientists and philosophers have argued that humans and the patterns of learning they exhibit are indeed qualitatively different from non-humans and non-human patterns.

Jean Piaget

Jean Piaget (1896–1980), a renowned Swiss psychologist, challenged many of the arguments of conventional conditioning theory, arguing that the formation of the human personality is more complex than indicated by the behaviouralist position. Piaget is also important because he offered a perspective on personality formation based on a recognition of the roles of both biology and society. For Piaget the biological component is self-evident, because humans are biological creatures who undergo processes of growth, development, and maturation. Much of our personal, intellectual, and moral development is predicated on a certain sequence of physical growth and maturation. The processes of becoming a mature, intelligent adult are a complex interaction of biology or heredity and experience or environment.

The role of physical biological maturation is apparent in Piaget's ideas about the human stages of development. Each stage involves both physiological or biological maturation and development of the individual as well as the emergence of unique and distinctive cognitive skills and methods of learning. Indeed, Piaget is best known for his arguments about cognitive structures, a notion that refers to the tendency of all human children to exhibit common or standard rules for problem-solving and reasoning at each stage of development. The discovery of sequential patterns of development that move a child from the use of one set of rules to another led Piaget to theorize that these changing patterns of cognition were tied to or related to the correlated physical and psychological development or maturation of the individual.

Based on observations of his own children and experiments with others, Piaget concluded that there were four distinct stages or periods of development:

1. Sensorimotor. A stage covering birth to about 2 years of age.
2. Preoperational. Lasting from about 2 years old to age 7.
3. Concrete operational. Years 7 to about 11.
4. Formal operational. Lasting from about age 11 to full maturity in adulthood.

Piaget associated unique or distinctive modes of cognition, reasoning, knowing, social and psychological development, and learning with each of these stages.

Sensorimotor Stage

In a collaborative work with Barbel Inhelder (Piaget and Inhelder, 1969), Piaget further subdivides the sensorimotor stage into six substages; here we need only note the general flow of their discussion. During the first stage, human infants gradually come to understand that they are unique and distinctive beings with an existence apart from others. Children tend to experience the world directly, that is, they physically manipulate objects they encounter by attempting to touch or hold

Renowned Swiss Psychologist Jean Piaget concluded that there were four distinct phases or periods of development. The first phase is the sensorimoter stage, from birth to two years of age. In this stage, children tend to experience the world directly, that is, they physically manipulate objects they encounter by touching and holding them. (Photograph courtesy of Phyllis Wilson)

them. In doing this they are essentially exploring the world and learning about their senses and motor capacities, as well as using their senses and motor capacities to learn about the world. Cognitive activity is at a low level, due in part to linguistic capacities.

Although early on in this stage children are not capable of comprehending things outside their immediate sight, they eventually develop a sense of the permanence of an object; they come to realize that an object continues to exist even if they do not actually see it at a given moment. For example, a typical 10-month-old child playing with a toy will immediately lose interest in that toy if the object is covered up. The child will simply transfer attention to something else. When the same experiment is done with older children, they will try to find the objects they had been playing with.

Imitation is a key part of the learning process during the sensorimotor stage. By the end of the period children are beginning to master the use of language, an important prerequisite for the process of symbolic thought that characterizes the child's cognitive capabilities in later stages. Piaget argues that the use of symbolic thought becomes apparent when a child uses one object as a substitute for another. The ultimate expression of the capacity for symbolic thought is the child's use of language.

Preoperational Stage

At about 2 years of age children mature to the point that they pass into the second stage of cognitive development, which lasts until they are about 7. The preoperational stage is marked by a dramatic increase in linguistic capacities; however, the children are literal in the use of language and the focus of all understanding still tends to be their own being. They are self-centred. At this age they are unable to fully understand the world from the perspective of others and unable to describe things from a hypothetical or abstract perspective that is different from the one they are physically located in. If you ask children in this stage a question about how something might look from a different perspective or angle, they tend to ignore your question because they simply cannot envision or comprehend the possibility of an alternative point of view.

At this stage children's understanding of language and physical perspectives is limited. They will use language in a way that seems to be unaware of the perspective of the listener. They will also use language in a quite literal fashion, accepting little or no ambiguity in terms. Their literal and limited cognitive capacity is illustrated by what Piaget calls conservation. For example, if you take two glasses of water that are the same size, each containing an equal amount of water, and show them to children in this stage, they will probably agree that the glasses contain the same amount of liquid. If you pour some of the liquid from one glass into a thinner and taller glass, the water level becomes higher in that

glass. The children will tend to argue that the taller, thinner glass with the higher water level contains more liquid. Similarly, if children are shown two rows of similar objects such as blocks or dominos that are equally spaced and equal in length, they will probably tell you that each row contains the same number of items. If you spread out the items in one row so that it appears longer, these children will tend to say that the new row contains a greater number of the objects. These responses indicate that the children have not come to understand the principle of conservation, namely that changes in the physical arrangements of objects do not change their quantity. The logical capacity of reversibility develops later, and children then come to realize that every action has a logical opposite.

Concrete Operational Stage

Around the age of 7 children pass into the last of Piaget's key *childhood stages* of cognitive development. During the concrete operational stage their cognitive capacities begin to illustrate the types of logic that we commonly associate with adult thinking. They begin to understand the logical principle of conservation, that all judgments cannot be merely based on how things appear.

While there are still limits on the cognitive abilities of children, especially in the area of abstract reasoning, they make great intellectual strides during this stage. Among the important cognitive capacities they develop is the ability to understand complex social relations. A child develops the ability to understand that the same person can be a mother, a sister, a daughter, an aunt, even a friend, depending on the position of the reference person. The world, the child comes to realize, is not nearly as simple and literal as it once seemed.

The children's increased cognitive capacities demonstrate a much more significant use of logic and a degree of abstract reasoning, but they are still somewhat limited and dependent on practical and concrete intelligence. This means that they can operate most effectively when there are actually objects in the immediate environment to be manipulated. Children move into the realm of fully abstract reasoning during the final stage of development.

Formal Operational Stage

According to Piaget, at about 11 years of age children pass into the last stage of development, which lasts through adulthood. The formal operational stage is the culmination of the development of cognitive capacities. It is the stage during which our full capacity for abstract and logical reasoning emerges.

Our final cognitive ability is the capacity to reason abstractly and to use hypothetical concepts and thinking. When confronted with a problem we are able to think through a wide range of possible solutions in advance. Because of our capacity for abstract thought and abstract reasoning, we do not have to experience things directly to be able to think about them and solve problems related to them. During this stage of our development we acquire the capacity to work with analogies and abstract ideas as well as to accept arguments that might appear to be contrary to the apparent facts. The full human capacity for using abstract thought, symbols, and logic becomes apparent. We can think in terms of hypothetical possibilities and communicate our ideas to others who readily accept them, even in the absence of immediate, concrete, experiential data.

Moral Development

In his studies of the moral development of children, Piaget found that children pass through two stages of development. He called the first period, which lasted from about years 4 through 7, the stage of moral realism. Children in this stage of development tend to take the presence and legitimacy of rules and regulations for granted. They tend not to question the origins of rules but accept them at face value and treat them as sacred and not to be questioned. In this stage children exhibit what Piaget calls unilateral respect for the adult or other person in charge of administering the rules.

In one case that Piaget describes as an example of typical behaviour of moral realism, children were told stories about two boys. When called for dinner the first boy went immediately, but on the way into the dining room he accidentally bumped into a teacart, breaking 15 cups. The second boy accidentally broke one cup while he was climbing on a cupboard to get some jam he had been told not to eat. When asked which boy deserved to be punished more severely, the children answered that the boy who broke 15 cups deserved more punishment because his actions had caused more damage. They apparently made no distinction between the intent of or reason for the actions and the outcome.

As they mature in a cognitive sense children gradually begin to develop a more sophisticated and complicated approach to moral issues. As this happens they move towards the stage of moral development called moral autonomy. Children exhibiting moral autonomy do not simply accept 'black-and-white' interpretations of rules and moral issues. They question the legitimacy of rules and regulations, asking why actions were undertaken before passing judgments on their outcomes. In a game situation, the moral autonomist might agree, providing all others involved have agreed, to change the rules of a game. Such an attitude, which exhibits a stronger sense of social being, develops as children mature in their physical and cognitive capacities.

What we find in Piaget, then, is an approach demanding that we pay attention to both intellectual and physical development and maturation in our efforts to understand the human personality. The individual human is a unique combination of a physiological developmental and maturation process that takes place within an equally unique social and learning situation. The theory argues that we all share something in common, in that we have all passed through a series of stages in both our physical and cognitive maturation. Our differences are understandable in terms of the uniqueness of the biological basis of our being and our experiences.

The Symbolic Interactionist Approach

The work of Piaget postulates a more complex learning process than the one found in the behaviouralist stream. The research of Charles Horton Cooley and George Herbert Mead, two contemporaries who influenced each other's work, presents an even more complex view of the human learning process. Mead and Cooley stressed the importance of human symbolic communication and interaction.

George Herbert Mead

It is difficult to characterize George Herbert Mead (1863–1931) within the usual boundaries of academic disciplines, because he was a philosopher, social psychologist, and sociologist. His studies cover a wide range of topics, but what is important to us here is his work as it relates to the process of socialization and social learning.

Mead's approach has been called biosocial, because it encompasses an analysis of both the biological and the social aspects of development (Morris, 1962: xv). Although there are similarities with the work of Piaget, Mead's analysis of the intersection of the biological and the social is somewhat more complicated.

In his posthumously published work, *Mind, Self and Society* (1934), Mead argues that there is an inherent connection linking the development of the human mind, the human self (or personality), and society. Mead's use of the term *mind* implies an important distinction between the physical organ called the brain and the social product he calls the mind. The brain, as a physical organ, is responsible for the many distinctive capacities that characterize human beings. The mind, more akin to the personality, encompasses complex stocks of knowledge somehow stored in the brain organ. Mead explicitly notes that the complexity and size of the human brain underpin human social existence by aiding our ability to undertake two important activities: the development of a temporal dimension; and communication (1962: 117–18, 145).

For Mead, temporal dimension refers to the human ability to arrange behaviour and action in a temporal order or sequence based on an understanding of the future consequences of what is being done at a given moment. The human animal possesses the ability for reflexive intelligence. That is, we do not merely and simply respond to stimuli in an automatic and immediate manner. Rather, after receiving a stimulus we reflect on it, think about it, and interpret its meaning. Then we reflect on the possible actions we could take, the responses we could make, and we consider the possible consequences. Finally, in the context of these interpretative and reflexive processes, we act (1962: 117–18). This temporal dimension has a physiological basis in our brain organs and a social basis in our minds.

In addition, Mead notes that one of the peculiar characteristics of human social activity is our extensive use of communication. Indeed, we are able to learn all that we are required to know to survive only because of our extraordinary ability to communicate—thanks largely to the role of our large and complex brain.

Communication is by no means unique to humans, although in animal life many visual and audible gestures that imply messages have proved to be instinctual responses. When a beaver senses danger and slaps the water with its tail, it is making an immediate, instinctual gesture, not one that has been thoroughly, even if quickly, considered from a number of angles. Non-human animals also use gestures in even more complicated communications, as in Mead's well-known example of the behaviour of dogs before a fight. When confronted with a hostile being, dogs instinctively respond with a gesture we call a growl. Mead calls this behaviour a 'conversation of gestures' and sees it as quite different from a human conversation, because the gestures tend to be simply stimuli followed by an instinctual response (1962: 63). In a non-human conversation of gestures, a stimulus produces an inborn and unlearned response, which can itself become a gesture, which produces another response in the animal making the first gesture, and so on. The key point is that gestures are instinctual responses to stimuli, and that gestures themselves become stimuli to further instinctual reaction.

Human communication is different because the gestures used are both significant and symbolic (Mead, 1962: 45). A gesture is significant, Mead argues, when it has an assigned or abstract meaning behind it, that is, when it is the result of thought or deeper reflection and intentionally communicates a meaning. Unlike dogs and their instinctual growl, when humans receive stimuli that they perceive as hostile they tend to respond only after considering the nature of the threat, possible courses of action, and the consequences of both. When humans respond, they tend to try to use gestures that both convey their understanding of the situation and indicate the subsequent actions they might take.

For instance, if you frighten me and I respond with a faint smile and say, 'Don't do that', I am passing along a good deal of information about how I interpret and understand your actions, how I intend to respond, how I expect you in turn to respond, and, finally, how I will probably respond to your response. If I respond by snarling, 'Back off, turkey', accompanied by a look of displeasure on my face, I pass on quite different information. My response, whatever it is, is not instinctually predetermined. Rather, it is dependent on how I understand your initial action, my relationship to you, the circumstances, and other factors.

The human response to a perceived threat is different from the animal response precisely because it includes the interpretation of the initial gesture and the use of significant gestures to respond. Significant gestures are thoughtful and deliberate actions intended to communicate a meaning from one human actor to another (Mead, 1962: 46). Meaning implies the use of symbols and gestures that are constructed and used by one actor with a clear 'eye' to the role of the other actor. The communicator has thought about and reflected on the meaning of the message, determined how to respond, and anticipated the response of the other actor. In communicating in this way with others we are imagining ourselves in the position of the other and attempting to judge how that other will react to our communication. This is indeed a complex process that requires humans to use complex systems of communication.

People and Communication

What are you doing at this precise instant in your life? The answer undoubtedly is reading a book written in the English language. While you may not be paying attention to every word, you are nevertheless reading a series of words in the English language. The words you are reading are nothing more than a particular set of written symbols that humans have developed for the purposes of communication. The specific shape and order of the symbols that make up the English alphabet have no basis in nature or human instinct. They are an arbitrary, even accidental, series of shapes that have become codified into a system of abstract symbols. The use of the English language involves the manipulation of these symbols in various combinations called words. Over the centuries those who came before us have developed systems of arbitrary sounds and arbitrary meanings that have become attached to these symbols.

Human communication is based on the use of these abstract symbols. The human being is a language-using animal. Without language, how could we acquire the vast amount of knowledge that we require to be functioning members of society? Without language and the communication that it makes possible, the process of socialization could not take place, and we would be unable to accumulate and pass on our culture. For Mead, it is impossible to contemplate the human animal without the use of some form of language, whether written or spoken. Language is a key to the development and survival of the species.

For Mead the mind and the symbol are inseparable and essential aspects of being human. An essential difference between the human animal and other animals is the intersection of the human mind between stimulus and response (Mead, 1962: 117). Much non-human behaviour is a matter of the reception of a stimulus followed by automatic response. In the case of human behaviour, we have the human mind with its vast stores of knowledge intervening between stimulus and response. The mind gives humans the capacity to interpret a stimulus and ascertain its meaning, then to consider various responses and the consequences of each possible response, and finally to determine a pattern of behaviour. The development of the capacity to do this, that is, the development of the mind, is an integral part of the emergence of the human personality, or of what Mead calls the self.

G.H. Mead's 'Self'

Without providing a succinct and tidy definition of the 'self', Mead's use of the term tends to suggest a meaning related to personality or character. His key point is that we should understand the self as an inherently social product. We are not born with a self, but rather the self develops (Mead, 1962: 135). The development of this self is in essence the process of personality formation.

Mead maintains that the self is essentially a product of the human capacity for reflexive thought. It is because we are capable of reflection and thought that we are also capable of consciously knowing that we are a self. Mead also maintains that the development of this capacity for thought and thus the development of the self are dependent on the acquisition of language (Natanson, 1973: 12). He argues that the self emerges through a series of distinct stages.

Mead's Stages of Personality Development

Reece McGee refers to Mead's first stage of development of the self as the self-consciousness stage (1975: 72). Mead discusses the necessity of a preparatory stage of development during which the human child acquires the capacity to use language in the process of reflection and thought. McGee notes that the self-

consciousness or preparatory stage occupies, roughly, the first two years of a child's life.

The key stage of self-formation begins, according to Mead, at about year two when the child enters the play stage of development. During the play stage the child begins to play at taking on the role of others. A child might play at being a teacher, a parent, or even a baby. Such behaviour obviously cannot occur unless the child has sufficient knowledge of language and the structures of the social situation to know that these various roles exist. Through playing at roles or pretending and imagining that they are other people, children begin to understand that there are statuses other than their particular positions. Getting outside one's own normal status is an important part of the process of coming to understand how to interact with others. Through play and imaginary interactions children further their knowledge and understanding of the social structure, its roles, norms, values, and statuses. At this stage in their development they may not yet have a firm concept of their self.

The play stage is followed by what Mead calls the game stage (Mead, 1962: 150–2). The interaction becomes more complex: children are in situations of interaction involving others, not just imagining those situations. Mead uses the example of a baseball game to illustrate (154). To interact successfully in baseball you have to know and understand the variety of different roles involved. The pitcher must know what is expected of that role and have a degree of knowledge about how each of the other players will act in a variety of different situations. For instance, the first time children are on the field playing a baseball game, they all have a tendency to chase the ball no matter where it is hit. Similarly, novice soccer players tend to be constantly crowded together and scurrying around the ball regardless of the position they are supposed to be playing. The coach's first job is often to teach the children that there are various positions, each with a specific role or expected behaviour attached to it. That is, the players have to 'stay in their positions'. Once the children learn these positions and roles the games proceed more effectively, with far better end results.

According to Mead, in our everyday and ordinary interactions in the game of life, we need to go through a similar learning process before we can interact properly (play). The learning necessary for acquiring the skills and knowledge required for interaction takes up our childhood and occurs during the play and game stages of personality formation. This learning involves the acquisition of a set of symbols that facilitates communication, that is, language, which then makes it possible to learn the specifics of a society's roles, statuses, norms, values, folkways, and mores.

Through the use of language and symbolic communication a person learns about the nature of the society's role structure, value system, and normative expectations. As this learning occurs, people become capable of interacting in complex, organized social activities requiring co-operation. What emerges in the individual's mind is an understanding of the general rules and regulations and modes of conduct that members of the society use and find acceptable and that facilitate the society's continuing interaction. In their minds people gain a conception or an understanding of what Mead calls the 'generalized other' (1962: 154–5). Once we have an understanding of the general expectations and rules that govern an interactive situation, we are in a position to become players in that situation. At this point in our development we definitively begin to develop a personality; or, to use Mead's terms, the self begins to emerge.

Mead's Concept of the Self

Mead argues that the human self has two essential components: the 'I' and the 'me'. The 'I' component of the self is the biological basis of existence, the biological creature, the sensual bodily structures, our physiological, organic being.

According to Mead, because we are more than mere biologically driven or programmed beings, our self or personality has another dimension or aspect: the 'me'. This dimension is the learned and acquired social component, made up of all we learn as we develop language, norms, values, folkways, and mores. In other words, the 'me' is the sum total of the learning that we have experienced up to a particular point in our lives. It is the stock of knowledge acquired through our social existence and has great importance in the overall makeup of our personalities. This 'me' is constructed and determined by the nature of the 'generalized other' that individuals acquire through social interaction in specific though varied social contexts.

Mead's concept of the self implies that personality development is a lifelong process that continues as long as our biological beings continue to develop and as long as we continue to engage in social interactions. Although we are not always aware of it on a day-to-day basis, our biological beings are in fact continually changing, and all of the various associated processes have an impact on our personalities. Similarly, as we go through life we are continually involved in new experiences that often involve new behavioural expectations, norms, and values, which in turn alter the 'me' part of the self and thus the whole personality.

We need only think about all the changed social expectations that people experience after graduation from high school or when they get married. In those cases, the expectations of society change dramatically. The graduates are suddenly no longer 'high school kids' but 'young adults' under increased pressure to look after all aspects of their own lives, to go on to higher endeavours. Newlyweds similarly have to live up to a whole new set of behavioural expectations. To the extent that these new expectations come to have an impact on personal attitudes and conduct—to use Mead's phrase, on the self—that self remains in a continual process of development and transformation.

Charles Horton Cooley

Charles Horton Cooley (1864–1929) was a contemporary of G.H. Mead's, and many of their ideas were similar. For instance, like Mead, Cooley understood that the individual and society cannot be separated. Cooley also shared Mead's views on the fundamental importance of communication in human existence and development. Cooley understood that the human mind is not the same thing as a physical brain organ because the mind is a social product that develops in a social context.

Among Cooley's concepts that help explain how our personalities emerge and continue to develop is 'the looking-glass self'. According to him, the looking-glass self is an important part of the process by which our self-image develops and is maintained. Furthermore, it very much influences our day-to-day interactions and behaviours. As Cooley says, there are three parts or components to the 'self-idea' or looking-glass self: 'A self-idea of this sort seems to have three principal elements: the imagination of our appearance to the other person; the imagination of his judgment of that appearance; and some sort of self-feeling, such as pride or mortification' (1956: 184).

According to Cooley, when we interact with others we form images in our mind of how we think we appear to them—most often without even being aware of it. This 'appearance' may not be merely physical. For example, a teacher can form an image of how she appears to others, not just as a physical being, but in her social role of teacher. After experiencing how others interact with her, our hypothetical teacher first forms an image of how the students in her class 'see' her. She then forms or develops another image, this one of how she thinks the other or others she is interacting with judge her. For example, in her mind they see her as a good teacher, a poor teacher, a fun person, a bore, or whatever. The final part of the looking-glass self is a self-image. Depending on the nature of her image of how others see her, and her further image of how they judge her, our teacher will feel good or bad, enthusiastic or depressed, and so on, both about herself and about her role as teacher. This self-image will have an important impact on her attitudes,

behaviour, and general pattern of interactions.

Cooley indicates that the images and feelings we have about ourselves are the product of the social interactions we engage in as we go about playing various social roles. Our self-image is a product of a myriad of social interactions, the responses of others to us, our judgments of what others are thinking about us, and resulting self-feelings.

Cooley's ideas in this area have stimulated considerable research in the area of interactions and behaviour. For example, Mark Snyder (1982) reports on research on self-fulfilling stereotypes that illustrates how our treatment of others elicits behaviour consistent with what our treatment tells them we expect of them. Snyder reports that some people chosen as research subjects were shown photographs of strangers they were about to talk to on the phone and asked what they thought the strangers would be like. Later, when the researchers watched the subjects talking to the strangers they saw that the subjects treated the strangers differently, depending on what they thought in advance the people would be like. The ones picked in advance as looking sociable, pleasant, and friendly were treated differently than the ones described in advance as unfriendly, distant, and so on. What is especially interesting is that the people being talked to answered in kind: that is, they responded in a manner consistent with what was expected of them. The expectations of certain behaviour or characteristics actually set in motion an interactive process that elicited that particular kind of behaviour (Snyder, 1982: 47–50).

Cooley also points out that not everyone we interact with has equal significance in terms of impact on our self-image. There are some 'significant others', such as those in our primary groups, who are very important and whose opinions of us as communicated in our looking-glass self are very important. Others, perhaps those in secondary groups, are less significant, and their opinions have less impact on our behaviour.

The work of Mead and Cooley locates the basis of human development in our communicative abilities and our capacity for reflexive intelligence, both of which require a social environment in order to develop. Although Mead clearly recognized that we are first and foremost biological creatures, the work of Mead and Cooley, which is often referred to as the symbolic interactionist approach because of their emphasis on symbol usage and interaction, can be criticized for downplaying the biological dimension of human personality. The social scientist who is interested in an approach that systematically incorporates the role of biological processes and forces in personality development should become familiar with the work of Sigmund Freud.

Sigmund Freud

The process of human personality development has been approached from enormously divergent perspectives, and one of the best examples of this is the Austrian psychiatrist, Sigmund Freud (1856–1939). The breadth and depth of his writings defy summary, simple or otherwise, but in his efforts to understand the development and structures of the human personality Freud contributed key theories and concepts to the growth of the social sciences.

In his work Freud argued that the human body is an energy system subject to the basic laws of nature that govern the universe. Like all life forms, the human being evolved after cosmic forces acted on inorganic matter. At a point in the distant past, Earth held only inorganic matter and the planet existed in a condition of stability. Cosmic forces that we may never fully understand acted on this inorganic matter, transforming it and giving rise to the conditions necessary for the development of organic matter. The end result was the beginning of life. Since the time that organic matter emerged a continuous evolutionary process has been at work, which ultimately resulted in the emergence of the human species. The human animal is, Freud argued,

an evolved dynamic energy system essentially 'powered' by the biological and physiological processes that sustain all life on the planet (Hall and Lindzey, 1970: 39).

Freud maintained that the human species, like other life forms, is influenced by instincts—although he did not use the term in the same way that biologists do. An instinct is, for Freud, a psychological representation of a source of tension. Duane Schultz notes that 'Freud's term in German, *Trieb*, is best translated as driving force or urge' (1975: 315). The tensions that are the basis of instincts have their origins in the biological and physiological processes of the body. In brief, our physiological existence produces various needs and drives, which yield excitations, which in turn are the real root of instincts (Freud, [1933] 1965: 85–6). Instinctual energy is deemed to be the driving force of the human personality whose structures we now want to explore.

Id, Ego, and Super-ego

It is possible, for analytical purposes at least, to think about the human personality as being composed of three interconnected and interrelated parts: the id, the ego, and the super-ego (Freud, [1933] 1965: lecture xxxi). The most basic part of the personality structure is the id, which is present at birth and is in closest touch with the physical or bodily processes. The id constantly strives to keep the human physiological and psychological systems in a situation of stable and low levels of energy or tension. This is a task of enormous difficulty, because the normal physiological functioning of the human body constantly yields fluctuating levels of energy and thus tension. This simply means that, under normal circumstances, we tend continually to get hungry, thirsty, and sexually stimulated. When tension of one kind or another increases, the id immediately attempts to address the problem through what Freud called the pleasure principle. The id, trying to solve the problems we are faced with, is concerned with immediate gratification of the drive or need because it desires an immediate reduction of the tension. It is constrained in this, however, because it is only capable of operating at the level of wishes and impulses. The id uses what Freud called the primary process, which involves the creation of images that would satisfy the need. It only dreams or imagines satisfaction, because it does not understand the difference between reality and the imagination. The fact of the matter is, however, that wishful thinking does not reduce the tension. If we are actually starving, no matter how hard we imagine food the hunger persists; and, ultimately, without real food we will die. The id cannot solve our problems or reduce our tensions.

Human survival, however, has been facilitated by the emergence of another part of the personality system called the ego, which relates to our need, if we are to survive as individuals and as a species, for contact with the objective world. The ego is the part of the personality that transcends the id and makes it possible for us to secure real satisfactions and real means of reducing tensions in the real world. Whereas the id operates under the auspices of the pleasure principle and the primary process, the ego is directed towards the reality principle and the secondary process.

The reality principle leads the organism to seek out and locate objects in the physical world that will satisfy the various tensions experienced at a given moment. The ego knows that imagining food or drink does not really deal with hunger or thirst, so, using the secondary processes, it develops a plan to secure actual satisfaction for the need or drive. The ego is not constrained by rules and regulations in its efforts to secure satisfaction, and thus the individual operating under the direction of an id and ego shows little constraint or social responsibility and is not bothered by moral or ethical concerns. In its continuing efforts to deal realistically with the fluctuating tension and energy levels that the body produces, the ego pretty much does whatever it thinks it can get away with. Reducing tension and achieving survival are its paramount concerns.

Although many disagreed with his controversial and sexist theories, Austrian psychiatrist Sigmund Freud is the father of modern psychiatry, and has had a great deal to offer sociology. One of the most influential theories, for sociology, was that of the three-part personality, comprised of the id, ego, and super-ego. (CP Picture Archive)

A world occupied by humans governed by their ids and egos would be unlike the social worlds we have come to accept. In his important book *Civilization and Its Discontents* (1930), Freud argued that humans come to realize that if they are to develop their higher facilities and engage in occupations and pursuits within a stable society, they must renounce the immediate gratification of all their needs and drives. Although it means less than complete and full reduction of all tensions, humans must learn to sublimate and displace some of their tensions in exchange for the larger benefits offered by living in society. The structure of the personality that facilitates the movement from an unstructured and uncivilized state of complete gratification to a civilized but constrained and not fully satisfied condition is the super-ego.

The super-ego is the part of the personality that understands that the ego must be constrained. It offers moral and social reasons for inhibiting the immediate gratification of all our needs and drives. Keep in mind that if all humans were to seek immediate and unconstrained gratification of needs and drives as they arise, life would be a jungle and Thomas Hobbes's famous description of life as being 'solitary, poore, nasty, brutish and short' would ring true (Hobbes, [1651] 1968: 186). As an intelligent species, however, we come to accept that such a situation is not in our individual or collective best interests. We come to realize that the full development of our individual and species potentials and capabilities requires some degree of social and moral regulation of conduct. As a result we develop collective restraints, moral codes, and rules of conduct that make it possible to substitute social peace and security for immediate gratification. These rules and regulations, which make society possible, become a part of our personality structure in the form of the super-ego, the internal agency of control that ensures our compliance. All this is similar to the way a military garrison governs a conquered city (Freud, [1930] 1982: 61). The super-ego is our conscience, the reason we have an internal feeling of guilt when we violate what we know are the established rules, even if no one else is aware of what we have done (61–4).

It is through the super-ego that the social and moral dimensions of our personalities are introduced. The regulations and constraints that the super-ego imposes do not originally come from within the individual but from society, in most cases passed on by parents. The values, norms, and ideals that the super-ego uses to constrain the actions of the ego are the values, norms, and ideals of the society in which the individual lives. Through socialization the individual comes to know what is appropriate and inappropriate, what actions will result in reward and what will be punished. Eventually each individual accepts these values, and as a result personal actions come to be guided by the internal operation of the conscience. Society's values and norms become the individual's, imposed on the ego through the operation of the conscience (Hall, 1979: 31–5).

The id, ego, and super-ego are among the central analytical concepts employed by Freud in his efforts to understand the human personality. In their study of human personality theory, Robert Frager and James Fadiman describe these as the three subsystems of the psyche. Each makes its own contribution to the distribution of energy and thereby facilitates an existence that balances pleasure and tension (Frager and Fadiman, 1984: 14).

In his later work Freud argued that there are two essential kinds of instincts, one directed to the enhancement of life and the other towards aggression and destruction (Freud, [1933] 1965: 92–5). The behaviour that arises out of the presence of the life instincts, Eros, serves to facilitate the survival of the individual and species. Eros directs our activities in the search to satisfy our need for nutrition, fluids, and reproduction. The death instincts are related to the original preorganic state of all living matter. They are rooted in the desire of all living matter to reduce tensions as much as possible, with the ultimate state of tension reduction being the return to non-organic existence after death (Freud, [1920] 1955: 36; Gay, 1988: 401).

Human instincts are also flexible. That is, while instincts have an aim—to remove the cause of an excitation or tension—there are usually many different objects that can accomplish that aim (Freud, [1930] 1982: 16). In the human animal, energy originally directed by a specific kind of tension can in fact be redirected or sublimated. For instance, in the case of sexual tension other kinds of activity can replace sexual activity and accomplish a measure of tension reduction. Sexual energy can, in effect, be redirected into sports, art, music, or even studying sociology. As a result of sublimation and displacement, human instinctual energies are redirected into the multiplicity of activities that characterize our species, and the pursuit of these varied activities results in the development and flourishing of our civilizations (Freud, [1930] 1982; Hall and Lindzey, 1970: 37–8). The means by which we come to develop modes of conduct based on processes such as sublimation and displacement are in essence the process of personality formation.

Instincts, the forces that drive the human personality, also change and develop as the organism matures and develops. What forms of energies and excitations the organism is confronted with and must deal with will change as it matures and develops. Maturation and development also give rise to learning and the development of the types of behaviour we mentioned above. Defence mechanisms are essentially adjustments that we make when we encounter situations and conditions that prevent us from discharging tensions. Freud refers to anything that prevents the organism from discharging tension as a frustration. Among the key methods of dealing with frustrations are identification, displacement, sublimation, and the development of defence mechanisms (see Hall, 1979, for an excellent overview of these complex processes).

Freud suggested that one of the most important forms of energy that the human organism and personality have to learn to deal with is sexual energy. As Hall points out, however, his definition of sexual energy was quite broad:

> Freud's conception of the sexual instinct is much broader than the usual one. It includes not only expenditure of energy for pleasurable activities involving genital stimulation and manipulation, but it also embraces the manipulation of other bodily zones for pleasure as well (1979: 102). The major areas of the body through which sexual energies are manifest and subsequently dissipated vary as we develop. The main centres of tension reduction, or erogenous zones, are the mouth, the anus, and the genitalia. As we mature and develop attention shifts from one zone to another, marking different stages in the development of our personality.

Stages of Development

Freud believed that as humans develop they pass through a number of distinct stages, each of them characterized by different sources of tension that require handling. Just how these tensions come to be handled during the various phases can affect subsequent personality characteristics.

The first stage of development is the oral stage. During the first year of our lives, because most of our interest is devoted to acquiring basic nourishment, the oral cavity is the centre of our tension-reducing activity. The common attempts of small infants to put anything and everything into their mouths are characteristic of this period. Later in life, personality traits such as excessive sarcasm, gossiping, and constantly nibbling or eating are manifestations of certain problems that a child encounters in reducing tensions during this period.

As children begin the second year of life, a new stage of development unfolds involving a dramatic change in the location of the tension-reducing activity. As they begin the process of toilet training, the major location of tension and tension-reducing activity shifts from the oral cavity to the anal cavity. The necessary biological process of waste removal becomes an important source of tension reduction. The elimination of wastes is made all the more pleasurable for the child after the process comes under conscious control. Once again the manner by which this tension-reducing process is handled by the parents or others taking care of the child has an impact on subsequent personality development. In the case, for example, of strict toilet training, the outcome can be an obstinate, retentive, and stingy character; but the element of parental praise can produce a more creative and productive individual (Hall and Lindzey, 1970: 51).

The third stage of development is the phallic stage. At about age three the major focus of tension reduction shifts to the child's genitalia. The ways in which sexually based energies and tensions are manifested and addressed differ in males and females, which Freud explains by citing the physiological differences between males and females. It is during this stage that children develop and resolve in some manner their Oedipus complex. The Oedipus complex, named after a character in the classical Greek tragedy *Oedipus Rex* who unknowingly kills his father and marries his mother, involves the emergence, among children, of sexual feelings for their parents. The precise manner in which these sexual feelings and attractions reveal themselves and are dealt with differs for males and females. (For an overview of these ideas, see Freud, [1933] 1965, lectures xxxii and xxxiii.)

In the male child the emergence of sexual tensions and energies results in a strengthening of his affection and love for his mother. Those feelings for the mother also change, with the love developing a potential sexual aspect. The male child is aware of a possible conflict over the love and affection of the mother, given the presence of another male in the form of the father. The boy develops a fear of his larger, more powerful rival, which manifests itself as a castration anxiety. The child is afraid that his rival will punish him for his secret love for the mother by removing the offending organ, the penis, through castration (Freud, 1965: 114–15). To avoid such a painful loss the boy decides that he must avoid antagonizing the father, and he represses his sexual feeling for the mother and seeks to identify himself with the father. By identifying with the father the male child is preparing himself for the eventual role of father, when at some point in the future he, too, will have a relationship with a mature woman like his mother.

Freud notes that in the case of the female child the process is quite different, owing to her different biology. In *The Longest War: Sex Differences in Perspective*, Carol Tavris and Carole Wade summarize Freud's arguments regarding the essentials of the process in females:

> Girls too go through an Oedipal stage, Freud supposed, but with far different results. Whereas the boy worries that he might be castrated, the girl, after seeing a penis for the first time, worries that she already has been castrated. As Freud described it, 'When she makes a comparison with a playfellow of the other sex, she perceives that she has "come off badly" and she feels this is a wrong done to her and a ground for inferiority'. . . . She is, to say the least, angry that she lacks the marvelous male organ and has an inferior clitoris. She blames her mother for this deprivation, rejects her, and seeks to displace her in the father's eyes. She becomes daddy's darling. (1984: 180–1)

The female child is ultimately forced to seek compensation for her lack of a penis through the act of mothering a child, ideally a male child who would indirectly make up for her shortcoming. The female child is thus cast for her role as a mother later in life.

After the boys' and girls' resolution of the Oedipus complex, a period of latency begins during which relatively little happens in terms of new sources of tension and energy. At the onset of puberty the adolescent passes into the genital stage, which offers the opportunity for development of a personality; and the characteristics and features that emerge are a result of the various stages the child has passed through. Significantly, most of us remain unaware that we have passed through the stages or that our personalities are composed of various components resulting from those stages. Many of the important psychic processes that influence our personality and its development occur at an unconscious level, and we may never be aware of them.

In recent times, scholars influenced by feminist thought have sharply criticized various aspects of Freud's analysis. Some notable examples are Michèle Barrett (1980), Sandra Harding (1986), Carol Tavris and Carole Wade (1984), and R.A. Sydie (1987). In *Natural Women, Cultured Men*, Sydie argues that because the major theories in sociology were formulated by men, the discipline is 'blinkered' and has neglected, ignored, and excluded the social realities faced by women and the general position of women in society (1987: 10). In specifically discussing Freud, she points out that feminist theory has found two central flaws in Freud's analysis: first, it assumes that patriarchal societies are natural and inevitable; second, the psychoanalytical treatment that developed out of Freud's work reinforced the unequal positions of men and women in Western societies (Sydie, 1987: ch. 5). Clearly, there are substantial grounds for questioning many of Freud's universal claims and the scientific legitimacy of his overall approach, although his ideas do remain influential and sociologists need to be familiar with them.

Towards a Sociological Synthesis

Most if not all sociologists agree that no single approach to socialization offers an adequate account of the complex process of human personality formation and development. As a result, sociologists have incorporated or modified various insights drawn from these thinkers into a perspective that both recognizes the biological basis of human existence and stresses the role of the environment in moulding the basic structures of the human character.

To summarize, the human animal is a biological creature with physiologically rooted needs and drives. Humans face a number of basic problems that must be solved if the species and its individual members are to survive. If we define instincts as species-wide, unlearned, biologically transmitted, and invariant complex behaviours, the human animal does not seem to be particularly well endowed instinctively. Humans do not seem to have much instinctual behaviour to assist us in dealing with hunger, fear, finding shelter, sexual drives, and so on, yet we still do find ways of dealing with our needs, problems, and drives. Indeed, if we did fail to deal with those aspects of life, we would cease to exist as living organisms and as a species. All of this raises questions about how we have managed not only to survive but also to prosper.

Human beings have used our species-specific capacities—everything from the upright posture to our constant sex drive and relative longevity—to develop systematic social behaviours to solve the many problems the species faces. Acting in concert with each other, humans have developed patterns of social interaction that represent cultural solutions and cultural behaviours.

Unlike instinctual behaviour, human cultural behaviour is diverse and learned, and it has produced a variety of material and non-material products, from the millions of human artifacts that surround us daily (material) to our languages, beliefs, customs, ideas, and ideals (non-material). These non-material and material products are the essential components of what social scientists call human culture.

An essential characteristic of human culture is its orderly, organized, patterned, and structured character. Human conduct is not random and accidental. Indeed, the most stressful moments in our lives occur in situations in which we don't know what to expect from others, or when there is a lack of structure and as a result we don't understand the behaviour of others.

For sociologists, culture is a concept that must be located within the context of an even larger set of social arrangements or structures. Culture is intertwined with these social structures: institutions, statuses, roles, norms, values, formal organizations, and groups.

Human infants are born into a social structure. They enter the world as sensual biological creatures with basic needs and drives that must be satisfied; but they are incapable of satisfying their needs or dealing with the problems they face without the assistance of other members of their species. To survive, human infants require a long period of systematic physical, emotional, and social support. The development and maturation take place within the context of social structures.

The shaping, moulding, and learning that the infant, the young child, the adolescent, the young adult, and the middle-aged and older person are exposed to is the process of socialization. Through a series of social experiences we come to acquire our characters and personalities—from what we eat to our values and attitudes towards others around us to our political beliefs and practices and the ways we act when we are angry, frustrated, or afraid. Through the social learning process our possibilities and potentials are developed—or not developed.

This tremendous amount of learning—of socialization—seems to be predicated on our capacity to communicate. The use of abstract written, vocal, and signed symbols for the systematic and deliberate transmission of knowledge and information is an essential characteristic of the human species, which means that the learning of language is considered an essential aspect of human development.

Many people assume that we are born with innate or natural talents or abilities, whether these are musical, athletic, or intellectual. This matter has been the subject of some very interesting studies that question some of our common-sense assumptions. In 'Expert Performance: Its Structure and Acquisition', K. Anders Rescission and Neil Charness review the evidence, noting the tendency for people to explain expert or exceptional performers in purely individualistic terms, sometimes even attributing these abilities to a divinity (1999: 203). They note that a lot of the support for this position is drawn from the study of child prodigies; however, they note that much of the literature that supports this approach is questionable. Moreover, they argue that the evidence they have gathered on prodigies suggests that 'early instruction and maximal parental support appears to be much more important than innate talent'. They continue that 'there are many examples of parents of exceptional performers who successfully designed optimal environments for children without any concern about innate talent' (209). After reviewing copious amounts of research they conclude:

> For a long time the study of exceptional and expert performance has been considered outside the scope of general psychology because such performance has been attributed to innate characteristics possessed by outstanding individuals. A better explanation is that expert performance reflects extreme adaptations, accomplished through lifelong effort, to demands in restricted, well-defined domains. By capturing and examining the performance of experts in a given domain, researchers have identified adaptive changes with physiological components as well as the acquisition of domain-specific skills that circumvent basic limits on speed and memory. Experts with different teachers and training histories attain their superior performance after many years of continued effort by acquiring skills and making adaptations with the same general structure. (1999: 247)

Another study titled 'Innate Talents: Reality or Myth' reviews some of the same evidence, but it also includes other studies. Among their conclusions is that autistic savants really do represent exceptional cases that are explainable by virtue of 'involuntary specialization of their mental functions' (Howe, Davidson, and Sloboda, 1999: 279). Their alternative to the innate talent argument for exceptional performers is this:

Large amounts of regular practice were found to be essential for excelling. Studies of long-term practice and training suggest that individual differences in learning-related experiences are a major source of the variance in achievement.

The evidence we have surveyed in this target article does not support the talent account, according to which excelling is a consequence of possessing innate gifts. This conclusion has practical implications, because categorizing some children as innately talented is discriminatory. The evidence suggests that such categorization is unfair and wasteful, preventing young people from pursuing a goal because of the unjustified conviction of teachers or parents that certain children would not benefit from the superior opportunities given to those who are deemed to be talented. (1999: 279)

In stressing the importance of the social learning process in moulding the personality, sociologists must be aware of the danger of adopting an over-socialized conception of human development. In a famous article, D.H. Wrong (1961) warns against adopting an oversimplified or purely culturally determined view of human beings. It is not possible simply to look at a set of agents of socialization and predict that those influences will produce a person with certain characteristics. Because each of us is the unique product of biological or genetic and sociological or environmental influences, our development must be understood as having been influenced by both factors. In a set of published lectures, R.C. Lewontin, a leading geneticist, has argued that a further complicating factor is what he calls 'developmental noise' or random-chance factors in development (Lewontin, 1991: 26–7). Lewontin argues that the precise manner by which an individual organism develops is subject to chance and random variations that are not immediately linked to its genes or environmental circumstances. He notes, for

example, that the way in which cells divide and produce the various organs of the central nervous system can be very much influenced by developmental noise. Thus, while we emphasize the environmental and social factors in sociology, we must still recognize that human development is the outcome of a complex process of environmentally mediated biological factors that are influenced by developmental noise.

In the context of his study of deviance Erich Goode makes a similar point, noting that although our species requires socialization and culture to survive the process by which we learn and internalize values and norms is not simple. He writes:

> We are not robots. We are not sponges that simply 'soak up' rules. There will always be a certain number of people who question the rules, even the entire social order. In fact, it is often difficult to determine just what 'the rules of society' are because there may be many competing sets of rules that are believed by different sets of people in society. However, it is often the case that a majority believe in the validity of one set of rules. And those who believe otherwise, or who do things that seem to contradict these rules, will be regarded with suspicion. These people are often seen as troublemakers who threaten the social order. They seem to offer an alternative way of looking at reality, at the world, at the rules. ([1978] 1999: 238)

Although the human individual is a creature with biological needs and drives and biologically based physical and psychological capacities and potentials, we require a social environment for our survival. We must learn how to solve our needs and deal with our problems, and as we learn to do so certain of our various complex potentials and capabilities come to be developed while others remain undeveloped. We may never know the precise nature of all of our potentials and capacities, and it is possible that we possess many capacities and potentials that for a variety of reasons never come to be realized. An inquiry into which of our individual capacities get developed and thus form a part of our 'self' must involve the use of our sociological imagination. To understand our strengths and weaknesses, we must look at our individual life stories or biographies, always within the context of the various existing social structures.

What Do Twin Studies Tell Us?

One of the most interesting, potentially valuable, and incredible controversial sources of information on the role of genes and/or environment is the study of twins, particularly identical twins. Indeed the phenomenon of twins has been the cause of much attention in various cultures through history. Judy Hagedorn and Janet Kizziar begin their book on twins by noting some of the culturally different responses, responses that vary from infanticide to reverence (1974: 11–12).

We know from basic biology that there are two types of twins. Monozygotic (MZ) twins are commonly referred to as identical twins because they are in fact genetically identical. MZ twins result from the splitting of a single embryo (fertilized egg) into two. Dizygotic (DZ) twins develop from the fertilization of two different eggs by two different sperm. DZ twins share the same numbers of genes in common as most siblings, that is, about half. For obvious reasons MZ twins have attracted the most interest by those interested in issues relating to the role of genetics in human behaviour.

A word of caution is advised before looking at some of the more important studies of identical twins. We have noted R.C. Lewontin's notion of developmental noise and the fact that no two cells develop in precisely the same manner. Perhaps a bit more detail on this matter is in order. Lewontin notes that fruit flies do not have the same number of bristles in each ear, not as a result of genetics or environment but rather as a result of the 'random

variation in growth and division of cells during development: *developmental noise*' (1991: 27, emphasis in original). If we apply this notion to the development of the embryos that become MZ twins we can see that they will in fact not be identical in the pure sense of the word.

The most famous, though perhaps infamous is a better word, study of MZ twins is that of Sir Cyril Burt (1883–1971). Burt was a British psychologist who studied the IQ of MZ twins reared apart. Burt published a series of studies, but the most important one was of 53 sets of twins. In order to measure the similarities in IQs Burt used the common statistical procedure of reporting correlation coefficients. He reported that the correlation of the IQs of identical twins reared apart was .771. Keep in mind that if two phenomena are perfectly related the correlation coefficient would be 1. If there is absolutely no relationship between two phenomena, then the correlation coefficient would be 0. Burt's .771 correlation means that there is a very strong relationship between the IQs of MZ twins reared apart, with the common causal factor appearing to be the virtually identical genetic makeup. There was a problem, however.

Although Cyril Burt became Sir Cyril Burt partly on the basis of this research, not everyone accepted his findings. Several critical voices emerged raising concerns about his findings; however, the issue of the credibility of the studies became a public issue after the *London Sunday Times* ran a front-page story on 24 October 1976 claiming that Burt's data was fraudulent. Although the debate still rages, a number of scholars are convinced that Burt's data should be considered worthless and discarded (Farber, 1981b: 34; Rose, Lewontin, and Kamin, 1985: 101–6).

One need not use Burt's data to engage in a debate about the relationship between IQ and genes as manifest in identical twins because there is a wealth of other data. Farber overviews a significant number of studies; however, she concludes that many of them are not useful because they were based on small samples; that is, of the 30 studies she summarizes that were reported between 1922 and 1973, 20 were based on 'samples' of one (1981a: 35). There is further significant data that has been widely reported on and whose legitimacy is not questioned. I am referring to an ongoing research project at the University of Minnesota. Nancy L. Segal is a former assistant director at the Minnesota Center for Twin and Adoption Research and is now director of the Twin Study Centre at the California State University at Fullerton. She has summarized many of the relevant studies in her book *Entwined Lives: Twins and What They Tell Us About Human Behavior* (1999).

Segal covers many dimensions of the lives of twins, including the extent to which twins share athletic abilities, various legal cases involving twins, the case of conjoined twins, and various stories about conflict and co-operation. As interesting as these stories are, it is her conclusions regarding the relationship between having identical genes and behaviour and personality that are of interest to us. Reflecting on a television experience during which she had no opportunity to explain her main point she wrote:

> Had there been time, I would have explained that more stable, reliably measured behavioral characteristics, such as general intelligence, show higher degrees of genetic influence (50 to 70 per cent) than less stable, less reliably measured behaviors, such as personality traits (50 per cent), occupational interests (40 per cent) and social attitudes (34 per cent). Greater genetic than environmental influence on behavior does not imply that behavior resists change. (314)

Later in the book, while responding to some criticisms of twin studies, she is equally definitive:

> Twin methods (and other behavioral genetic designs) have been disparaged for not

revealing the developmental processes linking genes and behaviors. Twin, sibling, and other family methods are first steps toward solving developmental mysteries. Once gene-environment contributions to behavioral differences are identified, elucidating genetic and environmental factors and the ways they are expressed over time will become possible. Twin studies have shown that genetic differences explain 50 per cent of personality differences among people. The biggest surprise has been that identical twins raised apart and together are equally similar, revealing that common genes, not common rearing, underlie relatives' resemblance. Separated parents and children may also resemble one another for genetic reasons. (321)

There are many other volumes that study both MZ and DZ twins, some of them more scientifically rigorous and some more geared to a general audience. Bard Lindeman's *The Twins Who Found Each Other* represents the latter in that it documents the life stories of two MZ twins separated at birth but who are brought together by accident only to discover how much they share (1969). *The New Yorker* staff writer Lawrence Wright's *Twins and What They Tell Us About Who We Are* is a more sustained account of the literature that covers both those who use twin studies to prove that much of our behaviour is biologically determined and those critical of such arguments.

Susan Farber provides one of the most through and systematic critiques of the conclusions of Segal and others who maintain that these studies prove a significant genetic basis for basic personality traits. In an early article in *Psychology Today* called 'Telltale Behaviour of Twins', she reviewed some of the evidence and found flaws in the methodologies of the studies. For example, she expresses concerns about the extent to which twins that were called separated really were separated. Of the 95 sets in one study, she notes that 'Overall, 27 pairs have to be described as hardly separated at all' (1981: 60). As a result of what she calls the 'contamination from the influence of meetings', any conclusions based on apparently identical genes but differences in environments are open to question. She writes 'when mutual contact is entered into the statistical analysis, the heritabilities for IQ drop so low as to negate any possibility that heredity is the predominant influence on intelligence' (60). We have noted her criticism of the small 'sample' size. To the small numbers in the studies she adds another criticism, the manner by which the twins were selected for study. In her book, *Identical Twins Reared Apart: A Reanalysis*, she writes: '*The approximately 90 per cent of the known cases of separated MZ twins have been studies precisely because they were so alike. This circular reasoning undermines the generalizability of patterns in the sample to the population at large*' (1981: 360, emphasis in original).

Rose, Lewontin, and Kamin are among the most persistent to critique the thesis that twin studies prove that much of our personality is the result of genes. Their rather long summary of their position reads:

> Though hereditarians attribute this difference to the greater genetic similarity of MZs, there are also some obvious environmental reasons to expect higher correlations among MZ than among DZ twins, especially when one realizes the degree to which an MZ pair creates or attracts a far more similar environment than that experienced by other people. Because of their striking physical similarity, parents, teachers, and friends tend to treat them very much alike and often even confuse them for one another. MZ twins tend to spend a great deal of time with one another doing similar things, much more so than is the case with same-sexed DZ twins, as established by many

questionnaire studies. The twins are much less likely to have spent a night apart from each other during childhood. . . . In an extreme example of this deliberate pattern, one of the most extraordinary social experiences of identical twins is the institution of the twin convention, to which identical twins of all ages go, or are sent by their parents, dressed identically, acting identically, to show off their identity, and, in a sense, to compete with other twins to see who can be the most 'identical'.

> There is no great imagination required to see how such a difference between MZs and DZs might produce the reported difference in IQ correlations. It is entirely clear that the environmental experiences of MZs are much more similar than those of DZs.

> Twin studies as a whole, then, cannot be taken as evidence for the heritability of IQ. They have been interpreted, of course, as if their proof were adequate, and hereditarian scholars have routinely ground out quantitative estimates of IQ heritability from the results of twin studies. Claiming validity for such calculations can only be done by willfully ignoring the obvious fact that MZ and DZ twins differ in environment as well as in genetic similarity. (115–16)

None of this is to make sweeping and untenable cultural determinist claims, because as we have seen, the fact that we are living creatures means we have a biological basis to our existence. There are some clear instances of behaviours or perhaps predispositions to behaviours that seem to have a significant biological component. For example, twin studies on the incidence of Tourette's Syndrome reported by Thomas Hyde and Daniel Weinberger indicate a significant concordance of the syndrome among MZ twins, although they also note environmental factors impact the expression of the syndrome (1995). Research on drug abuse reported by Patrick Zickler (1999) indicates that 'genetic factors play a major role in the progression from drug use to abuse and dependence' (1).

So what do the various studies of twins tell us? A careful study of the literature, and it is much more extensive than that reported here, leads us to conclude that the data is contradictory and confusing. There are claims and counterclaims, but more and more there is a realization that we must move beyond either/or claims. Perhaps appropriate last words are the title of the last chapter of Wright's study, 'Beyond Nature Versus Nurture'. Farber explains:

> No trait is independent of hereditary or environmental agents. Certain environmental conditions are necessary before a genetic potential becomes expressed (or, conversely, inhibited), while the genetic endowment of any individual is certain to influence the way he perceives, experiences, or processes environmental stimuli. Just as important, genetic endowment influences an individual's ability to mold the environment and shape his surroundings and the responses he receives. Thus the correct question to ask of data is how much of the variability among individuals for any given trait is due to hereditary differences. (1981: 5)

In a review essay titled 'What Did They Name the Dog?' Wendy Doniger (1998) discussed Wright's book. We will give her the true last word on this matter:

> Why not just demonstrate that some factors owe more to nature, others to nurture, and leave it at that? Because such an argument lacks the sharp edge that is the weapon of ideology. Humanistic studies of twins are not statistical but anecdotal, a dirty word in the laboratory. But since twin studies take place

in an area in which rigid statistical controls are impossible to maintain, all of them are ultimately anecdotal—indeed, mythological. Wright's book is full of fascinating anecdotes—which prove nothing but the selection criteria favoured by the researchers. Their studies fail not (only) because they do not, and cannot, establish reliable scientific controls, nor even because they are asking the wrong questions, driven by corrupt political agendas, but because they either forget or assume that they already know the answer to the question that gives perennial life to the myth of the separated twins: what is it that makes every human being unique?

Socialization as Unique and Shared

Linking biography and history reveals other aspects of human development. A central question that often emerges when we consider human personality and development relates to our differences and similarities. Sociologists are often asked, 'If your argument is that the social environment fundamentally influences our personalities and character structure, why are each of us so unique, so individual?' Another related question is: 'My sister and I must have had a similar socialization process because we had the same parents, shared a house for 18 years, went to the same school, attended the same church, and even played with the same kids when we were young. Why are we so different?'

These are important questions, and they relate to two essential points about socialization: first, socialization is both shared and unique; second, it is always a complex phenomenon.

The argument that each of us undergoes an individual and unique socialization process is a simple recognition of the reality of our lives. No two human beings have ever shared an identical environment. For instance, consider the fact that no other person has the exact social learning experiences that you have had. Even if you had an identical twin, there is no way that brother or sister could have shared every single one of your social learning experiences. It would be both a logical and physical impossibility. Even if two individuals have the same parents, share the same house, attend the same school and church, take vacations together, and read the same books, they do not share identical environments, because no matter how many of their experiences are similar, they will still have many totally different experiences. They may have had different friends, different teachers at school, watched different movies and television shows.

Indeed, a sociologist would argue that while siblings have the same biological parents, the personalities and character structures of the parents who raised and socialized them will have changed, matured, and developed during the period between the births of the children. Socialization is a two-way process, and while parents are socializing a child there is a reciprocal process at work that changes the parents themselves. In the normal course of living, people change and develop in countless ways, both in their physical beings and in their personalities. This is in keeping with George Herbert Mead's notion of the 'self' as being composed of a biologically based 'I' and a socially produced 'me'. As we develop and mature biologically, the 'I' goes through considerable change. Similarly, as society along with its values, norms, and folkways changes, so, too, does the social 'me'. Are you identical today in every way to what you were like a year ago, or two years ago? I suspect not—and I hope not, because the constant process of development and change is one of the reasons human beings are so interesting.

The building of the human personality is also an extremely complex phenomenon. Once our personalities or character structures begin to develop they become a factor in their own subsequent development. For example, because you are human you possess an amazing brain, with unbelievable capacities. Your brain allows you to think, reason, reflect, communicate, and learn. As you engage in these actions socialization occurs, and your personality and character emerge and develop. Your developing personality has an impact on how you respond to different experiences in your life, which in turn influences how and why you learn certain things and how and why you react to certain situations. As your personality develops and forms it becomes a part of the complex social interactions you participate in, social interactions that are an essential part of the ongoing socialization process. The result is a lifelong process of development, learning, and interaction.

When we speak of the socialization process as shared we refer to all the common learning experiences shared by members of a society. There are a great many things that people born and raised in North America have in common as a result of socialization. Many of the society's dominant values, norms, folkways, and mores have become part of our personalities simply because we grew up and live in this society. There are, for example, certain acts, words, or behaviours that most of us find acceptable or unacceptable in certain circumstances, and our definitions of what is acceptable or not under certain circumstances are learned. Socialization explains both our individual differences and our similarities.

A central issue that bears attention is the matter of how sex and gender relations impact the social learning process. We will have much more to say about this when we address the matter of feminist theory in Chapter 8; however, it is worth keeping in mind throughout this discussion. Deborah Tannen has examined the nature of gender and behaviour in large organizations as it relates to the matter of advancement in hierarchies (2001). Her analysis focuses on important structural considerations, but it also leads us to think about subtle behaviours and how we learn them.

As we think about the complex problems associated with understanding socialization, it is useful to keep a unique human characteristic in the forefront—the role of our mind. Much behaviour for most animals equipped with instincts behaviours tend to be relatively simple:

Stimulus ⟹ Response.

However for humans the mind intervenes so the situation looks like this:

Stimulus ⟹ Mind ⟹ Response

But what precisely is this 'Mind' that we are talking about?

There is an ongoing and vibrant debate about how we understand the Brain ⟷ Mind/Consciousness relationship. We know quite a lot about the brain as a physiological organ including the fact that humans have a huge cerebral cortex that seems to be site of many complex mental functions. The brain is truly a marvelous and complex physical organ with series of lobes and over 100 billion neurons. Each of these neurons is estimated to have hundreds to thousands of synaptic connections that are involved in the creation and recording of experiences as memory. We know that registering sensations is a very complicated process involving neurons (specialized cells) and electrical transmissions (messages) and the release of chemicals (neuron transmitters)—all the elements work together to produce a signal that I am, for example, burning my hand, eating something sweet, or listening to certain sounds that I define as music. As I think about what to write next these complex electrical and chemical processes that are associated with thinking are going on. The same processes happen when I taste something or see a colour. For some sociologists all of this leads to a question that we as of yet unable to answer. Some call it the 'qualia' problem.

We know that we possess states of consciousness, states of having feelings, and a certain awareness and various responses to stimuli. We know that we like or do not like some sounds (music), or colours, or tastes, or tactile feelings. But how do these immediate sensations become the qualitative experiences that become encoded in our character and personality. That is, what is the MIND? Is there a brain–mind dualism? Or is the mind just somehow the sum total of all these electrical impulses and chemical activity. The question really is: can we understand the mind through a reductionist approach that reduces complex phenomenon to its most simple elements to produce an explanation? Or is it more useful to use what one might term a generative approach? A generative approach would suggest that some phenomenon cannot be reduced to simple elements because there is something in the dynamics of how the elements come together that creates an entity or phenomenon that is more that the sum of the parts. Given that a brilliant group of scientist and philosophers (Sacks, 2004; 2001; Gardner, 1997; Searle 1995; 1997; Gopnic, 1999) are involved in this debate as you read this, no suggestions will be offered here other than the following 'thinking question': What can we even know about these issues?

As for the unabating complexity of socialization, how could a lifelong social learning process be anything but complex? The more we come to understand socialization, the more we realize that it is a process we may never fully understand. Every institution in my society, as well as scores of groups, organizations, and individuals, have influenced my own personality. If I am to understand this process I must also understand how the institutions themselves operate, how they are related to each other and the entire social structure. If I am to understand fully how my personality has been influenced by various norms and values I must also understand the nature of these phenomena. Where do they come from? What is their role in society? If I am to understand myself as the product of a unique socialization process, I must understand the nature of the larger social structures within which this socialization occurred. The full development of the sociological imagination requires an understanding of how those social structures work.

Critical Thinking Questions

- What was Sigmund Freud's most important contribution to understanding human behaviour?
- Are there universal forms or modes of human communication? If so, what are they? How about content of human communication?
- What per cent of your personaility or character can you attribute to socialization? To genetics? Are these even legitimate questions?
- Are there dimensions of your character structure that you can locate as being the result of some form of conditioned learning? Provide concrete examples.
- Explain why our personality cannot be the result of either nurture or nature.

Terms and Concepts

Classical conditioning—learning that involves the association or substitution of a new behaviour or response with a stimulus. Present a hungry dog with food and it will salivate. Classical conditioning occurs if you ring a bell each time you present the food; eventually the ringing of the bell will be enough to produce salivation: the dog has been conditioned to salivate at the sound of the bell.

Freud's concepts of id, ego, and super-ego—in Freudian theory, the three major dimensions of the human personality. The id represents our basic instinctual biological being and its behavioural tendencies, which mostly involve fantasies about reducing tensions. The ego is the dimension of our being that impels us to direct action in order to reduce various tensions without, however, moral or ethical guidelines. The super-ego represents the internalization of the social and moral controls that we have developed to facilitate an ongoing civilized social existence.

Generalized other—our knowledge and understanding of the attitudes, values, norms, expectations, and expected actions of others in different roles and the community at large in our social milieu. Our actions and interactions are affected by our understanding of the generalized other.

G.H. Mead's play and game stages—according to Mead, the two most important stages of development for the human self or personality. The play stage involves playing at various social roles, becoming aware of the complexities of social interaction, while in the game stage we actually occupy different roles and learn the appropriate behaviours for those and other roles.

G.H. Mead's 'self'—akin to the concept of personality; the total bundle of characteristics, attributes, and features that define a person as unique. Composed of an 'I' that is the sensual biological dimension and a 'me' that is the socially learned behaviours, values, norms, and attitudes. The biologically based 'I' and the socially constructed 'me' are not in isolation but rather are dynamically integrated in the 'self'. The 'I', 'me', and 'self' all tend to be dynamic and changing, yet there is a degree of consistency.

The looking-glass self—a concept developed by C.H. Cooley to illustrate how our self-image and the behaviours that emerge as a result of that image are socially constructed through interaction with others. The looking-glass self is essentially a process that involves: (1) forming images of how we think others perceive us; (2) making assessments as to how we think others judge us on the basis of these images; and (3) developing a self-image and/or self-feelings that influence our behaviours and actions in that situation.

Operant conditioning–learning that involves the association of a consequence, a reward or punishment, with some behaviour. If a specific behaviour produces a positive reward while another behaviour produces a negative reward, an organism will learn to behave in a manner that produces the positive reward and avoid the one that produces the negative reward.

Piaget's stages of development–the four stages that children pass through, in chronological order: (1) sensorimotor, birth to about 2 years; (2) preoperational, from 2 years to 7; (3) concrete operational, from 7 to 11; and (4) formal operational, from 11 to

maturity. Each stage reflects the dynamic relationship of physiological maturation and social environment as the child develops from a sensual being to a mature human being capable of abstract and hypothetical thinking.

Significant gesture–Mead's term for a gesture or symbol used deliberately and consciously in social communication.

Temporal dimension–the human capacity to understand the temporal ordering of events, which allows us to take into account the consequences of our actions prior to acting and to adjust our actions on the basis of our understanding of their perceived future consequences.

Related Web Sites

http://www.piaget.org/

This is the site of the Jean Piaget Society. The site contains news and links through which you can find bibliographical information on Piaget, notices of conferences, new books, previously unpublished essays by Piaget, and a special link for students.

http://www.cddc.vt.edu/feminism/psy.html

Linked to its homepage at the Center for Digital Discourse and Culture, Virginia Tech, this site is titled Feminist Psychology and Psychoanalysis. Stesha Day has assembled an impressive biography. The site also contains a number of links to notable feminist scholars in this area.

http://www.loc.gov/exhibits/freud/

This is Library of Congress Home Page that provides an excellent opportunity to learn about Freud. The links to 'Formative Years', 'The Individual: Therapy and Theory', and 'From the

Individual to Society' will be of particular interest to the readers of this book.

http://spartan.ac.brocku.ca/~lward/

The Department of Sociology at Brock University has done everyone interested in George Herbert Mead a huge favour with the creation of 'George's Page', which is listed as part of the Mead Project. The site gives access to original books and articles, some not previously available, which provide a full range of Mead's work.

http://users.rcn.com/brill/freudarc.html

Titled 'Sigmund Freud and the Freud Archives', this site is one of the many, many sites that result when one performs a web search using 'Freud' as the search term. There are many useful links on this site that will put the student in touch with historical and contemporary writings and debates concerning Freud's work.

Suggested Further Readings

Ehrlich, P. 2000. *Human Natures.* Washington, DC: Island Press. A detailed discussion of the various perspectives bears on the issue of human behaviour and personality. The subtitle is 'Genes, Cultures and the Human Prospect'.

Freud, S. [1933] 1965. *New Introductory Lectures*

on Psychoanalysis. New York: W.W. Norton. There is nothing like the original and this is a very readable set of major lectures covering many foundational concepts in Freud's work. It's accessible to the lay reader.

Mead, G.H. [1934] 1962. *Mind, Self and Society*. Chicago: University of Chicago Press. Always a bit of a tough read—students and followers compiled the book after Mead's death—it remains an essential contribution to understanding our 'selves'.

Peterson, C. 1988. *Personality*. New York: Harcourt Brace Jovanovich. An introductory book in the field of psychology, it overviews the theories or approaches covered in this chapter. This is a good one but there are others.

Steinem, G. 1994. 'What if Freud were Phyllis? *or, The Watergate of the Western World' in *Moving Beyond Words*. New York: Simon & Schuster. Here's a tongue-in-cheek, yet biting, look at some of Freud's major concepts and how they might have developed had he been a woman.

PART II

Theorizing Society

Chapter 1 presented a challenge for the student of sociology by advocating the development of our sociological imaginations. The sociological imagination is an intellectual capacity or frame of mind that allows people to better understand their lives, their behaviour, the behaviour of others, and the social world they live in. The first task involves arriving at an understanding of the impact that society has on our personality, character, behaviour, and lives in general. As Mills points out, however, this is not enough because the full development of the sociological imagination requires that we understand how our society is structured and organized, how women and men interact and behave, how and why it changes or remains stable, how wealth and power are distributed, and so on. In Part II the reader will be introduced to some of the ideas, arguments, and propositions developed over the past century and a half about how society works. The field you are entering is commonly known as sociological theory.

Students in introductory sociology courses sometimes have difficulty understanding the role of social theory. One problem is the confusion that often surrounds the term 'theory', and the fact that in many social science disciplines students are confronted with a range of different theories, all purporting to offer a basis for sociological analysis and explanation.

Let us begin by attempting to define 'theory'. The *Oxford Illustrated Dictionary* defines theory as: 'Scheme or system of ideas or statements held to explain a group of facts or phenomena, statement of general laws, principles, or causes of something known or observed' (860). *The Dictionary of Sociology* defines theory as: 'A set of interrelated principles and definitions that serves conceptually to organize selected aspects of the empirical world in a systematic way. The essence of theory is that it attempts to explain a wide variety of empirical phenomena in a parsimonious way' (Theodorson and Theodorson, 1969: 436–7). Theories are thus nothing more than sets of ideas, concepts, and propositions that purport to explain some phenomena. Social theories are those sets of ideas, propositions, definitions, and concepts that attempt to explain phenomenon as they relate to the dynamics and processes of human society.

Developing and applying social theory rests on some basic assumptions. The first is that human social behaviour and action is not typically random, chaotic, arbitrary, haphazard, or without purpose and intent. In fact, sociologists maintain that the structured, regularized, organized, patterned, and routine nature of most of our actions and behaviours are the very basis of human society. The systematic and scientific investigation and explanation of these actions and the social context in which they occur is one of the primary differences between sociological knowledge and common sense impressions.

There are several other basic assumptions that tend to inform the activity of developing, revising, extending, and using social theory. Some of these include:

- There is an *objective external reality beyond the observer*, some aspects of which can be known. This knowledge can be shared and evaluated even if there are a variety of possible perspectives, outlooks, and opinions about it.
- There are *patterns, regularities, and structures in the social world* that are amenable to observation, interpretation, and explanation.
- The *structures and processes* that comprise human society are *not preordained, natural, or inevitable*.
- The task of social theory is to *try and 'figure out' how the social world is structured and constructed* and how we, as humans, produce and are produced by these structures and processes.

The Project of Social Theory

The core issues that social theory must address, when one considers previous statements, are some macro questions relating to how 'society works' including, but not in any way limited to, the following:

- What gives a society its shape and character? Why do societies tend to differ from one another?
- How are various institutions related? What are the roles of the various institutional orders in society?
- How, why, and when do societies tend to change?
- What is the basis of social stability and order?
- How are individuals and social structures related and interrelated?
- How do we explain patterns of economic, sex, gender, and race inequality?
- How do we understand the nature, extent, and dynamics of the distribution of social power?
- What is the nature and role of political power and the political institutions?
- What roles do the various communication media play in society?

In addition to these macro questions, social theories seek to assist in providing answers to specific questions relating to various micro areas of specialization. For example, in this book we will attempt to develop questions and answers that relate to several of the subfields noted in Chapter 1 including the study of inequality, sex, gender and familial relations, deviance, mass communications and the polity.

As you begin to study social theory you will encounter a distinction between macro and micro. This distinction is intended to draw your attention to the fact that social theory is developed and used at several levels of abstraction. Sometimes we operate at a high level of abstraction, focusing on the general nature of society or a particular form of society without reference to empirical or historical detail. For example, we might attempt to understand the operation and dynamics of capitalism or industrial society in general. At other times we might be less abstract, examining and analyzing a specific advanced industrial or capitalist society such as Canada. When we do this we add empirical and historical detail while using the insights offered by the more abstract level to guide our understanding and investigation. At other times we might actually focus on the individual actor, placing the individual in the context of a particular society that is, in turn, understood in the context of what we know about that form of society in general. Perhaps this would be more easily understood if we think about social theory a kind of 'map'. Depending on your purpose—what you want to know or explain—it might be appropriate to use a globe, a world map, a continental map, a national map, a city map, or a street map of your neighborhood.

A final point that must be considered relates to the issue of alternate or competing theories and the process of comparing theories. There is a general assumption within the discipline that theories must be subject to empirical verification or must demonstrate some concrete and empirical applicability. It is not just a matter of choosing one theory over another on the basis of mere opinion, impressions, or personal preferences. To recognize that theoretical perspectives can direct our attention, impact our perceptions, and offer us different explanations and interpretations is not to say that everything is relative to one's perspective and that no rational evidence-based comparisons and evaluations are possible. You may think a room is hot (having come from outside where it is -30), while I (having just been in the sauna) think that the same room is cold. Nevertheless, as rational creatures, we can agree on a definition of hot or cold, and use a thermometer to actually determine the temperature. Similarly, as rational thinkers, we can engage in meaningful dialogue concerning the evidence with which we are presented and the way we interpret and understand it.

This section has three chapters. The first, Chapter 6, introduces what we might call the founding figures and the streams, or schools, of theory that developed out of their work. Chapter

7 considers how the ideas of the founders have been revised and reworked in the middle- and late-twentieth century to produce several streams of contemporary sociological theory. Chapter 8 casts serious doubt on the heuristic capacities of the three major streams or schools of sociological theory that were dominant prior to the late 1960s. The reason we question the adequacy of the arguments and theoretical positions that have dominated sociology has to do with their failure to include systematic efforts to theorize and explain an essential dimension of the human condition—sex and gender relations. In Chapter 8, therefore, the reader is asked to come to grips with the most important development in sociological theory in the twentieth century, namely, the emergence of feminist theory.

CHAPTER 6

Science, Theory, and the Origins of Sociology

Sociology is a social science that, as a first step, requires its practitioners to describe the world and the events that make up daily existence. For most of us that probably doesn't seem a difficult task. Indeed, much of our daily conversation is composed of providing others with descriptions of things we have observed or experienced.

For instance, take the book you are reading and close it. Then raise the book a metre or so off your table or desk and release it from your hand. Next, describe precisely what happened. In most cases your description would provide an image of the book falling and give an idea of the sound the book made when it hit the surface of the desk, table, or floor—possibly a good hard thump. According to one dictionary, to describe something is to 'set forth in words; recite characteristics of; qualify as' or to 'mark out, draw'. Description involves the systematic symbolic presentation of our perceptions of the characteristics of some phenomenon.

But sociology goes beyond this first step. It is fairly straightforward to describe what happens when you lift up a book and then let it go; but scientists must not only describe events, they must also seek to answer questions such as 'Why did the book fall to the table or floor?' When we ask this sort of question the focus of our intellectual energies shifts from describing to explaining. Although describing an event or phenomenon is an important part of understanding what happened, descriptions alone do not allow us to probe or answer the 'why'

questions. Most practitioners in virtually all disciplines and branches of scientific knowledge production seek to do more than merely describe the world: they also seek to explain it.

In the case of the dropped textbook you might offer a number of different answers to the 'why' question. You could argue that objects fall towards the ground because there are dragons in the centre of the Earth that suck all objects towards them. You could postulate that the weight of the air pushes objects down towards the Earth. Or you could contend that the pressure of lightwaves, most of which originate from above, pushes objects down. Finally, you could argue that all bodies in the universe exercise a force of mutual attraction towards each other, a force related to the mass of the body and the square of the distance between them. If you adopt this last explanation you would know that the force is called gravity, and you could note that because the mass of the Earth is greater than the mass of the book, this makes the book move towards the Earth as opposed to the Earth moving up to meet the book.

This admittedly simple example draws attention to a couple of essential points. First, explaining something—that is, dealing with 'why' questions—means more than merely describing things. Second, answering the 'why' questions can involve more than a single response. Both of these points in turn raise a series of further issues.

The argument that explanation is more than and different from description strikes at the core of what is commonly understood as the 'project' or the objective of science. For scientists, the task of answering the 'why' questions, of providing an explanatory capacity, falls to theory, which, in its simplest form, is nothing more than an attempt to offer an explanation of something. Most of us, for instance, have heard about the theory of gravity and know, even if vaguely, about the sets of assumptions and propositions commonly associated with that explanatory framework. In the case of the falling textbook, most of us would probably accept the explanation provided by that theory—a fact that raises a further important question: why would we find this particular theoretical explanation acceptable rather than, say, the idea that there are dragons in the centre of the Earth sucking objects towards themselves?

The question of which explanation should be selected for a given event or phenomenon is a major issue in the scientific production of knowledge. The scientific approach calls for the systematic use of empirical data to help determine how useful a theory is in explaining a problem. Part of how we judge theories is through their capacity not only to explain events in the world but also to stand up to empirical verification. The notion of empiricism refers to the commonly accepted assumption in science that there is a real and objective external world that serves as the basis for testing whether a theory is correct or not. A theory should be capable of generating hypotheses—predictions or provisional theories about what will happen under specified circumstances—that can be tested by some method of gathering data from the objective world. There are, however, endless debates around the issue of just how you test a theory and the extent to which accepting a theory predetermines the evidence you gather.

Since the beginnings of sociology, theory has been central to all sociological work. The social thinkers who influenced the emergence and development of sociology produced extremely complex sets of arguments and ideas about how human society works and how we should go about under-

standing it. What follows here will provide only a brief outline of how key theorists viewed the workings of human society and how they suggested we go about attempting to understand that society.

The Historical Background

Chapter 1 provided some background to the social, political, economic, and historical circumstances that were the context to the emergence of a new set of ideas about humans and society that became the basis of sociology. We noted that this overview of the circumstances that gave rise to the new discipline was in fact an exercise in the sociology of knowledge because the central concern of that subfield is the relationship between the social conditions and structures that exist at a given time and place and the process of the production of knowledge. The sociology of knowledge attempts to place the producer of knowledge and the process of knowledge production within its historical, cultural, political, economic, and religious contexts.

We know that the French thinker Auguste Comte (1798–1857) was the first to use the term *social physics* to describe the new science he was attempting to establish, later switching to the word *sociology*. We also know that Comte wrote in an era when the ideas associated with classical liberalism were still dominant although many scholars were concerned that they contained inadequate or mistaken conceptions of humanity and society. To review these, although the specifics of their conceptions of human nature varied, most of them maintained that there were fundamental, innate human behavioural tendencies that had to be acknowledged as the basis for the structuring of society. That is, most of the thinkers we commonly include in what is called the classic liberal tradition tended to believe that human beings were by nature competitive, acquisitive, possessive, and individualistic. As a result they supported the social relations connected to a market or capitalist economy because they believed those social relations would allow the blossoming of the natural behavioural tendencies of human beings. In developing his arguments about why a new approach to the understanding of human affairs was needed, Comte was reacting to the conceptions of humanity and society prevalent in his day. In his opinion, the existing conceptions of humanity and society were faulty, and the relationship between them needed reconsideration. This meant a complete revamping of how people explained the workings of the social world—a revamping of both the sources and methods of social knowledge.

Auguste Comte and the Emergence of a Discipline

The substantive work of Auguste Comte is little used or referred to in modern sociology, but his contribution to the development of the discipline was enormous—apart from his early use of the term *sociology*.

Many of the early social, economic, and political thinkers, in applying the methods of science to their fields of study, ended up being sharply critical of existing society. As a result of this tendency, science had taken on a 'critical edge', a tendency that greatly concerned Comte. He lived in France during the aftermath of the French Revolution, a period of enormous change, confusion, and turmoil. Not surprisingly, he became deeply concerned about the roles of confusion and chaos. From Comte's point of view, many of the radical changes and much of the social turmoil seemed to grow out of the findings of thinkers who claimed to be scientists, and who had become tied to an excessively critical project. Comte was not prepared to abandon science; he just wanted it to play a more positive role in social reconstruction. He also began to question some of the basic premises of the classical liberal thinkers, especially those relating to human nature.

Yet another concern was that most of the thinkers of the previous two centuries had been mistaken in what they identified as the object of their inquiries. The classical liberal thinkers had

studied 'man' in order to discover his basic 'nature'. They then went on to consider the sort of society that would be most appropriate given 'human nature'. Comte took exception to this approach, arguing that it was incorrect to postulate the existence of a fixed, universal, and unchanging human nature. Comte was working in an era during which European colonialists, missionaries, and military officials were providing a wealth of new knowledge about cultural diversities. In addition, the period was characterized by a growing body of historical data. When he put this new historical information together with the new knowledge about different cultures, Comte concluded that human beings were not and never had been static and unchanging creatures. Indeed, as he asserted in *The Positive Philosophy* (1838), what he saw in human history was a record of constant change, development, and improvement of both the physical condition and the intellectual faculties and abilities of humans. Comte believed that far from being the same the world over and across historical periods, human beings were quite different in different places and at different moments in history.

Comte was also concerned with the approach of the classical liberals at another level. The prevailing view of society understood it as an extension of the individual. This view led to a certain approach to social phenomena: it was considered appropriate and possible to first study individual people without reference to their society, and then to extrapolate the characteristics of society from the supposed natural characteristics of those individuals. Comte objected to this view on the grounds that society was not merely a collection of individuals. According to him, the 'social' was a realm of existence of its own, governed by laws unique to it, and therefore society and the social must themselves be the object of investigation. Comte explicitly argued that individual human beings, as parts of a larger social whole, must be understood within the context of that larger whole. He further argued that the social whole of which the individual is a part can itself be understood by means of an example drawn from biology—thus introducing an important analogy into sociological discourse: the organic analogy.

A living organism is clearly more than merely the sum of its parts. If we only examine, for example, the individual organs, tissues, and fluids that make up a human body, we cannot completely comprehend the complexity of the human organism as a totality. This is because once the various individual parts are arranged in a different way, what we see is a new entity altogether, and not a human body. Indeed, under certain conditions the totality of the parts takes on a life of its own, becoming a living organism and not just a collection of organs. Using this analogy, Comte argued that we must understand human society as more than just a collection of individuals. Human social phenomena are real, they have a reality and an existence of their own, and they represent an object of investigation for the new discipline of sociology.

Comte is important to the development of sociology, then, because he broke the mould of existing patterns of thought by systematically arguing against the prevailing idea of a fixed, static, inborn human personality, or the behavioural traits commonly called human nature. He said instead that humans are diverse and, as a species, capable of changing and improving their condition, character, temperament, behaviour, and ability. He argued that throughout history humanity had developed and passed through a series of stages, each stage different in how society was organized, how knowledge was produced, and what people were typically like. He maintained that society and the social are real, different, and distinct from the individuals within them. Further, he suggested that the social is a crucial factor in shaping and moulding the individual. Lastly, he argued that society and the social realm were the objects of investigation of an emerging new discipline called sociology. The objective of sociology was to be the discovery or uncovering of the natural laws that govern the social. The knowledge produced by the application of science to social improvement would provide a positive basis for even further human progress and development.

Comte's primary contribution was the development of a distinct discipline with a distinctive approach to the study of society and the social. What is most important about Comte, then, is the fact that he ignited the interest of subsequent thinkers who all, in their own ways, attempted to provide the kind of scientific basis of knowledge of society and the social that Comte had envisioned. Some of these thinkers explored ways of studying society that were at odds with Comte's approach, but nevertheless they still claimed to be producing scientific knowledge.

Marx and the Study of Human Society

The German theorist Karl Marx (1818–83) is one of three major thinkers, along with Emile Durkheim and Max Weber, who had a significant influence on the development of modern sociology. Each of these thinkers produced complex ideas that, once again, defy simple presentation. This problem is even more acute in the case of Marx because his name has become purposefully connected to various political agendas and regimes all over the world—an unfortunate situation, perhaps, because many of those regimes and societies bear little relationship to Marx's original ideas. In effect, the producers of a set of ideas lose control over the uses that others make of their work. The ideas and teachings of Christ, for example, have historically been used by Christians as a justification for waging war and murdering innocent humans, which seems distinctly contrary to the purpose of the original message.

If there is a single phrase that best characterizes Marx's analytical style, it is 'the materialist approach'. In this sense the term does not mean an obsession with the accumulation or possession of material artifacts and goods. As used in social theory, materialist refers to a distinctive approach to understanding human beings and human society.

Marx's materialist approach is based on a series of fundamental assumptions about what it is that makes humans unique and different from all other animals. He suggested that humans can be distinguished from other animals in a number of ways; but the central distinguishing characteristic is the fact that humans produce the material necessities of life. To survive, humans need to provide certain elementary material necessities such as food, clothing, and shelter, and what is unique about the human species is how these basic material needs are met (Marx and Engels, [1845] 1973: 42, 48). Non-human animals simply take what they find in nature or use what nature provides in the immediate environment, whereas humans actively and deliberately go about producing what they need to survive, intervening with nature to provide for the satisfaction of material needs.

Humans, through the application of our intelligence and physical capacities, alter and change nature to satisfy our needs through actions such as the domestication of animals, the creation of new plant strains, the raising of crops, the diverting of water channels, and even the creation of new artificial products that we eat, use for travel, or clothe ourselves in. All of our basic necessities, such as food, clothing, and shelter, are the outcome or the product of humans labouring to create satisfaction for our material needs.

Productive Forces and Relations of Production

The human activity of producing the material goods, products, and services that we require for survival involves the use of technology, tools, knowledge, and skills, which Marx called productive forces. Marx also argued that in addition to being characterized by the use of productive forces, human productive activity is also inherently social; that is, it involves other humans (Marx and Engels, [1845] 1973: 43, 50). His materialist method proceeds from these assumptions to provide a way of understanding human society. He argued that if

German theorist Karl Marx is one of the major sociological thinkers, along with Emile Durkheim and Max Weber. Although his name hs been unfortunately associated with totalitarian political regimes, the way Marx thought about society—specifically, his thesis of historical materialism—has altered sociology profoundly. Issues of power and domination, and the heart of inequality, are thoroughly investigated in his lengthy writings, cmposed in the latter quarter of the nineteenth century. His primary work was *Das Kapital*, the investigation of past, present, and future societies.

we want to understand human beings and human society we must investigate and understand how the production of society's material necessities is organized. We must examine the productive forces that are in existence at a particular moment in time as well as how material production is socially organized. He referred to this last point as the social relations of production.

The nature of the productive processes is determined by both the level of development of the productive forces and the nature of the social relations of production, that is, the patterns of ownership use and control of the productive forces. The nature of the economic institutions is of fundamental or prime importance in influencing the nature and character of the other social institutions. The character and shape of the various institutional orders—the family, polity, education, religion—are fundamentally influenced by the nature of the productive arrangements.

A substantial debate has emerged about just how much emphasis Marx put on this influence. Some theorists have argued, for example, that Marx advocated an economic-determinist position, meaning that the economy or economic institutions determined all other aspects of a society. Although Marx may not have advocated such a strong position, the essence of the materialist position is that economic institutions are the most important factor in a society's general shape and character. The various other institutional orders in turn have reciprocal influences on each other and the economy; but these reciprocal influences are not of the same magnitude as the influence of material production over the whole (Marx, [1857] 1973: 83–100).

Marx's Method Applied

The critical dimension of Marx's work is not necessarily found in his materialist approach, but rather in the outcome of his application of this approach to an analysis of capitalist society. Marx spent a major portion of his life engaged in a systematic and critical examination of the nature of material production and distribution within capitalist society. The major product of this work was his three-volume book called *Capital*.

Among Marx's essential conclusions concerning the social relations of production in capitalist society

was the argument that capitalist society is by necessity a class society. The class structure of capitalist society is, Marx argued, based on the specific social relations of production that characterize the society. The class relations in a capitalist society are based on people's different structural relations to the forces of production, that is, their position in the economic institutions. This means that there are some people who own, operate, and control the factories, mills, mines, land, and other facilities that produce material wealth, while there are other people who do not. Those in structural positions of ownership receive income by virtue of that ownership, while those who do not own productive resources are forced to sell their capacity to work, that is their labour power, in order to survive.

According to Marx, the class structure of capitalist society is also characterized by relations of economic domination and subordination: some people own and control the major production resources in the economy while others do not have a share in the ownership of or any control over economic resources. For Marx, an analysis of class was essential for understanding the general structures of capitalist society.

Relations of Domination and Power

Marx linked the existence of classes, based on different economic positions, with the existence of ideological domination. Here ideology refers to sets of ideas or beliefs that justify or legitimate the social structures and arrangements of capitalist society. It was in connection with a consideration of how certain sets of values, norms, ideas, or beliefs come to be accepted that Marx made his famous statement that 'The ideas of the ruling class are in every epoch the ruling ideas' (Marx and Engels, [1845] 1973: 64). By arguing that there are relations of ideological domination and manipulation, Marx was attempting to illustrate the pervasiveness of relations of domination within capitalist societies. The ruling class attempts to influence all aspects of the social structure, including the very way people think.

Marx also linked economic power and economic domination to political domination. Although he made several different arguments about the precise way in which economic and political power are linked, the key point for us here is his argument that the presence of overwhelming economic power in the hands of one class makes authentic democracy impossible. This is because the class with economic power is always able to influence the government and the state to ensure that the political order acts in its long-term interests.

What we find, then, in the work of Marx is an approach that is materialist in its general orientation. Marx suggested that if we want to understand human beings within a capitalist society or the overall structures of a capitalist society, we must begin our examination with a consideration of how material production is organized. Such an approach leads to more questions. What level of technological development has taken place? Who owns, controls, and directs the use of productive forces? The answers provide essential clues for understanding the entire social structure. In other words, an analysis of the economic or material basis of a society becomes a point of departure for understanding the rest of society, a master key that helps open a series of other doors in our exploration of social complexities.

In his basic assumptions regarding the nature of reality itself, Marx's thought was very much influenced by the German philosopher Frederick Hegel (1770–1831), who produced one of the most complex and comprehensive philosophical systems ever formulated. There was one key assumption of Hegel's that Marx held to firmly. For Hegel, and thus for Marx, an essential characteristic or attribute of the universe was constant change. Everything in the universe is in a constant process of change, development, and transformation, of unfolding, a process guided by the internal logic and structures of the phenomena themselves. Marx assumed that the social scientist must take this basic fact into account when examining and explaining a given phenomenon.

Emile Durkheim

The ideas and work of the French sociologist Emile Durkheim (1858–1917) were very much an extension of the project initiated by Comte. More specifically, Durkheim was attempting to establish the scientific legitimacy of the new discipline of sociology, and he wanted to use that new discipline to assist in the establishment and maintenance of social order. The persistent issue of social order and stability had continued to be of importance in Europe and France during his era. Durkheim was concerned that not only did society seem to be devastated by conflict, but that this situation was also being described as normal by Marx and his followers, who argued that the capitalist system was inherently prone to conflict and crisis. In a fundamental way he set out to develop both an alternative to the Marxian, materialist approach to the study of society and an alternative approach to the study of capitalist or, to use his term, *industrial society*.

The Division of Labour

One of Durkheim's most important books, *The Division of Labour in Society*, illustrates these two related objectives. Durkheim discusses and presents an approach to understanding human society, and in so doing he attempts to illustrate the nature of sociological analysis. The book examines the transition from pre-industrial to industrial society, although his specific focus is the role of moral codes and belief systems in social structures and changes. Durkheim seeks to demonstrate that the basis of social order is to be found in society's moral codes, by which he means belief systems, value systems, and normative orientations. As a society evolves, changes, and develops the basis of social order, its moral codes can change, and there can be periods of conflict as the new moral codes or belief systems develop. Over time there will be a tendency for order to return as the new belief systems become accepted and internalized within the population.

An Emerging Functionalist Approach

In his effort to understand how society works, Durkheim adopted and developed the organic analogy, making the role of functional analysis much more explicit. Functional analysis is a mode of thought that seeks to explain the parts of a system in terms of the overall needs of the system and the particular need that each of the parts or components deals with or solves.

The survival of an organic system such as the human body requires that a number of basic problems or needs be successfully solved or satisfied. In the human body there are specialized structures, such as the various organs, that meet these various needs. One way, for example, of explaining a human heart is to refer to its function as a pump that ensures the circulation of blood throughout the organic system. Similarly, the lungs and stomach could be explained by referring to the functions they perform for the entire body. Understood in this manner, the human body is a system with a series of basic needs that must be met if it is to survive. Each of the organs that make up the body performs a specialized function, allowing the entire system to continue to survive.

When this mode of analysis, called functionalism, is applied to human society, it holds that we should seek to understand the various aspects or components of a social system in terms of the functions they perform for the social whole. For instance, in his study of the division of labour, Durkheim announced that he would look at the division of labour by exploring the function it performs (Durkheim, 1933: 49).

One problem that social systems face, which an organic system does not, is social order. Social order was an acute problem for many of the classical sociological thinkers because they were operating in an era in which the transformation from the old feudal order to the new capitalist system had only recently occurred. The feudal system had been characterized by the existence of a widely accepted set of moral beliefs providing the basis of social stability. In the feudal system tradition was much more important and individuals tended to view themselves as one part of a larger God-given whole. In the emerging modern market system, individuals were no longer connected to each other by traditional bonds and ties, and some thinkers were concerned about how social order and stability would be assured. Durkheim eventually concluded that within the new society a situation similar to the one that prevailed in feudal society would eventually develop. That is, a new set of moral codes or beliefs would indeed emerge, and although the content of this new moral code would be different, its function would be the same: the new moral code would provide a social cement to hold the society together.

Durkheim thus provided an alternative view of society and an alternative approach for society compared to the one posited by Marx. A materialist would argue that economic order is at the core of society. The economic order, Marx argued, is the most important factor in shaping and influencing the structures of a society. For Durkheim the value system is the most important factor. The character and structure of a society will be, in a fundamental manner, determined by the nature of its moral codes, belief systems, and normative orientations.

One of Durkheim's essential tasks was to establish the legitimacy and value of the sociological approach. It was important, he maintained, to view social phenomena and processes as social and not individual. To illustrate this point he engaged in an extensive study of what many thought was the ultimate individualist act, suicide, intending to show how sociology could cast light on even this human extreme.

Suicide

The book *Suicide* ([1897] 1995) is perhaps Durkheim's best-known work. As a result of his investigation of the phenomenon, Durkheim concluded that suicide was not simply an individual act understandable in psychological terms. A person is, Durkheim suggested, connected to society through a series of bonds that regulate conduct and aspirations and provide purposes and ideals. If these bonds are weakened and the individual is not sufficiently integrated into society, that person could be prone to one of three types of suicide. First, when a person does not have firm bonds or connections to society, the act of suicide is caused by egoism. Second, under other circumstances a person may be too strongly integrated into society and have no autonomous self or thought for her or his self. Under such circumstances the person could commit altruistic suicide, which involves giving one's life for the collectivity, as in the case of a soldier who willingly throws himself on a bomb to save his comrades. Third, Durkheim identified a type of suicide that tends to occur when society as a whole has a weakened moral code. He characterized a society lacking a strong system of beliefs and values to hold it together as being in a condition of *anomie*. Under such circumstances people do not feel firm anchoring bonds with the social structure, and as a result anomic suicide can occur.

According to Durkheim, then, there are sociological explanations for many of the events and processes that we assume are individual acts and processes. As a discipline sociology focuses on the study of the social forces and processes that have an impact on individuals and influence their behaviour.

The Study of the Social

Whether he was studying the moral codes that change as the division of labour develops, the role of religion, or social factors related to the levels of suicide, Durkheim insisted that those social forces and processes, which he called social facts, were real and subject to scientific study. In a book that amounts to an instruction manual for sociologists, *The Rules of Sociological Method*, he wrote: 'The first and most fundamental rule is: Consider social facts as things' ([1895] 1964: 14). A social fact is something that has an impact on an individual's 'ways of acting, thinking, and feeling' and is 'external to the individual and endowed with a power of coercion,

Renowned French sociologist Emile Durkheim was attempting to establish the scientific legitimacy of the new discipline of sociology. Perhaps his most famous work was *Suicide* (1897). In this book, Durheim suggested that a person is connected to society thorugh a series of bonds that regulate conduct and aspirations and provide purposes and ideals. (© Bettmann/CORBIS/ MAGMA)

reason of which they control him' (3). Elsewhere in the same book he stated: 'A social fact is to be recognized by the power of external coercion which it exercises or is capable of exercising over individuals' (10). If we find, for example, that someone's religious values cause her or him to act in certain ways, we would have to recognize religion as a social fact and subject it to sociological investigation, an activity that Durkheim in fact spent much of his life doing.

Durkheim made a systematic attempt to develop an approach that would provide an alternative to both Marxism and the various other theories that characterized the social sciences of his day, including those offered in psychology. While Marx and Durkheim provided quite different approaches to understanding society, each introduced a kind of set of instructions about how we can at least begin to undertake social analysis.

Max Weber's New Blueprint for Analysis

Max Weber (1864–1920) was a contemporary of Durkheim, but as a German he was influenced by a very different intellectual environment. Weber set out to establish an approach to sociology that was different from both Marx's materialist approach and Durkheim's functionalism. As a result he provided a definition of sociology that was not so all-encompassing.

All of the early sociological thinkers possessed broad backgrounds and were not the narrow specialists that modern thinkers tend to be. However, even by the standards of classical thinkers, Weber's background was astounding. He studied, among other things, law, general history, politics, economic history, economics, political history, and religion before he began to formulate his unique approach in the developing discipline of sociology.

Weber's View of Sociology

Weber did not develop his systematic approach to sociology until late in his career and life. In his large and unfinished major treatise on sociology, published in German in 1922 and in English under the title *Economy and Society* (1968), Weber provided a definition of sociology that pointed the discipline in a direction quite different from that taken by the followers of Durkheim and Marx. Weber defined

sociology as 'a science concerning itself with the interpretive understanding of social action and thereby with a causal explanation of its course and consequences' (1968: 4). For Weber, the objective of sociology was to provide a basis for interpreting and understanding individual human social actions. The job of the sociologist was to provide a framework for answering important questions such as: Why did she or he do that? Why did they do that? Why do people act the way they do?

Fundamental to Weber's definition of sociology is the assumption that the subject matter of sociology, indeed of all the social sciences, is quite different from that of the natural sciences. The social or human sciences deal with human action and behaviour, and thus they are concerned with motivation. Human actions and behaviour, unlike the actions and 'behaviour' of inanimate phenomena such as atoms or electrons, are motivated and must be understood in terms of these motives. The driving forces for human action and behaviour are not, Weber suggested, only external coercive forces in the social structure. There are important internal subjective motives and factors that must be taken into account when we study, interpret, and explain the individual human actor. Religion, for example, is not so much an 'external social fact' as an internal and personal driving or motivating factor. As such it is one of the factors that must be examined when we attempt to develop an interpretative understanding of a particular social action.

Doing Sociology

If we accept Weber's definition of the goals of sociology, the next logical question is, how do we move in this direction? What sorts of issues must sociologists be concerned with as they attempt to offer an explanatory and interpretative understanding of individual social actions? In a collection of essays, *The Methodology of the Social Sciences*, Weber warned social scientists of the difficulties they faced in attempting to understand their particular subject matter. He argued that the world social scientists were attempting to understand was infinitely complex and presented 'an infinite multiplicity of successively and coexisting emerging and disappearing events, both "within" and "outside" ourselves' (1949: 72).

Weber warned that the people attempting to understand this infinitely complex world possessed only finite minds and were therefore capable of grasping only a finite portion of the infinitely complex reality that would confront them. In other words, social scientists would never be able to understand completely and fully the social world they were attempting to explain. He did not, however, suggest that they abandon the project. Instead, through the illustrative analysis presented in *Economy and Society*, he argued that it was necessary at least to begin the work. Just because we can never isolate causal explanations for all human actions and behaviours does not mean that we should not try. What we must do as social scientists, rather, is face up to our inherent limitations and then 'have a go at it' and begin the process of attempting to offer explanations for as many actions and behaviours as we can.

The approach that Weber suggested does not necessarily begin with the elaboration of a basic theoretical approach for the study of human society. Different societies work in different ways, so that rather than attempting to develop grand and abstract theories of human society, as sociologists we should examine the structures and workings of the society that is home to the individuals we are attempting to understand. Weber spent much of his time examining the structure and workings of capitalist or market society, because that was the society he lived and worked in. This led him to investigate and study a large number of different factors that he felt had to be taken into account in order to explain and interpret individual social action in a market society.

As the table of contents of *Economy and Society* indicates, Weber covered an enormous range of topics and issues: from economic action to status

German-born theorist Max Weber differentiated himself and his writings from both Karl Marx and his contemporary Emile Durkheim. In many ways, he adopted a much broader approach because he had an extensive background in a wide variety of areas. He had studied law, history, politics, economics, political history, and religion before he began to formulate his theories. In a nutshell, Weber directed sociologists to attempt an interpretive understanding of human social actions by analyzing the factors that motivate an individual actor. His most famous work was *The Protestant Ethic and the Spirit of Capitalism*, published in 1930. (The Granger Collection, New York)

groups and classes, from social norms to the sociology of law, from religion to politics, feudalism, and the ancient city. It is an intimidating array of subject matter, perhaps, but one way of looking at it is to see it as an instruction manual or blueprint for sociological analysis. The book illustrates the infinite number of possible factors that sociologists have to pay attention to as they attempt to develop interpretative understandings of human social actions. Some of our actions might be understandable in terms of our class positions, others in terms of our religious beliefs, others within the context of the legal system of our society, and still others by considering the current structures of authority. Although we can never explain all the social actions we confront or observe, we must still make a valiant effort to explain as many of them as we can.

Weber directed us to attempt an interpretative understanding of human social actions by analyzing the factors that motivate an individual actor. He listed a series of different possible factors that could explain our social action, and he provided insights into how we can actually proceed in the investigation. For example, assume for a moment that you are a religious person and that I am attempting to explain one of your social actions in terms of your religious beliefs. There are several things I must do. First, I must study and understand your religious beliefs. Second, I must offer a coherent summary of those beliefs. Finally, I must use this detailed analysis of your religion as part of my interpretative understanding of your actual behaviour.

There are no easy routes or shortcuts I can take in the first step: I must go out and study the particular set of religious beliefs you subscribe to. The second step, summarizing those beliefs, can be difficult, and for it Weber suggested a particular approach. Instead of attempting to present all of the details and specifics of the particular beliefs, Weber

argued that we use what he termed ideal types, defined in the *Modern Dictionary of Sociology* as 'a conceptualization or mental construction of a configuration of characteristic elements of a class of phenomena used in social analysis' (Theodorson and Theodorson, 1969: 193). I thus create an ideal-type representation of your religion and use this set of ideas as a basis for my explanation. I am able to make sense of your behaviour by comparing it to the ideal type. I can compare your behaviour with others in a similar position by referring to the ideal type, which provides a benchmark against which I can analyze and understand your behaviour. In what is perhaps the most widely read of his books, *The Protestant Ethic and the Spirit of Capitalism* (1930), Weber makes extensive use of ideal types in his discussion of both capitalist entrepreneurs and Calvinist religious beliefs (1958: 71, 98).

Following Weber and the other early thinkers, the task of the sociologist is to explain human social action in terms of its motives and causes. We are faced with a situation in which we will never know all the motives and causes of all behaviour, yet we can make a start. Our work will be facilitated by the use of ideal-type mental constructs or representatives of the factors we are examining. Such ideal-type constructs allow us to explain particular instances of social action and, perhaps more importantly, they give us a basis for making generalizations about the motivating factors under examination. Such generalizations, by providing systematic knowledge, will be of use to other sociologists and will contribute to the larger body of knowledge of the field of sociology.

Critical Thinking Questions

- Is the study of sociology a necessary part of the process of self-understanding?
- What is a 'social fact'? Provide some personal examples of the impact of social facts on your personality and behaviour.
- Is it possible to have an objective science of society?

- What do sociologists mean by the term *economic determinist*? Was Marx an economic determinist?
- Explain what Weber means by the term sociology? What must you study to engage in the kind of sociological analysis that Weber envisioned?

Terms and Concepts

Theory—a set of concepts, propositions, and arguments that attempts to offer an explanation of the dynamics, operation, characteristics, and features of some phenomenon or event. Theories are more than descriptions, because they seek to explain why and how 'things happen'. Theory is an essential part of science, because scientific work seeks to explain, not just describe, the world.

Inductive thought—a mode of thought or reasoning that moves from the specific or particular to the general. General principles are inferred from particular instances. For instance, you might study specific manifestations of some phenomenon and then make generalizations about all cases of this phenomenon.

Deductive thought—a mode of thought or reasoning that moves from the general to the specific or particular. You begin with general or even universal statements and deduce specific or particular conclusions. On the basis of some body of established knowledge or principles, you make deductions about some particular instance or case of that phenomenon.

Materialist approach—in sociology, an approach most often associated with Marx. Based on the assumption that humans are unique creatures because they produce satisfaction for their material needs, the materialist approach assumes that the level of technological development and the social organization of material production (economic activity) form the basis or core of society and influence all other aspects of society. A materialist would argue that sociological analysis must always begin with an examination of the basic economic institutions in a society and move from there to study the other institutions and structures.

Relations of production—within Marxian theory, the social arrangements and patterns of social interaction that have been developed to facilitate material production. Included are the patterns of ownership, use, and control of a society's productive resources and capacities. In an industrial society this refers to the people who own, control, and have the power to direct the use of the mines, mills, factories, and other productive resources. Throughout history humans have developed many different types of social relations of production as they have attempted to survive and prosper; and this factor, in part, helps explain the difference between hunting and gathering societies and advanced industrial societies.

Productive forces—within Marxian theory, sometimes referred to as the forces of production. Refers to the technology, tools, skills, and knowledge that a society possesses, which are applied to material production. Throughout history humans have survived and prospered using an incredibly diverse range of productive forces, which again, in part, helps explain the difference between hunting and gathering societies and advanced industrial societies.

Power—the capacity of human actors to influence

social structures, processes, and the conditions of their lives. But it is one of the most contested concepts in sociology. In its Marxian sense, power refers to the capacity of those who control the vital processes of material production to control and direct the overall structures, direction, and operation of society. Weber adopted a more individual approach, relating power to the capacity of individuals and groups to carry out their will even in the face of opposition.

Ideology—a system or set of ideas, beliefs, or values that serves to explain and justify social, economic, cultural, and political phenomena, structures, and processes from the perspective of a particular class or group. For example, a dominant ideology will explain and justify the socioeconomic and political system from the perspective of the ruling class.

Social facts—as used by Durkheim, those phenomena that have an impact on the actions and behaviour of individuals and are social and external to the individual. For example, because religion can have an important influence on society and individuals it can and must be studied as a social fact, in the same way that a physicist might study the influence and impact of gravity on physical bodies.

Labour power—in Marxian theory, the capacity or ability of human beings to engage in work and productive activity. In a capitalist society a worker sells this capacity to capitalists.

Functionalism—in sociology, a general approach that assumes society can be understood as a system with needs that must be met if the overall system is to survive. Institutions operate or function to meet one or more of these basic system needs. The function of an institution is the system need it meets or the problem it solves for the overall system. Normally systems exist in a stable and orderly condition.

Weber's definition of sociology—that the objective of sociology is the explanation of individual social actions and behaviours. As a social science, sociology deals with behaviours and actions that are both meaningful to the actor (usually we know why we are doing things) and caused by motivations (there are reasons for our actions). Sociology should seek to provide interpretations of social actions by offering an interpretation of the meaning the actions had for an actor and interpreting their motivation. Interpretations of meaning and motive are key parts of a causal explanation.

Ideal type—as used by Weber, an abstract or pure representation of some phenomenon people are interested in studying or understanding. Although we may never find a real or empirical example that is similar to an ideal type, the intellectual construction of ideal types will assist in understanding the concrete real-world phenomenon under study. The 'ideal' in no way implies a moral judgment, because we can create an 'ideal-type' personality profile of a serial killer as readily as that of a saint.

Related Web Sites

http://www.marxists.org/archive/marx/

Given the many different and contradictory interpretations of what Marx wrote or really meant, it is often a good idea to go to the original source. This site offers access to a wide range of Marx and Engel's original writings, organized in different ways including by date of production

and subject. It also includes biographical material, images, and extensive links to other writers who claimed to be following Marx.

http://www.pscw.uva.nl/sociosite/topics/weber.html

Albert Benschop has produced this site as part of a larger project 'Sociological Information

System Based at the University of Amsterdam'. The Web site should be of great interest to students interested in Max Weber because it allows one to read much of Weber's original work plus many secondary comments and analytical books and articles.

http://www.relst.uiuc.edu/durkheim/

Created by Robert Alum Jones at the University of Illinois (Urbana-Champaign), this site is also very comprehensive. You are able to access original writing, reviews, essays, a complete bibliography of Durkheim, lectures, and news for Durkheim scholars.

http://www.cla.sc.edu/socy/faculty/deflem/
Cybertheory.htm

Professor Mathieu Deflem from Purdue University is the Webmaster for the American Sociological Association's 'Comparative and Historical Sociology' section. This site is appropriately titled 'Cybertheory.htm Sociological Theory in the Internet'. It provides what might be the most comprehensive site for sociological theory, both classical and contemporary, with more links than I can mention, plus images and much more.

http://www2.pfeiffer.edu/~lridener/DSS/DEAD
SOC.HTML

Dr Larry Ridener established this site at James Madison University. In addition to the information associated with the 'Dead Sociologists Society', there are links to the 'Dead Sociologists Index' and the 'Dead Sociologists Gallery'. Much useful and interesting information is here on a variety of dead sociologists.

Suggested Further Readings

Giddens, A. 1986. *Social Theory and Modern Sociology*. Stanford, CA: Stanford University Press. This comprehensive and accurate documentation of the major ideas of Marx, Durkheim, and Weber is one of the best secondary sources for a beginning student.

Morrison, K. 1997. *Marx, Weber and Durkheim*. London: Sage Publications. Another fine and detailed secondary account of the ideas of these major founders, the book includes a glossary of major concepts.

Sydie, R.A., and B.N. Adams. 2001. *Sociological Theory*. Thousand Oaks, CA: Pine Forge Press. This is an excellent and current overview of both classical and contemporary theory. It is notable for a perceptive feminist critique and exposition of the weaknesses of the classics.

Zeitlin, I. 1990. *Ideology and the Development of Sociological Theory*. Englewood Cliffs, NJ: Prentice-Hall. This is an excellent summary of some of the main ideas of many major theories. The sections on Marx, Weber, and Durkheim stand out.

CHAPTER 7

Contemporary Sociological Theory

Since the beginning of the discipline, sociologists have had an abiding concern with developing theoretical frameworks to help explain the various phenomena and issues that come under their scrutiny. But although many of the insights and arguments developed by the founding figures in sociology were astute, indeed brilliant, few sociologists of the twentieth century have been willing to acknowledge that the 'classical thinkers' dealt adequately with all the key issues: indeed, an important stream of contemporary thought argues that the earlier theories are fundamentally flawed. As a result, the field of sociological theory has retained a dynamic core, with numerous new and quite complex theories emerging in the seemingly endless quest to provide a more adequate and contemporary approach to the issues of society.

The modern approaches to sociological theory involve a large number of thinkers, but the studies can be usefully broken down into a few major streams or schools of thought, most of them, not surprisingly, connecting back to the classical approach: structural functionalism (influenced by Comte, Durkheim, and others); neo-Marxism; and symbolic interactionism (influenced by G.H. Mead and Weber). But beyond these approaches—which at one time at least might have been considered various branches of the sociological mainstream—are other new challenges, particularly from the vital field of feminist thought and from the work on structuration theory as developed by Anthony Giddens. In the end, all of these various streams raise other questions: Is theory really necessary? Are there limits to abstract theory? And how, after critically evaluating the various approaches, can we use them to further the sociological imagination?

The Structural Functionalist Perspective

From the Great Depression of the 1930s until well into the turbulent decade of the 1960s, Western sociology was dominated by structural functionalism. As a stream of sociological theory, structural functionalism, which is also often referred to just as functionalism, was influenced by the ideas of Comte, Durkheim, and—to some degree—Weber, as well as by anthropologists such as Bronislaw Malinowski and A.R. Radcliffe-Brown and the economist-sociologist Vilfredo Pareto. In the United States contemporary functionalism was systematically developed by Talcott Parsons, altered somewhat by Robert Merton, and refined by, among many others, Kingsley Davis, Wilbert E. Moore, Neil Smelser, and Daniel Rossides.

The Organic Analogy Revisited

Harking back to the work of Comte and Durkheim, structural functionalists often use the organic analogy as their mode of explanation. That is, they have analyzed society in the same way others might view an organic system such as the human body. This overall approach is based, once again, on the recognition that if it is to survive, an organic system such as the human body has certain basic needs that must be met and problems that must be solved. For example, a minimal level of nutrients must be provided for all its organs; wastes of a variety of sorts must be removed; oxygen must be provided for the organs; sexual tensions must be released; and so on. Some structural functionalist thinkers use the phrase *system prerequisites* to refer to these basic needs and problems.

Similarly, social systems have system prerequisites: a number of basic and common problems that must be addressed and solved. Talcott Parsons and Robert Bales developed the first list of what these basic system prerequisites are for the human social system. They suggested that for a society to survive over time it must provide or make arrangements for biological reproduction, the provision of material needs, the establishment and dissemination of a value system, and the general co-ordination of all this activity (Aberle et al., 1967: 317–31; Parsons, 1951: 26–36; Rossides, 1968: 67–8; Skidmore, 1979: 137).

In the case of a complex organic system such as the human body, complex specialized organs have evolved or developed to deal with the various specific needs or problems. The heart, stomach, kidneys, central nervous system, and other specialized organs all have a specific task or function to perform within the system as a whole. The heart pumps blood throughout the body; the stomach and the digestive tract work to enrich the blood with nutrients; the lungs add oxygen to the blood and remove wastes; and so on. Each of the organs in the system performs a function, solves a problem, or meets a need for the whole organic system. In other words, an organic system is made up of specialized structures (organs) that perform specialized functions for the whole system.

When we apply this general framework to society, we can argue that society or the social

system faces certain basic problems that it must solve if it is to survive. The social system, like an organic system, is a complex phenomenon made up of component parts. While in the organic system the most important component parts are organs, in the social system the most important component parts are institutions. Like organs, institutions are complex structures that perform various functions for the entire social system. For example, one of the problems faced by a social system is biological reproduction and sexual regulation. The structure that takes care of this general system need is the family. Similarly, the economic institutions function for the entire social system by solving the problems associated with the production and distribution of the basic goods and services required for survival. The problems associated with establishing and maintaining a value system are dealt with by the educational and religious institutions, while the problems of social decision-making are handled by the political order, also called the polity.

The mode of analysis employed in the structural functionalist approach is quite commonly used in both scientific and non-scientific discourse. Pretend for a moment that a life form from another planet approaches you holding an animal heart in its hand (or whatever appendage it uses for what we would call a hand). The creature and you are somehow able to communicate, and it asks you what this object is. You answer that it is a heart, which prompts the question, 'What is a heart?' How do you reply? One approach would be to explain the heart as a mass of muscle tissue; but when the creature asks for more details you find yourself explaining the heart in terms of its function as a pump that keeps blood circulating throughout the body. You might elaborate, noting that by pumping blood the heart is ensuring that nutrients and oxygen reach the various other organs and tissues and that wastes are removed. As soon as your explanation takes this turn you have begun to practise classical functionalism. You are explaining a single part of a system in terms of the function it performs for the whole.

Social Order

One of the central concerns of the structural functionalist approach, especially as it developed in the United States under the influence of Talcott Parsons, is social order. In this case, moving beyond the simple organic analogy to understand society, we must ask how the entire complex of social institutions is organized, co-ordinated, and maintained as a working system. For example, how do people in the various institutions know what behaviours and actions are expected of them and their institutions? How is the whole social structure held together and maintained? That is, how is the multitude of complex interactions and institutions that make up an advanced industrial society co-ordinated and organized? In attempting to answer these questions structural functionalists have tended to borrow from Durkheim, adopting his arguments about the role of value systems or moral codes in binding social systems together. In his study of functionalism Mark Abrahamson notes the importance of value systems in the functionalist view of society: 'The entire social system, or at least its stability, is seen as resting heavily upon shared values, even though society is also seen as having a structure and organization' (1978: 41).

A shared set or system of values, norms, beliefs, and morals is seen as the basis of social order. Because the majority of members of a society share a moral code or belief system, they will know and understand what behaviours are appropriate and inappropriate under what circumstances, what the proper functions of institutions are, and generally 'how things work'. As a result of its members sharing values and beliefs, social systems will tend, under normal circumstances, to exist in a state of consensus and equilibrium. Indeed, functionalists argue that social order is the norm, and as long as there is a common value system holding or binding all the elements of the system together, social order

will be maintained. For this reason the structural functionalist perspective is often referred to as the consensus or order perspective.

In addition to providing the basis of social order, shared moral codes or value systems also tend to be important factors in giving social systems their general shape and character. In Parsons' work this discussion is posed in the context of a highly abstract discussion of a series of dichotomous value orientations (Parsons, 1951: 180–200). Here we can keep the language simpler. Daniel Rossides states that there are two factors regularizing human actions into the structures that sociologists call institutions: the type of technology as given in a society's cultural artifacts; and the society's sets of values and ideas. Rossides sees values and ideas as playing an important role in the overall structuring of the society (Rossides, 1968: 183). In *Social Structures and Systems* (1969) William Dobriner more forcefully developed an argument about the central role of norms in structuring society and social relationships. He explicitly argued that norms both define the very character of social relationships and provide a central cohesive force binding relationships together in a unified system (1969: 72–6).

Understanding Social Change

As a result of its key focus on institutions and other social practices and phenomena in terms of how they contribute to maintaining the social system, many social theorists have argued that structural functionalism is biased towards the existing social system and against the element of social change.

Various theorists have examined these criticisms. Two of them, John Wilson (1983: 75–6) and Percy Cohen (1973: 58–9), noted that advocates of functionalist analysis have in fact taken a variety of different positions that address the issue of social change, and that this criticism may not be as valid as the critics have claimed. Parsons explicitly addressed the issue of social change in one of his later books, *Societies: Evolutionary and Comparative Perspectives* (1966). In *Social Change*, a book also published in the 1960s, prominent functionalist Wilbert E. Moore noted that at a certain point functionalists had to make amendments to their approach to allow it to deal more adequately with the issue of social change (1963: 8). As suggested by the title of his book, Moore argued that functionalism is indeed interested in and capable of dealing with social change.

Another author, William Skidmore (1979), noted that structural functionalism is certainly capable of dealing with evolutionary change, that is, gradual changes in how a society or social system adapts to its environment and looks after the material needs of its members (179–80). As Skidmore suggested, this conception of change implies a certain degree of slowness in the process. Ruth Wallace and Alison Wolf (1986) also noted that, as presented in the classical formulation of Parsons, structural functionalism views social change as a slow process that occurs when social systems adapt to gradual changes among the component parts of the system. In the organic analogy, as the human body ages its various organs may not function in the same way as they did previously. In the case of the heart, for instance, the entire system is forced to make adjustments to the slightly changed capacity of that organ so that fresh blood can still be delivered effectively. In the case of social systems, changes to any of the institutional orders can result in adjustments and changes to other orders, although these changes tend to be slow, gradual, or evolutionary.

Robert Merton's work made significant advances in the capacity of structural functionalism to deal with change. Merton argued that it was not correct to assume that every aspect of a social system made a positive contribution to maintaining the overall system. He noted that it was possible for a component or a part of a system to be dysfunctional (1968: 105). Dysfunction refers to a situation in which a component or part of a social system operates in a manner that has the effect of actually lessening the system's capacity to survive.

Using the organic analogy, we can argue that a body will continue to exist in a healthy, stable condition providing all its various organs are functioning in a normal manner. If an organ does not, for any number of possible reasons such as age, infection, or disease, perform its functions normally it could be referred to as dysfunctional. The dysfunction of a particular organ could lead to a crisis situation that if not corrected would threaten the very existence of the system. Most of the dysfunctions associated with the organs in an organic system are corrected by the internal mechanisms of the body's immune system and other biological corrective mechanisms.

In the workings of a social system, consider the case of the presence of sexist ideas in a society's norms and values. Such ideas often mean that many important jobs become labelled as being outside the interest, domain, and possibilities of women. The result is that women in the society are socialized to not aspire to those jobs, and the positions are filled primarily by men. Half of the society's potential pool of talent is thus not available for jobs that could be vital to social development and prosperity. This is surely not a desirable situation, and it should be taken as an indication that a part of the society, in this case a part of its system of norms and values, is operating in a dysfunctional manner.

When a particular institution does not perform its allotted function, the stability and equilibrium of the social system can be threatened because of the failure to meet and solve a part of the system's basic needs or problems. Under such circumstances social systems tend to make adjustments, perhaps allocating the task or function that is not satisfactorily being addressed to another institution or facilitating the development of a new institution to carry out the function. If, for example, one of the central functions of the family is the provision of child care for young children, and if both parents in a traditional nuclear family become employed in the labour force, then a new institution, such as day care, could emerge to fill the void. Under these circumstances some form of social change occurs as the transformation of family structures brings about corresponding adjustments in other parts of the social structure. The change was brought about through an adjustment to the larger system to deal with a dysfunctional part. The larger, more important point, as a functionalist might argue, is that the social system's tendency to move towards equilibrium and stability facilitates the ability of the overall system to deal with dysfunction. Similarly, it could be argued that because structural functionalism tends to emphasize stability, equilibrium, and consensus, the theory is able to deal with social change, particularly if the change is slow and evolutionary.

Changing Social Values

In addition to social change that occurs as a result of the evolutionary adaptation of a society to its surroundings and the dysfunction of components of a social system, some social change occurs as a result of shifts in a society's value orientations and normative systems. Structural functionalists tend not to focus on the history and origin of a society's values and norms, because their concern is more with the ongoing functions of social phenomena. Because value systems and normative orientations are at the centre of society, shifts and changes in the core values are bound to have an impact on the entire social structure.

Understanding Social Conflict

For structural functionalism, the question of social conflict is even more difficult than the question of social change. The assumption that social systems normally exist in a condition of stability and are characterized by equilibrium and consensus tends to focus the attention of a structural functionalist away from the issue of social conflict. In addition, the approach does not have a well-developed conception of power, and as a result its ability to address the issue of conflict is diminished (Skidmore, 1979: 180).

For Parsons the issue of social order was not only important, but also one of the most fundamental issues facing society. Social order tended not to be a problem after a society had established a more or less stable value system and set of normative orientations. Once those values and norms were successfully passed on to individuals and ingrained in their personalities through the process of socialization, the problem of social order was solved (Hamilton, 1983: 104). There would always be conflicts of a more or less minor nature—that is, conflicts that were not system-threatening—but these could usually be handled within the system.

Arnold Rose presented a classic statement about the basis of social conflicts, in noting that values are usually at their centre. Rose argued that conflicts arise because individuals and groups engage in a clash of values or attempt to stop the actions of others holding different values (1956: 492). This approach would apply to industrial conflict, religious conflict, and even conflict between different racial groups. Most stable social systems have established mechanisms and procedures for dealing with such conflicts. These mechanisms and procedures, when successfully used, not only address the problem of a specific conflict but also add to the stability of the whole system.

In *The Functions of Social Conflict* (1956), Lewis Coser systematically developed the theme of conflict as contributing to the general stability of a social system. Coser argued that conflict is likely to occur in any large and complex society, but if it is limited and does not threaten the basic values and norms of the social system, it can serve to strengthen and stabilize the system. Indeed, a social system must tolerate a degree of conflict and provide the institutionalized means of dealing with it. If there are 'safety-valve' institutions that individuals and groups can use to address concerns and problems that might lead to conflict, the system will be able to make the adjustments necessary to prevent the conflict from threatening the overall system. In addition, the institutional expression of legitimate grievances gives individuals and groups a chance to 'let off some steam' and thus avoid a potentially

Arnold Rose presented a classic statement about the basis of social conflict, in noting that values are usually at their centre. Rose argued that conflicts arise because individuals and groups engage in a clash of values or attempt to stop actions of others holding different values. In this photo, police in Quebec City have just released tear gas to control the crowd that is demonstrating at the Summit of the Americas in May 2001. (CP Picture Archive/Stephan Savoia)

threatening build-up of discontent. Finally, the expression and emergence of limits to conflict can serve to revitalize the existing value and normative system by leading to a re-examination of existing elements and possibly introducing fresh and innovative ideas. A functionalist might argue that conflict can even have a positive function for the social system.

Social Inequality and Power

The structural functionalist perspective explains social inequalities in terms of either a society's value system or its division of labour. For some functionalists, such as Parsons, social inequalities result from individuals possessing or not possessing certain traits or characteristics deemed desirable within the context of the value system. For example, if the society's value system stresses the importance of material possessions, people with material possessions tend to have a higher social position or standing.

Kingsley Davis, Wilbert Moore, and others developed another explanation for social inequality from within the functionalist stream. This approach suggests that a degree of social inequality is necessary if a complex society is to allocate its various jobs and tasks to the individuals available in society.

In their approach to the polity or the political order, functionalists are interested in analyzing the functions that the political order performs for society. For North American political structures, functionalists tend to accept the approach known as pluralism. According to this approach, political power in Western liberal democracies is typically not concentrated but spread out among a plurality of centres of power. Among the unique features and strengths of liberal democratic systems are the opportunities available to all citizens to influence government and have an impact on the political process. According to the theory, even though there are individual inequalities in Western liberal democracies, they are still basically open and egalitarian societies.

We will be discussing the structural functionalist approaches to social inequality and the polity in Chapters 9 and 11 respectively.

Structural Functionalism and Social Theory

The set of general ideas and arguments presented here under the rubric of structural functionalism represents a sort of 'generic version' of the perspective. It indicates only some of the general assumptions and positions that characterize the broad theoretical stream or perspective called structural functionalism. A particular theorist would never, strictly, make all these arguments; but they do represent a summary of the key background assumptions, arguments, and propositions that inform the structural functionalist approach.

When grappling with somewhat abstract theoretical ideas and arguments, we need to keep in mind the key role that theory plays in social analysis. Theory provides the basis for explaining how something works; it provides answers to the 'why' questions that emerge as we try to get through each day. In attempting to provide the basis for explanations and answers to these questions, theories also provide the basis for ways of organizing and making sense—in our minds at least—of the phenomena we experience. The social and physical worlds present themselves to us as an incredibly complex series of events and experiences, and we are required to organize all of it in some manner if we are to survive those worlds, let alone understand

them. Theories provide a means of organizing the world in a way that renders it comprehensible, and the various perspectives that have emerged in the field of sociology have been developed in the attempt to make sense out of how society is organized and how it works.

A student of social theory must always keep the dynamic and developing nature of social theory in mind. For example, while functionalism has often been viewed as conservative and focused on the status quo, a group of contemporary scholars are busy revising the approach. Key figures in this undertaking are Jeffrey Alexander and Paul Colomy, who have undertaken a sympathetic yet systematic re-examination of many of the basic tenets of structural functionalism (1990). George Ritzer (2000: 118–19) has summarized their essential ideas in a series of points:

1. Neofunctionalism focuses on society as a system that must be differentiated from its environment.
2. Neofunctionalism devotes equal attention to action and order.
3. System integration cannot be viewed as an assumed reality, but rather it is possible to accomplish.
4. Social theory must analysis change and control in all key systems–social, cultural and personality.
5. Attention must be devoted to social change and differentiation within these systems.
6. The development and expansion of social theory must remain a core activity.

The overall logic of this approach is to retain core elements of functionalist thought while addressing some of its obvious weaknesses on which critics had focused.

Neo-Marxist Social Theory

The Materialist Perspective

Karl Marx's materialist approach to the understanding of human beings and human society was based on a series of ontological assumptions concerning the human species. Humans are unique, Marx argued, primarily because our physiological and psychological makeup allows us to produce satisfactions for our material needs and wants. As we have undertaken the act of material production, we have created a variety of productive forces: various tools, technologies, skills, and bodies of knowledge. Human material production is also a social act involving others, which leads to the concept of social relations of production. It is an elementary postulate of the materialist method that if we are to understand a particular society we must understand the nature and organization of its forces of production as well as of the social relations of production.

There is much academic debate among neo-Marxists about just how the social relations of production and the productive forces impact on each other and on society, but it is clear that Marx himself understood that they both make up the economic basis of society (Marx, [1859] 1977: 20). Although neo-Marxists tend to accept that the various non-economic institutions do have a reciprocal influence on the economic base, for the most part they assume that the economic basis or core is the essential or primary factor in influencing and structuring the various other components or parts of the social structure. More specifically, institutional orders such as the political order and state structures, as well as the educational order and its components, are influenced by the nature of the economic order. In addition, the family and even the religious order will, in some fundamental manner, have their shape, character, and structure influenced by the economic institutions.

For a neo-Marxist, the nature of a society's economic structures and institutions provides essential clues that will help unlock the dynamics, structures, and character of other components of the larger social structure. The relationship between the various institutional orders and institutions is not a simple one, but in the final analysis the key to

understanding the entire social structure is to understand the economic core.

Social Change

In using this basic method, neo-Marxists make an additional further assumption: human societies tend to be dynamic and constantly changing. To explain the importance of social change, neo-Marxist theorists might ask you to think about what has happened in human history over the past several millennia. Having done this, they might ask if you are impressed by the extent to which human societies have remained stable and constant over the past several thousand years. Or are you struck more by how change and development, often of a dramatic and radical nature, seem to have been the normal pattern of things? Neo-Marxists would suggest that human society is a dynamic phenomenon in which change and development are a constant. They argue that the constant changes in productive forces and social relations of production have led to constant changes in the various other institutional orders.

Materialist Analysis as Social Criticism

In engaging in the act of production, the human species is in essence creating itself. Production is an act of self-creation and an expression of our unique species' powers and abilities. It is an expression of our humanity. For the materialist, material production is the most important human activity.

In *The German Ideology* Marx and Engels discussed the importance of the act of production to human existence. They maintained that how we are situated in the process of production fundamentally determines the kind of people we are and that we become. A part of their argument holds that, since the act of production is central and essential to being a human, humans must control not only the process of production but also both the products of their production and the relationships they enter into as they produce. If people do not have this control they experience what Marx termed alienation. When material production is conducted under conditions characterized by alienation, its entire role in human development and existence changes. Rather than being an expression of our humanity and creativity, productive work under alienating circumstances becomes a process that distorts, destroys, and dehumanizes.

The issue of alienation remains a central concern for most neo-Marxist thinkers (Ollman, 1976). Additionally, the concept provides the basis for offering critical analysis of larger structures of capitalist society. It suggests that in any truly humane society the entire range of activities surrounding material production must be under democratic control, that is, under the control of the people who actually produce the physical wealth. Only under such circumstances will production be an activity that allows for the full development of all human potentials and possibilities.

In their analyses of the economic basis of capitalist society, neo-Marxists maintain that some mode of class analysis is essential. Although there are substantial, radical differences in how various neo-Marxists approach the study of class, there is agreement that class is a central concept that must be employed in the investigation of capitalist society. Neo-Marxists tend to assume that in a capitalist society there will be a dominant class and at least one (and very likely more) subordinate class. The dominant class is defined in terms of its structural position within the economic order; its position allows it to gain control of the bulk of the society's economic surplus. By virtue of its position as owner of the society's productive resources, the dominant class exploits other classes, most notably the working class, benefiting from their economic activities.

Ideology

Another central concept in the neo-Marxist approach—and one that is also still very much an issue of continuing debate, as well as being subject to widely differing usage—is ideology.

One usage of the term *ideology* follows quite directly from Marx's views. Marx suggested that ruling classes have a tendency to develop, or at least promote, views of the world that suit their interests and serve to justify their position. In stating that the ruling ideas of an epoch were the ideas of the ruling class, he was really arguing that ruling classes maintain their power through a number of different means, including ideas. A ruling class interested in maintaining its position within a particular set of social structures will attempt to ensure its position and prevent the emergence of opposition and conflict by articulating and promoting views of the world that justify the status quo. It should not be implied that the ruling class always does this in a conscious and deliberate manner, nor should we assume that the views expressed by the ruling class are always a deliberate and intentional attempt to manipulate the subordinate classes (although this cannot be ruled out). The neo-Marxists argue that the value systems, normative orientations, moral codes, and belief systems of a society such as ours are, in fact, in a direct and substantial manner connected to the larger process of class rule and domination. Winning the hearts and minds of the subordinate classes is an important part of maintaining control.

Neo-Marxists often use the term *dominant ideology* to refer to those sets of beliefs, values, and norms that support and justify the overall system and the position of the ruling classes in that system. The precise nature and content of dominant ideologies will, of course, vary over history. In a capitalist society the values and norms might typically place emphasis on individualism, individual initiative and responsibility, freedom of enterprise, the desirability of competition, the necessity of being aggressive in order to succeed, and respect for leadership. In addition, ideas that downplay the importance, or even existence, of class would be seen as supportive of the overall system. A neo-Marxist might argue that to the extent that all classes in the society accept these values and norms, the overall system is strengthened—and so, too, is the position of the ruling class, which benefits most from the operation of the system. The themes of ideological manipulation and domination play an important role in the thinking of some neo-Marxists. Others calling themselves neo-Marxists would disagree, arguing that placing too much emphasis on the notion of ideological manipulation is a mistake because it directs our attention away from an important characteristic of capitalist society, the tendency for the system to produce conflict.

If we assume that there are different classes in capitalist society, with different positions in the society's economic structures, it is possible to envision the emergence of conflicting systems of ideas or ideologies. Although the ruling class produces and promotes sets of beliefs, values, and norms that express its interests and concerns, and although it attempts through a variety of means to impose these elements on all classes, the subordinate classes will also generate their own ideologies and ideas about how the world works. For example, subordinate classes might begin to realize that the value system, norms, and beliefs they were taught in school or that are presented in the media really don't explain the world as they experience it. Workers who are told again and again that if they work hard they will get ahead might be finding out that after 20 years of hard work they will still be barely able to keep up with the escalating cost of living. Meanwhile, corporate profit margins increase and the major shareholders of large corporations become wealthy beyond belief. Under such circumstances, if workers become familiar with socialist ideas and critiques of the structures of inequality that characterize a capitalist society, they may find that such ideas and critiques make sense; and a counter-ideology postulating a radically different set of values, norms, beliefs, and ideas representing the interests and concerns of a subordinate class could gain credence. In such a situation there would then be a clash of ideologies; or, put differently, the conflict that is always a part of a class society would take on an ideological dimension.

When a structural functionalist discusses value systems and normative orientations and when a neo-Marxist discusses ideology, they are, essentially, referring to the same thing. But each perspective views the role of values, norms, ideas, or ideologies in a fundamentally different manner. For structural functionalists, a society's primary values are the social cement that binds society together in the interests of all. For neo-Marxists, a society's primary values represent the views and interests of the dominant class, and—to the extent that they hold society together—they serve the interests of the dominant class. The values, norms, ideologies, and so on are a part of a larger strategy of domination and manipulation. But if there are conflicting counter-ideologies, those elements are part of a larger process of class-based conflict, which is typical of class societies.

Many neo-Marxists follow the work of Antonio Gramsci (1891–1937). The issue of ideology was always important for Gramsci. In the following passage he explains that humans are complex creatures because we carry and formulate complex systems of ideas about the world and our place in it:

> Each man, finally, outside his professional activity, carries on some form of intellectual activity, that is he is a 'philosopher', an artist, a man of taste, he participates in a particular conception of the world, has a conscious line of moral conduct, and therefore contributes to sustain a conception of the world or to modify it, that is, to bring into being new modes of thought. (1975: 9)

The thinking, conscious actors must be understood as being imbued with ideas, beliefs, intellectual conceptions, and understandings, all of which must be taken into account and understood because of the fact that 'popular beliefs and similar ideas are themselves material forces' (165).

Gramsci uses the word *hegemony* to refer to this notion of ideological, social, and political domination. Although the concept has been subject to significant misunderstanding, Julia and David Jary provide a straightforward definition. They note that, according to Gramsci, hegemony is 'the ideological/cultural domination of one class by another, achieved through "engineering consensus" through controlling the content of cultural forms and major institutions' (1995: 279). Gramsci recognized the reality of differing modes of domination and control by the dominant class in capitalist society, one more indirect accomplished by controlling consciousness and knowledge, and one more direct in the sense of the use of state power:

> What we can do . . . is to fix two major super-structural 'levels': the one that can be called 'civil society', that is the ensemble of organisms commonly called 'private', and that of 'political society' or 'the State'. These two levels correspond on the one hand to the function of 'hegemony' which the dominant group exercises throughout society and on the other to that of 'direct domination' or command exercised through the State and 'juridical' government. (1975: 12)

The Polity or State System

The tendency to view capitalist society as a system fundamentally characterized by relations of domination and subordination extends to the overall neo-Marxist views about the nature of the state in capitalist society. Although there are major differences in how they see this happening, their common assumption is that the polity and the state structure in capitalist society tend to serve, over the long run at least, the interests of the dominant class. The state may serve the interests of the dominant class by direct actions, such as when state agents act to end a workers' strike, or the state may serve the interests of the dominant class in more indirect ways, by promoting general social and economic stability and legitimizing the system. A neo-Marxist might argue, for example, that the provision of social services to people out of work is a way of both

legitimizing the humane nature of the system—of seeing that no one goes without—while keeping at least a minimal purchasing power in the hands of the population, a situation that ultimately benefits the producers and sellers of consumer commodities. The state may also take actions that create a favourable climate for profitable investment, thus ensuring a measure of economic growth and social stability, which is in general most beneficial to the dominant class. The key questions that arise from such a position are: how and why does the state serve the interests of the dominant class? Recent developments in Marxian theorizing on the state are discussed further in Chapter 11.

Conflict and Contradiction

Neo-Marxists also usually hold one other assumption in their analysis of capitalist society: the presence of conflicts and contradictions. For neo-Marxists, the class structure of capitalist society ensures the existence of persistent and inevitable conflicts between different classes over a range of different issues. Class conflict is normal and expected.

The concept of contradiction relates to more structural features of the system. In the *Dictionary of Marxist Thought,* Ben Fine states that a contradiction involves a 'situation that allows the satisfaction of one end only at the cost of another' (1983: 93). For example, there would be a contradiction created when people with capital invested in manufacturing seek to reduce their costs of production and thus increase profits by replacing workers with machines. As more and more capitalists do this, more and more workers are replaced and become unemployed. As more and more workers become unemployed, their capacity to purchase the various goods that capitalists produce diminishes—which is a fundamental contradiction in a system based on the production and sale of commodities. The logical pursuit of the objectives of the system—an increase in profits—leads to a situation that is detrimental to the overall economic structure.

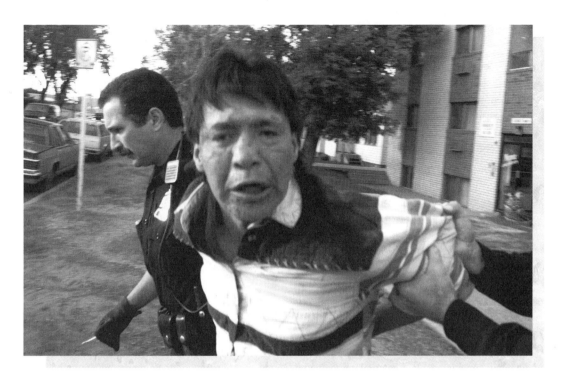

Neo-Marxists view capitalist society as a system fundamentally characterized by relations of domination and subordination. The polity and the state structure in capitalist society tend to serve the interests of the dominant class. Here, Constable Dean Hoover leads Hair Spray Jerry, a downtrodden Aboriginal male, to the police cruiser. Canada's treatment of Aboriginal peoples illustrates the Marxist notion perfectly. (John Morstad/Reprinted with the permission from The Globe and Mail)

Neo-Marxism and Structural Functionalism: One Similarity

A neo-Marxist might argue that the key to understanding the operation and functions of most institutional orders and institutions is to be found in how they contribute to the maintenance of the overall system and thus serve the interests of the dominant class. A fundamental, logical similarity between this approach and the approach of structural functionalism is that both tend to examine social institutions and orders in terms of their functions. Both approaches share common assumptions about society and the relationship between the individual and society. Both are macro approaches, meaning that they focus attention on the larger social structure, its character, and its features. Neither of them concentrates on the individual human actor or agent.

But there is a big, and essential, difference between the two theories as well. The difference appears most clearly in answer to the question: in whose interests do the institutions of a society operate? The structural functionalist answers: in the interests of the entire society and all its members. The neo-Marxist says: in the interests of the dominant class. Obviously, despite the similarity, sociologists choosing one of these approaches over the other will ask different kinds of questions and study different issues in the attempt to understand the structures, processes, and dynamics of society.

The Symbolic Interactionist Perspective

Just as Weber might have been critical of both Marx and Durkheim for focusing too much on structure and not enough on the individual, there is a school of thought in modern sociology that is critical of the macro approach because it ignores a number of fundamental issues, including how and why individuals come to act as they do on a daily basis.

This approach, commonly referred to as symbolic interactionism, accepts a definition of sociology more akin to the thought of Weber than to that of any other classical thinker. Symbolic interactionism focuses on understanding the microelements, the face-to-face, everyday actions and interactions of individuals. The major twentieth-century influences on the development of symbolic interactionism are Max Weber, George Herbert Mead, and Charles Horton Cooley. Following them, Herbert Blumer (1969) synthesized their ideas into a systematic statement of the symbolic interactionist approach.

Society and the Individual

A useful starting point for understanding the approach or, to use Blumer's own term, perspective of symbolic interactionism, is to consider how symbolic interactionists view humans.

The approach emphasizes the unique human capacity for abstract reasoning and thought. Because of our large, complex brain we have the capacity for a variety of intellectual processes, including reflective intelligence, abstract reasoning, and symbolic thought—abilities that are crucial for the development of the human mind. In turn, the human mind is important because it determines the everyday interactions and actions that make up our social existence. For example, we can compare a non-human animal's instinctual response to a stimulus to a human response. If I shout 'yo' at a beaver swimming in a pond, I know what will happen—the animal will slap its tail on the water and dive. The stimulus is received and the response is immediate and instinctual. That is, the response is inborn and unlearned and does not require any conscious thought on behalf of the beaver. If I shout 'yo' at a university student crossing a parking lot I cannot be sure what the response will be, because the student will first of all try to figure out what the stimulus was; then, using his or her mind, the student will attempt to interpret what the shout means before responding. The response, assuming the student chooses not to ignore me, will ultimately depend on an interpretation of what my 'yo' means. Is it a form of greeting? Do I know Tibetan and am I simply pleased with something that has happened? Am I in fact even directing the stimulus at that student, or at someone else? The essential point is that there is a direct connection between stimulus and response in instinctual behaviour, whereas in the case of human behaviour the mind intervenes.

Before they respond to a stimulus, human beings must first interpret that stimulus. They attach a meaning to it, and on the basis and within the context of that meaning they decide on an appropriate response. In the human world a stimulus could be a sound, a physical gesture, a written symbol, or even an object. The process of attaching meanings to these stimuli requires that the individual attempt to make sense out of it. An alien object, such as the Coke bottle in the movie *The Gods Must Be Crazy*, can, if it is not understood, lead to a series of unusual actions and interactions that could change the world of the interacting individual. The meanings we attach to various physical, visual, verbal, and written stimuli are fundamentally symbolic. In an important sense, then, our behaviour and interactions with others are always influenced by our use and understanding of symbols. There is a symbolic basis to all our social interactions.

For the symbolic interactionist, human society is made up of a series of interacting selves—that is, of interacting individuals whose behaviours and interactions are very much influenced by how they interpret the actions and intentions of people they are in social contact with. Society is not something that is external to and outside of the individual; it is created by human beings as they go about their daily actions and interactions. Society is not a fixed fact that exists apart and separate from individuals; rather, it is the product of a variety of interacting individuals going about their daily lives. The essence of society is individuals sharing symbols and, on the basis of those shared symbols, interacting with each other.

Symbolic interactionists are not particularly concerned with the origins of those symbolic systems that prove so important in our daily lives. It is clearly the case that the human capacity for the use of symbols and language developed over many thousands of years of human history, but the key element is an appreciation of the role the shared symbols play in facilitating continuing interaction and thus social life and society itself. This perspective argues that people are active participants in the daily creation of those forms of interaction that we have come to call society. It is in regard to this issue—of whether society exists 'out there', external to us—that the symbolic interactionist perspective is most clearly differentiated from functionalism and neo-Marxism.

Functionalists focus on the overall social structure, examining the social functions performed by various institutions and social practices. Neo-Marxists focus on the role of the economy in shaping and influencing the overall social structure. But symbolic interactionists examine the daily interactions of individuals to explain and facilitate understanding of how society works. Symbolic interactionists are interested in how people know what to do and how they act as they go about their everyday lives, and in what sorts of adjustments people make to facilitate the continued interactions that form the basis of society.

Although not necessarily directly connected to symbolic interactionism, ethnomethodology is an approach to understanding society that continues to be important. Often associated with the work of Harold Garfinkel, ethnomethodology tends to question the assumptions of a more-or-less orderly

social world that inform structural functionalism and various forms of power conflict theory in different ways. It might be said that even symbolic interactionists see an inherent order to the social world, albeit an order that we construct on a daily basis. Ethnomethodologists, by contrast, see the ongoing orderly nature of social interaction is much more tenuous, fluid, and subject to instant negotiation and change as we go about our activities. An ethnomethodologist would see ongoing interaction as an accomplishment, something we achieve and thus not to be taken for granted. At any given moment one of us may act in an unexpected manner, thereby violating the patterns of interaction others were expecting. If and when this occurs the end result is typically a breach of the 'normal' patterns of interaction. This breach can lead to chaos if normality and order is not restored. Malcolm Waters describes some of the breaching experiments Garfinkel and his followers would conduct to prove their point. Waters notes the ethical implications of experiments involved members of a family acting like billets rather than members of the family and then watching the behaviour of others as the normal patters of social interaction breakdown. Typically the point was made—social reality and the patterns of interaction that govern our daily lives are in fact very tenuous.

Both the functionalist and neo-Marxist approaches have developed criticisms of the symbolic interactionist perspective, which has never been as widely used (Ritzer, 1988: 316–17; Stryker, 1980: 145–6). Both of the major approaches argue that symbolic interactionism downplays the impact of larger social structures on the individual. A neo-Marxist might argue that symbolic interactionism ignores the key issues of class, domination, and power. Can we be sure, a neo-Marxist might ask, that the meanings attached to significant symbols do not come from and serve the interests of a dominant class? A social thinker influenced by Durkheim would be concerned about the extent to which central social forces, such as adherence to a set of norms and values, are ignored when the individual is understood to be quite freely interpreting stimuli almost at will.

The symbolic interactionist perspective does, however, alert us to the fact that while understanding social structures is important, we must not lose sight of the micro picture. Although we need, surely, to have an overall picture of the forest, nevertheless we must be aware that it is made up of individual trees, and we must understand both of these conditions.

Conclusion

When we study the development of sociological theory from its emergence in the middle of the nineteenth century through to the second half of the twentieth century, what we find is an impressive array of ideas, arguments, concepts, and propositions that were developed and mustered to guide sociologists as they attempt to explain the overall structures and organization of human society. As impressive and wide-ranging as these theories are, however, they have failed to address one of the central issues in human affairs—how to explain the nature and dynamics of sex and gender relations. Given the importance of these issues, it behooves us now to examine new directions in sociological theory that attempt to offer ways of explaining some of the most essential questions concerning human conduct and social organization.

Summarizing complex ideas is an inherently risky procedure because one can never do justice to the arguments and concepts; however this is partly what an introduction to a discipline such as sociology is about! With these caveats in mind the reader may be better able to understand the essential differences that emerge as these theories are applied to some of the issues we have discussed.

SIMPLE COMPARISON OF TWO MAJOR SOCIOLOGICAL THEORETICAL APPROACHES

The following comparision has been considered at a high level of abstraction, as applied to the analysis of the western capitalist/market society.

STRUCTURAL FUNCTIONALISM	POWER CONFLICT
Society	
Organic analogy	Materialist approach
Interdependent elements	Mode of production
Stability & order	Conflict and contradiction
Norms & values shape	Economic institutions as 'Prime Mover'
Shared moral codes key	Dominant ideologies common
Institutions	
Specialized structures performing functions for society	Economic order as core
All vital	In class structured society institutions tend to serve dominant class in some manner

Values & Norms

Based on shared moral codes
or belief systems
Significant impact in shaping society

Dominant classes impose their
world views as dominant ideologies
Possibility of conflicting ideologies

Core Concepts

Social system
Social order
Consensus
Integration
Function
Dysfunction

Mode of production
Conflit
Contradiction
Class
Power
Domination

Socialization

Necessary for social integration
Basis ofshared values & norms

Contradictory process
Inculcation of dominant ideologies. But
also potential for counter ideologies
from subordinate classes

Social Inequality

Theory of stratification
Based on Davis & Moore
Three dimensional reward
of stratification
Functional inequalities

Class analysis
Structural location in society's
productive institutions as basis
Multiple variations on theme in system basis
literature–All related to economy
Exploitation and alienation

Family

Functions for society
Internal roles
Role in socialization
Gender roles and scripts

Ask: How does nuclear family
serve the needs of the
dominant class? What are its
functions for dominant class?

Polity/State

Pluralist approach
Multiple centres power
Elections and lobbing basis of democracy
state

A version of power conflict theory
State serves interests of ruling class
Mechanisms of power allow class with
economic power to control

Critical Thinking Questions

- What, according to structural functionalist thought, makes society possible?
- Why do societies change? What factors have an impact on the rate and speed of social change?
- Why do some societies remain stable over extended periods of time? How would a structural functionalist and a neo-Marxist each explain social stability?
- Are you involved in the creation of the institutions in which you interact and that form part of the larger society? If you are, then how?
- Is human society an organic totality or just a totality? What is the difference?

Terms and Concepts

Organic analogy—as used in functionalist theory, a mode of analysis that compares society to a living organism. A living organism is assumed to have certain basic needs that must be met and problems that must be solved if it is to survive. The component structures of the organism, its organs and tissues, are understood to operate, work, or function in a way that solves the various problems and meets the various needs and thus allows the organism to survive. The analogy assumes we can understand society in a similar manner, that is, as a complex system made up of different parts, all of which meet some need or solve some problem for the whole system, thereby allowing it to survive.

System prerequisites—the basic needs that must be met and the problems that must be solved if the system is to survive. For example, if society is to survive, the material needs of its members must be satisfied, its culture must be transmitted from generation to generation, the spiritual needs of its members addressed, biological reproduction facilitated, some system of social decision-making developed, and so on. These are the system prerequisites for a social system, because if they are not met there can be no social system.

Function—the need or problem that a part of a social system deals with. For instance, if people have certain basic spiritual needs, then the function of religion and the religious order is to deal with those needs. The social function of religion is the satisfaction of the spiritual needs of members of society. The function of an institution or social practice is usually understood in terms of its contribution to the maintenance of the overall system, that is, its 'task(s)' or 'job(s)' within the overall system.

Dysfunction—when a part or component of a system ceases to perform its function or begins to operate in a manner that is harmful to the overall system. For instance, in an organic system an infected organ may be said to be dysfunctional. In a social system an institution not performing its allotted function would be considered dysfunctional.

Social inequality—in structural functionalism, it has three basic dimensions: (1) economic inequalities (commonly called class); (2) inequalities in social honour and prestige (occupational prestige); and (3) inequalities in power or authority (associated with a person's institutional position). These three forms of social inequality may very well arise out of completely different sources and need not be related.

Social change—in structural functionalism, it is slow, evolutionary, and orderly, unless there are catastrophic events. Although structural functionalists view the normal condition of society as being stable and characterized by social order, they recognize that social change does occur. There are several possible causes of social change, including shifts in values and norms, adjustments to the overall social structure necessitated by dysfunctioning components and external forces.

Alienation—in Marxian theory, a loss of control over the processes, products, and relations of material production. The concept is based on the assumption that the essential defining characteristic of human beings is their ability to labour and produce satisfaction for their material wants and needs. Humans express and realize their true humanity through their productive activity, and loss of control of the various aspects of this activity is a loss of an important part of their humanity. True freedom is deemed to involve control over the most important human activity: material production.

Dominant ideology—in Marxian and neo-Marxian theory, those sets of ideas, ideals, beliefs, and values promoted and advocated by the dominant class, which serve to justify the existing order and the position of the dominant class. Dominant ideologies can be complex sets of beliefs and ideals that permeate the entire culture and influence the operation of many different institutional orders. There are debates about how successful the use of a dominant ideology can be in the face of alternative ideologies that might arise from subordinate classes.

Contradiction—as commonly associated with Marxian and neo-Marxian theory, the structural incompatibility of certain features or processes within a society. For example, within capitalist society there is a contradiction between automation and economic stability. As individual capitalists automate production to improve their individual profit margins, they replace workers with machines, thus driving up the rate of unemployment. As a result, with more and more workers unemployed there are fewer and fewer people in a position to buy the commodities that capitalists produce, and the overall result is less economic activity and a loss of profits.

Related Web Sites

http://www.theory.org.uk/main.htm

This is a versatile Web site that provides access for those interested in some critical analysis of the media. There are links to a number of major contemporary theorists including options for 'Theory Trading Cards'!

http://www.soci.niu.edu/~sssi/

The Society for the Study of Symbolic Interactionism organizes sessions at various major sociological association meetings. Their Web site is an important source of information on virtually every aspect of symbolic interactionism as a perspective and an approach to research.

http://cepa.newschool.edu/het/schools/neomarx.htm

Subtitled 'Radical Political Economy', this site provides information on many of the most prominent neo-Marxist thinkers of the twentieth century. Although there is a certain emphasis on economics, there is information on international links, contemporary issues, and journal links.

http://www.hewett.norfolk.sch.uk/CURRIC/soc/Theory1.htm

This is a link from the 'Theory' icon at the 'Sociology and Hewitt' page. Mr S. Poore at The Hewett School has developed this excellent site that contains many links including an 'A–Z of

Sociologists', a map of sociological theory and links to most important contemporary schools of theory.

http://www.mcmaster.ca/socscidocs/ w3virtsoclib/theories.htm

Maintained under copyright by Carl Cuneo, McMaster University, this is an excellent source for virtually every major contemporary and classical theorist. With links to individual theorists as well as links to schools of thought, this is a valuable resource for the student of social theory.

Suggested Further Readings

Cuff, E.C., and W.W. Sharrock. 1991. *Sociological Perspectives*. Routledge: London. Without speaking down in any way, this book presents a more introductory or basic level treatment of key sociological theories, both contemporary and classical. Introductory students will find the boxed summaries and concept definitions useful.

Ritzer, G. 1988. *Sociological Theory*, 2nd edn. New York: Alfred A. Knopf. This text is virtually a classic by now in its comprehensive coverage of the work of the founders, as well as contemporary theory. New editions continue to add material, preserving the book's relevance.

Ritzer, G. 1991. *Frontiers of Social Theory: The New Synthesis*. New York: Columbia University Press. This edited collection includes essays by some of the leading theorists of the day. The book covers well-known and not-so-well-known approaches in sociology.

Turner, B. 1997. *Blackwell Companion to Social Theory*. Blackwell: Oxford. In the tradition of the Blackwell Companion series, this is a very comprehensive and contemporary review of major theoretical developments. It provides an opportunity to compare various approaches, albeit at an abstract level.

CHAPTER 8

Classical Sociology's Lacuna: Theorizing Sex and Gender

What dimensions or aspects of your life and experiences have been among the most important in terms of their impact on the development of your character and personality, general behaviour, and outlook on life? Although there are many possible answers, it has become apparent to many that sex and gender are among the most important. When we examine human societies, what is one of the most important aspects of social relations that interests us? For many of us the answer is the manner by which sex and gender relations are organized, that is, how women and girls, men and boys, are categorized, expected to behave, do behave, and are treated. As soon as we start to think systematically about questions relating to sex and gender, it becomes clear that sex and gender attributes and behaviours are a fundamental aspect of human existence. If you are still not convinced, think about the following questions for a moment. What does it mean in your society to be a woman? What is your conception of feminine? What traits do you attribute to femininity? How should girls, adolescents, young women, middle-aged women, and elderly women act? Would you rather be female or male? Why? What does it mean to be a man? What does it mean to be masculine? Should all men be masculine? Why?

One of the major reasons for questioning the appropriateness and pedagogical usefulness of the existing approaches in sociology is their inability to deal adequately with these important questions relating to sex and gender. Existing social theories have tended not to pay systematic attention to the impact of these fundamental dimensions of human existence on our social and individual being and on how societies are organized and structured. In some ways the history of the modern world is a history of a changing world with changing relationships between men and women; but the nature of these relationships and the changes in them have not been systematically included in traditional social science theories.

A logical question is, why not? A Canadian theorist, Mary O'Brien, uses the term *malestream thought* to characterize the nature of much of the theoretical thinking that has dominated Western social science and philosophical thinking (1981: 5, 62). She has made the important and accurate argument that much of the thinking that informs our efforts to understand and explain the world has been dominated by a male perspective, so that we have ignored the voice of women as well as the central issue of sex and gender relations.

The situation, however, is well on its way to being rectified. It is no exaggeration to state that the emergence of new streams of feminist theory over the past 30 years represents the most important development in sociological theory this century. The creativity and vitality of feminist scholarship, research, theorizing, and political activity has resulted in the emergence and development of a very complex and diverse literature. It is impossible to cover all the various streams of feminism that have emerged over the past three decades here. In her overview of feminist theorizing and theory, Rosemarie Tong (1989: 1) identifies the seven major streams of contemporary feminist thought as: liberal, Marxist, radical, psychoanalytic, socialist, existentialist, and postmodern. In what follows, no attempt will be made to cover all these streams of thought, since we focus only on the three or four varieties of feminist theorizing that have had the greatest impact on sociological theory. Prior to examining some tenets of liberal, Marxist, radical, and socialist feminist explanations we must make sure we understand the concepts we are employing and must also briefly examine an approach that remains firmly rooted in popular culture and common-sense knowledge and that receives more attention in the mass media than any of the sociologically oriented approaches—biologically oriented explanations of sex and gender. First, let us review the definitions.

Since much confusion surrounds the terms *sex* and *gender*, it is necessary to revisit some definitions. When sociologists use the term *sex* they are referring to biological attributes. Caplan and Caplan provide a definition that is acceptable to most sociologists: 'We shall use sex to refer to the biological sex of the individual—whether a person is born physically female or male. Sex is determined by the genes' (1994: 4). In virtually all human societies a person's sex, that is, the nature of their genetically determined reproductive and associated organs, has had a great deal to do with how their lives have unfolded and been lived. However, an equally important factor in the development of our personalities and behaviours is our gender. By gender we mean the personality and behavioural characteristics that are assumed to go with biological sex. Caplan and Caplan (1994: 4–5) once more provide an excellent summary:

We shall use gender to refer to the social role of being a woman or being a man. Gender

means 'being feminine' or 'being masculine', standards that look different in different societies. Gender is composed of a whole list of features that the society in question labels as appropriate for, or typical of one sex (but not the other, or more than the other), including feelings, attitudes, behavior, interests, clothing, and so on.

If we are interested in understanding human behaviour, a key question must be: what determines the characteristics of sex- and gender-related behaviour? As we noted above, the mass media and many people in society seem to be wedded to the idea that sex and gender behaviours are biologically or genetically predetermined and there is nothing we can possibly do about the fact that 'Boys will be boys'. As social scientists we must ask ourselves if this position has any credibility in the light of the evidence.

Perhaps a word of warning is in order before we begin to categorize, classify, and possibly even pigeonhole various feminist theories. In the introduction to her study of the key concepts used in feminist theory Judith Grant warns against stressing the differences among feminists, theories, and theorists rather than focusing on what they have in common. Grant is concerned that such a focus might impose a structure on feminist theory that results in key themes being ignored (1993: 3–4). In order to avoid the risk she identifies we are asked to focus on 'the development of feminist theory in terms of early feminist writings and practice' and to 'look as the similarities among various feminism' (4).

Biological Theories

Sociologists readily admit that most of our sexual characteristics are genetically determined. What we are less willing to acknowledge is that clear-cut personality and behavioural characteristics are attached to having certain sexual and reproductive organs. The essential question for sociologists, however, is: are gender differences genetically determined? The Caplans note that the question as to 'how much of our masculine or feminine behaviour is unavoidably determined by our physical sex—underlies most of the controversies in the science of sex and gender' (5). If we can be sure of one thing, it is the fact that the media are always quick to cover issues relating to sex and gender. The cover story for the 20 January 1992 edition of *Time* was entitled 'Sizing Up the Sexes'. The bold print under the title reads 'Scientists are discovering that gender differences have as much to do with the biology of the brain as with the way we were raised' (36). Not to be outdone, about a month later *Newsweek* ran a story on the relationship between genetics and sexual orientation under the title 'Born or Bred?' Even a cursory examination of how the mass media cover issues relating to sex, gender, and biology turns up stories with a similar orientation. Headlines and stories such as 'Boys found better at math' (*Regina Leader Post*, 28 May 1986), 'Researchers find link between genetic inheritance and aggression' (*Globe and Mail*, 23 October 1993), 'Brain studies yield clues on gays' (*Globe and Mail*, 17 November 1994) and 'Packing of nerve cells differs in men, women' (ibid.) typify the current trend of thought that attempts to use or find biological explanations for gender behaviour. It is worthwhile noting that some media stories present, as fact, issues and claims still very much open in terms of scientific debate.

The media use provocative headlines to grab our attention, but a critical appraisal of the substance of the claims often demonstrates a lack of logical or evidential connection between the headline and the actual evidence. As a case in point, the 27 January 2001 edition of the *Globe and Mail* ran a front-page story with the byline 'Must men fight? Probably'. The opening sentence makes reference to violence in hockey and barroom fighting, claiming that a recent study of a freshwater fish and fig wasps demonstrate, somehow, that all males are prone to violence. The story makes no reference to the fact that extrapolating complex human behaviour from the instinctual behaviours of fish or wasps is a very questionable undertaking. Again, on 24 November 2001 the *Globe and Mail* ran a major feature article with the banner headline: 'The brain is a sex organ'. While it is rich in descriptive detail, it is also shy on explanatory suggestions other than attributing the supposed differences to genes and hormones. Our society seems to seek simple biological explanations for complex social phenomenon, and often the media presents these uncritically.

Basic Biology and Biological Explanations

The physiological development of our sex organs is determined by information carried in the genes that make up the 23 pairs of chromosomes that humans normally possess. Although there was a debate and ongoing research into how many genes our chromosomes may carry, with speculation running at numbers between 50,000 and 100,000, we now know that the recent Genome Project findings point to a much smaller number, somewhere in the range of 30,000. Genes influence the structures and functioning of cells through the manufacture of proteins, which in turn act on cells. When a human egg and sperm unite to form a fertilized egg, each contributes 23 chromosomes. Prior to fertilization, the egg's 23 chromosomes include a sex chromosome, usually designated as the X chromosome. The sperm, on the other hand, as a result of random chance when it was formed, contains either an X or a Y sex chromosome. If the sperm happens to contain an X chromosome the fertilized egg will normally become female, with 46 chromosomes including an XX. If the sperm contains a Y sex chromosome, the fertilized egg will contain 46 chromosomes including an XY sex chromosome and it will normally develop into a male.

For many years it was thought that determining sex was a relatively easy matter; we now know it is not. In her recent study of the matter, Brown University biologist Anne Fausto-Sterling recounts the story of a world-class female Olympian who, although she possessed breasts and female genitalia, tested positive for the presence of a Y chromosome (2000: 1–3). As a result the International Olympic Committee ruled that, despite the fact that her external genitalia appeared to be those of a female and the fact that she had breasts, she was not biologically a woman and she was barred from participating in the women's competition. This ruling was eventually overturned, and Fausto-Sterling points out that this case is not as unusual as was once thought. Noting that our thinking that an issue of biological sex is a straightforward either/or, she states: 'A body's sex is simply too complex. There is no either/or. Rather there are shades of difference' (3).

The developing embryo shows no noticeable sexual differentiation for about the first 6 to 10 weeks of growth. After that time, the fertilized egg begins to show a difference. Depending on the chromosome structure, the formerly undifferentiated gonads begin to develop into either ovaries or testes. After this differentiation occurs, a new physiological dynamic begins to develop as the ovaries and testes begin to produce different sex hormones. The presence of androgens in a male leads to a change in the manner by which the sex organs develop, resulting in the formation of the typical male reproductive apparatus. The female fetus continues a development trajectory initiated at fertilization. Since many issues relating to sex and gender relations are potentially politically sensitive, it is worth noting that even biologically based explanations of the developmental trajectories of female and male embryos have resulted in controversy. In her excellent study of theories of female and male development, Anne Fausto-Sterling (1985: 81) points out that some of the so-called scientific literature seems to be predicated on sexist assumptions since female development was often cast in terms of females 'lacking' a hormone or as female development occurring in the 'absence' of something. Why not argue that the female developmental trajectory is normal, and the presence of a chemical substance leads to abnormalities in the developmental trajectory of males?

The issue of the impact of hormones on the development of the human organism once again becomes an important issue when we turn our attention to puberty. At this point in the physiological maturation process the presence of ovaries and testes results in the production of different types and levels of hormones. In females the ovaries typically begin to produce increased levels of estrogens and progesterones, while the testicles' production of androgens increases. It should be noted that the so-called sex hormones are present in both females and males, and, as Rose, Lewontin, and Kamin (1985: 151) suggest, it is the ratio of the various hormones to each other that differs. In any event, it is clear that the typical physiological changes we observe during puberty are largely the result of significant changes in the amounts and types of hormones.

From the perspective of the sociologist, the key issue is not the presence of physiological sexual differences (they obviously exist) but rather what these sex differences have to do with personality, character, and social behaviour. When thinking about sexual differences we must heed those who have argued that an emphasis on sexual differences tends to hide the simple fact that females and males are more alike in terms of basic physiology than they are different (Epstein, 1988: 39–41; Renzetti and Curran, 1992: 28). Assuming there is basic compatibility in blood types and such, the majority of organs can be transplanted from females to males and vice versa. Still, we are confronted with the type of media stories cited above, ancient mythologies about what little girls and boys are made of, and much common-sense 'knowledge' concerning what is 'natural' when it comes to female and feminine or male and masculine behaviour.

The question of how physiological differences might influence personality, character, and social behaviours seems to have many answers. An abundant literature suggests a variety of hormone-based explanations for what is often referred to as male aggressiveness and female passivity. The conclusion these arguments often have pointed to is that the male dominance characteristic of patriarchal societies is natural. In criticizing an advocate of this position, Rose, Lewontin, and Kamin (1985: 154) note that the argument holds that 'there is an unbroken line between androgen binding sites in the brain, rough and tumble play in male infants, and the male domination of state, industry and the nuclear family'. They also state that the counterpart to this argument about male dominance and testosterone concerns female passivity and the naturalness of mothering, an argument they, along with Tavris and Wade (1984: 162–3), convincingly reject on the basis of empirical evidence. Indeed, after examining the entire hormonal basis of behaviour, Rose, Lewontin, and Kamin (1985: 156) draw the following conclusion:

> All the evidence is that human infants, with their plastic, adaptive brains and ready capacity to learn, develop social expectation concerning their own gender identity, and the activities appropriate to that gender, irrespective of their genetic sex and largely independent of any simple relationship to their hormone levels (which can at any rate by themselves be substantially modified in level by social expectations and anticipations). Psychocultural expectations profoundly shape a person's gender development in ways that do not reduce to body chemistry.

Other biological or physiological explanations for different gender characteristics and behaviours have stressed the structures of the brain. Caplan and Caplan (1994: 32) undertake a detailed consideration of the arguments concerning apparent differences in the spatial abilities of females and males. They conclude that 'Most studies actually yield no difference at all', and further, when there are differences they are usually very small and appear near or after adolescence with great overlap between male and female scores. The implication of this position is that such differences emerge only after many years

of socialization. Fausto-Sterling reviews a wider literature dealing with a variety of brain functions ranging from IQ to mathematical ability. Her conclusion is that the effort 'bears witness to the extensive yet futile attempts to derive biological explanations for alleged sex differences in cognition'. She goes on to note that 'such biological explanations fail because they base themselves on an inaccurate understanding of biology's role in human development'. She concludes that 'unidirectional models of biological control of human behaviour misconstrue the facts of biology' (1985: 60).

The work of Caplan and Caplan, Epstein, Rose, Lewontin, and Kamin, and Fausto-Sterling all points to the need to consider the social context of our sex and gender development and behaviour. Renzetti and Curran summarize their findings in a section appropriately titled 'Sex Differences: The Interaction of Nature and Environment':

> In other words, biology rather than determining who we are as males and females, instead establishes for us the broad limits of human potential. How each of us eventually thinks and behaves as a man or a woman is a product of the inescapable interaction between the potential and the opportunities and experiences to which we are exposed in our social environments. That these environments are diverse and that humans as a species exhibit great adaptability account for the wide variations in behaviors and personalities not only between the sexes, but also within each sex. (1992: 37)

If we accept the arguments and evidence that our social environment plays an important role in structuring our sex and gender behaviours, we must once again return to sociological theory to better understand the dynamics involved. The remaining sections of this chapter will consider how various sociological feminist theories have sought to understand and explain sex and gender relations and behaviour. Since structural functionalism represents the dominant mode of theorizing for much of the past half-century we will first review how this approach might address the issues of sex and gender relations.

Structural Functionalist Thought

Although it is not necessary to restate the basic tenets of structural functionalist theory in detail, we should recall the importance of societal value systems and normative orientations in this stream of social theory. Structural functionalists maintain that every human society has a complex set of value systems and normative orientations at its core or centre. As we know, according to this theoretical perspective these sets of ideas, ideals, and beliefs are important because they provide the basis of social stability and integration, while also influencing the overall shape and character of the entire social structure. A complex society's value systems and normative orientations will typically contain an enormous amount of knowledge, information, and common-sense wisdom, not to mention mythology and lore. Structural functionalists tend not to be excessively concerned with the origins of these belief systems, as it is generally assumed they have evolved and developed over the history of a society with input from a variety of sources ranging from the religious to the secular and even the academic. Daniel Rossides suggests that it is appropriate to think about 'any given structure of values, ideas and practices as having emerged haphazardly during the course of history, much if not most of it, without conscious intent or design' (1968: 183). A central aspect or dimension of most societies' value systems and normative orientations are ideas and beliefs about sex, sex roles, gender, and gender behaviours.

It is clear, then, that ideas about sex and gender become an important part of the overall stock of knowledge that children acquire through the socialization process they are constantly exposed to in the various institutions to which they belong. In the family, in the education system, in religious institutions, via the media, and through their peers, children are constantly socialized according to the prevailing ideas about sex and gender roles and behaviours. Literally from the time of their birth, females and males both learn about being female and feminine, male and masculine. The knowledge we acquire through the ongoing, ever-present socialization process becomes a part of our personality and influences our attitudes, actions, and behaviour.

In discussing this approach to understanding sex and gender socialization, Epstein (1988: 104) uses Robert Merton's concept of 'status-set'. A status-set is similar to a role set (see Chapter 3) in that it refers to a set, or cluster, of statuses an individual may occupy at any one time. Epstein explains how this concept might be employed in understanding the perpetuation of sex and gender relations:

> Prevailing notions of properly feminine and masculine statuses lead to sex-typed status-sets in societies: A male-typed status-set might be father-husband-steel worker-veteran; a female status-set, wife-mother-primary school teacher-volunteer community worker. Although women and men share some common statuses, such as US citizen, member of a political party, and high school graduate, these statuses do not carry precise normative expectations regarding behavior (that is, what the associated role is), or they may be defined differently for men and women. A male political party member might run for office, whereas a female political party member would be expected to work for the male's campaign.

Sex and gender behavioural attributes, then, are to be explained and understood as emerging out of females and males being socialized to accept and incorporate into their behavioural repertoires and personalities certain ideas about what it means to be female and feminine and male and masculine. It is the society's value system that defines sex and gender roles and these are passed on via socialization. In classical functionalist thought no particular concern was paid to the origins of these values or to their negative or positive impact on females and males.

According to functionalist thought, the acceptance of a value system and set of normative orientations by the majority of a society's members is a prerequisite for a smoothly functioning and orderly social structure. As long as there is a general acceptance of the socially sanctioned and prescribed sex and gender behaviours, and as long as these beliefs are effectively transmitted via the socialization process, there should be a measure of stability when it comes to sex and gender relations. While there is debate concerning the degree to which sex and gender relations in Western industrial societies were ever marked by stability and order, some have argued that by the 1950s, just when the traditional nuclear family was reaching its zenith, it was also beginning to crumble.

John Conway argues that despite being idealized in the media and other institutions the golden days of the nuclear family were not all that golden. For one thing, as he points out, there were few roles available to many women. Conway notes that the traditional Western industrial nuclear family, which he describes as 'dads at work and mom at home with the kids', left few choices for women (1993: 13–14). Indeed, 'For women who wanted a choice, there was none, and the socialization process ensured that few wanted to be anything other than wives and mothers' (15). Epstein (1988: 107) points out that by the 1970s a growing body of literature and research had begun to demonstrate that the sex and gender roles and behaviours that accompanied the 'Happy Days' of the 1950s were not all that positive for women. She writes: 'It was widely recognized that the norms that defined women's roles were those regarded as expressive, nurturant, service-oriented, and ancillary to men's both in personality and behavior, in contrast to the norms for men's roles, which were clustered around instrumental,

dominant and goal-oriented qualities.' Epstein notes that as early as 1963 Betty Friedan had objected to the fact that the typical feminine roles prescribed in the Parsonian view of the family had a negative impact on women, 'narrowing women's horizons by isolating them in the home', and as a result these roles 'created psychological problems for women and wasted their talents' (108). As was the case in the study of the family, the dysfunctional impact of the existing sex and gender roles was instrumental in new and more critical analytical approaches that accompanied the re-emergence of the women's movement in the 1960s. The first of these new approaches, liberal feminism, represents a critique of functionalist thought more or less from within.

Liberal Feminism

In their excellent summary of the development of feminist theory, Patricia Madoo Lengermann and Jill Niebrugge-Brantley (1988) note that women have been protesting their social position for centuries, although much of this activity has not been preserved on the printed page. In spite of this, in recent centuries there is an impressive record of scholarship dealing with the position of women in Western society. For instance, the eighteenth-century writings of Mary Wollstonecraft along with those of John Stuart Mill and Harriet Taylor Mill in the nineteenth century mark the beginning of the systematic development of a stream of feminism called liberal feminism.

The liberal feminist approach has much in common with structural functionalism. Among the essential points of similarity is a stress on the role of values, norms, and ideas in the structuring of society and its inequalities. Although they use a different term to describe the approach and are not within this tradition, Pat Armstrong and Hugh Armstrong (1984) provide an excellent description of it. According to Armstrong and Armstrong, liberal feminist ideas underlie many of the positions and publications of government departments and government-sponsored agencies. In their discussion of feminism, Lengermann and Niebrugge-Brantley identify Jessie Bernard as a key representative of this approach, while Rosemarie Tong (1989) notes that Betty Friedan is often classified as a liberal feminist.

The essence of the liberal, and functionalist, approach is its acceptance of the basic structures of Western society as appropriate, while recognizing the existence of a dysfunctional element: the emergence of sexist ideas in the society's value system. Those sexist ideas refer to the beliefs or values that attribute behavioural characteristics or personality attributes purely on the basis of biological sex. When this happens people are more or less automatically streamed into jobs, careers, and roles on the basis of gender rather than ability. Many women face insurmountable barriers in attempting to enter so-called non-traditional occupations and roles.

For women, the situation of not having a fair chance to develop all their abilities and potentials by being streamed into traditional roles and behaviours is clearly not in accordance with the premises of freedom and opportunity for all. For society, a major potential talent pool made up of half of the society is lost. For example, how many potential scientists have been denied an opportunity to contribute to the search for a cure for cancer as a result of women's systematic exclusion from particular jobs?

As Armstrong and Armstrong point out, this approach places a great deal of emphasis on socialization. Values, norms, beliefs, and behaviours are passed on from one generation to another through the process of socialization. Because the essence of the problem is located in the society's value and belief system, changes have to be made in that system. Sexist ideas and behaviours have to be confronted and altered. New non-sexist ideas have to be disseminated through the socialization process, while some cases will call for resocialization.

In liberal feminist thought, the general picture is far from hopeless. Because liberal feminists accept the basic soundness of the current social structures, they conclude that all that is really needed is some 'fine-tuning'. The society's belief system and moral codes have become corrupted with sexist ideas; but the current institutional arrangements are strong enough to ensure that the required reforms and adjustments can be made and that these changes will lead to the eventual development of egalitarian relations between men and women.

Marxian Feminism

Much has been written about the relevance and usefulness of Marx and the concepts he developed for our understanding of sex and gender (Donovan, 1992; Tong, 1989). While opinions on this issue vary, one thing is quite clear—for Marx, sex and gender relations were not of primary significance in understanding the overall structures and dynamics of human society. In Marx's work we find systematic accounts of many key sociological issues, including the essential character of human beings, the nature and operation of the capitalist economic order, the nature of human consciousness, the dynamics of political power, and so on; however, we find little explicit treatment of sex and gender. There is, however, one original work dating to the era that Josephine Donovan refers to as 'first wave' Marxism.

Engels and the Origin of the Family
Frederick Engels (1820–95) was a close collaborator, lifelong supporter, and friend of Karl Marx. In 1884, one year after Marx died, Engels published *The Origins of the Family, Private Property and the State*, in which he attempted to provide the basis of a materialist approach to the development of the family. The study draws heavily on the work of a nineteenth-century anthropologist, Lewis H. Morgan. Engels argues that as human society develops and evolves we witness the development and evolution of different forms of familial organization. During the earliest period of human history, referred to as a stage of 'savagery', sexual and reproductive relations were organized on the basis of group marriages. The second major stage, barbarism, was marked by the

For women, the situation of not having a fair chance to develop all their abilities by being streamed into traditional roles, such as nurses or teachers, is clearly not in accordance with the premise of freedom and opportunity. Sexist ideas, such as only boys can excel in maths and science, must be confronted and altered. New non-sexist ideas have to be disseminated, while some cases will call for resocialization. Here, two young women excel in the science lab. (Harry Cutting Photography— www.harrycutting.com)

development of pottery, the domestication of animals, and the cultivation of cereal grains. By the end of the period, the smelting of iron and the use of an alphabet had come into being. During this second stage of development group marriages gave way to paired families.

Engels notes that the development of paired families and of restrictions concerning who could marry whom was in part due to the biological problems associated with close biological relatives reproducing ([1884] 1972: 47). There were, however, other reasons for the definitive emergence of monogamy—reasons that, Engels argues, were social and economic. As human society evolved there was an increasing social surplus; that is, there was an increasing difference between the total wealth produced in society and the wealth required for subsistence—for keeping the population alive and reproducing. Subsistence living implies a 'hand-to-mouth' existence with no surplus that can be stored and used later. As humans became more productive, a surplus developed and the basis for a class structure emerged, because with a surplus comes the possibility of someone or some group controlling that surplus and thereby acquiring a measure of economic power. At a certain moment men began to appropriate and control the economic surplus, and as a result they came to have more power. Accompanying this process was the development of a concern, among those men who controlled the society's economic surplus, with the disposition of the surplus. They wanted to both protect their material wealth on a day-to-day basis and arrange for its intergenerational transfer: the disposition of the wealth after death. Engels argues that men established a system of monogamy and patriarchy in order to control the disposition of their wealth. By controlling women and attempting to ensure that women only had sexual relations with their designated husbands, men could be sure that their wives bore only their own children and could be confident that those children would be legitimate heirs to their properties.

According to Engels, the development of a social surplus and the subsequent appropriation of that surplus as private property provided the basis for the emergence of both a system of social class and a system of patriarchy. The root cause of class and patriarchal domination is to be found in the economic structures and processes of the capitalist system. Given that, the elimination of class and male domination can only come through the transformation of class relations. And because men's domination of women is fundamentally rooted in men's desire to provide legitimate and true heirs for their private productive property, Engels argues, the abolition of private productive property will logically mean that there will be no more need for men to oppress women ([1884] 1972: 71).

Debates concerning the strengths, weaknesses, and relevance of Engels' arguments have been legion (see Sayers, Evans, and Redclift, 1987). The emergence in the 1960s of yet another surge in the ongoing struggles of women for equality and the creation of an egalitarian society produced a renewed interest in the potential insights of the work of Marx and Engels. Among the first to plumb the works of Marx for insights into the nature of contemporary sex and gender roles was Margaret Benston. In a 1969 essay entitled 'The Political Economy of Women's Liberation' Benston argued that to understand fully the dynamics of sex and gender relations we must look more closely at the nature of housework and its relationship to material production in capitalist society.

Benston's analysis of the relationship between housework and the position of women in society draws on the distinction in Marxian economic theory between use value and exchange value. Commodities or items that have a use to somebody are said to embody use value. If you are hungry and I make you a sandwich and give it to you at no charge, the sandwich can be said to have use value only. Exchange value refers to the amount of value that can be received for an item or commodity if it is exchanged for money or traded for another commodity. If I prepare and give away my sandwiches they are said only to have use value; on the other hand, if I sell them (exchange them for money) they are said to have exchange value. Since capitalist market economies are based on production for sale and profit, commodities produced that embody exchange value are more highly prized and are deemed to be more socially important.

The work that women typically do in the home is unpaid and involves the preparation of meals, childcare, house-cleaning, and other family service and support work. Benston argues that this work results in the creation of use values for family members, but no exchange value is produced since women do not charge or get paid for what they produce. Housework is, Benston argues, a form of pre-capitalist work. The problem for women is that the labour they engage in at home is undervalued and not deemed socially important because no exchange value is produced. As a result both women and the work they do are deemed less important than is the profit-producing work of men. Benston notes that in terms of the perpetuation of the capitalist system the work that women do in the home is essential since it involves the consumption of various commodities the capitalist system produces for sale. In addition, by providing a stable and healthy home life they make it possible for men to continue to work and produce surplus value. Women also are available to enter the work force during times of need, composing a reserve army of labour, a concept we will discuss later.

The key issue Benston raises—the relationship between women's work in the household and the overall nature of sex and gender relations in the society—became a topic of considerable debate during the 1970s. Peggy Morton (1972) drew our attention to a new issue involved in connecting women and their domestic labour to the larger society when she argued that women actually produce one of the most important commodities involved in capitalist production—labour power. Morton does not disagree with the claim that women produce use values that are not sold on the market; she argued that what is important, however, is the fact that women also produce the essential commodity that capitalists require if they are to appropriate surplus value—labour power. As we know, within the Marxian approach labour power is the essential commodity, as it is the

source of surplus value and, thus, profits. According to this argument one of the key social roles the family plays is making it possible for workers to return to work day after day, week after week, month after month, and even year after year by providing them with a place where they get proper nutrition and can rest and relax and get their 'batteries re-charged'. Others, including Mariarosa Dalla Costa (1972) and Wally Seccombe (1974), supported this position, even emphasizing in stronger terms the role of housework in the production of surplus value in capitalist society. The question of the precise nature of the relationship between domestic labour and the production of surplus value became the topic of what has become known as the domestic labour debate, the details of which need not concern us here. (For an excellent summary of the various positions, see Armstrong and Armstrong, 1990: Chapter 5.)

What is important about the debate over the precise nature of domestic labour (housework) in capitalist society is that it pointed out some important weaknesses in Marxian theory in regard to understanding sex and gender relations. Armstrong and Armstrong (1990: 88) note that at a certain point many interested in more fully understanding the nature of sex and gender relations 'became increasingly disillusioned by a domestic labour debate that seemed to have reached a dead end'. The dead end related less to the role of domestic labour than to the fact that too little attention was being devoted to the question of why it is that domestic labour is predominantly the domain of women. One answer to this question came out of what is commonly called radical feminism.

Radical Feminism

Among the most powerful of the feminist treatises of the past few decades is Shulamith Firestone's *The Dialectic of Sex: The Case for Feminist Revolution* (1970). Firestone maintains that men and women must be understood as being members of separate and distinctive classes. For Firestone, the basis of class is biological and, as in the Marxian analysis, one class has historically been dominant and exploitative. Firestone argues that men have dominated and exploited women largely because of the biological role that women play in species reproduction. The fact that women give birth is at the root of the problem. The biological processes of childbirth are such that women are forced to depend on men for long periods of time, and this dependency has resulted in the emergence of the larger patterns of domination and subordination characteristic of patriarchal society.

The central theme of Firestone's work, that the systematic oppression of women is one of the central characteristics of patriarchal capitalist society, has been taken up by other feminist thinkers, although many of them have disagreed with Firestone's specific explanation. For instance, the work in Lydia Sargent's book (1981) and in a reader edited by Annette Kuhn and AnneMarie Wolpe (1978) illustrates diverse explanations of women's oppression. Among the many innovative theoretical approaches are the efforts by scholars such as Michèle Barrett (1980) and Heidi Hartmann (1981) to develop a feminist analysis borrowing from the traditions of both Marxian and radical feminism. Such writers have worked at developing a mode of analysis that directs attention to the structural characteristics of capitalist society and the patriarchal system as they have developed within the context of Western society. The work of scholars such as Barrett and Hartmann is generally referred to as socialist feminism, which will be examined later.

Yet another, more recent, discussion in feminist thought has centred on the question of 'diversity and commonality' (see, for instance, the article by Code, 'Feminist Theory', in Burt, Code, and Dorney, 1993). While feminists of various streams have 'rallied around a common cause in their opposition to patriarchy', celebrating the sisterhood of all women, the idea of 'difference' has also become prominent as new theories of race have been added

to the older theories of gender. It has been argued that women have 'failed to take into account the effects of institutionalized racism' and that factors of ethnic, racial, and sexual diversity have to be more adequately considered. As Canadian theorist Lorraine Code puts it, 'The historical goal of achieving equality for women has to be refined and redefined if it is to retain any legitimacy as a feminist project' (Burt, Code, and Dorney, 1993: 48). For some feminists an adequate understanding of the nature of sex and gender relations, a precondition to the creation of egalitarian relations, was not possible as long as our thinking was confined to the logic of functionalism, Marxism, or any of the biologically oriented approaches. New and innovative directions were required. Some of these feminists were unwilling to jettison Marxism totally, although they did argue that traditional Marxism was of limited value. The outcome of these developments was what we call socialist feminism.

Socialist Feminism: Hartmann and Barrett

In her important essay, 'The Unhappy Marriage of Marxism and Feminism: Toward a More Progressive Union', Heidi Hartmann lays out the rationale for the development of a new analytical approach that incorporates insights from and builds on the strengths of both Marxism and feminism. She notes that while Marxism provided potentially powerful analytical tools, it is essentially flawed: 'while Marxist analysis provides essential insight into the laws of historical development, and those of capital in particular, the categories of Marxism are sex blind' (1986: 2). On the other hand, 'feminist analysis by itself is inadequate because it has been blind to history and insufficiently materialist'. Her proposed solution was a 'more progressive union of Marxism and feminism' (3). The analytical fruit of this more progressive union would be a mode of analysis that simultaneously examined the structures and dynamics of both capitalism and

In her ground-breaking essay, 'The Unhappy Marriage of Marxism and Feminism', leading feminist Heidi Hartmann established the rationale for the development of a new analytical approach that incorporates insights from and builds on the strengths of both Marxism and feminism. (Institute for Women's Policy Research)

patriarchy. Such an analytical approach would allow us to understand the dynamics of class exploitation that Marxian analysis holds is a key feature of capitalism and also the dynamics of sex- and gender-based exploitation and domination that feminists see as integral to patriarchy. Since feminists and Marxists are not supposed merely to analyze and engage in intellectual debates about inequality, oppression, and exploitation, a new theoretical orientation such as this would offer something more practical. Hartmann explains: 'As feminist socialists we must organize a practice which addresses both the struggle against patriarchy and the struggle against capitalism' (33).

The essential project that Hartmann outlines is very much the same as that attempted by Michèle Barrett in *Women's Oppression Today: Problems in Marxist Feminist Analysis*. Barrett offers a more detailed outline of the analytical logic of a socialist feminist approach and is critical of traditional Marxian, liberal feminist, and radical feminist analyses because they fail to provide an adequate way of understanding and explaining the nature of women's oppression in complex relations that comprise capitalist society. An adequate analytical approach must take into account 'the economic organization of households and its accompanying familial ideology, the division of labour and its accompanying relations of production' (1985: 40).

Barrett musters a convincing set of arguments against any form of biological determinism, radical feminist or otherwise. She then engages in an examination of the concept of ideology that is critical in her analysis. Barrett is careful not to suggest that ideology can be used in any simplistic manner, yet she maintains it is central to understanding the structuring of notions of sexuality and gender in capitalist society. After examining the role of the educational system in transmitting ideology, she looks at the dynamics of family life. Barrett is critical of the concept of 'the family' because it tends to be ahistorical and ideological, meaning that as capitalism has developed there have been various forms of family organization and to postulate the nuclear family as the norm is to impose an unrealistic model or standard on everyone. 'The family' is an ideological concept because it includes ideas about what the 'normal' sex and gender relations are supposed to be. Important to her understanding of family relations is what she terms the *ideology of familialism*, which involves, among other things, 'ideologies of domesticity and maternity for women, of breadwinning and responsibility for man' (206–7). Such powerful ideological formulations of the 'normal' family with associated sex and gender roles become a part of the dominant ideology and they come to impact the thinking, character, and lives of people.

Barrett's analysis of the operation and dynamics of families and households makes it clear that the institution and the assumptions about sex and gender behaviours contained therein do not operate in the best interest of women. She explicitly asks who seems to benefit from the nature of patriarchal family relations and the attendant sex and gender relations? Her answer is, as we have stated, not most women and not the working class, though perhaps working-class men get some benefits. As for the ruling class, she concludes that they seem to gain the most from the operation of these social structures, though even in this case the benefits are not

exactly unambiguous (222–3). Barrett also examines the role of the state in maintaining and reinforcing the structures and dynamics of the patriarchal family, noting that throughout history there is evidence that the state has participated in creating social conditions and regulations that foster the oppression of women.

Barrett and Hartmann both draw our attention to an important analytical problem when it comes to understanding sex and gender issues. Can sex and gender relations in our society be understood purely within the context of the patriarchal system, with no reference to the fact that we live in a capitalist society? Or, are sex and gender relations in our society to be understood primarily as the outcome of the operation and dynamics of the capitalist system, and thus if that system were changed would we tend to see the emergence of more egalitarian sex and gender relations? Or must we, as Barrett and Hartmann suggest, turn our analytical attention to understanding both capitalism and patriarchy and the intersections between the two?

Third Wave Feminism

In 1997 Leslie Heywood and Jennifer Drake published a collection of essays titled *Third Wave Agenda: Being Feminist, Doing Feminism*. The editors note their debt to earlier feminism but they see their agenda as different:

A 'Report on the 1981 National Women's Studies Association Conference', argues for a feminist movement defined by difference: 'What U.S. third wave feminists are calling for is a new subjectivity, a political revision that denies any one perspective as the only answer, but instead posits a shifting tactical and strategic subjectivity . . . no simple, easy sisterhood for U.S. third world feminists.' . . . Third Wave Agenda acknowledges how fully third wave feminism comes out of this groundbreaking work, and how U.S. third world feminism changed the second wave of the women's movement for good. (1997: 9)

In their discussion of Third Wave feminism, Lengermann and Niebrugge explain further:

Third-wave feminism's focal concern is with differences among women. Anchored in this concern, third-wave feminists reevaluate and extend the issues that second-wave feminists opened for general societal discourse while at the same time critically reassessing the themes and concepts of those second-wave theories. Third-wave feminism looks critically at the tendency of work done in the 1960s and 1970s to use a generalized, monolithic concept of 'woman' as a generic category in stratification and focuses instead on the factual and theoretical implications of differences among women. The differences considered are those that result from an unequal distribution of socially produced goods and services on the basis of position in the global system, class, race, ethnicity, age, and affectional preference as these factors interact with gender stratification. (332–3)

They go on to note that Third Wave feminism addressed three important issues: diversity of feminist voices, the need to critique some of the categories used by both feminist and non-feminist social analysis, and the relations of subordination and privilege that exist among women (333).

The issue of diversity refers to the fact that there are differences and diversity even among women as a disadvantaged or oppressed category. In simpler terms, while all women might be considered oppressed by the overall structures of patriarchy, when one adds the dimensions of race, ethnicity, class, age, sexual orientation, and nationality there are significant numbers of women who are even more non-privileged or marginalized. Because many women have very different lived experiences,

their voices must be heard and their situations understood.

Nelson and Robinson use the term *inclusive feminism* to refer to those feminists whose focus is on the inclusion of those often left out or marginalized. They note that inclusive feminism is critical of the fact that earlier feminists seemed to be searching 'for the essential experience of generic "woman" when there were many quite different experiences' (2002: 96). Patricia Elliot and Nancy Mandell's overview of various feminist theory and approaches included a section on postmodern feminism. Among the issues of the postmodern feminists is the need to include the voices and perspectives of 'women of color and women from developing countries' as well as 'lesbian, disabled and working-class women' (1995: 24).

The second activity that Lengermann and Niebrugge identify as important to Third Wave feminism is critiquing many of the orthodox mainstream social science concepts that Second Wave feminists might have used. This is an activity that has much in common with the other postmodern critiques of the styles of thought, theoretical assumptions, and approaches to science and knowledge that characterized most social science in the second half of the nineteenth century. In their schema Nelson and Robinson identify postmodern feminism under a separate heading, but it seems clear that one of the features of the larger tendency we are calling Third Wave feminism is this critique. Nelson and Robinson note that postmodern feminists maintain that 'the theoretical claims emanating from liberal, Marxist, radical, cultural and socialist feminisms, which assert a single or even a limited plurality of causes for women's oppression are flawed, inadequate'. Further, these feminisms might actually be engaged in suppressing those women suffering from forms of oppression that the theories cannot address (98). Any theory that claims to be 'fully explanatory, it is argued, is assuming a dominant oppressive stance' (98).

The third characteristic of Third Wave feminism that Lengermann and Niebrugge identify follows from what we know already. According to Lengermann and Niebrugge, Third Wave feminism maintains that not all suffering is equal and that the fact is that a working-class lesbian woman of colour will be oppressed and exploited in ways that are both qualitatively and quantitatively different. Lengermann and Niebrugge quote Lourdes Arguelles to the effect that there is a 'calculus of pain' that is 'determined by the intersection of one's individual life of global location, class, race, ethnicity, age, affectional preference, and other dimensions of stratification' (334). Lengermann and Niebrugge refer to this as the notion of vectors of oppression and privilege.

An overview of the basic ideas associated with Third Wave feminism is, in the end, impossible because Third Wave feminism represents an approach to women's oppression that is inherently opposed to thinking or theorizing that can easily be summarized. The Third Wave Agenda contains a variety of articles on a wide range of issues and topics, all relating to the role, position, status, oppression, liberation, freedom, and subjugation of some women in America. Perhaps the best way to provide the reader with a sense of the approach is to quote the editors, Heywood and Drake, on someone they see as important and representative of the Third Wave attitude:

> One public figure who demonstrates some of the contradictions that third wave feminism brings together is Courtney Love, the punk rock musician who bridges the opposition between 'Power feminism' and 'victim feminism'. She combines the individualism, combativeness, and star power that are the legacy of second wave gains in opportunities for women (which arrived in conjunction with cultural backlash against such gains), with second wave critiques of the cult of beauty and male dominance. Love is a proto-type of female ambition and a sharp cultural critic of both the institutions that sustain that ambition and those that argue against it. Glamorous and grunge, girl and boy, mothering and selfish put together and taken apart, beautiful and ugly, strong and weak, responsible and rebellious, Love bridges the irreconcilability of individuality and femininity within dominant culture, combining the cultural critique of an earlier generation of feminists with the backlash against it by the next generation of women, legacies of Reagan Republicanism who are busy reclaiming the province of beauty for female power in ways that can only fail because they have been critiqued too thoroughly. (4–5)

Conclusion

In this chapter we have reviewed some of the approaches developed to allow us to better understand the complex issues associated with the important topic of sex and gender relations. We examined biologically based explanations and the research that claimed to support them, but found them inadequate. The fact that structural functionalist theory sees the issues of sex and gender as merely aspects of how a society's value system and normative orientations are organized suggests that this approach is not capable of making this a primary issue in its theorizing and explanations of human conduct. As Armstrong and Armstrong (1990: 45) point out, those adopting this general approach 'have not provided a systematic explanation of how or why ideas and behavioural patterns develop or how and why they change'. Moreover, as Armstrong and Armstrong further indicate, it is also problematic to assume that value systems and normative orientations represent 'a neutral set of beliefs uniting society' because sometimes these ideas and beliefs serve to justify various relations of domination and power (41). On the other hand, the tendency of theorists influenced by Marxian thought to focus on material production, economic processes, and class relations has resulted in this stream of thought downplaying the issues of sex and gender or just adding them on as a secondary issue.

After examining the mainstream efforts to address the questions surrounding sex and gender relations we turned to feminist theory. It is imperative that sociologists account for the challenges and incorporate the insights of feminist theory into future theorizing. We need to adopt new modes of theorizing about human society that take us beyond the limitations of orthodox functionalism and orthodox Marxism and include the various elements of sex and gender relations in all our thinking about every aspect of human conduct and social organization. Fortunately, the basis for such an approach exists in the various streams of feminist theory, although much work remains to be done.

Critical Thinking Questions

- Discuss the following comment: 'The emergence of a feminist critique of sociology was inevitable.'
- Discuss the relationship of liberal feminism to structural functionalism.
- What is domestic labour? Who benefits from domestic labour?
- Why is radical feminism called radical feminism?
- Explain the difference between socialist feminism and Marxist feminism.
- Why did Third Wave feminism develop?

Terms and Concepts

Feminism—a complex term used to describe diverse sets of beliefs, political practices, social practices, social movements, and sociological theories. As used here it refers to a set of underlying assumptions and principles that recognize the historical subordination and oppression of women; it seeks to explain this phenomenon and provide alternative non-oppressive modes of social organization.

Liberal feminism—a stream of feminist thought that focuses on inequalities between men and women. Liberal feminists primarily locate their explanation of women's inequalities in a dysfunctioning of the existing social institutions. Liberal feminists argue that sexist ideas and beliefs are a central cause of women's inequalities and that these can be corrected through the introduction of non-sexist ideas, values, and norms and intensive resocialization without any major or radical change to the basic institutional orders.

Marxian feminism—tends to see the inequality and exploitation of women as a historical process and part of the overall system of class exploitation of capitalist society. Although there are a variety of different streams of Marxian feminism, they all tend to view the position of women as a special case of subordination understandable only within the context of capitalist society, and thus they focus more on class exploitation and domination than on the exploitation and domination of women *per se*. They generally argue that once the capitalist relations of class domination and exploitation are eliminated, the stage will be set for the emancipation of women.

Radical feminism—describes an extremely diverse set of thinkers who argue that neither liberal nor Marxian feminism really understands the basis of women's oppression. Although there are radically different positions, ranging from biologically based arguments to others closer to Marxian feminism, radical feminists stress the need to understand that women's oppression predates capitalism and has continued to exist in non-capitalist societies; therefore, it cannot be simply a matter of sexist ideas or an offshoot of class domination. Radical feminists call for a systematic empirical and theoretical rethinking of all dimensions of human relations, with the issues of sexual and gender differences at the centre of this process. We must, they argue, begin with sex and gender relations and not merely add them on as we think about human relations and social structures. No existing theory has done this.

Third Wave feminism—by definition defies and denies the possibility of simple definition. A complex set of ideas that emphasize the necessity of recognizing the complexities of women's situations and experiences. Third Wave feminism explicitly rejects any simple notion of women as a homogeneous category or group noting that class, race, ethnic, age, geographic, national, and a host of other differences and divisions prevent the emergence of any singular, totalizing, or universal feminist theory.

Related Web Sites

http://www.criaw-icref.ca/indexFrame_e.htm

This is the homepage for The Canadian Research Institute for the Advancement of Women. To quote from the page: 'CRIAW is a research institute which provides tools to facilitate organizations taking action to advance social justice and equality for all women. CRIAW recognizes women's diverse experiences and perspectives; creates spaces for developing women's knowledge; bridges regional isolation; and provides communication links between/among researchers and organizations actively working to promote social justice and equality for all women.'

http://www.cddc.vt.edu/feminism/

Under the leadership of Dr Kristin Switala from Virginia Tech University, this feminist theory Web site contains access to nearly 5,500 bibliographic entries plus nearly 600 other Web sites. You can choose English, French, or Spanish before beginning your search.

http://www.eskimo.com/~feminist/
nownetin.html

Associated with the Washington State chapter of the National Organization of Women, this basically liberal feminist site, 'Feminism on the Net (HTML)', describes itself as providing a 'short primer' on feminist resources. There are many links and resources on this site, including mailing lists, information on newsgroups, and advice on navigating the world wide web.

http://womens-studies.osu.edu/

Although this site is partially a report on a video project, it is really an excellent resource on issues relating to lesbian feminism. There are links that can be used to connect to historical issues, politics, lesbians of colour, and a contemporary snapshot.

http://www.io.com/~wwwave/

One of many excellent and informative sites most search engines will turn up if you enter 'Third Wave feminism'. This site has informative links under 'What Every Woman & Girl Should Know', 'Women, Men, and Feminism', 'Our World Our Lives', and 'Second and Third Waves'. The site makes it clear that Third Wave feminists have important contributions to make in terms of analyzing contemporary events like the terrorist attack on the World Trade Centre.

Suggested Further Readings

Barrett, M. 1981. *Women's Oppression Today: Problems in Marxist Feminist Analysis*. London: Verso. Barrett offers an opportunity to understand the creative process of theory revision. The subtitle gives away the main issue addressed but not the creative solutions offered.

Jaggar, A., and P.S. Rothenberg, eds. 1993. *Feminist Frameworks: Alternative Theoretical Accounts of the Relations Between Men and Women*. New York: McGraw-Hill. In its third edition, this is a collection of original essays and statements of various feminist frameworks or approaches. It is an excellent resource, providing the original works of key individuals who have had an impact on feminist theory.

Mackie, M. 1991. *Gender Relations in Canada.* Toronto: Butterworths. An important book, it offers both theoretical discussions and empirical studies of key issues in feminism and the lives of women in Canada.

Nelson, A., and B. Robinson. 2002. *Gender in Canada.* Toronto: Prentice-Hall. This is one of the most current treatments of a range of theoretical, social, and political issues in the field of gender studies in Canada. The treatment of gender across the life cycle is particularly important.

Tong, R. 1991. *Feminist Thought: A Comprehensive Introduction.* Boulder, CO: Westview Press. A very comprehensive overview of a variety of feminist theories and schools of thought is given. It is an excellent source book for those first encountering some of these ideas.

PART III

Applying Sociological
Theories and Concepts

The promise of the sociological imagination goes well beyond being forced to learn new concepts and wrestle with abstract theoretical ideas and debates. The promise of the sociological imagination is that these concepts and theories must somehow assist in your ongoing efforts to understand yourself, others, and the social world around you. For that to happen, you must be able to take the concepts and theories we have been discussing and apply them to real issues and events. No introductory book or course will fully develop your sociological imagination or even introduce you adequately to the complexities of the discipline. All we can hope to do is illustrate how sociologists view and understand the social world.

In this section you will be introduced to several important social issues. In each case you will be asked to think about these issues in several different ways, using different theoretical perspectives. No effort will be made to convince you that one approach is necessarily better or more adequate—that judgment is left up to you. The issues considered in the following chapters are: (1) social inequality; (2) mass communications; (3) the nature of political power; (4) race and ethnicity; (5) deviance and social control; (6) the nature of family relations; and (7) globalization. In each case you will be asked to consider some historical and empirical matters, but most importantly you will be asked to try to make sense of the world. As will become obvious, this is not an easy task, but what in life that is really worthwhile is easy? The crucial tasks are to use, expand, revise, and evaluate the theoretical perspectives we have in hand, keeping in mind the importance of developing your own critical analytical capacities.

CHAPTER 9

Explaining Social Inequality

'The social inequalities that characterize Canadian society are as stark and deeply rooted as you will find anywhere in the world.'

Many Canadians would disagree with this statement, because a part of our society's common-sense stock of knowledge maintains that although there are some people who are rich and some who are poor, Canada is, after all, an egalitarian society. Before we jump to the conclusion that there is a significant degree of equality in Canadian society we should look at some empirical data.

Social Inequality in Canada

Income Inequality

Statistics Canada regularly measures income among Canadians, and using this data we can trace patterns of income distribution in Canada. Among this data is the average income of Canadians by social group. For example, in 2002 the average income for two-parent families with children under 18 was $67,700, while the average income for lone parents with children under 18 was $33,000—and just $30,800 for female lone parent families (Statistics Canada, 2002). While these incomes might seem significant, and by world standards they are significant, as we will see in Chapter 15 there are others in Canadian society whose incomes make these average incomes insignificant. The 30 April 2004 *Globe and Mail* contained a major feature on the incomes of some of the top-earning chief executive officers in

Canada. The article notes that the top earner in terms of salaries, bonuses, and stock options earned $56.6 million dollars in 2003. Second on the list was totalled $52.4 million. In terms of just salary income, the top registered at $3.5 million.

Statistics Canada also breaks the population into what are called 'quintiles', meaning one-fifth of the population. In the first Statistics Canada graph on page 181 you can see the share of various kinds of income (market, total, and after tax) that go to each quintile. Keep in mind that each quintile represents an equal number of people so the bars for the highest group do really say that 20 per cent of the population is getting more that 40 per cent of income while at the bottom 10 per cent of the population is getting about 5 per cent of the income!

Data available from Statistics Canada also illustrates a relatively stable pattern of income inequality in Canada. The second Statistics Canada chart illustrates how, over time, the share of total income going to the highest 20 per cent has remained consistently significantly higher than that received by the bottom quintile.

Canadian society is clearly characterized by significant structural inequalities in income. In Canada there are rich folk, there are poor folk, and there are folk in the middle. However, while the data describes certain features of Canadian society, the phenomenon of inequality remains unexplained. A logical question that follows the presentation of

Income share

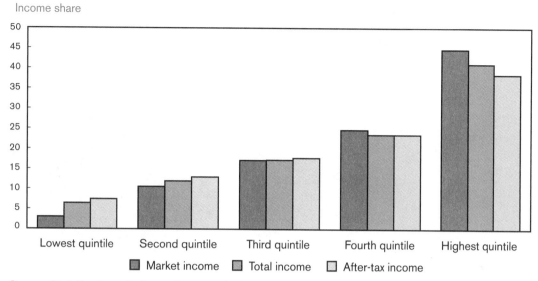

Source: Statistics Canada. 'Lower income quintile families had larger shares of aggregate income, after transfers and taxes, 2002', *Analysis of Income in Canada*, 2002. Catalogue 75-203, 20 May 2004. Available at http://www.statcan.ca/english/freepub/75-203-XIE/00002/ct024_en.htm.

Income share

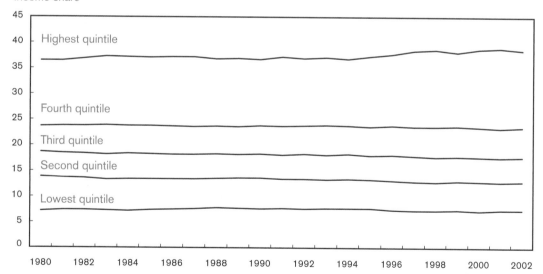

Source: Statistics Canada. 'Shares of aggregate after-tax income by quintiles, 1980 to 2002', *Analysis of Income in Canada*, 2002. Catalogue 75-203, 20 May 2004. Available at http://www.statcan.ca/english/freepub/75-203-XIE/00002/ct015_en.htm.

such data is: Why? Why do some people in Canada have incomes in excess of a million dollars a year while a significant number of others live below the poverty line? Why does the top 20 per cent of the population receive over 43 per cent of the country's income while the bottom 20 per cent receives less

Almost one-quarter of Canadian families live below the poverty line. That means that over 5 million Canadians live below the poverty line. Living on the street has become a desperate alternative for some. (Dick Hemingway)

than 5 per cent? How do we explain income inequalities in our society?

Prestige or Status Inequality

In addition to the structural economic inequalities in Canadian society, there also exist what sociologists call prestige inequalities. There is a tradition in sociology of using the terms *status*, *prestige*, and *honour* interchangeably. Because in this book we consistently use the term *status* in a different context—to refer to positions within an institution or group—we will use the word *prestige* for the purpose of examining structures of inequality. What, then, do we mean by *prestige*?

The *Modern Dictionary of Sociology* defines prestige in terms of social recognition, respect, and even admiration and deference (Theodorson and Theodorson, 1969: 312). In their *Dictionary of Sociology*, Abercrombie, Hill, and Turner (1988:

194) note that the concept of prestige has a long tradition in American sociological studies of occupational rankings. They indicate that a consistent pattern has emerged when people in capitalist societies are asked to rank different occupations according to 'social standing or desirability'. It seems that people in Western societies agree that some jobs are more prestigious than others. Sociological researchers have found that many people think that there is more prestige attached to being a judge, a priest, and even a university professor than there is to being a construction worker, a janitor, or a trapper.

If we accept that there are certain commonly held ideas in our society about the prestige, honour, or social recognition attached to various occupations and positions, we can also argue that a person in a given occupation might be located above or below another person in a different occupation. The questions that emerge from this type of research relate to the general importance that such a ranking plays in the society's structures of inequality. There is significant disagreement about the basis of these apparent prestige-related inequalities.

Power

In addition to economic and prestige inequalities, sociologists have found substantial evidence indicating an unequal distribution of power in society. The very fact that you have bought and are reading this book may in itself be an indication of a power difference. In all likelihood you purchased and are reading this book because you have to, whether you like it or not, that is, because someone told you to get it and read it. The fact that instructors can influence your behaviour in this way means they have power over you. This particular concept of power refers to different relations between individuals within an institution, yet the concept can also be used to refer to larger social processes at a macro level, as in the case of power vested in the government to make certain decisions that have an impact on the lives of most if not all members of the society. These two 'levels' of power indicate that although social scientists frequently use the concept of power, they do so in different ways. As a result the concept is often subject to confusion and misunderstanding.

The definition of power most widely adopted in sociology is based on the classical definition provided by Weber, who noted that power means the ability of an individual or a number of individuals to realize their will in a communal action even when that will is resisted by others (Weber, 1946: 180). Weber's use of the term *communal action* implies that power tends to be related to social collectivities such as groups and classes more than to individual situations. This raises the further issue of how we understand power at the micro level of an individual within an institution. If we are to understand the connection between the macro and micro dimensions of power, we must first consider

how different theoretical perspectives have handled the issue.

The 'Discovery' of Class in North America

When we examine the extent of the inequalities in our society, some obvious questions should come to mind. Why do these significant differences in income levels exist? Why are some jobs, occupations, or positions considered more prestigious than others? Why are people not equal in terms of the power they exercise?

The issue of social and economic inequality was not a pressing concern for most North American social thinkers until midway through the twentieth century. While there were exceptions, such as the work of Thorstein Veblen, the idea that North America consisted of open and basically classless societies was a pervasive aspect of the worldview held by most academics and non-academics alike. Other societies, such as those in Europe, were viewed as having traditions of class inequalities, but the United States in particular was a part of the New World where all individuals were supposed to have an equal opportunity to better themselves. According to this belief system, people were able to determine, to a large extent, what their lives would be like. As Harold Kerbo (1983) points out, the founders of American sociology ignored the issue of social inequality until the trauma of the Great Depression forced social scientists to undertake investigations that began to question the mythology of the United States as a classless society.

During the 1930s and 1940s two different types of studies pointed to the existence of social and economic inequalities in the United States. The first important empirical investigation of inequality, by Robert and Helen Lynd, found significant differences in the economic and social positions of Americans.

Middletown: The Economic Basis of Class

Robert and Helen Lynd conducted a detailed investigation of the patterns and structures of inequality in an Indiana city they thought was typical of the United States in the mid-1920s. They called the city Middletown, which was also the title of the 1929 published account of their work.

The Lynds used a variety of techniques to gather data on the social structure and patterns of interaction and behaviour in the city. They found not only that Middletown was a class-divided city, but also that class position was one of the most important factors influencing an individual's life chances there. They concluded that there were essentially two classes: the working class, made up of about 70 per cent of the population; and the business class, made up of the remaining 30 per cent.

A key aspect of their initial study was its historical dimension. The Lynds collected as much data as they could on Middletown, since it was founded in 1890 about 35 years before their study, to provide an indication of what was happening to the overall structures of the society. On the basis of their data, they concluded that the class structure of Middletown was becoming more pronounced. The Middletown of the 1920s was considerably more industrialized, and the development of industry had altered the previous class structure. The working class had grown in size. In 1890 Middletown had been more of a typical pioneer city, with considerable equality of opportunity for people to improve their situation providing they had the initiative and were willing to work hard. As American society became more industrialized, the amount of capital required to engage in business grew rapidly. By 1920 the situation had developed to the point that it took more capital than most individuals could muster to engage in any industrial or manufacturing enterprises. As a result, the majority of people found themselves in the working class.

The Lynds later returned to the city and produced a second important study of social inequality in the United States, *Middletown in Transition* (1937). The second book painted a slightly different picture of the class structure, although the two basic classes remained the same.

The class structure had become somewhat more complex, because Middletown had developed a more substantial industrial base and a considerably larger service sector. As a result, the Lynds concluded that there were essentially six classes:

- Group I: wealthy owners of large local businesses. Manufacturers, bankers, local heads of major corporations.
- Group II: smaller local manufacturers, merchants, professionals. High-paid salaried officials in local and national businesses.
- Group III: medium-sized and smaller local businesses, professionals, white-collar workers, clerical workers, civil servants.
- Group IV: aristocracy of local labour. Supervisors, highly skilled craft workers, and trades people.
- Group V: working class. Average and typical blue-collar workers in skilled and unskilled jobs. Average wage-earners.
- Group VI: marginated people. Seasonally employed, unemployed.

The work of the Lynds provided firm evidence that despite the views held and espoused by many Americans, especially politicians and the wealthy, there was indeed a class structure in the United States. Their research, by concentrating on the economic basis of class, tended to push the analysis of social inequality in the direction of a Marxian theory—although there were many US sociologists who were not at all interested in that mode of analysis.

W. Lloyd Warner and Associates: Prestige as Social Class

In the early 1930s a group of sociologists led by W. Lloyd Warner began a series of community studies destined to have an enormous impact on the study of social inequality in the United States. Warner and his associates produced a large number of different studies in addition to a manual that presented their method of analyzing social inequality in a formal manner (see Warner, 1949). An approach—we will call it stratification analysis—developed out of this work.

This stratification analysis refers to an approach to the study of social inequality that assumes that society is layered or divided into strata. The strata or layers are made up of people who share a common characteristic or attribute such as income or social prestige and honour. Thinkers adopting this approach tend to see the strata or layers in society as forming a ladder or continuum on which people are placed higher or lower, depending on how much of some measurable 'characteristic', 'attribute', 'possession', or 'quality' they possess. Because many different criteria could be used to define strata, it was important to define as precisely as possible just what the basis of the stratification system was.

Warner and his associates studied the city of Newburyport, Massachusetts, which they called Yankee City. They, too, were interested in the issue of inequality, although their studies were based on a different set of assumptions from that of the work of the Lynds. The approach Warner adopted assumed that the most important types of inequality were related to social status, and so the Yankee City studies were geared to investigating inequalities in prestige rather than the economic dimensions of social inequality.

The assumption that a society's value system is the basis of its stratification system was compatible with the basic tenets of structural functionalism—the dominant theoretical orientation at this time—and as a result the work of Warner and his associates became widely known and accepted. Based on their investigation of people's beliefs, attitudes, patterns of social interaction, and consciousness of inequalities, the Warner group identified six distinct classes in Yankee City: the upper-upper class; the lower-upper class; the upper-middle class; the lower-middle class; the upper-lower class; the lower-lower class.

The Warner researchers used a number of different research methods to arrive at this schema. As Dennis Gilbert and Joseph Kahl (1987) note, their main method became known as *evaluated participation*. This method attempts to place families and individuals in one of the classes on the basis of their reputations, patterns of social interactions, community participation, and memberships in formal networks and associations. Warner and his group eventually developed another system for determining class position, a system they hoped would be easier to administer than the evaluated participation approach. The second method was based on four major factors: an individual's occupation, source of income, house type, and dwelling area. They established an index or ranking of occupations, income sources, house types, and dwelling areas based on the standards and values of the community being studied, and ranked individuals and families according to their combined standing in these four scales. On the basis of these criteria the group argued that the class structure of Yankee City, and North America in general, looked like this:

- Upper-upper: old established families. Biggest houses, in exclusive areas. Strong sense of lineage and belonging to this class.
- Lower-upper: newer wealth. Less secure in income, identity, and sense of lineage. Manners and habits less polished and 'natural'.
- Upper-middle: businesspeople and professionals. Individuals and families in affluent areas, self-maintained houses (no gardeners and servants). Value education and community participation and service.
- Lower-middle: smaller business, white-collar salaried semi-professions (such as teachers), supervisors in factories. Own modest middle-class houses in middle-class areas. Churchgoers and lodge members.
- Upper-lower: blue-collar and clerical workers. Own or rent small and average houses

in working-class areas. Hardworking and respectable people who stay out of trouble.

- Lower-lower: marginally and seasonally employed. Spend time on relief of various kinds. Less respectable than upper-lower workers. Seldom own houses. Rent in poorest areas of town.

The arguments developed by Warner and his associates became widely accepted, although some scholars disagreed that the study of social prestige was an appropriate mode of understanding class. Perhaps the most serious criticism was that the approach tended to ignore the relationship between status inequalities and power structures and economic position. The Warner approach focused on social and community beliefs and values as related to the amount of prestige attached to an occupation and source of income, while it ignored the actual amount of income. The approach was based on subjective appraisals of an individual's social position. The Lynds had advocated an alternative position, arguing that an individual's or family's position within the actual economic processes determined class position. From the very beginning of their studies of inequality, American sociologists were unable to agree on the basis and nature of social class.

The Structural Functionalists: Parsons, Davis, and Moore

The work of the Lynds and the Warner group was significant because the studies clearly demonstrated the existence of structured patterns of inequality in American society. Despite the widespread popular belief that the United States was a society without classes, in their own ways the Lynds and the Warner group demonstrated that there were indeed classes, and that class was an important part of social structure. Although there were important differences in how they understood the term *class* and what formed the basis of class differences, American

sociologists subsequently had to address the issue of class. That issue was taken up by three well-known and important sociologists, Talcott Parsons, Kingsley Davis, and Wilbert E. Moore.

Talcott Parsons

Talcott Parsons first addressed the issue of social stratification in 1940 and continued to explore the issue in his subsequent work. Not surprisingly, his explanation of social inequalities follows the overall logic of the structural functionalist perspective.

Given that structural functionalism assumes that every society has at its core a complex set of values, norms, beliefs, ideas, and ideals that give the society its shape and character and serve as a major source of social stability and order, it follows that certain individual qualities or attributes will be highly valued and that others will be less valued. For example, in a particular society at a specific historical moment physical strength and endurance may be valued, while in another society at another moment in history people with intellectual prowess may be highly valued. Yet another society may consider the possession of material wealth to be most important and desirable.

As a result, in almost all societies certain people have come to attain a higher status, honour, or prestige than others. The opposite is also true, that there are some people whose characteristics and attributes are the opposite of those considered desirable or valued highly, and as a result those people are ranked lower in the social hierarchy. It is inevitable that there will be a system of status or prestige stratification. This hierarchy leads to structured inequalities in wealth and power. People who rank high on the prestige scale can use that position to acquire, enjoy, and maintain economic rewards and power.

Parsons' explanation of social stratification has become less important than other aspects of his work. However, as Peter Hamilton argues, Parsons' line of thinking was important because of the direction it gave to structural functionalist thinking on the issue (1983: 88). Parsons continually argued that

American functionalist Talcott Parsons first addressed the issue of social stratification in 1940. Not surprisingly, his explanation of social inequality follows the overall logic of the functionalists. He claimed that in all societies, certain people need to attain status, honour, and prestige, and as a result, others must suffer a life of economic struggle. (HUP Parsons, Talcott (1b), courtesy of the Harvard University Archives)

we must examine the functions that social phenomena play for the entire social system. Kingsley Davis and Wilbert E. Moore adopted the logic of this argument and undertook an alternative way of analyzing the function of social differentiation in a social system.

Kingsley Davis and Wilbert E. Moore

The seminal Davis and Moore essay, 'Some Principles of Stratification', first published in 1945, has become the classical statement of the fundamentals of a structural functionalist explanation of

social inequality. As the essay's title suggests, the authors developed an approach to why systems of stratification exist in most societies. They argued that modern complex societies are characterized by the existence of complicated and specialized institutions that contain various positions. That is, the institutions include a division of labour, with different roles attached to various positions. The reason why complex societies have stratification systems is related to the nature of these different roles or tasks.

As Davis and Moore pointed out, an examination of the different positions within most major complex institutions indicates that the positions are not all the same. They differ in a number of ways. Some of them are more important than others in terms of both the functioning of the institutions and, by implication, societal stability and survival. Some institutional positions are more pleasant than others, and some require special skills and training. If the institution is to operate at maximum efficiency, competent, committed, and qualified individuals must be attracted into the important, difficult, and less pleasant jobs. For example, within the structures of a modern university the job of president is usually considered to be important, difficult, and even—because it may on occasion involve firing or disciplining employees—unpleasant.

If the institutions that make up society are to function to the maximum benefit of society, some means of motivating individuals to take on the important, unpleasant, and difficult jobs must be developed. It is also important to develop a means of encouraging individuals to acquire the special skills and training that some of these jobs require. The question is, how can society motivate people to take on important, sometimes unpleasant jobs that may require the acquisition of special skills and training? The answer, according to Davis and Moore, is to develop a system of rewards.

Society has at its disposal, they argued, a number of different rewards it can allocate to entice or motivate individuals to take on the difficult and important jobs and acquire the necessary skills and training. Although Davis and Moore did not specify in detail what those rewards are, they did note that there are three different kinds of rewards. These relate to what they call things that contribute to 'sustenance and comfort', things that contribute to 'humour and diversion', and things that contribute to 'self-respect and ego expansion' (1945: 65).

The Davis and Moore argument stimulated a major debate among social scientists, which eventually produced a further refinement of the precise nature of the rewards society allocates to individuals. The key for us here is their contribution to the study of social stratification: they systematically laid out what they thought were the reasons for and causes of social stratification. Their conclusion is quite simple: by providing a basis for motivating individuals to take important, difficult jobs that require the acquisition of special skills and training, social stratification performs a function for society. Not only is a system of social stratification functional for society, in all likelihood it is necessary and inevitable. In essence, Davis and Moore argued that without a system of unequal rewards, society would not be able to motivate people to take on those difficult and specialized jobs that are so important to society.

Davis and Moore Elaborated: Society's Reward System

After Davis and Moore presented their theory, an exchange took place between Davis and Melvin M. Tumin (Davis, [1953] 1974; Tumin, [1953] 1974). Others, such as Richard Simpson (1956) and Dennis Wrong (1959), also contributed to the ongoing discussion. Wrong's intervention raised a central issue in the developing functionalist approach, namely, what are the precise rewards that society has to allocate or offer? Wrong referred to power, prestige, and wealth as the central elements of the reward system, taking up a position that became an essential aspect of the emerging functionalist approach to social stratification.

In 1957 another functionalist, Bernard Barber, published a book that became a classic in the field. In *Social Stratification* Barber used arguments based on the work of Parsons and Davis and Moore, pointing out that social stratification performs an integrative function. First, he suggested that the process of rewarding people for upholding or representing the values and norms of the community really serves to reinforce those very same values and norms. Second, he pointed out that a system of differential rewards is necessary to motivate people. Barber emphasized that prestige is the primary reward, with the other rewards being somehow related.

The precise nature of the connections between the various rewards was more fully developed in the following decade. In 1967 Melvin M. Tumin produced an important study in the prestigious 'Foundations of Modern Sociology Series'. Tumin's book *Social Stratification: The Forms and Functions of Inequality* presented a systematic account of the revisions that had been made to the functionalist theory of stratification. One of his most important points related to the system of rewards (Tumin, 1967: 40). The rewards that individuals receive can be classified, he suggested, under three general headings. First are the rewards related to property and material wealth. Second are those associated with power in society, which allow certain people to secure their will even when others oppose that will. Third are the rewards associated with psychic gratification or, to use language familiar to us by now, prestige and honour.

In the functionalist perspective, wealth, power, and prestige are the three essential rewards that, first, society allocates to those who excel in conduct that is socially desirable, and that, second, are used as motivation to ensure that some people are willing to perform socially important tasks that may be difficult, unpleasant, and require special skills and training. In their introduction to a book of readings on social stratification in Canada, James Curtis and William Scott (1979) made explicit reference to these three rewards, and their book includes sections examining each of the rewards. In his important analysis of social stratification in the United States, first published as *The American Class System*, then republished as *Social Stratification: The Interplay of Class, Race and Gender* (1997), Daniel Rossides explicitly referred to the three dimensions of social stratification, which he refers to as class, prestige, and power. The position that the stratification system of Western society involves three dimensions or components has become a widely accepted tenet of functionalist theory, and Rossides' advice that these 'areas' of inequality be considered analytically separate has been heeded (Rossides, 1976: 33).

The Dimensions of Social Stratification

Wealth and Income as Social Class

The first dimension of the stratification system relates to social divisions based on economic criteria. Within the functionalist perspective the terms *class* and *social class* are generally used when discussing the economic differences in people's lives. Although functionalist class analysis includes a large number of different positions, here we will focus on one example.

In *The American Class System*, Rossides used class to refer to social positions determined by economic criteria and forming recognizable groupings within the stratification system. Using economic criteria as the main determinant of a person's class position, supported by associated characteristics related to education and overall style of living, Rossides argued that there are five classes in America.

1. Upper class: very high incomes. Old established wealth and money. Owners of major corporations. 1 to 3 per cent of population.
2. Upper-middle class: high income. Upper-level professionals. Highest level of civil service and military. Corporate executives

and owners of medium-sized national businesses. 10 to 15 per cent of population
3. Lower-middle class: average incomes and above. Small business owners. Lower-level professional, white-collar workers, small farmers, civil servants. Some modest personal savings. 30 to 35 per cent of population.
4. Working class: average incomes and below. Skilled and unskilled blue-collar workers in factories, mines, stores, and service industries. 40 to 45 per cent of population.
5. Lower class: income close to or below poverty level. Unemployed or seasonally and marginally employed. Some on social security. 20 to 25 per cent of population.

Rossides' criteria, which are quite general, tend to relate to income and how that income is earned. There is no implied relationship between the classes, other than the fact that the people at the top of the class system have more or earn more income than those at the bottom; as a result the groupings exhibit different personal and lifestyle characteristics. In the final chapter of the reissued version of his book Rossides essentially maintains the same schema; however he places more emphasis on the role of what he calls 'Racial-Ethnic' minorities and gender (1997: Chapter 20). In addition to adding these dimensions, Rossides is also more explicitly critical of the implications of this quite clearly defined class structure. He notes, for example, the class system is marked by what he calls 'significant amounts of powerlessness, exploitation, waste and privilege' that these are deeply institutionalized and systemic (1997: 493). Thus we see the dynamic nature of social analysis as theorists, such as Rossides, continuously adjust and update their work.

In summary, although Rossides does not make the argument, a more 'pure' functionalist might argue that those near the top are in all likelihood being rewarded for the tasks they perform for society. According to this theory, the jobs of the high-income earners and the wealthy are by and large not only more important but also more difficult: they require special skills and training.

Prestige

There is a long tradition in North American sociology of viewing prestige or social honour as being central to stratification analysis. The work of Parsons exemplifies this tradition. In more recent functionalist analysis, prestige has come to be viewed as an analytically separate dimension of stratification; one of the rewards society has at its disposal. This argument holds that the status or prestige reward becomes built into the society's value system, and as a result we all come to know that being a Supreme Court justice or university president has more honour and prestige attached to it than being a logger or garbage handler. According to the logic of this theory, some of us are then willing to take on the 'difficult, important jobs' and even stay in school for many years, in part because we know one day we will have a position that rewards us with social status or prestige. In their efforts to better understand the specifics of how social honour or prestige fits into the stratification system, sociologists have generally concentrated on occupational prestige, that is, the generally accepted social attitudes and values concerning different jobs and occupations.

In the United States, researchers have been interested in occupational prestige for at least four decades. In 1947 the National Opinion Research Center (NORC) conducted a study of how Americans rated various occupations in terms of their prestige. The NORC investigation set the stage for a series of other works in the United States and Canada, and this research further developed our understanding of occupational prestige.

The various assessments of occupational prestige have all adopted a more or less similar approach. People are interviewed and asked to rank a variety of different occupations according to how they perceive the social standing or position of the occupation. On the basis of these various rankings, researchers look to find patterns and, given these patterns, establish a ranking of occupations. Significantly, the studies conducted in both the United States and Canada indicated a shared perception among the citizenry about the social standing of various occupations and led to a series of scales ranking various occupations according to prestige.

Rossides introduced a reproduction of part of the 1963 NORC occupational prestige ratings from the United States. Among the highest-rated occupations in this scale were US Supreme Court justice, scientist, governor, and college professor. Among the lowest were janitor, soda fountain clerk, garbage collector, and shoe shiner (1976: 244–5).

Two major studies were conducted in Canada, one by Peter Pineo and John Porter (1967) and the other by Bernard Blishen (1967). In his study Blishen ranked 320 different occupations. In the top 10 positions of this socioeconomic index he placed chemical engineers, dentists, college professors, physicians and surgeons, geologists, mining engineers, lawyers, civil engineers, architects, and veterinarians. The bottom 10 positions included spinners and twisters, weavers, teamsters, labourers, winders and reelers, sectionmen and trackmen, labourers in textiles, shoemakers, fish canners, and trappers (1967: 42, 50).

In addition to ranking occupations in a more or less systematic manner, sociologists have also examined other forms of stratification. Peter Pineo (1980) reported on how Canadians rank individuals from various national and ethnic groups. Similar studies have been conducted in the United States, with similar results (Ogmundson, 1990: 241).

The first two dimensions of the stratification system raise important questions. Can we conceive of an individual whose income and thus class position might be high, yet whose prestige position is much lower? Conversely, is it possible to think about an individual with a relatively low income, and thus a lower class position, but with a very high level of social honour or prestige? For instance, where on the scale of prestige would you place a wealthy individual widely recognized as a slum landlord, as compared to a member of the local clergy?

As important as occupational prestige or social honour may be, like income or wealth these elements are not the only rewards society has at its disposal. Some people relish the prestige attached to their positions, while others are more interested in what comes with a high income. Possibly, still others are satisfied with the power that comes with their position in the social scale.

Power

For centuries the issue of how to define and understand power in society has been at the centre of considerable debate within the social sciences. The question of power has been a particular thorn in the side of the functionalist tradition, because the discussion of power inevitably leads to the argument that power is concentrated in the hands of a ruling class, and this is a view that many functionalist sociologists have wanted to distance themselves from (Aron, 1966: 201).

In any case, in attempting to deal with the complex issue of power, functionalists tend to differentiate between personal or individual power and social or political power. The first level, that of the individual, emphasizes a person's position within a particular institution or set of statuses. The second level, the level of society as a whole, emphasizes power as it occurs in the political system.

At the second, broader social level, power tends to be understood as political power, or, as Tumin stated, it relates to the ability to influence general social policy (1967: 41–2). The institutional order we call the political or the polity is the setting for decisions concerning general social policy and debates concerning broad social issues. Within the structural functionalist approach, one of the essential functions of the polity is the establishment of collective goals and objectives that influence and

have an impact on the entire social structure (Dobriner, 1969: 122).

Authority

In functionalist thought, authority refers to the concept of legitimate influence, in which influence is understood as the capacity to affect the thinking and actions of another person or social grouping (Barber, 1957: 234).

In this sense, authority is seen as a relatively benign and necessary form of power. It is benign because it flows from or is located within formally established and socially sanctioned structures and relations. Functionalists tend to argue that authority is necessary in a modern industrial society because the complexity of most institutional orders requires a division of labour. In other words, complex institutions include job or task specializations, with some roles or positions being responsible for co-ordinating the overall operation of the institution. For example, according to functionalist thought, institutions like modern Western universities, with their intricate divisions of labour, require hierarchical decision-making. Functionalists would argue that for a university to perform its functions for society, some measure of authority must be granted to various positions to ensure that administrators administrate, teachers teach, cleaners clean, and students do their work. They apply the same logic to a variety of other institutions, from the family order to the economy.

Authority is not only necessary for the smooth operation of institutions but is also an important part of the social reward system. Some people find that the authority associated with a difficult position is a key part of their reward for undertaking that job. Functionalists could argue that one of the reasons why people are willing to take on difficult and important jobs requiring the acquisition of special skills and arduous training is because they know that eventually they will be rewarded with a measure of personal power (Tumin, 1967: 40–1).

For functionalists, authority is the institutional dimension of power and the reward system; as such, it is necessary for institutional functioning, and in that sense its role is not particularly difficult to understand (Parsons, 1966: 249).

Within the functionalist approach there is broad acceptance of the necessity for the stratification or layering of relations of authority in complex societies. Bernard Barber states that because there are role differences and role specialization, some degree of stratification based on the authority of position is inevitable (1957: 232). But functionalists also maintain that the element of stratification does not mean society as a whole must be authoritarian or undemocratic. It is possible to have a society that has differential amounts of individual power and is also open, egalitarian, and democratic. Their explanation for this has to do with their particular understanding of the nature of the polity and political power.

Marxist Theories of Class

The structural functionalist approach, which was dominant in North American sociology from the mid-1930s through the 1960s, created a new subfield—the study of stratification—through its varied attempts to answer the questions raised by social inequality. Although the different positions taken up were often subtle and complex, the structural functionalists did share a general set of premises and assumptions in their interpretations of the whys and hows of social stratification.

In the 1960s an alternative approach emerged as scholars began a systematic re-evaluation and re-examination of the ideas and theories of Marx. Through that process some of them hoped to separate or distance Marx's ideas and theories from their association with political regimes like the ones that had developed in the Soviet Union and Eastern Europe. Many neo-Marxists believed that Marx's name had become associated with governments that had nothing in common with Marx's original commitment to social criticism of capitalist society

and the creation of a truly humane, free, and democratic society.

The broad stream of thought referred to as neo-Marxism encompasses a great many different theorists and thinkers who emphasized and focused on different aspects of Marx's work. Despite having some differences, the theorists' approaches have enough in common so that, as a way of beginning the process of understanding this mode of analysis, we can paint a general picture of their basic assumptions.

Marx's View of Class

There is perhaps no more important concept for Marxist and neo-Marxist social analysis than the concept of class. The reasons for this are closely related to the general analytical approach taken up by the thinkers who have followed a Marxian approach.

Marx, and later his followers, approached the study of society by adopting a materialist approach. An essential tenet of both the classical and contemporary versions of Marxism is the assumption that the most important human social activity is material production; and all Marxists insist that the most appropriate point of departure for social analysis is an investigation of the society's economic order. A society's economic basis is itself determined by the stage of development reached by that society's productive forces (its level of technological and scientific development) and its social relations of production (the patterns of ownership and control of the productive forces).

The Two Major Classes

Marx examined the social relations of production in the most advanced capitalist society of his day, Britain, investigating the patterns of ownership and control of the society's productive resources. He concluded that capitalist societies are, by definition, class societies. In a capitalist society, he found, there are some people who own and control the factories, mines, mills, and other productive resources, and these people receive income and make a living by virtue of that ownership of productive property. But not everyone in capitalist society owns a share of the society's productive resources. Indeed, most people survive only by selling the one thing they do own, something they can sell again and again, day after day, month after month, year after year: their capacity to work, known as their labour power.

The people who own the society's productive resources (or at least hold some share in them) are usually not in a position to operate those resources themselves. They require the help of others, and wage labourers supply that help. Both groups—those who own society's productive resources and those who do not—exist in a symbiotic relationship: each needs the other in order to survive. Those selling labour power require someone who needs to purchase labour power, and those wanting to purchase labour power require someone who offers labour power for sale. The key to Marx's understanding of class is his analysis of the relationship between these two classes.

Marx used several different terms to refer to these two main social groups. He referred to the owners of society's productive resources as the capitalist class, the bourgeoisie, the owning class, and capital. He referred to the others who sell their labour power as the working class, the proletariat, or labour. In addition, when Marx wrote of ownership of property he was not referring to personal property such as houses, clothing, or other purely personal items; rather, he meant the productive resources of society, which are by definition part of the economic infrastructure that produces and distributes wealth.

Surplus Value and Exploitation

For neo-Marxists, a key question is: what is the essential nature of the relationship between the capitalist class and the working class? For Marx the answer was: it is a relationship of exploitation. The capitalists, by virtue of their ownership of a portion of society's productive resources, are in a structural position to exploit the working class, and they do so because of how the entire economic system works.

The key to Marx's explanation of why and how the capitalist class exploits the working class is found in the concept of surplus value and his understanding of the key dynamic of capitalist society.

Capitalism is, Marx contended, a system predicated on the assumption that the most important goal in life for those with money is to use that money to make more money. In a capitalist society those with wealth do not merely 'sit on their laurels' and enjoy what they have. Instead, they take their wealth and invest it with the objective of eventually accumulating even more wealth. For Marx, the central dynamic of capitalism is the accumulation of wealth on an expanding scale.

To understand the essence of Marx's analysis of class relations, we must bear in mind that he was examining an industrial capitalist society in which the most effective way for an individual with money to make more money was to invest in some form of industrial production. Marx argued that investing in industrial production involves the purchase of certain commodities with the ultimate objective of turning a profit. The key to the process, he maintained, was to be found in the nature of the commodities purchased by the capitalist class.

When people with capital invest their money in an industrial enterprise, they purchase several different kinds of commodities. First, they must acquire a factory within which production can occur. Next, they must acquire raw materials that can form the basis of the manufacturing process, and they need machines and technology they can use to process the raw materials into a final product. But, according to Marx, if investors just purchase these three types of commodities they find that rather than making money they lose money, because raw materials and machines sitting in a factory cannot by themselves produce profits. Before they can create the basis for profits, investors must purchase the additional, and most vital, commodity required in the productive process: labour power. To make a profit the owner of capital must bring together the raw materials, machines, and labour power in a factory. Once they have assembled these commodities, the capitalists produce and sell new commodities (the factory output) and thereby make more money.

For Marx, a major interest was the precise nature of the process by which industrial capitalists were able to make money by hiring workers to run their factories. Who actually produced the wealth that the owners were able to claim as profits? His answer to the question might be easier to understand through an example. Assume for a moment that I am in possession of a substantial sum of money and I want to invest it so I will make more money. Further, I have determined that an investment opportunity exists in the manufacture of a new style of jogging shoe. I go out and invest by purchasing all the necessary raw materials, a factory, and the necessary machinery and technology. I find out that the total daily costs of my raw materials will be $40, and the payments on my factory and depreciation on my machines will cost another $20 a day.

Lastly, I hire students to work in my factory. The agreement I make with them specifies that I must pay them $10 an hour for an eight-hour day. Suppose that in eight hours of work they create eight pairs of shoes. At the end of eight hours they get $80 and I get the eight pairs of shoes. If I go out and sell the eight pairs of shoes for $10 each and realize a total return of $80, I will be losing money, because at that price I have not been able to recover my costs of production.

We live in a capitalist society, so I am not involved in the productive process just because I want to provide people with jobs; I am involved because I want to make money, and if I am not making money I will shut my factory down, sell the assets, and invest somewhere else. So let's assume a different outcome, one that will enable me to continue in production. Assume that I sell the shoes for $20 each. After I sell the shoes I have $160. Given the total daily costs of my raw materials and the payments on my factory and depreciation on my machines, at the end of the day my balance sheet looks like the following table:

Total value of commodities produced:
   8 pairs of shoes @ $20 each = **$160**

Total costs of production:	
Wages for labour power	$80
Raw material costs	40
Depreciation and factory costs	20
Total	**$140**

Subtract the total costs of production from total value of commodities produced	$160
	−140
Equals surplus value appropriated by capital	**$20**

The origin and disposition of the surplus that arises out of this productive process were, for Marx, the key to understanding the nature of class in a capitalist society. Marx used the term *surplus value* to describe this amount, arguing that although the working class, through their productive activity, produces surplus value, it ends up being appropriated by the capitalist class. This forms the basis of class exploitation. The working class is exploited because they work and labour to produce and create wealth, which is subsequently claimed and appropriated by another class.

Marx concluded, then, that capitalism is, by definition, a class society and relations of exploitation are a basic and fundamental characteristic of this class structure. The two classes must be understood in terms of the different structural positions they occupy in the economic institutions. The method of defining and understanding these classes is quite different from the method used in stratification theory. It is not that the owners necessarily have or make more money that puts them in a different class position; it is their different structural position in the economic order.

Other Classes in Marx's Schema

Although Marx believed that understanding the relationship between the capitalist class and the working class was essential to understanding the overall dynamics of the system, he never claimed these were the only classes. In fact, there has been a good deal of debate among those interested in Marx's analysis about just how many other classes he thought there were. The last volume of his major work, *Capital*, breaks off just when he was about to begin to engage in a systematic analysis of the class structure of his society. At that point he refers to four major classes. In addition to what have sometimes been called the two great classes, Marx also referred to the landlords and the petty bourgeoisie.

The landlords essentially represent a remnant of the previous mode of economic organization, feudalism, although they had been an important part of the processes involved in the initial development of capitalism. The petty bourgeoisie are in a structural location between the capitalist class and the working class. Like the major capitalist class the petty bourgeoisie own productive resources, but the magnitude or size of those resources is limited, and they are able to operate those productive resources themselves or with the aid of unpaid labour (such as family labour). The capacity to engage in some productive activity without the employment of paid wage labour is an essential characteristic of the petite bourgeoisie and an important difference between them and the major capitalist class. Also, unlike the working class, the petite bourgeoisie do not have to sell their labour power in order to make a living. Their income comes from the small productive resources they own; however, the fact that they are able to operate these resources themselves, without paid labour, means that, unlike the capitalist class, they do not directly exploit the working class.

How Many Classes?

No attempt at class analysis has caused as much debate and controversy as Marx's. There are a number of reasons for this, one of them related to the political implications of his analysis. Marx concluded that class relations involve more than an unequal distribution of wealth: they also involve relations of domination, subordination, exploitation, and even a lack of real freedom for the subordinate classes. The other reason Marx's analysis has stimulated a lot of debate is because it was unfinished—interrupted by his death in 1883.

At no point in any of his works do we find an adequate theory of class. As Bertell Ollman (1968) pointed out, there are a number of seemingly contradictory statements about class scattered throughout Marx's work. A common theme is the argument that the basis of a person's class position must be understood in terms of the social organization of material production. Class positions are determined by structural positions in the economic order; however, there is some confusion relating to the question of the number of classes in a capitalist society. Statements can be found in Marx that there are 2, 4, and even more than 10 classes—the last kind of statement being found in historically specific analyses such as those dealing with the political events in France in the early 1850s (Marx, [1852] 1972). In those historical works he referred to many different subclasses within the major capitalist, petit bourgeois, and working classes. Marx used the term *fraction* to refer to internal class divisions based on economic interests. For example, he argued that the capitalist class is subdivided into industrialists, bankers, financiers, and large-scale merchants. He argued that in the end class analysis is meaningful only when it is carried out in the context of a specific historical social structure. Marx was interested in understanding class structures and dynamics in real historical circumstances and not in producing abstract schemas and theories.

What do we make of Marx's seeming confusion? There are two possibilities. One is simply that he was confused and could not decide how many classes there were. The other is that he was examining classes at different levels of abstraction, and when he worked at a very abstract level, as in writing *Capital*, he was only trying to provide a theoretical view of the most general features of capitalist society. At this high level of abstraction his discussion of class was limited to an enunciation of the general principles on which class membership is based. In other more historical and empirical works he elaborated on those abstract principles, painting in the actual details of a historically situated, concrete society. Performing social analysis at this lower level of abstraction, that is, of a particular society at a specific moment in time, led him to make refinements to his general and abstract theory. He still understood classes primarily in terms of people's position in the economic structures, but he then tried to account for and describe specific historically determined internal divisions within the various classes.

In either case, as far as providing a solid and well-developed basis for subsequent class analysis, the legacy of Marx was laced with a good deal of confusion. For this reason, Western scholars interested in re-examining Marx and separating his approach from the stultified dogma of 'official Marxism' began to revise and update his approach to class.

Neo-Marxism and Class Analysis

The decades of the 1970s and 1980s saw the emergence of a number of new approaches in the study of class from within the Marxian tradition. The neo-Marxist approach accepted many of the basic premises and assumptions of Marx's overall approach, but also argued that revisions were necessary to make his analysis relevant to late twentieth-century capitalist society (Baran and Sweezy, 1966). Significantly, many of the scholars attempting to revise Marx disagreed with one another, and as a result a variety of schools or approaches emerged within the general approach that we are calling neo-Marxism. Among the central issues of contention and disagreement was the question of how the class structure of capitalist society had changed in the hundred or more years since Marx had studied it—

or of what the concept of class meant in advanced capitalist society.

Classes and Class Fractions

One of the many attempts to further elaborate on and develop the legacy of Marx involved the rethinking of Marx's notion of class fractions. In *Marx and History*, D. Ross Gandy provided a concise summary of an updated Marxian understanding of class. Gandy noted that a Marxist understanding of class involves the explicit recognition that nowhere does Marx himself provide a systematic account of class. He also suggested that a Marxist conception of class must locate and define classes in terms of positions within the economic structures and processes (1979: 96).

Central to the Marxian approach is the recognition of the existence of three main classes in an industrial capitalist society. In typical Marxian fashion, Gandy used the terms *bourgeoisie*, *petty bourgeoisie*, and *proletariat* to refer to the three major classes in capitalist society. He stated the importance of recognizing the existence of these classes, but he also argued for the importance of recognizing internal divisions within them. Within the bourgeoisie, for example, Gandy saw key differences between people with investments in different sectors of the economy such as industrial production, finance, banking, and merchandising. Each of those fractions has different economic interests and concerns that can lead to situations of conflict. For instance, with the issue of rent controls the different sectors of the capitalist class may take up different positions. An industrialist may be in favour of rent controls because they decrease the cost of living for workers, thus producing less upward pressure on wages. An investor in real estate would undoubtedly be opposed to rent controls.

Similarly, within the ranks of the petty bourgeoisie there are many different economic positions or fractions—farmers, small merchants, independent artisans, self-employed professionals—that must be accounted for in any class analysis.

The last major class, the working class or proletariat, can also be divided internally, and the many different occupations and levels of skills must be accounted for in class analysis. Gandy noted the potential for the emergence of divisions within the proletariat between workers in different areas of production.

Gandy also discussed the role of additional classes in society. In addition to the three major classes, he noted that social analysis must take into account the existence of people not directly involved in productive activities. What he refers to as vagabonds, beggars, thieves, and others making a living more or less illegally are commonly referred to as the *lumpenproletariat*, and they, too, have to be accounted for because they play a role in society.

The potential role of the lumpenproletariat raises a central point in Marxian class analysis. Marx was first and foremost a revolutionary. He was interested in understanding society so it could be changed in a manner that would allow the vast majority who he believed laboured under exploitative and alienating conditions to be truly free. For Marx, class analysis had as its objective an understanding of the political and material interests of different classes. Such an analysis would make it possible to determine which classes and groupings had an interest in changing the existing social order—and thus to understand what kinds of political positions and actions the various classes might adopt. Social criticism aimed at social change remains a vital aspect of neo-Marxist social analysis.

C.H. Anderson's Subclasses

Not all scholars working within the Marxian tradition used the notion of class fractions in their efforts to elaborate on Marx's analysis of class. In *The Political Economy of Social Class* (1974), C.H. Anderson argued for the need to refine Marx's rather simplistic schema. He maintained that class distinctions are based on the ownership of productive property and on the income source, but he also suggested that what occurs in an advanced capitalist

society is the emergence of new classes, including a new working class composed of white-collar workers. These members of the working class are different from the traditional Marxian industrial working class. While they do sell their capacity to work in order to make a living, they also work in production-related scientific and technical jobs as opposed to directly productive ones on the factory floor (Anderson, 1974: 125). Anderson also referred to a service-producing class made up, for example, of workers involved in providing health and educational services. Finally, he discussed the class position of those directly tied to the capitalist class, whose income is dependent on providing various services to that class. In this class, which he called subcapitalist, Anderson included lawyers, accountants, and financial managers.

In his approach Anderson developed an analysis that involved the examination of the emergence of new classes in industrial capitalist society. He did not really provide an adequate explanation of the precise basis for those new subclasses, but his work pointed in a new direction that was to be explored by a number of other scholars.

Nicos Poulantzas and Non-Productive Labour

The work of Nicos Poulantzas (1936–79) is commonly associated with a stream of Marxian thought referred to as French structuralism. Poulantzas (1975) argued that the major development in the class structure of capitalist society since Marx's time was the emergence not of a new working class but of a new petty bourgeoisie. He insisted on the necessity of defining the working class strictly in terms of the concept of exploitation. The working class are those people who produce actual commodities and in so doing produce surplus value; therefore, they are exploited by capital in the process of production. It is not the selling of labour power that determines class but whether or not a person engages in the production of surplus value. That is, class depends on whether a person

Marx and the neo-Marxists tend to divide the populace into major classes such as the proletariat, the bourgeoisie, etc. What was important and different about Erik Olin Wright's argument was his contention that between the major classes were smaller classes occupying what he called contradictory class locations: groupings that do not fit into any of the major classes. Many, thousands and hundreds of thousands in North America, slip through the cracks and find themselves in need of assistance. (Harry Cutting Photography—www.harrycutting.com)

engages in what Poulantzas refers to as productive labour, defined as the labour that is involved in physical production of commodities. It is as a result of doing productive labour that a person is directly exploited by the capitalist class.

For Poulantzas, some of the workers Anderson had discussed, such as managers, teachers, health workers, and commercial and service workers, are not members of the working class. These people do not produce commodities and therefore do not produce surplus value and are not exploited in a manner similar to the productive workers. Because these others do not fit into any of the traditional Marxian classes, Poulantzas suggested that they could be best understood as composing a new class, the new petty bourgeoisie. He suggested that there are four basic classes plus various class fractions in a capitalist society. But his arguments were not widely accepted.

E.O. Wright and Contradictory Class Locations

Erik Olin Wright was one of many to develop a critique of Poulantzas. In addition, he developed an alternative way of understanding the class structures of advanced capitalist society. Wright's revision of Marx was more radical, that is, it went deeper and more to the core, than the work of either Anderson or Poulantzas. Interestingly, after developing this alternative approach during the late 1970s Wright became engaged in a process of self-criticism that led to the rejection of his initial arguments (Wright, 1985).

Wright's first published efforts to reformulate Marx were based on a re-examination of the basis of class (see Wright, 1978). He argued that class membership is primarily determined by three factors: control over investment and resources; control over the actual physical production of commodities; and control over the labour power of others. On the basis of these factors he postulated that there were three major classes in capitalist society: the traditional Marxian bourgeoisie (controls all three factors); the proletariat (controls none of the three); and the petty bourgeoisie (controls some investments/resources and some production but not the labour power of others). What was important about Wright's argument was his contention that between the major classes were smaller classes occupying what he called contradictory class locations: groupings that do not fit into any of the major classes. Wright suggested there were at least three major contradictory class locations.

Between the bourgeoisie and the petty bourgeoisie Wright located a class of small employers. This class position represents those who own enough productive resources to require the hiring of wage labour to operate their enterprises, but whose holdings are not equivalent to that of large-scale capital, which dominates the economy. Small employers represent a distinctive class because they have economic and political interests that are distinct from any of the other major classes, although at certain times and on certain issues they might form alliances with other classes. Small employers form a contradictory class position between the bourgeoisie and the petty bourgeoisie.

Wright suggested that there are two additional contradictory class locations, one between the bourgeoisie (capital) and the working class and the other between the working class and the petty bourgeoisie.

He locates managers, supervisors, and technocrats between capital and the working class. This class position involves control over the actual process of production on a daily basis, but no fundamental control over investment decisions. People in this class do not share exactly any of the features of the other classes and warrant being recognized as a distinctive class. Finally, Wright suggested that people who work sometimes for themselves and sometimes as wage labourers should be understood as occupying a contradictory class location between the petty bourgeoisie and the working class.

Wright has continued to develop his theoretical and empirical understanding of class. The class schema discussed earlier came under significant criticism from a variety of sources including Wright himself. In a subsequent study of class, aptly called *Classes*, Wright engages in serious self-criticism, arguing that the notion of contradictory class positions was in fact flawed because it relied too much on the notion of domination at the expense of an analysis based on exploitation. In *Classes* Wright seeks to rectify his mistake by broadening the Marxian concept of exploitation to include the possibility that exploitation could occur as the result of the ownership of the means of production and of what he calls 'organizational assets and skill credential assets' (1985: 87). When Wright applies this new approach, he concludes that the class divisions in capitalist societies are typically such that there are actually 12 classes. Wright presents his schema in the form of a grid that illustrates the complex division of labour in industrial capitalism. The schema illustrates the manner by which the ownership/ possession of the means of production, organizational assets (authority and power in a hierarchical organization), and skill assets intersect and vary so as to produce a complex class system. His 12 classes include 3 classes who own productive assets (bourgeoisie, small employers, and the petty bourgeoisie), 3 classes of managers (expert managers, semi-credentialled managers, uncredentialled managers), 3 classes of supervisors (expert supervisors, semi-credentialled supervisors, and uncredentialled supervisors) and finally, expert non-managers, semi-credentialled workers, and the proletarians (88). Wright maintains that this new conception of class returns his analysis to the critical Marxian notion of exploitation as the root of the class system (77). It is important to understand that Wright, as a thinker influenced by Marx, works at a variety of levels of abstraction. As a result, the precise nature of the concepts he employs and the nature of these concepts will vary depending on whether he is addressing an abstract general issue or a particular and historical matter. For example, in a recent analysis of the power differential between workers and capitalists he basically uses a two-class model because the object of his analysis and investigation are the relations between these two classes. This does not mean he thinks there are only two classes; it is just that this particular study focuses on these two classes (2000b).

Although the work of Gandy, Anderson, Poulantzas, and Wright represents only a small sample of the positions taken up in the neo-Marxist literature, these few sketches should help to illustrate the nature of the discussion of class within the Marxist tradition. Above all, neo-Marxists understand class in terms of people's positions in society's economic structures and not in terms of stratified positions in a continuum. In addition, the theoretical approach of neo-Marxism also sees class as being systematically related to even larger patterns and processes of domination and subordination.

The Study of Social Inequality in Canada: New Directions in Class Analysis

For the past several decades the study of social inequality in Canada has been an important element in Canadian sociology. A number of scholars have engaged in an analysis of social class in Canada, and their diverse work illustrates the relationship between abstract debate and the actual practice of sociological analysis. Not only have some of these

theorists attempted to further develop the existing approaches, but also in some cases they have worked to synthesize ideas from different perspectives.

John Porter's Vertical Mosaic

In 1965 John Porter's *The Vertical Mosaic: An Analysis of Social Class and Power in Canada* appeared, and the more than 600-page book soon became a classic in Canadian sociology. Its basic approach is more in the tradition of elite theory than class analysis. Porter suggested that the development of capitalism during the twentieth century had changed the nature of the system Marx studied and that, as a result of developments such as institutional specialization, power not property should become the focus of studies of inequality.

Porter argued that we recognize people with power as forming elites and those without power as forming the non-elites (1965: 27). Because the elites form the group with power, they are important factors in shaping and influencing the general development and character of society. Porter used this basic tenet of elite theory to study the major elites he found to be controlling Canadian society. He investigated their family backgrounds, attitudes and values, social connections, education backgrounds, religious affiliations, and ethnic and national backgrounds. His findings proved surprising to many Canadians.

Porter suggested that there are five important elites in Canada: economic, political, bureaucratic, ideological, and labour. These elites represent people in the decision-making or power positions in key institutions in Canada. The economic elite is made up of the major decision-makers in the corporate sector. The political elite is composed of federal cabinet ministers, provincial premiers, and top members of the judiciary in Canada. The bureaucratic elite is composed of the top decision-makers in the federal public service and administrative structures. The ideological elite includes those in control of the mass media, as well as top decision-makers in the educational sector and the major churches. The labour elite is made up of top labour leaders, that is, the heads of major unions and labour federations.

The data that Porter presented illustrate two important facts about these elites. First, with the possible exception of the labour elite, the membership of the various elites is drawn from a narrow sector of the population. In essence, Porter concluded that the majority of elite members were white Anglo-Saxon men with middle-class and upper-class backgrounds. Second, there seems to be a pattern of systematic interaction among elite members—not only with members of their own elite but also with member of other elites. The general picture is of a society dominated and run by a relatively small number of powerful people who have common backgrounds, values, and education and who are not representative of most Canadians.

Porter's work remains extremely important for several reasons, not the least of which is the response it stimulated from other scholars.

Wallace Clement: From Elite Theory to Class Analysis

Exactly 10 years after *The Vertical Mosaic* came out, the results of research that, in part, updated Porter's study were published. In *The Canadian Corporate Elite: An Analysis of Economic Power*, Wallace Clement continued to look at the roles of power and class in Canada, but what was different about Clement's work was his greater focus on the issue of economic power and his use of both class and elite analysis. He examined both those in command or in positions of power in the major corporations in Canada and the role of the media and of the elite that controls the media. Clement noted that economic power was becoming more and more concentrated; as a result the role of the economic elite was becoming more and more important. Clement also discussed the existence of divisions within the economic elite: between the people who controlled Canadian corporations (the indigenous elite) and the ones who controlled branch plants of multinational corporations in Canada (the comprador elite).

Like Porter, Clement found that there is anything but open recruitment into the corporate or economic elite. The elite tends to be drawn from specific class, ethnic, national, religious, and regional backgrounds. There were still important similarities in educational background and continuing interactions at both formal and informal levels. By formal levels of interaction, Clement was referring to the tendency for various elite members to sit on each other's corporate boards of directors.

Clement became one of Canada's most productive scholars. His second book, *Continental Corporate Power* (1977), was dedicated to John and Marion Porter and it studied the economic and corporate linkages between Canada and the United States. Later, in a collection of essays called *The Challenge of Class Analysis* (1988), Clement made it clear that in his opinion some form of class analysis continues to be an essential part of any adequate sociological approach to Canadian society. Clement's approach to class, as shown in these essays, is very much influenced by the neo-Marxist approach. He defined class largely in terms of property, noting that there continue to be two major classes in Canada, capitalists and workers, along with a declining petty bourgeoisie (1988: 171). Clement also noted that within these classes there are fractions or economic divisions, although he said the precise nature of these divisions would only become apparent when researchers engaged in concrete, historical investigation of the dynamics of class in Canada.

Similarly, the argument that the Marxian legacy is still the most appropriate approach to class analysis continues to inform the work of a number of other Canadian scholars, although not all of them explicitly adopt a Marxian framework.

The Canadian Class Structure: Forcese and Veltmeyer

The fact that Dennis Forcese's *The Canadian Class Structure* has been updated several times since its original publication in 1975 attests to its importance and acceptance by Canadian social scientists. Forcese argues that social inequality is a fundamental fact of life in Canada, although he does not explicitly spell out what theoretical approach he thinks is most appropriate. His analysis is that social class has to do with wealth, prestige, and power—and the resources those elements command (1975: 13). He notes that measuring social class is a difficult task, but that wealth seems to be the key factor (15). Wealth, he further argues, is tied to occupation and property; but because meaningful class analysis must take place at the micro level, we must also take into account local dimensions, city/farm relations, regionalism, ethnicity, and gender.

Forcese demonstrates that the reality of class is manifested in issues as diverse as the level of our health care, our daily quality of life, how we are affected by the processes of crime and the operation of the justice system, and our quality of living or working conditions as well as our religious and political attitudes and level of education. Forcese suggests that a Marxian approach is a good point of departure; but by presenting a wealth of important data he also illustrates the complexity of class, warning us not to adopt a simple abstract schema. His book reminds us that class analysis is ultimately about the real world and therefore must proceed on the basis of an approach that is capable of recognizing the complexities of that world. The latest edition (1997) of this Canadian classic contains the following statement of the reality of class and why it is important that we, as sociologists, understand it:

> Classes, therefore, are aggregates of persons distinguished in the first instance by inherited relations to wealth or income. Power and educational achievement are factors that may reinforce or modify such wealth. In large part, inherited wealth or property and occupation are crucial to a person's class and the class membership of a dependent. But class origins can be transcended. Classes are not formally demarcated, and the boundaries are fluid. But they do represent distinctive shared or common positions of relative privilege, and that privilege is in large measure inherited, whether directly as wealth or indirectly as opportunity to acquire wealth. Especially to the degree that such aggregated individuals are conscious of their common positions, even as the classes are not formalized, they constitute social classes. (1997: 20–1).

While Forcese tends to use, but not elaborate on, the theoretical boundaries of a Marxian approach, Henry Veltmeyer explicitly attempts to present a systematic neo-Marxist approach to social class. In *Canadian Class Structure* (1986) Veltmeyer presents a systematic revision of Marx, arguing that class position is determined by whether a person, first, owns property or the means of production, second, sells labour power, and, third, controls the labour power of others. A fourth determinant is a person's source of livelihood (1986: 16). On the basis of these economic criteria Veltmeyer suggests that there are three major economic classes: the bourgeoisie or capitalist class, the petty bourgeoisie or middle class, and the proletariat or working class (21). In addition, he suggests that we must recognize the existence of internal class sectors or subclasses. In Canada this means dividing the bourgeoisie into the monopoly and lieutenant sectors and the petty bourgeoisie into the small business, independent producer, managerial, and professional sectors. Finally, the working class can be divided into the semi-professional, office, service, and productive sectors (25).

In addition to these major classes, which are defined primarily by economic criteria, Veltmeyer notes that some members of the working class, such as older and younger workers, are often not in the labour force at particular moments. As well, there is a major marginalized class called, in Marxian fashion, the lumpenproletariat. This group is made up of those more or less permanently out of the labour force, on relief, and otherwise destitute.

SOCIAL STRATIFICATION OR SOCIAL CLASS

Social inequality is a fundamental issue that demarcates the differences between structural functionalism and neo-Marxism. At its most simple level, the issue is one of stratification versus class analysis. According to stratification theory, one's position along or in a continuum is determined by the nature of one's occupation. Class analysis, on the other hand, holds that it is one's structural position in the society's productive institutions that determines one's share of the social surplus and therefore one's class.

Stratification Theory

Kingsley Davis and Wilbert E. Moore's original essay, 'Some Principles of Stratification', remains a classic statement of the functionalist position. This excerpt is drawn from a section titled 'The Functional Necessity of Stratification'.

Functional Inevitability of Stratification

Curiously, however, the main functional necessity explaining the universal presence of stratification is precisely the requirement faced by any society of placing and motivating individuals in the social structure. As a functioning mechanism a society must somehow distribute its members in social positions and induce them to perform the duties of these positions. It must thus concern itself with motivation at two different levels: to instill in the proper individuals the desire to fill certain positions, and, once in these positions, the desire to perform the duties attached to them. Even though the social order may be relatively static in form, there is a continuous process of metabolism as new individuals are born into it, shift with age, and die off. Their absorption into the positional system must somehow be arranged and motivated. This is true whether the system is competitive or non-competitive. A competitive system gives greater importance to the motivation to achieve positions, whereas a non-competitive system gives perhaps greater importance to the motivation to perform the duties of the positions; but in any system both types of motivation are required.

If the duties associated with the various positions were all equally pleasant to the human organism, all equally important to societal survival, and all equally in need of the same ability or talent, it would make no difference who got into which positions, and the problem of social placement would be greatly reduced. But actually it does make a great deal of difference who gets into which positions, not only because some positions are inherently more agreeable than others, but also because some require special talents or training and some are functionally more important than others. Also, it is essential that the duties of the positions be performed with the diligence that their importance requires. Inevitably, then, a society must have, first, some kind of rewards that it can use as inducements, and, second, some way of distributing these rewards differentially according to positions. The rewards and their distribution become a part of the social order, and thus give rise to stratification.

One may ask what kind of rewards a society has at its disposal in distributing its personnel and securing essential services. It has, first of all, the things that contribute to sustenance and comfort. It has, second, the things that contribute to humor and diversion. And it has, finally, the things that contribute to self-respect and ego expansion. The last, because of the peculiarly social character of the self, is largely a function of the opinion of others, but it nonetheless ranks in importance with the first two. In any social system all three kinds of rewards must be dispensed differentially according to positions.

In a sense the rewards are 'built into' the position. They consist in the 'rights' associated with the position, plus what may be called its accompaniments or perquisites. Often the rights, and sometimes the accompaniments, are functionally related to the duties of the position. (Rights as viewed by the incumbent are usually duties as viewed by other members of the community.) However, there may be a host of subsidiary rights and perquisites that are not essential to the function of the position and have

only an indirect and symbolic connection with its duties, but which still may be of considerable importance in inducing people to seek the positions and fulfil the essential duties.

If the rights and perquisites of different positions in a society must be unequal, then the society must be stratified, because that is precisely what stratification means. Social inequality is thus an unconsciously evolved device by which societies insure that the most important positions are conscientiously filled by the most qualified persons. Hence every society, no matter how simple or complex, must differentiate persons in terms of both prestige and esteem, and must therefore possess a certain amount of institutionalized inequality.

From Kingsley Davis and Wilbert E. Moore, 'Some Principles of Stratification' in Kurt Finsterbusch and Janet Schwartz, eds, *Sources: Notable Selections in Sociology* (Guilford, CT: The Dushkin Publishing Group, [1945] 1993).

COUNTERPOINT: NEO-MARXIAN CLASS ANALYSIS

In *Canadian Class Structure,* Henry Veltmeyer offers an overview of the main theoretical elements of a neo-Marxian approach to class. Note the emphasis on structural location and social relations as opposed to the characteristics of one's job. Veltmeyer's first chapter is titled 'The Structure of Class'.

Structural Position and Claiming the Wealth

This approach to analysis is not without controversy. Some critics, even some who are Marxist-oriented, object to treating class as something that can be analysed in its own terms without reference to lived experience. They fear that objectifying the economic structure of class relations may lead analysts to ignore or miss the political dimension of class struggle. On the other hand,

Marxists who take a structuralist position insist that classes exist and must always be understood in terms of their relations to other classes. In the organisation of production, people enter into relations under conditions that they do not choose; with reference to these conditions, it is useful to treat individuals as supports of an underlying structure rather than as free agents.

After discussing the concepts of capital, labour, and land and their roles in understanding material production, Veltmeyer explains how class is linked to material production.

What is produced and the details of doing so vary from society to society but the need for all three factors does not. Neither does the presence of two other important factors that Marx pinpointed: (1) the *forces of production,* the physical and social technology a society uses in economic activity; and (2) the *relations of production,* the social organization for this activity. The two combine to form the society's *mode of production (13).*

The key to the capitalist system is that its mode of production permits—in fact, is based on—the *exchange of labour–power for a wage.* Thus the mode of production defines a capitalist system's two basic classes: the *bourgeoisie,* who own (or control) land and capital, and the *proletariat or working class,* who have only their labour-power.

   Given that Marxists also posit inherent social struggle for the possession of wealth, this class structure is intrinsically rife with conflict and inequity. Except in a frontier setting. The

proletariat have no access to the land and capital necessary to produce anything. The only way they can obtain subsistence is to sell their labour-power, and thus they become exploited, oppressed, and alienated. Some definitions and distinctions are in order here. A basic concept is that of *surplus value,* which rests on the difference between something's value in use and its value in exchange *(14).*

Understanding the concept of surplus value is essential to understanding *exploitation,* which can be defined as the difference between the amount of wealth or surplus value provided by workers and the amount of wealth returned to them in the form of wages. For example, a worker who produces $50.00 worth of goods or services per hour and is paid $10.00 per hour is more exploited than a worker who produces $10.00 worth of goods per hour and is paid $4.25 per hour *(15).*

Abridged from Henry Veltmeyer, *Canadian Class Structure* Garamond Press, Toronto, 1986. Reprinted with permission of Garamond Press.

Throughout his book Veltmeyer makes clear that for him the real purpose of class analysis is to assist in the process of understanding and explaining the dynamics of Canadian society. He indicates that a correct analysis of economic classes can form an important part of how we come to understand the real lives of real people (1986: 107).

Towards a Synthesis: Hunter and Grabb

Alfred A. Hunter's *Class Tells: On Social Inequality in Canada* (1981) illustrates an important direction for class analysis in Canada. The book outlines the major competing theoretical perspectives in the areas of class and stratification analysis. It also presents a

massive amount of empirical data on economic, gender, and ethnic inequality in Canada. By examining issues such as the role of merit in determining income level and the relationship between inequality and education, Hunter demonstrates how social inequality influences virtually every dimension of our lives. The book also contains an overview of the historical emergence of class in Canada and the relationship between class and political activities.

   As the title implies, one of Hunter's major points is the fact that class does indeed tell, that is, it influences virtually every aspect of our being. Although Hunter summarizes the major perspectives, he does not overtly embrace or adopt either a

Marxian or structural functionalist approach; but in his conclusion, having demonstrated the importance and persuasiveness of structured inequality, he does use some concepts usually associated with the neo-Marxist perspective. He reminds us that structured inequality is a dynamic and changing phenomenon and that the historical record shows that some classes come into being while others fade away and become less important. Hunter's study implies that no matter what approach we use, we must be capable of dealing with the complexities of economic, gender, and ethnic inequalities.

One of the most ambitious attempts to develop a fresh approach to the study of social inequality is found in the work of Edward Grabb. In *Theories of Social Inequality* (1990) Grabb presents a systematic overview of various classical and contemporary perspectives. After introducing students of society to these debates Grabb argues that the study of economic inequality must be integrated with an analysis of power and domination. He suggests that once we do this we will realize that control over economic matters is but one aspect of inequality. In addition to economic power and control, we must account for political power and domination as well as ideological power and domination. Grabb does not argue for a three-dimensional system, as in orthodox functionalism; it is clear that he is interested in the phenomenon of social domination and power as it unfolds through a class system in a capitalist society that is, at its core, based on three classes. For Grabb the three classes are the upper class, a heterogeneous middle class, and a working class, although he does not provide a detailed account of the basis of his class positions. Grabb ends his book by reminding us of the importance of moving beyond economic analysis to understanding the nature of gender inequalities as well as other structured inequalities that are related to ethnic and national considerations.

Can Class Analysis Be Salvaged?

'Can Class Analysis Be Salvaged?' was the title of a provocative article written by David Grusky and Jesper Sørensen in 1998. The article postulates that there has been a retreat from class analysis, and their stated aim is to 'rebuild it in ways that may usefully direct future research' (1188). According to Grusky and Sørensen, those still engaged in some form of class analysis operate within one of three general approaches. The first eschews traditional notions of class and uses other measures of cleavage in society such as educational levels, organizations affiliation or even employment sector (public vs. private). The second approach they identify with a kind of postmodernist analysis that sees various new social movements such as feminism or environmentalism replacing traditional class-based social movements. The last approach, the one they identify with their position, seeks to renew and reinvigorate class (1188–9). The type of class analysis they ultimately propose involves what they refer to as 'ratcheting down' the units of analysis from very general aggregates of people, such as E.O. Wright employs, to much finer units of analysis based on occupation (1191–2). In the final analysis the article does not attempt to paint a picture of the class structure but instead it offers some methodological and theoretical advice as to what units of analysis we should examine when we study class. They argue that by disaggregating occupations one can begin to understand the real issues that class analysis should draw our attention to, namely, attitudes, behaviours, and lifestyles (1223).

Sørensen and Wright are the primary participants in an ongoing debate about class analysis. In a 'Symposium on Class Analysis' recently published in the *American Journal of Sociology* each presents their case for a particular mode of class analysis. Sørensen makes a clear distinction between those conceptions of class that are based on the idea that class is really about exploitation as opposed to those who claim that it is mostly about different life conditions (2000a: 1525). Sørensen then reviews various positions on class and argues that a reformulated concept of rent is the most appropriate tool for understanding the dynamics of income distribution in advanced capitalist society. Sørensen's notion of rent involved an abandonment of the labour theory of value and thus the traditional Marxian conception of exploitation; however, it retains the notion that 'class concepts should be based on property rights to assets and resources that generate economic benefits' (1553). In his rejoinder Wright agrees that it is possible to understand exploitation without accepting the labour theory of value but he disagrees with Sørensen's notion of rent. Wright argues that exploitation occurs when three conditions are satisfied. The first is that the material benefits of the exploiter depend on the exploited getting less. Second, the exploited are excluded from some benefits that accrue to the exploiter. Thirdly, there is some appropriation of the 'labour effort of the exploited' (1563).

It is not important that the reader fully come to grips with the technicalities of the Sørensen–Wright debate on rents and their calculations. What is important is the fact that the debate is open, vibrant, and ongoing. What is important is that the reader accepts the challenges of these various ideas and attempts to arrive at an appropriate understanding of class that is theoretically sound and empirically supportable.

A New Issue: Globalization and Class

As we all know from our exposure to the mass media, politicians, or business leaders, we live in a global era. The issue of how class relations express themselves across international boundaries has been of interest to sociologists for some time. Although Wallace Clement's *Continental Corporate Power* (1977) was not the first analysis of the impact of American economic power on Canadian society and the Canadian class structure, it remains one of the most systematic examinations of the relationships between the business elite in Canada and the United States. A more recent study by Joseph Roberts concludes that the Canadian capitalist class is made up of two major fractions, one composed of domestic or Canadian capitalists, the other repre-

senting foreign interests (1998: 42). Robert Brym offers a different interpretation of the importance of the position of foreign capitalists in the overall structure of the Canadian capitalist class. Brym notes that there is significant empirical evidence presented by William Carroll (1982) that suggests, although there is considerable foreign investment in Canada, there is a powerful domestic ruling class (Brym, 1993: 36). Edward Grabb also addressed the issue noting that there is a strong intellectual tradition in Canada that focuses on the high level of foreign investment, but he too notes that it was decreasing during the past quarter century (1993: 12).

A new perspective on the issue of international class relations is a recent essay by William Robinson and Jerry Harris entitled 'Towards a Global Ruling Class: Globalization and the Transnational Ruling Class' (2000). In the essay, Robinson and Harris argue that a transnational ruling class has emerged in recent years. They claim that this class is composed of owners of major transnational and financial institutions and 'elites that manage supranational economic planning agencies, major forces in dominant political parties, media conglomerates and technocratic elites and state managers in both North and South' (12). As can be seen, the essay does not contain a particularly focused or adequate theoretical conception for what constitutes class membership. It would seem not to have anything to do with patterns of ownership and control. The notion of class as defined by lifestyle is not here. Despite the apparent lack of theoretical rigour to their argument, perhaps there is an issue worthy of investigation here?

Towards an Alternative Materialist Approach

If we assume that the most appropriate mode of analysis for understanding the class structures of our society is one that directs our attention to the economic structures, it makes sense to look to both Marx and Weber for insights into how to conceptualize and understand class. In recent years two important groups of authors have attempted to use both Marx and Weber as the basis for an understanding of class in capitalist society (Bilton et al., 1987; Clegg, Boreham, and Dow, 1986).

The class structure of capitalist society is understandable in terms of the organization of material production and distribution. A central characteristic of capitalist economic structures is the role of the market in the distribution of wealth. People's claim to a share of society's wealth is fundamentally determined by their positions within the structures of the market. Their positions within the structures of the market in turn depend on the resources they bring to the market. Some people come to the market in possession of wealth and capital, and as a result they become the owners of the major productive resources of society. Such people can be designated as the corporate ruling or upper class (Bilton et al., 1987: 55; Clegg, Boreham, and Dow, 1986: Chapter 5). This class enjoys economic power and is able to accumulate the major share of the social surplus. Although there can be important divisions within the ranks of this class—between, for example, those who control the banking sector and those who dominate the manufacturing sector—we cannot specify the nature of such divisions except by examining a specific society.

The other major class that shares in the ownership of society's productive capacities is the petty bourgeoisie. According to Stewart Clegg and his co-authors, it is more useful to distinguish the petty bourgeoisie from the corporate ruling class by the scale of operation involved than by the strict Marxian distinction between those who employ and those who do not employ labour. Clegg, Boreham, and Dow suggest that the petty bourgeoisie can be best understood as those employing fewer than 10 employees, arguing that such a number indicates a scale of enterprise that results in a different capacity to claim social surplus and thus accumulate wealth.

In addition to the corporate ruling or upper class and the petty bourgeoisie, there is the new

middle class. Clegg, Boreham, and Dow suggest that this is a heterogeneous class made up of numerous different occupational positions. The common thread is that all these structural positions tend to help the corporate ruling class or some sections of the petty bourgeoisie realize or claim their portion of the social surplus. In addition, the middle class facilitates the reproduction of the conditions necessary for continued social stability. Tony Bilton and his co-authors note the existence of a middle class broadly made up of those who bring non-manual skills to the market. As a result, these people are in a position to claim greater economic rewards than those who bring manual skills to the market; they can thereby increase their chances of claiming economic benefits.

Both the Clegg and Bilton books note that in capitalist society one of the largest classes is the working class. In the abstract, Clegg, Boreham, and Dow refer to the working class as the sellers of labour power who produce the economic wealth in society. According to Bilton and his co-authors, the working class is made up of non-owners of wealth who bring mostly manual skills to the market. Again, both books agree that there will be internal splits and differences based on factors such as the level of skills and the specific occupation, but all such splits and internal divisions must be examined within the context of a particular society.

What these scholars are attempting to do is provide a conceptual map or guide to assist in the understanding of class in modern capitalist society. The precise nature of the classes—their internal divisions, histories, patterns of development, and relationships with each other and the state—is a central issue that must be addressed. But this central issue has to be addressed in the context of an analysis of a specific society.

In the end these conceptions of class structure will prove to be useful only if we can apply them to the concrete investigation of class formation and struggle in a particular society. After all, the final test of the adequacy of any theoretical construction is its usefulness in facilitating empirical and historical analysis. We must always ask ourselves: to what extent does this theory help us make sense of the complexities of class in our society? The challenge for students, then, is to take these ideas and apply them to the study of class in their own society.

Critical Thinking Questions

- Discuss two possible explanations for the fact that, in capitalist society, typically some people are rich and some are poor.
- Is North America a socially stratified or a class-divided society? What is the difference?
- Is there class-based exploitation in North America? Explain your answer.
- What bearing does one's class position have on one's life chances?
- What is your class position? Explain the basis of your answer in sociological terms.

Terms and Concepts

Stratification theory—associated with the functionalist perspective, assumes that individuals in society are layered or arranged in strata. According to the stratification theorists, there are three quite distinct dimensions of the stratification system: class, status, and power.

Class—based largely on income (amount or source), a category of people who share similar economic characteristics. The relationship between different classes is usually understood in terms of a layering situation in which one class has more income and is placed higher in a hierarchy while another class has less income and is ranked lower. There is no implied antagonistic relationship between and among classes. The terms *lower, middle, upper-middle, upper*, and so on are typically used.

Status—perhaps more appropriately called social prestige or honour; not necessarily related to class, although it is often associated with an occupation. Surveys have shown that people rank some occupations with quite low incomes as more prestigious and carrying more social honour, and therefore as more desirable than others with higher incomes.

Members of the clergy are typically cited as examples of people with high status but low incomes.

Power—when viewed at the individual level, power is associated with a person's position in a particular institution. To function properly, many institutions contain a division of labour, and not all positions within the institution contain equal amounts of authority and power. Some people will accept a position because of the power and authority it carries.

Surplus value—in Marxian theory, the difference between the total costs of producing a commodity and the amount that the capitalist gets for the commodity. If the total costs (including labour costs, raw materials, depreciation on machinery, and factory costs) of producing a car were $10,000 and the company producing the car sold it for $12,000, the difference ($2,000) is the surplus value. According to the Marxian perspective, because this wealth was produced by the workers who actually made the car but goes to the owners of the company, the appropriation of this surplus wealth is the basis of class exploitation.

Exploitation—used to describe the process by which the owning or capitalist class appropriates wealth produced by the working class. According to the Marxian perspective, the real producers of wealth are those who actually engage in productive activities in the mines, mills, and factories. It is the labour power of the working class that produces the commodities; however, the workers receive only a portion of the wealth they produce in the form of wages, while the difference between the total costs of production and the amount the capitalists get for the commodity (surplus value) is appropriated by capital. The appropriation of surplus value is the basis of class exploitation.

Capitalist class—usually associated with Marxian class analysis; those who, in a capitalist society, own and control the society's productive and distributive resources, that is, the factories, mills, mines, as well as the financial and distributive capacities. Other terms are also used, including *bourgeoisie*, *capital*, and *owning class*.

Working class—as opposed to the capitalist class, the term used within Marxian theory to refer to those who do not own and control any productive and distributive resources within capitalist society. In order to make a living the working class, or proletariat, is forced to sell its labour power, and within the productive process these workers end up being both alienated and exploited. In Marx's view the proletariat was the class with an interest in radical social change and thus in ending the exploitation and alienation inherent in the capitalist relations of production.

Fraction—originally used by Marx in the context of class analysis: an internal division within a major class based on some economic criterion. For example, the bourgeoisie might be subdivided into an industrial fraction (ownership of major industrial enterprises), a resource-capital fraction (major investors in resource and extractive industries), a financial fraction (banking, insurance, and financial services), and a commercial fraction (both wholesale and retail businesses). Similarly, the petty bourgeoisie and the capitalist class might be internally divided.

Petty (or petite) bourgeoisie—along with the capitalist class and the working class, the third major class in a classical Marxian class schema. The petty bourgeoisie are owners of some productive resources, but unlike the capitalist class the resources they own are so small that they tend not to require hired labour to operate them. Unlike the working class the petty bourgeoisie do not sell their labour power. The classical example of the petty bourgeoisie is farmers who own the productive resources and produce goods with their own and unpaid family labour.

Lumpenproletariat—as used by Marx, those people who are in a sense outside the normal productive arrangements in society. Made up of people without regular incomes who live off crime or by begging, or by wandering about with no systematic role in society. The political role of the lumpenproletariat was worrisome to Marx because they could not be counted on by the proletariat to assist in ending class rule, alienation, and exploitation in capitalist society.

Related Web Sites

http://www.statcan.ca/english/freepub/
11-516-XIE/sectiona/toc.htm
    Statistics Canada is the primary data source for information on almost every aspect and dimen-

sion of Canadian society. This massive link includes access to various indicators of class and/or stratification and other dimensions of inequality in Canada.

http://www.inequality.org/whowearefr.html

This is the starting point that can lead you to a rich data set dealing with income distribution and inequality in the United States. Links provide data and graphs on individual and household incomes and much more. There are also reading lists and other resources to use in your investigation and explanation of the social inequality in the United States.

http://www.policyalternatives.ca/

This is the Web page for the Canadian Centre for Policy Alternatives. The centre conducts social policy related research and engages in what one might term 'left of centre' analyses of important issues in Canadian society. Many of the centre's publications deal with the social implications of inequality.

http://www2.fmg.uva.nl/sociosite/topics/inequality.html

Dr Albert Benschop (Social & Behavioral Sciences/Media Studies, University of Amsterdam) maintains this site under the 'Sociosite'. The specific site noted above is called 'Social Inequality and Classes' and contains many links that provide empirical and theoretical information and analysis on an international scale.

http://www.aber.ac.uk/media/Sections/gender.html

To assist with your comparative studies, we include this British 'Media and Communications Studies' site. Links to 'Ethnicity', 'Gender', 'Representation', 'Social and Personal Identity', as well as 'Social Class' allow you to develop a comprehensive sense of the impact of inequalities.

Suggested Further Readings

Curtis, J., E. Grabb, and N. Guppy, eds. 1994. *Social Inequality in Canada*. Scarborough, ON: Prentice-Hall. This collection of theoretical and empirical essays approaches the issue of social inequality across a number of dimensions including class, education, age, ethnicity, and occupation. A valuable concluding section deals with the implications of inequality.

Grabb, E. 1998. *Theories of Social Inequality*, 3rd edn. Toronto: Harcourt Brace. This remains one of the very best overviews of various theories of class from Marx to the most contemporary contribution. The reader comes away knowing a lot more about sociological theory in general.

Nakhaie, M.R. 2000. *Debates on Social Inequality*. Toronto: Harcourt Brace. This edited collection of point–counterpoint essays deals with a variety of dimensions of social inequality as related to issues such as class, gender, and ethnicity.

Sørensen, J., and E.O. Wright. 2000. Contributions to the 'Symposium on Class Analysis', *American Journal of Sociology* 105 (6) (May). This detailed and sometimes technical exchange focuses on the notion of class exploitation. Sørensen argues for a modified concept of rent while Wright disagrees, offering to defend a more Marxian notion of exploitation.

CHAPTER 10

Sociology of Mass Communications

If there is one common experience we can assume every reader of this book has had, it is exposure to what is commonly referred to as the mass media. Even if you claim to never watch television, the fact that you are conscious enough to be reading this book means that you have heard a radio, glanced at a magazine, seen a billboard, or read at least one story in a newspaper. Given that exposure to some aspect of mass communication—the business of the 'mass media'—is an evitable experience in modern society, undertaking a sociological analysis of these experiences is obviously a worthwhile and important endeavour.

Before we can think systematically about the so-called mass media, we must clearly understand what the concept means. A useful point of departure might be a review of some common definitions. An online encyclopaedia, WorldiQ.com, provides the following definition: 'The mass media is the whole body of media reaching large numbers of the public via radio, television, movies, magazines, newspapers, and the World Wide Web. The term was coined in the 1920s with the advent of nationwide radio networks, mass-circulation newspapers, and magazines.' While this is a good start that includes a historical note, it is limited to identifying specific modes of communicating messages. The National Public Radio outlet in Northern California, KQED, maintains a Media Literacy site that goes one step further:

Any form of communication produced by a few people for the consumption by many people. Mass media are channels of communication through which messages flow. As the messages go through the channels, they are distorted. When people receive media messages they have no opportunity for immediate feedback with the producers of the messages.

The *Concise Oxford Dictionary of Sociology* introduces the sociology of the mass media with the following statement: 'A medium is a means of communication such as print, radio, or television. The mass media are defined as large-scale organizations that use one or more of these technologies to communicate with large numbers of people ("mass communication")' (Marshall, 1994: 313). It would probably be appropriate to extend the definition to include recorded material such as compact discs, various forms of advertising billboards, as well as video and other electronic games.

To complicate the definitions even further they all introduce an associated concept—communications. Indeed, communication has increasingly become a central concept in the analysis of the media as the title of a popular book, *Mass Communication in Canada* (2001) by Rowland Lorimer and Mike Casher illustrates. In this book they suggest an approach that will be adopted here.

As the title implies, rather than focusing on the medium or media they focus on the social process of communication. The study of the particular medium or various media is subsumed under the broader study of the social process of communication. So, while the media—the actual channels or conduits for passing on the messages—is mass communications, it is the processes it entails that are of primary interest to the sociologist.

We should note that such an emphasis does not negate the importance or the impact of new technologies. Indeed, most students of the mass media will be familiar with the work of one of Canada's best-known scholars in the field—Marshall McLuhan. McLuhan is famous for his oft quoted statement: 'This fact merely underlies the point that "the medium is the message" because it is the medium that shapes and controls the shape and form of human association and action' (1965: 9). While the precise meaning of the phrase 'the medium is the message' is open to interpretation, one plausible meaning is that the content may be less important than the medium through which that content in carried. Stanley Baran (1999) suggests that McLuhan is pointing out that if a family is watching television during dinner the fact that the TV is on and, thus, influencing conversations and interactions, is more important than the actual content of the program being watched (446). As Baran noted, McLuhan made a distinction between media technologies that are 'hot' and 'cool', or, how media 'provide a lot of information, leaving the consumer with little to do other than interpret what is presented. Cool media, in contrast, require the consumer to "fill in the blanks" to make meaning' (Baran, 1999: 446). Television is considered cool while newspapers are hot. As noted, the approaches we will examine in this chapter tend to focus on the content more than the technology; however the insights of McLuhan need to be kept in mind.

Lorimer and Casher are among those focusing on the content and its production and presentation. They define mass communications in two ways: '(1)

practice and product of providing leisure entertainment and information to an unknown audience by means of corporately financed, industrially produced, state regulated, high-technology, privately consumed commodities in the modern print, screen, audio, and broadcast media; (2) communication to large audiences' (2001: 332). The authors treat the mass media as a 'subset' of their analysis. They follow a pattern found in the work of Denis McQuail who identified the mass media as a set of distinct *activities* that use specific *institutionally organized technologies* governed by certain *rules and laws* and operated by *individuals in defined roles* who convey '*information, entertainment, images and symbols*' to a *mass audience* (quoted in Lorimer and Casher: 38). These definitions would have us approach the study of the media by focusing on the patterns of social action and institutional activity that result in the production and transmission of messages and on the nature of those messages and their possible impact on the audiences who consume or receive them. This seems like a useful approach to follow and so we will use it to try to make some sense out of these various aspects of the mass media.

What, then, are some forms of communication that the sociology of mass communications might study? Some—such as television radio, movies, audio and video recordings of all types, and the print media (newspapers, magazines, books, etc.)— are obvious; however, others might not typically be considered mass communications: the internet, video games, and billboards. While we might take the presence of these forms of mass communications for granted, it is important that we step back and think systematically about the fact that these various modes of communication convey virtually unfathomable quantities of information, entertainment, representations, images, and even emotions and sentiments. If we pause to take notice of the omnipresence of various forms of mass communication in our lives, we might actually be led to begin to think more critically about the potential social roles and impacts. Let us start by first briefly considering the history of the mass media, and then the actual magnitude of the presence of mass communications.

Historical Overview of Mass Communications

While a history of the mass media is well beyond the limits of this chapter, a brief look at the history and development of mass communications is in order and in keeping with the overall project of developing our sociological imagination. While one could go back to pre-industrial societies and begin with the invention of writing and paper, our approach will focus on relatively more recent times.

Johannes Gutenberg is typically credited with the invention of the printing press in the mid 1400s. The importance of this development was that, for the first time, written materials could be mass-produced, as opposed to being hand written one copy at a time. Among the first mass circulation documents produced was Gutenberg's Bible. Gutenberg's technology was obviously necessary for what then followed—the mass production of a variety of literary materials in the form of pamphlets and news broadsheets. These broadsheets carried a range of news, including sensational accounts of the activities of Count Dracula! The first newspaper seems to have appeared in England in the late 1600s and the first North American paper was in Boston in 1690. As literacy rates increased there was a virtual explosion in the number and type of newspapers on both sides of the ocean. The first newspaper in Canada seems to have been the *Halifax Gazette,* which first published on 2 March 1752 (Kesterton, 1983: 3). The subsequent growth and transformation of the newspaper industry has been well documented by others (Hall, 2001; Kesterton, 1983; McPhail and McPhail, 1990; Vivian and Maurin, 2000; and Lorimer and Gasher, 2001). What one should particularly note is the persistent debate over the last few decades about the growing concentration and centralization of holdings and control a small number of large corporations have over the print media.

The ownership structure of the newspaper industry today seems to reflect a pattern characteristic of many industries in an advanced capitalist society. As technology develops and market competition takes its toll, a trend of fewer and fewer, though larger and larger, companies can be traced. It is important to note that this is not a new trend. As early as 1970 the Canadian Government was concerned enough to establish a Special Senate Committee to investigate the industry. The Committee's Report (the Davey Report) was followed by a full Royal Commission on Newspapers (the Kent Commission). While each Report recommended a range of actions to ensure ownership of this medium did not become too concentrated, no systematic action has been taken to stem the tide of concentrated corporate ownership and control (Romanow and Soderlund, 1992: 105–14, 263–70). As David Hall notes, the number of daily newspapers has steadily declined over the past century while the concentration of ownership has reached a point where over three-quarters of Canadian daily newspapers are produced by four companies: Southam, Thompson, Sun Media, and Hollinger (2001: 14). Tracing the intricate patterns of ownership and control in the newspaper industry is virtually a full-time job: announcements of acquisitions, stock trades, and divestitures are an almost daily occurrence. Our only recourse is to advise the reader to use the Internet to investigate the actual extent of the holdings of the organizations.

Other forms of mass communications have equally fascinating histories. The electrical technology that eventually produced radio dates back almost two centuries to the earlier work done in the 1840s with both electrical impulses that produced telegraph messages and a transatlantic cable. Before the turn of the twentieth century radio waves were being used to transmit messages—a technology that the American navy found interesting. Eric Barnouw's *Tube of Plenty: The Evolution of American*

Television is a nearly definitive source that documents the interaction of individuals, corporations, the military, and the government in the development of both the radio and television industries. While the first radio stations were actually run by the companies that manufactured radios—if there were no messages there was no reason to buy a radio—the potential of commercial radio was soon apparent, and the rest, one might say, is history (see also Baran, 1999).

The history of radio in Canada dates to the immediate post-First World War period when a station was started in Montreal. Newspapers soon followed and set up self-promotion stations, however, owing to British influence, the subsequent history of radio in Canada took a different path from that in the United Stated. In Canada there was a significant debate about whether the 'air waves' were the realm of unfettered private enterprise or whether they were a public resource to be developed in the public interest. There are dozens of books on this matter—a online listing can be seen on the Ontario DX Association's home page at http://www.odxa.on.ca/archives/timelinebooks.html—but for our purposes the important point is that the industry did, in fact, unfold differently in Canada where a much more active and government-present regulator—in the form of the Canadian Broadcasting Corporation—eventually emerged (Hall, 2001; Kesterton, 1983; Hall and Siegal, 1983; Boyle, 1983).

The history of television, as Barnouw notes, is different in terms of the technology but not in terms of the players: corporate advertisers and production companies exist for both programs and hardware. A similar historical pattern of growth from small independent enterprises to multinational conglomerates can also be traced in the other major areas of mass communications—movies, music recording, and magazines.

So what do we know about the sources of the messages we noticed above? Although it is not universal, the overwhelming pattern is mass media integration with large corporations increasingly owning and controlling a variety of different forms of mass communication at every level, from production to distribution to public sale. What precisely this means to the average citizen is not immediately apparent because an analysis of the meaning of these developments and the messages alluded to above requires a framework. As we have seen in the preceding chapters, in sociology such an analytical framework involves the utilization of social theory.

The Omnipresence of Mass Communications

In 2001, 99.2 per cent of Canadian homes had a colour television, 68 per cent had cable television, and 92 per cent had a video player. Canadians over two years of age watched an average of 21.6 hours of television per week in 2003. Statistics Canada surveyed Canadians on their use of time in 1998 and found that other mass media-related activities were also significant: 82 per cent of respondents reported they read a newspaper, 71 per cent read magazines, and 61 per cent read books. Nearly 60 per cent attended movies, 73 per cent watched movies on video, 77 per cent listened to recorded music. The statistics continue to point to the extent of our exposure as a society to mass media. According to Newspaper Audience Databank Inc., Canadian adults spent 47 minutes a day, during the week, reading newspapers and 88 minutes on weekends. They also report that, during a given week, about 80 per cent of Canadians report reading a paper. Media use is even more significant in the United States where the US Census Bureau projects that in 2004, for those 18 and over, the average number of hours per year spent watching television, listening to the radio, reading newspapers, books and magazines, watching movies, surfing the Internet, and playing video games will reach 3,715—over 71 hours a week.

The importance of video games over the past decade has resulted in some researchers turning their attention to study this dimension of mass communications in greater detail. In 2003 the University of

Michigan conducted a study of video game usage among students in grades five, eight, and eleven in Michigan and Indiana. Students in grade eight played the most, averaging about 23 hours a week for males compared to 12 hours for females. The survey also considered college-aged males, who averaged about 16 hours a week (Greenberg, 2003).

Does It Matter?

While these numbers may surprise some, for a sociologist they are only an illustration of a social process that requires further analysis in order to supply an acceptable explanation. Among the most important questions: 'So what?' What impact does all this exposure to mass communications have on individuals and on society as a whole? Questions regarding the impact and implications of what Todd Gitlin calls 'the ever-present torrent' and the 'swarming enormity of popular culture' (9) will depend somewhat on the subfield one is engaged in studying. If you were to consider the subfields mentioned in Chapter 1, it is clear that mass communication, as an ever-present phenomenon will impact virtually every field of sociological study. We referred to some of these impacts in the discussion of agents of socialization in Chapter 4; however, it is necessary to consider the potential role of mass communication as an agent of socialization more fully.

A lively debate has emerged—beginning in the 1950s and lasting several decades—around the impact of television and movies on human behaviour, including violence. John Murray reviewed the many sides of this debate in an article titled 'The Impact of Televised Violence'. He notes that in the United States there have been almost continuous congressional hearings on the issue and a series of reports including:

National Commission on the Causes and Prevention of Violence; Surgeon General's Scientific Advisory Committee on Television and Social Behavior; the report on children and television drama by the Group for the Advancement of Psychiatry; National Institute of Mental Health, Television and Behavior Report; National Research Council violence report; and reports from the American Psychological Association's Task Force on Television and Society and the Commission on Violence and Youth. (Murray, 1994)

Murray goes on to note that the issue has been studied, debated, and researched from many different angles with many different research techniques. The result has been thousands of articles and hundreds of books drawing very different, indeed diametrically opposed, conclusions. For example, on the day I was writing this I entered the words 'television violence' into the Google search engine, which resulted in approximately 8.7 million results! In order to provide you with a sense of the flavour of this literature I will comment on a few differing conclusions; not necessarily the most rigorous or best known, but sources you might use for follow up research and reading.

As might be expected, the results themselves have produced debate and discussion. On the one side there is the position that television violence does have implications for social behaviour. John Murray summarized the results of different types of studies in the following series of conclusions: 'The weight of evidence from correlational studies is fairly consistent: viewing and/or preference for violent television is related to aggressive attitudes, values and behaviors.' As for the experimental studies: 'The results of these early studies indicated that children who had viewed the aggressive film were more aggressive in the playroom than those children who had not observed the aggressive model.' Lastly, on some field studies that observed children after they had been watching different types of programs: 'The overall results indicated that children who were judged to be initially somewhat aggressive became significantly more so, as a result of viewing the Batman and Superman cartoons. Moreover, the children who had viewed the prosocial diet of Mister Rogers' Neighborhood were less aggressive, more cooperative and more willing to share with other children.'

In 1994 researchers at The Center for Communication and Social Policy at the University of California (Santa Barbara), in conjunction with colleagues in several other universities, began a longitudinal study of television violence. The study produced a series of reports, Volume 3 of which concluded that violent behaviour typically has no single determinate and that televised violence does not have a uniform impact on viewers. However, the study does consider some foundational premises, including the assumption that television violence contributes to harmful effects such as learning aggressive behaviours, becoming desensitized to violence, and increasing fear. These findings, which the reader can easily locate at the Center for Communication and Social Policy's web site (http:// www.ccsp.ucsb.edu/ntvs.htm for further reading), mirror the summaries found on the American Psychological Association's web site: violence on television increased children's fear, level of aggressive behaviour, and level of sensitivity to pain and suffering among others. An APA task force on violence on television found that by the time they leave elementary school a typical American child will have witnessed 8,000 murders on television. The APA has also turned its attention to violent video games and their conclusion is no less disturbing: 'violent video games may be more harmful than violent television and movies because they are interactive, very engrossing and require the player to identify with the aggressor' (Anderson, 2000).

The Department of Canadian Heritage sponsored a Canadian study that found the impact of television violence varies with the age of the child (Josephson, 1995). Given what we have previously outlined about the stages of personality development (Chapter 5), the findings that an infant will view and understand a violent act in a different way than an elementary school child, and that a secondary school student will view and understand

the act in yet another way, is not surprising. We know that as the mind develops it becomes a filter through which our perceptions are interpreted and understood. The Canadian Radio-television and Telecommunications Commission (CRTC)—the Federal government body that regulates these matters in Canada—has a web site at http:// www.crtc.gc.ca/eng/social/tv.htm that provides a highly informative and worthwhile article titled 'RESPECTING CHILDREN: A Canadian Approach to Helping Families Deal With Television Violence'.

The debates over the potential negative effects of television violence on behaviour are, of course, not the only controversy surrounding media images. The issue of how the various media portray images of sex (female and male) and gender (feminine and masculine) is as contested as the issue of violence. Once again the literature and topics are so widely varied that an attempt to summarize would be futile. Instead, I will point to some directions that students are encouraged to follow.

If you consider the issue of sex and gender images in various mass communication media the first question becomes 'Which media do I investigate?' Given the steady and rapid birth and death cycle of magazines it is impossible to determine how many magazines are published every week. At the time of this writing, one web site, Metagrid (http:// www.metagrid.com), characterized itself as 'The Newspaper and Magazine Database on the Web' and claimed to facilitate access to 4,000 newspapers and 2,500 magazines. Study of the magazine market is further complicated because it is more specialized than any other medium: there are magazines catering to every age, sex, gender, class, level of physical fitness, occupation, interest, language, activity, sporting preference, hobby, lifestyle, pet owner, and food preference. And that list just provides a brief summary!

While there are thousands of magazines to choose from, one particular genre that has been studied with emphasis on images of sex and gender are so-called 'men's magazines'. This label covers a great variety of readily available magazines from hard to soft-core pornography, to sporting, hobby, business, fitness, and health magazines of every possible ilk. Some of the most interesting analyses of sex and gender imagery and content is available through a web site—Theory.org.uk—maintained by David Gauntlett from the Bournemouth Media School. The 'Media, Gender and Identity' section contains some excellent analytical information including materials on potential negative implications of the sex and gender images found in magazines produced for both young women and young men. Lucy Brown's article 'Are magazines for young men likely to reinforce stereotypical, "macho" and sexist attitudes in their readers?' is particularly important, in part because the answer to the question posed in the title is affirmative. The work of Jean Kilbourne is very important in terms of analysing and understanding the images presented by advertisers. Her films, particularly the various versions of 'Killing Us Softly' and her recent book *Can't Buy My Love: How Advertising Changes the Way We Think and Feel* both have a common side-effect—you will never again look at an advertisement in the same light!

Consider the role mass communications plays to provide you with basic information about current events. Did you watch the news on television today, or read a newspaper? If you did, do you think that the 15 or 20 minutes you viewed, or the 20 or 30 pages you read really covered all that was happening? Since the answer is surely no—who do you think made the decision as to what was important enough to be included and on what criteria was that decision made? Are you a rational consumer? Marc Grimier has collected an interesting series of essays that examine the process of selectivity in news media when it comes to covering social events such as strikes, sports, violent events such as the Montreal Massacre, or conflicts involving minorities. The picture is clearly not one of neutral objective coverage (Grenier, 1992). The same selectivity creeps into other aspects of everyday life. Do you buy neutrally objective day-to-day items such as the least expensive

no-name toothpaste of shampoo? Most of us don't. But why don't we? Perhaps we would be well served to heed the advice of Sam Femiano and Mark Nickerson (2002) who warn us in 'How do Media Images of Men Affect Our Lives? Re-Imagining the American Dream' that we need to engage in constant critical thinking to make sure we understand the dangers of stereotypes.

But surely by now you are saying, 'Wait a minute, I just watch television or movies, read magazines, or play video games for entertainment or to be better informed, or to escape the humdrum of my existence. What can be wrong with that?' The answer might be nothing, expect that the sociologists always insist on keeping Peter Berger's insight in mind—nothing is what it seems to be! The reality of your world is that while we are watching television, going to the movies, playing video games, and reading magazines and newspapers we are also being socialized, we are learning about roles, behaviours, values, modes of conduct, possibilities, and solutions to life's problems and dilemmas.

A particularly interesting new literature is emerging around the issue of watching television and physiological development. The interesting part of this literature goes beyond the concerns that watching too much television can substitute for healthier physically active lifestyles (although this issue should not be ignored), to focus on the actual physiological development of the brain. We noted in the discussion of Genie in Chapter 4 that there is some evidence that language acquisition can impact brain development. In 'Understanding TV's effects on the developing brain', Dr Jane M. Healy reviewed some recent findings from the field of neuroscience that connect experiential stimuli with the actual physiological development of the brain. She suggests that excessive television at an early age can potentially negatively impact the development of particular portions of the brains such as the language circuitry in the left-hemisphere and predispose children to having short attentions spans. A *Times of*

London story reprinted in the *Washington Times* (6 April 2004) contained a similar warning about the potential negative impact on brain development, although organizations such as the Citizens for Media Literacy warned against taking this line of reasoning too far. A 2003 *Globe and Mail* story by Gloria Galloway—'Too Much TV impairs reading, study suggests' reports on an American study of the same nature; however the implication is not so focused on a physiological impact on the brain, but rather than the concern should be the deflection of time from other activities.

Among the many studies of the impact of mass communications is Neil Postman's classic *Amusing Ourselves to Death: Public Discourse in the Age of Show Business*. While the typical 18-year-old student reading this book may find the notion of the 'Age of Show Business' an amusing anachronism of their grandparent's age, Postman develops a very convincing argument around one of his main themes— 'that the form in which ideas are expressed affects what those ideas will be' (31). As technology has developed and revolutionized the form in which ideas and entertainment are presented—from verbal to print to photography to various electronic media—those very ideas transmitted and communicated have been, and are being, impacted by the media. The nature of political and public debate was very different in a pre-television society composed of avid book and newspaper readers. The advent of electronic communications changed society so that we became 'consumers' of news and views that were, in every sense of the word, disconnected from our everyday lived experience but which we came to feel were connected. We know that all humans must learn, however Postman reminds us that the form in which ideas are presented is not innocent, and will impact what we learn. In a fascinating discussion of 'Teaching as an Amusing Activity' he has the reader think about whether the format of the television show 'Sesame Street' is conducive to creating the attention span necessary for a child to engage read a full-length novel? Could it be, he has us wonder,

that 'Sesame Street' will make us prefer television to the process of learning subjects such as math and writing? Televised 'debates' have become a standard part of most major elections; however the format is strictly controlled and the objective often seems to be to generate the best 'sound bite'—a short quip often devoid of substance. Postman makes reference to past political debates that were laden with both content and substance. One such debate, in a series between Abraham Lincoln and his rival Stephen Douglas, lasted over seven hours not including a break for supper (44)! Postman reminds us of the great dystopian writings of George Orwell and Aldous Huxley. He warns us that Orwell's 'Big Brother' is not watching us: we are watching him. Further, he reminds us of Huxley's warning that in the brave new world we would come to enjoy what oppressed us, reminding us that more and more we do not seem to know why we laugh or that we seem to have actually stopped thinking. If this is the case, one is led to wonder how we arrived at this point.

Social Theory and the Media

As we have been arguing throughout this book, one of the key distinguishing features of sociology is the requirement that social analysis go beyond mere description. While we quite often look to the so-called founders discussed in Chapter 6 for theoretical frameworks, on the matter of mass communications we must look to more recent theory. This is not to say that Marx's notion of ideology and the power of the ideas of the ruling class, or Durkheim's focus on the role of shared consciousness, or Weber's analysis of the growing role of rational forms of control have no relevance. While these ideas will emerge either directly or indirectly, our focus here will be on more recent developments. What follows will present an overview of some of the different theoretical frameworks that sociologists have attempted to use to explain the role, operation, and impact of mass communications in modern industrial society. We will begin with the theoretical approach that was dominant for most of the last half of the twentieth century—structural functionalism. It is important to note that the overview of how mass communications might be viewed from the perspective of major sociological theories differs from the specialized models of mass communication that one might find in texts on mass communications. In all likelihood such specialized models might be grounded in these broad social theories, but their focus is more specialized.

Structural Functionalism

Perhaps it might be useful to first briefly review the central tenets of functionalist thought before illustrating how this approach would view the role of the media.

For functionalists, human society can be understood by using an organic analogy. Societies have certain basic needs and problems that must be satisfied and solved if they are to survive. For example, if a society is to survive its culture must be transmitted, biological reproduction facilitated, the young cared for and socialized, the spiritual and material needs of individuals met, and so on. Societies (social systems) are composed of specialized structures, called institutions. Institutions function to deal with one or more of the system's prerequisites for survival. Institutions are best understood in terms of the functions they perform for society, that is, the need, problem, or system prerequisite they solve. Society is a system of interconnected structures and institutions each performing some function for the whole and contributing to the maintenance of the entire system.

Traditionally functionalists also assume that social systems are complexly integrated wholes that normally remain stable. Societies tend to remain orderly as long as their members share similar values, norms, beliefs, moral codes, and stocks of knowledge. A society's moral codes and belief systems are essential because they do two things. First, they provide society with its 'shape and character',

influencing how institutions are organized and how people act. Secondly, shared values, norms, and beliefs provide the basis for social order. As long as the majority of members of a society share or accept a system of values, the society will tend to be stable. Stability, homeostasis, equilibrium, and consensus are words that describe the typical condition of society.

As a functionalist undertakes an analysis to explain a social institution such as the media he or she would typically ask the following questions: What are the functions of mass communications or the mass media? What system prerequisites do these institutions address? What is their function?

Given the dominant position of functionalist thought in North American sociology over much of the last century, it is not surprising that there is a well-developed functionalist literature on mass communications and the media. Charles R. Wright's classic, *Mass Communications: A Sociological Perspective* has been republished several times since its initial appearance in the 1950s. Wright lays out the various functions of mass communications, differentiating how these functions serve society, individuals, specific subgroups, and the culture as a whole. Wright presents his analysis of the functions of mass communications under four main headings with a number of sub headings under each:

Surveillance—includes providing warnings of dangers, news, assistance in setting social agendas, and legitimating certain issues as priorities.
Correlation—includes impeding threats to social stability, assisting mobilization as required, and once again agenda setting.
Socialization—includes dissemination of norms and values thereby assisting social cohesion, continuing socialization to ensure on-going sense of belonging and sharing of values and norms.
Entertainment—includes providing respite from the daily routines of life. (15–17)

Given the centrality of norms and values for a functionalist's understanding of human society, the emphasis on the positive functions of the media for society and individuals is to be expected; however Wright also notes that there are potential dysfunctions associated with these functions. For example the surveillance function of providing news of imminent danger can produce panics, correlation can produce excessive conformism, the socialization function of mass communication can produce a mass society in which everyone leads a totally predictable but colourless life. The 1998 movie *Pleasantville* depicts life in a mass society through a view of the world based on a 1950s soap opera: life unfolds day after day in perfect harmony, no differences, no tensions, no emotions, just a very 'pleasant', albeit stultifying, routine in which everyone is pretty much the same. Entertainment can excessively divert attention away from reality and reduce social activity.

Wright's list of functions is very similar to more recent functionalist literature. Michael W. Gamble and Teri Kwal Gamble (1986: 11) list the functions of the media as:

Inform!
Set Agendas!
Connect!
Educate!
Persuade!
Entertain!

David Knox provides a somewhat longer list of the functions of the mass media but the logic is the same. The various social institutions and practices that make up the mass media perform a variety of mostly positive and necessary functions in advanced industrial society. Knox's list includes: warning, companionship, status conferral, agenda setting, reality construction, surveillance, correlation, socialization and education, propaganda, mainstreaming, entertainment, and advertising (442–9). Perhaps a word of explanation is in order for several of these functions. The notion of 'reality construction' refers to the role of the media in providing a context and

meaning to particular events in the interest of social order and society as a whole. 'Mainstreaming' is a mild form of propaganda such that watching a television program may provide a common basis for interaction and communication. The advertising function is very important in a market society (a form of social and economic organization that most functionalists would support) because it involves providing information for consumers regarding new products and services that, presumably, will make their lives better.

While functionalists are interested in the overall functions of mass communications and their role, some specific studies—often by scholars influenced by social psychology and/or symbolic interactionism—focus on particular aspects of the mass communication process.

The work of Harold Lasswell is very well known among those interested in mass communication. In a famous 1948 article, 'The Structure and Function of Communication in Society' Lasswell laid out what he thought were the essential questions to be answered by the sociologists interested in mass communications. The key issues were:

Who
Says What
In Which Channel
To Whom
With What Effect?

The work of Lasswell and others generated further interesting research on the function and social impact of the media. A variety of studies focused on several of these issues in interesting but largely descriptive studies. Elihu Katz and Paul Lazarsfeld's *Personal Influence: The Part Played by People in the Flow of Mass Communications* (1955) is an excellent example of the type of work that grew from the functionalist tradition. The volume documents how information on matters as diverse as fashion and political leadership flows from the media of mass communications through opinion leaders and makers on to the public at large. Other studies such

WHAT THE MASS MEDIA DO—A FUNCTIONALIST PERSPECTIVE

There are a number of ways in which the mass media make daily life easier for us. First, they inform and help us keep a watch on our world; they serve a surveillance function. The media provide us with the news, information, and warning we need to make informed decisions. They gather and pass on information we would be unlikely or unable to obtain on our own. They also inform us about conditions or happenings that they determine could threaten our day-to-day existence. Of course, not all the information provided to us by the media is serious; much of the information they offer focuses on sources of entertainment, the home, fashion tips, or menu suggestions.

By relying on the media to perform the information and surveillance function, we reap benefits as well as risks. To be sure, we do find out things quickly, but the rapidity of the dissemination can itself lead to problems. For example, on January 4, 1984, the following warning went out across the state of Pennsylvania: 'The USA is under attack.' The warning, intended for use in case of a nuclear war, was relayed to forty-four of Pennsylvania's sixty-seven counties—all because a technician made a mistake while installing a computerized teletype system. Though the alert was cancelled within four to five minutes, at least one county had already broadcast the news to the public. Mistakes and distortions travel as quickly as accurate information.

Second, the media set our agendas and help structure our lives. By deciding what stories are given coverage in newspapers and magazines and what programs are aired on radio and television, the mass media schedule what we talk about and what we think about; in other words, our conversations tend to be media-current. Along with this 'selection' aspect, each medium also provides us with a specific perspective on each event. The range of

analyses and evaluations we open ourselves to can affect whether or not we will be exposed to differing points of view and whether or not we will be in a position to evaluate all sides of an issues before we ourselves take a position.

Third, the mass media help us to connect with various groups in society. Although we may not get the same pleasure from them as we might get from interacting face-to-face with other human beings, the media do enable us to keep in contact with our politicians, keeps a finger on the pulse of public opinion, and align ourselves with others who have the same concerns and interests.

Fourth, the media help to socialize us. Through the mass media we supplement what we have learned about behavior and values in direct encounters with other people. The media show us people in action; their portrayals help us assess what the preferred patterns of behavior and appearance are. By so doing, they teach us norms and values, and they participate in our socialization.

Fifth, the media are used to persuade us and to benefit the originators of messages. For example, advertising and public relations are filled with people whose task is to use the media to further their persuasive goals. Thus, the media provide platforms for idea and product advocates. It is their ability to persuade and sell so effectively that sustains and nourishes most of our media. Let us not forget that the media are predominantly industries that must turn a profit to stay in business.

Sixth, the media entertain. All of the media expend a portion of their energies trying to entertain their audiences. For instance, even though the newspaper is a prime medium of information, it also contains entertainment features; most newspapers offer their readers at least some of the following: comics, a crossword puzzle, games, and horoscopes. Television, motion pictures, recordings, fiction books, and some radio stations and magazines are devoted primarily (though not exclusively) to entertainment. As our free time increases–the typical adult now has almost thirty-four hours a week of leisure time–and people seek relief from boredom, escape from the pressures of daily life, or emotional stimulation and release, the entertainment function served by the mass media will become even more important than it is a the present time *(10–11)*.

From Michael W. Gamble and Teri Kwal Gamble, *Introducing Mass Communication* (New York: McGraw Hill Book Company, 1968).

WHY DOES ADVERTISING EXIST?

The prime contention of the critics is that advertising *creates demand* among consumers. The neoliberal position is that a managed economy is desirable, but within such an economy advertising is seen as unnecessary and disadvantageous to the public welfare. The Marxist position sees advertising as essential to the maintenance of the exploitative relations of advanced capitalism. (*16*)

The Marxist Critique

. . . In Marxist theory, advertising is such a vital and integral part of the *system* of capitalism that the one could not survive without the other. Capitalism's productive capacity is so great that it would threaten its own existence were it not for the aid it gets to stave off he threat of overproduction from institutions such as advertising. The problem is this: Although the process of production places value in goods (the value of labor and raw materials), profit is only extracted when those goods are sold in the marketplace and the value in goods is converted into a usable form (money). Once he basic needs of food, shelter, and clothing are satisfied for most people, capitalism faces the problem of 'realization', of making sure that they huge numbers of goods produced beyond this minimal level are consumed. If capitalism cannot overcome this, it will collapse, because if goods cannot be sold, there will be no further investment in production, resulting in a stagnant economy. In the absence of counteracting forces, advanced capitalism would sink into a permanent depression. The problem is one of overproduction–of 'too much'. (*15–16*)

In his critical study of the beginnings of national advertising, *Captains of Consciousness* (1976), Stuart Ewen comments on the way a fledgling advertising industry reacted to the role thrust upon it in the first decades of this century. The crisis of overproduction created the imperative to expand markets to the poorer social classes and on a national scale, and the advertising industry offered business a means of 'creating' consumers and controlling the consumption of products.

> *Such social production of consumers represented a shift in social and political priorities which has since characterized much of the 'life' of American industrial capitalism. The functioning goal of national advertising was the creation of desires and habits. (Ewen 1976, 37)*

The tremendous growth in the scale of national advertising in the period from 1890 to 1920 is seen by Ewen as an indication of the way that capitalist domination and control would seek to affect the mass of the working population beyond the boundary of the factory gate. (16–17)

The Marxist critique sees advertising as a response to the needs of advanced capitalism for a solution to the problem of realization. Advertising is a willing accomplice in creating and perpetuating the unhealthy features of the social system in which it evolved, and moreover has become indispensable to its continues existence; therefore, one cannot contemplate its abolition except in the context of rejecting capitalism as such. (17)

Extracts from: William Leiss, Stephen Kline, and Sut Jhally. 1986. *Social Communication in Advertising* (Toronto: Methune).

as Herbert Gans's, *Deciding What's News: A Study of CBS Evening News, NBC Nightly News, Newsweek, and Time* follow this tradition. Gans presents a fascinating study of roles, organizational structures, and power in the news business.

Before moving to consider alternate perspectives, a final word on the notion of the dysfunctional aspects of mass communication is in order. Wright warns that the socialization function of the mass media can have a dysfunctional aspect to it—the production of mass society. The theme is even more important in 'Mass Communication, Popular Taste and Organized Political Action' by Paul Lazarsfeld and Robert Merton. This article identifies public concern with the potential role of the media and the possibility of powerful groups such as advertisers using it for their ends. They also worry about what they call the 'narcotizing dysfunction' and the possibility of creating an apathetic population rather than involved citizens (1964: 105).

The capacity of the media to impact the masses led to another concern, even among functionalists—the emergence of mass society. While some argued that the emergence of mass society is equivalent to the emergence of modernity as all sorts of progress moved humanity from folk or traditional society toward mass society (Rose, 1956), other later functionalists equated the notion of mass society with the

emergence of a form of society in which individuals lacked individuality partly because there was a excessive reliance on, or over exposure to, mass communications. The fact that more and more people are spending more and more time watching the same television programs and reading the same magazines and newspapers could result in the emergence of an excessively strong collective consciousness. Shared values and normative orientations are necessary, but ideally there should also be a role for local variations, subcultures, and some variety of style, opinion, and behaviour. When this variety is lost, and only mass opinions, tastes, styles, and behaviours exist, something is lost in terms of the varieties of human cultures and experiences that characterize our past, not to mention the potential for mass communications to facilitate manipulation and social control.

Although this strain of argument is present, the dominant motif in the functionalist literature is a view of mass communication as facilitating the smooth functioning of a complex industrial society. We will now discuss a view that emerged from the power conflict tradition that radically contrasts with the functionalist approach.

Power Conflict

The stultification of many of Marx's ideas under the pressure of the political leadership of the former

Soviet Union and the concomitant lack of theoretical refinement or development resulted in the dominance of functionalist thought in North America during the post-Second World War. There were two important exceptions to the lack of innovation in the Marxian tradition: 1) the work of the Frankfurt School and 2) the work of Antonio Gramsci.

Frankfurt School

Of all the difficult and complex ideas that you may encounter in this book, those associated with what is generally referred to as the Frankfurt School are among the most difficult and complex, and therefore they are virtually impossible to summarize. What we are calling the Frankfurt School actually originated as the Institute of Social Research at Frankfurt University in 1923. Although many individuals were attached to the School at various times, the three individuals most commonly associated with it are Max Horkheimer, Theodor Adorno, and Herbert Marcuse. There is some debate as to whether there was sufficient agreement among the various figures associated with the School to really call them a 'School', however, David Held (1980), Douglas Kellner (1989) and Martin Jay (1973) have written important books arguing that there was significant commonality among the group to view their contribution to social analysis as distinct. Among the varied intellectual, theoretical, and political projects of the Frankfurt School was the liberation of the Marxian legacy from those who viewed it as a form of economic determinism or used it to justify the political agendas and machinations that were unfolding in the Soviet Union. The restoration of the true analytical and political potentialities of the Marxian legacy would, these thinkers agreed, require an integration of Marx's core ideas with newer insights into the human condition such as were coming from Freud and a return to his Hegelian heritage.

The core notion of the Frankfurt School that interests us in this chapter is their work on what they called the culture industry. As Kellner points out, the analysis of mass communications that the Frankfurt School (like many others, he refers to their work and approach as Critical Theory) developed connected mass communications with the culture industry and a sweeping broad process of social domination that was unfolding as capitalism developed: 'Their analysis included new theories of consumerism and the development of the consumer society, of the culture industries, of the incorporation of science and technology into relations of production and new forms of social control, of changing patterns of socialization, personality development and values, and of the decline of the individual' (1989: 5–6). An important part of this analysis is the argument that the drive for ever-increasing profits, part of the inherent logic of the capitalist system, leads to the systematic application of science and technology to all aspects of production including culture and art. As a result the culture industry become a commodity like everything else; however it is a special commodity whose function is to indoctrinate the population with a particular understanding of the world. The complex and multidimensional arguments of the Frankfurt School would eventually lead some of them to a critique of the Enlightenment, science, technology, and the notion of the domination of nature. Kellner argues that the School's analysis of the role of 'culture, ideology and the mass media are among its most valuable legacies' (121).

So what, according to the Frankfurt School, is the social role or function of mass communications? Nothing short of total social control and manipulation in the service of the economic interests of those in control of the emerging monopoly capitalist system. The total control will involve the penetration of the consumer ethic into the very personalities of citizens so that they think that never-ending consumption is both what freedom means and the only purpose in life. Further, the omnipresent bombardment of the culture industry will ensure that the citizens of capitalist society come to think that this is human nature and that there is no other acceptable, possible, or conceivable system other than capitalism. Later works of the Frankfurt School came to use phrases such as 'one-dimensional man' and 'totally administered society' to describe the condition of the total incorporation into a consumer and commodity based society in which citizens really do think that consuming is the highest form of conduct, an appropriate leisure activity, and that the lives, trials, tribulations and fantasies of rich celebrities are worthy of conversation! In such a world consumption is guaranteed while opposition is unimaginable.

Antonio Gramsci

The Italian Marxist Antonio Gramsci (1891–1937) was a contemporary of the Frankfurt School. Gramsci seems to have become a socialist during his time at Turin University and he remained politically active even after being imprisoned by the fascist Mussolini. He died a political prisoner. As was the case with the Frankfurt School, Gramsci worked to develop Marxian theory by distancing it from any form of simple economic determinism. Although the ideas of what we refer to as elite theory in Chapter 11 were an important part of the intellectual landscape in Italy, Gramsci was interested in investigating the process by which subordinate classes were incorporated into the very system that exploited them. This project resulted in Gramsci eventually formulating the concept that is most often associated with his name—hegemony.

Gramsci observed that class relations and class struggle almost always had an ideological component to them, and it was necessary to go beyond some of Marx's rather simple notions about the ideas of an epoch being the ideas of the ruling class. While he did not dispute the general nature of this claim, as a result of some of his own political experiences he understood that a more systematic and elaborate analysis was required if the political struggles of the working class were to succeed. He came to understand that a ruling class could not succeed on the basis of force or coercion alone;

somehow it must convince the subordinate or oppressed population to consent to and support the system. This, Gramsci argued, was accomplished through the establishment and imposition of ideological hegemony.

What does Gramsci mean by ideological hegemony? The concept refers to a situation in which the dominant class has been able to convince the majority of a society that the its ideas, world view, beliefs, practices, philosophy, and overall understanding of the world are 'common sense' and the only possible and reasonable way understand the world. Ideological hegemony is a process of manipulating the public opinion so that one's views are widely accepted, viewed as normal, and received with an 'of course' reaction when explained to someone. Gramsci's notion of ideological domination left room for alternate or counter ideologies emanating from the subordinate classes. Indeed, a key part of any class struggle is the efforts of the subordinate classes to present alternate or counter worldviews to those of the dominant classes. While Gramsci understood that many institutional orders (education, religion, the press) are part of the process by which certain ideologies become hegemonic, he did not specify the mechanisms by which mass communications are a part of this process. In summary, '[f]rom a "Gramscian" perspective, the mass media have to be interpreted as an instrument to spread and reinforce the dominant hegemony... although they could be used by those who want to spread counter-hegemonic ideas too' (Stillo, 1998). Dominic Strinati provides a worthwhile concluding statement in his 1995 volume *An Introduction to Theories of Popular Culture*:

> ...Pop culture and the mass media are subject to the production, reproduction and transformation of hegemony through the institution of civil society which cover the areas of cultural production and consumption. Hegemony operates culturally and ideologically through the institutions of civil society

that characterises mature liberal-democratic, capitalist societies. These institutions include education, the family, the church, the mass media, popular culture, etc. (168–9)

The Political Economy of Mass Communications

Given that Marx and Marxism are often viewed as an analytical approach predicated on the study of political economy, it is not surprising that many within this tradition have focused on the economic role of mass communications. Among the important works that could be termed the 'political economy approach' are Vincent Mosco's *The Political Economy of Communications* and the analysis of the media found in Paul Baran and Paul Sweezy's attempt to update Marx. We will focus on *Monopoly Capital* in which Baran and Sweezy argue that the mass media play a central economic role in sustaining capitalism.

As an economic system based on the production of commodities, capitalism is incredibly successful. Indeed, it is so successful that the overproduction of commodities is a constant problem simply because the system is so productive that it can produce more of any given commodity than can typically be sold. An alternate way of stating the situation is that because the system is so capable of producing commodities, the possibility of underconsumption is an ever-present problem. Keep in mind, though, that the problems of overproduction or underconsumption do not mean that people in capitalist society have all the necessities of life they need. If capitalist firms cannot sell commodities for a profit they will not produce them. If capitalist firms slow down or terminate production the economy will move into recession or depression.

The problem is exacerbated by the fact that in advanced capitalism a small number of very large companies control production. When there is overproduction (underconsumption) these firms tend not to reduce prices in order to stimulate sales, but rather they curtail production, which leads to economic slowdowns, loss of jobs, unemployment, and eventually a depression. Since the logic of the system dictates that commodities will only be produced if they can be sold for a profit, capitalist companies have a vested interest in expanding sales and consumption. Baran and Sweezy argue that large multinational corporations typically avoid the kind of 'knock-down-drag'em-out' price wars that characterized an earlier stage of capitalism, and thus they seek alternate ways of attempting to stimulate sales and consumption such as advertising and demand creation.

Baran and Sweezy go on to argue that advertising, the creation of new needs, and efforts to promote product and brand loyalty become key activities in capitalist society. Indeed the sales effort becomes a key part of their analysis (1966: Chapter 5). If a company can create a new need for a particular product by, for instance, convincing us that the very natural process of perspiring is to be avoided at all costs, then as a society we will very likely go out and spend millions of dollars annually on a variety of chemical concoctions called deodorants to prevent this process from occurring. If a car manufacturer can convince us that a particular brand of automobile will get us the right kind of mate, make us look sexually attractive, or provide the freedom to be ourselves, then we, as a society, will go out and spend billions of dollars acquiring this environmentally destructive mode of transportation. And how best to get these messages across to potential consumers—the various modes of mass communications of course!

The essential logic to this approach is that the central role of mass communications in a monopoly capitalist system is the stimulation of consumption and sale of commodities through advertising and demand creation. The notion that the ultimate purpose or meaning of life is consuming becomes the dominant motif of our lives in advanced capitalism. Baran and Sweezy set this out over 40 years ago:

The strategy of the advertiser is to hammer into the heads of people the unquestioned desirability, indeed the imperative necessity, of owning the newest product that comes on the market. For this strategy to work, however, products have to pour on the market in a steady stream of 'new' products, with none daring to lag behind for fear his (sic) customers with turn to his (sic) rivals for their newness. (1966: 128)

Although Baran and Sweezy also examine the overall negative social implications of a media-dominated culture with, for example, their observation that one can be a 'sports fan' without ever having played a game or even knowing anything about the game (246–7), the focus of their analysis is on the necessity of demand creation. Clearly mass communications play a vital economic role in the interests of dominant corporations by creating demand and consumer loyalty to their products.

Audience as Commodity: An Alternate Political Economy

A somewhat different focus, although still in the Marxian tradition, is found in the work of Dallas Smythe. In an article 'Communications: Blind spot of Western Marxism' and later in his book, *Dependency Road: Communications, Capitalism and Consciousness, and Canada*, Smythe laid out the basis for what we might call the 'audience as commodity approach'.

The difference in Smythe's approach is his focus on the audience and its precise role in the capitalist economic system. Smythe is critical of most of the approaches that social scientists have developed to analyze the role of mass communications in contemporary capitalism. Some, he argued, focused on the content of programs and ignored advertisers, while Lasswell and other functionalists tended to view all the content as benign. For Smythe, the essential point of departure for understanding mass

communications in advanced capitalism is the acknowledgment that capitalism is a system that transforms more and more aspects of the world around us into commodities that are bought and sold on the market. Further he argues that if we are to understand mass communications and the media we must understand that it plays both economic and ideological roles.

Starting with the economic role, Smythe acknowledges that mass communications and advertising are about creating demand and consumer loyalty for the various products of capitalist industry. However, what Smythe attempts that others had not, is to explain precisely how the audience, the mass media industries and advertisers (and the companies the serve) interact.

According to Smythe, mass communications media produce particular types of communications, for example, magazines, newspapers, or television programs. The actual non-advertising content of that communicative product is designed to, or will tend to, attract a certain type of audience. The non-advertising content represents a kind of 'free lunch' that attracts you to the product so you buy the magazine, read the paper, watch the television show, or listen to the radio station. A host of specialized service companies such as Nielsen Media Research or BBM Canada undertake surveys of viewers, readers, and listeners to determine how large the 'audience' is and what its demographics (age, sex, income, occupation, geographic location, etc.) are. These audience survey companies then sell their data to mass communications organizations that determine who and how many are reading, listening, or watching. The mass communication outlets, in turn, negotiate blocks of advertising time or space with particular advertisers and their corporate clients. Smythe argues that what is happening is that the media is offering a 'free lunch' to create an audience and then it is selling that audience to advertisers and their clients. In essence, when you read a magazine or watch a television program you are being sold as a commodity. An example might clarify his point. A television network decides to broadcast a sporting event such as a football game. The audience survey company tells the network that typically x number of people with specific demographics (typically males of a certain age, income range, locale, etc.) will be watching at a particular time. The sales representatives for the network then contact a truck manufacturer who might be interested in creating demand for its product and offers the manufacturer an audience of x many males with particular demographics at a particular time and date. The truck manufacturer agrees and, as these men sit in their living rooms watching the football game and the advertisements it contains, they are actually being bought and sold like any other commodity. In a similar fashion one might create an audience of children with Saturday morning cartoons and sell them to toy manufacturers, or an audience of domestic workers with afternoon serials and sell them to soap companies (hence the name soap operas!).

Smythe hastens to add that the ideological content of the messages, the 'free lunches', are typically not ideologically innocent when it comes to supporting and legitimating the capitalist system. Indeed, Smythe refers to the Consciousness Industry as operating to both motivate people to consume, consume, consume, and to legitimize the status quo (1981: Chapter 1). And, to repeat, perhaps most insidious for Smythe is the fact that in a capitalist society, even as you enjoy your 'free time' watching your favourite television show you are being turned into a commodity and being actively sold and bought on the market!

Thus far we have been reviewing alternate analytical frameworks that are rooted in the mainstream perspectives discussed in Chapters 6 and 7. The time has come to face the overarching critique of these ideas that we encountered at the end of Chapter 7—namely these ideas are typically innocent of any consideration of the role of mass

communications with regard to sex and gender relations. As noted above, this lacuna is potentially fatal to the efforts of sociologists to explain the contemporary world, so we now turn our attention to feminist analyses of mass communications.

Feminist Theory and Mass Communications

There is perhaps no topic more important to feminists and feminist analysis than the issues of communication, portrayal, and imagery. Indeed it is a key issue, as Liesbet van Zoonen starkly put it: 'The media have always been at the centre of feminist critique' (1994: 11). She goes on to note that the women's movement was about rights, but also about symbolic issues and definitions of femininity, with the warning that this literature is characterized by an 'enormous heterogeneity' (12). We noted above that over the past several decades there have been volumes of studies that examined and documented the negative, subordinate, and stereotypical portrayal of women across the spectrum of mass communications.

We have noted the work of Jean Kilbourne and her *Killing Us Softly* films. Jane Tallim of the Media Awareness Network has produced an article titled 'Sexualized Images in Advertising' that further develops the point that sexual images and suggestions playing off girls and women continue to be common in advertising (Tallim, 2003). The United Nations Division for the Advancement of Women has attempted to take action on the issue of women's employment in the media. A collection of essays edited by Pamela Creedon, *Women in Mass Communication: Challenging Gender Values* (1989) looks at the roles and participation of women across a wide spectrum of mass communications institutions. *Women and Media: Content, Careers and Criticism*, (Lont, 1995) contains a series of excellent articles that examine the presence, or lack thereof, of images and the portrayal of women in front page stories, fashion magazines, prime time television, advertising, television news, movies, and the music industry. While these last two references are somewhat hopeful voices, others are less sanguine that much has changed over the past several decades. In an excellent summary of many studies on the portrayal of women in the media Shari Graydon begins by noting that in the past the typical motifs for presenting women across the various media were: objectification, irrelevant sexualization, infantization, domestication, and victimization (2001: 179–80). In 'How to Evaluate Media Images of Women' Linda Seger (2002) suggests not much has changed:

> If images of women were only limiting, if would be sad, but not tragic. Unfortunately, most of the images of women are not just restricted, but negative. These images misrepresent who we are, demean us, and make it harder to see women as people. When women are only shown as beautiful and passive or rich and bitchy, it becomes more difficult for both men and women to accept them as the diverse, multifaceted people they really are.

In a collection of essays focusing on politics, *Gender, Politics and Communication* (2000), the editors Annabelle Sreberny and Liesbet van Zoonen are forced to note that while some changes have occurred, there remains a 'depressing stability in the articulation of women's politics and communication' (17). Their point is that a common trend across the diverse studies in the collection is 'the underlying frame of reference is that women belong in the family and domestic life and men to the social world of politics and work; that femininity is about care, nurturance and compassion, and that masculinity is about efficiency, rationality, and individuality' (17).

One could go on indefinitely reviewing the findings of those who have looked at images of girls and women in music, video games, television, music videos, movies, novels, newspapers, magazines, and billboards. Indeed, web sites such as the Women's Media, Communication, and News Sources provide virtually limitless resources and possibilities; however I assume our point has been made—the portrayal, presentation, depiction, and imagery of women continues to be, to say the least, problematic. The issue then becomes explaining the persistence of these images and portrayals after many years of feminist agitation for change, and in the presence of liberal democratic charters of rights and freedoms.

In Chapter 9 we saw that the field of feminist analysis was characterized by different approaches and foci. While everyone calling herself or himself a feminist would probably agree that the systems of mass communications in patriarchal society will tend to portray women in a different manner than men—as subservient, less rational, more emotional, and dependent—the reasons they provide to explain these portrayals will be quite different. One of the challenges involved in learning to think critically about the phenomenon from a sociological perspective is learning how to put ideas together when considering complex phenomenon. Given that feminist scholars typically have not approached the study of mass communications from an explicitly identified perspective within the larger field of feminist theory, we need to think back to the distinctions between various schools of feminism identified in Chapter 9. Having done that, the challenge becomes thinking creatively about how these various schools would approach the issue of women and mass communication in patriarchal society.

The following comments on the various approaches within feminism directed towards the media is partly informed by van Zoonen's approach in *Feminist Media Studies*, although it is important to explicitly note that she also argues that the manner by which feminism has been categorized, mainly around distinctions between liberal, radical, Marxian/socialist feminism, is increasingly becoming tenuous as the complexity of feminist theorizing and politics become more apparent (1994: 12–13). This warning notwithstanding, we will briefly examine how the trends in feminist theory we noted above play themselves out in media analysis.

We will begin with liberal feminism. Given that liberal feminism tends to focus on the normative value dimension of society and locates the basis of women's inequality in the existence of sexist ideas, values, norms, and beliefs, it is not surprising that this approach would focus on media content. Indeed some of the most trenchant critiques of the sexist nature of media content come from within this tradition. Volumes such as Cynthia Lont's collection, *Women and Media: Content, Careers and Criticism*, provide both criticism and hope—a common feature of liberal feminists. The criticism is found in the various chapters that examine the portrayal of women in a wide range of media, noting everything from the exclusion to women to the excessive use of traditional stereotypes. The hope is found in the conclusion, where Lott makes an explicit plea for more education on the issue of the role of women and the use of women's political and economic power to change the situation. Working within the system, reform, education, and the use of existing levels of power and influence to change sexist ideas and practices are all very much part of the liberal feminist agenda. Margaret Gallagher's report on the work and successes of those involved in media advocacy, *Gender Setting: New Agendas for Media Monitoring and Advocacy*, is an important illustration of a liberal feminist approach. As the title of the first chapter illustrates, the book makes a strong, well-argued, and well-supported case for media monitoring and international advocacy. Gallagher argues that monitoring, documenting, and then advocating for change are all effective in the struggle to improve the position and representation of women in the mass communications. Jean Kilbourne's work also represents this approach in that her films tend to advise the use of consumer power and lobbying to change the sexist,

demeaning, and even dangerous portrayal of women in advertising.

The approach and focus of what we have termed 'radical feminism' will, of course, be different. As van Zoonen points out, scholars operating from this standpoint have been very active in the debates and struggles against pornography. Recall that the radical feminist perspective's core arguments typically include the notion that men and women must be understood as being members of separate and distinctive classes and that the basis of these class distinctions is biological. The perspective also assumes that men, as a class, have been historically dominant and exploitative largely because of the biological role that women play in species reproduction. If one considers that women's role in biological reproduction is a root cause of patriarchal domination, it is not surprising that radical feminists have focused on pornography as 'a form of sexual violence against women, simultaneously a source and product of a deeply misogynistic society' (van Zoonen, 1994: 19).

While pornography is not the only issue that a radical feminist might address, it is an important part of how this tendency would address mass communications. The fact that male domination is ingrained in virtually every institution in patriarchal society obviously will have significant implications for how we approach and understand mass communications. The media representation of the so-called typically normal nuclear family that has been in place since the era of the *Flintstones* would be seen as part of the process by which patriarchal social structures and institutions are seen to be unchanging, if not sacred.

Socialist feminists tend to have a more comprehensive analysis of the status of women in modern capitalist society than either liberal or radical feminists. This is because they see females facing two different forms of oppression and exploitation. Socialist feminists would argue that when women enter the labour force in capitalist society they are exploited and alienated in the same manner as anyone forced to sell their labour power in the 'free' market (Chapter 6). On the other hand when they engage in domestic labour they may be exploited by capital (as they produce and reproduce labour power), however, they are also exploited by men who directly benefit on a daily basis by virtue of having their meals cooked, clothes washed, children cared for, and so on.

There are many social forces that enforce, reinforce, and legitimatize this dual system of oppression; however, as we saw in Chapter 8, the work of scholars such as Michele Barrett points to the key role that ideology and ideas play in this process. Obvious important agents of socialization that carried the dominant ideologies of both capitalism and patriarchy are the various forms of mass communication. While socialist feminists would use various forms of content analysis to examine the images, portrayals, and representations of women in the media, they would also be interested in the extent to which these images both seek to mask the reality of class and class conflict while presenting women as occupying roles that are appropriate to their so-called natural inclinations as domestically inclined nurturers and mothers (Enriques, 2000).

As is always the case in an introductory overview, these comments are sketchy and simple. There is much more to feminist media analysis than could be summarized in one book let alone in a few pages. The point of this brief encounter, like all encounters in this book, is to whet the reader's appetite so that he or she will follow up with courses in these areas, additional readings, self-study, and further reflection. As we leave this section it is important to keep van Zoonen's warning about these traditional typologies of feminist discourse in mind and make an effort to examine some more recent directions. As was pointed out in Chapter 8, feminist theory is a vibrant ever-changing field and analysis defies summary because it changes on a daily basis. Readers are advised to pay attention to the role that cultural studies and the so-called post-structuralist and post-

modern analysis is playing in feminist media studies.

The approaches we have discussed tend to be relatively straight-forward. Each one attempts to explain women's inequality and/or oppression in capitalist and patriarchal society with reference to some more-or-less real social processes and dynamics. These perspectives might see mass communication as responsible for the transmission of dysfunctional sexist ideas or the dissemination of oppressive ideologies in the interests of males as a class, or the ideological manipulation of women and men in the interests of the capitalist class and the concomitant ideological domination of women in the dual system of capitalist and patriarchal oppression. In each case the process is seen as open to investigation, analysis, and explanation as something that we can study and understand.

As we will see in the final chapter of *Introducing Sociology: A Critical Perspective*, the view of the social world as amenable to some form of scientific investigation, analysis, and understanding that can be quite easily reported and debated is very much a matter of contention today. The assumption that ideas such as those surrounding sex and gender can be simply transmitted and received surely flies, at least partially, in the face of our analysis of the role of the human mind in interpreting the meaning of signs and symbols. The symbolic interactionists are correct is arguing that humans, as active creators, users, and interpreters of symbolic communications, perform an active role in how we use, don't use, accept, reject, and respond to the messages we get via the instruments and media of mass communications. Since we at least partially construct our social realities on the basis of communications—mass and otherwise—we need to carefully reflect on this process.

Towards a Conclusion

It is important to heed the warning of van Zoonen, who ends her analysis of various directions and trends in feminist analysis of the media with recognition that attempting to produce a conclusion to a discussion of ideas and materials that are heterogeneous and diverse is, at best, a contradictory task. This chapter has attempted to establish that mass communications are an integral dimension of your life and the structures and processes of your society. In the interests of developing our sociological imagination, we must pay explicit attention to the diverse processes that we call mass communications.

This chapter has attempted to remind you of the ubiquitous nature and omnipresence of mass communications in our lives. As agents of socialization these forms of communication must be considered important. However, note that there is an on-going debate around what is often called the 'effects model'. The very useful web site I have referred to several times, Theory.org.uk, contains an article by David Gauntlett titled 'Ten Things Wrong with the "effects model"'. While Gauntlett makes a number of important points, the aspect of the issue I want you to think about relates to the nature of social reality and the extent to which we are active in constructing our social realities on an ongoing basis. Some of the theories reviewed imply that there is a media-sent message that is received and absorbed by a more-or-less passive receiver. The approach to socialization and personality development found in Chapters 4 and 5 surely mitigate against any such view. This is not to say that the various agents of mass communication do not attempt to influence our thinking, perception, character, and behaviour through their messages, but it is to say that we need to ensure that we have a sufficiently sophisticated understanding of socialization and the social construction of reality so that we can avoid casting ourselves as passive sponges.

The human mind, like the human brain, remains a marvellous, complex, and not very well understood phenomenon. To the extent that our minds mediate the sensations and perceptions that constantly bombard us, we must make sure we understand the manner in which mass communications and mass communicators might attempt to provide us with particular kinds of messages—messages that have been 'mediated'. Additionally, we need to think critically about the warnings noted in Neil Postman's work and Todd Gitlin's convincing argument that we live in a omnipresent torrent of images and sounds that threaten to overwhelm us in content, in volume, and in the speed at which they cross our consciousness.

Critical Thinking Questions

- Given what you know about the process of socialization, explain whether or not it is possible to argue that the various portrayals of violence in the contemporary media of mass communications have no impact on behaviour in our society.
- What, according to structural functionalist theory, are the positive social functions of the mass media? What are the potential dysfunctions associated with these activities?
- How might Gramsci's concept of hegemony be used in an analysis of the political role that the media of mass communications plays in modern liberal democracies?
- What, according to the arguments developed by Baran and Sweezy, is the central economic role of mass communications in advanced capitalist society?
- How, according to Smythe, do you become a commodity as you sit and watch your favourite television program?

Terms and Concepts

Mass communications–various modes of communication (all print and electronic forms from radio to the internet) that are produced and presented in an effort to communicate some message to mass audiences. The various media of mass communications are typically institutionalized and exhibit patterns of social organization.

Functions of the media–structural functionalists are typically interested in the social and individual functions of various social activities and phenomenon. While different scholars describe the functions of the media of mass communications in slightly different terms, Gamble and Gamble's list is a suitable summary of the key functions: 'Inform; Set Agendas; Connect; Educate; Persuade; Entertain'.

Hegemony–popularized by Gramsci and widely used by critical sociologists hegemony typically is understood to refer to a situation in which the dominant class is able to convince the majority members of a society that the its ideas, world view, beliefs, practices, philosophy, and overall understanding of the world are 'common sense', natural, and the only possible and reasonable way understand the world. The media of mass communications are seen are part of the efforts of ruling classes to establish ideological hegemony. This means manipulating public opinion so that the views of the dominant class are widely accepted and received with an 'of course' reaction when explained to someone. Gramsci did leave room for the emergence of alternate ideologies representing the ideas and viewpoints of subordinate classes to present counter world views to those of the dominant classes.

Audience as a commodity–according to Smythe the media of mass communications, like all capitalist industries, produce commodities for sale on the market. In the case of mass communications the commodity is an audience that is produced by offering the equivalent of a 'free lunch'. The 'free lunch' is the television program, magazine article, particular music, or whatever leads to you reading, watching, or listening. Once created the audience is then measured, quantified, and then sold to advertisers. As members of the audience read, listen, and watch the various media of mass communications they typically do not even know that they are being bought and sold like any other commodity.

Culture industry–a complex concept typically associated with the work of the Frankfurt School. The notion of the culture industry is often associated with the idea of a mass society in which most, if not all, aspects of life have been made into commodities and the population has become convinced that the most worthwhile human activity is consuming commodities. The media of mass communications are central to the promotion of consumer society as the natural condition of humans; however the full notion of the culture industry includes and impacts virtually all forms of human communication from art to everyday conversation.

Related Web Sites

http://www.americancomm.org/studies/mediaculture.html#Mass%20Media

The American Communication Association maintains this site titled 'Mass Media and Culture'. The site contains links to many resources under four headings: Mass Media, Culture, Film/Television, and Radio. Each has multiple entries, many of which have other links.

http://www.theory.org.uk/

This useful site has been noted in connection

with other topics; however the 'Media, Gender and Identity' link is a must for sociology students interested in mass communications.

http://www.mediastudies.com/

Peter Clayton from Richmond, British Columbia, is responsible for this excellent site. Its stated purpose is 'to help advance research and education in media studies and critical thinking'. It does this by providing an impressive range of international media sites and media criticism resources.

http://www.cddc.vt.edu/feminism/com.html

Kristin Switala holds copyright for this 'Feminist Theory Website: Communication and Media' site that is hosted by the Center for Digital Discourse and Culture at Virginia Tech University. The site contains a good bibliography, links to individual feminist scholars whose work addresses the issues of feminism and the media, as well as some international links.

http://www.library.wisc.edu/libraries/WomensStudies/media.htm

The University of Wisconsin System Women's Studies Librarian maintains this site that provides a rich variety of sources on virtually every aspect issues relating to women and mass communications.

http://www.aber.ac.uk/media/sections/gen01.php

This is a very interesting site that contains more search possibilities than most. The home page for the site describes itself in the following manner: 'The MCS (pronounced "mix") site is an award-winning portal or "meta-index" to internet-based resources useful in the academic study of media and communication. . . . It is British-based and is intended to give priority to issues of interest to both British scholars in the field and to others who are interested in media in the UK.' I would only add that the links provide ideas and information of interest beyond the UK!

Suggested Further Readings

Smythe, Dallas W. 1981. *Dependency Road: Communications, Capitalism, Consciousness, and Canada*. Norwood, NJ.: Ablex Publishing Corp. Although the empirical data maybe dated, this is the classical statement of the 'audience as commodity' thesis, an idea that still deserves attention.

Gitlin, Todd. 2001. *Media Unlimited: How the Torrent of Images and Sounds Overwhelms Our Lives*. New York: Metropolitan Books. The title of this book lays out its central thesis—we are being overcome with a torrent of images and sounds that threatens our capacity for independent thought and feeling. Todd Giltin's four

other books are also highly reccommended.

Gumpert, Gary, and Robert Cathcart, eds. 1986. *Inter/Media: Interpersonal Communication in a Media World*. New York: Oxford University Press. A collection of 40 essays that touch almost every important aspect of the sociology of mass communications.

Erik Barnouw. 1982. *Tube of Plenty*. New York: Oxford University Press. Although the recent and on-going mergers and consolidations render this a history of television, it is perhaps the best history of the electronic media in the United States written to date.

CHAPTER 11

The Polity and Political Power

Although the study of the polity—of the structures, operation, and processes of government and social decision-making—is usually deemed to be within the purview of political science, sociologists have always maintained a keen interest in the issue. The study of the polity is more than the study of political parties and voting patterns. It includes the social decision-making process—a process that has an impact on every member of a society.

Complex modern industrial societies have developed or evolved formal mechanisms and political structures to facilitate social decision-making. In most Western societies these structures are among the most visible, complex, and formal institutions. The polity is often formally structured and organized on the basis of codified rules and procedures called constitutions; and these constitutions are really just sets of rules and regulations that govern the structures and processes of social decision-making. Most often sociologists leave the study of the formal constitutional arrangements and processes to the political scientists and focus instead on the functions of the polity and the social dynamics of the decision-making process.

The polity performs a series of essential social tasks. The process of social decision-making includes setting a number of general and specific social goals, priorities, and initiatives. Social policy can include everything from domestic issues such as the availability of unemployment insurance to abortion to spending on education. Social policy

issues can also include matters as different as international relations and the funding of space research programs. The polity or the political order is particularly important for the members of a society because the decisions made within political institutions touch on the lives of virtually everyone. When a decision is made within one of the educational institutions, it usually has an impact only on those immediately involved with that institution. Similarly, when a religious institution changes its policy on an issue such as abortion, not everyone in the society is necessarily affected. The situation is different when important decisions are made within the political order. When the government decides to implement free trade or a comprehensive goods and services tax, for example, every member of the society feels the effect. Given the far-reaching impact of decisions made within the political order, it is not surprising that the study of the polity is an important part of the discipline of sociology.

As we have seen, when sociologists attempt to understand and explain social phenomena, they often use different theoretical perspectives. In the field of political sociology we can identify at least three general frameworks: (1) the pluralist approach, commonly adopted by structural functionalists; (2) a class analysis model associated with some version of a Marxian orientation; and (3) some version of elite theory. In recent years scholars influenced by feminist theory have also been turning their attention to the polity, so we will examine some of these developments as well. We will begin by examining the basic tenets of the pluralist approach.

Pluralism

When structural functionalists undertake an analysis of the operations of the political order in Western societies, they tend to adopt an approach that is commonly called pluralism. The pluralist perspective appeals to them because it maintains that social systems such as ours—and the political structures within them—are basically stable, democratic, and open (Rossides, 1968: 157; Tumin, 1967: 45–6). Functionalists argue that the development of a democratic, pluralist political system has been the essential means of preventing individual inequalities from being translated into systematic social or political inequalities. What is unique about Western capitalist societies, they would argue, is the fact that although such societies recognize the necessity and functional value of individual inequalities, they do not allow those individual inequalities to affect the overall process of social decision-making.

According to Tumin, the essential features of a pluralist, democratic political order are the opportunities that all members of a society have to use formally established electoral procedures to select the personnel who operate the political institutions. In addition, all members of society can compete to influence the decision-making process between elections through actions such as lobbying the decision-makers (Tumin, 1967: 44–5). The most important aspect of Western democracies, a pluralist functionalist would argue, is the extent to which all members of society have an opportunity to participate in attempting to influence the policies of the government through these activities. The income levels or class positions of individuals may well vary considerably. The amount of status an individual enjoys may vary according to occupation, ethnic group, or gender. But when it comes to the social decision-making process, all people are equal. In all

liberal democratic societies the creed is 'one person, one vote', and thus on election day all are essentially equal: the people with high income and the people on social assistance are equal in the polling booth. The same basic structural situation exists in the area of lobbying, because regardless of a person's class or status position, all are equal in having the right to make their opinions known to the decision-makers.

In an open and democratic society the citizens tend to know what the government or other parts of the polity are doing. If a decision that carries broad social implications is about to be made, all of the people interested should know about it, because key elements of a democratic polity are a free press and an informed citizenry. If people feel strongly about an issue, they have the right to contact members of Parliament, the Senate, the cabinet, or the head of the government to express their opinions. There are no rules preventing any person, regardless of income level or status, from engaging in this activity. The element of lobbying—the opportunity to approach people who have been democratically elected to operate the political institutions—is another of the structures that makes it possible to have a society in which there are individual differences in wealth, status, and authority.

Although in theory all individuals have the opportunity to influence the polity through the electoral process and lobbying, the pluralist approach tends to pay more attention to the activities of organized groups in the political process than it does to the actions of individuals. People often find that they can be more influential if they organize themselves and act collectively, and thus it is common in liberal democratic societies to see the emergence of organized groups representing different sectors and interests in society. The groups that emerge may represent interests grounded in the institutional orders, from the economic to the religious, the educational, or the family. Among those groups, we typically find parent-teacher associations, church associations, anti-poverty organizations, university alumni associations, environmentalists, business interests (large and small), women's organizations, and labour unions. The continuing debates in North America over the issue of abortion represent a situation in which many different interest groups representing many different viewpoints and sectors of society have competed to influence the policies and actions of the government.

Perhaps the best-known and most prolific writer among pluralists is Robert Dahl. Dahl outlined the basic tenets of pluralism in his 1972 classic, *Democracy in the United States: Promise and Performance*. Dahl argues that 'the best government for a state is a government of the people based on political equality and the consent of all' while avoiding the pitfalls of majority rule democracy and rule by the few (21). The term Dahl applies to what he believes is the best possible system is *polyarchy*. Polyarchy, for Dahl, means a system of government that 'incorporates certain aspects of both democratic and elitist theories, presents a critique of both, and offers an alternative way of understanding politics in different systems, particularly systems ordinarily called "democratic"' (46–7). The polyarchy is a system that recognizes the importance of consent and political equality as processes requiring 'that every citizen have unimpaired opportunity to formulate and indicate his or her preferences and have them weighted equally in the conduct of government' (47). Furthermore, the polyarchy requires a number of institutional guarantees to ensure that its principles are upheld in the actual working of government. A polyarchy differs from both majority rule democracy and elite rule in its definition of 'the people', guaranteeing of minority rights, modes of addressing inequalities, role allotted to opposition, and reliance on the electoral process for the settlement of conflicts. Dahl does not provide a concise definition of polyarchy, in part because the term refers to a general structure of government with many possible variations in details and specifies (1972: 38–40).

In a recent spirited defence of pluralism, *Reconstructing Political Pluralism*, Avigail Eisenberg

warns that groups in liberal democracy represent a double-edged sword. Eisenberg writes:

> On the one hand, groups are the means to sort out self-development often identified as the raison d'être of democracy. On the other hand, groups can stifle and distort development through socialization processes that seek to control and oppress the individual. (1995: 5)

She goes on to note that since groups are essential to the fabric of society, while being a means to political power, and important for personal development, they continue to be a core concept in contemporary pluralism. Eisenberg's volume is a conservative reconstruction of pluralism that devotes considerable time and attention to developing a critique of the communitarian side of what she terms the liberal-communitarian debate. While the study provides many insights into new and classical debates within pluralist and liberal theory circles, its overriding concern is individual or personal development and the extent to which pluralism and liberal democracy provide the most effective means for facilitation.

Eisenberg's conclusion presents nine lessons drawn from the extensive discussions of core pluralist ideas that form the bulk of the text. Among the lessons are the need to understand that political power plays an important role in facilitating personal development; however, she reminds us that pluralism must always keep in mind that it 'aims at securing individual well-being and, as such, is individualistic' (Eisenberg, 1995: 187). Other lessons include the stricture that pluralism must be explicitly normative, that it must recognize the plurality of group contexts that individuals are involved in, and that it seeks to 'avoid state intervention in shaping substantive values that define communities' (188). Further, it is important to acknowledge that healthy individual development is predicated on the realization that individuals are the best judges of

The most important aspect of Western democracies is the extent to which all members of society have an opportunity to participate in attempting to influence the policies of the government through activities. (Dick Hemingway)

what is good for their self-development. The final lessons include warnings about the need to maintain pluralism among groups requesting special protections in 'the cultural marketplace', and to watch for external forces that might impose values on the collectivities to which we belong, values that might result in individuals finding themselves 'hostage to the standards of others which aim to determine' key aspects of ourselves (191).

While Eisenberg's reconstructed pluralism seems not to be excessively concerned with the obvious presence of enormous and growing disparities in wealth and income that we witness in most Western societies, one of Robert Dahl's later works looks at pluralism in the context of the post-Soviet world and the collapse of Soviet-style communism. In *After the Revolution? Authority in the Good Society* Dahl offers a sympathetic, yet realistic and even critical, re-examination of the contemporary status of pluralist theory. After reviewing some possible basis

for authority in modern society Dahl concludes that his analysis demonstrates two conclusions: 'that no single form or authority is the most desirable in all associations and that possible combinations of various forms in any concrete association must be nearly endless'. He goes on: 'Consequently, it would be folly to think that a single mass-produced model stamped out according to eternal patterns can possibly fit all the kinds of associations we need in order to cope with our extraordinarily complex world' (1990: 44).

The complex world that Dahl refers to is one that he describes as involving enormous and politically significant structured inequalities. He examines the significant inequalities of resources (wealth and income) in American society, as well as the fact that the economy is dominated by what he refers to as 'corporate leviathans' that represent a form of public authority but under the control of private rulers (96–101). Although he pauses to lament the fact that there is no tradition of socialist thought in America, Dahl ends up concluding that polyarchy offers the nearest thing to a system capable of offering some measure of democracy in the world we live in, even if it's because he sees no alternatives!

> Although polyarchy shows up badly compared with unrealized ideal forms, it looks very much better when it is compared with other political systems that have actually existed to the present. In particular, when it is placed alongside rival political forms that have been tried out this century—waves of the future that swept people overboard—polyarchy looks to be not only incomparably closer to genuine rule by the people but much more humane, decent, tolerant, benign, and responsive in dealing with citizens. (1990: 116)

So pluralists continue to argue that a reconstructed pluralism and/or a realistic polyarchy represents the best options for a democratic polity in the modern era.

An essential feature of political decision-making in liberal democratic societies, pluralists argue, is the extent to which the outcomes tend not to systematically favour any particular individual or group. As individuals and groups compete with each other to influence the decision-making process, over time, supposedly, no one group wins all the time or loses all the time. The phrase 'you win some, you lose some, and some are draws' summarizes the expectations of this approach. Indeed, the term *pluralism* itself draws attention to the sense of having more than one interest group competing for political influence. Political power and influence are scattered throughout the society in the myriad of interest groups and individuals competing through elections and lobbying tactics to influence the social decision-making process.

The concept of pluralism, then, is used to explain the nature of political processes in liberal democratic societies. These societies are characterized by a stratification system in which there are individual inequalities in income (class), status (prestige), and power (authority). These inequalities are, structural functionalists maintain, both necessary and inevitable. But their existence does not mean that these societies are undemocratic and authoritarian. The strength of the liberal democratic system is to be found in the political structures that have developed and evolved. These political institutions have proved capable of facilitating a political process that allows all individuals an opportunity to influence the political decision-making process and thus ensure that individual inequalities cannot be translated into systematic inequalities at the level of social decision-making.

Power and the Ruling Class: The Marxian Perspective

For Marx and those following his mode of analysis, the relationship between capital and labour involves relations of exploitation, domination, and subordination. The capitalist class is the class with economic power. The capitalist class is in a structural position to make society's major economic decisions and ultimately to determine whether economic expansion or contraction occurs—to determine whether jobs are created as plants are built and expanded or if jobs are lost as plants are closed or relocated. Neo-Marxists also argue that the class possessing economic power is able to translate that power into political and ideological power. In short, the class with economic power is, in reality, a ruling class because of its capacity to convert its economic power into other kinds of power.

Political Power: The Realm of the State
Given Marx's concern with understanding the patterns of domination in capitalist society, it is not surprising that political power and the state were issues of concern to him for his entire adult life. His early works were devoted to a critique of the

conception of the state developed by the German philosopher Georg Wilhelm Frederick Hegel (Marx, [1844] 1970). He first began to undertake a more systematic analysis of the state in *The German Ideology*, co-authored with Engels in 1845 to 1846.

Marx and Engels first discussed the position of the institutions we call the state by using or applying the materialist perspective they were in the process of developing. After repeated statements outlining the basic premises of their materialist approach, Marx and Engels identified the state as an institutional order distinct from, though related to, other social structures such as the economy and civil society. In their analysis, civil society refers to a variety of institutional orders, including the family and religion. Although they did not specify the precise nature of the relationship of the state to the economy, the state is clearly linked, they argued, to the structure of class relations. Indeed, Marx and Engels noted that all struggles involving political power are really nothing more than an expression or manifestation of class struggles.

In their subsequent polemical works, such as *The Communist Manifesto* (1848), Marx and Engels further developed this point, suggesting that the state is really nothing more than a structure that directly serves the interests of the capitalist class and its fractions (Marx and Engels, 1952: 43–4). The implication is that the capitalist class somehow directly controls and manages the state, ensuring that the state looks after its interests.

In other works Marx presents a more complex picture of the relationship of the state to the capitalist class. In *The Eighteenth Brumaire of Louis Bonaparte* (1852), Marx presented a picture of the state as having considerable autonomy from the capitalist class, yet in the long run serving its interests. Again, in the first volume of *Capital* (1867), he pictured the state as autonomous though still, over the long run, serving the interests of the capitalist class. What he did not systematically present, however, in any of these works is an argument about how the state comes to serve the capitalist class, or

how the capitalist class controls and dominates the state and the political process.

We have noted that Gramsci's notion of hegemony made an important contribution to the neo-Marxist conceptions of ideology. Gramsci also contributed to the development of a Marxian view of the state in capitalist society. In his *Notebooks* he begins the section on Italian history with this observation: 'The historical unity of the ruling classes is realised in the State, and their history is essentially the history of States and groups of States' (52). In an earlier 1919 piece, which he wrote as a practising journalist, he noted:

> In fact, the laws of historical development were laid down by the property-owing class organized in the State. The State has always been the protagonist of history. In its organs the power the propertied class is centralized. Within the state, the propertied class forges its own discipline and unity, over and above the disputes and clashes of competition, in order to keep intact its privileged position in the supreme phase of competition itself: the class struggle for power, for pre-eminence in leadership and ordering society. ([1910–20] 1977: 73–4)

He also discussed the role of law and the two primary functions of the state. The first function is clear: 'The Law is the repressive and negative aspect of the entire positive, civilising activity undertaken by the State' (247). The second function is referred to in this sentence as the 'civilising' activity, and has to do with the role of the state in terms of providing education and basic knowledge to its citizens. Gramsci understands that this role is contradictory because such knowledge typically includes the elements of a hegemonic ideology and as such it serves to benefit the dominant class:

> . . . the cultural state, is this: every State is ethical in as much as one of its important

functions is to raise the great mass of the population to a particular cultural and moral level, a level (or type) which corresponds to the needs of the productive forces for development, and hence to the interests of the ruling class. (1975: 258)

Revising Marx: Neo-Marxism on the State

One of the first substantial efforts by neo-Marxists to understand the state in capitalist society is found in the work of Ralph Miliband. In 1969 Miliband published *The State in Capitalist Society*, in which he attempted to accomplish two objectives: to offer a critique of the pluralist approach; and to develop the outline of a neo-Marxist alternative. Miliband argued that the various branches or agencies of the state, such as the government, the administrative arm, the military, and even state agencies, are staffed, at their upper decision-making levels at least, by personnel drawn from the business and propertied class as well as the professional middle class. The class background, educational training, and general value orientations of these people lead them to believe that the proper role of government is to oversee the maintenance of social, economic, and political stability and thus the existence of the status quo. Miliband argued that the overwhelming economic power wielded by members of the capitalist class makes it possible for them to dominate the electoral and lobbying processes. In addition to these factors he examined the role played by ideology in the larger political processes, arguing that the vast majority of people in command positions in the state tend to accept capitalist society as the most appropriate if not the best of all worlds; as a result, they work for the continuance and stability of the system. The end result of all these processes and structures, Miliband argued, is a political system controlled and dominated in a variety of ways by the economically dominant class. In the final analysis, according to Miliband, the capitalist class

is able to influence the state in a number of ways, and ensure that it continues to act in their own long-term interests.

The Poulantzas Challenge

About the same time that Miliband was working on his book, Nicos Poulantzas was developing an alternative neo-Marxist approach. This approach was quite different, stressing the logic and functioning of the structures of capitalist society and not the personal and personnel connections between capital and the state, which had been Miliband's focus. When used in this context, personal connections between the capitalist class and the state would involve the capitalist class promoting candidates for state positions that share its ideology and value system, with common educational backgrounds and social connections. Personnel connections would involve members of the capitalist class actually occupying positions of power in the state system.

The Poulantzas approach became associated with a particular variation of neo-Marxism called French structuralism, and it bore a strong resemblance to more orthodox functionalist thought. The key was his assumption that, because capitalism is a class-based society, it is in constant danger of breaking down as a result of class-based conflict and tension. In such a society some means of providing social stability is essential if the society is to continue to exist and operate relatively smoothly. For Poulantzas, the function of the state is to provide a basis of social order. The state, he argued, is a powerful factor of cohesion that attempts to bind together the conflict and contradiction that riddle society (1972: 246). The essential reason why the state acts in the interests of the dominant or capitalist class is because some institution must perform this function or the society will disintegrate.

Poulantzas explicitly criticized Miliband for dwelling on personal and personnel connections (1972: 246). For Poulantzas, the capitalist class itself is divided into internal fractions that can have differing economic interests and political agendas. Given this situation, the possibility of instability exists if one of the fractions directly controls the state and uses it to secure its narrow interests. The state must be capable of accommodating the demands of the various fractions or segments of the dominant class, all the while overseeing as much as possible the smooth functioning of the whole system. A key issue for Poulantzas is the question of state autonomy. He argued that the state in capitalist society is relatively autonomous of the capitalist class, yet the logic of the structures results in the state functioning to stabilize the system.

The differences in the positions developed by Miliband and Poulantzas resulted in a series of journal articles that turned into a debate between the two. What is important for our purposes is that this debate ultimately produced and stimulated a number of different directions and approaches within the neo-Marxist school. Many of those differences are still apparent today in the neo-Marxist literature, although there is some indication of a move towards less abstract approaches that allow for the analysis of actual historical and concrete events.

Neo-Marxist Theory and Social Research

As the debate among neo-Marxists continued, many new positions emerged. These positions or approaches were quite varied in their degree of sophistication and theoretical complexity (Carnoy, 1984; Jessop, 1982; Knuttila, 1992). One of the interesting outcomes was a demand that critical or neo-Marxist approaches must be capable of stimulating actual social analysis if they are to be useful in the process of social criticism (Skocpol, 1985). The arguments of Albert Szymanski are especially illustrative of efforts to develop an approach that has the possibility of being used in historical and empirical research and analysis.

In his 1978 book *The Capitalist State and the Politics of Class*, Szymanski discussed the state in capitalist society while avoiding the problems associated with relying on the personal/personnel

linkages of Miliband and the abstract functionalism of Poulantzas and others. Szymanski argued that in a liberal democratic state there are mechanisms of power through which individuals and members of classes can attempt to influence or control the state (1978: 24–5). He noted that there are two different types of mechanisms of power that individuals belonging to various classes could use to try to influence the operation and decisions of the state: direct and indirect. His argument was not that the pluralist approach is completely wrong; it is just that it only addresses a couple of the means through which the state can be influenced. Among the direct mechanisms are:

- direct participation in the operation of the state by individuals and members of classes;
- the lobbying process;
- the policy formation process; for instance, various 'think tank' organizations that offer policy advice to governments; by establishing or funding such organizations, classes and individuals can influence the state.

In addition to these direct mechanisms of power, Szymanski outlined four indirect modes of controlling the state:

- *The ideological environment.* State officials are constrained in their actions and policy initiatives by the overall ideological environment. Those making decisions within the state are always aware of and concerned with public opinion, and they simply will not take actions that would be deemed to represent a violation of some aspect of the dominant ideology. Ideological power is a mechanism of political power, because by influencing public opinion people can indirectly influence the state.
- *Economic power.* The state operates as part

of a set of social structures that depend on the economy for their existence. Without a healthy and expanding economy the entire social structure, including the state, will encounter difficulty. A growing economy provides the elected state representatives with a better chance of re-election, not to mention an expanding tax base. The capitalist class makes the major economic decisions relating to investments and economic growth or decline, and if the state undertakes actions deemed to be against the interests of capital, capital can close plants and curtail investment and thereby cause instability in the economic basis of society.

· *Financing of the electoral process.* To win elections, politicians need substantial amounts of money, and through financial contributions, or the withholding of same, the policies and actions of parties and candidates can be influenced.

· *The presence of the military as a mechanism of last resort.* Usually a conservative force dedicated to the status quo, the military will defend the existing order should its ultimate stability be threatened. Szymanski argues that the military has close ties to the dominant class.

In his discussion of specific linkages or mechanisms of power through which the state can be influenced, Szymanski was attempting to avoid the functionalist logic of Poulantzas by providing concrete examples of the means by which the capitalist class could influence the state. In a constitutional liberal democratic society these mechanisms of power had theoretically become available to all citizens; but it was clear that the capacity to use them requires economic power and resources. Given the fact that neo-Marxists assumed that economic power and resources are largely in the hands of the capitalist class, they maintained that there is an unequal distribution of economic power.

The kind of work done by Miliband, Poulantzas, and Szymanski indicates, first, that in more recent years neo-Marxists have attempted to develop an alternative to the functionalist and pluralist approach to the study of the polity in capitalist society. Second, it shows that, given the various positions within the neo-Marxist camp, not all of those who have disagreed with the functionalist and pluralist approaches have agreed among themselves about exactly what approach to take. As a result, various schools or streams of thought have developed within the Marxian tradition.

New Directions and Beyond Neo-Marxism

The Miliband–Poulantzas debate and Szymanski alternative approach do not come close to exhausting the literature. Indeed in recent years many others, including Eric A. Nordlinger and Theda Skocpol, have sought to understand the relationship between various classes and the state in capitalist society. Although it would not be appropriate to place all these thinkers within the Marxian tradition, they all do accept that 'the state is a force in its own right and does not simply reflect the dynamic of the economy and/or civil society' (Jessop, 1990: 279). The 'state-centred' approach obviously directs our analytical attention to the structures and operation of the state as an independent 'actor' in the complex interplay of economic, social, and political forces. Such an approach does not assume that the state is tied to or will reflect any class forces. Skocpol summarizes the argument: 'States conceived as organizations claiming control over territories and people may formulate and pursue goals that are not simply reflective of the demands or interests of social groups, classes or society' (Skocpol, 1985: 9). She goes on to note that 'Bringing the state back in to a central place in analyses of policy making and social change does require a break with some of the most encompassing social-determinist assumptions of pluralism, structural functionalist developmentalism, and various neo-Marxisms' (20).

In his 1990 volume Jessop offers a substantial critique of what he calls 'state-centred' theorists; however, he goes on to note that the work of scholars such as E. Laclau and C. Mouffé represents an even more serious challenge to current thinking and theorizing about the state. According to Jessop, Laclau and Mouffé do not just question the manner by which scholars operating for a variety of perspectives have understood the state; the logic of their work challenges the very existence of the state. Mouffé and Laclau represent an approach to understanding social processes that holds that 'the social has an open, unsutured character and that neither its elements nor its totality have a pre-given necessity' (Jessop, 1990: 289). As a result, the various relations that compose the social result in 'societies that are tendentially constituted as an ensemble of totalizing effects in an open relational complex' (290). If one accepts this conception of the state it becomes, at most, one part of a larger set of social relations that are constantly contested, produced, and reproduced. Jessop summarizes: 'even if their [Mouffé and Laclau's] approach does not require the total deconstruction of the state, it does deny states any positivity and de-privileges them as sites of political struggle' (293).

An alternative contemporary approach to the state has been developed by thinkers associated with an approach commonly referred to as regulation theory. While, as Jessop points out, many complex and sophisticated different ideas and arguments are associated with regulation theory, there are some common assumptions that inform these thinkers. Central among the underlying principles is the assumption that the social and economic structures that typically characterize capitalist society are unstable and incapable of maintaining themselves in the long term without some significant transformations and interventions. It is argued that regulatory mechanisms are the basis of the transformations and interventions that make it possible for the capitalist system and its concomitant institutional structures and arrangements to

survive. Jessop summarizes: 'they all focus on the changing social forms and mechanisms in and through which the capital relation is reproduced despite its inherent economic contradictions and emergent conflictual properties' (1990: 309).

Regulation theorists tend to examine both the economic and extra-economic processes and structural conditions that allow different accumulation regimes to exist and function despite the inherent contradictions and class conflicts that characterize the system. They further assume that there are no abstract necessary or typical systems of regulation that work in all or most capitalist systems. The modes of regulation that characterize a particular society or nation will be the outcome of historically specific institutional arrangements, modes of conduct, and normative rules (309).

Jessop explains that there are variations on this theme among those scholars working within this tradition. Some regulation theorists use concepts such as 'regimes of accumulation' or 'modes of regulation' to describe historically and nationally specific institutional arrangements and institutions that might characterize the structures and operations of capitalism in specific locals at specific moments in history. For example, one might have used the general descriptor of Keynesian welfare state (see Chapter 15) to describe both Canada and the United States at a certain moment; in actual fact, there were significant differences in the forms and structures of the welfare state in the two nations. In each case there were different sets of policies and institutional arrangements (regimes of accumulation or modes of regulation) that reflected the strength or weakness of labour, various fractions of capital, the role of state agencies and so on. In Canada, for example, one might argue that the stronger British Fabian socialist influence in farmers' and workers' movements resulted in a mode of regulation that included a significant government role in the provision of medical services. Despite its apparent tendencies to be abstract, regulation theory draws our attention to the need for concrete analysis by denying 'that there is a single objective logic of capitalist development that transcends all particularities: the development of capitalism is always mediated through historically specific institutional forms, regulatory institutions, and norms of conduct' (1990: 309).

The state is able to provide the required modes or systems of regulatory mechanisms because it is 'neither an ideal collective capitalist whose functions are determined in the last instance by the imperatives of economic production nor is it a simple parallelogram of pluralist forces' (1990: 315). The process of establishing the necessary regulatory system to facilitate continued capitalist accumulation is deemed to be very complex:

[S]ecuring the conditions for capital accumulation or managing an unstable equilibrium of compromise involves not only a complex array of institutions and policies but also a continuing struggle to build consensus and back it with coercion.... [T]he state itself can be seen as a complex ensemble of institutions, networks, procedures, modes of calculation and norms as well as their associated pattern of strategic conduct. (Jessop, 1990: 315)

According to Jessop, the regulationist perspective offers a useful antidote to the simplistic or economic reductionism arguments, conventional functionalist positions, and approaches that exaggerate the separateness of the formal state apparatus from the less formal political processes that surround the processes of capital accumulation.

Julia O'Connor and Gregg Olsen have also commented on the issue of functionalist logic permeating non-functional-structuralist analyses of the state (1998: 5–6). In their edited work *Power Resource Theory and the Welfare State: A Critical Approach*, O'Connor and Olsen introduce an alternative approach commonly referred to as power resource theory. They explain its origins: 'Power resources theory emerged in the late 1970s and early

1980s in an attempt to redress some of the problems with existing mainstream and radical accounts of the welfare state' (6). The approach, which seeks to direct more attention to the potential role of various classes in influencing state policies and actions without, emerged out of the work of Gösta Esping-Andersen and Walter Korpi. O'Connor and Olsen further note that the approach rejects the pluralist notions that power is not concentrated, but rather is widely dispersed. The approach also takes umbrage with the tendency among those within the Marxian tradition to see power absolutely concentrated in the hands of the capitalist class. They note that this approach suggests 'that the balance of power between labour and capital was fluid, and therefore variable' (6). They go on:

While capital would always have the upper hand within a capitalist framework, labour had the potential to access political resources which could increase its power, and thereby allow it to implement social reform and alter distributional inequities to a significant degree. (6)

Walter Korpi explains that power must be conceptualized as a resource that shifts over time, and cannot be readily understandable simply in terms of immediately observable behaviours, just as an iceberg cannot be understood by observing the tip that presents itself to us (1998: vii). He goes on to describe an essential feature of the approach:

The power resources approach therefore focuses not only on the direct, but also the indirect consequences of power, indirect consequences mediated through various alternative strategies and actions available to the holders of power resources. (1998: vii)

Korpi goes on to explain that the exercise and distribution of power occurs within specific institutions, with markets, the polity and the family being the three main institutional sites in which the distribution of power takes place. As power relations and dynamics change, the precise configuration and operation of institutions will change. Power resource theory analyzes how institutions in which power is exercised and distributed, such as those associated with the welfare state, change and evolve (see Bashevkin, 2000; Olsen, 1999). If we return for a moment to the regulation theory argument that different political, cultural, and historical circumstances generate different regimes of accumulation and modes of regulation, it becomes obvious that power resource theory arguments are not very different. Both of these positions draw our attention to the need for historical and empirical research that is viewed through a theoretical prism that provides insights into actual mechanisms and modes of exercising power.

While this cursory overview only touches some of the recent approaches, it should alert the reader to a simple fact, namely, that the project of understanding the state and developing an adequate theoretical framework is still ongoing, open, and incomplete.

Classical Elite Theory

Alongside the structural functionalist, Marxist, and feminist theories, there has been one other major approach in Western sociology that has focused explicitly on the issue of social inequality. Although elite theory is not as important in terms of its use by contemporary sociologists, it does warrant a brief introduction. Among the first of the classical elite thinkers was Vilfredo Pareto.

Vilfredo Pareto

Although Pareto (1848–1923), an Italian born in Paris, was trained in engineering and mathematics, he later turned to the social sciences and eventually developed a complex theory of society. A part of his theory sought to explain the persistence of social

and economic inequalities. His major sociological work, translated as *The Mind and Society: A Treatise on General Sociology*, was published in Italy in 1916.

Pareto argued that the social and economic inequalities that had always characterized all human societies are because of the simple fact that the human beings who make up society are not themselves equal. Pareto developed a complex series of arguments to explain the basis of human inequalities. The essence of his position is that individual inequalities are based on the biologically determined distribution of personal attributes, abilities, talents, and aptitudes. Not all individuals are equally endowed in terms of their capacities and propensities. When unequally endowed individuals engage in the competitive situations that typically characterize human social existence, some will always tend to exhibit superior traits and over time they will emerge as a special group, which Pareto called the elite ([1916] 1976: 248).

The superior performers assume control of the realm of human affairs or conduct in which they operate. Pareto argued that there are two different kinds of elites, the governing and non-governing. The governing elite is composed of those directly involved in politics and political rule, while the non-governing are superior performers not directly involved in politics. The majority of the population, however, are not in either of the elites, and they make up what Pareto refers to as the 'lower stratum', 'lower classes', and 'the commonality' (1976: 158, 249). The elites constitute a minority that rules over the majority—what elite theorists call the masses. This is as it should be, since members of the elite hold their positions by virtue of their special abilities.

The basic fact that human individuals are unequal led Pareto to pose fundamental questions about the logic and possibility of democracy. Indeed, if we follow Pareto's elitist approach to its logical conclusion, democracy, which implies the rule of the masses, is an undesirable state. It is not surprising, then, that the Italian dictator Mussolini found Pareto's ideas attractive (Coser, 1977: 406).

Another Italian social theorist, Gaetano Mosca (1858–1941), took Pareto's core ideas one step further. In his major work, *The Ruling Class* ([1896] 1939), Mosca developed a less biologically based explanation of why there are elites. But he nevertheless retained a strong element of the biological argument for individual superiority, which from the perspective of a sociologist means his arguments are highly flawed. The most powerful statement of elite theory that contained an explicitly sociological thrust would be developed by Robert Michels.

Robert Michels

Robert Michels (1876–1936) was a German-born academic who spent most of his adult life in Italy, where he became familiar with the arguments of Pareto and Mosca. Michels, too, was interested in

the same phenomenon, that is, the tendency for human society and all other forms of human organization to become dominated and governed by small groups of people. He was interested in how and why elites always emerged.

Michels is best known for his study of the internal operation of the social democratic party in Germany. In *Political Parties* (1911) he reached disturbing conclusions for all who value and cherish the democratic ideal, because he argued that there is something inherent in organizations and organizational activity that leads to the emergence of elites.

According to Michels, if individuals or groups want to have an impact on any aspect of a modern complex society, they must first organize themselves. This is so because of the very nature of a modern society. All the groups attempting to gain power and influence in society are themselves highly

PLURALIST DEMOCRACY, ELITE RULE, OR A CLASS STATE?

Political thinkers, philosophers, and theorists of all kinds have been contemplating and debating the nature of the state or polity for thousands of years. We seem no closer to determining what is the most appropriate form of the state—perhaps we never will. The debate you are encountering here is less about the nature of the polity in the abstract than about the polity in capitalist or Western liberal democratic society. We present three radically different perspectives. The pluralist approach argues that Western democratic societies really are democratic, while the Marxian position holds that the inequalities of class make that impossible because there is one class with the capacity to translate its economic power into political power. Elite theory, of course, suggests that the structures and dynamics of complex modern societies make the very notion of democracy a *non sequitur*.

Pluralism

Pluralism has been the dominant theoretical approach in North America for many decades, and during that time Robert Dahl has been the dominant political theorist of the pluralist tradition. Here are two excerpts from his work, one written in 1969 and the other in 1998.

A Pluralist Democracy

In his classic *Pluralist Democracy* in the United States, Dahl outlines what he sees as the inevitable political problems that every society faces. He then discusses what he calls the 'pluralistic solution' outlining its basic premises.

The fundamental axiom in the theory and practise of American pluralism is, I believe, this: Instead of a single center of sovereign power there must be multiple centers of power, none of which is or can be wholly sovereign. Although the only legitimate sovereign is the people, in the perspective of American pluralism even the people ought never to be an absolute sovereign; consequently no part of the people, such as a majority, ought to be absolutely sovereign.

Why this axiom? The theory and practise of American pluralism tend to assume, as I see it, that the existence of multiple centers of power, none of which is wholly sovereign, will help (may indeed be necessary) to tame power, to secure the consent of all, and to settle conflicts peacefully:

- Because one center of power is set against another, power itself will be tamed, civilized, controlled, and limited to decent human purposes, while coercion, the most evil form of power, will be reduced to a minimum.

- Because even minorities are provided with opportunities to veto solutions they strongly object to, the consent of all will be won in the long run.

- Because constant negotiations among different centers of power are necessary in order to make decisions, citizens and leaders will perfect the precious art of dealing peacefully with their conflicts, and not merely to the benefit of one partisan but to the mutual benefit of all the parties to a conflict.

These are, I think, the basic postulates and even the unconscious ways of thought that are central to the American attempt to cope with the inescapable problems of power, conflict, and consent. How a system reflecting these views came about, how its main institutions operate, what forces sustain it, and how it meets the problems of power, conflict, and consent are the subjects of this book (*24*).

From Robert Dahl, *Pluralist Democracy in the United States* (Chicago: Rand McNally, 1967), 24. Reprinted by permission of the author.

In his 1998 book, *On Democracy,* the theme was the same, but there are more details. Dahl asks the question: how can we reasonably determine what political institutions are necessary for large-scale democracy? He offers some ways to approach the issue, but concludes that the approach does not really matter.

Fortunately, all three methods converge on the same set of democratic political institutions. These, then, are minimal requirements for a democratic country.

THE POLITICAL INSTITUTIONS OF MODERN
REPRESENTATIVE DEMOCRACY
Briefly, the political institutions of modern representative democratic government are:

1. Elected officials. Control over government decisions about policy is constitutionally vested in officials elected by citizens. Thus modern, large-scale democratic governments are representative.

2. Free, fair, and frequent elections. Elected officials are chosen in frequent and fairly conducted elections in which coercion is comparatively uncommon.

3. Freedom of expression. Citizens have a right to express themselves without danger of severe punishment on political matters broadly defined, including criticism of officials, the government, the regime, the socioeconomic order, and the prevailing ideology.

4. Access to alternative sources of information. Citizens have a right to seek out alternative and independent sources of information from other citizens, experts, newspapers, magazines, books, telecommunications, and the like. Moreover, alternative sources of information actually exist that are not under the control of the government or any other single political group attempting to influence public political beliefs and attitudes, and these alternative sources are effectively protected by law.

5. Associational autonomy. To achieve their various rights, including those required for the effective operation of democratic political institutions, citizens also have a right to form relatively independent associations or organizations, including independent political parties and interest groups.

6. Inclusive citizenship. No adult permanently residing in the country and subject to its laws can be denied the rights that are available to others and are necessary to the five political institutions just listed. These include the rights to vote in the election of officials in free and fair elections; to run for elective office; to free expression; to form and participate in independent political organizations; to have access to independent sources of information; and rights to other liberties and opportunities that may be necessary to the effective operation of the political institutions of large-scale democracy (*84–6*).

From *On Democracy* by Robert Dahl. © 1998 Yale University Press. Reprinted by permission of the publisher.

Neo-Marxism and the Class-dominated State

Given that a central concern of neo-Marxist theory is societal domination by the class with overwhelming economic power, we should not be surprised that neo-Marxists see pluralism as more myth than reality. In what follows, Albert Szymanski explains what he sees as the reality of politics in capitalist society with its inherent class inequalities.

Class Control of the 'Democratic' State

Unlike the elite theorists, Marxists do not maintain that the capitalist class fully controls the other classes in society, nor do they maintain that it can have the state do anything it wants. Rather, the capitalist class is considered to be politically dominant or hegemonic. It normally either gets its way or is able to so deflect and integrate the pressures coming from other classes as to turn them to its own uses, but it does not control all aspects or society. It is merely the typical dominant force' in the class struggle, and the force that is dominant within the state.

There are two fundamentally different ways by which the interests and will of the capitalist class are realized against the state. First, through *direct* means or 'input' channels, and second, through the *indirect* means of structuring the environment in which the state must operate. In most cases both forces are operating at once to guarantee doubly that the state does the bidding of the capitalist class.

One of the direct mechanisms by which the state in capitalist society is directly dominated by the capitalist class is through the actual selection of the incumbents for top governmental office. Leading officials tend to be either leading members of the capitalist class (such as Franklin Roosevelt, John Kennedy, or Nelson Rockefeller); famous celebrities who have been carefully picked and closely advised by members of the upper class, who finance and manage their campaigns and surround them with advisers; . . . or small-time politicians who have worked their way up the ladder by years of service to big business interests, who reward and promote them by funding campaigns and opening doors for them *(23)*.

A second direct mechanism of achieving dominance is through the process of lobbying. Business interests employ thousands of people who have considerable resources at their disposal to influence members of Congress and members of the regulatory and administrative agencies. A third mechanism is the process of forming public policy. Exclusive capitalist-class organizations, such as the Council on Foreign Relations (CFR), actually formulate public policies. . . .

The capitalist nature of the state is also guaranteed by another set of processes. Even if the capitalist class exercised no direct control over the state by any of the three mechanisms described earlier, the state would behave in the same way (at least in 'normal' conditions). Although if this were the case the state might be more willing to experiment with different policies before settling on those most advantageous to the largest segments of the business community

if not the capitalist class as a whole. The state must operate within an ideological, economic, military, and political environment structured by capitalist relations of production. If state officials are to succeed in their careers, if the agencies they command are to operate smoothly, if the state is to prevent social crisis and promote prosperity, and if it is to be successful militarily, then there are certain imperatives that it must follow. This is true as long as it stays within the parameters established by the nature of the capitalist system.

There are four mechanisms of indirect control over the state:

1. Capitalist values permeate the society and are propagated through the schools, military, media, and churches. Officials typically accept capitalist ideology as their own and authentically act as if capitalist rationality were the only rationality. Attempts by state officials to enact measures that would violate capitalist ideology would generate considerable opposition, even from the oppressed, as long as they accept capitalist ideas.

2. If the state attempts to follow policies that business doesn't like, businesses can move to other countries or they may curtail production, lay off workers or follow other restrictive policies, thereby promoting an economic crisis for which the state would be blamed. Businesses can refuse to invest unless the state follows probusiness policies. Banks have the special advantage of refusing to make loans to the state unless the state follows policies directed by them. Such actions by business might not be malicious, but might be merely economically rational and dictated by the necessity of maximizing profits.

3. States that attempt anticapitalist policies are subjected to the threat of military intervention, either by foreign states that want to prevent the abolition of capitalism, or by their own military, which may well be closely tied to the capitalist class.

4. Officials who follow anticapitalist policies may be cut off from campaign financing, slandered in the capitalist-class-controlled media, and forced to face well-financed and promoted opponents in their campaigns for reelection as well as being confronted with embarrassing demonstrations, disruptions, and possible social and political crises (24–5).

From Albert Szymanski, *The Capitalist State and the Politics of Class* (Cambridge: Winthrop, 1978).

Elite Theory or the Impossibility of Democracy

Neo-Marxist social theory is also critical theory with a Utopian political project geared to emancipation attached to it. But this is not the case with elite theory. The reason for this is simple. According to elite theory, the rule of the many by the few, the masses by an elite, is inevitable and necessary. In his classic study, *Political Parties*, Robert Michels makes this clear.

The Inevitability of Elite Rule

LEADERSHIP is a necessary phenomenon in every form of social life. Consequently it is not the task of science to inquire whether this phenomenon is good or evil, or predominantly one or the other. But there is great scientific value in the demonstration that every system of leadership is incompatible with the most essential postulates of democracy. We are now aware that the law of the historic necessity of oligarchy is primarily based upon a series of facts or experience. Like all other scientific laws, sociological laws are derived from empirical observation. In order, however, to deprive our axiom of its purely descriptive character, and to confer upon it that status of analytical explanation which can alone transform a formula into a law, it does not suffice to contemplate from a unitary outlook those phenomena which may be empirically established; we must also study the determining causes of these phenomena. Such has been our task.

Now, if we leave out of consideration the tendency of the leaders to organize themselves and to consolidate their interests, and if we leave also out of consideration the gratitude of the led towards the leaders, and the general immobility and passivity of the masses, we are led to conclude that the principal cause of oligarchy in the democratic parties is to be found in the technical indispensability of leadership.

The process which has begun in consequence of the differentiation of functions in the party is completed by a complex of qualities which the leaders acquire through their detachment from the mass. At the outset, leaders arise SPONTANEOUSLY; their functions are ACCESSORY and GRATUITOUS. Soon, however, they become PROFESSIONAL leaders, and in this second stage of development they are STABLE and IRREMOVABLE.

It follows that the explanation of the oligarchical phenomenon which thus results is partly PSYCHOLOGICAL; oligarchy derives, that is to say, from the psychical transformations which the leading personalities in the parties undergo in the course of their lives. But also, and still more, oligarchy depends upon what we may term the PSYCHOLOGY OF ORGANIZATION ITSELF, that is to say, upon the tactical and technical necessities which result from the consolidation of every disciplined political aggregate. Reduced to its most concise expression, the fundamental sociological law of political parties (the term *political* being here used in its most comprehensive significance) may be formulated in the following terms: 'It is organization which gives birth to the dominion of the elected over the electors, of the mandataries over the mandators, of the delegates over the delegators. Who says organization, says oligarchy.'

From Robert Michels, *Political Parties: A Sociological Study of the Oligarchical Tendencies of Modern Democracy* (New York: The Free Press, [1911] 1962).

organized, and to compete with them requires a sophisticated degree of organization. But the need for organization brings with it certain problems and dynamics. The existence of complex organizations brings on problems related to the logistics of organizing mass meetings, communicating with a mass membership, and organizing debates in the presence of hundreds or even thousands of members. Even in an organization formally committed to democratic procedures these logistical problems give rise to an interesting tendency: after an organization struggles with these logistical problems for a while it becomes apparent that it needs some form of delegation of authority and decision-making rights to function properly or to the highest degree of effectiveness. There is, Michels argued, an organizational imperative or logic that leads to the emergence of delegation of authority, which in turn leads to a specialization of tasks. Once this process begins, the organization is well on its way to becoming dominated by an elite.

Michels argued that once the specialization of internal tasks develops and the delegation of authority begins, a universal process takes place. The people specializing in various tasks tend to become 'experts' in their areas and very soon they come to assume leadership positions within various parts of the organization. These specialists and leaders increasingly make decisions on their own,

and they become more and more separated from the majority of the members, that is, from the masses. A further dynamic develops as well. As the leaders and specialists carry out their tasks, their personalities and behavioural patterns are changed by their experiences. Those who see themselves as representing the masses tend to become involved in meetings with representatives from other organizations; they travel to various centres to meet government officials and other powerful individuals. As the process carries on, these specialists and leaders increasingly come to constitute an elite that gradually assumes control of the organization.

These tendencies, Michels said, are exacerbated by apathetic tendencies among the masses. Many of those not directly involved in decision-making have a desire to be led. As a result the masses not only go along with their organization being taken over by an elite, but they also want it—although Michels gave no adequate explanation of why the masses would possess this characteristic.

For Michels, the tendency for elites to emerge is so strong that it can be referred to as a law: the 'Iron Law of Oligarchy'. In a forceful and much-quoted summary of his argument, he stated, 'It is organization which gives birth to the domination of the elected over the electors, of the mandataries over the mandators, of the delegates over the delegators. Who says organization, says oligarchy' (1962: 365).

Beyond Class Politics: Feminism and the State*

Thus far, we have examined two major analytical approaches to the study of the polity in capitalist society. In the case of the pluralist and structural functionalist approach, the polity is seen as a part of a social decision-making process in which there are no dominant forces, interests, or players who consistently get their way at least in the long run. According to the various Marxian positions, the state in capitalist society is either instrumentally, structurally, or through mechanisms of power 'connected' to the capitalist class and as a result the state tends to work in the interests of that class. As a result of its ability to influence the state, the capitalist class is truly a ruling class, having both economic and political power. As we have seen, however, the adequacy of functionalism and Marxism have been very much questioned in recent years, and this applies to their understanding of the state as well.

The most important and systematic critique of the analytical and explanatory capacities of the approaches discussed above has come from thinkers, scholars, and activists associated with various schools of feminist thought. As new questions were posed concerning the nature and role of the state, especially as it relates to sex and gender relations, the existing approaches were found wanting in two related, but different aspects. First, convincing arguments supported by overwhelming evidence showed that the state played a central role in the subordination of women and the domination of men. This evidence then led to the second important development, namely, demands that the existing theoretical frameworks that had informed the study of the state be radically rethought so as to account for the role of the state in maintaining a society based on patriarchal and heterosexual relations. Let us first look at the literature that illustrated the role of the state in maintaining unequal sex and gender relations.

If there was any doubt about the extent to which the actions and policies of the Canadian State have an immediate impact on relations between the sexes and are gendered, a collection of essays edited by Janine Brodie, *Women and Canadian Public Policy*, represents the *coup de grâce*. The volume contains numerous essays and studies that examine the extent to which the policies and actions of neo-conservative states of the 1990s impact women and men differently. The conclusion, as summarized by Brodie, is inescapable: 'The essays in this book point to the new emerging order as fraught not only with new dangers for Canadian women, but also with contradictions' (1996: 24). The latter, of course, opens the door to resistance and struggles for equity and democratization.

While the essays and their findings are too voluminous to review in detail, a few illustrations are in order. Patricia McDermott examines what many people would assume are state policies that would necessarily be beneficial for women—pay and employment equity legislation. However, McDermott demonstrates how the Ontario decision to treat the wage gap between women and men and the various discriminatory labour practices that segment the labour force as separate problems amenable to different legislative and policy solutions resulted in neither being satisfactorily addressed. The end result is, after much public debate and political posturing, a very real danger that the long-sought-after goal of fairness and equity will slip though the cracks (1996: 102). In her study of a central issue for Canadian women, new reproductive technologies, Barbara Cameron demonstrates that it is not so much that the Canadian state is developing or intending to develop policies in this area that are detrimental to women, but rather that the new global era is preventing the Canadian state from doing anything. Cameron argues that the provisions of the North American Free Trade Agreement 'contains

---

* Material in this section is from Murray Knuttila, 'The State and Social Issues: Theoretical Considerations', in Wayne Antony and Les Samuelson, eds, *Power and Resistance: Critical Thinking about Canadian Social Issues* (Halifax: Fernwood, 1998).

provisions that can be used to limit the capacity of member states of NAFTA to regulate commercial activity within its territory' 123–4). It matters not that such regulations impact pay or equity or new reproductive technologies, NAFTA very likely forbids them!

Several essays in the collection address the issue of how the neo-conservative and neo-liberal eras of fiscal restraint and deregulation have adversely impacted women. Pat Armstrong concluded her essay on the destruction of the health care system, 'Unravelling the Safety Net: Transformations in Health Care and Their Impact on Women', with a pointed conclusion. She notes: 'Meanwhile, states are reducing the capacity of women to remain healthy by dismantling social-security programs, by deregulating industries, and by moving away from an equity agenda' (1996: 145).

A section of the book entitled 'Restructuring Private Life' contains a number of powerful essays addressing issues relating to issues such as same-sex couples, obscenity law, and pornography, and violence against women. In each case the conclusion is inescapable, namely, that the state levels in Canada are powerful forces in the structuring of relations between women and men and in the gendering of our society.

These essays, and others in collections such as that edited by M. Patricia Connelly and Pat Armstrong, *Feminism in Action: Studies in Political Economy*, demonstrate definitively that the state is an important player in constructing and regulating sex and gender in advanced capitalist society. The question they tend not to answer is *why*. As important as these historical and empirical studies are, they tend to neglect the larger issue of what sort of theoretical explanations might be most appropriate for explaining these developments and offering answers to the essential why questions.

An early work that argued that the state played an important role in sex and gender relations was Mary McIntosh's 1978 essay, 'The State and the Oppression of Women'. McIntosh claimed that the

state is involved in the oppression of women through its support of the household system, which in capitalist society is intimately linked to the accumulating of capital. Her thesis holds that the household is the site of the production and reproduction of the essential commodity in the production and appropriation of surplus value in capitalist society—labour power. Further, she argued that the state plays a central role in the maintenance of the specific household form in which women produce and reproduce labour power and thus the state oppresses women through various measures that serve to maintain patriarchal family relations in its efforts to provide the conditions that are necessary for the maintenance and continuation of the system.

Numerous feminist writers elaborated on these themes. As we have seen, Michèle Barrett (1985) warned us not to try to explain the persistence of patterns of male dominance and the patriarchal family just in terms of economic factors, arguing that we need to consider the role of ideology. In a powerful essay, 'Masculine Dominance and the State', Varda Burstyn (1985) questions the value of a Marxian-based concept of class in addressing sex and gender oppression. Indeed, she argues that we need to develop the concept of 'gender class' to understand the full extent of the oppression of women, which is not just a matter of women in capitalist society being oppressed but rather is part of a larger transhistorical pattern of sexual oppression. Burstyn suggests that the state has played a central role in both economic class domination and gender class domination. Further, she maintains that the state has acted to enforce these dual patterns of domination because state structures have tended to be dominated by men.

A somewhat different argument was developed by Jane Ursel (1986), who advocated the development of an analytic approach that recognized the importance of both material production and biological reproduction in determining the shape and character of human society. Ursel argued in effect that the concept of capitalism as understood in Marxian analysis is useful for understanding the nature of material production in Western society, while the concept of patriarchy is most appropriate for an analysis of reproduction. She notes that the state has played a central role in facilitating the continuance of the various modes of material production and biological reproduction, and thus the state has served the interests of those who benefit from the class-based relations of production in capitalist society and the sexual oppression of patriarchal society.

Two important articles, Norene Pupo's 'Preserving Patriarchy: Women, The Family and The State' (1988) and Jane Jenson's 'Gender and Reproduction, or Babies and the State' (1992), illustrate the complexities of the relationship between the state and sex and gender relations. Pupo examines the rise and role of what we might term family-related legislation in Canada, noting its contradictory nature. She writes:

> Through its vast system of laws, regulations, and the institutional structure of the welfare state, the state shapes both personal and social lives. Historically women have both welcomed and resisted the encroachment of the state in the family home. The state at once is regarded as a source of protection and justice and as the basis of inequality. Such contradictions are inherent in a state under capitalism. (229)

She goes on to note that although the actions and policies of the state may appear to be liberating in its actions and policies, 'in the long run it reproduces patriarchal relations'.

A similar analysis of the sometimes contradictory nature of state policies and actions is found in Jane Jenson's work. Jenson reviews some of the efforts of feminists who opted to use a Marxian approach to the state to understand the oppression of women, though the major portion of the article is devoted to presenting valuable comparative data drawn from the experiences of women in France and England. On the basis of this data she concludes that it is not possible for her to make generalized theoretical statements. However, '[b]eginning with the logic of the capitalist state's location in any conjuncture, and mapping the articulation of power relations such as those of class and gender in the politics of any social formation, it is possible to understand the ways in which the state contributes to the oppression of women' (229). Then Jenson makes a very important point: 'Moreover, it also points to the space for resistance.'

The notion that people have opportunities to resist is central, as is the argument that there are even opportunities to use the contradictions in the system in a positive way. This argument is developed by two Canadian scholars, Pat and Hugh Armstrong, who have contributed greatly to the advancement of feminist scholarship. They note that 'more and more feminists have come to realize that the state is not simply an instrument of class or male rule: that it can indeed work for the benefit of at least some women' (1990: 114). They go on to reiterate the idea that the state remains very complex and contradictory.

In *Toward A Feminist Theory of the State* (1989), Catharine Mackinnon focuses on the negative impact many state actions have for women. In her discussion of the actions and logic of the liberal state in capitalist society Mackinnon notes that 'the state, through law, institutionalizes male power over women through institutionalizing the male point of view in law. Its first state act is to see women from the standpoint of male dominance; its next act is to treat them that way' (169). She later concludes with a powerful claim: 'However autonomous of class the liberal state may appear, it is not autonomous of sex. Male power is systemic. Coercive, legitimized and epistemic, it *is* the regime' (170, emphasis in original).

Though we have barely scratched the surface in terms of the available literature that empirically illustrates the role that the state plays in sex and gender oppression, an important point made by R.W. Connell (1990: 519) should now be clear:

This adds up to a convincing picture of the state as an active player in gender politics. Nobody acquainted with the facts revealed in this research can any longer accept the silence about gender in the traditional state theory, whether liberal, socialist or conservative.

As Connell then goes on to argue, concepts of sex and gender must be included from the beginning in all theorizing and thinking about the modern state. The task of theorizing and understanding that sex and gender relations are integral to the polity and the state means that we must break with existing approaches.

Critical Thinking Questions

- Why is the polity a 'special institution'?
- What is hegemony? Does this concept help you understand your society? Explain your answer.
- What are three essential tenets of political pluralism? Do these apply to the nature of political activity in the society you live in?
- Why do some neo-Marxists claim that the state in capitalist society is a capitalist state?
- Explain why elite theory claims democracy is impossible. Was Michels correct in his famous claim?
- Is democracy possible? Is your society democratic?

Terms and Concepts

Pluralism—argues that Western liberal democracies are among the best political systems because they recognize that there are different interests in society that must be given an opportunity to influence government. Pluralists argue that a democratic electoral system and an open process of decision-making that allows for group lobbying are the most appropriate systems for ensuring a democratic decision-making process. It is assumed that all groups and interests in society have a more or less equal opportunity to influence the government through electoral and lobbying activities.

State system/polity—as used in sociological theory, all the institutions, organizations, and agencies connected with the political processes in societies with formally organized political institutions. In Western liberal democracies the state system or polity includes not only the formal elected apparatus of government, but also the appointed officials, all arms of the state bureaucracy, the judiciary, police and military, and the various national and international agencies.

Instrumentalist view of state—used to describe a neo-Marxist view of the state in capitalist society that stresses the personal and personnel connections between the capitalist class and the state. According to the logic of the instrumentalist view, the capitalist class is able to control and direct the activities of the state because the people operating the state either come directly from the capitalist class or share the values, ideologies, and objectives of the capitalist class. The state is seen as an 'instrument' of the capitalist class because of such direct connections.

Structuralist view of state–a neo-Marxist approach to the state that is critical of the supposed simplicity of the instrumentalist approach. The structuralist position draws on a kind of functionalist logic and focuses on what the state must do to maintain the capitalist system. It argues that the state's major role is in attempting to prevent the conflicts and contradictions from destroying the system, and its operations are defined by the logic and structures of the system, not the connections that state personnel have to the capitalist class. For example, the fact that the state needs tax revenues to operate means that state managers, no matter what personal political affiliations they have, must attempt to ensure that profits remain high and the economy healthy because economic slowdown might mean no re-election. The structural importance of maintaining 'business confidence'–of preventing capitalists from moving their production to another country and attempting to ensure continued investment–is a pressure that leads to the state acting in a manner that pleases the capitalist class.

Mechanisms of power–as opposed to pluralism, instrumentalism, or structuralism, stresses the need to understand that there are a number of different means that can be employed to influence the state in a capitalist society. In a liberal democratic system there are both direct (personnel and personal connections, lobbying, and impacting policy formation) and indirect (using economic power, ideological power, and political funding) mechanisms of power. Although all classes and individuals are able to use these mechanisms of power, the class with overwhelming economic power is best placed and for this reason is better able to exercise the various mechanisms of power.

Elite theory–emphasizes, in several different streams, that society always has been and always will be controlled by a small group called the elite. The elite is composed of those individuals who are superior performers in some area of human endeavour. Eventually these superior performers rise to positions of power, authority, and control, and the masses of people are content to have these superior performers 'run the show'. Some elite theorists such as Pareto argued that there was a biological reason for elite superiority, while others such as Michels looked for an organizational basis for the emergence of elites. The focus for all elite theorists is the small group that controls and runs society and holds wealth and power.

Related Web Sites

http://eserver.org/govt/theory.html

Found on an English Server 'Government, Law and Politics', this site offers more than 40 links to key issues in the theory of the state, politics, and the polity. The links cover a wide range of approaches, and the analysis is substantial and challenging.

http://vos.ucsb.edu/index-netscape.asp

The 'vos' refers to 'Voice of the Shuffle', a Web site devoted to facilitating learning and research across the humanities and related disciplines. Under the guidance of Alan Liu (University of California, Santa Barbara), this amazing site offers links to an array of issues in the humanities and social sciences including, for our immediate purposes, a very good 'Politics and Government' link. This page is the most comprehensive I have encountered in terms of breadth of issues and depth of coverage.

http://www.uta.fi/valogos/theories.html #approach

A Finnish Web site, it includes multiple links to a range of social science approaches to the state and the polity. In addition to covering functionalist and Marxian-inspired approaches, the site offers links to some very contemporary approaches including postmodernism.

http://www.sociologyonline.co.uk/soc_essays/
Marxism.htm

Written by Tony Fitzgerald, this summary of key
points with some good links is part of 'Sociology
Online'. The links cover key concepts in Marxian
theory generally.

http://www.marxists.org/archive/gramsci/
works/prison_notebooks/state_civil/
ch01.htm

This site contains a selection from Gramsci on
the state plus some additional links and interpretative material.

Suggested Further Readings

Brodie, J., ed. 1995. *Women and Canadian Public Policy.* Toronto: Harcourt Brace. This very important collection of essays addresses a range of political issues from the perspective of theory and offers numerous important empirical case studies of women and the polity.

Eisenberg, A. 1995. *Reconstructing Political Pluralism.* New York: State University Press of New York. This is an important recent contribution that updates and expands the frontiers of pluralist theory.

Held, D. 1995. *Democracy and the Global Order: From the Modern State to Cosmopolitan Governance.* Cambridge, UK: Polity Press. This book makes a major contribution to the development of state theory in the global era by a scholar with an international reputation. Some important and innovative insights into the issue of global governance are given.

Jessop, B. 1991. *State Theories: Putting the Capitalist States in Their Places.* University Park, PA: Pennsylvania State University Press. A very detailed treatment is presented of major ideas in the development of state theory. Jessop makes a cogent argument in favour of a form of regulation theory.

Kubik, W., and M. Knuttila. 2000. *State Theories.* Halifax: Fernwood and ZED. The expanded third edition attempts to overview major theories of the state in capitalist society.

CHAPTER 12

Race and Ethnicity and Difference

Wherever you are at this moment, pause and look around you. Chances are good that there are some other human beings in sight. Next, carefully observe and describe the physical appearance of the *other* human beings that happen to be nearby. Now count the ways in which these *others* appear to be different. What characteristics did you focus on? Did you focus on obvious physical characteristics such as eye or hair colour and style? Nose shape? Clothing style? Weight and height? Sex? Skin colour? Now think about what concepts you would use to classify or categorize these people if you were asked to describe them. If you used size or weight, what sorts of different 'types' of people would you describe? If you used eye colour or hair texture, how many types did you observe and classify? If you used clothing style, what sorts of types would you categorize people into? If the difference you noticed was as a result of skin pigment, did you use the concept of race or ethnicity in your classification schema? If you were to use the notion of race, on what basis would you make distinctions? Did you use skin colour as the basis of your classification? If the answer is yes, then why? What precisely does the term *race* imply for you? What is the basis of race? What do you mean by race? Or, did you focus on clothing, noting in particular those people not dressed in the conventional costumes of your locale? Did you identify these folks as ethnic groups?

Defining Race, Ethnicity, and 'Other'

When we are asked to define a concept or word we generally start with a nominal definition, that is, a simple definition that uses other words or concepts to try to explain what it is we are interested in. Of course, the way we currently define a particular term may be quite different from the way we defined it twenty years ago, or the way we will define it twenty years from now. The *Oxford Illustrated Dictionary*, published in 1970, defined *race* this way:

> Group of persons, animals, or plants connected by common descent; posterity of (person); house, family, tribe, or nation regarded as of common stock; distinct ethnical stock; any great division of living creatures; descent, kindred; class of persons etc. with some common feature; (biol.) subdivision of a species; variety.

Compare this definition of *race* with the one found in *The New Oxford Dictionary of English*, published in 1998:

> each of the major divisions of humankind, having distinct physical characteristics. ■ a group of people sharing the same culture, history, language, etc.; an ethnic group. ■ the fact or condition of belonging to such a

division or group; the qualities or characteristics associated with this. ■ a group or set of people or things with a common feature or features. (*Biology*) a population within a species that is distinct in some way, especially a subspecies. ■ (*in non-technical use*) each of the major divisions of living creatures. ■ (*poetic/literary*) a group of people descended from a common ancestor. ■ (*archaic*) ancestry.

The two definitions, written nearly 30 years apart, are quite different, yet we can see how the more recent one evolved from the earlier one, reflecting the way our use of the word has changed over time. One thing that both definitions show is the fact that the concept of race has multiple, complex, and somewhat confusing meanings attached to it.

When we turn to *ethnicity* in these two dictionaries we notice something even more striking. While the *New Oxford Dictionary* defines *ethnicity* as 'the fact or state of belonging to a social group that has a common national or cultural tradition', the *Oxford Illustrated* does not define it at all. This suggests that 30 years ago the word *ethnicity*, if it was used at all, was not used in mainstream written English.

Thomas Hylland Eriksen (1997) and Werner Sollors (1996) both suggest the word *ethnicity* is relatively modern. Sollors locates its origins in the United States in the sociological community studies of W. Lloyd Warner and Paul Hunt conducted in the 1940s (x). Eriksen notes that *ethnicity* first appeared in the *Concise Oxford Dictionary* in 1972, although the word is actually much older than that. Indeed, the volume of essays that Sollors edited on the topic, *Theories of Ethnicity: A Classical Reader*, contains a chapter that attempts an etymology of the word. Eriksen notes that during the fourteenth century the adjective *ethnic* had come to mean *pagan* or *heathen*, and thus as part of a social structure dominated by religion, it referred to an other, an outsider of some sort (33).

As well, the sociological literature is inadequate in providing a concise definition. Indeed, Wsevolod

W. Isajiw reviewed 65 sociological and anthropological studies dealing with some dimension of ethnicity but found only 13 definitions of *ethnicity*, leaving 52 with none (1980: 13)! After reviewing these definitions, he suggested that ethnicity be used to refer to 'an involuntary group of people who share the same culture or to descendants of such people who identify themselves and/or are identified by others as belonging to the same involuntary group' (1980: 24). One of the most prolific Canadian scholars in the area of ethnic studies is Leo Driedger. He suggests that ethnic identification emerges as a result of the interplay of six factors: ecological territory, culture, institutions, ideology, leadership, and some historical awareness or symbols (1978: 21–2). Driedger's emphasis on the subjective factors as the basis of ethnic identification is a useful point of departure but it is necessary to add the dimension of power if we want to consider ethnic in the social context. Augie Fleras and Jean Leonard Elliott (1999) remind us that ethnicity is often part of political struggles between outsiders and insiders and their definition reflects this: 'Broadly speaking, ethnicity consists of a *shared awareness of ancestral differences as a basis for engagement or entitlement*' (108, emphasis in original). There is a subtle difference here between Fleras and Elliott's definition and that found in Marshall's *Dictionary of Sociology*. The latter states: 'Ethnicity defines individuals who consider themselves, or are considered by others, to share common characteristics which differentiate them from the other collectivities in a society within which they develop distinctive cultural behaviour' (157). Peter Li's important studies of ethnicity, class, and race draw attention to the necessity of always including power as a vital dimension of the process by which some become identified as ethnic or other (1988, ch. 2). Although Marcus Banks (1996) notes that the confusion surrounding the word might be the basis for a cogent argument to kill the term off completely, he concludes that the term, like *race*, has become so much a part of our social experience that we cannot simply stop using it. What we need to do is to try to understand how it is used. Before we do this we need to establish more clarity surrounding the notion of race, and thus we need to examine the history and development of the concept in more detail.

Race in Western Thought: Early Views of Difference, Inequality, and Race

Although we may not understand the precise connotations intended, the term *race* has a long heritage in Western thought. For example, we find it in one of the first works of Western literature, Homer's *Odyssey*. Menelaus uses the term in reference to his friend Odysseus: 'I had meant to favour him above all others of our race when he came back, if all-seeing Zeus had allowed the two of us to bring our good ships safely home across the sea' (50). We know that various philosophers in classical Greek society pondered and offered explanations for human physiological difference. In his interesting study *Race: The History of an Idea in the West*, Ivan Hannaford points out that Herodotus, the Greek philosopher and observer of history, provided considerable detail regarding various physiological and behaviourial characteristics of Egyptians, Mesopotamians, southern Russians, and north Africans in the fifth century BC. Hannaford notes, however, that Herodotus did not use a concept similar to race to explain the differences he observed, preferring rather to see differences in behaviours as the outcome of differing moral and political values (1996: 25–7).

The notion that humans possess vital inherent differences is central to Plato and the vision of society he articulated. As Harry Elmer Barnes explains, Plato's just society was founded on the acceptance of a 'social division of labour among the crafts and the major classes. He worked out a hierarchy of social classes—the workers who supplied material needs, the guardians or warriors who protected the state, and the rulers, preferably

philosophers, who directed political life' (1965: 13). Leo Strauss makes the same point when he observes that according to Plato, 'men differ from one another by nature, that is, different men are gifted in different arts' (1972: 17). As he did with Herodotus, Hannaford argues that, despite what some have argued, Plato's conception of human difference and inequality are not based on a racial analysis.

Plato's student Aristotle followed his master on the matter of human differences and inequalities, arguing for the creation of what he saw as an ideal state. As was the case with Plato, Aristotle's ideal state was predicated on the acceptance of various forms of difference as inequality including slavery. Aristotle wrote, 'from the hour of their birth, some are marked for subjection, others for rule'. Elsewhere he added: 'It is clear, then, that some men are by nature free, and others slaves, that for these latter slavery is both expedient and right.'

Although he does not explain the precise basis of the differences that give rise to some people naturally being slaves, he might have understood it to be biological because with regard to another issue he notes that biological sexual differences are a source of inequality between men and women: 'Again, the male is by nature superior, and the female inferior; and the one rules, and the other is ruled; this principle of necessity extends to all mankind' (80). Biologically based inequalities might result in some humans naturally being slaves, but as Hannaford (1996: 50) concludes, these differences and the resulting inequalities were not based on a concept of race. The notion that humans are somehow inherently, at birth, different and unequal—the roots of Plato and Aristotle—disappears in the work of the early Christian writers. St Augustine explicitly uses the term *race*, but in a unifying manner noting that Adam and Eve were the 'two first parents of the human race'. However, because of human sin, the human race has become divided. 'This race we have distributed into two parts, the one consisting of those who live according to man, the other of those who live according to God' (177–8). Although this division is radical in the true sense of the word, it is not necessarily permanent. There is a route for reunification of the race via the behaviours outlined in various Christian theologies.

The notion that the world and our place in it is the result of preordained divine will became one of the defining characteristics of life in Europe after the fall of Rome and the emergence of feudal society. Although feudal society was characterized by significant inequalities in wealth, lifestyles, and power, in its heyday it tended to be relatively stable. The prime source of this stability was the widespread acceptance of a set of religious and secular beliefs that emphasized natural and divinely sanctioned hierarchies such as the feudal class system. Custom, tradition, acceptance, and acquiescence to authority were hallmarks of Western European feudalism with the Church playing a key role in providing the overall ideological justification for the system (Hunt, 1990: 3–7). Kenan Malik provides a detailed description of how difference was viewed, understood, and accepted:

> The pre-Enlightenment view of the world was characterized by its irrational premises, static nature, and parochial scope. . . . The serf, the slave, the peasant, the artisan, the lord, the king—all were allotted their place in the world by divine sanction. In this world of fixed relations and limited experiences, irrational prejudices attached themselves to anything and everything out of the ordinary. In communities that were ethnically homogeneous, geographically isolated, technologically backward, and socially conservative, prejudice and superstition were the natural responses to the strange and the unknown. What we would today call racial prejudices were certainly common. (43)

Malik goes on to note that 'fixed relations and limited experiences, irrational prejudices attached themselves to anything and everything out of the ordinary'. As a result those individuals who were different in any manner were viewed as 'other'. He states that what might be called racial prejudice was common; observers have to take care not to judge one historical era and context through the lens or perspective of another (43–4). Certainly the Church was able to mount massive social/military movements as in the Crusades when thousands of Western Europeans marched off in a campaign that was ostensibly about freeing the Holy Land from the infidels. Whether this was primarily a clash of religious beliefs or whether it also had elements of racial undertones seems somewhat uncertain.

What are we to make of these early uses of the term *race*? What precisely did Homer mean when he had Menelaus identify Odysseus as from the same race? When Aristotle laments the phenomenon of Greek slaves in his remark 'Wherefore Hellenes do not like to call Hellenes slaves, but confine the term to barbarians', was he just referring to those who had been conquered? Is Ivan Hannaford correct in arguing that the classical Greek thinkers were focused on differences in political and moral ability and not anything physiological? Did what some would call racial differences play a role in the treatment of 'others' during the feudal era? Although there may not be definitive answers to these questions, they point out the need for a careful definition, understanding, and use of the analytical concepts to explain the social world.

There is a significant body of literature that holds that the concept of race is relatively new. International expert in the study of race, British sociologist Michael Banton, points out that there is some obscurity surrounding the linguistic origins of the term *race*. In his earlier work he suggests that the first recorded English use of the word is found in a William Dunbar poem written in 1508 (1975: 13). He also points out that the term began to become associated with lineage in a 1570 Biblical study of Abraham's lineage (1997: 30).

Raymond Williams has developed a useful resource for any investigation of the meaning of many words and concepts used in the social sciences and humanities. In *Keywords* Williams notes that the word *race* came into English usage in the sixteenth century in association with lineage or lines of descent and the notion of stock—from the same stem or trunk. However, the word became problematic, all the more so after it was used in classification systems in biology. As we will see, this use led to efforts to classify humans into differential groups based on some physical characteristic of another. In the opening sentences of his co-edited book *Race*, Roger Sanjek was definitive in terms of the lineage of the concept: 'Let's be clear from the start what this book is about. Race is the framework of ranked categories segmenting the human population that was developed by Western Europeans following their global expansion beginning in the 1400s' (1994: 1).

In a study of the use of the concept in France, Colette Guillaumin (1995) argues that prior to the French Revolution the term distinguished the common lineage of the various classes or estates, as they tended to be called. By 1778, following the Revolution, the use of the term had changed from being mostly self-attributed to one that was attributed by others. In particular, the emerging new middle class or bourgeoisie, although lacking the formal lineage of the aristocracy with whom they were engaged in a struggle for political power, still sought some means of establishing a hierarchy of identities. Apparently, establishing that there were 'others' who were not just different but inferior assisted in the process. In his overview of the history of the concept, Vic Satzewich summarized Guillaumin's arguments by noting that the change in use to designate others brought with it some significant and unfortunate connotations: 'Categorizing certain groups as races became linked with the negative evaluation of the "other's" social and biological capacities' (1998: 28).

Perhaps it would be useful to approach the concept in a manner similar to that suggested by Banton in his more recent work. He set out some of the essential issues surrounding the concept in the following manner:

'What is race?' seems a simple question, and those who ask it often think there should be a simple answer. Some make the mistake of assuming that because there is a word in the language there must be something in the natural world that corresponds with that word. This is a philosophical error. There is also a historical dimension, because the word race is less than five hundred years old. There have been physical differences between humans for thousands of years, but it is only within the last two centuries that these differences have been conceptualized as racial. The use of ideas about race to organize evidence about human variation has entered popular consciousness and influenced relations between groups. (1997: 1)

In this passage Banton suggests that the historical uses of the word are not relevant for contemporary sociology. Despite what we have been discussing, the salient issue may not be the history of the concept or even its changing application throughout human history, but its contemporary use and meaning.

Race and Modernity

As we have seen in Chapter 1, one of the essential features of modernity and the intellectual revolutions that characterized the Enlightenment was the new way of knowing called science. Among the branches of human knowledge to adopt the new approach was biology, a science that focused on the study of living organisms, including humans. Among the first activities of this new science was the development of various systems of 'description, classification and systematization' (Barnes, 1965: 686).

One must read a detailed study, such as Ivan Hannaford's *Race: The History of an Idea in the West*, to fully understand the development of the concept of race. Having offered this advice, and without any pretence of comprehensiveness, we review the concept as it emerged from early efforts to classify people.

Carolus Linnaeus (1707–78), often referred to as the 'father of taxonomy', is best known for his work in botany and the classification of living things. His *Systema Naturae*, first published in 1735, was republished as his findings grew. The volume eventually included a descriptive classification for humans or what he called *Homo diurnis*. Hannaford summarizes the scheme that arranges humans on the basis of Linnaeus's assessment of differing moral principles:

> *Homo ferus*: wild, savage, cruel man
>
> *Europaeus albus*: ingenious, white, sanguine, governed by law
>
> *Americanus rebescus*: happy with his lot, liberty loving, tanned and irascible, governed by custom
>
> *Asiaticus luridus*: yellow, melancholy, governed by opinion
>
> *Afer niger*: crafty, lazy, careless, black, governed by the arbitrary will of the master (204)

Some of Linnaeus's students travelled with Captain James Cook; however, their major interest was plant life. This was not the case with Georges Cuvier (1769–1832) who, Banton and Harwood report, provided written instructions to French expeditions to the Pacific 'on how they should study savage people' (1975: 26). Banton and Harwood note that Cuvier arranged men into three major races—whites, yellows, and blacks—attributing the differences in social position in part to different skull shapes. While Cuvier was writing in France, Johann Friedrich Blumenbach (1752–1840), a professor of medicine at Gottingen, Germany, who is sometimes referred to as the 'father of physical anthropology', was proposing another classification schema. Blumenbach used geological variables as the basis of

his system that subdivided the human species into races. He initially divided humans into four subdivisions—Mongolian, Caucasian, American, and African; however, he later added a fifth, Malayan, a development that Stephen Jay Gould argues required a somewhat arbitrary shift in the alleged basis for membership in one of the races (Gould, 1997: 5; see also Colliers Encyclopedia, vol. 4 CD-ROM).

Cuvier's ideas had an impact in North America through the work of two individuals, Louis Agassiz (1807–73) and Samuel George Morton (1799–1851). Agassiz was a naturalist from Switzerland who immigrated to the United States where he took up a position as comparative zoologist at Harvard University. In his classic study, *The Mismeasure of Man*, Stephen Jay Gould argues that Agassiz changed his opinions concerning the origins and nature of different humans, moving from monogenism (single source origin for all humans) to polygenism (separate or distinct biological origins for different races). Gould quotes Agassiz as arguing that the races 'cannot have originated in single individuals, but must have been created in that numeric harmony which is characteristic of each species' (1981: 46). Agassiz's work provides a good illustration of how the apparently new scientific knowledge that was being produced contained important political subtexts. Not only did Agassiz postulate the existence of different species of humans, he connected their apparent different traits to various positions in the social structure. As Gould notes before quoting Agassiz, he employed recognizable stereotypes when he made the following claim:

> The indominable, courageous, proud Indian—in how very different a light he stands by the side of the submissive, obsequious, imitative negro, or by the side of the tricky cunning, and cowardly Mongolian! Are not these facts indications that the different races do not rank upon one level in nature. (quoted on 46)

As outrageous as this claim may seem, in the

argument that followed, Agassiz went on to claim that, given that some species of human are innately superior and others innately inferior, we should construct educational policies that recognize this fact of nature.

Agassiz was a contemporary of Samuel George Morton, a physician who engaged in the study of human skulls and cranial capacity. Morton engaged in detailed studies and calculations of human cranial capacity, proceeding from a polygeny point of departure. Gould claims that, as a polygenist, Morton had a point to make or a hypothesis to test 'that a ranking of races could be established objectively by the physical characteristics of the brain' (51). At the end of the day Morton did claim to have established what Gould argues he set out to do. Morton claimed to have demonstrated that the different races (Caucasian, Mongolian, Malay, American, and Ethiopian) did in fact have different cranial capacities with the Caucasians having, on average, the greatest cranial capacity (Gould, 1997: 54).

A full census of all the various efforts to establish a biological basis for various races or even species of humans is well beyond this chapter. I refer the reader again to Ivan Hannaford's detailed study for a much more adequate overview. I also refer the reader to the excellent summary of this literature by Raymond Scupin and Christopher DeCorse in their *Anthropology: A Global Perspective*. They summarize efforts ranging from those of the ancient Egyptians to some from the 1970s. Their summary points out the range of criteria that have been used (skin, eye and hair colour, body build, blood types, and geographical boundaries) to produce schemas with from 3 to 30 different races (1995: 113). Daniel Blackburn also summarizes what he calls 'Some Classifications of Human Race' covering thinkers whose work ranges over two hundred years (2000: 5).

Despite the fact that dozens of scientists representing many different disciplines have not come close to agreeing on just what physical difference is the basis of race, the concept of race continues to be used as the basis of ranking humans. Among the contemporary advocates of the notion of a racial hierarchy is the Canadian psychologist J. Philippe Rushton.

Although the issue remains salient with ongoing efforts to differentiate racial groupings on the basis of various physical characteristics, in order to move the discussion forward we will now consider some of the most recent information regarding biological differences. Rushton's work has been widely debated, condemned by some but praised by others. His basic assumptions are quite simple. First, he claims that race is defined as 'a recognizable (or distinguishable) geographic population' (1996: 2). He indicates that there are over 60 anatomical and social variables that serve to aggregate Asians and Africans into quite different aggregations; indeed, he says 'at opposite ends' of a continuum. These include 'brain size, intelligence, sexual habits, fertility, personality, temperament, speed of maturation and longevity' (1969: 2). In his detailed study, *Race, Evolution and Behaviour*, he tends to focus on a few of these differences including brain size, size of the genitalia, speed of maturation, and some personality attributes. His claims are quite stunning. With regard to brain size and, he concludes, intelligence, he writes:

From weighing wet brains at autopsy and calculating cranial capacity from skulls and external head measurements, it will be seen from modern as well as historical studies that Mongoloids and Caucasoids average larger brains than Negroids. The Mongoloid > Negroid finding is especially striking. When adjustments are made for body size, Mongoloids have even larger and heavier brains than do Caucasoids. Although sampling and methodological difficulties may be identified in particular studies, results obtained from multimethod comparisons allow a triangulation of probable truth. (113)

His findings with regard to genitalia are no less definitive. Rushton claims that on average both male and female Orientals tend to have smaller genitalia, with Caucasians somewhat larger and blacks (he uses small case 'b') the largest of all (1997: 167). Sexual activity follows, he states, an associated pattern:

> In sum, college-educated whites tend to be the most sexually restrained and college-educated blacks the least sexually restrained, with non-college-educated whites intermediate. This pattern was observed on measures made of the speed of occurrence of premarital, marital, and extramarital sexual experiences, number of sexual partners, and frequency of intercourse. For women, measures of the speed and incidence of pregnancy, the rapidity of the menstrual cycle, and the number of orgasms per act of coitus also differentiated the groups. (176)

Given that Rushton explicitly notes that he writes in the historical tradition of the founder of eugenics, Sir Francis Galton (1997: 9), it is not surprising that he explicitly draws our attention to the social and political implications of his conclusions. Genes, Ruston claims, have far-reaching social implications:

> From an evolutionary point of view, individual differences are the alternative genetic combinations and adaptations that compete through the mechanism of natural selection. A mountain of data has now accumulated showing that genes bias the development of complex social behavior in one direction over alternatives, even of political attitudes and choice of marriage and other social partners. (43)

With regard to the social implications of the differential intellectual capacities he claims to have demonstrated, he writes:

The central role of intelligence in law abidingness is demonstrated by the finding that IQ has an effect on delinquency independent of family background, race, or class. Siblings reared together in the same families show almost the same degree of association between IQ and delinquency as is found in the general population (Hirschi and Hindelang, 1977). The relation between IQ and delinquency was measured by self-reports as well as by incarcerations, so the result is not just due to clever people evading capture. Less intelligent people often lack behavioral restraint, marriage-bonding techniques, adequate parenting styles, and moral rules, and are less capable of creating stable personal circumstances or of predicting their environment. (269)

As Rushton himself acknowledges, his arguments provoked a major controversy that included input from the then premier of Ontario and investigations by the provincial police and the Ontario Human Rights Commission (1997: xiv). Many members of the academic community reacted with equal vigour. One of the most detailed of many critiques is Leonard Lieberman's 'How "Caucasoids" Got Such Big Crania and Why They Shrank: From Morton to Rushton' (2001). Lieberman addresses several genetic or biological determinist arguments, but Rushton is the major focus. Lieberman presents his critique in a point-by-point form, starting by arguing that 'Rushton uses "race" despite decades of findings that invalidate it' (9). Lieberman reviews a significant literature by renowned scholars dating from 1938 to 1999 that casts serious doubt on the legitimacy of race as a biological concept. Lieberman's conclusion that Ruston 'does not discuss the weaknesses of the concept of race' is important because Rushton's entire analysis is based on the legitimacy of this concept. Lieberman's second criticism is slightly more technical in that it related to the manner by which Rushton manipulates and aggregates his and others' data. On a key point Lieberman concludes that 'empirical similarity has not been established between the populations that Rushton aggregates into three "races", and therefore aggregation of the mean IQ scores or correlation in not justified' (11). Lieberman presents further evidence to support his third critique that 'Rushton's cranioracial variation is contradicted by evolutionary anthropology' (12). The fourth critique is again methodological in that Lieberman demonstrates that Ruston failed to utilize appropriate controls to account for variables well established in the work of other researchers. Lieberman's fifth systematic point is that 'Rushton did not relate environment, nutrition, cranial size and IQ' (15) in spite of a wealth of evidence that nutritional factors are key in both brain size and IQ. Lieberman's final point-by-point criticism relates to Rushton's tendency to subsume diverse and complex behaviours under single labels. For example, what Rushton labels 'cultural achievement, personality traits, marital stability, law-abidingness' and so on are really many different and complex behaviours and they cannot be aggregated in the manner that Rushton does.

Lieberman's essay is presented with a series of supporting commentaries from others in the field, followed by a reply by the author. Lieberman's critique is, I would argue, devastating, but it was not by far the only response. Zack Zdenek Cernovsky starts his critique with the observation that 'old-fashioned racist doctrines of the inferiority of blacks have recently been resuscitated in psychological terminology by J.P. Rushton' (1990: 337). Cernovsky goes on to argue that Rushton uses nineteenth-century methods already discredited because Rushton fails to correct for difference in body weight and height and thus his brain/body mass comparisons are invalid. In their critique 'Rushton on Race and Crime: The Evidence Remains Unconvincing', Thomas Gabor and Julian Roberts point out that not only is Rushton's data questionable from a scientific point of view, the potential conclusions that a policy-maker might derive from

it are horrific. Gabor and Roberts acknowledge that genes influence behaviour, but in a very different way than Rushton suggests (1990: 337–8).

Rushton's work is not, the only contemporary effort to link some notion of race to complex social behaviours in a largely negative manner. In a much debated book, *The Bell Curve: Intelligence and Class Structure in American Life*, published at about the same time as Rushton's, Richard Herrnstein and Charles Murray argue that many of the inequalities and problems that beset American society are understandable by reference to intelligence. Early on, the authors declare that 'Jobs sort people by their IQs, just as college does' (52). They go on to note that 'No one decreed that occupation should sort us by our cognitive abilities, and no one enforces the process. It goes on beneath the surface, guided by its own invisible hand.' So intelligence is everything, but what determines intelligence? For Herrnstein and Murray the answer is quite easy: 'Ethnic differences in measured cognitive ability have been found since intelligence tests were invented' (270). This claim follows one at the beginning of a chapter titled 'Ethnic Difference in Cognitive Ability': 'Despite the forbidding air that envelopes the topic, ethnic differences in cognitive ability are neither surprising nor in doubt' (269). As to the meaning of 'ethnic', Herrnstein and Murray explain that they call people what they prefer to be called and they seem to like ethnic. As to what the major so-called 'ethnic groups' are, these sound a lot like Rushton's racial dividers in that Herrnstein and Murray note that they will use the terms *black*, *white*, and *Asian* (271):

> As far as anyone has been able to determine, iq scores on a properly administered test mean about the same thing for all ethnic groups. A substantial difference in cognitive ability distributions separates whites from blacks, and a smaller one separates East Asians from whites. These differences play out in public and private life. (315)

And, we might ask, just how do these differences play themselves out? According to Herrnstein and Murray, they affect levels of poverty, the effectiveness of schooling, employment, unemployment, family relations and dynamics, welfare dependency, parenting skills and success, propensity to engage in criminal activity, an overall level of civility, and citizenship responsibilities. Indeed, most of these issues comprise chapters in their book. Having claimed to establish the reality and inevitability of inequalities in American society, Herrnstein and Murray are not bashful when it comes to following through to consider the public policy and social implications of their conclusion. A major section of the book addressed the various forms of affirmative action that have been attempted in order to deal with inequality in American society. In the conclusion, mistitled 'A Place for Everyone', Herrnstein and Murray begin by restating that there are 'twin realities' that must be faced. These are: (1) people are unequal in intelligence and this is not their fault; and (2) these inequalities have 'a powerful bearing on how people do in life' (527). Given that these inequalities are inevitable and that trying to 'pretend that inequality does not exist has led to disaster' (551), all Herrnstein and Murray can do is recommend acceptance of these racial inequalities and somehow live through them!

Herrnstein and Murray's efforts were the object of much critical attention. Not surprisingly, Rushton liked the book but he thought it should have gone further. Rushton writes, 'My admiration of the *Bell Curve* was overshadowed by the fact that it did not deal thoroughly enough with the genetic basis of racial differences' (1997: 278). Many others were far less impressed. Indeed, the responses were so significant and varied that some of them have been collected into a separate volume titled *The Bell Curve Wars*. The book contains two types of criticism, one scientific and the other political. Both are important.

Among the important critics of the book is the internationally known Harvard professor of geology, Stephen Jay Gould. In his essay 'Curveball', Gould takes exception to the manner in which Herrnstein and Murray apply a research technique, factor analysis, which is central to their book. Gould is also critical of their use of statistical methods, arguing that they are less than rigorous in their application of these techniques and that their conclusions do not necessarily flow from the data (1995: 18–20). Howard Gardner, a Harvard professor of education and author of an important book on intelligence, is also critical. He notes that 'the science in the book was questionable when it was proposed a century ago, and it has not been completely supplanted by the development of the cognitive science and neurosciences' (1995: 23). University of Michigan psychology professor Richard Nisbett also criticizes the science. After offering detailed and specific objections, he summarized his concerns:

> Let me be clear about what I am asserting about *The Bell Curve*'s treatment of evidence. For the question of genetic contribution to the IQ gap, almost all the direct evidence has been left out, and the single study treated at any length is the only one consistent with a genetic component to the gap. Moreover, that study is presented without even its author's qualifications. (53)

An important issue in any work that purports to have the status of science is the treatment of data to cast doubt on one's claims. In his intervention, journalist and researcher Dante Ramos notes that 'the authors choice of contrary evidence is bizarre' (1995: 65). A persistent criticism of Herrnstein and Murray's data is their use of correlation. Thomas Sowell explicitly draws our attention to the difference between correlation and causality. To link two phenomena might be enough to establish correlation, but it is not the same as establishing a causal connection (1995: 77–8). The critics typically were not accusing Herrnstein and Murray of malfeasance or deliberate and willful falsification—a point made by Mickey Kaus. Rather the issue is the efficacy of the arguments and the use of the data. Kaus notes that the standards of evidence required to support the political claims are wanting (1995: 132).

But why are books such as this emerging and receiving support at this moment in history? Stephen Jay Gould offers some suggestions:

So, when a book garners as much attention as *The Bell Curve* we wish to know the causes. One might suspect the content itself—a startlingly new idea, or an old suspicion newly verified by persuasive data—but the reason might also be social acceptability, or even just plain hype. *The Bell Curve*, with its claims and supposed documentation that race and class differences are largely caused by genetic factors and are therefore essentially immutable, contains no new arguments and presents no compelling data to support its anachronistic social Darwinism, so I can only conclude that its success in winning attention must reflect the depressing temper of our time—a historical moment of unprecedented ungenerosity, when a mood for slashing social programs can be powerfully abetted by an argument that beneficiaries cannot be helped, owing to inborn cognitive limits expressed as low IQ scores. (1995: 11)

Michael Lind concurs:

The controversy about *The Bell Curve* is not about *The Bell Curve* only. It is about the sudden and astonishing legitimation, by the leading intellectuals and journalists of the mainstream American right, of a body of racialist pseudoscience created over the past several decades by a small group of researchers, most of them subsidized by the hereditarian Pioneer Fund. *The Bell Curve* is a layman's introduction to this material, which

had been repudiated by the responsible right for a generation. (1995: 172)

Lind's point is that the politics of exclusion supporting these arguments are not from the 'responsible right' of the political spectrum, but rather they represent what he calls the 'Brave New Right'.

Genome Science and Race

If race is indeed primarily a genetic concept, surely the recent findings of human genetics and DNA have something to say about the notion. On 26 June 2000 leaders of two research groups, one working under the auspices of the Human Genome Project (a consortium of 16 institutions) and the other connected with Celera Genomics (a private company) jointly announced the mapping of virtually the entire human genome. The significance of the event was such that President Clinton of the United States of America was in attendance. The project had cost more than $3 billion US to get a rough draft of all 24 human chromosomes. One of the first startling findings was that humans have far fewer than the 100,000 genes that conventional wisdom expected. Apparently, we have about 30,000 genes, about twice as many as a fruit fly, 300 more than a mouse, and about the same number as an ear of corn!

It is important to note something about the methods that were used to select the DNA to be examined. If, as some have suggested, the various so-called human races really are genetically different, surely the selection of DNA donors would make a difference. According to a publication from the US Department of Energy Human Genome Program, *Human Genome News* (vol. 11, nos. 1–2, November 2000), the DNA tested was 'from donors representing widely diverse populations' and 'neither donors nor scientists know whose genomes are being sequenced.' The bulletin states that the private company, Celera Genomics, collected samples from individuals who identified themselves as 'Hispanic, Asian, Caucasian, or African-American'. We are told that additional samples were secured from 'anonymous donors of European, African, American (north, central, and south) and Asian ancestry'. It would seem that the scientists involved were not concerned with the geographic origin or the physical characteristics of the donors.

The findings, however, are very striking. Story by-lines such as 'Do Races Differ? Not Really Genes Show' and 'Race Is an Unscientific Concept Experts Say' (*New York Times*, 23 and 30 August 2000) tell the story. In the 30 August report, Natalie Angier quotes J. Craig Venter, the head of Celera Genomics, as saying that 'Race is a social concept, not a scientific one.' Elsewhere, Venter states: 'No serious scholar in this field thinks that race is a scientific concept. It is just not' (quoted in Philipkoski, 2001). He was able to say this because the results of the genome mapping or sequencing project demonstrated conclusively that, in the words of Eric Lander, director of the human genome sequencing laboratory at the Whitehead Institute, 'Any two humans on this planet are more than 99.9 per cent identical at the molecular level. Racial and ethnic differences are all indeed only skin deep' (quoted in Philipkoski, 2001). The same article notes that what geneticists call single nucleotide polymorphisms are responsible for the obvious physiological differences but they make up a small part of the fractional genetic differences among people. Angier's *New York Times* story also makes this point, quoting another expert who notes that external appearance seems to be accounted for by about 0.01 per cent of our DNA. In an analysis of the impact of these findings in *Science* (vol. 286, October 1999) Kelly Owens and Mary-Claire King suggest that even the small variations noted are more significant among particular geographic populations than across different continents. This leads them to conclude: 'The possibility that human history has been characterized by genetically relatively homogenous groups ("races") distinguished by major biological differences is not consistent with genetic evidence.' Moreover, simple physiological traits such as skin or hair colour 'are literally superficial, in that they affect exposed surfaces of the body. It is reasonable to suggest that variations in these traits may reflect differential selection by climate in various parts of the world.'

So we are left with concepts that are widely used, scientifically disputed, politically sensitive, and/or dangerous and very much contested. The issue that we must now face is how sociologists use these concepts.

Sociological Theory, Race, and Ethnicity

Structural Functionalism: Basic Tenets

As you will recall, structural functionalism commonly draws on an organic analogy in order to understand and explain the structures and functioning of human society. Living organisms are deemed to face a number of basic problems that must be solved and addressed if they are to survive. For example, in order for a complex organism like the human body to survive, blood must circulate throughout the system and be cleaned and replenished with oxygen, nutrition must be provided to all organs and tissues, a central nervous system must co-ordinate various processes, wastes must be removed from the body, and so on. Living organisms are understood to be composed of a number of interrelated parts or structures (organs, tissues, etc.) that deal with these various problems. The function of the heart is to ensure the circulation of blood throughout the system, while the kidneys clean the blood, the lungs oxygenate the blood and the central nervous system and the brain co-ordinate the entire operation. Each of these structures (organs) performs some function, does something, functions for, and contributes to maintaining the whole system.

Human society can be understood by using an organic analogy. Societies have certain basic needs that must be dealt with and problems that must be solved in order to survive. Functionalists refer to these as system prerequisites. For example, if a society is to survive, its culture must be transmitted, biological reproduction facilitated, the young cared for and socialized, the spiritual and material needs of individuals met, and so on. Societies (social systems) are composed of specialized structures, called institutions. Institutions operate or function to deal with one or more of the system's prerequisites for survival. Institutions are thus best understood in terms of the functions they perform for society, that is, the need, problem, or system prerequisites they solve or deal with. Society is a system of interconnected structures and institutions each performing some function for the whole, and contributing to the maintenance of the entire system by dealing with one or more system prerequisites.

Social systems are complex integrated wholes that normally remain stable. Societies will remain orderly and smooth functioning as long as their members share values, norms, beliefs, moral codes, and stocks of knowledge. A society's moral codes and belief systems are essential and central because they do two things. First, they provide society with its 'shape and character', influencing how institutions are organized and structured and how people act. Secondly, shared values, norms and beliefs provide the basis for social order. As long as the majority of members of a society share and accept a system of values, normative orientations, beliefs, etc., the society will tend to be stable. Stability, homeostasis, equilibrium, and consensus are words that describe the typical condition of society.

Functionalists are not typically concerned with the origins and history of values, norms, and belief systems, since their major focus is on the role or function of such belief systems. Structural functionalists will downplay social conflict.

Structural functionalists will typically recognize the possibility of an institution dysfunctioning. If we return to the organic analogy for a moment we can envision the possibility of an organ becoming infected and, as a result, dysfunctioning (not functioning properly). When this occurs, the entire system can be disrupted. Similarly, it is possible that an institution, for some reason, might not perform its functions properly and as a result social order and stability might be jeopardized. When this happens measures might have to be undertaken to restore social order or the system will evolve or develop new arrangements to account for the new realities. For example, if for some reason the normal functioning of an institution such as the family is disrupted, new patterns of providing the services (functions) typically provided by the family might have to be worked out.

Structural Functionalism, Race, Ethnicity, and Other

We have seen that human cultures are diverse and different. This is not surprising, given the power of the human intellect to develop behaviours, practices, and institutions to deal with society's and our individual needs and problems. We also know that humans are mobile on a global scale and that some relatively new societies such as Canada, Australia, and the United States have literally been created as a result of massive population movements over the past several centuries. Virtually every complex society in existence today is an amalgam of different people with different ancestors and cultural histories. What we typically find in most modern complex societies are dominant or mainstream cultures, as well as a range of smaller, non-dominant subcultures.

When we examine the norms, values, beliefs, and ideas that characterize the dominant cultures in advanced industrial societies we find that they are complex compendiums or collections of ideas, beliefs, values, norms, behaviours, and viewpoints that have evolved and developed over time. It is very difficult to trace the sources and origins of these various ideas and notions because they are many, varied, and diverse. They might have their origins in religion, arts, literature, secular philosophy, social and political theory, common-sense knowledge, and so on. What is important for the structural functionalist, however, is not the origin but the role, function, and content of these value systems and normative orientations.

We know something of the functions of norms and values. We also know that the dominant values and norms contain ideas about how the world works, how people behave, and what is appropriate and inappropriate. It is very likely that these values and norms come to contain ideas about people who are different in their appearance or dress. This is all the more likely if these people in fact exhibit some particular and even peculiar dress habits, religious practices, tastes in food or social mannerisms. If a group of people does indeed possess some such characteristics and if these are an important part of that group's daily activities we most likely would refer to them as a subculture. Indeed many people would refer to Canada and the United States as pluralistic societies, characterized by the existence of a dominant or mainstream culture but containing many subcultures that are based on national origin, geographic locale, or even religious beliefs. Such a structural circumstance presents several possible scenarios that could lead to social dysfunction and even conflict.

It is possible to envision a situation in which the dominant or mainstream value system or normative orientations have absorbed beliefs or opinions that are detrimental to some members of society. For example, the racist belief that some individuals are inferior and therefore do not have the same claim to basic human rights as others could become part of a society's value system. If this were to happen, the lives and opportunities of this group could be severely affected. In such a society we would expect to find discrimination, inequalities, differential treatment before the law and a series of similar negative social practices. We would also expect to find individuals and groups subject to such treatment involved in resisting and opposing their unequal status, especially if the mainstream values were premised on official declarations of the equality of all human

beings. A dysfunctional situation exists when there is a major inconsistency between a society's official or formal values and the actual lived experiences of its members. A functionalist might explain race or ethnic-based conflict in such a situation as the outcome of a social dysfunction, racist ideas producing dysfunctional social institutions and practices. The obvious solution so such a situation is legitimate collective and social action to eliminate the sources of the dysfunctions, first the racist ideas and then the discriminatory or unfair social and institutional structures and practices.

Whenever mainstream values, norms, and beliefs become excessively strong and binding, the potential for deviance from the norm is exaggerated. This claim can hold true for groups just as easily as individuals. It is possible that the majority of members of a society could label as deviant an entire subculture just because they are different and outside the norm. Under such circumstances, members of the mainstream culture may exhibit ethnocentric attitudes and engage in exclusionary or discriminatory behaviours associated with this particular dysfunction.

Most Western liberal capitalist societies claim to be founded on principles of equality of opportunity. Individuals are deemed to be equal in terms of their opportunities to succeed; the actual extent of one's success is thus the outcome of individual ability, initiative, and effort. If such a society is characterized by ascribed status and not achieved status, one would expect dysfunctions. Put somewhat differently, when an individual's social position or roles in society is assigned or allocated on the basis of their apparent race or ethnicity and not their achievement, then we have ascribed and not achieved status. In a modern democratic society the ascription of status is potentially dysfunctional.

Conflict Theory: Basic Tenets

As was the case above, we will begin with a review of some of the basic tenets of power-conflict theory. The conflict perspective adopts the general tenets of

Power-conflict theory maintains that racist ideas and beliefs have long been a part of dominant ideology in North America. Racist ideas have been a significant part of a divide and rule tactic that has split the subordinate classes into conflictual factions. Racist ideas might be seen to benefit the dominant classes by justifying slavery and the appropriation of the land of the First Nations while hiding the contradictions inherent in a society based on class and exploitation. (John Morstad/Reprinted by permission from The Globe and Mail)

the materialist approach. This means that its supporters argue that there is a central process or factor that moulds, shapes, and for some, determines the overall character of society. The central process in question relates broadly to the manner by which the material requirements and needs of the members of society are met. It is deemed that societies have a material basis or core composed of the economic institutions that are primary in terms of giving the society its overall shape. Though society as a totality is understood as a complex set of structures and institutions with connections among institutions, the manner by which material production is organized is the most important element. Despite the fundamen-

tal differences between the two approaches, conflict theory can share a common element with functionalist theory. Both perspectives argue that institutions can be understood in terms of the functions they perform. The major difference relates to the question of 'in whose interests' do institutions function? Rather than holding that institutions function for the society as a whole, conflict theorists argue that institutions function for and in the interests of the dominant class or classes.

Since conflict theorists argue that a society is primarily determined by the nature of its economic order, they do not deem that norms, values, and belief systems are as important. These they view as systems of ideology or dominant ideologies, and as such must be understood in the context of larger structures of power and domination. Conflict theorists might typically argue that most societies have had ruling classes that have attempted to impose their views and ideas about the world on the entire society through a process of ideological domination.

Conflict Theory, Race, Ethnicity, and Other

As one might expect, power-conflict theory approaches the issues of race and ethnicity in a manner that is quite different form that used within the functionalist perspective. In North America we begin by examining the historical development of capitalism in this part of the world. Such an examination would include an analysis of the changing class structure, the changing role of the state, and the changing forms and content of the dominant ideology.

As outlined in Chapter 9, there are a number of different specific approaches to the study of class within the power-conflict tradition; however, they all are predicated on the assumption that a dominant class is in a structural position to appropriate the majority of the wealth in the society. The approach also assumed that there are associated subordinate classes that are involved in the creation and production of wealth, but who are not in a structural position to appropriate the entire benefit of the wealth they create and produce. An associated set of assumptions applies to the issue of political power and class. As Chapter 11 notes, there are several different specific approaches to the study of the state within the power-conflict approach, but again all are predicated on some common assumptions. Central among these is the notion that the state in capitalist society serves the interests of the dominant or ruling class.

None of this, of course, tells us anything about how this perspective would explain the persistence of racism or ethnic conflict in a manner different from that presented above. In order to address this issue we must return to the notion of dominant ideology.

We have seen that power-conflict theory uses the concept of dominant ideology rather than referring to a society's norms and values. When we first encountered social theories we introduced the concept of hegemony. The reader will recall that hegemony can refer to both a set of ideas, beliefs, norms, values, and opinions and the fact that in a hegemonic situation a ruling class is able to maintain its power in part by having the subordinate classes accepts its view, beliefs, values, and so on. Power-conflict theory maintains that racist ideas and beliefs have long been a part of the dominant ideology in North America that has held a hegemonic position. Racist ideas have, power-conflict theory would argue, been a significant part of a divide and rule tactic that has both divided and split the subordinate classes into conflictual factions. Racist ideas might be seen to benefit the dominant classes by justifying slavery and the appropriation of the land of the First Nations while hiding the contradictions inherent in a society based on class and exploitation.

The notion that there are superior races and more advanced ethnic groups could be seen to justify the four major sources of so-called racial and ethnic divisions in North America. Two brief booklets, *The Roots of Racism* and *Patterns of Racism*, explicitly make the argument that racism and racist ideologies were part and parcel of the pillage of Africa that resulted in the slave trade and the subsequent agricultural and industrial development of both England and the United States. These volumes point out that even after the official abolition of slavery, ingrained racist ideas continued to serve the dominant classes.

Although not all of the scholars we are about to mention identify themselves with the tradition we are calling power-conflict, their work could be used to support the claim that First Nations and aboriginal people in Canada have had their culture and society destroyed by European and Canadian colonialism. Further, it seems clear that as a result these very people have been the object of state actions and ideological distortions that have caused and justified their marginated and exploited status. Francis Henry, Carole Tator, Winston Mattis, and Tim Rees (2000) trace both the actions of the Canadian state and the systematic ideological undertakings that resulted in the destruction of pre-Contact society. They refer to 'Canada's racist policies toward Aboriginal peoples' but make it clear that the cause is not merely a case of a dysfunctional value system (128). In his essay 'Race and Racism', Rick Ponting examines a number of dimensions of racism in Canada concluding that it is 'structured into the major institutions of society' and thus its elimination will demand significant political action (2001: 68–9). Fleras and Elliott provide powerful evidence that racism in Canada and elsewhere must be understood in the context of European expansion, colonialism, and imperialism. Among the most definitive studies in this regard is Peter Li's *Ethnic Inequality in a Class Society*. Although Li presents abundant and irrefutable empirical data to demonstrate that ethnic groups often experience structural inequality in Canadian society, he is clear in his conclusion that ethnicity and race serve to fragment class divisions and that therefore an understanding of class is essential (1988: 140–1).

Chances are if you were to ask a Canadian on the street what he or she thinks are the two most pressing issues in Canada as far as so-called race and ethnic relations are concerned, the answer would be Indian/First Nation relations and the Quebec issue.

Race, Ethnicity, and Colonialism in Canada

Surely the term *colonialism* has no relevance in any analysis of Canada, or does it? A careful study of Canadian history (something that will not be attempted here) reveals, as careful analysis often does, a picture that is somewhat different than what casual impressions might indicate.

Canada is a product of colonialism. As Chapter 15 argues, Canada is the outcome of a period of

European colonial expansion when the new nation-states of Europe sought colonial empires. Colonies were sought after, valued, and acquired because they were a source of various forms of wealth and they served to enhance the power and prestige of the states and their rulers. The search for fish brought the first sustained wave of Europeans to the east coast of what is now Canada. As the fishing and colonial expansionist activities intensified, Europeans made more and more systematic contacts with the indigenous peoples and aboriginal societies and communities. There is considerable debate about the precise origins and pre-history of the aboriginal peoples and societies that came into contact with the Europeans, we know that they had been in what we now call North America for thousands and thousands of years. The Creation Story of the Ojibwa has a familiar ring to those from the Judaeo-Christian tradition:

> In the beginning, before there was anything, in the vast emptiness where there was a never-ending darkness and deep, deep silence; in this beginning before the beginning there was One who dreamed of creations yet to be. One who struggled to send out the first thought, who sought to draw together the vastness into a bound whole and focus the great silence into sounds. This is He for whom there is no explanation—only the knowledge that He is.

The Hurons and Iroquois had a creation story of their own that begins like this:

> In the beginning, there was nothing but water—nothing but a wide, wide sea. The only people the world were the animals that live in and on the water.
>
> Then down from the sky world a woman fell, a divine person. Two loons flying over the water happened to look up and see her falling. Quickly they placed themselves

beneath her and joined their bodies to make a cushion for her to rest upon. Thus they saved her from drowning

While they held her, they cried with a loud voice to the other animals, asking their help. Now the cry of the loon can be heard at a great distance over water, and so other creatures gathered quickly.

The volume from which these stories are drawn contains a detailed account of the complex institutional structures and dynamics of the various indigenous peoples prior to contact with the Europeans. This rich and important history is ignored because, quite frankly, the Europeans turned out not to just be trading partners and allies, they were colonizers and conquerors and as such became the dominant force in writing history. David Bedford and Danielle Irving discuss the role that the *Great Law of Peace*, a codified record of the nature of pre-Contact Iroquois society, played, comparing it to the role of Homer's poetry in ancient Greece (2001: 18). Among the aspects of pre-Contact society that the *Great Law of Peace* documents are the political structures of the Five, then Six Nations Confederacy (19–21). Bedford and Irving point out that while this was not a state in the sense of Western liberal democratic theory, it was the basis of a 'society held together by a clan system and a spiritual sense of obligation and thanksgiving' (21). The authors of *Survival of a People* provide a similar account of pre-Contact society:

From time immemorial, centuries before the Europeans set foot in North America, Indian societies existed as distinct sovereign nations. Each nation was identified as occupying specific territories whose borders were respected by other Indian Nations. Each nation also exercised sovereignty rights such as: the power to make and enforce laws, the power to determine membership and citizenship, the power to regulate trade within its borders, the power to make war and peace, and the power to regulate domestic relations (including marriage, divorce, and adoption). True, some nations did not possess imposing structures such as churches and parliament buildings in which to house their institutions, but these institutions existed all the same. It is also true that certain practices (e.g., the collective decision-making procedure) were carried out in a manner foreign to the Europeans, but nonetheless they too existed and served the purposes set out by the Indian Nations.

In short then, Indian Nations were autonomous entities which exercised the powers of sovereignty and freedom enjoyed by other governments around the globe. While Indian Nations were ruling their own lands, however, European nations were seeking ways in which to secure the land of North America (as well as other land which had not been 'discovered') under their own sovereign jurisdictions. Thus, the Doctrine of Discovery was born.

In what would soon prove to be seen as an ironic twist of history, the French were the first to colonize and appropriate the lands along the lower reaches of the St Lawrence. As the focus of European wealth appropriation expanded to include both fish and furs, the European presence spread farther and farther inland. Given that European powers were competing for power and wealth in Europe, it is not surprising that North America soon became a front. As the English, Dutch, and Spanish were expanding their empires to the south, the French moved to consolidate their position along the St Lawrence. Efforts to establish permanent settlements were underway as early as 1543 but the use of private charter companies proved ineffective. Faced with increased competition from the English to the south the French government took control and New France became a royal colony in 1663. Despite its best efforts, the

French were unable to compete with the English in North America or elsewhere. The establishment of the Hudson's Bay Company in 1670 showed the growth of English power. It is astounding that the English, who under the terms of the Treaty of Utrecht in 1713 had secured these lands, were able to grant the Hudson's Bay Company full state powers over a huge landmass that included the entire watershed of Hudson Bay. With the stroke of a pen, and without any negotiations with them, the land, economic assets and political rights of thousands of indigenous people were given over to a private company.

The international rivalry between the British and the French reached a climax in North America in 1759 when the British defeated the French in the famous Battle of the Plains of Abraham. The formal treaty that ended that particular war, the Treaty of Paris (1763), ceded all French lands on the mainland of what is now Canada to the British. For the French it was a bitter turn of events as they went from being conqueror to conquered.

Key Events in Post-1763 Aboriginal History

Some of the first British actions following the conquest of Quebec would have different implications for the two colonized peoples under the terms of The Royal Proclamation of 1763. As James Frideres points out, the Proclamation recognized the land rights of the indigenous people with some limitations. The Proclamation seemed to provide some basis upon which the indigenous peoples could build a future, albeit a very different future than would have been the case if the Europeans had not arrived. Henry, Tator, Mattis, and Rees describe the situation:

Aboriginal–English relations had stabilized to the point where they could be seen to be grounded in two fundamental principles. . . . Under the first principle, while Aboriginal peoples were regarded as British subjects, they also were generally recognized as autonomous political units capable of having treaty relations with the Crown. The second principle acknowledged that Aboriginal nations were entitled to the territories in their possession, unless or until they ceded them to others. (2000: 122)

A series of events in quick succession changed world history and with it the fate of indigenous people in what would become Canada. In 1774 the British Parliament passed the *Quebec Act*, a precipitating factor in the American Revolution and the emergence of the United States of America as an independent nation-state in 1776. This was followed by a significant influx of political refugees (United Empire Loyalists) into Canada. The resulting increase in the population of the remaining colonies of British North America changed the demographic mix with those of British ancestry growing in number. As industrialization proceeded in England some benefits accrued to its colonies and thus the period between the American Revolution and the middle of the 1800s was one of substantial growth. As we will see, this period brought with it significant political tension and economic problems. The creation of a new nation, Canada, in 1867 was seen as providing a framework for solving them.

The implications of these developments for the indigenous peoples were not positive. Henry, Tator, Mattis, and Rees describe what emerged as change from a relationship that was 'mutually beneficial co-operation and practical accommodation' to 'a pervasive and sustained attack on the respectful egalitarian nation-to-nation principle' (2000: 123). *The Survival of a People* documents a change in the nature of the treaties from what were called 'The Treaties for Friendship and Peace' to treaties such as the Robinson Huron Treaty and the Robinson Superior Treaty that involved the ceding of lands in order for Canadian and British interests to access mineral deposits (1986: 94–5).

In the years following Confederation in 1867 the focus of Canadian economic development shifted to the West (Fowke, 1957). As the idea that Canada could become an industrial nation through the creation of markets for its industrial goods in an agricultural west included a series of steps to dispossess the indigenous people from these lands. The new Government of Canada moved decisively in this regard by first buying the lands of the Hudson's Bay Company in 1869 and then by beginning a process of removing the indigenous population through the treaties.

If there was any doubt that the federal government was moving to dispossess, administer, make marginal, and render people dependent, the *Indian Act* of 1876 confirmed it. The paternalism and negative implications and impact of the *Indian Act* have been well documented; however, Bedford and Irving make the important point that according to the Act 'Indian' is thus a legal classification, not a cultural or ethnic concept (25).

The authors of *Survival of a People* provide a detailed description of the treaty signing process that followed the passing of the *Indian Act*. Through these treaties virtually all of Western Canada was ceded to the federal government, which subsequently made it available to immigrant settlers under the auspices of the *Dominion Lands Act*. The loss of the land base of their societies, the onslaught of the systematic efforts to extinguish their cultures, and the destruction of the traditional political, social, and economic institutions ushered in a period of unimaginable social upheaval for indigenous peoples. *Survival of a People* refers to the initial period of reserve life, 1879–84, as the starvation period. The years that followed brought continual hardship and deprivation. Confined to reserves, governed by the terms and conditions of the *Indian Act,* with their children forced into residential schools, indigenous peoples fell on hard times. Henry, Tator, Mattis, and Rees summarize:

> throughout this period of displacement and assimilation, Aboriginal peoples were denied access to their traditional territories and often forced to move to new locations selected by colonial authorities. They were also displaced socially and culturally by being subjected to intense missionary activity and the establishment of schools that undermined Aboriginal parents' ability to pass on traditional values to their children. They had imposed upon them male-oriented Victorian values, while traditional activities such as significant dances and other ceremonies were attacked and made unlawful. They were also displaced politically, forced by colonial laws to abandon or at least disguise traditional governing structures and processes in favour of municipal-style institutions. (2000: 132)

Although the post-Second World War boom did not bring many benefits to indigenous peoples in Canada, it did usher in a period of somewhat more liberal thinking and social-political activism that forced the federal government to take some action. Amendments to the *Indian Act* passed in 1951 marked small improvements; however, no major developments occurred until after Jean Chrétien, the minister of Indian Affairs, issued a *White Paper on Indian Policy*. That paper and the 1984 Nielson Task Force provoked major debate and discussion and might have been factors that gave rise to a renewed political, social, and economic organization among indigenous peoples. Not until 1985 was the *Indian Act* brought into conformity with the Canadian *Charter of Rights and Freedoms* (Henry et al., 2000: 203). One of the outcomes of the political activism of the past two decades was the move towards settling land claims that remained outstanding from the government's failure to abide by treaty conditions or the dishonest and corrupt allocations of lands under the treaties (Frideres, 1993: 73–4). Bedford and Irving summarize the complex situation facing persons of indigenous or aboriginal ancestry:

> The rejection of their identity as Canadian and the retention of an Aboriginal identity

leads to an important, and as yet unresolved, problematic. Self-governing Aboriginal communities that wish to preserve an Aboriginal identity and culture must face the question that Aristotle argued all communities must face: 'how to live well'. In this case the issue is compounded because what it means to be Aboriginal in the new millennium is not at all clear. As Gerald Alfred (1995) has pointed out, there are divisions in communities based on strategies for achieving common goals. In many communities there is also conflict over what goals to pursue. The question of 'how to live well Aboriginally' is almost by necessity extraordinarily difficult to answer. (2001: 34)

Key Events in Post-1763 Quebec History

We have seen that the Royal Proclamation of 1763 recognized the existence of indigenous peoples; however, it had the opposite intent for the Quebecois, that is, the people of Quebec. The Proclamation was a radical document in terms of its proposed treatment of the Quebecois because its intent was the replacement of the existing French legal codes with English law and the replacement of the Roman Catholic Church with the Church of England. In short, the Proclamation was intended to make sure that British North America was *British* North America. John Conway refers to the Proclamation as a draconian program (1997: 14). The Proclamation was never enacted, partly because the British were increasingly concerned with the impending American Revolution. In what amounted to a major shift in policy, the British passed the *Quebec Act* in 1774 in an effort to keep the Quebecois from joining the Revolution if something bad happened to the south. The *Quebec Act* recognized the legitimate existence of the established Church and allowed for the continuance of the French Law in civil areas, although it did impose English criminal law. Elements of the traditional feudal land-holding system that represented a core

institution in rural Quebec, commonly referred to as the seigneurial system, were retained.

Without attributing any necessary notion of causality, the fact is that the population of Quebec did not join with the Thirteen Colonies at the time of the American Revolution. As a result, Quebec became an important and distinct part of British North America after the United States of America was created. As we have seen, one of the political outcomes of this was an influx of British citizens into British North America who wanted to remain loyal. Although historians tend not to use the word, what happened was a significant inflow of political refugees into British North America. Conway notes that it is estimated that about 40,000 arrived in total, with about 7,000 of these settling in Quebec. Hubert Guindon has considered the role of the Church in these processes and concludes that it was important, not because it kept the Quebecois from joining the Revolution but because of its role in the aftermath. Guindon argues that the *Quebec Act*, by allowing the Church to retain its prominence, created the conditions for the continued survival of the Quebecois, but ultimately that survival relied on the maintenance of a myth (2001: 290–1). The core of Guindon's argument is that the Church in Quebec became the agent of the survival of the Quebecois as a rural, Catholic, and traditional society. It was a myth that was to have considerable power for over a century.

The Post-Revolutionary period in British North America was one of significant population and economic growth. The economic growth involved a shift in the class structure as merchants and aspiring industrialists emerged alongside an emerging wage labour or working class. The urbanization that accompanied this development became the cradle for new professions, small businesses, and the homes of the workers. In the immediate aftermath of the Revolution, many immigrants from Britain who previously might have gone to the Thirteen Colonies now came to one of the northern colonies, typically to the St Lawrence region. As a result of the increase in population growth, Britain was forced to realign the political structures creating the colonies of Upper and Lower Canada in 1871, each with its own non-democratic government structures. The decades that followed saw continued economic growth, to the point that by the 1820s and 1830s, a new middle class began to challenge the undemocratic structures and processes that characterized the colonial governance of British North America.

The phenomenon of an emerging 'middle class', also sometimes called an aspiring bourgeoisie, demanding and struggling for political power is a common feature of the development of capitalist society. This is precisely what happened in British North America with the Rebellions of 1837. As Conway points out, the Rebellion in English Upper Canada does not get much attention in Canadian history. He notes, however, that 'the Rebellion in Lower Canada was a different matter' (1997: 25). Stanley Ryerson's account of the aftermath of this middle-class effort to gain more power by military means remains one of the most detailed. Ryerson notes that 501 people were imprisoned in Montreal, 116 on the serious charge of treason. Eventually, 108 were brought to trial, 12 were executed, and 59 deported to the penal colonies in Australia (1975: 80).

By some accounts of Quebec history this amounts to the second military conquest of the Quebecois by the British Army. The British response to the Rebellions was to have Lord Durham investigate, and then to act on the Durham Report by passing the *Act of Union*. Durham claimed to find 'two nations warring within the bosom of a single state' (quoted in McRoberts, 1988: 51). As McRoberts notes, Durham's recommendations centred on the notion of assimilation. To this end, the *Act of Union* reunified Upper and Lower Canada into one political unit with equal political representation from each part. The trouble was that the population of French-speaking Lower Canada was greater, so in fact the English population of Upper

Canada was overrepresented. The response of the Quebecois to the military defeat and the subsequent creation of political structures that appeared to treat them unfairly have been described as a form of retreat into survival mode. To the extent that those supporting the Rebellion wanted to create a democratic state governed by the French, that dream was gone. Alain Gagnon describes the retreat to survival in the following passage:

> *La survivance* is premised on the idea that Quebec's national culture faces continual threats and the threats, historically, have been perceived as taking many forms. There have been infringements by federal and other provincial governments on the rights and privileges of French Canadians outside Quebec. Canada's links to Britain meant the participation of French Canadians in imperial campaigns. Within Quebec the forces of industrialization challenged traditional anti-materialism and the rural ideal. Although French Canadians established control over their political, social, cultural, and religious institutions, the economic penetration of Quebec—led by foreign interests attracted, by low labour, costs and, government policies— resulted in the progressive exclusion of Quebecois from increasingly powerful economic institutions. In the larger context of the Canadian political system, demographic trends have operated to the disadvantage of francophones. For nationalists, their minority status in federal institutions offers insufficient protection for Quebec's interests, notwithstanding the significance of Quebec support for the electoral success of federal political parties. The collective impact of these and other threats have given traditional nationalism its 'culture under siege' quality.

Although the power of this myth, to use Guindon's term, may have been significant, there were major changes occurring in the real world. Industrialization continued to move ahead in British North America during the 1840s and 1850s, bringing with it significant population growth. By the 1860s the population of English-speaking Ontario was greater than that of Quebec and the overrepresentation/underrepresentation situation was reversed. As a result, demands from the English for increased representation in the Assembly, which had taken on greater significance since democratic responsible government had evolved, were resisted by the representatives from Quebec. The colony of Canada was mired in political deadlock that became a contributing factor to the creation of a new nation-state in 1867.

The creation of Canada as a federal system with two levels of government was seen as a solution because each province would have its own legislative assembly. Although the provinces were given few powers by the *British North America Act* that created Canada in 1867, they did have control over key issues for those interested in preserving their language and culture. Conway summarizes the situation:

> Canada would be divided into two provinces, Ontario and Quebec. Thus, the Quebecois would again be granted a political and constitutional home in which they would enjoy a certain hegemony within the considerable constitutional limits of Confederation. The French language and civil law would prevail in Quebec, and significant powers would be granted to all provinces—education, health, local government, property, resources, civil rights, a large say in agriculture—powers sufficient to defend the cultural and linguistic foundation of the Quebecois nation. The powerful English minority in Quebec would be reassured by Article 80 of the *British North America Act*, which established 17 protected English provincial constituencies in the

Eastern Townships, the Ottawa Valley, and northwestern Quebec. These constituencies were to remain protected until a majority of the 17 sitting members agreed otherwise. And, for the first time since 1837, the Quebecois nation would be able to express its democratic political will, however circumscribed by the *British North America Act*, through a National Assembly. (1997: 35)

As we have seen, the period following Confederation was one of significant economic development albeit development focused on industrialization via tariffs and the creation of a market through the settlement of the West. This process required the removal of the indigenous population from the land and the settlement of that land by immigrant farmers. The process by which the land was 'cleared' of the various elements of the indigenous population resulted in two political events that had an impact on French-English relations. In 1870 and again in 1885, Louis Riel spearheaded military resistance to the expansion of the Canadian state. In each case he was unsuccessful, and in the latter case the undertaking resulted in his execution in Regina. Conway summarizes the significance for the Quebecois and their relations with the rest of Canada: 'The message to Quebec was obvious. The Quebecois nation could play no significant role in westward expansion. The west belonged to English Canada' (1997: 40).

The West may have been the focus of the national policy of economic development that Canada was pursuing but Quebec was changing along with the rest of Canada. As the twentieth century unfolded, investment from the United States and English Canada poured into Quebec. Its industrial presence grew and demand for its raw materials grew. Although the real world and the face of Quebec were changing, the myth of Quebec articulated by the Church and the educational system it controlled persisted. Social, political, and cultural tensions emerged. Perhaps we can liken it to the movements of the Earth's tectonic plates when pressure builds and builds until there is a sudden release in the form of an earthquake. The term *Quiet Revolution* has been applied to the situation in Quebec during the 1960s and into the 1970s when a series of new, mostly Liberal, governments set the stage for the emergence of Quebec into the twentieth century. Michael Behiels describes the events in the following manner:

> The term *Quiet Revolution* was used first by a journalist to refer to the administration of Jean Lesage's Liberal Party, which narrowly defeated the Union Nationale in June 1960 and retained power until 1966. Yet it is now becoming increasingly clear that the social, economic, and ideological forces that set the Quiet Revolution in motion were not dissipated with the defeat of the Liberal government in 1966. Those forces found expression in successive governments, the most prominent being the Parti Québécois. The Quiet Revolution had two dimensions, the first internal and the second external. Achieving reform within Quebec proved considerably easier than enhancing Quebec's power within Confederation or in international affairs. The first dimension involved using the Quebec state to modernize, as quickly as possible, Quebec's outmoded social, economic, administrative, and political institutions at all levels. (1987: 47)

One of the dimensions of the Quiet Revolution that was not so quiet was the rise of a complex, at times militant, at times terrorist, but always dedicated independence movement. The fall of 1970 marked a crisis in Canada when several terrorist cells of an organization called the Front du Libération du Québec (FLQ) kidnapped a representative of the British government and a minister in the Quebec government. The latter individual, Pierre Laporte, was murdered while in captivity. The fact that the Canadian government enacted the most repressive legislation at its disposal, the *War Measures Act*, must have meant that there was a real threat to Canada. But why did the FLQ resort to these tactics and why does the project they represented—an independent—Quebec not go away? However, we understand the nature of the transformation of Quebec during the last half of the last century, this is certain—the changes and conflict are not over. Many in English Canada tend to breathe a huge sigh of relief every time there is a negative vote on an independence referendum; however, they seem at a loss to explain why the population of Quebec keeps electing governments dedicated to this objective.

Some Further Theoretical and Empirical Considerations

This introductory discussion of the concepts of race and ethnicity and how sociologists study them should make one issue crystal clear—these remain contested concepts. However, let's move our analytical capacity forward by reconsidering some of the points discussed in the context of the historical data presented above.

Given the important questions that the recent genome research raises with regard to the scientific validity of the concept of race, we will focus on the notion of ethnicity. To the extent that ethnic groups are defined with reference to a common culture and a sense of shared historical or ancestral origins, virtually every nation in existence today is multiethnic. The 2001 *World Factbook* contains a list of over 230 countries and islands and the proportion of various ethnic groups in each. While the definitions are less than clear, fewer than 10 are listed as being composed of only one ethnic group. Wsevolod Isajiw has studied ethnic relations and the ethnic composition of Canada for many years. In one of his recent studies he noted that it is difficult to draw a precise picture of the ethnic composition of Canada because of changes to the nature of the census questions on which the data is based, and because many Canadians (36 per cent) indicate they are of mixed ethnic background (1999: 53). Isajiw notes that in 1996 the largest single group, nearly 19 per cent, comprised those who identified their ethnicity as 'Canadian'; however, those identifying themselves as British were numerically the largest. There was no group with a numerical majority.

This data clearly illustrates that Canada, like all nations today, is multiethnic, with no group being numerically dominant. The fact that Canada is multiethnic has long been recognized. Indeed, the potential for conflict based on national background which included language was a factor that led the federal government to create the 1963 Royal Commission on Bilingualism and Biculturalism. As it turned out, the act of investigating the two founding cultures and languages—French and English—brought the deeper reality of the importance of other ethnic groups to the surface and the government responded (Isajiw, 1999: 246). In 1971, the Government of Canada formally declared that Canada was a multicultural society. This policy was later enshrined in legislation in the form of the 1988 *Canadian Multiculturalism Act*. These actions allowed Prime Minister Jean Chrétien to declare in June 2000 that Canada is 'a post-national, multicultural society [that] . . . contains the globe within its borders' (quoted in 'What Is Multiculturalism?').

But what of the relations between these groups? Does the presence of multiple ethnic groups and nationalities foster the development of a diverse and interesting mix of cultures, religions, languages, and national traditions or does it foster divisions, hostilities, and the absence of a sense of nation and place? When John Porter published his definitive study of class and power in Canada, *The Vertical Mosaic*, in 1965, he documented in significant detail what many Canadians knew—that

economic, political, and other resources and the power that accompanies them are not equitably distributed. Porter studied what he saw as the five major elites in Canadian society: economic, political, labour, ideological, and bureaucratic. Porter documented a clear relationship between class/wealth/power and ethnicity, with the so-called dominant charter groups (the British and French) overrepresented in every one of the five elites he studied.

Porter's groundbreaking analysis established the need to add new concepts to our repertoire because inequality clearly characterized relations among ethnic groups in Canada. Richard Schemerhorn suggests that, rather than using the concept of ethnic group to understand social relations in a multicultural society, we examine groups in terms of their size and power. If we do this, concepts such as 'dominant group' and 'subordinate group' must be included (1996: 17). Schemerhorn suggests the concept of 'minority group' under the rubric of subordinate group. The position of a dominant or subordinate group need not be predicated on ethnicity, but as Porter's analysis illustrates, ethnicity can be an important factor. If we understand relations among ethnic groups as not just benign cultural, linguistic, religious, or historical differences but rather as relations of power and subordination, then we need to consider the implications of this dimension for sociological analysis. Since the object of sociological inquiry is not simply description but explanation and analysis, we need to return to the issue of how the theories we have been considering might account for this added dimension.

A sociologist employing a form of structural functional analysis might argue that the Canadian approach of explicitly acknowledging and celebrating cultural and ethnic differences is an appropriate response. Such an argument would be based on accepting the official government position that multiculturalism creates respect and acceptance of difference and results in a society that is interesting, diverse, and culturally rich. The fact that we accept as equals the many varied ethnic and cultural traditions and practices that immigrants bring to Canada makes us less prone to the racism and bigotry that ignorance of other cultures can generate. The recognition and celebration of ethnic subcultures, this argument would maintain, generates integration, acceptance and ultimately stability.

This same theoretical tradition might support a different policy orientation more akin to notion of the American 'melting pot approach'. As opposed to the Canadian notion of multiculturalism with its emphasis on dual or hyphenated identities (e.g., Finnish-Canadian), there seems to be a tradition in the United States of emphasizing becoming and being an American. The immigrant to the United States becomes an American first and foremost, albeit one with certain ethnic roots; but those ethnic roots tend to be merely part of his or her past. A structural functionalist might argue that this is an appropriate and effective way to create the shared values, normative orientations, moral codes, and belief systems that are necessary for a smooth functioning, integrated, and stable society.

If we operate from within the power-conflict tradition, our analysis would pay more attention to the phenomena of power and domination. Multiculturalism might be seen as a mode of social integration that works to cover up class divisions and relations of exploitation by encouraging division and difference among subordinate classes. The fact that I pay more attention to my ethnic origins than I do to my class membership tends to mute possible class conflict. As well, the society is made to appear to be open to difference and accommodating.

As far as the melting pot approach is concerned, it is clear that the ideological barrage that is necessary in order to change my ethnicity provides the dominant classes and groups with an opportunity to manipulate my consciousness. The act and fact of becoming an American involves a significant resocialization effort that affords an opportunity to try and convince me that classes really don't exist, we are all equal, and that the Western model of a capitalist free market is the best of all possible worlds.

As is always the case in social analysis, the relative explanatory capacity of these, and other, approaches cannot be determined by sitting in a classroom or office. What is required is some detailed empirical, historical, and comparative research. We need to study and investigate these processes and determine how well these approaches work and how well they can explain actual social events.

In summary, we are still left with the question: what do we make of the concepts of race and ethnicity? Are they so badly misused and scientifically discredited that we abandon them altogether? Or is such an argument itself a form of racism that seeks to deny history, deny diversity, deny difference, and impose a monolithic dominant culture? If we retain the concepts, how do we address the issues raised by those who would use them to identify an 'other' and attach inferior status to same? How do we address the arguments of the genome scientists who argue that biological differences are so small as to be negligible and that our differences really are 'skin deep'? And what of ethnicity? Many of us marvel at and admire the diverse cultures our species has produced over the past few thousands of years. How do we continue to celebrate this diversity without losing and avoiding the possibility that difference becomes the basis for exclusion and subordination?

These are tough questions indeed and well beyond the scope of this little study. The preceding pages were intended to introduce some ideas, some history, and some debate. As intelligent and human citizens of the world, all we can hope to do is approach the reality of our planet and our species with all the information possible and a willingness to learn from our history.

Critical Thinking Questions

- What does the term race mean to you? What is ethnicity? Should we still use these concepts in sociology?
- Is your society racist? Explain.
- What are the political implications of claiming that certain forms of inequality are genetic?
- Does the concept of colonialism have any saliency for the study of Canadian society?
- What was the Quiet Revolution? How did it affect Canada as a whole? Is it over?

Terms and Concepts

Race—the most common contemporary incorrect usage of the word to refer to a group or category of people who are socially, politically, culturally, or economically differentiated on the basis of some biological or genetic characteristic or feature. The notion that biological characteristics alone produce social differentiation has been scientifically discredited, leading to arguments in favour of abandoning the concept altogether. The only connection to biology is the fact that so-called racial differences involve the arbitrary selection of a physical feature as the signifier of a 'race'. It has been suggested we use quotation marks for such usage to ensure readers understand we are not using the concept in the traditional manner.

Racism—a system of thought, action, practice, and beliefs that assigns inherent social, cultural, political, or economic characteristics, rights, and behaviours to a social group on the basis of some arbitrary physical or biological characteristic. Because racism usually implies a distinctive hierarchy of people and cultures, it has often been the case that racist categorizations have been used to justify colonial conquests and various forms and regimes of social, political, cultural, and economic inequality and domination.

Ethnicity—a group of people who identify themselves, or are identified by others, as sharing some common characteristics. These common character-istics are typically based on differences that we might define as involving culture, language, nationality, ancestry, or geographic location. The characteristics might also be more related to customs and processes of group self-identification.

Gene and Genome—*gene:* the basic unit of genetic material; *genome:* the entire genetic material that composes an organism or some part of it. It is now estimated that about 30,000 genes make up the human genome. Recent research has reminded us that genomes are much more alike than previously thought. Your genome is pretty much 99.9 per cent the same as mine and, as Hilary and Steven Rose remind us, the fact that 'we share 98 per cent of our DNA with chimps and 35 per cent with daffodils potentially changes not only how we think about ourselves but also our connection with other live forms' (2000: 5).

Colonialism—as used here, the establishment of political, economic, social, and cultural control of one people by another. What is often called the 'expansion' of European nations to many other parts of the world between the sixteenth and twentieth centuries was really a part of a process of colonialism. In Canadian history there have been several forms of colonialism starting with the French conquest of the indigenous peoples, the British conquest of the French, and then again when the

Canadian government completed the conquest of the remaining indigenous peoples after 1867.

Quiet Revolution—in Quebec, the period from 1960 to 1966. Although the material reality of the Quebec economy and society changed during the first half of the twentieth century, the cultural, political, and social fabric was mired in the past. In 1960, a more progressive Liberal government set off a period of modernization, secularization, nationalism, cultural revival, and political, social, and educational reforms that marked the beginning of the Quiet Revolution. It has been referred to as a 'decolonization' process because of the intensity and radical nature of the social changes that occurred as the Quebecois caught up and, some argue, passed the rest of North America.

Related Web Sites

http://www.clearinghouse.fsin.com/

The homepage of the Federation of Saskatchewan Indian Nations—which represents 74 First Nations in the province—provides links and information on the history of First Nations in Canada, treaties, self-govenrment issues and much more. The information is as relevant to students outside Saskatchewan as to those in province.

http://dmoz.org/Society/Issues/
Race-Ethnic-Religious_Relations/
Race_and_Racism/

Described as a 'DMOZ' 'Open Directory Project', this site has international links with a number of articles that focus on the issue of how race is lived in everyday lives. There is historical and contemporary coverage.

http://www.crr.ca/EN/default.htm

This is the home page for an important albeit relatively young Canadian organization, the Canadian Race Relations Foundation. The site contains news releases, information on programs, publications and commentaries on current issues.

http://www.afn.ca/

This is the web site of the Assembly of First Nations in Canada. It's a good point of departure for those not familiar with current First Nation political, economic, social, and cultural issues. The amount of information here is as overwhelming as the need for most Canadians to spend time at this site.

http://www.ainc-inac.gc.ca/index_e.html

These are the Department of Indian and Northern Affairs, Government of Canada Web sites. A good critical thinking exercise is to compare this site with the home page of the Assembly of First Nations.

Suggested Further Readings

Conway, J. 1996. *Debts to Pay*. Toronto: Lorimer. Written from the perspective of a Western anglophone, this is an excellent summary of the history of Quebec within Canada and a sobering appraisal of what English Canada has to understand if Quebec is to remain part of the nation.

Fraser, S., ed. 1996. *The Bell Curve Wars*. New York: Basic Books. A wide range of essays and arguments are critical of the basic thesis of the Herrnstein and Murray volume, *The Bell Curve*.

Hannaford, I. 1997. *Race*. Washington, DC: Woodrow Wilson Center Press. This is a must read if you are to fully understand the evolution of the use and meaning of this concept. The subtitle 'The History of an Idea in the West' says it all.

Saskatchewan Indian Federated College. 1987. *Survival of a People*. Regina: SIFC at the University of Regina. Probably the best history of indigenous peoples to be found, this book is written by a group of scholars associated with SIFC, the only First Nation Controlled post-secondary institution in Canada.

Satzewich, V., ed. 1996. *Racism and Social Inequality in Canada*. Toronto: Thompson Educational. This edited collection of essays includes some of the pre-eminent scholars in the field of race and ethnic relations in Canada.

CHAPTER 13

Deviance and Social Control

Have you ever done anything that someone in a position of authority or power considered wrong? The chance is great that for most of us an honest answer to this question is yes. According to sociological wisdom, when we act in a manner that contravenes the dominant norms that govern a given society or social situation we are engaging in deviant behaviour. There are a great many different sociological definitions of deviance, including: (1) 'any social behavior that departs from that regarded as normal or socially acceptable within a society or social context' (Jary and Jary, 1991: 120); (2) 'behavior which fails to conform with the accepted norms and standards of a social group or system' (Martin, 1976: 21); and (3) 'behaviour which violates institutionalized expectations, that is, expectations which are shared and recognized as legitimate within a social system' (Cohen, 1959: 462). As you think about these definitions a fundamental sociological proposition regarding deviance should become apparent—that deviance tends to be socially defined and constructed. As we know from our discussion of culture, values, and norms, when it comes to human behaviour, there are enormous variations in what we might consider normal and appropriate.

In sociology, deviance and deviant behaviour are generally distinguished from crime and criminal behaviour. As we know from our discussion of norms, folkways, and mores, sometimes norms (especially mores) become codified into laws and legal codes. A crime is generally considered to be a violation of a criminal law or a formal, legally sanctioned social norm. Crimes are sometimes categorized as being against property, violent, white collar, and victimless. Criminal behaviour tends to be subject to penalties and sanctions as specified or laid out in the laws and legal codes. As is the case with deviance and deviant behaviour, crime and criminal behaviour are socially constructed. A specific behaviour can be made a crime simply by changing the laws and legal codes.

Implicit in sociological definitions of deviance and crime is the notion of social control. Who or what social institution or agency defines what is normal and acceptable or abnormal, unacceptable, and therefore deviant? Who or what social institutions or agencies determine what sanctions are appropriate for a particular case of deviant behaviour? As Jary and Jary put it, 'the question of by whom, and how, deviance is labeled becomes crucial to its explanation' (1991: 120). Similar questions emerge when we consider the legal system, crime, and criminal behaviour. The issues of who makes laws, how laws are made, how they are enforced, and who determines and implements punishments and sanctions are essential if we want to understand the social phenomenon of crime. By now the reader should be sensitive to the fact that when sociologists raise who, what, why, and how questions, they will look to theory, in particular sociological theory, for the answers.

There are many different sociological definitions of deviance including 'any social behaviour that departs from that regarded as normal or socially acceptable' to 'behaviour which fails to conform with the accepted norms and standards of a social group.' Teen rebellion is deviance-based. (Dick Hemingway)

Biological Explanations

On 22 October 1993, the *Globe and Mail* ran a story about a family whose male members demonstrated a propensity towards violence and aggressive behaviour under the banner, 'Researchers Find Link Between Genetic Inheritance and Aggression'. The story reports that a study of one particular family's history had found that the presence or absence of a particular enzyme seemed to influence the behaviour of some males. The intimation that there is a biological basis and explanation for deviant or criminal behaviour is an ancient idea. Early in the twentieth century Cesare Lombroso (1835–1909) popularized the idea that criminal behaviour was inborn. In 1876 he published the first edition of *The*

Criminal Man in which he presented his theories of crime. Lombroso was particularly interested in the physical features of prison inmates because he thought these would allow him to identify the characteristics of the typical criminals. Among his list of typical characteristics were shifty eyes, high cheekbones, oversized ears, and scanty beards. Ronald Akers describes his work in the following passage:

Lombroso believed that certain physical features identified the convict in prison as a 'born criminal'. The born criminal comes into the world with a bodily constitution that causes him to violate the laws of modern society. The born criminal is an 'atavism', Lombroso theorized, a throwback to an earlier stage of human evolution. He has the physical makeup, mental capabilities, and instincts of primitive man. The born criminal, therefore, is unsuited for life in civilized society and, unless specifically prevented, will inevitably violate its social and legal rules. Lombroso maintained that this born criminal can be identified by the possession of certain visible 'stigmata' for example, an asymmetry of the face or head, large monkey-like ears, large lips, receding chin, twisted nose, excessive cheekbones, long arms, excessive skin wrinkles, and extra fingers or toes. The male with five or more of these physical anomalies is marked as a born criminal. Female criminals are also born criminals, but they may be identified with as few as three anomalies. (1994: 43)

Although there were some who apparently found this work interesting, it was soon pointed out that there was a problem in his investigative techniques because he had not compared the prison population to the general population. Were these characteristics indeed representative of only the prison population or were they common in the general population? When it was discovered that these so-called criminal characteristics were in fact quite common, and present in many non-criminals, Lombroso's work became less credible.

Among the more interesting attempts to relate physical attributes to behaviour and intellectual attributes was the work of a physician named Franz Gall (1758–1828) and a student of his, Johann Spurzheim (1776–1832). Gall was initially interested in the relationship of a variety of physiological characteristics, such as the shape of the forehead and jaw, but later he focused on the overall shape and features of the skull. To Gall's credit, he did focus on the brain as the central organ in understanding human behaviour, but we now know that his claims that the various bumps and indentations of the skull were the key to understanding the brain were misguided and, shall we say, wrong-headed.

Other notable efforts to associate and explain deviant and criminal behaviour with physiological characteristics are found in the work of William Sheldon, who published a typology of human body types in 1940 and followed this study with an effort to determine the extent to which these general body types were represented among a small sample of youth in Boston defined as juvenile delinquents (1949). During the 1950s two researchers, Eleanor Glueck and Sheldon Glueck, conducted a follow-up study that tended to support Sheldon's conclusions; however, they were never able to point out any plausible causal connections between body type and deviant behaviour. It seems as if this is an idea that will not easily go away, because in 1985 yet another study claimed to find a relationship between biology and deviant behaviour. In *Crime and Human Nature*, James Q. Wilson and Richard J. Herrnstein argue that there is a connection between physical attributes, what they term *intelligence*, and personality traits that seems to predispose certain people to deviant and criminal behaviour. As I point out in Chapter 12, Herrnstein later teamed up with Charles Murray to produce their infamous *The Bell Curve* volume. Herrnstein and Murray begin the chapter dedicated to the issue of crime with the following claim:

Among the most firmly established facts about criminal offenders is that their distribution of IQ scores differs from that of the population at large. Taking the scientific literature as a whole, criminal offenders have average IQs of about 92, eight points below the mean. More serious or chronic offenders generally have lower scores than more casual offenders. The relationship of IQ to criminality is especially pronounced in the small fraction of the population, primarily young men, who constitute the chronic criminals that account for a disproportionate amount of crime. Offenders who have been caught do not score much lower, if at all, than those who are getting away with their crimes. Holding socioeconomic status constant does little to explain away the relationship between crime and cognitive ability.

> *High intelligence also provides some protection against lapsing into criminality for people who otherwise are at risk. Those who have grown up in turbulent homes, have parents who were themselves criminal, or who have exhibited the childhood traits that presage crime are less likely to become criminals as adults if they have high IQ. (235, emphasis in original)**

After examining a range of data dealing with IQ and crime statistics and making an obligatory and condescending observation that not all citizens with low cognitive ability engage in criminal activity, they offer the following conclusion:

> The caveats should not obscure the importance of the relationship of cognitive ability to crime, however. Many people tend to think of criminals as coming from the wrong side of the tracks. They are correct, insofar as that is where people of low cognitive ability disproportionately live. They are also correct insofar as people who live on the right side of the tracks—whether they are rich or just steadily employed working-class people— seldom show up in the nation's prisons. But the assumption that too glibly follows from these observations is that the economic and social disadvantage is in itself the cause of criminal behavior. That is not what the data say, however. In trying to understand how to deal with the crime problem, much of the attention now given to problems of poverty and unemployment should be shifted to another question altogether: coping with cognitive disadvantage. (251)*

For a sociologist, one of the difficulties of many of these types of analysis is the lack of causal

mechanisms that actually explain the connections between these apparent individual differences and deviant or criminal behaviour. In a review of Wilson and Herrnstein's book, Christopher Jencks states: '*Crime and Human Nature* is a book about the way individual differences affect criminality in one particular kind of society, namely our own, not about the way societies can alter—or eliminate— the effects of individual difference' (1987: 38).

Jon Shepard presents an excellent summary of why sociologists do not accept biological explanations when he notes that such explanations ignore culture and social learning, and are often based on data gathered by questionable and flawed research methodologies. In addition, they are ideologically suspect in that they can be interpreted as justifying existing patterns of social inequality that might produce what is defined as deviant behaviour (Shepard, 1990: 151). As we have seen in the definitions above, sociologists insist that deviance must be studied in its social context; therefore, we must turn our attention to the role society has been deemed to play in fashioning and defining deviant behaviour.

Emile Durkheim

Emile Durkheim devoted the bulk of his intellectual life to establishing the legitimacy of sociological explanations for social phenomena, so it is appropriate to begin with his analysis of deviance and crime. Durkheim was very much concerned with the question of how to establish and maintain social order and stability. He emphasized the role that shared moral codes and values, sometimes referred to as 'collective representations', played in shaping and influencing our social life and the overall characteristics of society (1964: xli). As long as the majority of individuals in a given society shared a belief system or a moral code, the society would be stable and social order would prevail. Durkheim acknowledges, however, that it is impossible to conceive of a situation in which all members of a society totally share a belief system and agree on everything. In *The Rules of Sociological Method* Durkheim employs insights from the organic analogy in his chapter titled 'Rules for Distinguishing Between the Normal and the Pathological' to explain why such an occurrence need not be fatal for society. The arguments advanced could be summarized in the following fashion. Every normally functioning organism will experience periods during which there are temporary disturbances, morbidities, or occurrences that are potentially pathological and disruptive to the functioning of the whole. Such disturbances to the normal functioning of a healthy organism need not be fatal because compensations occur that typically return the organism to a normal healthy state. In society, the presence of individuals who do not share the beliefs and values of the majority might seem to be akin to a virus infecting normal tissue in an organism.

ARE CRIMINALS INDIVIDUALLY CREATED OR SOCIALLY CONSTRUCTED?

Biological Explanations of Crime

The idea that some people are born defective and therefore we can expect them to behave differently is a human prejudice that has been applied to criminal and deviant behaviour for several centuries. Among the more famous supporters was Lombroso. This approach views crime and criminal behaviour as largely individual phenomena, understandable by reference to individuals and their characteristics.

The alternative approach looks to the social structure for the causes of individual behaviour. Conflict theory represents one such structural approach. The first summary below is from James Wilson and Richard Herrnstein's *Crime and Human Nature*. Although the explanation offered is quite different from that of earlier biological approaches, look for a common thread. Wilson and Herrnstein title Chapter 3 'Constitutional Factors in Criminal Behavior', and in the introduction to it they preview some of the arguments that are to follow.

It's Mostly in the Genes

Some individuals are more likely to become criminals than others. As we shall see in the next two chapters, males are more disposed than females to criminal behavior, and younger males are more likely than older ones to commit crimes at high rates. It is likely that the effect of maleness and youthfulness on the tendency to commit crime has both constitutional and social origins: That is, it has something to do both with the biological status of being a young male and with how that young man has been treated by family, friends, and society.

When we speak of constitutional factors, we are referring to factors, usually present at or soon after birth, whose behavioral consequences appear gradually during the child's development. Constitutional factors are not necessarily genetic, although they may be. A genetic factor, if not a mutation, is inherited from one or both parents. There is no 'crime gene' and so there is no such thing as a 'born criminal', but some traits that are to a degree heritable, such as intelligence and temperament, affect to some extent the likelihood that individuals will engage in criminal activities . . . . Other constitutional factors are not hereditary. An individual may be born with a trait that is caused by a chromosomal abnormality—a defect in the arrangement of the genes—that is not acquired from either parent and is not passed on to any offspring. One such abnormality—the XYY chromosome—will be discussed later in this chapter. And some constitutional factors may be the result of prenatal or perinatal accidents. If, for example, the mother smokes heavily, takes drugs, is malnourished, or is exposed to environmental toxins while pregnant, this may affect the infant in ways that influence the chances of later displaying aggressive or criminal behavior. Similarly, if the infant experiences some trauma during birth—sustained oxygen deprivation, for instance—or is improperly fed and cared for immediately after birth, some organic damage may result that also may affect subsequent behavior, including criminal behavior. The evidence on the influence of such nongenetic

constitutional factors is quite sketchy.

In this chapter, we wish only to establish the fact that individuals differ at birth in the degree to which they are at risk for criminality. The evidence of this is of two sorts. First, certain human features that are indisputably biological—an individual's anatomical configuration—are correlated with criminality. We do not argue that these anatomical features cause crime, only that they are correlated with criminal behavior. But the fact of their correlation indicates that there is some psychological trait, having a biological origin, that predisposes an individual to criminality. In chapters 6 and 7, we consider various traits that are leading candidates for this role. Second, studies of the degree to which criminal behavior runs in families shed light on the extent to which some individuals are more prone to commit crime than others. These studies examine the prevalence of crime in twins and among the adopted children of criminal parents *(69–70)*.

A bit further on they review some of the evidence that points to genetic factors and crime:

A number of secondary but informative findings in this critical study should not be overlooked. We mention them briefly without dwelling on details. Adoptee crime was predicted by biological-parent crime no matter what the crime category, at least when the categorization was no finer than violent versus property. As far as this dichotomy is concerned, the genetic disposition is toward crime in general, not toward specific offenses. Over the period covered by the study (adoption from 1924 to 1947) no change in the major findings could be detected, despite the upheavals of a deep economic depression, a world war, and occupation by a foreign power, suggesting that the biological

links in the chain of causation are strong. About a quarter of the adoptees were placed in adoptive homes immediately after birth, about another half by the end of the first year, and another 13 percent by the end of the second year. The age of placement exerted no effect on the relationship between biological-parent-male-adoptee criminality. Finally, the transmission of criminality from biological parents to their sons was unaffected by whether the biological parents committed their crimes before or after the children were placed in adoptive homes, or by whether the adoptive parents knew the biological parents' criminal records *(99)*.

A CONFLICT PERSPECTIVE

Crime in Canadian Society is one of the most popular academic books on the topic. The editors are prominent Canadian criminologists, Robert Silverman, James Teevan, and Vincent Sacco. In their introduction to Part 3, 'Theories of Crime and Delinquency', they summarize the core ideas of what they call conflict theory. Note the different focus.

Crime as an Expression of Class Conflict

Conflict theories see social conflict as central to any theoretical explanation of crime and delinquency. These theories reject the assumption that societies are based upon a shared consensus about important norms and values. Instead, they assume that the most noteworthy feature of any complex society is the presence of conflict between segments of that society that differ from each other in terms of the social power and other resources to which they have access. The important task for criminological theory, conflict theorists argue, is to understand processes of lawmaking and lawbreaking in a manner that takes the conflict-oriented nature of society into account.

At the risk of oversimplification, it is possible to recognize two broad categories of conflict theory. Conservative conflict theorists tend to view social conflict as involving a wide variety of groups in society. They conceptualize conflicts as emerging in response to particular situations or particular events that bring into sharp relief their competition for social or economic advantage. In contrast, radical theories of social conflict, which derive primarily from the writings of Marx, conceptualize social conflict primarily in terms of a struggle between social classes in the context of the structured inequalities of capitalist societies.

George Vold provided an early example of conservative conflict theory in criminology. Vold's argument begins with the assumption that people are fundamentally 'group involved' in that their lives are both a part of, and a product of, group belonging. Groups are formed because individuals have common interests and common needs that are best met through collective action. Moreover, Vold maintained, groups come into conflict with each other as 'the interest and purposes they serve tend to overlap, encroach on one another and become competitive'.

Building upon these assumptions (and upon the insights provided by the writings of more conservative conflict theorists), Marxian criminologists have attempted to understand the relationship between crime and social control, and the structured inequalities of capitalist societies. Consistent with much Marxist scholarship, they have argued that capitalist forms of economic production contain within them the elements of a conflict between a capitalist class, which controls the mode of production, and a labouring class, which must sell its labour in order to survive.

During the 1970s, many Marxian scholars argued that processes of criminalization could be understood as the means by which the capitalist ruling class attempts to control the labour class and thereby maintain its advantage. Criminal law, as a social institution, was thus viewed as an instrument of class oppression, and behaviour that threatened the interests and privileges of the ruling class was seen as subject to criminalization. Moreover, it was argued that, while 'capitalist crimes' such as price-fixing, union busting, the pollution of the environment, or the endangerment of worker safety may result in greater harm than the garden-variety offences of robbery or assault, they are either ignored by the state or defined as less serious regulatory offences.

However, their presence need not represent a radical threat to overall social order.

Durkheim goes on to define crime as a potentially pathological phenomenon in society; however, he notes that this is not necessarily the case because crime can be understood as being a normal part of every society: crime is present not only in the majority of societies of one particular species but also in all societies of all types. There is no society that is not confronted with the problem of criminality (1964: 65).

Further, he argues that 'crime is normal because a society exempt from it is utterly impossible' (67). Durkheim's definition of crime is as follows: 'Crime, as we have shown elsewhere, consists of an act that offends certain very strong collective sentiments' (76).

Given the complex nature of our lives in an advanced industrial society, we cannot all possibly be and think alike; therefore, some individuals will very likely come to hold beliefs and opinions that contravene those dominant in society as a whole (69–70). The presence of sentiments, opinions, and patterns of behaviour that go against the grain of the dominant collective sentiments can actually result in social progress because such challenges to the status quo are 'indispensable to the normal evolution of morality and law' (70). Durkheim is explicit about the fact that morality and law must change and evolve as the conditions of human life change. Referring to society's belief systems, which he calls collective sentiments, he writes:

Nothing is good indefinitely and to an unlimited extent. The authority that the moral-

conscience enjoys must not be excessive: otherwise no one would dare criticize it; and it would too easily congeal into an immutable form. To make progress, individual originality must be able to express itself. In order that the originality of the idealist whose dreams transcend his century may find expression, it is necessary that the originality of the criminal, who is below the level of his time, shall also be possible. One does not occur without the other. (71)

There are, of course, limitations, and excessively high rates of serious crime might become a social pathology.

In *The Rules of Sociological Method* Durkheim argues that crime might actually serve a positive social function by facilitating the development and evolution of collective sentiments and thus preventing the ossification and stagnation of society. In *The Division of Labour in Society* he returns to the issue of crime. In this later work Durkheim once again illustrates why he is considered one of the founding figures in sociology, defining crime in the context of society: 'In other words we must not say that an action shocks the common conscience because it is criminal, but rather that it is criminal because it shocks the common conscience. We do not reprove it because it is a crime, but it is a crime because we reprove it' (1964: 81). He goes on to argue that in order for society to continue to exist in a stable and orderly manner, violations of collective sentiments must be dealt with, that is, punished. The punishment of violators is really about affirming the collective sentiments and/or conscience. By punishing those who are deviant we reaffirm the validity of the values and norms that are the basis of social order. When discussing punishment Durkheim declares that '[i]ts true function is to maintain social cohesion intact, while maintaining its vitality in the common conscience' (1964: 108).

What we find in the writing of Durkheim is an analysis of deviant and criminal behaviours that places an emphasis on the social context. Whether a behaviour or action is deviant and/or criminal will depend on the value system of the society, that is, on the collective conscience of the community and the extent to which those sentiments have been codified into law. According to Durkheim's analysis, deviant behaviour can actually have several positive functions, including preventing social ossification by facilitating social change and development, and reinforcing social stability by having the beliefs of the collectivity reinforced when punishment is meted out to violators of the collective conscience. The general principles that informed Durkheim's work were influential in the subsequent development of functionalist thought.

Parsons and Merton

As was noted in Chapter 7, Talcott Parsons is generally recognized as the founder of twentieth-century American structural functionalism. While Parsons incorporated ideas from a wide array of sources in the formulation of his theories, Durkheim was one of the most important influences. A common thread throughout all of Parsons' writings is the central position that values and roles play both in guiding the actions of social actors and in stabilizing the overall social system. An integrated and stable social system requires that the individual actors within the system be adequately socialized, that is, they must be familiar with and accept the legitimacy of the society's value orientation. In one of his earlier major works, co-authored with Edward Shils, Parsons wrote: 'Internalization of patterns of value

is crucial in the integration of an actor in a role system' (Parsons and Shils, 1952: 156). According to Parsons and Shils, an individual characterized by 'faulty internalization' of society's value system might tend: (1) to withdraw from social interaction; (2) 'to evade the fulfillment of expectations'; or (3) 'to rebel by openly refusing to conform' (156–7). Deviance and deviant behaviour is thus something that develops or occurs when, for some reason, an individual is not properly socialized and as a result has not adequately internalized society's value system. Elsewhere, Parsons and Shils had referred to this as a problem of 'mal-integration' (151).

In his much denser theoretical work, *The Social System*, Parsons devoted considerable attention to the study of deviant behaviour and social control (see Parsons, 1951: Chapter 7), although the basic logic of approach outlined earlier remained intact. He defines deviance 'as a disturbance of the equilibrium of the interactive system' (250) and reminds us that 'all social action is normatively oriented, and that the value-orientations embodied in these norms must to a degree be common to the actors in an institutionally integrated interactive system' (215). If an individual social actor (Parsons tends to use the term *ego*) does not fully internalize the society's value orientations and as a result is not fully integrated into the social system, she or he might begin to manifest abnormal behaviours, which Parsons categorizes as compulsive in the performance of duties or status expectations, rebelliousness, or withdrawal (257). Whatever the type of abnormal or deviant behaviour that is manifest, its origins are to be found in an inadequate internalization of the dominant value system and the consequent lack of integration of the individual into the overall social system.

In his concluding remarks Parsons sounds remarkably like Durkheim: 'The conformity-deviance "dimension" or functional problem is inherent in social structures and systems of social action in a context of cultural values.' He also states that 'tendencies to deviance' are socially structured.

Further, Parsons reiterates Durkheim's point about the role that deviance plays in social change and the need for society to have mechanisms of social control to ensure that deviant tendencies are maintained within acceptable bounds (320–1).

As important as are Parsons' insights for the development of the structural functionalist approach to deviance, it is the work of his student, Robert K. Merton, that has had the greatest impact. Originally written in 1938, Merton's celebrated essay 'Social Structure and Anomie' has become one of the most-quoted and referenced works in the study of deviant behaviour. Merton begins with a critique of those theories of deviance that have sought to explain the phenomenon in biological terms. As a sociologist Merton finds such explanations unacceptable, and he definitively states that his approach will locate the primary causal processes that explain deviant behaviour in the social structure. He writes: 'Our primary aim is to discover how some *social structures exert a definite pressure upon certain persons in the society to engage in non-conforming rather than conforming conduct*' (1968: 186, emphasis in original).

Two central concepts in Merton's analysis of deviant behaviour are culturally defined goals and the means for achieving these goals (186–7). Merton defines goals as the socially legitimized and sanctioned objectives for which we strive. The means for achieving these goals are simply the 'allowable procedures for moving toward these objectives' (187). According to Merton there need not necessarily be a relationship between how much emphasis a culture places on given values and the actual or practical means available to individuals in their efforts to achieve goals. If some goal is highly valued while many people lack socially sanctioned or legitimate opportunities to achieve that goal, non-conformist or deviant behaviour may develop as individuals strive to achieve the valued goal. In Merton's words:

> It is when a system of cultural values extols, virtually above all else, certain *common*

Functionalist Talcott Parson's best known student, Robert K. Merton, investigated deviance in his celebrated essay, 'Social Structure and Anomie', written in 1938. He explained the goal of his research: 'Our primary aim is to discover how some social structures exert a definite pressure upon certain persons in the society to engage in non-conforming conduct.' (Courtesy of the Estate of Robert K. Merton)

> success-goals *for the population at large* while the social structure rigorously restricts or completely closes access to approved modes of reaching these goals *for a considerable part of the same population,* that deviant behavior ensues on a large scale. (200, emphasis in original)

Merton went on to examine some typical types of deviant behaviour that might emerge under these circumstances. He briefly comments on conformist behaviour, which occurs when an individual accepts a culturally defined goal and has access to the means through which to achieve that goal; however, he points out that this is not really a form of deviant behaviour and therefore not of particular interest. He refers to the four major forms of deviant behaviour that arise from a disjunction between a socially emphasized goal and the lack of means to achieve it as being innovation, ritualism, retreatism, and rebellion.

Innovation is a behavioural pattern that occurs when an individual accepts the social values and goals but lacks the legitimate means of achieving a goal and turns to innovative, non-conformist, and deviant means to achieve it. Imagine a situation in which an individual accepts the idea that the accumulation of wealth is the supreme objective in life. If individuals lack access to the normal means of accumulating wealth, such as job or business opportunities, they might resort to innovative and deviant behaviours such as theft, fraud, or the sale of illegal substances in order to make money.

Ritualism is a form of adaptation that Merton notes might not be considered deviant, but since it is 'departure from the cultural model' he suggests we treat it as such (204). The ritualist is an individual who comes to reject the goal, but ritualistically clings to socially sanctioned behaviours that typically lead to achieving that goal. The example Merton provides is of an individual who has given up on, or is not interested in, upward mobility in an organization, yet slavishly works away at his or her job just as hard as the upwardly mobile individual. The individual exhibiting ritualistic behaviour appears to be satisfied with what he or she has and is not seeking higher status, more power, or wealth like so many in capitalist society do.

The adaptation Merton calls retreatism might appear to be more akin to our typical understanding of deviant behaviour. The individual adopting this approach rejects both the culturally or socially sanctioned goal and the culturally and socially legitimized means of achieving the goal. The retreatist might typically be the 'drop out'. Merton provides some examples:

> In this category fall some of the adaptive activities of psychotics, autists, pariahs, outcasts, vagrants, vagabonds, tramps, chronic drunkards, and drug addicts. They have relinquished culturally prescribed goals and their behaviour does not accord with institutional norms. (207)

Lastly, there are Merton's rebels. Rebellion is a behavioural pattern that involves rejection of society's goals and means of achieving those goals; however, unlike those engaged in retreatism the rebel postulates an alternative system of goals and means. The rebel might end up producing a counterculture, that is, postulating a new set of values, institutions, and social practices that will achieve those goals. The rebel might reject the competitive ethos of market society and the work ethic and practices that are supposed to facilitate monetary success in favour of a communal and co-operative value orientation and lifestyle.

Merton's ideas proved to be extremely important in the subsequent development of structural functionalist theory. Indeed, in his discussion of Merton's work, Edwin Schur states that 'Virtually all subsequent theorizing about deviance has built on, or had to take account of, his major formulations' (1979: 138). Others, such as Albert Cohen, sought to extend Merton's concepts as they examined the role of subcultures in producing deviant behaviour.

Deviant Subcultures

If you ever enrol in a social problems or deviant behaviour course and study theories of deviance in some detail, you will discover that introductory books simplify complex arguments. In what follows we will take several approaches that are, in fact, different and combine them. It is possible to do this because these approaches share a number of common assumptions and propositions. For the student of sociology, these approaches are relatively easy to understand because they simply combine what we know about the impact of subcultures and socialization on human behaviour. The approaches we are combining are variously referred to as the cultural transmission approach, the subcultural approach, the social-bonding approach, the differential association approach, and modelling theory. They share a common focus, namely, the existence of subcultures characterized by values and norms that are significantly different from those of mainstream society. Individuals who are exposed to or are a part of these subcultures become socialized or resocialized into these values and as a result begin to act in ways that are deviant from the mainstream culture.

Although a great deal more could be said about how functionalists have explained deviance, these brief comments provide some indication of the general tenor of the arguments. The emphasis on values and deviation from established values differentiates this approach from the more class-oriented focus of Marxian or conflict theory.

Conflict Theory and the Study of Deviance

The term *conflict theory* is a difficult one because it has been used by different writers to mean different things. The well-known American sociologist Lewis A. Coser notes this when he observes: 'The term is sometimes simply used as a code word for Marxism.' He suggests that the terms can also refer 'to sociologists who have made a contribution to the sociological study of conflict and who have highlighted the importance of conflict-ridden interaction in society without, however, claiming that "conflict theory" presents an encompassing theoretical scheme' (1977: 579). When addressing the issue of deviant or criminal behaviour it is important to distinguish the difference between conflict theory and neo-Marxist/power-conflict theory.

In this rather long quote, Randall Collins lays out the general principles of conflict theory in the form of a set of instructions for how you, as a sociologist, might study any empirical issue or phenomenon:

The general principles of conflict analysis may be applied to any empirical area. (1) Think through abstract formulations to a sample of the typical real-life interactions involved. Think of people as animals maneuvering for advantage, susceptible to emotional appeals, but steering a self-interested course toward satisfactions and away from dissatisfactions. (2) Look for the material arrangements that affect interaction: the physical places, the modes of communication, the supply of weapons, devices for staging one's public impression, tools, and goods. Assess the relative resources available to each individual: their potential for physical coercion, their access to other persons with whom to negotiate, their sexual attractiveness, their store of cultural devices for invoking emotional solidarity, as well as the physical arrangements just mentioned. (3) Apply the general hypothesis that inequalities in resources result in efforts by the dominant party to take advantage of the situation; this need not involve conscious calculation but a basic propensity of feeling one's way toward the areas of greatest immediate reward, like flowers turning to the light. Social structures are to be explained in terms of the behavior following from various lineups of resources, social change from shifts in resources resulting from previous conflicts. (4) Ideals and beliefs likewise are to be explained in terms of the interests which have the resources to make their viewpoint prevail. (5) Compare empirical cases, test hypotheses by looking for the conditions under which certain things occur versus the conditions under which other things occur. Think causally; look for generalizations. Be awake to multiple causes—the resources for conflict are complex. (60–1)

Weber has been identified as one of the intellectual inspirations for modern conflict theory. There is no doubt that he was interested in social conflict and one of the many subjects he studied was law. Indeed, law appears in one of the sections in the opening chapter of his magnum opus *Economy and Society*. Thus, first mention of law is in the context of Weber's discussion of different ways in which the social order is provided legitimacy. Keep in mind what Weber was interested in doing— explaining individual social action. Given this objective, it was obvious to Weber that our individual social action will be significantly affected when we understand that there is 'the probability that physical or psychological coercion will be applied by a *staff* of people to bring about compliance or avenge violation' (1978: 34, emphasis in original). He returns to law later in Volume 1 (311–38) and Volume 2 dedicates an entire chapter to economy and law.

Given what we know about Weber, we can see how and why such an approach must be viewed differently than traditional Marxian approaches. There is surely no prime mover or causal determinacy here. In his treatment of conflict theory Rick Linden notes that there are several streams including those he terms cultural conflict, group conflict, Weberian conflict, and non-partisan conflict theory (1996: Chapter 10). Although power is a central issue in all these approaches, the criticisms levelled against Marxism cited by Linden seem important to understanding what we are calling conflict theory. Society is seen as an arena that inherently involves various forms of conflict but there are no absolute standards for determining who or what is right and wrong.

Akers (2000) points out that when conflict theory is applied to issues of deviance and criminal

behaviour it focuses on how not why, that is, it asks how is it that some behaviours become defined as deviant and criminal rather than why certain people engage in these behaviours (169). An excellent example of how difficult it can be to pigeonhole theorists is the work of William Chambliss, especially his study of societal treatment of young offenders. In 'The Saints and the Roughnecks', Chambliss compares the treatment meted out to two groups of young men. His conclusion was that it was class background more than the act committed that determined the severity of the treatment, with those from lower-class backgrounds being treated more harshly ([1973] 1999). The issue of social control is very important for conflict theory with its assumption that dominant or powerful groups will attempt to control the behaviour of others either through law or through ensuring the internalization of its definitions of what is appropriate via agents of socialization (Akers, 2000: 165–6).

Neo-Marxist or Power-Conflict Theory

Needless to say, the conflict approach to explaining deviance will be predicated on a materialist approach. In an essay titled 'Toward a Marxian Theory of Deviance', Steven Spitzer notes that for the Marxian the crucial unit of analysis is the mode of production. He then spells out what the point of departure must be: 'If we are to have a Marxian theory of deviance, therefore, deviance production must be understood in relationship to the specific forms of socio-economic organization' (1978: 351). The mode of production dominant in our society is, of course, capitalist, and thus an analysis of deviance must begin with an understanding of the socioeconomic organization of capitalism.

We need to remind ourselves of the basic assumptions that inform such social analysis (see Chapters 6 and 7 for a review of Marxian theory). The social relations of production that typically characterize the capitalist mode of production are predicated on patterns of ownership and control that generate a class system. Although there are ongoing debates among neo-Marxists concerning the precise nature of the class structure and the number of classes in advanced capitalist society, these scholars generally agree that a dominant class controls the major economic institutions and benefits from the operation of these institutions. The dominant class is typically made up of those who own and control the forces of production and who, as a result of this structural position, are able to draw off social surplus such as profit and rent. There is also general agreement that other classes are defined by different relationships to the forces of production. Members of the non-dominant class typically survive by selling their capacity to work, their labour power. These class relations generate relations of power, domination, subordination, alienation, and conflict. According to neo-Marxian theory, the dominant class is able systematically to translate its economic power into ideological power and political power. Ideological power will, of course, allow the dominant class to influence definitions of normal and abnormal, acceptable and deviant behaviour. Control over the institutions of the polity give the dominant class a large measure of control over the codification of its values into law and the implementation and enforcement of those laws by the agencies of social control such as the police. The existence of a class structure in which the various classes are defined by different structural locations in the economic order will produce economic, ideological, and political conflict as different classes struggle to improve, enhance, and protect their economic and political interests.

Those adopting a neo-Marxian or conflict approach will tend to assume that the capitalist system is also characterized by a series of fundamental and radical contradictions. Not the least of these contradictions is the tendency for the dominant class to attempt to improve the economic productivity of its workers through the application of new technologies, while workers might resist technologies because they know that one of the costs of technological change is workers' jobs. As more and more workers are replaced by technology, the overall, or aggregate, capacity of the people in a society to buy the goods and services that capitalists offer on the market are reduced and thus there is a fundamental contradiction between technologically based economic change and the health of the economy as characterized by consumer activity. The end results of technological change can be rising unemployment, declining sales, and economic stagnation, all of which threaten the economic foundation of the society. Eventually, these processes will result in a more polarized class structure, with growing pockets of poverty and misery amid potential plenty and opulence. Under such circumstances theft, violence, and other criminal behaviour are to be expected.

When the economic foundation of a society is characterized by class relations that generate conflict, and when a dominant class has access to state and ideological power in order to maintain its position, the inevitable result will be conflict. And when there is conflict, those with power will likely seek to define those opposing their interest as abnormal, unreasonable, and deviant. Spitzer argues that those who steal from the rich, question the operation of the system, try to escape the relationships of alienation and despair via drugs, or question the sanctity of capitalism and the dominant ideologies that reinforce it become defined as problem populations (1978: 352–3). Schur (1979) points out that according to conflict theory those who might question the dominant values in society are not necessarily maladjusted because their opposition might arise from 'systematic class oppression and arbitrary definition of "their" behaviour as deviant' (143).

Whereas more 'traditional' conflict or neo-Marxian theory focused on the role of class domination, conflict, and resistance, this theory could be revised to include the possibility of dealing with the conflicts and contradictions that arise from race, sex, and gender relations. Although such a task will not be attempted here, it is possible to envision an analysis of how behaviours arising out of efforts to overcome sexual, gender, ethnic, or racial oppression come to be defined by the dominant ideology as deviant.

Conflict theory focuses much of its attention on social forms, modes, and agencies of control. Spitzer notes that state agencies use a variety of approaches in attempting to deal with deviant behaviour. Among them are efforts to absorb deviant populations into the general population by co-optation, thereby diffusing or normalizing their actions and criticisms of the system. He argues that efforts are also made to convert potential 'troublemakers' by hiring them as police, guards, and social workers who then have responsibility for social control themselves. As he puts it: 'If a large number of the controlled can be converted into a first line of defense, threats to the system of class rule can be transformed into resources for its support' (1978: 361). Other approaches include containment, that is, segregation or placing people into ghettos in order to manage them more effectively. Finally, as a last resort, there is outright repression and greater support for law enforcement and punishment, key elements of what Spitzer calls the 'crime industry' (362).

The functionalist and conflict perspectives offer radically different explanations for deviant behaviour and quite different answers to the questions posed at the beginning of this chapter. These two approaches, however, also share something in common once again—their focus on the macro picture, on how society (with its value system in one case and its ruling class and structures of power in the other) defines and creates deviance. There is, of course, an alternative approach that derives from symbolic interactionism.

Symbolic Interactionism and Deviance: Labelling Theory

Structural functionalist and power-conflict theory both focus on issues and processes pertaining to the larger social structures and society as a whole and thus we refer to them as macro perspectives. As you have seen, some sociologists, including Weber, warn not to place excessive emphasis on social structures and society because this may deflect attention from what sociologists should be concerned with—issues of human social behaviour. Chapter 7 noted that the symbolic interactionism perspective (many have claimed it is more a perspective or viewpoint for understanding human social behaviour than a theory of society) warns against reification—the process of thinking about or approaching something that is not real as if it had an objective existence. To reify society is to make it something 'real', 'out there', 'external' to us, with a power and a reality above and beyond those individual human beings who compose it.

A symbolic interactionist would typically remind us that human beings are unique for a number of reasons, not the least of which are our intellectual powers, our capacity for symbolic and abstract thought, and our communicative capacities. Human society is nothing more than the totality of patterns of interactions undertaken by individuals. Complex patterns of human interaction are possible because we can think and communicate and thus develop regularized patterns of social interaction. The patterns of human social interaction that make up our institutions and social structures, the reality of our daily lives, do not occur automatically or without human effort. As human actors we create our family, educational, economic, political, and religious institutions as we go about interacting with others in the process of solving our problems and meeting our needs. Each time we are in an interactive situation we must think, interpret symbols, determine responses and behavioural pattern, use our communicative skills, and create the situation. We are active in creating and recreating the basis of our institutions. Because of this fact, institutions and social structures cannot be studied as real, objective structures 'out there' and apart from us.

Therefore, symbolic interactionists argue that sociologists should focus on the study of micro behaviour and social interaction to understand how human social actors create and recreate the patterns of interaction and behaviour that make up social institutions and structures. As applied to the study of deviance, this approach would examine how individuals interpret the behaviours and symbols of other actors and how these interpretations influence their interactive process. For example, if I introduce myself and explain that I am nervous about meeting new people because I have just spent 10 years in prison for murder, a symbolic interactionist would be interested in how this information might influence your reaction to me and our subsequent interaction. She or he would be more interested in that interaction than in finding out why I committed the initial deviant act, why I was punished in the manner I was, what my punishment had to do with maintaining social order, and so forth. Interactionists always focus their attention on the interpretations and meanings that actors bring to an interactive situation and how this knowledge affects the interactive process. When they study deviance, symbolic interactionists will look at the effects that being labelled a deviant has on the interaction of the deviant and others once they know about the presence of a person labelled as deviant. The very title of Howard Becker's classic study using this approach is descriptive: *Outsiders: Studies in the Sociology of Deviance*.

This notion of labelling is important enough in the study of deviance to warrant the designation of an approach called 'Labelling Theory' (see Akers, 2000: Chapter 6). Wayne Morrison summarizes the approach in the following manner: 'At the core of the labelling orientation is the assumption of process: deviance and social control always involve processes of social definition and reaction' (1995: 321). As Akers explains, a core assumption of this approach is that the act of being labelled in a certain manner will actually produce the kind of behaviours that the person labelled deems appropriate to the label. Therefore, having been labelled a delinquent and a troublemaker, an individual will manifest behaviours that are appropriate to that label. It

is a self-fulfilling prophecy of the kind discussed in Chapter 5. Akers refers to these actions as '*secondary deviance* created by the societal reactions and by stigmatizing labels' (2000: 125, emphasis in original).

Admittedly, these sketchy comments do not do justice to the interactionist approach. However, like all the material in this introductory volume, they are designed to whet the reader's appetite. Many of the studies of deviance that employ this approach are more exploratory than explanatory. It could be argued that the strength of the symbolic interactionist perspective is its capacity to explore the interesting, complex, and subtle nature of human interaction at the micro level and, therefore, that criticisms of its lack of explanatory power are misguided.

Feminist Theory

As is the case in every field of sociological inquiry and investigation, feminism and feminist theory have affected the study of crime and deviance. In the introduction to their edited volume *Feminist Perspectives in Criminology*, Loraine Gelsthorpe and Allison Morris discuss recent contributions and explain why a feminist criminology was necessary: 'They have exposed criminology to be the criminology of Men. Theories of criminality have been developed from male subjects and validated on male subjects. Thus they are man-made' (1990: 3). They note that there is not necessarily anything wrong with these theories unless one assumes that they automatically and simply apply to all humans, male and female alike. Meda Chesney-Lind puts the issue more bluntly: 'Criminology has suffered from what Jessie Bernard has called the "stag effect". It has attracted male scholars who wanted to study and understand outlawed men, hoping perhaps that some of the romance and fascination of this role would rub off' (1995: xii).

The argument that criminology has to pay attention to females informed what Kathleen Daly and Lisa Maher describe as the first phase of the development of feminist criminology (1998: 2–4). Such a phase would have involved using the ideas, concepts, and arguments of several of the feminisms that emerged during the Second Wave (liberal, Marxist, socialist, and radical). Roslyn Muraskin and Ted Alleman's edited book *It's a Crime: Women and Justice* (1986) adopts such an approach. In the first chapter, Alleman overviews these four streams of feminist thought and comments on their application to the study of crime and criminal justice. He points out that the impact of liberal feminism was apparent in works that argued that women had indeed been liberated from their 'traditional home-bound social role into positions of power and influence' and as a result they were beginning to behave and act more like men, that is, women were becoming 'more competitive and aggressive' (14). This 'masculinity thesis of women's liberation' suggests that women are taking on new roles that are similar to those traditionally occupied by men, and as a result women are starting to commit more of the same types of crime that males have traditionally been involved in (Alleman, 1986: 16). Alleman discussed another approach also related to liberal feminism developed by Rita Simon. According to this argument, women's liberation provided women with more opportunities to commit crime because their roles and positions became more varied and complex (16–17).

Alleman's discussion of the application of Marxian theory to female criminality is quite brief since it—being sex- and gender-blind—did not really have much to confront. Female criminal activity is attributed to women being part of relations of exploitation, domination, and alienation (28). According to Alleman, socialist feminism had a bit more to say about women and crime because its explanatory concepts included patriarchy and the attendant understanding that women are controlled and dominated by men. This approach focused more attention on crimes, such as sexual assault, child abuse, and domestic violence, where women

were victims. The socialist feminist approach would see such crimes not just as the outcome of class domination and alienation but also of the oppression inherent in a patriarchal system. Alleman's account of how radical feminism approached crime is an extension of the notion that male domination is a central cause of women's involvement in the criminal justice system. Radical feminists were successful 'at showing the law and its application to be male-dominated, male-centered, as well as male serving' (38). Crimes such as rape were understood as crimes of domination, violence, power, and control. Radical feminists also focused our attention on issues such as pornography and sexual harassment, again linking them to the inherent injustices of a male-dominated social system.

The remaining twenty-two chapters of Muraskin and Alleman address specific issues in the field of criminology without necessarily making further contributions to these theoretical approaches. Akers focuses only on two of the four approaches discussed above and concludes: 'No distinctive feminist theory on the etiology of crime has yet been formulated' partly because 'Feminist theory is still in formation' (234).

If we recall the discussion of what was referred to as Third Wave feminism in Chapter 8, the issue of future directions in feminist criminology becomes somewhat easier to understand. You will recall that Third Wave feminists are concerned that existing feminist theories are predicated on an inadequately simple conception of the experiences of women. The notion that there are no simple explanations of women and crime is not new. In a 1985 study of the autobiographies of four women who became involved in criminal activity, Pat Carlen arrived at an important conclusion, namely, 'that the complexity of the accounts should call into question *all* accounts of the monocausal and global theories of crime' (1985: 9). She went on:

as a result of the persistent assumption that a *special* theory of women's criminality is called for, theorists have not only been caught on the horns of the misleading 'masculine or feminine' dilemma, they have also, for much longer than has been the case in relation to 'crime in general', persisted in the quest for a global, ahistorical, monocausal and essentialist explanation. (9, emphasis in original)

The argument that the ideas and theories of the past are inappropriate for the present represents a core notion in what Daley and Maher call the second phase of feminist criminology (1998: 4). They note that this second phase, as they call it, actually encompasses two tendencies, one that explores 'women as agents in constructing their life worlds including their lawbreaking and victimization'. The other 'explores how women are constructed in and by particular discourses, including criminal law, medicine, criminology, and even feminism itself' (4). Daley and Maher go on to argue that what is needed is a new approach that recognizes that women are sometimes their own subjects and sometimes they are characterized in certain ways as a result of social discourse. In addition, they add that scholars have come to realize that 'terms such as *women* (or *men* or *blacks* or *lesbians*) should reflect non-essentialist, socially constructed, and variable character' (5). As a result, there can be no single unified and unifying feminist criminology; rather, the perspectives we use must recognize the intersections of race, gender, age, ethnicity, and so on with the various social practices that comprise the legal and justice systems (5).

When examining theories of social deviance the reader should consider to what extent each approach can explain the empirical manifestations of deviant behaviour they encounter in their daily lives, including what they learn from the mass media. In using theory, we consider whether it is logical and also its capacity to allow us to make sense of the real world we confront on a daily basis.

Critical Thinking Questions

- What is deviance? Why did Durkheim claim that some deviance is normal?
- Are patterns of crime and socialclass related? If you answered yes, explain how.
- Is there a need for a feminist criminology? Explain your answer.
- What are deviant subcultures and how do they relate to crime and deviance?
- Explain Merton's understanding of deviant behaviour.

Terms and Concepts

Deviance—social actions and behaviours that violate commonly acceptable, dominant, or mainstream values, norms, folkways, and mores. Sociologists will, depending on the theoretical orientation they adopt, explain and interpret deviance and deviant behaviour very differently.

Social control—the mechanisms, agencies, and practices through which conformity to social accepted values, norms, and beliefs is enforced. Social control can be: (1) understood to be largely internal, involving individual acceptance of society's values and norms; or (2) seen as external, involving the use of formal state and other agencies of enforcement. Usually sociologists understand it to include both.

Subculture of deviance—commonly associated with a structural functionalist approach, characterized by values, norms, beliefs, and social practices that deviate from those of the mainstream or dominant culture. It is assumed that subcultures of deviance are perpetuated through socialization.

Merton's typology of individual adaptation—R.K. Merton argues that deviant behaviour very often occurs when there is a disjunction between an individual's acceptance of a cultural goal and her or his capacity to achieve that goal. The individual responses include: (1) innovation (acceptance of goal but lack of access to normal institutional means to achieve it so alternative innovative means are developed); (2) ritualism (rejection of cultural goal but dogged maintenance of prescribed behaviours to reach it); (3) retreatism (rejection of both goals and socially sanctioned behaviours to achieve them,

which thus involves dropping out and existing at margins of society); (4) rebellion (rejection of cultural goals and means for achieving but involves the postulation of alternative goals and means).

Labelling theory—associated with symbolic interactionist understanding of deviant behaviour, labelling theory focuses on the implications for interaction that follow from individuals being labelled in certain ways. Social labelling typically involves the ascription of positive or negative characteristics to an individual. Labelling theory might study the implications for subsequent social interaction that follow from an individual being labelled a murderer, a pedophile, or a Communist.

Related Web Sites

http://www.statcan.ca/start.html

This is an official Statistics Canada web site that has data on, in their words, 'crimes, victims, suspects, criminals, police and the courts'. A very useful source of primary data, it needs, of course, your interpretation in order to turn it into understanding.

http://laws.justice.gc.ca/en/index.html

At your very fingertips are major laws and statutes in Canada, including the *Criminal Code* of Canada with a very user-friendly web site that lists major statutes and sections.

http://www.critcrim.org/feminist.htm

The American Society of Criminology and the Academy of Criminal Justice Sciences have a Division and/or Section on Critical Criminology. A part of those Divisions/Sections is devoted to

feminist criminology and this web site allows you to keep up-to-date with recent developments.

http://www.douglas.bc.ca/crimweb/sites.html

The folks at Douglas College maintain this detailed listing of web sites of interest to those interested in criminology. The sites listed cover the field from research, to police, the courts and law, corrections, and other search engines.

http://www.stthomasu.ca/research/youth/index.htm

This site links you to the Centre for Research on Youth at Risk at St Thomas University. There are links that provide empirical evidence that debunks a number of myths, and others that raise key issues about youth in contemporary society.

Suggested Further Readings

Akers, R. 1995. *Criminological Theories*. Los Angeles: Roxbury. A major figure in American criminology, Akers presents a comprehensive introduction to most major theories in the area of

criminology. His analysis is detailed yet accessible.

Comack, E., ed. 1995. *Locating Law*. Halifax: Fernwood. This collection of essays is largely written from a critical perspective, covering a wide range of issues. The essays are strong both in their theoretical contribution and their empirical content.

Daly, K., and L. Maher, eds. 1998. *Criminology at the Crossroads*. New York: Oxford University Press. Subtitled 'Feminist Readings in Crime and Justice', scholars offer the basis of a substantial feminist and postmodern critique of much of the field. The notion of crossroads is central and the contributors are convincing that a new direction is required.

Linden, R. 1998. *Criminology*. Toronto: Harcourt Brace. This is the third edition of the successful Canadian text. The book covers the field, addressing a range of issues in a comprehensive manner for an introductory volume.

CHAPTER 14

Sociological Approaches to the Study of Familial Relations

As important as class is, it is only one aspect of inequality in our society. Indeed, we could argue that issues of class are not even the most important dimension of inequality, and that class distinctions pale when compared, for instance, to inequalities in relationships between men and women or inequalities based on differences of ethnicity or colour.

An issue of central concern for both sociologists and the general public is the set of social relations and interactions we commonly refer to as 'the family'. By looking at how sociologists have analyzed and explained familial relations and interactions we can learn a number of things. First, a discussion of how sociologists analyze something as common and 'everyday' as familial relations provides us with an opportunity of seeing just how the sociological approach differs from the way we usually understand the world. Most Canadians have, by virtue of personal experience at least, some understanding of the nature and character of familial relations. But our common-sense understanding is not the same as a systematic view of the phenomenon, and as a result sociologists would maintain that such a view is inadequate.

The second benefit we can gain by studying familial relations is connected to the question of social theory. The precise differences, strengths, and weaknesses of the various theoretical positions become clearer when the theories are applied to specific issues. Sociologists using the major perspectives of structural functionalism and neo-Marxism,

as well as those influenced by feminist thought, have developed an extensive literature on the family, and a quick overview of the basic arguments each position has put forth should allow us to develop our understanding of the issues of gender and familial relations.

Although there are any number of other social issues or institutions that could be used to illustrate the nature of sociological analysis, familial relations are appropriate for discussion here for a number of reasons.

1. It has often been argued that some form of organized familial relations is a universal feature of human society. If some form of family is found in all societies, the study of families is surely of fundamental importance.

2. Concern for and and interest in familial relations pervades our society. Politicians, people in the media, representatives of organized religion, as well as social scientists and town gossips all articulate a professed interest in the structures, conditions, and future of families.

3. An understanding of familial relations is a necessary precondition for understanding the larger patterns of sex and gender relations in society. Much of what defines our femininity and masculinity is rooted in our families.

A nuclear family usually refers to a couple who, along with any dependent children, share a residence and form a social union. The family is the most basic and elementary social union. (Photograph courtesy of Phyllis Wilson)

4. Families are important agents of socialization and are therefore important in the development of our overall personalities.

Thousands of books, articles, and collections deal with various aspects of familial relations. There are studies dealing with cross-cultural perspectives, marriage rites and family relations, different family forms, mate selection dynamics, the stages of family life, sexual relations in and out of marriage, marriage and family dissolution, and parenting. Here we are going to focus briefly on a narrow and particular aspect of the sociology of the family: the general structure and operation of the nuclear family in industrial capitalist society. We will see how structural functionalists and neo-Marxists have addressed these relations, keeping in mind our goal of seeing how sociological analysis works and how the adoption of a specific theoretical perspective influences the questions asked, the research performed, and, finally, the analysis produced.

Basic Definitions

There is much debate in sociology about whether it is appropriate to use the term *the family*, because, strangely enough, in a complex industrial society such as ours there is no such thing as 'the family'. There are instead a number of different types or forms of family, including primary, secondary, single parent, nuclear, and extended. To the extent that there is a workable definition of family, it usually includes ideas such as a group of people related or connected by bloodline, marriage rite, or adoption, who live together or view themselves as a unit and who perform caretaking services for others, especially the very young (for example, see Robertson, 1981: 350; Schaefer, 1989: 321).

'Nuclear family' generally refers to a couple who, along with any dependent, unmarried children, share a residence and form a social unit. This definition incorporates most of the features of the various definitions found in the literature. Nuclear families are differentiated from extended families by the fact that extended families typically include, in addition to the couple and any dependent children, other relatives such as grandparents, aunts, or uncles. We could define an extended family as three or more generations connected by either blood or marriage relationships forming a social unit and living together. A single-parent family refers to an individual who, for whatever reason, is living with a child or a number of children.

In discussing families we often encounter the word *kinship*, which refers to networks of people who define themselves as being related by virtue of ancestry, marriage, or adoption. Marriage generally refers to some socially or culturally sanctioned arrangement for sexual relationships and the care and rearing of the young. There are many historically and culturally specific rules and forms of marriage.

The Structural Functionalist Approach

The Nuclear Family in Industrial Society

Structural functionalists would say that to understand the position and role of the nuclear family within a developed industrial society such as Canada we must remind ourselves of the nature of the overall social structure. When functionalists examine any aspect or component of a society they begin by asking what is perhaps the most important sociological question: what function does the social phenomenon we are investigating perform for society and its members? It is a question predicated on an important basic assumption, namely, that most if not all social institutions and practices perform functions for society. What, then, are the functions of the family?

To answer this question we must remind ourselves that social systems face a number of problems that must be solved if they are to survive.

Functionalists typically refer to these problems as system prerequisites, and they use the notion of system prerequisite as a basis for explaining the typical functions of the nuclear family in modern industrial society.

For the most part, functionalists agree that the functions of the family have changed over time. As industrial society emerged and developed, the entire social structure changed. In pre-industrial society the family was a pivotal institution, because within its confines a great amount of economic activity occurred, children and the young were educated, and in some cases political decisions were made. As society developed and evolved its various structures became more complex, complicated, and specialized. With the emergence of an industrial economy came new economic structures in the form of factories, a development that removed economic activity from the home. The demands of an industrial economy led to the widespread establishment of a formal educational system outside of the home. What in fact occurred was a significant and systematic narrowing and specialization of the functions that the family typically fulfilled. The end result of this evolutionary and developmental process was the typical nuclear family, which came to characterize industrial societies (Parsons, 1971).

The Functions of the Nuclear Family

Just as in structural functionalist theory there are several different 'lists' of system prerequisites, in the functionalist literature on the family there are also a number of opinions on just how many central functions the family performs. F. Ivan Nye and Felix Berardo note that the family has been seen as performing at least seven essential functions for society and its individual members: producing economic goods and services, allocating status, educating the young, providing religious training, and offering recreation, protection, and affection (1973: 8). Adrian Wilson notes that all families tend to perform four core functions: facilitating reproduction and the regulation of sexual conduct, socializing the young, providing a site for the provision of material necessities, and providing emotional support (1985: 10). In their book on the family, Bryan Strong and Christine Deffault state that the family performs four functions: the production and socialization of children, the facilitation of economic co-operation, the assignment of status and roles, and the provision of an environment for the development of intimate relationships (1986: 5–6). Lastly, Talcott Parsons and Robert Bales argue that the number of functions the family performs diminishes as society develops and evolves and that as a result the modern nuclear family has only two essential functions: the socialization and training of the young and the provision of an environment within which adults can maintain stable personalities (1955: 16). According to Parsons and Bales, the family provides for a socially acceptable and legitimate outlet for sexual energies and the fostering of relationships based on intimacy (19–20).

Although their lists of functions vary greatly, all of these scholars are making a similar point: that the family is best understood in terms of the functions it performs for society as a whole and for individual members of that society. The articulation of a list of functions, however, is just the beginning of the analysis of familial relations. When we understand something of the family's functions we can move on to try to find out precisely how the family performs those functions.

The Internal Dynamics of the Nuclear Family

Let's assume for a moment that we accept the argument that the essential functions of the nuclear family in our society are facilitating biological reproduction and the regulation of sexual conduct, the socializing of and caring for the young, and providing economic and emotional support for adults. We must then move on to studying how the family accomplishes these functions. In a functionalist analysis it becomes readily apparent that the family is like every other complex institution in society: it contains within it a division of labour.

Given that the family is the institutional arrangement that provides for children's socialization and care and for some of the material needs (food, for example) of adults, it follows that some family member or members must look after the children and some other member or members must provide the food. The increasing specialization of the family's functions means that it is increasingly removed from economic activity, and the survival of the family unit and its members relies on someone working outside the family to bring in the resources required to provide the family's material necessities. That is, some members of the typical nuclear family must earn income to support the family unit. The next question is: how is the division of labour to be determined? Who provides internal services such as child care and socialization, and who engages in work outside the family to acquire the necessary resources for living (Zelditch, 1955)?

In a controversial argument Parsons suggests that the basis for the allocation of roles is at least partly biological. He notes that the fact that women bear and nurse children strongly predisposes them to roles within the family that have to do with the nurturing and care of the young. At the same time, men, by virtue of being exempted from the biological processes associated with birthing and nursing, come to specialize in roles that take them outside the family (Parsons, 1955: 22–3). Following this logic—although Parsons does not specifically make this argument—once these roles become established and accepted, the knowledge of these behavioural patterns becomes incorporated into the society's value system and normative orientations. Definitions of female and male roles become part of what young children learn through the socialization process, and thus girls and boys will begin to see and define themselves in terms of specific types of roles.

Expressive and Instrumental Roles

The work of Parsons and the other contributors to *Family, Socialization and Interaction Process* (1955) established the usage of the terms *expressive* and

According to Talcott Parsons, the 'expressive roles' of the family are chiefly assoicated with caring, nurturing, emotional support, family integration, and group harmony. In the past, the majority of emotional support was given to the child from the mother, but today's fathers are taking a more active role in child care and nurturing. (Photograph courtesy of Saskia Mueller)

instrumental to describe the two essential roles within the nuclear family (see, for example, 22–3, 313–15). The expressive roles are associated with caring, nurturing, emotional support, family integration, and group harmony and are mostly internal to the family. Instrumental roles involve connecting the family to the larger social environment and typically include qualities associated with leadership, achievement, securing resources, or goal attainment. Instrumental roles can operate both within and outside the family, although they also connect the family to the external world (Bourricaud, 1981: 88; Leslie and Korman, 1985: 197).

The ideas of expressive and instrumental roles, when added to those concerning male and female roles, provide an analysis suggesting why it is that women and men do what they do within the family structure. Many functionalists would argue that the allocation of different roles for men and women becomes less of a biologically determined process and more of a cultural and social process. That is, the movement of women into expressive roles and men into instrumental roles is something that relates more to society's values and norms than to some biologically based destiny. Once certain ideas and conceptions concerning what it means to be male and masculine or female and feminine become entrenched in the value system, they are passed on from generation to generation through socialization, thus influencing the personality characteristics and decisions that men and women make about their lives.

Functionalists would argue, then, that the processes by which female and male personalities develop are intimately connected to the structures and functions of the family, through the division of labour, socialization, and the allocation of expressive and instrumental roles. Other complicating factors can enter the picture—for example, when prevailing religious beliefs specify appropriate roles for women and men. When the definitions of masculinity and femininity contained in religious belief systems reinforce the values that have developed in the family and the larger society, this means that yet another agent of socialization is at work. In addition, the broader values, norms, folkways, and mores of a society are also transmitted through agents of socialization such as the educational system and the mass media. As a result, children come to acquire from an early age a systematic understanding of what is appropriate for males and females. Definitions of what it means to be masculine and feminine become a key part of our character structures, and as a result they have a great impact on our actions and behaviours.

Family Dysfunctions

In a 1965 article entitled 'The Normal American Family', Parsons delineated the general patterns of the nuclear family as 'normal'. To the extent that such a portrayal was part of what C.W. Mills called the great American celebration, it failed to address the possible element of dysfunction in the nuclear family. We now know that problems were developing within the North American family even in the postwar period of prosperity and its accompanying 'good life'.

By the early 1970s the mass media were becoming aware that not all was well with the American family. For example, in October 1971, the popular women's magazine *McCall's* included an article called 'Why Good Marriages Fail'. A major story in the 12 March 1973 *Newsweek* was 'The Broken Family: Divorce US Style'. In the September 1974 issue of *Redbook*, Margaret Mead contributed to the developing awareness of crisis in the American family with her article, 'Too Many Divorces, Too Soon'.

Added to the stories about more and more 'normal families' dissolving was evidence that some of the relationships within the traditional nuclear family were dysfunctional, to say the least. The August 1971 edition of *Psychology Today* contained the article 'Families Can Be Unhealthy for Children and Other Living Things' by Arlene Skolnick, an expert on family relations. The story was part of a process then under way that involved making public the so-called private issue of domestic violence. The decade of the 1980s brought the issue of domestic violence and sexual abuse into the realm of full public discourse, although even now there are still those who would deny its severity as a public issue. The first systematic revelations of this aspect of the nuclear family have caused considerable controversy.

In addition to the evidence of severe dysfunction, the typical nuclear family came under attack from other sources during the sixties and seventies. The emergence of a youth counterculture with its 'hippies' and 'drop-outs' brought with it a series of innovations in sexual and child-rearing practices. There seemed to be an increase in the number of single-parent families, as well as experimental, communal, and extended families. All of this led to more questions about the 'normalcy' of any specified family form.

Although structural functionalists recognize the possibility of dysfunctioning elements in a social system, their actual analysis of such occurrences leads to difficulties. Many functionalists engaged in examining the family began to recognize the existence of dysfunctions and malfunctions, but their explanations of these processes proved less than convincing. In many cases dysfunction was linked to individual problems such as drug use and addiction. Or it was linked to the family's need to adjust to external changes, such as economic dislocation, or to changes in society's views of appropriate roles for males and females. In short, structural functionalists had no systematic theoretical means of explaining the dysfunctionings. What did emerge, however, was a systematic challenge to the entire functionalist approach from those adopting a radically different perspective.

The Neo-Marxist Approach

The Twentieth-Century Marxian Analysis of the Family

Despite Engels' work on the subject, reviewed in Chapter 7, there was little systematic development of a Marxian approach to the family in the period from the turn of the century through the 1960s. This was due, in part, to the fact that Marxism tended to be associated with the Soviet Union and Stalinism, a development that did not particularly foster original and innovative revisions in areas like the analysis of familial relations. During the period since the 1960s the emergence of the women's movement and a renewed interest in Marx and Marxian theory both served to provide an impetus for the re-examination and re-evaluation of the Marxian approach to the analysis of familial relations. In the late 1960s especially, a number of scholars attempted to revise and reformulate the Marxian position regarding the family in capitalist society, carrying the thought beyond Engels' original position.

The Nuclear Family: Serving the Capitalist Class

The initial spate of neo-Marxist writings maintained in essence that the nuclear patriarchal family that characterized advanced capitalist society was perfectly suited to serve the interests of the capitalist or dominant class. Although the neo-Marxists did not dispute the argument that the family performs key functions in the social structure, for them the issue was 'In whose interests?'; that is, who or what class benefits from the particular role of the family? How, in particular, does the nuclear patriarchal family benefit capitalists?

Although the neo-Marxist writings cover a range of issues, there are three important arguments we can tease out of them (see, for example, Armstrong, 1984; Armstrong and Armstrong, 1984; Benston, 1978; Himmelweit and Mohun, 1977; Reed, 1978; Seccombe, 1974). These arguments are that the nuclear family serves capital by: producing and reproducing labour power; providing a site for the maintenance of a reserve army of labour; and facilitating the consumption of vast amounts of consumer goods.

Production and Reproduction of Labour Power

One of the essential commodities within the capitalist system is labour power, which is a commodity because, like any other commodity, it is bought and sold on the market, in this case the labour market. If the capitalist system is to function, and if capitalists are to appropriate surplus value and thus gain profits, they must have workers to operate their factories, mills, mines, stores, and offices. These workers sell their capacity to work, their labour power, for a wage or salary. If workers are to stay healthy and come to work for a specified period, say eight hours, day after day, month after month, year after year, those workers must have certain needs met. If they are to be efficient and effective, they must be properly nourished and rested. They must, when off work, have an opportunity to 'recharge' their physical and emotional batteries, to relax and enjoy life, which often involves producing children.

The process by which workers are prepared physically, emotionally, and mentally for the next day of work and by which workers, by having children, reproduce future generations of workers is called the production and reproduction of labour power. The central questions for this mode of analysis are: where is this done, and who performs the work?

The answer to the first question is in the family. The family in capitalist society, especially the working-class family, is in essence a social factory in which the commodity of labour power is produced and reproduced. The work that goes on in the family—work called domestic labour—is geared to both maintaining the life and fitness to work of the current generation of workers and caring for and preparing future generations of workers. In providing a worker with meals, emotional and physical support, and a place to rest and relax and generally to get ready to go forth to work the next day, the domestic worker in the family is really producing and reproducing labour power.

Complex debates have developed among neo-Marxists about the exact role of domestic labour in the production and appropriation of surplus value by capital. For instance, does domestic labour actually produce value or just use value? But the essential point here is how neo-Marxist theorists understand the role of the family. In its function of producing and reproducing labour power, they see the family as serving the interests of the capitalist class. It was, after all, the capitalist class that required a steady and reliable supply of labour power; by providing this supply family structures serve the interests of the dominant class.

The task of performing the required domestic labour has overwhelmingly been the domain of women. The question this leads to—how and why women came to be primarily responsible for the sphere of domestic labour—has itself spawned an enormous debate. (See, for example, Armstrong and Armstrong, 1984; Himmelweit and Mohun, 1977; Luxton, Rosenberg, and Arat-Koc, 1990; Oakley, 1974; Reed, 1978; Seccombe, 1974.) But one set of answers involves the role of ideology, the actions of the state, and even the role of biology.

Ideology enters the process in the form of sexism. Neo-Marxists are interested in the historical evolution of sexist ideologies in both the pre-capitalist and capitalist eras. Ideologies of male domination and sexism have been present in Western culture since the time of classical Greek and Roman society. During the period after the fall of Rome, when the Christian church was emerging, some of the tendencies became enshrined in official church teachings and dogmas—teachings that coincided with particular views of men and women that emerged in the codes of chivalry of feudal Europe, for instance. Before the emergence of capitalism, then, there was a long tradition of patriarchal and sexist thought in the West, and those modes of thinking became a part of the social, political, and economic processes of the capitalist system.

Added to these ideological factors is the role of the state. There is significant evidence that the state in various Western capitalist nations has been a decisive factor in the development of the patriarchal nuclear family (Dickinson and Russell, 1986; McIntosh, 1978). Through legislative actions that reinforce the male breadwinner role and the female domestic role, the state has helped to establish and maintain the structures of the nuclear family. These state actions include everything from the restrictions on women's work in the early English factory laws to more modern laws concerning child custody and family support. By limiting women's participation in certain sectors of the labour force, legislative initiatives served a double function. First, by being excluded women were more likely to be at home producing and reproducing labour power. Second, men were placed in a structural position of having others dependent on them. In theory, workers who are conscious of others depending on them tend to be more reliable; they are less likely to quit and move, or even go on strike, and risk the loss of job security and income.

The Nuclear Family: A Reserve Army of Labour

Given the neo-Marxist notion that labour power is a special and essential commodity in the capitalist system and that there is therefore a market for labour power, the people in a position to purchase labour power—the capitalist class—have an interest in a stable and adequate supply in the market. If there are shortages of labour power, the price of the commodity, in this case expressed as wages, can be forced up.

Some degree of unemployment—which creates an oversupply of labour power—is thus in the interests of the capitalist class. Marx examined the role of surplus labour pools in the early development of capitalism, and in applying his approach to modern capitalism neo-Marxists have suggested that women in the family can serve as a labour pool to be drawn on during times of acute labour shortage.

A neo-Marxist might argue that women within the nuclear family serve as an ideal reserve army of labour or surplus labour pool. During times of labour shortage brought on by a period of rapid economic expansion or other crises, such as war, various actions can be taken to encourage women to participate in the labour market. For example, ideological campaigns undertaken during the Second World War tried to convince women that it was their patriotic duty to go out and work in factories. Then, when the war was over, 'public relations' (or ideological) campaigns carried the opposite intent, encouraging women to return to their homes and unpaid domestic labour.

The Nuclear Family: An Ideal Consumption Unit

Another neo-Marxist argument concerning how the traditional nuclear family functions in the interests of the dominant class takes up the question of commodity consumption. Capitalism, neo-Marxists would argue, is a system based on the production and sale of material commodities, and one of its inherent problems is overproduction, which could also be termed a problem of underconsumption. The problem arises because in their never-ending pursuit of profits corporations develop levels of technology and productivity that are capable of producing more commodities than can be sold. In modern capitalist society oversupply is a constant problem, and corporations must continually attempt to increase their business, to sell as many consumer goods as they can. What better system to promote sales than one based on a nuclear family?

Picture in your mind a typical Western suburban neighbourhood composed of middle-class and working-class houses. In each of these homes there are several radios, perhaps several televisions, a washing machine, a dryer, a lawn mower, and other products. Given how many hours a week some of these items, such as the lawn mower or even the washing machine, are actually used, wouldn't it make sense for two or more families to share the items? The answer to that question, in capitalist society at least, is no. For Western families, part of the accepted social definition of success and the enjoyment of the 'good life' is having their own consumer durables. Indeed, as a result of massive advertising campaigns supported by the corporate sector, the possession of consumer durables has come to be equated with the meaning of life. The more stuff we have, the better off we are in every respect. Consume, consume, consume: this becomes the doctrine that drives our lives, and we can never have enough of the material goodies. If you are a producer of consumer commodities, what better system than one composed of hundreds of thousands of small-sized consumption units in the form of isolated nuclear families, which all compete with each other to have the latest and best of every possible household and personal consumer item?

The neo-Marxist tradition, then, understands the nuclear family within capitalist society as an institutional order or arrangement that functions primarily in the interests of the capitalist class. To be sure, the family looks after the individual and personal needs of its members, but to the extent that the family unit is a part of the process of producing and reproducing the capacity of the working class to sell its labour power, those activities also benefit capital. Neo-Marxists would argue that there are important class dimensions to this process, in that the structures and operations of working-class families will be different from those of the capitalist and middle-class or petty-bourgeois families. Among the essential differences will be the likelihood of the presence of paid domestic workers in upper-class families, a situation that changes the role of family members in terms of domestic work. In addition, the role of the upper-class family, and domestic labour therein, as regards the supply and provision of labour power for the capitalist system is different than it is for the working-class family.

The Feminist Challenge to Sociological Thought

Most of the important new directions in sociological thinking and analysis during the past two decades have been stimulated and informed by feminism. In the case of sociological analysis of familial relations, there has been an explosion of new ideas, arguments, theories, and empirical studies, and most of them have challenged both the structural functionalist and neo-Marxist positions.

In recent years both the Marxist and functionalist approaches have been criticized for failing to address numerous central issues in familial relations. Among those issues are the history of familial relations, especially patriarchal relations, the nature of household organization, sex and gender relations in the family, the extent and causes of domestic violence, and the role of the state in structuring familial relations and reproductive relations.

Although feminist scholars have not completed the task of developing the basis for systematic analyses of these issues, there are several excellent collections of readings that illustrate the new directions in family studies. In *Family Matters* (1988), Karen Anderson, Hugh Armstrong, Pat Armstrong, and other authors present a series of essays that deal with issues ranging from defining family to theories of the family, state policy, and domestic violence. Another significant collection, edited by Nancy Mandell and Ann Duffy, is *Reconstructing the Canadian Family: Feminist Perspectives* (1988). Essays in this collection deal with mothers and mothering, fathers and fathering, children, different family forms, women, family and work, issues surrounding reproductive technologies, and the role

of the state. Barrie Thorne and Marilyn Yalom have edited a collection of equally broad-ranging papers under the title *Rethinking the Family: Some Feminist Questions* (1982).

A central concern in feminist studies is the subordination and oppression of women (see, for instance, Barrett, 1980). Functionalism and Marxism both recognize and acknowledge that men and women tend to occupy different roles and positions in many institutions and that as a result men tend to have higher incomes, more power, and greater status. However, as Patricia Lengermann and Jill Niebrugge-Brantley (1988) argue, it is possible for an analytical approach to acknowledge that there are differences between people's income and their positions in terms of power without acknowledging that these conditions involve relations of subordination and oppression. The functionalist approach clearly sees inequality in this problematic way, and it can also be argued that the neo-Marxist approach fails to address the oppression of women because it concentrates on the issue of class.

In their analyses of domestic work and the relations typical of the traditional nuclear family, feminists have pointed out in detail the existing relations of subordination and oppression. They argue, for instance, that male members of a nuclear family benefit when women are in a structural situation of having to provide meals, undertake child care, do laundry and housecleaning, and engage in a whole range of domestic work that is necessary to produce and reproduce labour power (Hartmann, 1986). As the work of Meg Luxton (1980, 1988) indicates, even when women are employed full-time outside the household, they still tend to do the vast majority of domestic and household labour.

In addition to researching and analyzing domestic labour and familial relations, feminist scholars have also developed a compelling picture of the role of the state in the development and perpetuation of patriarchal family forms. Writers such as Jane Ursel (1986, 1992), Varda Burstyn (1985), and Norene Pupo (1988) have provided convincing arguments and evidence that the state in Canada has systematically acted in a way that promotes and bolsters patriarchy. Drawing on historical data, they show how a range of different state actions and acts dealing with issues from family allowances and support to employment measures all serve to maintain patriarchy and thus the oppression of women.

The important issue of reproductive relations has also emerged as central in recent feminist-inspired attempts to understand familial relations. Although many feminists deny that there is a biological basis to the oppression of women, some have suggested that the biological differences between women and men must be addressed in our efforts to understand the dynamics of patriarchal families. Mary O'Brien's *The Politics of Reproduction* (1981) has become a key source for those thinking about the role of biological differences in male and female relations.

Many sociologists who have been influenced by feminism have found that the concept of ideology is also a necessary tool for examining familial relations. Luxton notes that it is necessary and important 'to differentiate between ideology and the actual ways in which people interact, co-reside, have sexual relations, have babies, marry, divorce, raise

ONE HAPPY FUNCTIONAL FAMILY? SERVING THE INTERESTS OF CAPITAL? PATRIARCHAL OPPRESSION?

It is no exaggeration to say that Parsonian functionalism was the dominant approach in Western sociology for three or four decades following the Second World War. This was certainly the case in applied fields such as the study of the family. The following selection is from Parsons' famous essay 'The Normal American Family', first written in 1965.

The Normal American Family: A Model

It is of course commonplace that the American family is predominantly and, in a sense, increasingly an urban middle-class family. There has indeed been, if not a very great equalization of income (though there has been some in the present century), a very substantial homogenization of patterns of life in the population with reference to a number of things. Basic to this are the employment of one or more family members outside the home; the nuclear family household without domestic service except for cleaning and baby-sitting; and the basic constituents of the standard of living, including in particular the familiar catalogue of consumer durable goods, which constitute the basic capital equipment of the household . . .

It can then be said that, in a sense that has probably never existed before, in a society that in most respects has undergone a process of very extensive structural differentiation, there has emerged a remarkably uniform, basic type of family. It is uniform in its kinship and household composition in the sense of confinement of its composition to members of the nuclear family, which is effective at any given stage of the family cycle, and in the outside activities of its members, e.g., jobs for adult men, some participation in the labor force for women, school for children, and various other types of community participation. Indeed it is also highly uniform in the basic components of the standard of living, e.g., the private dwelling, the mechanical aids, the impingement of communications from the outside through the mass media, etc. *(53).*

On this background I may now turn to a few functional and analytical considerations. More than any other influence, psychoanalytic psychology has, during the last generation, made us aware of two crucial things. The first is the fundamental importance for the individual personality of the process of growing up in the intimacies of the family. Not only is mental illness to a large, though by no means exclusive, extent generated in the relations of a child to members of his family, but normal personality development is highly contingent on the proper combination of influences operating in the family situation. Of course the family stands by no means alone, and as the child grows older, influences from the neighborhood, then the school and beyond become increasingly important. The family, however, lays the essential foundations and continues always to be important.

There has been a good deal of discussion of the importance of psychological 'security' in this whole context. An individual's sense of security naturally depends on his experience in his family of orientation. It remains, however, an essential problem throughout life. We have become increasingly aware that for the adult, in psychologically very complex ways, his family of procreation is dynamically most intimately linked with his family of orientation. The experience of parenthood is of course a recapitulation in reverse of that of the child in relation to his parents, and in important ways reactivates the psychological structures belonging to that period. Just as much, marriage is a complex organization of components in the personality which are derived from childhood experience—the common involvement of eroticism

in both is the surest clue to the relationship.

For the normal adult, then, his marriage and his role as parent constitute the primary going reinforcement of his psychological security. The family can thus be seen to have two primary functions, not one. On the one hand it is the primary agent of socialization of the child, while on the other it is the primary basis of security for the normal adult. Moreover, the linkage of these two functions is very close. The point may be put by saying that their common responsibility as parents is the most important focus of the solidarity of marriage partners, and that the desire for children is the natural outcome of a solid 'romantic' attraction between two persons of opposite sex. The primary link between these two functions in terms of agency is clearly the feminine role in its dual capacity as mother and as wife.

I think it reasonable to suggest that the broad pattern of the contemporary American family fits this functional analysis. It seems to be a case of a process of differentiation through which the central functions of early socialization and giving individuals a psychological security base have become separated out from others to which they have been ascribed in less differentiated societies. The sharing of the common household as the place to 'live' with all its implications is the fundamental phenomenon—it is this sharing which makes the normal nuclear family a distinctive unit which cannot be confused with any others, based either on kinship or on other criteria. The home, its furnishings, equipment, and the rest constitute the 'logistic' base for the performance of this dual set of primary functions *(55–6)*.

From Talcott Parsons, 'The Normal American Family' in Bert Adams and Thomas Weirath, eds, *Readings in the Sociology of the Family* (Chicago: Markham, 1965).

COUNTERPOINT 1
THE MARXIST CHALLENGE:
THE FAMILY IN CAPITALIST SOCIETY

The last 40 years have witnessed efforts to revitalize Marxian analysis in many areas, including family studies. Adrian Wilson has produced an excellent summary of several theoretical approaches to the study of the family including a section titled 'A Marxist Approach: Is the Family the Tool of Capitalism?'

The Nuclear Family in Capitalist Society

Marxism has had a major impact on the development of sociology. Within the Marxist approach is an account of historical development, a theory of social class, and an analysis of capitalist society. Economic relationships are considered to be the central force that drives the development of a society, while at the same time they are also the means of keeping control over the members of that society.

For many years Marxists largely ignored the family as a political and social issue. It was believed that any faults in the family would be corrected by the creation of a socialist society. The revival in the Marxist theory of the family came with the examination of the issues raised by feminists about the nature and causes of sexual inequality. At the same time, Marxist academics were writing about the detailed economic and social controls that exist in capitalist society. The importance of the family as part of this process of social control was quickly recognized.

There has been a major debate between Marxism and feminism over the nature of the work that the woman does for the family. It is often referred to as 'the domestic labour debate'. Writers have argued that the capitalist economy needs to have women working in the home. The housewife services the needs of her husband, feeding and comforting him so that he can go refreshed to work each day. In a similar fashion, the mother ensures that the young children of

the community are brought safely through childhood to become workers in their turn.

Women are also part of what Marxists have called the 'reserve army of labour'. When the economy booms there is a need for more workers. Many women are available to be brought into industrial work as required. This was clearly illustrated by the way women were recruited into the factories during two world wars. Women have a second economic advantage to capitalism: they are cheap labour. Women are not seen as chief breadwinners of the family, therefore they can be paid a lower wage.

The 'domestic labour debate' is still continuing. Marxists have yet to resolve the precise way in which the labour of women fits their economic model. Nor have they really explained why domestic work and childcare have to be reserved largely for women. Feminists point out that it is not only capitalism that benefits from having women doing domestic work, it is also men! Those who recognize both sides of the debate have to cope with the problem of changing capitalism at the same time as improving the position of women.

There is less argument over the role of the family as part of the process of social control. This is not a new idea in sociology. Functionalist sociology has a very strong emphasis on the family as the main agent of socialization. Marxists recognize this role of the family but, unlike the functionalists, do not see it as beneficial. The family transmits the dominant bourgeois culture of capitalist society, preventing people from seeing the world as it really is (26–7).

From Adrian Wilson, *Family* (London: Tavistock Publications, 1985), pp. 26–7. Reprinted by permission of Taylor & Francis Group.

COUNTERPOINT 2
THE FEMINIST CHALLENGE:
THE FAMILY IN PATRIARCHAL SOCIETY

Feminism challenges both neo-Marxism and orthodox functionalism. In her summary, Ann Doris Duffy points out some key elements of feminist analyses of the family.

Patriarchy, Women, and the Family

Modern feminist analysis of women and the family emphasizes four basic themes. First, the economic and social structure of the family is based upon and reinforces the power and authority of the husband/father. Second, the content of family life—the roles of wife/mother—function to restrict and inhibit women's lives. Third, the prevailing system of ideas concerning marriage and the family deny women real choices about whether or not to marry and whether or not to bear children. Finally, the subordination of women in the family—as wives, mothers and daughters—accounts for the generalized powerlessness of women in society at large.

Echoing Engels' concerns, feminists point out that the basic structure of the modern family assumes the secondary and subordinate status of' women. Most women, even those who work outside the home, are to some degree economically dependent on their husbands, particularly if they have young children. This economic dependence is reinforced by social dependence embodied in the customs and traditions surrounding family life. The bride is 'given' in marriage by her parents and 'taken' by her husband; she usually is 'given' his name and is 'accepted' into his social class.

The economic basis of this inequality is perpetuated by the roles women are required to play within the family. As wife and mother, the woman is expected to perform most of the domestic and childcare work generated by the family. Since her time and physical and emotional energy are consumed by these tasks, she cannot undertake other more creative and more personal activities. Even if the husband has the best intentions, once the young woman becomes a mother, her household duties overwhelm her, just as they did in past historical periods. The home with its endless tasks becomes a trap which excludes women from the real world of creative work and serious challenges.

Feminists point out that women's subordination in the family is not simply the product of outmoded customs, burdensome household work and economic inequality. They stress that the ideology surrounding femininity and the family locks women into their traditional role in the home. Prevailing ideas about women's lives, including the dogma of romantic love and the cult of maternalism, are so pervasive and powerful that they discourage women from exploring alternative ways of living.

From a very early age, women are socialized into the culture of romance. Fairy tales, television, magazines, films and books tell women that they will achieve not only personal fulfilment but ecstasy and transcendence once they form a romantic relationship with the right man. The implied message is that failure to fall in love is the mark of an unworthy woman. She may love herself only if a man finds her worthy. As a result, most women devote a considerable part of their life to the pursuit of love. Cosmetics, aerobics, clothes, fashion magazines, even plastic surgery are employed to create an attractive and desirable image. Predictably, a recent survey of Canadian teenagers finds that young women are far more likely than their male counterparts to express concern about their appearance.

Energy consumed by this preoccupation with appearing desirable and finding romance is lost to other ventures. . . . Dreams of romance deflect young women from confronting the realities of their educational and occupational futures. By late adolescence the typical young woman has tailored her educational and occupational plans to suit the romantic script, disregarding the likelihood, whether she marries or not, that she will devote most of her life to some form of paid employment.

Through the process of dating and courtship, women are further socialized into both the culture of romance and the subordinate female role. Today, the male is still expected to formally initiate and then orchestrate the dating relationship. The woman's part is often reactive rather than active. . . . Recent research indicates that many young men do not accept women's right to sexual self-determination. Studies of male college students in Winnipeg and Los Angeles find that an average of 35% of these young men indicate some likelihood of forcing sexual relations on a woman, provided they can be assured of not being caught and punished. In a recent survey of American college students, more than one-quarter of the men report trying to coerce women into sexual relations and one in seven state that they have forced a woman to have sexual intercourse at least once in the past. Though the majority of young women do not encounter such directly oppressive situations, many discover that the courtship game has as much to do with power as with romance.

Indoctrinated into the culture of romance from their earliest years, many women cannot imagine personal happiness and happy endings except in terms of marriage and family. Once inside marriage, women often learn that romance appears more frequently in romance novels, soap operas and commercials for diamond rings than in the day-to-day routine. . . . Feminists strive to expose popular notions of romantic love as an ideology that functions to groove women into marriage and domesticity and out of an independent vision of their lives.

Coupled to the ideology of romance is the cult of maternalism. Once married, women find that motherhood is increasingly emphasized. Glamorized and romanticized by the media, motherhood appears to offer women a meaningful, life-long enterprise around which to build their lives *(113–16)*.

From Ann Duffy, 'Struggling with Power: Feminist Critiques of Family Inequality' in Nancy Mandell and Ann Duffy, eds, *Reconstructing the Canadian Family: Feminist Perspectives* (Toronto: Butterworths, 1988). Reprinted by permission of Ann Duffy.

children and so on' (1988: 238). She points out, as does Barrett, that the ideology of family tends to involve powerful notions of traditional 'oughts' in the views of the nuclear family. As Luxton argues, these ideological frames of reference or belief systems have an impact because they influence how people think things ought to be done and how they should go about organizing their lives, as well as influencing government policy and action.

Feminist theorists have also looked at domestic and family violence, incest and sexual abuse, the role of familial relations in constructing gender identities, different and changing family forms, and the precise historical patterns of family-form development—illustrating graphically how new approaches in sociology can offer alternative or extended perspectives.

These new approaches are necessary, because it is clear that women have long been excluded from the corridors of power—excluded from positions of power and leadership not just in politics, but in the home and workplace as well, including academia. In the past, women were not often included in the making of the sociological imagination—where men and male theory have long held sway. In the current day, new approaches to theory must play their part in dealing with this history of oppression and exclusion.

Critical Thinking Questions

* Is there such a thing as a 'normal family' in North America?
* Who tends to perform domestic labour? Why?
* Is the nuclear patriarchal family the most appropriate to suit the needs of capitalist society?
* What is patriarchy? Is our society patriarchal?
* Why, according to Parsons, do women and men perform different roles in the family?

Terms and Concepts

Family—a concept virtually impossible to define, in part because of its loaded ideological history. Conventional sociological definitions usually include references to 'basic kinship unit', or to people related by blood or adoption living together in some kind of recognized social unit. We may be well advised to use the concept only in reference to specific forms of family, as in nuclear family. Familial relations are those related to biological reproduction and extended child care.

Nuclear family—an arrangement or set of established social relationships between female and male biological or adoptive parents and their dependent children (biological or adopted).

Instrumental and expressive roles—relates to the traditional functionalist approach to the family, which

argued that there were two essential roles within the typical nuclear family. Instrumental roles are those associated with goal-directed behaviour, more external in orientation, involving authority, achievement, and leadership. Expressive roles are related to a family's more internal emotional matters dealing with nurturing, emotional support, or family integration. The classical functionalist work of Parsons and others suggested that men tend to occupy instrumental roles and women expressive roles.

Functions of the family—in structural functionalism, relates to the view of the family as a universal institution, found in every society because it performs several vital social functions, meeting basic system prerequisites including the regulation of sexual behaviour, facilitating biological reproduction, and providing early child care and socialization of the young, as well as providing a site for the provision of basic material and emotional support for its members.

Functions of the family—in Marxian theory, the assumption that the family tends, like all other social institutions, to operate in the interests of the ruling or dominant class. It has been argued that the traditional nuclear family serves the interests of the capitalist class by functioning to produce and reproduce labour power, by providing a site where a reserve army of labour (a labour pool) can be maintained at no cost to capital, and by being an ideal consumption unit for the commodities produced by capitalists. Although there are variations in the Marxian analyses of the role women play in the overall system, there is acceptance of the position that the nuclear family itself is well suited to meet the needs of the capitalist class and the capitalist system.

Related Web Sites

http://www-sul.stanford.edu/depts/ssrg/kkerns/family.html

Thanks to Stanford University Libraries anyone interested in studying any aspect of family relations has an instant annotated bibliography and source list available. It is actually more than a bibliography because it contains indexes and quick links to statistical sources.

http://sobek.colorado.edu/SOC/RES/family.html

Thanks to the Department of Sociology at the University of Colorado for this well-connected site that allows one to access information in issues ranging from family violence to many issues relating to parenting.

http://www.hc-sc.gc.ca/hppb/familyviolence/

This is the site for the National Clearing House on Family Violence sponsored by Health Canada. New publications are listed and available as they come out with extensive links for researchers and victims.

http://www.statcan.ca:8096/bsolc/english/bsolc?catno=85-224-X

A recent report (June 2001) from Statistics Canada, the fourth annual *Family Violence in Canada*, is available at this site. It is of vital interest to Canadian women and men.

http://dmoz.org/Society/Gay,_Lesbian,_and_Bisexual/Family_and_Relationships/

Another 'Open Directory Project', this site is an important source for understanding issues and perspectives relating to gay, lesbian, and bisexual families.

Suggested Further Readings

Armstong, P., and H. Armstrong. 1990. *Theorizing Women's Work*. Toronto: Garamond Press. This important summary and contribution to the ongoing debate about the nature of domestic labour is written by two of Canada's most important contemporary thinkers.

Connelly, P., and P. Armstrong, eds. 1992. *Feminism in Action: Studies in Political Economy*. Toronto: Canadian Scholars Press. This collection of essays represents viewpoints on a variety of issues. Most of the authors would be located within the Marxian and socialist feminist traditions.

Hartmann, H. 1986. 'The Unhappy Marriage of Marxism and Feminism: Towards a More Progressive Union'. In L. Sargent, ed., *The Unhappy Marriage of Marxism and Feminism: A Debate on Class and Patriarchy*. London: Pluto Press. One of the classical statements of the socialist feminist perspective, it includes a compelling critique of the gender blindness of traditional Marxism.

Mandell, N., and A. Duffy. 1996. *Canadian Families*. Toronto: Harcourt Brace. A comprehensive, edited volume, it covers issues ranging from the history of families to law, ethnicity, poverty, and violence.

Parsons, T., and R.F. Bales, eds. 1955. *Family, Socialization and Interaction Process*. Glencoe, IL: The Free Press. The original and fundamental statement of how structural functionalists view the family, this book framed the debate on the issue for many decades.

CHAPTER 15

Globalization

Some of you reading this book may have participated in political action or even political protest around the issue of free trade and globalization. Most of you will certainly have noticed these issues being debated in the media and in our political institutions. An often-asked question is: what are the issues? It seems as if two primary issues worry the opponents of global-ization and unfettered free trade. One has to do with the global distribution of wealth and income and the other has to do with the threat that globalization and global trade agreements bring to democracy at the national or local levels. A further question might be: why are some people opposed to globalization and free trade, while others endorse what are called the 'new realities'? Perhaps we can begin by considering that globalization is really not a new phenomenon. Indeed, capitalism is in fact a world system. Understanding why this is so requires some histori-cal background.

In Chapter 9 we examined some of the dimen-sions of income inequality in Canada. Perhaps some readers were surprised by the significance of the inequalities. An even more dramatic picture emerges when we examine global patterns of inequality. The extent of global inequalities makes it difficulty to produce comparative data; however, here are some statistics:

- The 225 richest individuals have wealth that totals the total annual income of the poorest 47 per cent of the world's population.

- The assets of the three richest people in the world are greater than the combined assets of the 49 least-developed countries.
- The assets of the richest 15 people in the world are greater than the total Gross Domestic Product (GDP) of sub-Saharan Africa.
- The consumption rate of the richest 20 per cent of countries is 16 times that of the poorest 20 per cent.
- In Canada the average life expectancy is just over 79 years; in Sierra Leone it is just under 35 years. (*1998 United Nations Human Development Report*)

It is interesting to compare the size of national economies around the world as measured by Gross Domestic Product with corporate sales figures. For example, General Motors ranks 23rd on such a list with sales greater that the individual GDP of all but 22 countries. Wal-Mart, ExxonMobile, Ford Motor, and DaimlerChrysler are 25th to 28th respectively, all with annual sales greater than Poland, Norway, and Indonesia, which rank 29, 30, 31 (*Labour Reporter*, November 2001: 8).

A Brief History of World Capitalism

To understand the role of the state in the global era and the issue of the international distribution of wealth, we need to review the nature of capitalism. To do this we will summarize some key developments of the past several centuries.

Over the past decade much has been made about how capitalism is a global, or world, system. Interestingly, this observation is being touted as a new insight. In fact, scholars as diverse as Adam Smith, Karl Marx, Immanuel Wallerstein, W.W. Rostow, Karl Polanyi, and Eric Wolf agree on one characteristic of the capitalist system—it is a world system driven by a primary dynamic.

The Canadian philosopher and theologian George Grant summarized the essence of the capitalist system in the following manner: 'Capitalism is, after all, a way of life based on the principle that the most important activity is profit-making' (1965: 47). In his essay 'The Drive for Capital', Robert Heilbroner (1992) uses the phrase 'the rage for accumulation' to describe the inner logic of the system (32). He notes that it is the ceaseless accumulation of wealth that drives the system and is the central dynamic that leads to the continual changes that characterize capitalism:

> Capital thus differs from wealth in its intrinsically dynamic character, continually changing its form from community into money and then back again in an endless metamorphosis that already makes clear its integral connection with the changeful nature of capitalism itself. (1992: 30)

Thinkers such as E.K. Hunt (1990), Broadus Mitchell (1967), Paul Baran and Paul Sweezy (1966), S.B. Clough and C.W. Cole (1967), and Robert Heilbroner (1968) all argue that capitalism has passed though a series of distinct stages, each marked by different levels of technical development and social relations of production, and each characterized by different forms of international exchange relations and roles for the state. The following represents a periodization schema distilled from their writings:

1500–1770s	Mercantilism or Merchant Capitalism
1770s–1860s	Industrial Capitalism
1860s–1930s	Corporate Industrial Capitalism
1930s–1970s	Keynesian State/Corporate Capitalism
1970s–Present	Neo-Liberal/Corporate Capitalism

Cough and Cole (1967) use the term *mercantilism* to describe the initial phase of modern capitalism, although the term *merchant capitalism* is also appropriate since trade and commerce were the central processes though which capital was accumulated. The era witnessed the rise of nation-states across Western Europe via a union of merchants and monarchs. During the mercantilist era, colonies were important for both merchants and the monarchs because they were a source of wealth and power. As a result of this, the era of mercantilism was one of feverish colonialism during which various European states and their merchant allies explored and invaded virtually every part of the globe. The successful capital accumulation that characterized the mercantilist era produced the conditions that gave rise to its transformation into the next stage of capitalist development. It is generally recognized that some time between the late 1770s and the 1850s, a revolution occurred that transformed, along with almost everything else, the class structure, conceptions of wealth and how wealth was produced and appropriated, and the role of the state in facilitating capital accumulation.

The Industrial Revolution, which ushered in the second stage of capitalist development, brought further radical changes as factory-based mechanized production came to dominate wealth creation. The new technologies and ways of organizing production resulted in productivity and output increases that would have been unimaginable just 50 years prior. As Thomas and Hamm (1944) point out, for a variety of reasons, during the

50 years following the Napoleonic Wars 'there was little interest in colonies' (566) and a concomitant lessening of the importance of the state. Indeed this was the era that would witness the emergence of laissez-faire with its emphasis on the necessity of a free market, unrestrained by state regulation.

In his discussion of the development and dynamics of this first period of industrial capitalism, E.K. Hunt points out that this 'classical' phase of industrial capitalism was relatively short-lived. He writes that the period from the mid-1840s to 1872 has been called the 'golden age of competitive capitalism'; however, he points out that it contained the seeds of its transformation:

> Just as competitive capitalism seemed to be achieving its greatest successes, the forces Marx had predicted would lead to the concentration of capital began to show themselves. Improvements in technology were such that larger-sized plants were necessary to take advantage of the more efficient methods of production. Competition became so aggressive and destructive that small competitors were eliminated. Large competitors, facing mutual destruction, often combined themselves in cartels, trusts, or mergers in order to ensure their mutual survival. In the United States the competition was particularly intense. (1990: 98–9)

Heilbroner (1968) makes a similar point when he notes that: 'A system originally characterized by large numbers of small enterprises was starting to give way to one in which production was increasingly concentrated in the hands of a relatively few, very big and very powerful business units' (109). Clough and Cole also describe this process as one that 'was definitely away from individual ownership to corporate ownership' (1967: 639). Numerous scholars have argued that we can date the emergence of the modern corporation from the post-Civil War period (Baran and Sweezy, 218; Heilbroner, 109; Mitchell, 155). E.K.

Hunt collaborates, commenting on the important changes that occurred during this period:

> During the late nineteenth and early twentieth centuries, capitalism underwent an important and fundamental transformation. Although the foundations of the system—the laws of private property, the basic class structure, and the processes of commodity production and allocation through the market—remained unchanged, the process of capital accumulation became institutionalized in the large corporation. (1990: 121)

Most scholars acknowledge that the emergence of the modern corporation transformed the capitalist system and brought forth a series of new tendencies and dynamics. The large-scale production made possible by the concentration and centralization of capital soon encountered obstacles of its own making as raw material supplies began to decline. In addition, the productivity of the modern corporation soon meant that domestic and local markets became saturated, and as a result profitable local or domestic investment outlets became harder and harder to find, especially in more industrialized nations such as Britain and the United States. Hunt further notes that this change in the basic structures of the accumulation process that saw 'the accumulation process rationalized, regularized, and institutionalized in the form of the large corporation' and was accompanied by a further important change, namely, 'the internationalization of capital' (121).

These changes to the structures and dynamics of capitalism led to the emergence of what is commonly referred to as the age of the 'new imperialism'. The geographical expansion associated with the new imperialism differed from mercantile colonialism in that it involved an unprecedented internationalization of capital as the corporations competed on a global scale for raw materials, markets, and investment outlets. Clough and Cole agree, suggesting that after about 1875 a number of factors produced a renewed interest in colonial expansion:

> There was a need for new markets to absorb the goods produced by Europe's ever-expanding productive equipment. There was a need for raw materials to satisfy the maws of European industry and of foodstuffs to feed Europe's ever-growing population. There was a need, so it was believed, for places to invest capital where the return would be high and the danger of default for political reasons would be slight. And there was thought to be a need for colonies to relieve the pressure of population—of overpopulation—in Europe. (1967: 618)

Thomas and Hamm summarize the characteristics of the new imperialism: 'These, then—markets for manufacturers, sources of raw materials, above all, places for investment of surplus capital—are the main reason for imperialism' (1944: 571).

The internationalization of capital and the global competition for raw materials, markets, and investment outlets were key factors leading to the First World War. The War proved to be a turning point in global relations marking the beginning of the end for the British Empire, and the emergence of the United States as the hegemonic world economic and military power. Despite the unimaginable tragedy of the War, Western Europe and North America experienced prosperity and economic growth throughout the first three decades of the twentieth century. Indeed, it is possible to argue that the boom period from the turn of the century to the Great Depression was a kind of golden age of corporate capitalism, although some scholars, such as Baran and Sweezy, maintain that this prosperity was based on a series of unique historical contingencies. In any event, in 1929 the system suffered a nearly total collapse as the international capitalist system entered a severe worldwide crisis.

The Rise of the Welfare State

Though the Depression wrought many changes, perhaps none was as important as the revolution in economic theory and the role of the state. The Keynesian revolution ushered in a new era of capitalism in which there was widespread acceptance of the notion that during periods of crisis, state intervention in the economy is both legitimate and essential. Government expenditures as a means of increasing aggregate demand were coupled with increased government regulation designed to smooth out some of the contradictions and excesses of the market, producing what Heilbroner refers to as 'guided capitalism'. The potential impact of government expenditures on the economy was demonstrated by the fact that the Depression ended and was replaced by prosperity as a result of massive state spending associated with the preparation for, and the conduct of, the Second World War. Students of history use various terms such as 'warfare economy' and the 'military industrial complex' to describe the new institutional structures and economic arrangements that characterize the intimate relationship that developed between large industry and the state.

The eventual Allied victory did not bring an end to government economic intervention, as the Marshall Plan and the related Bretton Woods Conference established a framework for sustained government expenditures geared to rebuilding shattered economies and keeping them firmly within the capitalist fold. The bulk of the financial and other resources used in the massive postwar rebuilding process originated in the United States, now the unchallenged leader of the capitalist world. The outbreak of the Korean War, the emergence of the Cold War, the massive expenditures necessary to provide an infrastructure for the postwar baby boom, the spread of suburbia, and the developing space race all contributed to two decades of prosperity. In addition to, and perhaps more important than, these specific expenditures was the emergence of what has become known as the welfare state.

The age of 'New Imperialism', at the end of the nineteenth century, involved an unprecedented inter-nationalization of capital as the corporations competed on a global scale for raw materials, markets, and investment outlets. Today's global economy continues to divide the world. (Copyright © 2000 Jean Pierre Gauzere/The Image Bank)

Gary Teeple provides an excellent explanation:

> Although sometimes used as a generic term for government intervention 'on many fronts', the welfare state can also be seen as a capitalist *society* in which the state has intervened in the form of social policies, programs, standards, and regulations in order to mitigate class conflict *and* provide for, answer, or accommodate certain social needs for which the capitalist mode of production in itself has no solution or makes no provision. (1995: 15, emphasis in original)

Teeple goes on to argue that the typical welfare state involved state intervention in four distinct areas that were all vital to the maintenance of the overall system and the postwar boom. According to Teeple these areas included, first, actions and policies in the areas of education and health care to facilitate '*the physical propagation of the working class and its preparation for the labour market*' (1995: 15, emphasis in original). The second area of activity involved 'regulations on the minimum wage, hours of work, child labour, retirement age, education/training, injury insurance, immigration' and other dimensions of labour market control (15). The state's third major focus was attempting to minimize labour–capital conflict in the actual arena of production through the provision of an 'institutional framework for class conflict (collective bargaining) and to protect the workers from the worst effects of the exploitation by capital' (15). The fourth and last form of state intervention was the 'provision of income assurance for the *unproductive and after productive life*' (1995: 16, emphasis in original). By this he means pensions, social assistance, and the like.

Stephen McBride and John Shields refer to the same set of policies as the 'Keynesian Welfare State', arguing that in the aftermath of the Great Depression and the Second World War it was essential to humanize capitalism and the state undertook

to 'provide a better integration of the working class into a reconstituted capitalism' (1993: 9). They note that the provision of direct social benefits, regulation of labour and the economy, and the provision of a range of welfare benefits, while often secured only after forms of class struggle, was actually 'part of the terms of a peace formula involving labour and other previously socially disenfranchised groups' (14).

The Fall of the Welfare State

Just as there was something in the logic of the system of competitive capitalism that led to its transformation to corporate capitalism, so too it can be argued that the logic of the era we are calling Keynesian corporate/state capitalism contained the seeds of its own transformation. Among the contradictions was the fact that the prosperity and stability of the postwar welfare state was predicated on high levels of government spending and an associated growth in government deficits. In addition, by the end of the 1960s the success of the Marshall Plan began to create problems and tensions in the international market as Western European and Japanese corporations started to challenge the traditional markets of American-based multinationals. Added to this were the problems associated with growing government debts, debts to be sure that had in large part been incurred as a result of spending in areas that directly benefited the corporate sectors as in the expansion of the military and the space race. Other international events such as the emergence of OPEC accentuated the instability of the international system until by the 1970s another crisis loomed.

The growing international competition, which accompanied the fiscal crisis of the state in many Western nations, gave rise to a sustained and well-articulated critique of Keynesian economics and the state practices that have sustained the system since the Great Depression. The popularization of supply-side and monetarist economics and governments committed to state cutbacks under the banner of neo-conservative (which are actually neo-liberal) philosophies ushered in a new era of capitalist development.

The rhetoric of deregulation, fiscal responsibility, and freeing the market from the fetters and burdens of government intervention and interference began to dominate the actions and policies of more and more governments. As governments undertook massive withdrawals from previous responsibilities and initiatives, they also faced restrictions and limitations on their actions as a result of the terms and conditions of international agreements such as the GATT and the ongoing authority and power of agencies such as the International Monetary Fund. The power of nation-states and capital with a regional or national base paled in the face of global capital supported by transnational international accords. The accumulation strategies and plans of giant multinational corporations became increasingly based calculations concerning securing the lowest possible input and labour costs as well as the largest possible markets, all of which are truly global in scope. Gary Teeple describes the emerging era and how it is distinguishable from the previous period:

> we have entered a transitional era between two phases in the development of capitalism. In this period there has been a profound shift from a mode of production based on semi-automated processes, sometimes referred to as advanced Fordism, to a more automated mode based on microelectronics and computer applications. In this transition, in which nationally based economic development has been more or less transfigured into self-generating global economy, all the social and political institutions associated with the national economy come into question, indeed begin to undergo a commensurate transformation. (1995: 5)

Even these cursory comments make it clear that capitalism has indeed passed through a series of distinctive stages or epochs as it evolved and changed. Throughout these various stages of development the inner logic or raison d'être of the capitalist system has remained unchanged—the pre-eminent drive of capital to accumulate. While the goal of capital has remained constant, its precise form and structure have changed as a result of the unmistakable tendency towards the concentration, centralization, and internationalization of capital.

Beyond the Welfare State?

The question then becomes: is there still a role for the contemporary nation-state in the so-called global era? As one could surmise, given the developments sketched out above there are some that argue that the nation-state is a relic of the past and has become largely irrelevant. For example, several speakers at a 1996 symposium on the future of Canada succulently summarize the position that Canadians have little choice but to adjust our public policy for the global era. The first noted 'The success of the current globalization experiment depends on many factors which are not guaranteed. First, developed nations must maintain open borders to imports from developing nations. This is best ensured by an economic system which is not susceptible to political pressure within those countries' (Brown, 1996: 114). As astounding as this justification for placing deliberate limitations on democracy is (with its recognition that this is an 'experiment' without controls!), it was still more qualified than another claim made at the conference:

> The Canada that we have come to know and love no longer exists! There is no viable status quo! We have to remake our nation and society in the light of irreversible external forces of globalization and of the knowledge/information revolution. (Courchene, 1996: 45)

Politicians of a neo-conservative inclination, and the mass media have also popularized the general notion that we are in a global era in which nation-states are somehow impelled by the constraints and strictures of a global market. Provincial and national budgets present the media with an opportunity to warn politicians that they are no longer really in control. For example, at the time of the 1995 federal budget, the *Globe and Mail* (6 March 1995) ran a column in which the president of a Chicago investment house asked rhetorically 'Is Moody's the Newest Superpower?' less than a week after running a commentary from the *New York Times* entitled 'Don't Mess with Moody's' (*Globe and Mail*, 27 February 1995). Between the time that these articles ran, in another commentary entitled 'Dollar Shows What World Thinks of Budget', Terence Corcoran reminded Canadians that the really important measure of the budget was the reaction of international finance markets (3 March 1995). Writing in the *New Left Review*, Linda Weiss summarized the message of these spokespersons of inevitable and unfettered globalization:

> According to this logic, states are now virtually powerless to make real policy choices; transnational markets and footloose corporations have so narrowly constrained policy options that more and more states are being forced to adopt similar fiscal, economic and social policy regimes. Globalists therefore predict convergence on neo-liberalism as an increasing number of states adopt the low-taxing, market-based ideals of the American model. (1997: 4)

Academics have also argued that we are in a new era in which the traditional role and power of the nation-state has been radically altered. For example, although he operates at a much more sophisticated theoretical level, in his *The Global Age,* Martin Albrow takes the point one step further by suggesting that a new global state is in fact emerging. He writes:

> The global shift leads necessarily to a reconceptualization of the state. It desegregates the

linkage of nation and state which national elites managed to effect and focuses attention on the development of institutionalized practices operating at the transnational level, and on the operation of global relevancies in the day-to-day activities of ordinary people. (1997: 172)

Albrow argues that the emergence of a world society is accompanied by the emergence of a world state, however, he fails to provide much conceptual clarity for either concept.

Several other important scholars have articulated the argument that the nation-state is in fact losing its efficacy to govern in recent years. In his important study of the decline of the welfare state in Canada, Gary Teeple sounds a warning about the potential political implications of globalization. He states: 'For the state the consequences of economic globalization are above all those of erosion of its functions and redefinition at the international level' (1995: 68). After commenting on how the nation-state is made somewhat unnecessary or redundant because transnational capital has superseded and/or replaced national capital, he goes on:

> Without fear of exaggeration it can be said that the national state has lost and continues to lose much of its sovereignty, although the degrees of independence vary with the degree of remaining integrity to national economic and military formations. It is not so much that a political state cannot act independently because of the erosion or usurpation of its powers, but that its raison d'être—the existence of a nationally defined capitalist class—has been waning. Taking its place has been the rise of an international capitalist class with global interests. (Teeple, 1995: 68–9)

In *When Corporations Rule the World* (1995), David Korten sounds a similar warning when he notes that 'Corporations have emerged as the

Politicians of a neo-conservative inclination have popularized the general notion that we are in a global era in which nation-states are somehow impelled by the constraints and structures of a global market. Writing in the *New Left Review*, Linda Weiss predicts that an increasing number of states of countries will adopt the low-taxing, market-based ideals of the American model. Here, Prime Minister Paul Martin welcomes US President George W. Bush to a press conference held during the US President's 2004 visit to Canada. (CP Picture Archive/Fred Chartrand)

dominant governance institutions on the planet' (54). He goes on to note that among the problems we face as a result of the growth of transnational corporations is the fact that the marketplace that governs more and more dimensions of our existence is itself governed by a special kind of democracy: 'In the market, one dollar is one vote, and you get as many votes as you have dollars. No dollar, no vote' (66). Korten aptly summarized his concerns

and warnings: 'The greater the political power of the corporations and those aligned with them, the less the political power of the people, and the less meaningful democracy becomes' (140).

Is the Nation-State Still Relevant?

Although some claim the state has lost virtually all its power, and scholars such as Teeple and Korten are both concerned that the nation-state is losing some power, others maintain that it is erroneous to place too much emphasis on the new globalization and the apparent attendant loss of national state power. Perhaps the most vigorous proponents of this view are found in the pages of *Monthly Review*. The title of William Tabb's article 'Globalization is *an* Issue, The Power of Capital is *the* Issue' (his emphasis) tells the story as he warns that it is defeatist for workers to accept that the power of global capital is supreme (Tabb, 1997: 21). Harry Magdoff and Ellen Meiksins Wood have engaged in a series of debates with other scholars. They repeatedly argue that, although capitalism is changing, as it always has, its essential nature and character remain and as such the nation-state remains essential to its continued functioning. Meiksins Wood writes:

> Besides I don't accept the premise of the 'globalization thesis'—which Piven and Cloward never quite contradict—that the importance of the state and political power declines in proportion to globalization. On the contrary, I think (as I have been repeating far too often, and as Harry Magdoff explains in this issue's 'Review of the Month' more clearly than I have even been able to do) that capital now needs the state more than ever to sustain maximum profitability in a global market. (Wood, 1998: 42)

In their analysis of the possibilities of worker resistance to globalization, Judy Fudge and Harry Glasbeek concur, noting that 'we observe that despite repeated assertions about nation-states being outmoded political units, the very roles that governments of nation-states are asked to play on behalf of the forces that favour the development of a differently structured capitalism—a globalized one—make them a pertinent and vital site of struggle' (1997: 220). In an analysis of the role of the nation-state in regulating banking and financial transactions, Ethan Kapstein stated the objective of

his study: 'If I can show that states are responding to the challenges posed by globalization in this area and that they remain the single most important actors, then we will expect to find them playing a key role in governing other sectors of the global economy as well' (1994: 2). In his conclusion, Kapstein notes that his findings in fact support the initial contention that what is emerging are nation-states that have developed a two-level structure 'with international cooperation at the upper level and home country control below' (177–8).

Robert Boyer and Daniel Drache bring together an important set of essays in *States Against Markets: The Limits of Globalization*. The collection contains several well-articulated arguments detailing why we must continue to pay attention to the state. In his essay, Boyer concludes that free markets simply have not been able to provide the goods that the majority of the population requires and therefore: 'The state remains the most powerful institution to channel and tame the power of the markets' (1996: 108). In her analysis of the impact of deregulation on the manner by which the spheres of the public and private are impacted, Janine Brodie (1996a) convincingly argues that it is not that the state has lost its relevance and power, it is rather that states have adopted quite radically different policies. Her argument meshes well with that presented by Claus Offe in his 'Aspects of the Regulation-Deregulation Debate' where he argues that deregulation is itself a form of state intervention. Offe notes: 'To be sure . . . invocations of market-liberal pathos of freedom fail to notice that a politics of deregulation, no less than one of regulation, has a character of massive state "intervention". For both cases involve a decisive change in the situations and market opportunities brought about by public policy' (1996: 75).

B. Mitchell Evans, Stephen McBride, and John Shields have also argued that, while the role and function of the nation-state are being transformed by the processes of globalization, it is a mistake to underestimate the continued importance of the nation-state. The position that claims the nation-state is irrelevant or has lost most of its power serves 'to mask the active role the state has played in establishing the governance mechanisms and the new state form congruent with a system of neo-liberal regionalized trading and investment blocks' (1998: 18). They buttress their claim that 'nation-states, however, are far from irrelevant' (19) with a variety of arguments concerning the new roles that the nation-state must take on in the global era.

David Held remains one of the most important political thinkers of our day. In recent years he has added to his impressive contribution with one of the most systematic and thoughtful theoretical treatises on globalization and the state yet produced. The volume, *Democracy and the Global Order: From the Modern State to Cosmopolitan Governance*, builds on his outstanding capacity to summarize difficult and complex arguments. Held offers an innovative model of global governance and notes that the nation-state has not become totally irrelevant: 'If the global system is marked by significant change, this is perhaps best conceived less as an end of the era of the nation-state and more as a challenge to the era of "hegemonic states"—a challenge which is as yet far from complete' (1995: 95). The task that Held undertakes, so important to twenty-first–century political theory, is to examine the consequences and implications of the rise of international and intrastate entities for democratic theory and the state. He notes that his efforts are 'motivated by the necessity to rethink the theory of democracy to take account of the changing nature of the polity both within pre-established borders and within the wider system of nation-state and global forces' (144).

In a sense, the gauntlet that Held throws down is almost as radical as the challenge that existing theory faces from feminism. Held suggests we have no choice other than to think our way through the existence of global structures and relations of power. Such centres and relations of power now exist—it is just that we do not theorize them, control them, understand them, or even realize they exist (138–9). Held encourages us to conceive of new ways to understand contemporary multi-dimensional relations of power. He argues that there are seven essential sites of power that range from the personal level of our bodies, through our cultural and civic associations, to the legal and regulators agencies that formulate and regulate law (Chapter. 8). In his final chapter he outlines what he terms a cosmopolitan model of democracy and postulates the possibility of radically new international governance structures and processes that integrate democratic governance principles into what must be termed the structures of a global polity.

How Do We Make Sense of the World Economy?

Globalization as Modernization

Much of the literature drawn on to present this brief view of the history of capitalism comes from the power-conflict tradition. There is, of course, another side to the story. We know that one of Emile Durkheim's important books, *The Division of Labour in Society*, was a study of the transition from pre-industrial to industrial society, and Talcott Parsons studied the evolution of society. Perhaps the most systematic attempt to understand the process of industrialization from outside the power-conflict tradition is the important work of W.W. Rostow, *The Stages of Economic Growth*, subtitled *A Non-Communist Manifesto*. The book presents an evolutionary-style argument that in the course of their development most societies pass though distinct stages: they move from a traditional society, through a 'Precondition', then to 'Take-Off', and finally to the 'Drive to Maturity' stage, with all culminating in the last stage, 'The Age of High Mass Consumption'. Although the polemical nature of Rostow's conclusions seem peculiar in the current era, there is no doubt that they were seen as a roadmap that Rostow expected most societies to follow (1960: 166). A similar argument was developed at about the same time by Daniel Lerner in *The Passing of Traditional*

Society. As the name implies, this book also saw non-industrial, typically non-Western societies pass though a development process that would eventually result in them becoming modern, that is, Western. Lerner notes that 'the Western model of modernization exhibits certain components and sequences whose relevance is global' (2000: 120). Although his study is of the Middle East, Lerner thinks that the model he has developed based on the Western experience has wider applicability.

Despite the optimistic expectations of those who saw world societies progressing through the stages that Western societies were claimed to have experienced, much of the world remained poor and undeveloped. In order to address this issue new theories emerged.

Globalization as Dependency

In 1969 Andre Gunder Frank published the first of a series of important works on the issue of development and underdevelopment. The essay, titled 'The Development of Underdevelopment', explicitly criticized the notion that most if not all societies pass through a series of virtually identical stages along their way to modernization. Frank criticized this notion in no uncertain terms, referring to 'our ignorance of the underdeveloped countries' history that leads us to assume that their past and indeed their present resembles earlier stages of the history of the more developed countries' (1970: 4). In a book, *Capitalism and Underdevelopment in Latin America*, published the same year, he stated: 'It is fruitless to expect the underdeveloped countries of today to repeat the stages of economic growth passed through by modern developed societies' (1969: xvi). He explained why:

> My thesis is that . . . the historical development of the capitalist system have generated underdevelopment in the peripheral satellites whose economic surplus was expropriated, while generating economic development in the metropolitan centers which appropriate

that surplus—and further that this process still continues. (3)

So, according to Frank and the advocates of dependency theory—the approach to development that he was instrumental in popularizing—underdeveloped societies do not just happen to find themselves so, their underdevelopment is a direct consequence of development elsewhere. It is what he calls the 'capitalist contradictions of polarization and surplus expropriation/appropriation' that causes underdeveloped countries to remain poor and underdeveloped. They are not just underdeveloped; they were made so by the international capitalist system.

Frank's work and overall thesis were the subject of intense debate and criticism including those on the left of the political spectrum (Laclau, 1971). Some within the Marxian tradition argued for an approach to development and underdevelopment that was more directly tied to the work of classical Marxists such as Lenin (Cardoso, 1972). Others such as Immanuel Wallerstein began to examine and theorize capitalism as a more unified complex world system. In the conclusion of his 1974 classic, *The Modern World System*, Wallerstein explained that 'capitalism as an economic mode is based on the fact that the economic factors operate within an arena larger than that which any political entity can totally control' (348). He goes on to note that the capitalist world system is 'one in which there is extensive division of labour' that is unevenly distributed and thus the economic benefits are unevenly distributed (349).

Conclusion

So, how are we to make sense of this world? We know that there are conflicting theoretical explanations and perspectives offering very different analyses of the role and relevance of the state and the nature of the world economy. First, perhaps the most prudent advice is to undertake still more study and research. There are empirical historical studies that might cast light on what is actually happening with regard to state policy and action. Why not begin to examine these for yourself? Second, sometimes positions become polarized and little or no attention is paid to the merits and strengths of the various viewpoints, and synthesis and development are given short shrift. Engage each of these theses and attempt to determine their value for your self-understanding. In short, carry on with your reading in this area. Undertake empirical research and try to figure out for yourself where you fit in the world economy and why.

Critical Thinking Questions

- How new is globalization?
- Is capitalism inherently global? Explain what might make it so?
- Explain the emergence of what we call the welfare state.
- Explain the decline of the welfare state during the latter part of the last century.
- Explain whether globalization and free trade are a threat to democracy or the logical extension of modernization and prosperity.

Terms and Concepts

Globalization—refers to the processes by which an international system of economic production has emerged. The chief actors are multi- or transnational corporations with production, finance, and distribution activities in many different nations and with production, finance, and distribution integrated across national borders. The contentious issues relate to the social, cultural, political, and economic implications of this.

Welfare state—an outcome of ideas associated with the political and economic response to the Great Depression of the 1930s. John Maynard Keynes and others argued that it was legitimate for the state to spend money during times when the aggregate demand for goods and services was insufficient to maintain economic stability. Such government spending, typically on public works and social infrastructure development, would provide a stimulus to the rest of the economy by creating demand for goods and services and thus increasing investment and employment. The post–Second World War era witnessed the development of many new government social programs to provide health care, education, unemployment insurance, social welfare and assistance, family allowances, pensions, and other forms of social security.

Neo-liberalism/Neo-conservatism—criticism of the welfare state came from those associated with what is called a neo-liberal or neo-conservative agenda. Joyce Green points out that these two descriptors refer to slightly different phenomena:

'Neoliberalism' is an ideology that advocates an economic arena free of government regulation or restriction, including labour and environmental legislation, and certainly, free of government action via public ownership. It advocates retreat from welfare's publicly funded commitments to equity and social justice. It views citizenship as consumption and economic production. This, not coincidentally, is compatible with and advances in tandem with 'neoconservatism', an ideology advocating a more hierarchical, patriarchal, authoritarian, and inequitable society. (1996: 112)

Related Web Sites

http://www.ifg.org/

According to the site the Forum is composed of 60 scholars and activists from diverse backgrounds, all of whom are concerned about the impacts of globalization. The Web site offers many links and much information.

http://globalization.about.com/mbody.htm

This is another site dedicated to globalization, but one that offers both pro- and anti-globalization links as well as links on the global media and global governance issues.

http://www.corpwatch.org

Typical of the issues that this site provides infor-

mation on are articles with titles such as 'Who Owns the WTO?', or 'A Citizen's Guide to the Globalization of Finance'. A great deal of information from an anti-globalization perspective is available.

http://www.wto.org/

The official Web site of the World Trade Organization offering, it goes without saying, the WTO's pro-free trade and pro-globalization perspectives. See also http://www.imf.org/, which is the official site of the International Monetary Fund, another arm of the pro-globalization forces.

Suggested Further Readings

Boyer, R., and D. Drache, eds. 1997. *States Against Markets*. London: Routledge. An impressive array of international scholars discuss theoretical, historical, and empirical issues about globalization, drawing on perspectives and data from across the globe.

Conway, J. 1984. *The West*. Toronto: Lorimer. This book presents a very readable account of the role that Western Canada has played in the development of Canada and the shaping of major debates about Canada's future.

Fowke, V. 2001. *The National Policy and the Wheat Economy*. Toronto: University of Toronto Press. No understanding of Canadian history is complete without reading this account of

Canadian history. Fowke explains how the project of industrialization via tariffs and the settlement of the West created many of Canada's key institutions.

Kapstein, E. 1996. *Governing the Global Economy: International Finance and the State*. Cambridge, MA: Harvard University Press. Kapstein examines the relationship of globalization to various international monetary and finance institutions over the post–Second World War period.

Mander, J., and E. Goldsmith. 1996. *The Case Against the Global Economy*. San Francisco: Sierra Club Books. Over 40 mostly short essays cover about every possible issue related to the globalization debate.

The Sociological Imagination and New Directions in Social Theory

Beyond the Existing Approaches

As sociology students first encounter basic sociological concepts and the different theoretical perspectives, two important questions often emerge. The first centres on what these abstract debates and discussions have to do with the development of the sociological imagination, that is, with the student's capacity to understand everyday social existence. The second question has to do with the fact that students often find themselves agreeing with key points from each perspective, and so they begin to ask if it is possible to synthesize the positions in order to arrive at a more adequate approach.

First, how does seemingly abstract social theory relate to our understanding of everyday social existence? Theory is an essential part of the scientific project: it is the basis of the intellectual process of explaining why and how things happen. Description and explanation are quite different. There are people, it is true, who are not interested in explaining and understanding their world and who are therefore not interested in theory. Sociologists, by definition, do not fall into this category because they have accepted the importance of attempting to understand and explain the social world. As a result of our commitment to the development of a sociological imagination, we accept the necessity of understanding and using social theory. We understand that without the study and use of theory we cannot fully understand our society or ourselves.

If we accept this argument—that understanding and using social theory are necessary parts of developing the promise of the sociological imagination—we must still confront the issue of which theory is most adequate or most appropriate. Because each of the major approaches undoubtedly has its strengths and weaknesses, we are not likely to accept any of them in its entirety. Perhaps it is possible to formulate an eclectic approach that adopts key elements of the major existing approaches.

Structuration Theory and an Alternative Framework

Over the past two decades some of the most innovative social theory has been developed in Europe and Britain. In France the work of Michael Foucault and Pierre Bourdieu has challenged many of the ideas presented in this book, while the British sociologist Anthony Giddens has developed a series of critiques of the existing sociological theories. The following comments attempt to outline how some of the insights of these thinkers might be incorporated into our attempts to construct a possible alternative framework suitable for the emerging century.

Agency and Structure
The central problem faced by any social theory is to explain the relationship between individuals and their society. As biological creatures with unique

physiological features—including our huge and complex brains and prehensile hands, for example—human beings have become active, conscious, intelligent, and social problem-solvers. Once we have solved a problem or met a need—accidentally or deliberately—we have the intellectual capacity to remember what we did, and then by using our communicative capacities we can pass this knowledge on to other individuals and future generations.

The social activities we develop and engage in as we attempt to solve our problems and meet our needs can be referred to as social practices. Whether it is the noun *practice* or the verb *practise*, we are referring to an action that is habitually performed. Taken together, these words suit the idea of human action, because it seems that once humans discover or develop a mode of conduct that solves a problem, we keep it. Our conduct becomes regularized, routinized, patterned, structured, and habitualized—in other words, institutionalized. When we say human practice becomes institutionalized, we mean it has developed into a structured and organized way of doing things.

In dealing with individual and species needs and problems we also develop stocks of knowledge and modes of understanding to explain 'how things work'. Such knowledge, ideas, belief systems, and consciousness become part of the social environment. An integral part of this knowledge has been the development of modes of communicating and of storing this knowledge, a process we commonly call the development of language. Significantly, all of these human practices occur in the context of a particular geographic location and a particular moment in history.

Human social structures, with their institutions, statuses, roles, value systems, groups, and so on, develop, then, as a result of humans acting socially to solve their individual and species needs, drives, and problems. Without doubt, human beings produce their social structures. Once these structures develop and emerge they in turn become the central determinant of subsequent behaviour. Giddens refers to the fact that we are simultaneously the product and producer of our social structures as the duality of structure (1984: Chapter 1).

Given the logic of the arguments presented thus far, none of this should be new or surprising; however the issue of if and how we incorporate these rather banal observations into a mode of social analysis remains to be completed. Before commenting on this it is useful to consider how we might use some concepts from the work of Pierre Bourdieu. Sociology was both an art and a craft for Bourdieu. He felt that as an art sociology brings to light what is hidden or disguised, while as a craft it requires skill and care. At its core, sociology is about critique—not just gathering information. The kind of critical thinking involved can make sociology an antidote for totalitarian forms of social organization. Thus sociology becomes about both understanding and exposing social, historical, economic, and political conditions and power struggles.

A key underlying intellectual project for Bourdieu was overcoming the individual/society or agent/structure duality. To offer an alternate, and more integrated, way of understanding our interconnectedness with society he popularized some new concepts: *habitus, field* and *practice*. I will try to explain these beginning with *habitus*.

Habitus refers to the basic stock of knowledge that people carry in their heads as a result of their social circumstances and experiences. It is an individual's disposition that impacts his or her understanding and preferences. Derek Layder, in *Understanding Social Theory,* explains: 'Thus habitus is a cognitive and motivating mechanism which incorporates influence of a person's social context and provides a conduit or medium through which information and resources are transmitted to the activities they inform' (156). Think about it as structural dispositions of thought and action, or mindsets, that have been socially acquired, shared, and associated with, among other things, one's class background.

For Bourdieu social practice is the actual form of the social activities that are grounded in or emerge from habitus. Our social practices are the totality of our activities! It is very much about the flow of our social lives. He uses an analogy of both playing a game and getting a feel for a game—the interaction with, learning from, and impacting on the environment in which we move. Your practice as a student is your presence and impact on your fellow students as you talk and ask questions.

Field is a concept we encountered in the discussion of institutions in Chapter 4. Field refers to the larger social environment in which social practice occurs. A field—usually inhabited by various groups—is the social space in which interaction occurs, as opposed to the typical notion of society as an overarching entity. Fields are socially structured spaces in which social practice, with all its complexities, conflicts, and dynamics, occurs.

We will look at one last concept—capital. The social actors who are characterized by their particular habitus and who engage in social practices across fields, do so in the possession of various forms of capital. Indeed the outcome of these social practices will be fundamentally determined by the nature of the capital's employ. Bourdieu's conception of capital is considerably broader than that employed in traditional Marxian analysis. For Bourdieu there are many forms of capital with the three main ones being economic, cultural, and social/symbolic.

Economic capital is the simplest form in that it is expressed through a variety of material resources such as money or the ownership of means of production. Economic capitals generate the capacity we call economic power. The second main type of capital is cultural, which has a variety of representations including art, education, language, and tastes. It is connected to dominant ideas about what is culturally valuable and can be manifest in the mastery of the dominant cultural practices of a given field. It is linked to, but not quite the same as, educational level, and its various iterations and definitions are subject to challenge, conflict, and struggle. Symbolic or social capital refers to the capacity of an agent to access authority, status, and social prestige (see Bourdieu and Wacquant, 1992).

For analytical purposes we can therefore understand the world of our everyday lives as one in which we engage in a wide range of social practices through which we, as humans, solve our various problems and address our needs. Since these practices can be understood as oriented to various objectives, in sociology we can analytically understand them as comprising fields that are organized into institutions and institutional orders. As we engage in the analysis of the relationships that comprise fields and institutions we must keep a simple fact in mind—an essential element of these human social relationships are relations, or circuits, of power. One of the most interesting refinements to traditional notions of power is found in the work of Michael Foucault (1997). Foucault argues that power is not some kind of force that people apply to each other, but instead it is something that operates in an omnipresent manner within society and human relations (29). Just as you cannot have a chain without its links, you cannot have human relations without some form of power. Power need not be malicious or conflictual, but it is ever-present in human social interactions. With these assumptions in mind we now need to consider the relationships between these clusters of actions.

Social Causation

Human society is an enormously complex phenomenon whose shape and character cannot be attributed to any single factor or process. It is clear, however, that the structure and organization of some human practices have a fundamental impact on the nature of the overall social structure. If human beings are to survive as individuals and as a species, we must deal with two basic problems. First, we must provide ourselves with the necessary material basis of our physical existence: food, clothing, and shelter. In addition, if we are to survive as a species we must reproduce in order to ensure that the present generation will not be the last. The future of any species is contingent on biological reproduction. The continuation of most of the activities we associate with being human—activities that might include art, philosophy, or even thinking about God—requires the species to ensure that its material needs are met and that the processes of biological reproduction are facilitated.

Besides being necessary for individual and species survival, these practices also seem to be central factors in influencing the general structures of the entire society. The organization of material production and biological reproduction has a profound impact on the entire range of institutionalized practices and structures that exist in a particular society. These key practices represent a kind of social basis, or core, around which other activities emerge and revolve.

Once again, the relationship between these practices and the larger social structure is complex. All institutions or fields of social practice in a social structure are part of a larger whole, and, as such, they are connected through a complicated reciprocal set of relationships. The practices we commonly associate with economic order, family, polity, religion, and educational order are each characterized by sets of particular habitus, ideas, stocks of knowledge, and ideologies. Each of them has its own internal structures, patterns of organization, and relationships with other institutional orders.

Both structural functionalism and neo-Marxist theory suggest that institutions are best understood in terms of their functions for either the society as a whole or the dominant class. The structural functionalist maintains that society has needs and problems that institutions function to solve. The neo-Marxist maintains that most institutions function in the economic interests of the dominant class. According to the alternative approach, institutions are better understood as emerging out of the social efforts of people to solve their individual and species problems across various fields of social

practice, employing various forms of capital. Society as a whole, as well as particular classes, may very well benefit from how institutions have come to be arranged, but this fact alone does not cause or explain the existence of institutions.

The alternative approach maintains that the point of departure for social analysis must be the organization of biological reproduction and material production. Used in this context, organization refers to the patterns of social relations taken up by human actors involved in the practice. In the case of production in a capitalist society, the organization of production refers to the class relations; and in the case of biological reproduction it refers to the relationships between the sexes. Included in the organization of social relations are the various stocks of knowledge, ideas, and ideologies that emerge as part of these activities which are always concretely located at a particular geographical location and at a particular moment in history.

The Limits of Abstract Theory

In the end, abstract theoretical discussions serve only a limited role in sociology because the final objective of the discipline is not to build abstract theoretical frameworks. When we study theory, it is always necessary to remember that the ultimate purpose of social theory is to explain a certain aspect of the real world. When it comes right down to it, sociologists are interested in the nature of the concrete, real social processes that occur in Canada, Australia, the United States, or some other specific society. Social analysis is about the emergence and development of social practices, processes, and structures that are by definition located firmly in time and space. It is about the habitus that characterize the various fields of practice, the power relations involved, and the forms of capital that characterize these fields. Social analysis is, in each and every case, about specific fields and societies, at specific moments in time. Thus all abstract theory can do is assist sociologists by guiding them in their investigations. Social theory can only suggest points of departure and establish priorities for what should be investigated.

This serves to raise the question of how the approach adopted here relates to concrete social analysis. And we must remember that individual sociologists may be interested in understanding any number of different societies at different points in time. A sociologist could be interested in understanding some aspect of classical Greek society, feudal Europe, England in the 1780s, France in 1850, or Canada in 2005. In each case, if the investigator were to follow what I've called the alternative approach, the point of departure would be an analysis of the fields of practice, habitia, forms of capital, and relations of power that characterized the organization's material production and biological reproduction and, in turn, the other fields in the social totality.

Point of departure is important. While understanding that the organization of material production and biological reproduction is a necessary condition for studying these societies, that understanding remains just that: a beginning point for sociological analysis. After explaining the workings of these aspects of the society, sociologists will still need to understand the nature of the larger social structure, including the polity, the role of religion, the manner by which culture is enhanced and transmitted (media, education), and the impact of geographical factors at a given historical moment.

Sociology is, after all, more than abstract deliberations on the nature of society. Sociology is more than the gathering of descriptive data about the social world. Sociology is the analysis and explanation of concrete and empirical social events. Sociological analysis and explanation become possible through the development of adequate theoretical guidelines, which provide the organizing principles necessary for making sense out of historical and empirical data.

One last issue that warrants particular comment relates to the possibility of developing a theory applicable to all societies in all places, at all times. Over the centuries, theorists have claimed to have found universal principles upon which an all-encompassing theory of society can be established. Although the approach being advocated here does make some claims—such as those relating to the necessity of humans producing and reproducing—which might seem like universal claims, it is clear that a transhistorical theory of human society is not a realistic or desirable goal.

To say that human beings must produce satisfaction for their material needs and engage in reproductive behaviour if they are to survive as individuals and as a species is not to make any claims about how these activities are organized or carried out. To argue that how material production and species reproduction are organized and structured has an impact on other dimensions of a social structure is not to make any claims about the precise nature of that impact. As we know, material production and species reproduction have been organized in a multitude of different ways over the span of human history, and no theoretical approach could possibly address them all. What we may require are, in fact, a multitude of quite specific theories addressing, for example, the structures of Greek society, feudal society, early capitalist society, liberal democratic society, and so on. In each case the task of sociologists is to study how material production and biological reproduction are organized and structured, and to consider what ideas and stocks of knowledge have emerged as a part of this process. How do these practices relate to each other and the surrounding institutional orders that characterize the society at a certain moment in time?

This book is written for those who live in a capitalist society. To understand a capitalist society we should begin by looking to those who have attempted to understand and explain material production in capitalist societies. The works of Durkheim, Marx, and Weber are obviously of interest. But sociologists must also direct their attention to the processes of biological reproduction and examine the efforts of social thinkers to understand those processes. In doing this, the work of feminist scholars is essential.

The scope of our investigation will become even more focused as we realize that our social analysis is not just with material production in general, but with material production in Canada. We are not simply interested in species reproduction in the late twentieth century, but with reproductive relations in Canada in 2005 and beyond. The specification of our precise research agenda makes our task more difficult and easier at the same time. It is more difficult because we must deal with the complexities and intricacies of the institutional orders and specific institutions that make up twenty-first century Canada. It is easier because we are dealing with concrete historical and empirical processes that we can actually come to know and that can be invaluable in determining the adequacy of our theoretical thinking.

As sociology moves forward into another century, new and innovative modes of theorizing will be required. There is good reason to think that an adequate approach must build on the insights of the materialist and feminist approaches. The materialist claim that the manner by which humans produce satisfaction for their material problems has a significant impact on the rest of society is compelling. The insights of feminist theory are even more forceful since we must consider the relationship between men and women to be a basic element of all our theoretical thinking. These considerations—of sex and gender relations—should never be simply treated as secondary or as issues that can be somehow 'added on'.

The Postmodernist Critique

In Chapter 1 we noted that the core ideas of both the Enlightenment and scientific models of knowledge production that emerged along with modern capitalism included notions such as that of a link between knowledge and progress and the possibility of producing objective knowledge of an objective world. Western science also assumed that it was possible to produce universal holistic knowledge that is based on rational shared premises and agreed upon procedures that are independent of the values and social status of the producer. As we have seen, this era—commonly referred to as the modern era—produced the major theoretical frameworks that have defined many of the major directions for sociological and other social scientific analysis and inquiry. This is the era that produced Marx, Weber, and Durkheim and those latter-day thinkers who revised the ideas and frameworks of these founders. Whatever their disagreements, the intellectuals who were producing these major theoretical frameworks agreed on some common ground rules, the most important one being that science was a legitimate undertaking that, when conducted properly, could yield objective knowledge that had the status of truth.

We have already seen how and why feminism and feminist scholars challenged the adequacy of the theoretical frameworks developed largely by men. These approaches were found to be either sex- and gender-blind—that is, they ignored issues related to sex and gender—or they were actually sexist. The historical period during which the Second Wave of feminism emerged was also an era of changing population patterns across the entire globe. The processes of immigration, emigration, and migration changed the nature of the population of every nation and society on Earth. As a result, societies became more diverse and complex in terms of the ethnic, religious, cultural, and national characteristics of their populations. The latter part of the twentieth century also witnessed the emergence of a series of new social and political movements and public concerns relating to issues such as the environment, world peace, international justice, national liberation, gay and lesbian rights, and global hunger, to name a few. The explanatory and analytical capacity of existing social theory became an issue for some scholars. A related but somewhat different issue was the extent to which the very success of

Enlightenment itself had produced social structures, institutions, beliefs, and practices that were beginning to undermine the possibilities of progress and greater human freedom. We have seen that Marx, Weber, and Durkheim, each in his own way, raised concerns about the nature of the new social order that had emerged. By 1959, when he wrote *The Sociological Imagination*, C. Wright Mills was openly declaring that the world was in a transitional era. He wrote: 'We are at the ending of what is called The Modern Age' (1959: 195). Mills was not sure what the next epoch would be called but he initially referred to it as 'a postmodern period' (166).

Sociology was not the only discipline that faced critical questions regarding the heuristic effectiveness of the existing approaches. In many fields of human endeavour, from art to architecture, from literature to literary criticism, from philosophy to popular culture, scholars began to pronounce the end of grand theory, the eclipse of what were termed totalizing theories and the replacement of the grand narrative with the particular, the specific, and the local. As it turns out, the term *postmodern* that C. Wright Mills used back in 1959 became a watchword of the late twentieth century. By very definition, the concept of postmodernity defies definition. Derek Layder, however, provides a summary of what he terms the three dimensions of postmodernism. According to Layder, postmodernism refers in part to a distinctive new form of society characterized by an advanced level of urbanization, technological development, and knowledge (1994: 50). To this I would add it is complex and diverse to the point of fragmentation and lacking widely accepted integrating value or normative orientations.

Layder points out that postmodernism can also refer to the type of social analysis required to even attempt an understanding of such a society. Such an analysis cannot be predicated on a grant or meta-theory claiming to provide the basis for a scientific objective analysis. Postmodern social analysis will focus on the diverse particular voices and perspectives that emerge out of a complex fragmented

social world and it will remind us that none of them is necessarily privileged with a monopoly on the truth. Knowledge is contingent, limited, partial, and incomplete. Indeed, there is and must be, a plurality of possible knowledges concerning any issue in the world because there is a plurality of perspectives from which the world is experienced.

The final use that Layder identifies with the concept of postmodern relates to what he terms *cultural style*, particularly as related to art and architecture (51). Following from the theme of there being multiple potential perspectives and different bases for knowing about something, there are multiple styles, approaches and genres of art, literature, and other forms of human creativity. We have seen a form of postmodern thought in our discussion of feminist theory when we noted that what we called the Third Wave and its critique of Second Wave feminism was too closely tied to one model of knowing and one voice.

Without fully endorsing Neil Postman's view that those adopting these modes of thought 'keep confusion at bay by writing books in which they tell us that there is nothing to write books about' (1999: 10), it is necessary to be as critical of the postmodernist turn as of established scholarship and thought. Surely it is important to be critical of grand theories that purport to explain everything, and to recognize that our world is extremely complex and diverse. However, such recognition need not preclude the use of theoretical schemas and frameworks to organize and make sense out of our daily interactions, observations, and experiences.

The Sociological Imagination Revisited

The famous dictum of Socrates that 'the unexamined life is not worth living' should remind us of what it means to be a human being, rather than just another animal. My cat and dog are incapable of examining their lives, and as a result they just seem to live from day to day, no doubt enjoying their life, but nevertheless without appreciating and understanding what their existence means. It seems they are not particularly concerned about behaving in a way that will help them leave the world a better place than they found it, or at least temporarily altered. All of this raises a question: is there anything wrong with just existing and enjoying life? Perhaps not, especially if it is all a given species is capable of. In the case of humans, however, merely existing is not at all close to what we are capable of.

Given the enormous and incredible potential and possibilities that each and every human is endowed with, isn't it a waste and a pity if we do not strive to develop that potential and thus attempt to improve and better our condition and that of the entire species? Isn't it a waste and a pity if we don't examine life, analyze it, and think about it with an eye to improving the human condition—for the sake of both ourselves as individuals and our species as a whole? C.W. Mills thought it was, and that is why he advised us to seek an understanding not only ourselves, our lives, and our biographies, but also others, their lives, and their biographies. In a fundamental way Mills, like Socrates, was telling us something about what it means to be human.

But how do we begin to examine and analyze our lives and biographies? Again, Mills provides some answers. He says that to understand ourselves we must be capable of answering questions that draw our attention to the impact of the social environment on ourselves and others. Further, he notes, we must be capable of understanding how our society is structured and how it operates. Lastly, we must know something about the processes by which that society has developed and is developing. This introduction to sociology, I hope, provides some initial concepts, arguments, perspectives, and tools that will allow readers to begin to ask and to answer these questions.

It is impossible to develop the capacity we are calling the sociological imagination by taking one university or college course or by reading one book. Indeed, such a capacity takes at least a lifetime to develop—and most likely will never be entirely satisfied. But we must begin sometime, and there is no time like the present. I hope the studies you are undertaking—and this book—will whet your appetite for more systematic and comprehensive sociological analysis; and I hope they will provide some of the tools you need to begin the process of undertaking such an analysis.

References

Abercrombie, Nicholas, Stephen Hill, and Bryan S. Turner. 1988. *The Penguin Dictionary of Sociology*, 2nd edn. London: Penguin Books.

Aberle, D.F., A.K. Cohen, A.K. Davis, M.J. Levy, Jr., and F.S. Sutton. 1967. 'The Functional Prerequisites of a Society' in N.J. Demerath and R.A. Peterson, eds, *System, Change and Conflict*. New York: The Free Press.

Abraham, Carolyn. 2001. 'The Brain Is a Sex Organ', *Globe and Mail*, 24 November, F1 and F8.

Abrahamson, Mark. 1978. *Functionalism*. Englewood Cliffs, NJ: Prentice-Hall.

Adie, Nelson, and Barrie W. Robinson. 2002. *Gender in Canada*. Toronto: Prentice-Hall.

Akers, Ronald. 2000. *Criminological Theories*. Los Angeles: Roxbury.

Albrow, Martin. 1997. *The Global Age*. Stanford, CA: Stanford University Press.

Alexander, Jeffery and Paul Colomy. 1990. 'Neofunctionalism Today: Reconstructing a Theoretical Tradition' in George Ritzer, ed, *Frontiers of Social Theory: A New Synthesis*. New York: Columbia University Press.

Alleman, Ted. 1993. 'Varieties of Feminist Thought and Their Application to Crime and Criminal Justice' in Roslyn Muraskin and Ted Alleman, *It's a Crime: Women and Justice*. Englewood Cliffs, NJ: Prentice-Hall.

Anderson, Charles H. 1974. *The Political Economy of Social Class*. Englewood Cliffs, NJ: Prentice-Hall.

Anderson, Craig A., and Karen E. Dill. 2000. 'Video Games and Aggressive Thoughts, Feelings, and Behavior in the Laboratory and in Life', *Journal of Personality and Social Psychology*, 78 (4). Available at: http://www.apa.org/journals/psp/psp784772.html.

Anderson, Karen L., Hugh Armstrong, Pat Armstrong, Janice Drakich, Margrit Eichler, Connie Guberman, Alison Hayford, Meg Luxton, John F. Peters, Elaine Porter, C. James Richardson, and Geoffrey Tesson. 1988. *Family Matters: Sociology and Contemporary Canadian Families*. Toronto: Nelson Canada.

Andreski, Stanislav, ed. 1974. *The Essential Comte: Selected from Cours de philosophie positive*. New York: Barnes and Noble.

Angier, Natalie. 2000. 'Race Is an Unscientific Concept, Experts Say', *New York Times*, 30 August.

APA Online. 'Violence in the Media – Psychologists help protect children from harmful effects'. Available at http://www.psychologymatters.org/mediaviolence.html.

Ardrey, Robert. 1961. *African Genesis*. New York: Atheneum.

———. 1969. *The Territorial Imperative*. New York: Atheneum.

Aristotle. 1969. *Politics*, in William Ebenstein, *Great Political Thinkers*. New York: Holt, Rinehart and Winston.

Armstrong, Pat. 1984. *Labour Pains: Women's Work in Crisis*. Toronto: Women's Press.

———. 1984. *The Double Ghetto: Canadian Women and Their Segregated Work*, rev. edn. Toronto: McClelland & Stewart.

———. 1990. *Theorizing Women's Work*. Toronto: Garamond Press.

———. 1996. 'Unraveling the Safety Net: Transformations in Health Care and Their Impact on Women' in Janine Brodie, ed, *Women and Canadian Public Policy*. Toronto: Harcourt Brace.

———, and Hugh Armstrong. 1983. 'Beyond Sexless Class and Classless Sex', *Studies in Political Economy* 10 (Winter).

Aron, Raymond. 1966. 'Social Class, Political Class, Ruling Class' in Rinehard Bendix and Seymour Martin Lipset, eds, *Class, Status, and Power*. New York: The Free Press.

Baker, John R. *Race*. 1974. New York: Oxford University Press.

Baldwin, John D. 1986. George *Herbert Mead: A Unifying Theory for Sociology*. Beverly Hills, CA: Sage Publications.

Banks, Marcus. 1996. *Ethnicity: Anthropological Constructions*. London: Routledge.

Banton, Michael. 1987. *Racial Theories*. Cambridge, UK: Cambridge University Press.

———. 1997. *Ethnic and Racial Consciousness*. London: Longman.

———, and Jonathan Harwood. 1975. *The Race Concept*. New York: Praeger.

Baran, Paul A., and Paul M. Sweezy. 1966. *Monopoly Capital*. New York: Monthly Review Press.

Baran, Stanley. 1999. *Introduction to Mass Communication: Media Literacy and Culture*. Mountain View, CL: Mayfield Publishing Company.

Barber, Bernard. 1957. *Social Stratification: A Comparative Analysis of Structure and Process*. New York: Harcourt Brace.

Barnes, Harry Elmer. 1965. *An Intellectual and Cultural History of the Western World*. New York: Dover Publications.

Barnouw, Erik. 1982. *Tube of Plenty: The Evolution of American Television*. New York: Oxford University Press.

Barrett, Michèle. 1980. *Women's Oppression Today: Problems in Marxist Feminist Analysis*. London: Verso.

Bashevkin, Sylvia. 2000. 'Rethinking Retrenchment: North American Social Policy during the Early Clinton and Chrétien Years', *Canadian Journal of Political Science* 33 (March).

Becker, Howard S. 1963. *Outsiders*. New York: The Free Press.

———, and Blanche Geer. 1980. 'The Fate of Idealism in Medical School' in Joel Charon, ed., *The Meaning of Sociology: A Reader*. Sherman Oaks, CA: Alfred.

Bedford, David, and Danielle Irving. 2001. *The Tragedy of Progress*. Halifax: Fernwood.

Behiels, Michael, ed. 1987. *Quebec Since 1945*. Toronto: Longman.

Bem, Sandra L., and Daryl Bem. 1982. 'Homogenizing the American Woman: The Power of an Unconscious Ideology' in Leonard Cargan and Jeanne H. Ballantine, eds, *Sociological Footprints*. Belmont, CA: Wadsworth.

Bendix, Rinehard, and Seymour Martin Lipset, eds. 1966. *Class, Status, and Power: Social Stratification in Comparative Perspective*, 2nd edn. New York: The Free Press.

Benedict, Ruth. 1934. *Patterns of Culture*. New York: Mentor Books.

Benston, Margaret. 1978. 'The Political Economy of Women's Liberation' in Alison M. Jaggar and Paula S. Rothenberg, eds, *Feminist Frameworks*. New York: McGraw-Hill.

Berger, Peter. 1963. *Invitation to Sociology: A Humanistic Perspective*. Garden City, NY: Anchor Books.

———. 1969. *The Sacred Canopy: Elements of a Sociological Theory of Religion*. Doubleday: New York.

———, and Thomas Luckmann. 1967. *The Social Construction of Reality*. Garden City, NY: Anchor Books.

Bilton, Tony, Kevin Bonnett, Philip Jones, Michelle Standworth, Ken Sheard, and Andrew Webster. 1987. *Introductory Sociology*, 2nd edn. London: Macmillan.

Blackburn, Daniel. 2000. 'Why Race Is Not a Biological Concept' in Berel Lang, *Race and Racism in Theory and Practice*. Lanham, MI: Rowman & Littlefield.

Blau, Peter, and Richard C. Scott. 1963. *Formal Organizations: A Comparative Approach*. San Francisco: Chandler.

Blishen, Bernard. 1967. 'A Socio-Economic Index for Occupation', *Canadian Review of Sociology and Anthropology* 4 (1).

Block, Ned. 1996. 'How Heritability Misleads about Race', *The Boston Review* 20 (6) (January).

Blumer, Herbert. 1969. *Symbolic Interactionism: Perspective and Method*. Englewood Cliffs, NJ: Prentice-Hall.

———. 1978. 'Society as Symbolic Interaction' in Alan Wells, ed, *Contemporary Sociological Theory*. Santa Monica, CA: Goodyear.

Bolaria, Singh, and Peter S. Li. 1988. *Racial Oppression in Canada*. Toronto: Garamond Press.

Bourdieu, Pierre, and Loic Wacquant. 1992. *An Invitation to a Reflexive Sociology*. Chicago: University of Chicago Press.

Bourricaud, François. 1981. *The Sociology of Talcott Parsons*. Chicago: University of Chicago Press.

Boyer, Robert. 1996. 'State and Market: A New Engagement for the Twenty-First Century' in Robert Boyer and Daniel Drache, eds, *States against Markets: The Limits of Globalization*. London: Routledge.

———, and Daniel Drache, eds. 1996. *States against Markets: The Limits of Globalization*. London: Routledge.

Boyle, Harry. 1983. 'The Media Controls Institution in Canada and the United States Compared' in Benjamin Singer, ed, *Communications in Canadian Society*. Don Mills: Addison-Wesley Publishers.

Bredemeier, Harry C., and Richard M. Stephenson. 1962. *The Analysis of Social Systems*. New York: Holt, Rinehart and Winston.

Brodie, Janine. 1996a. 'New State Forms, New Political Spaces' in Robert Boyer and Daniel Drache, eds, *States against Markets: The Limits of Globalization*. London: Routledge.

———, ed. 1996b. *Women and Canadian Public Policy*. Toronto: Harcourt Brace.

Brown, Laura Kimberley. 1996. 'Canada, Globalization and

Free Trade: The Past Is New' in Raymond-M. Hebert, ed, *Re(Defining) Canada: A Prospective Look at our Country in the 21st Century.* Winnipeg: Presses universitaires de Saint-Boniface.

Brym, Robert. 1993. 'The Canadian Capitalist Class' in James Curtis, Edward Grabb, Neil Guppy, and Sid Gilbert, eds, *Social Inequality in Canada.* Scarborough, ON: Prentice-Hall.

Burstyn, Varda. 1985. 'Masculine Dominance and the State' in Varda Burstyn and Dorothy Smith, *Women, Class, Family and the State.* Toronto: Garamond Press.

Burt, Sandra, Lorraine Code, and Lindsay Dorney. 1993. *Changing Patterns: Women in Canada*, 2nd edn. Toronto: McClelland & Stewart.

Calzavara, Liviana. 1988. 'Trends and Policy in Employment Opportunities for Women,' in James Curtis, Edward Grabb, Neil Guppy, and Sid Gilbert, eds, *Social Inequality in Canada.* Scarborough, ON: Prentice-Hall.

'Canadian Diversity: Respecting our Differences', Canadian Heritage Department. Available at: http://www.pch.gc.ca.

Canadian Global Almanac: A Book of Facts. 1992. Toronto: Global Press.

Caplan, Arthur L., ed. 1978. *The Sociobiology Debate: Readings on Ethical and Scientific Issues.* New York: Harper & Row.

Caplan, Paula J., and Jeremy B. Caplan. 1994. *Thinking Critically About Research on Sex and Gender.* New York: HarperCollins.

Cardoso, Fernando. 1972. 'Dependency and Development in Latin America', *New Left Review* 74 (July/August).

Cargan, Leonard, and Jeanne H. Ballantine. 1982. *Sociological Footprints: Introductory Readings in Sociology.* Belmont, CA: Wadsworth.

Carlen, Pat. 1985. *Criminal Women.* Cambridge, UK: Polity Press.

Carnoy, Martin. 1984. *The State and Political Theory.* Princeton, NJ: Princeton University Press.

Carroll, William. 1982. 'The Canadian Corporate Elite: Financiers or Finance Capitalists?', *Studies in Political Economy* 8.

———, Linda Christiansen-Ruffman, Raymond Currie, and Deborah Harrison, eds. 1992. *Fragile Truths: Twenty-five Years of Sociology and Anthropology in Canada.* Ottawa: Carleton University Press.

Case, James, and Vernon Stiers. 1971. *Biology.* New York: Macmillan.

Cassirer, Ernst. [1944] 1977. 'A Clue to the Nature of Man: The Symbol' in Dennis H. Wrong and Harry L. Gracey, eds, *Readings in Introductory Sociology.* New York: Macmillan.

Ceci, Stephen. 1999. 'Schooling and Intelligence' in Stephen Ceci and Wendy Williams, eds, *The Nature-Nurture Debate: The Essential Readings.* Oxford: Blackwell.

———, and Wendy Williams, eds. 1999. *The Nature-Nurture Debate: The Essential Readings.* Oxford: Blackwell.

Cernovsky, Zack. 1990. 'Race and Brain Weight: A Note on J.P. Rushton's Conclusions', *Psychological Reports* 66.

Chambliss, William. [1973] 1999. 'The Saints and the Roughnecks' in Joel Charon, ed, *The Meaning of Sociology.* Upper Saddle River, NJ: Prentice-Hall.

Charon, Joel M. 1979. *Symbolic Interactionism.* Englewood Cliffs, NJ: Prentice-Hall.

Chesney-Lind, Meda. 1995. 'Preface' in Nicole Hahn Rafter and Frances Heidensohn, eds, *International Perspectives in Feminist Criminology.* Buckingham: Open University Press.

Chomsky, Noam. 1989. *Necessary Illusions.* Montreal: CBC Enterprises.

Clark, Ann, and Alan Clarke. 1999. 'Early Experience and the Life Path' in Stephen Ceci and Wendy Williams, eds, *The Nature-Nurture Debate: The Essential Readings.* Oxford: Blackwell.

Clark, William, and Michael Grunstein. 2000. *Are We Hardwired? The Role of Genes in Human Behaviour.* New York: Oxford University Press.

Clegg, Stewart, Paul Boreham, and Geoff Dow. 1986. *Class, Politics and the Economy.* London: Routledge & Kegan Paul.

Clement, Wallace. 1975. *The Canadian Corporate Elite: An Analysis of Economic Power.* Toronto: McClelland & Stewart.

———. 1977. *Continental Corporate Power.* Toronto: McClelland & Stewart.

———. 1988. *The Challenge of Class Analysis.* Ottawa: Carleton University Press.

Clough, Shepard Bancroft, and Charles Woolsey Cole. 1967. *Economic History of Europe.* Boston: DC Heath.

Cohen, Albert. 1959. 'The Study of Social Disorganization and Deviant Behavior' in Robert K. Merton, ed, *Sociology Today.* New York: Basic Books.

Cohen, Bruce J., and Terri L. Orbuch. 1990. *Introduction to Sociology.* New York: McGraw-Hill.

Cohen, Percy. 1973. *Modern Social Theory.* London: Heinemann.

Collins, Randall. 1975. *Conflict Sociology.* New York: Academic Press. [Reprinted with permission from Elsevier.]

Comack, Elizabeth, ed. 1999. *Locating Law.* Halifax: Fernwood.

Comte, Auguste. 1853. *The Positive Philosophy.* New York: D. Appleton.

Connell, R.W. 1987. *Gender and Power.* Sydney: Allen & Unwin.

———. 1990. 'The State, Gender and Sexual Politics', *Theory and Society* 19.

———. 1995. *Masculinities*. Berkeley, CA: University of California Press.

Connelly, M. Patricia, and Pat Armstrong, eds. 1992. *Feminism in Action: Studies in Political Economy*. Toronto: Canadian Scholars Press.

Conway, John. 1993. *The Canadian Family in Crisis*. Toronto: James Lorimer.

———. 1997. *Debts to Pay*. Toronto: James Lorimer.

Cook, Joan Marble. 1975. *In Defense of Homo Sapiens*. New York: Dell.

Coole, Diana H. 1988. *Women in Political Theory: From Ancient Misogyny to Contemporary Feminism*. Hampstead, UK: Harvester Wheatsheaf/Lynne Rienner.

Cooley, Charles H. [1909] 1956. *Social Organization: A Study of the Larger Mind*. Glencoe, IL: The Free Press.

———. [1922] 1956. *Human Nature and the Social Order*. Glencoe, IL: The Free Press.

Coser, Lewis. 1956. *The Functions of Social Conflict*. New York: The Free Press.

———. 1977. *Masters of Sociological Thought: Ideas in Historical and Social Context*, 2nd edn. New York: Harcourt Brace Jovanovich.

Courchene, Thomas J. 1996. 'Globalization, Free Trade and the Canadian Political Economy' in Raymond-M. Hebert, ed, *Re(Defining) Canada: A Prospective Look at Our Country in the 21st Century*. Winnipeg: Presses Universitaires de Saint-Boniface.

Cowan, Philip A. 1978. *Piaget: With Feeling*. New York: Holt, Rinehart and Winston.

Creedon, Pamela. 1989. *Women in Mass Communications: Challenging Gender Values*. Newbury Park: Sage Publications.

Crider, Andrew, George Goethals, Robert Kavanaugh, and Paul R. Solomon. 1989. *Psychology*, 3rd edn. Glenview, CA: Scott, Foresman.

Cuneo, Carl J. 1985. 'Have Women Become More Proletarianized Than Men?', *Canadian Review of Sociology and Anthropology* 22 (4).

Curtis, James E., and William G. Scott, eds. 1979. *Social Stratification: Canada*. Scarborough, ON: Prentice-Hall.

———, Edward Grabb, Neil Guppy, and Sid Gilbert, eds. 1988. *Social Inequality in Canada: Patterns, Problems, Policies*. Scarborough, ON: Prentice-Hall.

Curtiss, Susan. 1977. *Genie: A Psycholinguistic Study of a Modern-day Wild Child*. New York: Academic Press.

Dahlie, Jorgan, and Tissa Fernando. 1981. *Ethnicity, Power and Politics in Canada*. Toronto: Methuen.

Dahl, Robert. 1967. *Pluralist Democracy in the United States*. Chicago: Rand McNally.

———. 1990. *After the Revolution? Authority in the Good Society*. New Haven: Yale University Press.

———. 1998. *On Democracy*. New Haven: Yale University Press.

Dalla Costa, Mariarosa. 1972. 'Women and the Subservience of Community' in Mariarosa Dalla Costa and Selma James, eds, *The Power of Women and the Subservience of Community*. Bristol, UK: Falling Wall Press.

Daly, Kathleen, and Lisa Maher. 1998. *Criminology at the Crossroads*. New York: Oxford University Press.

Davis, Kingsley. 1949. 'Final Note on a Case of Extreme Isolation' in Logan Wilson and William Kolb, eds, *Sociological Analysis*. New York: The Free Press.

———. [1953] 1974. 'Reply to Tumin' in Joseph Lopreato and Lionel S. Lewis, eds, *Social Stratification*. New York: Harper & Row.

———, and Wilbert E. Moore. 1945. 'Some Principles of Stratification', *American Sociological Review* 10 (2).

Demerath, N.J., and R.A. Peterson, eds. 1967. *System, Change and Conflict*. New York: The Free Press.

Dickinson, James, and Bob Russell, eds. 1986. *Family, Economy and the State: The Social Reproduction Process under Capitalism*. Toronto: Garamond Press.

Djao, Angela Wei. 1983. *Inequality and Social Policy: The Sociology of Welfare*. Toronto: John Wiley.

Dobriner, William M. 1969. *Social Structures and Systems: A Sociological Overview*. Pacific Palisades, CA: Goodyear.

Doniger, Wendy. 1998. 'What Did They Name the Dog?', *London Review of Books* 20 (6) (19 March).

Donovan, Josephine. 1992. *Feminist Theory: The Intellectual Traditions of American Feminism*. New York: Frederick Ungar/Continuum.

Dover, Gabriel. 2000. 'Anti-Dawkins' in Hilary Rose and Steven Rose, eds, *Alas Poor Darwin*. New York: Harmony Books.

Driedger, Leo. 1978. *The Canadian Ethnic Mosaic*. Toronto: McClelland & Stewart.

———. 1989. *The Ethnic Factor*. Toronto: McGraw-Hill.

Duffy, Ann. 1988. 'Struggling with Power: Feminist Critiques of Family Inequality' in Nancy Mandell and Ann Duffy, eds, *Reconstructing the Canadian Family: Feminist Perspectives*. Toronto: Butterworths.

Durkheim, Emile. [1895] 1964. *The Rules of Sociological Method*. New York: The Free Press.

———. [1897] 1995. *Suicide: A Study in Sociology*. New York: The Free Press.

———. 1933. *The Division of Labour in Society*. New York: The Free Press.

Ehrlich, Paul. 2000. 'The Tangled Skeins of Nature and Nurture in Human Evolution', *The Chronicle of Higher Education* (22 September).

Eisenberg, Avigail. 1995. *Reconstructing Political Pluralism*. New York: State University Press of New York.

Eisenstein, Zillah. 1981. *The Radical Future of Liberal Feminism*. Boston: Northeastern University Press.

Elliot, Patricia, and Nancy Mandell. 1995. 'Feminist Theories' in Nancy Mandell, ed., *Feminist Issues: Race Class and Sexuality*. Scarborough, ON: Prentice-Hall.

Elshtain, Jean B., ed. 1982. *The Family in Political Thought*. Amherst: University of Massachusetts Press.

Endleman, Robert. 1977. 'Reflections on the Human Revolution' in Dennis Wrong and Harry Gracey, eds, *Readings in Introductory Sociology*. New York: Macmillan.

Engels, F. [1884] 1972. *Origin of the Family, Private Property and the State*. Moscow: Progress.

Enriques, Elizabeth. 2000. 'Feminisms and Feminist Criticism: an overview of feminist strategies for reconstructing knowledge', Originally in *Women in Action*. Available at: http://www.isiswomen.org/wia/wia100/com00014.html.

Epstein, Cynthia Fuchs. 1988. *Deceptive Distinctions: Sex, Gender, and the Social Order*. New Haven: Yale University Press.

Ericsson, K. Anders, and Neil Charness. 1999. 'Expert Performance: Its Structure and Acquisition' in Stephen Ceci and Wendy Williams, eds. *The Nature-Nurture Debate: The Essential Readings*. Oxford: Blackwell.

Eriksen, Thomas. 1993. *Ethnicity and Nationalism: Anthropological Persectives*. London: Pluto Press.

———. 1997. 'Ethnicity, Race and Nation' in Montserrat Guibernau and John Rex, eds, *The Ethnicity Reader*. Cambridge, UK: Polity Press.

Eshleman, J. Ross. 1975. *The Family: An Introduction*. Boston: Allyn & Bacon.

Farber, Susan. 1981a. *Identical Twins Reared Apart: A Reanalysis*. New York: Basic Books

———. 1981b. 'Telltale Behaviours of Twins', *Psychology Today* 15 (1) (January).

Fausto-Sterling, Anne. 1985. *Myths of Gender: Biological Theories about Women and Men*. New York: Basic Books.

———. 2000. *Sexing the Body*. New York: Basic Books.

Femiano, Sam, and Mark Nickerson. 2002. 'How do Media Images of Men Affect Our Lives?: Re-Imagining the American Dream', Center for Media Literacy. Available at: http://www.medialit.org/reading_room/article39.html#bio.

Fine, Ben. 1983. 'Contradiction' in Tom Bottomore, ed, *A Dictionary of Marxist Thought*. Cambridge, MA: Harvard University Press.

Firestone, Shulamith. 1970. *The Dialectic of Sex: The Case for a Feminist Revolution*. New York: William Morrow.

Fleras, Augie, and Jean Leonard Elliott. 1999. *Unequal Relations*. Scarborough, ON: Prentice-Hall and Allyn & Bacon.

Forcese, Dennis. 1975. *The Canadian Class Structure*, 3rd edn. Toronto: McGraw-Hill Ryerson.

———. 1997. *The Canadian Class Structure*, 4th edn. Toronto: McGraw-Hill Ryerson.

Foucault, Michael. 1997. *Society Must be Defended*. New York: Picador.

Fowke, Venon. 1957. *The National Policy and the Wheat Economy*. Toronto: University of Toronto Press.

Frager, Robert, and James Fadiman. 1984. *Personality and Personal Growth*, 2nd edn. New York: Harper & Row.

Frank, Andre Gunder. 1969. *Capitalism and Underdevelopment in Latin America*. New York: Monthly Review Press.

———. 1970. 'The Development of Underdevelopment' in Robert Rhodes, ed, *Imperialism and Underdevelopment*. New York: Monthly Review Press.

———. 1976. 'Feudalism and Capitalism in Latin America', *New Left Review* 67 (May/June).

Fraser, Steven, ed. 1995. *The Bell Curve Wars*. New York: Basic Books.

Freud, Sigmund. [1920] 1955. *Beyond the Pleasure Principle. In The Standard Edition*, vol. 18. London: Hogarth Press.

———. [1924] 1970. *A General Introduction to Psychoanalysis*. New York: Pocket Books.

———. [1930] 1982. *Civilization and Its Discontents*. London: Hogarth Press.

———. [1933] 1965. *New Introductory Lectures on Psychoanalysis*. New York: W.W. Norton.

Frideres, James. 1993. *Native Peoples in Canada*. Toronto: Prentice-Hall.

Frisby, David, and Derek Sayer. 1986. *Society*. New York: Tavistock.

Fudge, Judy, and Harry Glasbeek. 1997. 'A Challenge to the Inevitability of Globalization: The Logic of Repositioning the State as the Terrain of Contest' in Jay Drydyk and Peter Penz, eds, *Global Justice, Global Democracy*. Winnipeg/Halifax: Society for Socialist Studies/Fernwood.

Gable, Sara, and Melissa Hunting. 2000. 'Nature, Nurture and Early Brain Development', *Human Environmental Sciences* (31 January).

Gabor, Thomas, and Julian Roberts. 1990. 'Rushton on Race and Crime: The Evidence Remains Unconvincing', *Canadian Journal of Criminology* (April).

Gagnon, Alain, ed. 1984. *Quebec: State and Society*. Toronto: Methuen.

Gallagher, Margaret. 2001. *Gender Setting: New Agendas for Media Monitoring and Advocacy*. London: ZED Books and WACC.

Galloway, Gloria. 2003. 'Too much TV impairs reading, study suggests', *Globe and Mail*, 29 October.

Gamble, Michael, and Teri Kwal Gamble. 1968. *Introducing Mass Communications*. New York: McGraw Hill Book Company.

Gandy, D. Ross. 1979. *Marx and History: From Primitive*

Society to the Communist Future. Austin: University of Texas Press.

Gannage, Charlene. 1987. 'A World of Difference: The Case of Women Workers in a Canadian Garment Factory' in Heather Jon Maroney and Meg Luxton, eds, *Feminism and Political Economy.* Toronto: Methuen.

Gans, Herbert. 1980. *Deciding What's News: A Study of CBS Evening News, NBC Nightly News, Newsweek, and Time.* New York: Vintage Books.

Gardner, Howard. 1995. 'Cracking Open the IQ Box' in Steven Fraser, ed, *The Bell Curve Wars.* New York: Basic Books.

———. 1997. 'Thinking about Thinking', *New York Review of Books,* 9 October.

Gauntlett, David. 'Ten Things Wrong with the "effects" model', Available at: http://www.theory.org.uk/effects.htm.

Gay, Peter. 1988. *Freud: A Life For Our Times.* New York: Anchor Books/Doubleday.

Gelsthorpe, Loraine, and Allison Morris. 1990. *Feminist Perspectives in Criminology.* Philadelphia: Open University Press.

Gerth, Hans, and C. Wright Mills. 1964. *Character and Social Structure: The Psychology of Social Institutions.* New York: Harcourt Brace.

Giddens, Anthony. 1979. *Central Problems in Social Theory: Action, Structure and Contradiction in Social Analysis.* Berkeley, CA: University of California Press.

———. 1981. *A Contemporary Critique of Historical Materialism.* Berkeley, CA: University of California Press.

———. 1984. *The Constitution of Society: Outline of the Theory of Structuration.* Cambridge, UK: Polity Press.

———. 1987. *Social Theory and Modern Sociology.* Stanford, CA: Stanford University Press.

———. 1990. *The Consequences of Modernity.* Stanford, CA: Stanford University Press.

Gilbert, Dennis, and Joseph A. Kahl. 1987. *American Class Structure: A New Synthesis.* Belmont, CA: Wadsworth.

Giner, Salvador. 1976. *Mass Society.* London: Martin Robertson & Company.

Gitlin, Todd. 2001. *Media Unlimited: How the Torrent of Images and Sounds Overwhelms our Lives.* New York: Metropolitan Books.

Gleitman, Henry. 1986. *Psychology,* 2nd edn. New York: W.W. Norton.

Glueck, Sheldon, and Eleanor T. Glueck. 1959. *Predicting Delinquency and Crime.* Cambridge, MA: Harvard University Press.

Goode, Erich. [1978] 1999. 'An Introduction to Deviance' in Joel Charon, ed., *The Meaning of Sociology.* Upper Saddle River, NJ: Prentice-Hall.

Gopnik, Alison. 1999. 'Small Wonders', *New York Review of Books,* 6 May.

Gordon, Milton M. 1950. *Social Class in American Sociology.* New York: McGraw-Hill.

Gould, Stephen Jay. 1981. *The Mismeasure of Man.* New York: W.W. Norton.

———. 1995. 'Curveball' in Steven Fraser, ed, *The Bell Curve Wars.* New York: Basic Books.

———. 1997. 'The Geometer of Race' in E. Nathaniel Gates, ed, *The Concept of 'Race' in the Natural and Social Sciences.* New York: Garland.

Grabb, Edward. 1990. *Theories of Social Inequality: Classical and Contemporary Perspectives.* Toronto: Holt, Rinehart and Winston.

———. 1993. 'Who Owns Canada' in James Curtis, Edward Grabb, Neil Guppy, and Sid Gilbert, eds, *Social Inequality in Canada.* Scarborough, ON: Prentice-Hall.

Gracey, Harry L. [1977] 1999. 'Learning the Student Role: Kindergarten as Academic Boot Camp' in Joel Charon, ed., *The Meaning of Sociology.* Upper Saddle River, NJ: Prentice-Hall.

Gramsci, Antonio. [1910–20] 1977. *Selections from the Prison Notebooks,* Quintin Hoare and Geoffery Smith, eds. New York: International Publishers.

———. 1975. *Selections from the Prison Notebooks.* New York: International Publishers.

Grant, George. [1965] 1991. *Lament for a Nation.* Ottawa: Carleton University Press.

Grant, Judith. 1993. *Fundamental Feminism.* New York: Routledge.

Green, Joyce. 1996. 'Resistance *Is* Possible', *Canadian Woman Studies* 16 (3).

Greenburg, Bradley. 2003. 'Children Spend More Time Playing Video Games than Watching TV', *Science of Mental Health.* Available at: http://mentalhealth.about.com/cs/familyresources/a/videotv404.htm.

Greenspan, Stanley. 2000. 'Parents DO Matter', *Washington Parent Magazine,* 13 October. Available at: http://www.washingtonparent.com/articles/9901/Green.htm.

Grenier, Marc, ed. 1992. *Critical Studies of the Canadian Mass Media.* Toronto: Butterworths.

Grusky, David, and Jesper Sørensen. 1998. 'Can Class Analysis Be Salvaged', *American Journal of Sociology* 103 (5) (March).

Guillaumin, Colette. 1995. *Racism, Sexism, Power and Ideology.* London: Routledge.

Guindon, Hubert. 2001. 'Quebec's Social and Political Evolution Since 1945: A View from Within' in Dan Glenday and Ann Duffy, eds, *Canadian Society: Meeting the Images of the Twenty-First Century.* Toronto: Oxford University Press.

Gurevitch, Michael, Tony Bennett, James Curran, and Janet Woollacott, eds. 1982. *Culture, Society and the Media.* London: Methune.

Hagedorn, Judy, and Janet Kizziar. 1974. *Gemini: The*

Psychology & Phenomena of Twins. Anderson, SC: Droke House/Hallux.

Hall, Calvin S. 1979. *A Primer of Freudian Psychology.* New York: Mentor Books.

———, and Gardner Lindzey. 1970. *Theories of Personality.* New York: John Wiley & Sons.

Hall, David, and Arthur Siegel. 1983. 'The Impact of Social Forces on the Canadian Media' in Benjamin Singer, ed, *Communications in Canadian Society.* Don Mills: Addison-Wesley Publishers.

———. 2001. 'The Growth of the Mass Media In Canada' in Craig McKie and Benjamin Singer, eds, *Communications in Canadian Society.* Toronto: Thompson Educational Publishing Inc.

Hall, Edward, and Mildred Reed Hall. 1982. 'The Sounds of Silence' in Leonard Cargan and Jeanne H. Ballantine, eds, *Sociological Footprints.* Belmont, CA: Wadsworth.

Hall, Stuart, David Held, Don Hubert, and Kenneth Thompson, eds. *Modernity: An Introduction to Modern Societies.* Cambridge, MA: Blackwell.

Hamilton, Peter. 1983. *Talcott Parsons.* London: Ellis Horwood and Tavistock.

Hannaford, Ivan. 1996. *Race: The History of an Idea in the West.* Washington: Woodrow Wilson Center Press.

Hansen, Karen V., and Ilene J. Philipson, eds. 1990. *Women, Class and the Feminist Imagination: A Socialist-Feminist Reader.* Philadelphia: Temple University Press.

Harding, Sandra. 1986. *The Science Question in Feminism.* Ithaca, NY: Cornell University Press.

Harlow, H., et al. 1976. 'Social rehabilitation of separation-induced depressive disorders in monkeys'. *American Journal of Psychiatry* 133 (11), 1279–85.

———. 1976a. 'Effects of maternal and peer separations on young monkeys'. *Journal of Child Psychology & Psychiatry & Allied Disciplines* 17 (2), 101–12.

Harp, John. 1980. 'Social Inequalities and the Transmission of Knowledge' in John Harp and John Hofley, eds, *Structured Inequality in Canada.* Scarborough, ON: Prentice-Hall.

Harris, Judy. 1998. *The Nurture Assumption: Why Children Turn Out the Way They Do.* New York: The Free Press.

Harris, Leonard, ed. 1999. *Racism.* Amherst: Humanity Books.

Harris, Marvin. 1980. *Cultural Materialism: The Struggle for a Science of Culture.* New York: Vintage Books.

Hartmann, Heidi. 1986. 'The Unhappy Marriage of Marxism and Feminism: Towards a More Progressive Union' in Lydia Sargent, ed, *Women and Revolution.* London: Pluto.

Heilbroner, Robert. 1968. *The Making of Economic Society.* Englewood Cliffs, NJ: Prentice-Hall.

———. 1992. *Twenty-First Century Capitalism.* Toronto: Anansi.

Held, David. 1980. *Introduction to Critical Theory: Horkheimer to Habermas.* Berkley: University of California Press.

———, ed. 1991. *Political Theory Today.* Stanford, CA: Stanford University Press.

———. 1995. *Democracy and the Global Order: From the Modern State to Cosmopolitan Governance.* Cambridge, UK: Polity Press.

Heller, Agnes. 1979. *On Instincts.* Assen, Netherlands: Van Gorcum.

Henry, Francis, Carol Tator, Winston Mattis, and Tim Rees. 2000. *The Colour of Democracy.* Toronto: Harcourt Brace.

Herrnstein, Richard, and Charles Murray. 1994. *The Bell Curve.* New York: The Free Press.

———, and James Wilson. 1985. *Crime and Human Nature.* New York: Simon & Schuster.

Heywood, Leslie, and Jennifer Drake. 1997. *Third Wave Agenda: Being Feminist, Doing Feminism.* Minneapolis: University of Minnesota Press. [Extracts copyright 1997 by the Regents of the University of Minnesota.]

Himmelweit, Susan, and Simon Mohun. 1977. 'Domestic Labour and Capital', *Cambridge Journal of Economics* 1.

Hirschi, T., and M.J. Hindelang. 1977. 'Intelligence and Delinquency: A Revisionist Review', *American Sociological Review* 42.

Hobbes, Thomas. [1651] 1968. *Leviathan.* Harmondsworth, UK: Penguin Books.

Hockett, Charles F., and Robert Ascher. 1964. 'The Human Revolution', *Current Anthropology* 5.

Hollingshead, A.B. 1949. *Elmtown's Youth: The Impact of Social Classes on Adolescents.* New York: John Wiley & Sons.

Holmes, Lowell D. 1985. 'South Sea Squall' in Phillip Whitten and David E. Hunter, eds, *Anthropology.* Boston: Little, Brown.

Homer. 1991. *The Odyssey.* London. Penguin Books.

Howe, Michael, Jane Davidson, and John Sloboda. 1999. 'Innate Theories: Reality or Myth' in Stephen Ceci and Wendy Williams, eds, *The Nature-Nurture Debate: The Essential Readings.* Oxford: Blackwell.

Hoyenga, Katharine B., and Kermit T. Hoyenga. 1979. *The Question of Sex Differences.* Boston: Little, Brown.

Human Genome News. 2000. Department of Energy Human Genome Project, 11 (1–2) (November).

Hunt, E.K. 1990. *Property and Prophets: The Evolution of Economic Institutions and Ideologies.* London: Harper & Row.

Hunt, Elgin F., and David C. Colander. 1984. *Social Science: An Introduction to the Study of Society.* New York: Macmillan.

Hunter, Alfred A. 1981. *Class Tells: On Social Inequality in Canada.* Toronto: Butterworths.

Hyde, Thomas, and Daniel Weinberger. 1995. 'Tourette's

Syndrome: A Model Neuropsychiatric Disorder', *Journal of American Medical Association* 8 (February). Available at http://www.tsa-usa.org.

Institute for Race Relations. 1982. *The Roots of Racism (Book 1); Patterns of Racism (Book 2)*. London: Institute of Race Relations.

Isajiw, Wsevolod. 1989. 'Definitions of Ethnicity' in Jay Goldstein and Rita Bienvenue, eds, *Ethnicity and Ethnic Relations in Canada*. Toronto: Butterworths.

———. 1999. *Understanding Diversity*. Toronto: Thompson Educational Publishing.

Jaggar, Alison M., and Paula S. Rothenberg, eds. 1993. *Feminist Frameworks: Alternative Theoretical Accounts of the Relations Between Men and Women*. New York: McGraw-Hill.

Jary, David, and Julia Jary. 1991. *Collins Dictionary of Sociology*. Glasgow: HarperCollins.

———. 1995. *Collins Dictionary of Sociology*, 2nd edn. Glasgow: HarperCollins.

Jay, Martin. 1973. *The Dialectical Imagination: A History of the Frankfurt School and the Institute of Social Research 1923–1950*. Boston: Little Brown and Company.

Jencks, Christopher. 1987. 'Genes and Crime', *New York Review of Books*, 12 February.

Jenson, Jane. 1992. 'Gender and Reproduction, or Babies and the State' in M. Patricia Connelly and Pat Armstrong, eds, *Feminism in Action*. Toronto: Canadian Scholars Press.

Jessop, Bob. 1982. *The Capitalist State*. Oxford: Martin Robertson.

———. 1990. *State Theories: Putting the Capitalist States in Their Places*. University Park, PA: Pennsylvania State University Press.

Johnson, Willis. 1969. *Essentials of Biology*. New York: Holt, Rinehart and Winston.

Jones, Peter. 1995. 'Contradictions And Unanswered Questions In The Genie Case: A Fresh Look At The Linguistic Evidence'. Available at: http://www.feral-children.com/en/ pager.php?df=jones1995.

Josephson, Wendy L. 1995. 'Television Violence: A Review of the Effects on Children of Different Ages', Department of Canadian Heritage. Available at: http://www.cfc-efc.ca/docs/mnet/ 00001068.htm.

Kapstein, Ethan B. 1994. *Governing the Global Economy: International Finance and the State*. Cambridge, MA: Harvard University Press.

Kaus, Mickey. 1995. 'The "It-Matters-Little" Gambit' in Steven Fraser, ed, *The Bell Curve Wars*. New York: Basic Books.

Kerbo, Harold R. 1983. *Social Stratification and Inequality: Class Conflict in the United States*. New York: McGraw-Hill.

Kellner, Douglas. 1989. *Critical Theory, Marxism and Modernity*. Baltimore: Johns Hopkins University Press.

Kesterton, Wilfred. 1983. 'The Press in Canada' in Benjamin Singer, ed, *Communications in Canadian Society*. Don Mills: Addison-Wesley Publishers.

Kilbourne, Jean. 2000. *Can't Buy My Love: How Advertising Changes the Way We Think and Feel*. New York: Free Press.

Knuttila, K. Murray, and Wendee Kubik. 1992. *State Theories: Classical, Global and Feminist Perspectives*, 2nd edn. Halifax: Fernwood.

———. 2001. *State Theories: Classical, Global and Feminist Perspectives*, 3rd edn. Halifax: Fernwood.

Korpi, Walter. 1998. 'The Iceberg of Power Below the Surface: A Preface to Power Resource Theory' in Julia O'Connor and Gregg Olsen, eds, *Power Resource Theory and the Welfare State*. Toronto: University of Toronto Press.

Korten, David C. 1995. *When Corporations Rule the World*. San Francisco: Berrett-Koehler Publications and Kumarian Press.

Kuhn, Annette, and AnneMarie Wolpe, eds. 1978. *Feminism and Materialism: Women and Modes of Production*. London: Routledge & Kegan Paul.

Labour Reporter. 2001. Saskatchewan Federation of Labour, November.

Laclau, Ernesto. 1971. 'Feudalism and Capitalism in Latin America', *New Left Review* 67 (May/June).

———. 1990. 'Post-Marxism without Apologies' in Ernesto Laclau, ed., *New Reflections on the Revolution of Our Time*. London: Verso.

———, and Chantal Mouffé. 1985. *Hegemony and Socialist Strategy*. London: Verso.

Lang, Berel, ed. *Race and Racism in Theory and Practice*. New York: Rowman & Littlefield.

Lasswell, Harold. 1948. 'The Structure and Function of Communication in Society' in Lyman Bryson, ed, *The Communication of Ideas*. New York: Cooper Square Publishers.

Layder, Derek. 1994. *Understanding Social Theory*. London: Sage Publications.

Lazarsfeld, Paul, and Robert Merton. 1948. 'Mass Communication, Popular Taste and Organized Political Action' in Lyman Bryson, ed, *The Communication of Ideas*. New York: Cooper Square Publishers.

———, and Elihu Katz. 1955. *Personal Influence: The Part Played by People in the Flow of Mass Communications*. New York: The Free Press.

Leahey, Thomas H. 1980. *A History of Psychology*. Englewood Cliffs, NJ: Prentice-Hall.

Leakey, Richard, and Roger Lewin. 1992. *Origins Revisited: In Search of What Makes Us Human*. New York: Anchor Books/Doubleday.

Lengermann, Patricia Madoo, and Jill Niebrugge-Brantley. 1988. 'Contemporary Feminist Theory' in George

Ritzer, ed, *Sociological Theory*. New York: Alfred A. Knopf.

Lerner, Daniel. 2000. 'The Passing of Traditional Society' excerpts in J. Timmons Roberts and Amy Hite, eds, *From Modernization to Globalization*. Oxford: Blackwell.

Leslie, Gerald R., and Sheila K. Korman. 1985. *The Family in Social Context*. New York: Oxford University Press.

Lewontin, R.C. 1991. *Biology as Ideology*. Toronto: Anansi.

Li, Peter. 1988. *Ethnic Inequality in a Class Society*. Toronto: Thompson Educational Publishing.

Li, Peter S., and B. Singh Bolaria. 1983. *Racial Minorities in Canada*. Toronto: Garamond Press.

Lieberman, Leonard. 2001. 'How "Caucasoids" Got Such Big Crania and Why They Shrank', *Current Anthropology* 42 (1) (February).

Lind, Michael. 1995. 'Brave New Right' in Steven Fraser, ed, *The Bell Curve Wars*. New York: Basic Books.

Lindeman, Bard. 1969. *The Twins Who Found Each Other*. New York: William Morrow.

Linden, Rick. 1996. *Criminology: A Canadian Perspective*. Toronto: Harcourt Brace.

Lopreato, Joseph, and Lionel S. Lewis, eds. 1974. *Social Stratification: A Reader*. New York: Harper & Row.

Lorenz, Konrad. *On Aggression*. 1966. New York: Harcourt Brace.

Lorimer, Rowland, and Jean McNulty. 1991. *Mass Communications in Canada*. Toronto: McClelland & Stewart.

———, and Mike Gasher. 2001. *Mass Communications in Canada*. Toronto: Oxford University Press.

Lott, Cynthia. 1995. *Women and the Media: Content, Careers and Criticism*. Belmont: Wadsworth Publishing.

Lowe, Graham. 1988. 'Jobs and the Labour Market' in James Curtis, Edward Grabb, Neil Guppy, and Sid Gilbert, eds, *Social Inequality in Canada*. Scarborough, ON: Prentice-Hall.

Lukes, Stephen. 1974. *Power*. London: Macmillan.

Luxton, Meg. 1980. *More Than a Labour of Love: Three Generations of Women's Work in the Home*. Toronto: Women's Press.

———. 1988. 'Thinking About the Future of the Family' in Karen Anderson et al., *Family Matters: Sociology and Contemporary Canadian Families*. Scarborough, ON: Nelson Canada.

———, Harriet Rosenberg, and Sedef Arat-Koc. 1990. *Through the Kitchen Window: The Politics of Home and Family*. Toronto: Garamond Press.

Lynd, Robert S., and Helen M. Lynd. 1929. *Middletown*. New York: Harcourt Brace Jovanovich.

———. 1937. *Middletown in Transition: A Study in Cultural Conflicts*. New York: Harcourt Brace Jovanovich.

———. [1939] 1967. *Knowledge For What?* Princeton, NJ: Princeton University Press.

McBride, Stephen, and John Shields.1993. *Dismantling a Nation: Canada and the New World Order*. Halifax: Fernwood.

McDermott, Patricia. 1996. 'Pay and Employment: Why Separate Policies?' in Janine Brodie, ed, *Women and Canadian Public Policy*. Toronto: Harcourt Brace.

McGee, Reece. 1975. *Points of Departure: Basic Concepts in Sociology*, 2nd edn. Hinsdale, IL: Dryden Press.

McIntosh, Mary. 1978. 'The State and the Oppression of Women' in Annette Kuhn and AnneMarie Wolpe, eds, *Feminism and Materialism*. London: Routledge & Kegan Paul.

Macionis, John J., and Nijole Benokraitis, eds. 2001. *Seeing Ourselves*, 4th edn. Upper Saddle River, NJ: Prentice-Hall.

Mackie, Marlene. 1991. *Gender Relations in Canada*. Toronto: Butterworths.

Mackinnon, Catharine. 1989. *Toward a Feminist Theory of the State*. Cambridge, MA: Harvard University Press.

McLaren, Arlene T., ed. 1988. *Gender and Society*. Toronto: Copp Clark Pitman.

Maclean, Charles. 1977. *The Wolf Children*. New York: Hill and Wang.

McLuhan, Marshall. 1964. *Understanding Media: The Extensions of Man*. New York: McGraw Hill.

Macpherson, C.B. 1968. 'Introduction' in Thomas Hobbes, *Leviathan*. Harmondsworth, UK: Penguin Books.

———. 1973. 'Natural Rights in Hobbes and Locke' in *Democratic Theory*. London: Oxford University Press.

McRoberts, Kenneth. 1988. *Quebec: Social Change and Political Crisis*. Toronto: McClelland & Stewart.

Malik, Kenan. 1996. *The Meaning of Race: Race, History and Culture in Western Society*. New York: New York University Press.

Malson, Lucien. 1972. *Wolf Children and the Problem of Human Nature*. New York: Monthly Review Press.

Mandell, Nancy. 1995. *Feminist Issues*. Scarborough, ON: Prentice-Hall.

———, and Ann Duffy, eds. 1988. *Reconstructing the Canadian Family: Feminist Perspectives*. Toronto: Butterworths.

———, eds. 1995. *Canadian Families: Diversity, Conflict and Change*. Toronto: Harcourt Brace.

Mander, Jerry, and Edward Goldsmith, eds. 1996. *The Case against the Global Economy*. San Francisco: Sierra Club Books.

Maroney, Heather Jon, and Meg Luxton, eds. 1987. *Feminism and Political Economy: Women's Work, Women's Struggles*. Toronto: Methuen.

Marshall, Gordon, ed. 1994. *The Concise Oxford Dictionary of Sociology*. Oxford: Oxford University Press.

Martin, David, ed. 1976. *50 Key Words: Sociology*. London: Lutterworth Press.

Marx, Karl. [1844] 1970. *Towards a Critique of Hegel's Philosophy of Right*, Joseph O'Malley, ed. Cambridge, UK: Cambridge University Press.

———. [1852] 1972. *The Eighteenth Brumaire of Louis Bonaparte*, Robert Tucker, ed., *The Marx-Engels Reader*. New York: W.W. Norton.

———. [1857] 1973. *Grundrisse*. Harmondsworth, UK: Penguin Books.

———. [1859] 1977. *A Contribution to the Critique of Political Economy*. New York: International Publishers.

———. [1867] 1967. *Capital: A Critique of Political Economy*. New York: International Publishers.

———. 1964. *The Economic and Philosophical Manuscripts of 1844*. New York: International Publishers.

———, and Frederick Engels. [1845] 1973. *The German Ideology*. New York: International Publishers.

———. [1848] 1952. *Manifesto of the Communist Party*. Moscow: Progress.

May, Tim. 1996. *Situating Social Theory*. Buckingham: Open University Press.

McPhail, Thomas, and Brenda McPhail. 1990. *Communications: The Canadian Experience*. Toronto: Copp Clarke Pitman.

Mead, G.H. [1934] 1962. *Mind, Self and Society*. Chicago: University of Chicago Press.

Mead, Margaret. [1935] 1971. *Sex and Temperament in Three Primitive Societies*. New York: William Morrow.

Merton, Robert K. 1968. *Social Theory and Social Structure*. New York: The Free Press.

Michels, Robert. [1911] 1962. *Political Parties: A Sociological Study of the Oligarchical Tendencies of Modern Democracy*. New York: The Free Press.

Miliband, Ralph. 1973. *The State in Capitalist Society*. London: Quartet Books.

Mills, C.W. 1951. *White Collar: The American Middle Classes*. New York: Oxford University Press.

———. 1956. *The Power Elite*. New York: Oxford University Press.

———. 1959. *The Sociological Imagination*. New York: Oxford University Press.

Milner, Henry. 1978. *Politics in the New Quebec*. Toronto: McClelland & Stewart.

Milner, Sheilagh, and Henry Milner. 1973. *The Decolonization of Quebec*. Toronto: McClelland & Stewart.

Miner, Horace. 1985. 'Body Ritual Among the Nacirema' in Phillip Whitten and David E. Hunter, eds, *Anthropology*. Boston: Little, Brown.

Mitchell, Broadus. 1967. *Postscripts to Economic History*. Totowa, NJ: Littlefield, Adams & Company.

Mitchell Evans, B., Stephen McBride, and John Shields. 1998. 'National Governance Versus Globalization: Canadian Democracy in Question', *Socialist Studies Bulletin* 54 (October/December).

Montagu, Ashley. 1972. *Statement on Race*. New York: Oxford University Press.

Moore, Wilbert E. 1963. *Social Change*. Englewood Cliffs, NJ: Prentice-Hall.

Morris, Charles W. [1934] 1962. 'Introduction' in G.H. Mead, *Mind, Self and Society*. Chicago: University of Chicago Press.

Morris, Desmond. 1969. *The Naked Ape*. Toronto: Bantam Books.

Morrison, Ken. 1996. *Marx, Weber and Durkheim*. London: Sage Publications.

Morrison, Wayne. 1995. *Theoretical Criminology*. London: Cavendish Publishing.

Morton, Peggy. 1972. 'Women's Work Is Never Done' in *Women Unite*. Toronto: Women's Press.

Mosca, Gaetano. [1896] 1939. *The Ruling Class*, Arthur Livingstone, ed. New York: McGraw-Hill.

Mosco, Vincent. 1996. *The Political Economy of Communications*. London: Sage Publications.

Muraskin, Roslyn, and Ted Alleman. 2000. *It's a Crime: Women and Justice*. Englewood Cliffs, NJ: Prentice-Hall.

Murray, John. 1994. 'The Impact of Televised Violence', *Hofstra Law Review* 22: 809–825. Available at: http://communication.ucsd.edu/tlg/123/murray.html.

Nagle, James. 1984. *Heredity and Human Affairs*. St Louis: Times Mirror.

Nakhaie, M. Reza. 1999. *Debates on Social Inequality*. Toronto: Harcourt Brace.

Natanson, Maurice. 1973. *The Social Dynamics of George H. Mead*. The Hague: Martinus Nijhoff.

Nelson, Adie, and Barrie Robinson. 2002. *Gender in Canada*, 2nd edn. Toronto: Prentice-Hall.

Nelson, Brian R. 1982. *Western Political Thought: From Socrates to the Age of Ideology*. Englewood Cliffs, NJ: Prentice-Hall.

Nelson, Joyce. 1987. *The Perfect Machine: TV in the Nuclear Age*. Toronto: Between the Lines.

———. 1989. *Sultans of Sleaze: Public Relations and the Media*. Toronto: Between the Lines.

Newton, Michael. 2002. *Savage Girls and Wild Boys: A History of Feral Children*. London: Faber and Faber Ltd.

New York Times, 23 and 30 August 2000.

Nisbett, Richard. 1995. 'Race, IQ, and Scientism' in Steven Fraser, ed, *The Bell Curve Wars*. New York: Basic Books.

Nye, F. Ivan, and Felix Berardo. 1973. *The Family: Its Structure and Interaction*. New York: Macmillan.

Oakley, Ann. 1974. *The Sociology of Housework*. London: Martin Robertson.

O'Brien, Mary. 1981. *The Politics of Reproduction*. Boston: Routledge & Kegan Paul.

O'Connor, Julia, and Gregg Olsen. 1998. 'Understanding the Welfare State: Power Resource Theory and Its Critics' in Julia O'Connor and Gregg Olsen, eds, *Power resource Theory and the Welfare State: A Critical Approach*. Toronto: University of Toronto Press.

Offé, Claus. 1996. *Modernity and the State, East, West*. Cambridge, MA: MIT Press.

Ogmundson, R. 1990. 'Social Inequality' in Robert Hagedorn, ed., *Sociology*. Toronto: Holt, Rinehart and Winston.

Ollman, Bertell. 1968. 'Marx's Use of Class', *American Journal of Sociology* 73 (5).

———. 1976. *Alienation: Marx's Conception of Man in Capitalist Society*, 2nd edn. London: Cambridge University Press.

Olsen, Gregg. 1999. 'Half Empty or Half Full? The Swedish Welfare State in Transition', *Canadian Review of Sociology and Anthropology* 36 (2).

Owens, Kelly, and Mary-Claire King. 1999. 'Genomic Views of Human History', *Science* 268 (October).

Oxford Illustrated Dictionary. 1970. London: Oxford University Press.

Paabo, Svante. 2001. 'The Human Genome and Our View of Society'. Available at: http://www.sciencemag.org/cgi/content/full/291/5507/1219 (7/27/01).

Pareto, Vilfredo. [1916] 1976. *Sociological Writings*. Oxford: Basil Blackwell.

Parsons, Talcott. 1949. *Essays in Sociological Theory*. New York: The Free Press.

———. 1951. *The Social System*. New York: The Free Press.

———. 1955. 'The American Family: Its Relations to Personality and the Social Structure' in Talcott Parsons and R.F. Bales, eds, *Family, Socialization and Interaction Process*. Glencoe, IL: The Free Press.

———. 1965. 'The Normal American Family' in Bert Adams and Thomas Weirath, eds, *Readings in the Sociology of the Family*. Chicago: Markham.

———. 1966. *Societies: Evolutionary and Comparative Perspectives*. Englewood Cliffs, NJ: Prentice-Hall.

———. 1971. *The System of Modern Societies*. Englewood Cliffs, NJ: Prentice-Hall.

———, and Edward Shils, eds. 1952. *Toward a General Theory of Action*. Cambridge, MA: Harvard University Press.

———, and R.F. Bales, eds. 1955. *Family, Socialization and Interaction Process*. Glencoe, IL: The Free Press.

PBS Nova Series # 2112G. 'Secret of the Wild Child', aired 4 March 1997. Transcript available at http://www.pbs.org/wgbh/nova/transcripts/2112gchild.html.

Peterson, Christopher. 1988. *Personality*. New York: Harcourt Brace Jovanovich.

Petras, James, and Henry Veltmeyer. 2001. *Globalization Unmasked*. Halifax: Fernwood and Zed Books.

Philipkoski, Kristen. 2001. 'Gene Maps Presents Race Concerns', 'Researchers Cut Gene Estimate', 'Human Genome Showdown' and 'Gene Map: Help or Hype', *Wired News*. Available at: http://www.wired.com/news/technology/0,1282,41610,00.html (7/23/01 and 7/23/01, 7/27/01).

Piaget, Jean, and Barbel Inhelder. 1969. *Psychology of the Child*. New York: Basic Books.

Pineo, Peter. 1980. 'The Social Standing of Ethnic and Racial Groupings' in J. Goldstein and R. Bienvenu, eds, *Ethnicity and Ethnic Relations in Canada: A Book of Readings*. Toronto: Butterworths.

———, and John Porter. 1967. 'Occupational Prestige in Canada', *Canadian Review of Sociology and Anthropology* 4 (1).

Pines, Myra. 1977. 'The Civilizing of Genie' in Kasper, Loretta F. ed, *Teaching English through the Disciplines: Psychology*. New York: Whittier Publications. Also available at: http://kccesl.tripod.com/genie.html.

———. 1981. 'The Civilizing of Genie', *Psychology Today* 15 September.

Polanyi, Karl. 1944. *The Great Transformation*. Boston: Beacon Press.

Ponting, J. Rick. 1998. 'Racism and Stereotyping of First Nations' in Vic Satzewich, ed, *Racism and Social Inequality in Canada*. Toronto: Thompson Educational Publishing.

———. 2001. 'Racism and Resistance' in Dan Glenday and Ann Duffy, eds, *Canadian Society: Meeting the Images of the Twenty-First Century*. Toronto: Oxford University Press.

Porter, John. 1965. *The Vertical Mosaic: An Analysis of Social Class and Power in Canada*. Toronto: University of Toronto Press.

Postman, Neil. 1985. *Amusing Ourselves to Death*. New York: Penguin Books.

———. 1999. *Building a Bridge to the 18th Century*. New York: Alfred A. Knopf.

Poulantzas, Nicos. 1972. 'The Problem of the Capitalist State' in Robin Blackburn, ed, *Ideology in Social Science: Readings in Critical Social Theory*. London: Fontana/Collins.

———. 1973. *Political Power and Social Classes*. London: NLB and Sheed and Ward.

———. 1975. *Classes in Contemporary Capitalism*. London: NLB.

Pupo, Norene. 1988. 'Preserving Patriarchy: Women, the Family and the State' in Mandell and Duffy, eds, *Reconstructing the Canadian Family*. Toronto: Butterworths.

Rafter, Nicole Hahn, and Frances Heidensohn, eds. 1995. *International Perspectives in Feminist Criminology*. Buckingham: Open University Press.

Ramey, Craig, and Sharon Landesman Ramey. 1999. 'Prevention of Intellectual Disabilities: Early

Interventions to Improve Cognitive Development' in Stephen Ceci and Wendy Williams, eds, *The Nature-Nurture Debate: The Essential Readings*. Oxford: Blackwell.

Ramos, Dante. 1995. 'Paradise Miscalculated' in Steven Fraser, ed, *The Bell Curve Wars*. New York: Basic Books.

Randall, J.H. 1940. *The Making of the Modern Mind: A Survey of the Intellectual Background of the Present Age*. New York: Houghton Mifflin.

Reasons, Charles, and Robert Rich. 1978. *The Sociology of Law: A Conflict Perspective*. Toronto: Butterworths.

Reed, Evelyn. 1978. 'Women: Caste, Class or Oppressed Sex?' in Alison M. Jaggar and Paula S. Rothenberg, eds, *Feminist Frameworks*. New York: McGraw-Hill.

Renzetti, Claire M., and Daniel J. Curran. 1992. *Women, Men, and Society*. Boston: Allyn & Bacon.

Rex, John. 1961. *Key Problems of Sociological Theory*. London: Routledge & Kegan Paul.

Rioux, Marcel. 1971. *Quebec in Question*. Toronto: James, Lewis and Samuel.

Ritzer, George. 1988. *Sociological Theory*, 2nd edn. New York: Alfred A. Knopf.

———. 1990. *Frontiers of Social Theory: The New Synthesis*. New York: Columbia University Press.

———. 2000. *Modern Sociological Theory*. New York: McGraw Hill.

Roberts, Joseph. 1998. *In the Shadow of the Empire: Canada and the Americans*. New York: Monthly Review Press.

Robertson, Ian. 1981. *Sociology*. New York: Worth.

Robinson, William, and Jerry Harris. 2000. 'Towards a Global Ruling Class: Globalization and the Transnational Capitalist Class', *Science and Society* 64 (1) (Spring).

Romanow, Walter, and Walter Soderlund. 1992. *Media Canada: An Introductory Analysis*. Mississaugua: Copp Clark Pitman.

Rose, Arnold M. 1956. *Sociology: The Study of Human Relations*. New York: Alfred A. Knopf.

Rose, Hilary, and Steven Rose, eds. 2000. *Alas Poor Darwin*. New York: Harmony Books.

Rose, S., R.C. Lewontin, and Leon Kamin. 1985. *Not in Our Genes*. Harmondsworth, UK: Penguin Books. [Extracts reprinted by permission of the authors.]

Rossides, Daniel. 1968. *Society as a Functional Process*. Toronto: McGraw-Hill.

———. 1976. *The American Class System*. Atlanta: Houghton Mifflin.

———. 1978. *The History and Nature of Sociological Theory*. Boston: Houghton Mifflin.

———. 1997. *Social Stratification: The Interplay of Class, Race and Gender*. Upper Saddle River, NJ: Prentice Hall.

Rostow, W.W. 1960. *The Stages of Economic Growth*,

excerpts in J. Timmons Roberts and Amy Hite, eds. 2000. *From Modernization to Globalization*. Oxford: Blackwell.

———. 1965. *The Stages of Economic Growth*. Cambridge, UK: Cambridge University Press.

Rushton, J. Philippe. 1996. 'Race as a Biological Concept'. Available at: http://www.leconsulting.com/arthurhu/97/06/rushtonracebio.htm.

———. 1997. *Race, Evolution and Behaviour*. New Brunswick, NJ: Transaction. [Extracts copyright © 1997 by Transation Publishers. Reprinted by permission of the publisher.]

Rutter, Michael, and the English and Romanian adoptees study team. 1999. 'Development Catch-up, and Deficit, Following Adoption after Severe Global Early Privation' in Stephen Ceci and Wendy Williams, eds, *The Nature-Nurture Debate: The Essential Readings*. Oxford: Blackwell.

Ryerson, Stanley. 1975. *Unequal Union*. Toronto: Progress Books.

Rymer, Russ. 1992. 'Annals of Science: A Silent Childhood I & II', *The New Yorker*, 13 and 20 April.

———. 1993. *Genie: Escape from a Silent Childhood*. London: Michael Joseph.

———. 1994. *Genie: a Scientific Tragedy*. New York: Harper Collins

Sacks, Oliver . 2001. 'Inside the Executive Brain', *New York Review of Books*. 26 April.

———. 2004. 'In the River of Consciousness', *New York Review of Books*. 15 January.

Salkind, Neil J., and Sueann Robinson Ambron. 1987. *Child Development*, 5th edn. New York: Holt, Rinehart and Winston.

Sanderson, Stephen K. 1988. *Macrosociology*. New York: Harper & Row.

Sanjek, Roger. 1994. 'The Enduring Inequalities of Race' in Roger Sanjek and Steven Gregory, eds, *Race*. New Brunswick, NJ: Rutgers University Press.

Sargent, Lydia, ed. 1981. *Women and Revolution: A Discussion of the Unhappy Marriage of Marxism and Feminism*. London: Pluto Press.

Saskatchewan Indian Federated College. 1986. *The Survival of a People*. Regina: Saskatchewan Indian Federated College Press.

Satzewich, Vic, ed. 1998. *Racism and Social Inequality in Canada*. Toronto: Thompson Educational Press.

———, and Terry Wotherspoon. 1993. *First Nations: Race, Class and Gender Relations*. Toronto: Nelson Canada.

Sayers, Janet, Mary Evans, and Nanneke Redclift, eds. 1987. *Engels Revisited: New Feminist Essays*. London: Tavistock.

Schaefer, Richard. 1989. *Sociology*. New York: McGraw-Hill.

Schemerhorn, Richard. 1996. 'Ethnicity and Minority

Groups' in John Hutchinson and Anthony D. Smith, eds, *Ethnicity*. New York: Oxford University Press.

Schultz, Duane. 1975. *A History of Modern Psychology*, 2nd edn. New York: Academic Press.

Schur, Edwin M. 1979. *Interpreting Deviance: A Sociological Introduction*. New York: Harper & Row.

Schusky, Ernest L., and Patrick T. Culbert. 1967. *Introducing Culture*. Englewood Cliffs, NJ: Prentice-Hall.

Scupin, Raymond, and Christopher DeCorse. 1995. *Anthropology: A Global Perspective*. Englewood Cliffs, NJ: Prentice-Hall.

Searle, John. 1995. 'The Mystery of Consciousness' and 'The Mystery of Consciousness Part II' *New York Review of Books*, 2 and 16 November.

———. 1997. 'Consciousness and Philosophers', *New York Review of Books*, 6 March.

Secombe, Wally. 1974. 'The Housewife and Her Labour Under Capitalism', *New Left Review* 83 (January/February).

Segal, Nancy. 1999. 'New Twin Studies Show the Career of Your Dreams May Be the Career of Your Genes', *Psychology Today* (October).

———. 2000. *Entwined Lives: Twins and What They Tell Us About Human Behavior*. New York: Plume.

Seger, Linda. 2002. 'How to Evaluate Media Images of Women', *Media Awareness Network*. Available at: http://www.medialit.org/reading_room/article44.html #bio.

Seidman, Steven. 1983. *Liberalism and the Origins of European Social Theory*. Berkeley, CA: University of California Press.

Shapiro, Martin. 1979. *Getting Doctored: Critical Reflections on Becoming a Physician*. Kitchener, ON: Between the Lines.

Sheldon, William H. 1949. *Varieties of Delinquent Youth*. New York: Harper.

Shepard, Jon M. 1990. *Sociology*, 4th edn. St. Paul: West.

Silcoff, Sean, and Peter Brieger. 2001. 'The Richest 50', *National Post*, 6 May.

Silverman, Robert, James Teevan, and Vincent Sacco. 2000. *Crime in Canadian Society*. Toronto: Harcourt Brace.

Simpson, Richard. 1956. 'A Modification of the Functional Theory of Social Stratification', *Social Forces* 35 (December).

Skidmore, William. 1979. *Theoretical Thinking in Sociology*, 2nd edn. London: Cambridge University Press.

Skocpol, Theda. 1979. *States and Social Revolutions*. Cambridge, UK: Cambridge University Press.

———. 1980. 'Political Response to Capitalist Crisis: Neo-Marxist Theories of the State and the Case of the New Deal', *Politics and Society* 10 (2).

———. 1985. 'Bringing the State Back In: Strategies of Analysis in Current Research' in Peter B. Evans, Dietrich Rueschemeyer, and Theda Skocpol, eds, *Bringing the State Back In*. Cambridge, UK: Cambridge University Press.

Smith, Adam. [1776] 1969. *An Inquiry into the Nature and Causes of the Wealth of Nations*. Port Washington, NY: Kennikat Press.

Smith, Anthony D. 1973. *The Concept of Social Change: A Critique of the Functionalist Theory of Social Change*. London: Routledge & Kegan Paul.

Smith, Dorothy. 1981. 'Women's Inequality and the Family' in Allan Moscovitch and Glenn Drover, eds, *Inequality: Essays on the Political Economy of Social Welfare*. Toronto: University of Toronto Press.

———. 1985. 'Women, Class and Family' in Varda Burstyn and Dorothy Smith, *Women, Class, Family and the State*. Toronto: Garamond Press.

Smith, Lillian. 1971. 'Killers of the Dream: When I was a Child' in Edgar Schuler, Thomas Hoult, Duane Gibson, and Wilbur Brookover, eds, *Readings in Sociology*. New York: Thomas Y. Crowell.

Smythe, Dallas. 1977. 'Communications: The Blindspot of Western Marxism', *Canadian Journal of Political and Social Theory*. 1 (3) (Fall).

———. 1982. *Dependency Road: Communications, Capitalism, Consciousness, and Canada*. Norwood, NJ: Ablex Publishing Corporation.

Snyder, Mark. 1982. 'Self-Fulfilling Stereotypes' in Leonard Cargan and Jeanne H. Ballantine, eds, *Sociological Footprints*. Belmont, CA: Wadsworth.

Sollors, Werner, ed. 1996. *Theories of Ethnicity: A Classical Reader*. New York: New York University Press.

Sørensen, Jesper. 1996. 'The Structural Basis of Social Inequality' in *American Journal of Sociology* 101 (5) (March).

———. 2000. 'Toward a Sounder Basis for Class Analysis', *American Journal of Sociology* 106 (6) (May).

Sowell, Thomas. 1995. 'Ethnicity and IQ' in Steven Fraser, ed, *The Bell Curve Wars*. New York: Basic Books.

Spitzer, Steven. 1978. 'Toward a Marxian Theory of Deviance' in Ronald A. Farrell and Victoria Lynn Swigert, eds, *Social Deviance*. Philadelphia: J.B. Lippincott.

Sreberny, Annabelle, and Liesbert van Zoonen, eds. 2000. *Gender, Politics and Communication*. Cresskill, NJ: Hampton Press Inc.

St Augustine. 1996. *The City of God*, in William Ebenstein, *Great Political Thinkers*. New York: Holt, Rinehart and Wiston.

Standley, Arline R. 1981. *Auguste Comte*. Boston: Twayne.

Statistics Canada. 1998. General Social Survey—Time Use. Available at: http://www.statcan.ca/english/sdds/4503.htm.

———. 2002. Average income after tax by economic family types. Available at: http://www.statcan.ca/english/Pgdb/famil21a.htm.

Statt, David. 1990. *Concise Dictionary of Psychology*. London: Routledge.

Stellar, Eliot. 1988. 'Instincts' in *Collier's Encyclopedia*. New York: Macmillan.

Stewart, Brian. 1983. 'Canadian Social System and Canadian Broadcasting Audiences' in in Benjamin Singer, ed, *Communications in Canadian Society*. Don Mills: Addison-Wesley Publishers.

Stillo, Monica. 1998. 'Antonio Gramsci'. Available at: http://www.theory.org.uk/ctr-gram.htm.

Strauss, Leo. 1972. *The History of Political Philosophy*. Chicago: Rand McNally.

Strinati, Dominic. 1995. *An Introduction to Theories of Popular Culture*. London: Routledge.

Strong, Bryan, and Christine Deffault. 1986. *The Marriage and Family Experience*. St Paul: West.

Stryker, Sheldon. 1980. *Symbolic Interactionism*. Menlo Park, NJ: Benjamin/Cummings.

Sydie, Rosalind A. 1987. *Natural Women, Cultured Men: A Feminist Perspective on Sociological Theory*. Toronto: Methuen.

Szymanski, Albert. 1978. *The Capitalist State and the Politics of Class*. Cambridge, MA: Winthrop.

Tabb, William. 1997 'Globalization is an Issue, The Power of Capital is the Issue', *Monthly Review* (June).

Tallim, Jane. 2003. 'Sexualized Images in Advertising', *Media Awareness Network*. Available at: http://www.media-awareness.ca/english/resources/articles/advertising_marketing/sex_images_in_ads.cfm?RenderForPrint=1.

Tannen, Deborah. 2001. 'The Glass Ceiling' in Robert Brym, ed, *Society in Question*. Toronto: Harcourt Brace.

Tavris, Carol, and Carole Wade. 1984. *The Longest War: Sex Differences in Perspective*, 2nd edn. San Diego: Harcourt Brace Jovanovich.

Teeple, Gary. 1995. *Globalization and the Decline of Social Reform*. New Jersey and Toronto: Humanities Press and Garamond Press.

Terkel, Studs. 1974. *Working*. New York: Pantheon Books.

Theodorson, George A., and Achilles G. Theodorson. 1969. *A Modern Dictionary of Sociology*. New York: Thomas Y. Crowell.

Thomas, Harrison Cook, and William Albert Hamm. 1944. *Modern Europe*. Toronto: Clarke, Irwin.

Thompson, Kenneth. 1976. *Auguste Comte: The Foundations of Sociology*. London: Nelson.

Thorne, Barrie, and Marilyn Yalom, eds. 1982. *Rethinking the Family: Some Feminist Questions*. New York: Longman.

Tiger, Lionel. 1969. *Men in Groups*. New York: Random House.

⸻. 1972. *The Imperial Animal*. New York: Holt Rinehart.

Tinbergen, N. 1951. *The Study of Instincts*. Oxford: Clarendon.

Tong, Rosemarie. 1989. *Feminist Thought: A Comprehensive Introduction*. Boulder, CO: Westview Press.

Torrance, James. 1979. *Higher Biology*. London: Edward Arnold.

Tumin, Melvin M. [1953] 1974. 'Some Principles of Stratification: A Critical Analysis' in Joseph Lopreato and Lionel S. Lewis, eds, *Social Stratification*. New York: Harper & Row.

⸻. 1967. *Social Stratification: The Forms and Functions of Inequality*. Englewood Cliffs, NJ: Prentice-Hall.

⸻, ed. 1970. *Readings on Social Inequality*. Englewood Cliffs, NJ: Prentice-Hall.

Turner, Jonathan H., and Leonard Beeghley. 1981. *The Emergence of Sociological Theory*. Homewood, IL: Dorsey Press.

United Nations Human Development Report. 1998. Available at: http://www.undp.org.

United States Census Bureau. *Statistical Abstract of the United States*. Available at: http://www.census.gov/prod/www/statistical-abstract-03.html.

Ursel, Jane. 1986. 'The State and the Maintenance of Patriarchy: A Case Study of Family, Labour and Welfare Legislation in Canada' in James Dickinson and Bob Russell, eds, *Family, Economy and the State*. Toronto: Garamond Press.

⸻. 1992. *Private Lives and Public Policy: One Hundred Years of State Intervention in the Family*. Toronto: Women's Press.

van Zoonen, Liesbet. 1994. *Feminist Media Studies*. London: Sage.

Veltmeyer, Henry. 1986. *Canadian Class Structure*. Toronto: Garamond Press.

Vivian, John, and Peter J. Maurin. 2000. *The Media of Mass Communications*. Scarborough: Allyn and Bacon Canada.

Walizer, M.H., and P.L. Wienir. 1978. *Research Methods and Analysis: Searching for Relationships*. New York: Harper & Row.

Wallace, Ruth A., and Alison Wolf. 1986. *Contemporary Sociological Theory*. Englewood Cliffs, NJ: Prentice-Hall.

Waller, Willard, ed. 1942. *Charles Horton Cooley*. New York: Dryden Press.

Wallerstein, Immanuel. 1974. *The Modern World System*. New York: Academic Press.

Warner, W. Lloyd. 1949. *Social Class in America: A Manual of Procedure for the Measurement of Social Status*. New York: Harper Torchbooks.

Waters, Malcolm. 2000. *Modern Sociological Theory*. Sage Publications: New York.

Weber, Max. [1930] 1958. *The Protestant Ethic and the Spirit of Capitalism.* New York: Charles Scribner's Sons.

———. 1946. *Max Weber: Essays in Sociology,* Hans H. Gerth and C.W. Mills, eds. New York: Oxford University Press.

———. 1949. *The Methodology of the Social Sciences,* E. Shils and H. Finch, eds. Glencoe, IL: The Free Press.

———. 1968. *Economy and Society: An Outline of Interpretative Sociology.* New York: Bedminster Press.

Webster's Encyclopedic Dictionary. 1988. New York: Lexicon.

Weiss, Linda. 1997. 'Globalization and the Myth of the Powerless State', *New Left Review* 225 (September/October).

Westby, David. 1991. *The Growth of Sociological Theory.* Englewood Cliffs, NJ: Prentice-Hall.

White, Leslie. (1949) 2001. 'Symbol: The Basic Element of Culture' in John Macionis and Nijole Benokraitis, eds, *Seeing Ourselves: Classic, Contemporary and Cross Cultural Readings in Sociology.* Upper Saddle River, NJ: Prentice-Hall.

Whitten, Phillip, and David E. Hunter. 1985. *Anthropology: Contemporary Perspectives.* Boston: Little, Brown.

Williams, Raymond. 1976. *Keywords: A Vocabulary of Culture and Society.* London: Fontana Paperbacks.

Williams, Thomas R. 1972. *Introduction to Socialization.* St Louis: C.V. Mosby.

Wilson, Adrian. 1985. *Family.* New York: Tavistock.

Wilson, James, and Richard Herrnstein. 1985. *Crime and Human Nature.* New York: Simon & Schuster, Touchstone Books.

Wilson, John. 1983. *Social Theory.* Englewood Cliffs, NJ: Prentice-Hall.

Wilson, Logan, and William Kolb. 1949. *Sociological Analysis: An Introductory Text and Casebook.* New York: Harcourt, Brace and World.

Wilson, Susannah Jane. 1981. *Women, the Family and the Economy.* Toronto: McGraw-Hill Ryerson.

Wood, Ellen Meiksins. 1995. *Democracy against Capitalism: Renewing Historical Materialism.* Cambridge, UK: Cambridge University Press.

World Fact Book (The). 2001. Published by the CIA. Available at: http://www.cia.gov/cia/ publications/factbook.

Wright, Erik Olin. 1978. *Class, Crisis and the State.* London: Verso.

———. 1985. *Classes.* London: Verso.

———. 2000a. 'Class, Exploitation, and Economic Rents: Reflections on Sørensen's "Sounder Basis"', *American Journal of Sociology* 106 (6) (May).

———. 2000b. 'Working-Class Power, Capitalist Class Interests, and Class Compromise', *American Journal of Sociology* 105 (4) (January).

Wright, Charles. 1986. *Mass Communications: A Sociological Perspective.* New York: Random House.

Wright, Lawrence. 1997. *Twins and What They Tell Us About Who We Are.* New York: John Wiley.

Wrong, Dennis. 1959. 'The Functional Theory of Stratification: Some Neglected Considerations', *American Sociological Review* 24 (December).

———. 1961. 'The Oversocialized Concept of Man in Modern Society', *American Sociological Review* 26.

Zeitlin, Irving M. 1990. *Ideology and the Development of Sociological Theory.* Englewood Cliffs, NJ: Prentice-Hall.

Zelditch, Morris, Jr. 1955. 'Role Differentiation in the Nuclear Family: A Comparative Study' in Talcott Parsons and R.F. Bales, eds, *Family, Socialization and Interaction Process.* Glencoe, IL: The Free Press.

Zickler, Patrick. 1999. 'Twin Studies Help Define the Role of Genes in Vulnerability to Drug Abuse', *National Institute on Drug Abuse (NIDA) Notes,* 14 (4).

Index